U0940616

西安统计年鉴

中国统计出版社
China Statistics Press

西安市统计局
XI'AN MUNICIPAL BUREAU OF STATISTICS
国家统计局西安调查队
NBS SURVEY OFFICE IN XI'AN

(总第18期 NO.18)

（京）新登字 041 号

图书在版编目（CIP）数据

西安统计年鉴.2010：汉英对照 / 西安市统计局，国家统计局西安调查队 编.
—北京：中国统计出版社，2010.8
ISBN 978-7-5037-6050-1

Ⅰ.①西…
Ⅱ.①西… ②国…
Ⅲ.统计资料-西安市-2010-年鉴-汉、英
Ⅳ.①C832.411-54

中国版本图书馆CIP数据核字（2010）第165002号

西安统计年鉴—2010

作　　者/ 西安市统计局　国家统计局西安调查队
责任编辑/ 余竞雄
责任校对/ 赵群洁
封面设计/ 西安市丰润广告有限责任公司
出版发行/ 中国统计出版社
通信地址/ 北京市丰台区西三环南路甲6号 中国统计出版社
邮　　编/ 100073
电　　话/（010）63376907
E-mail / yearbook@gj.stats.cn
印　　刷/ 西安煤航信息产业有限公司
经　　销/ 新华书店
开　　本/ 890×1240毫米 1/16
字　　数/ 107万
印　　张/ 34.25
印　　数/ 800册
版　　别/ 2010年8月第1版
版　　次/ 2010年8月第1次印刷
书　　号/ ISBN 978-7-5037-6050-1/C · 2407
定　　价/ 260.00元

《西安统计年鉴—2010》编辑部

XI'AN STATISTICAL YEARBOOK-2010
EDITORLAL STAFF

编者说明

一、《西安统计年鉴—2010》是一部全面记载西安市国民经济和社会发展情况的大型连续性统计文献资料。其内容全面丰富、信息高度密集，真实地记录了西安一年来经济社会发展变化情况，是国内外各界人士了解西安、认识西安、研究西安经济和社会发展的重要工具书。

二、本《年鉴》收录了2010年西安经济社会全方位的统计数据和重要历史年份、改革开放以来的主要数据。全书内容包括十九个篇目：（一）综合；（二）国民经济核算；（三）人口、从业人员与职工工资；（四）固定资产投资；（五）财政；（六）物价指数；（七）人民生活；（八）城市公用事业；（九）环境保护；（十）农业；（十一）工业和能源；（十二）建筑业；（十三）运输和邮电；（十四）国内贸易；（十五）对外经济贸易和旅游；（十六）金融和保险；（十七）教育和科技；（十八）文化、体育、卫生、社会福利和其他；（十九）企业调查。另外，作为插页还包括统计图表。

三、为便于国内外读者查阅，本《年鉴》全部内容均采用中英文对照编辑，并针对各部分内容编制了简要说明和主要指标解释。具备数据快速查询和加工的功能。

四、按照国际惯例，本《年鉴》依据西安市第二次经济普查结果已对主要历史数据予以调整，主要包括国民经济核算、工业、能源、建筑业、房地产开发、国内贸易等篇目，调整年限为2005-2008年，2005年以后均为可比数。依据2007年农业普查结果，对2006年农业统计数据进行了衔接调整。

五、本《年鉴》各篇资料均为正式年报数，除经济普查因素外，我们还根据最新掌握的统计资料以及国家新的统计制度规定，对历年年鉴相关数据重新予以核实，并对部分历史数据进行了调整和修订。因此，凡与本《年鉴》有出入的部分均以本《年鉴》为准。

六、本《年鉴》中对主要指标编制了定基指数、环比指数和年平均增长速度。

七、本《年鉴》中的部分数据由于单位取舍不同产生的计算误差均未作机械调整。

八、本《年鉴》使用的符号说明："空白"表示该项统计指标无数据或数据不详；"#"表示其中项；"*"表示另有注解。

感谢社会各界长期以来对《西安统计年鉴》的广泛关注和大力支持。为进一步做好工作，更好地为广大读者服务，希望社会各界提出宝贵意见。

PREFACE

I. *Xi'an Statistical Yearbook 2010* is a periodical statistic yearbook which records economic and social development of Xi'an all-around, with its features of comprehensive and intensive information, which pratically provides data covering the situation of social and economic development and change of 2009 in Xi'an. The book is an excellent publicity material to introduce Xi'an City to different people from home and abroad.

II.*The yearbook* covers the Xi'an's various aspects of economic and social development in 2010 and some selected data series in historical important years and since 'reform and opening'. The book contains nineteen parts, 1.General Survey; 2.National Economic Account; 3.Population, Employment and Wages; 4.Investment in Fixed Assets; 5. Government Finance; 6.Price Indices; 7.People's Livelihood; 8.Urban Public Utilities; 9.Environmental Protection; 10.Agriculture; 11.Industry and energy; 12.Construction; 13.Transportation, Post and Telecommunication Service; 14.Domestic Trade; 15.Foreign Trade; 16.Banking and Insurance; 17.Education, Science and Technology; 18.Culture, Sports, Public Health, Social Welfare Institutions and Other Social Activities; 19.Enterprises Investigation. As insert pages including statistical graphs and charts.

III. For the convenience of being consulted by foreigners, the book is Chinese-English bilingual edition, while provides brief introduction and explanatory notes on main indicators at end of each part. Also, the Yearbook has the foundation of processing data、drawing data-map and inquirying data quickly.

IV. According to international regulation, some important historic dates of 2005-2008 on national economy account, industry, energy resources, construction, real estate development, domestic trade and other related fields, published in the book have been verified according to the results of Economic Census in Xi'an.So datas after 2005 are comparable with each other. We made some adjustments on agriculture statistical of 2006 to connect with the result of agriculture survey in 2007.

V. All the datas in this yearbook are from formal annual report. According to the latest statistic and the new national statistical regulations, some important statistic published in the past except date related with Economic Census have been verified again in this yearbook, and parts of the historic datas have been adjusted. So if there are some differences between the historic information and the datas of this yearbook, we should take the data in this book as the standard.

VI. The yearbook provides fixed base index, chain index and annual average growth rate for main indicators.

VII. Statistical discrepancies due to rounding are not adjusted automatically in this yearbook.

VIII. Explanations on symbols used in this yearbook:

(blank) indicates the data not available;

# indicates the items of the total.

* indicates some other explanatory notes.

Here we would like to express our sincere thanks to the people for their concerning and supporting to the Xi'an statistical yearbook. In order to do perfectly and provide better service to readers, we hope that the whole society fields can propose constructive advices.

生产总值(亿元)

Gross Domestic Product(100 million yuan)

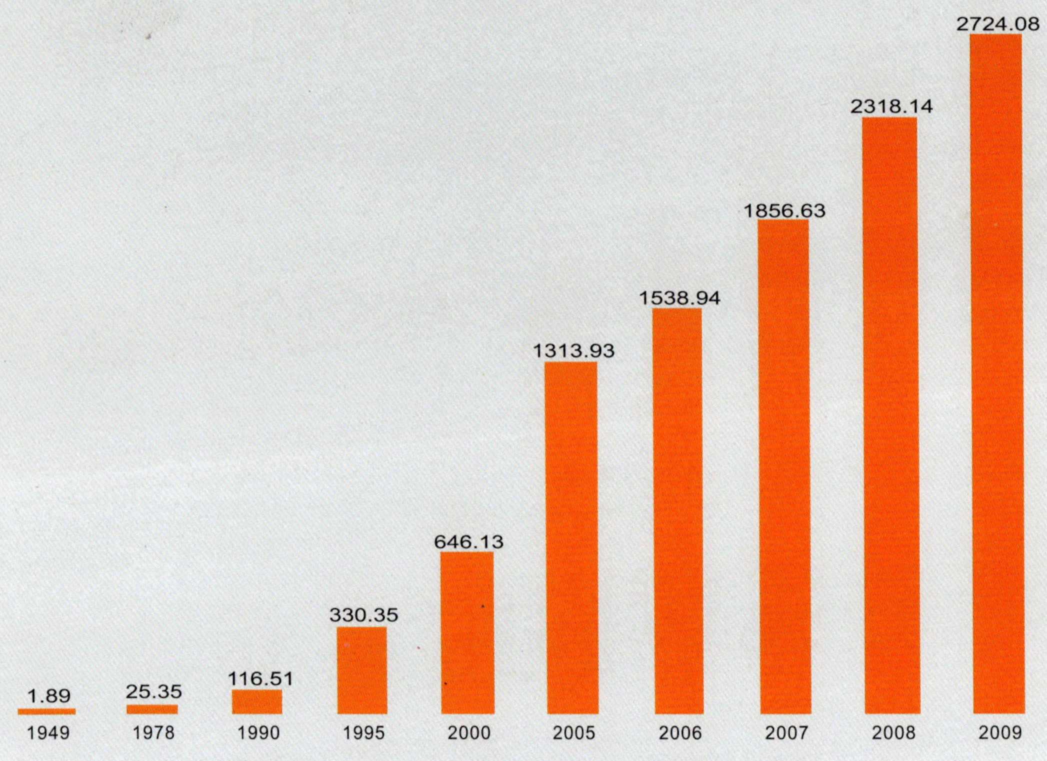

生产总值指数（以上年为100）

Indices of Gross Domestic Product(preceding year=100)

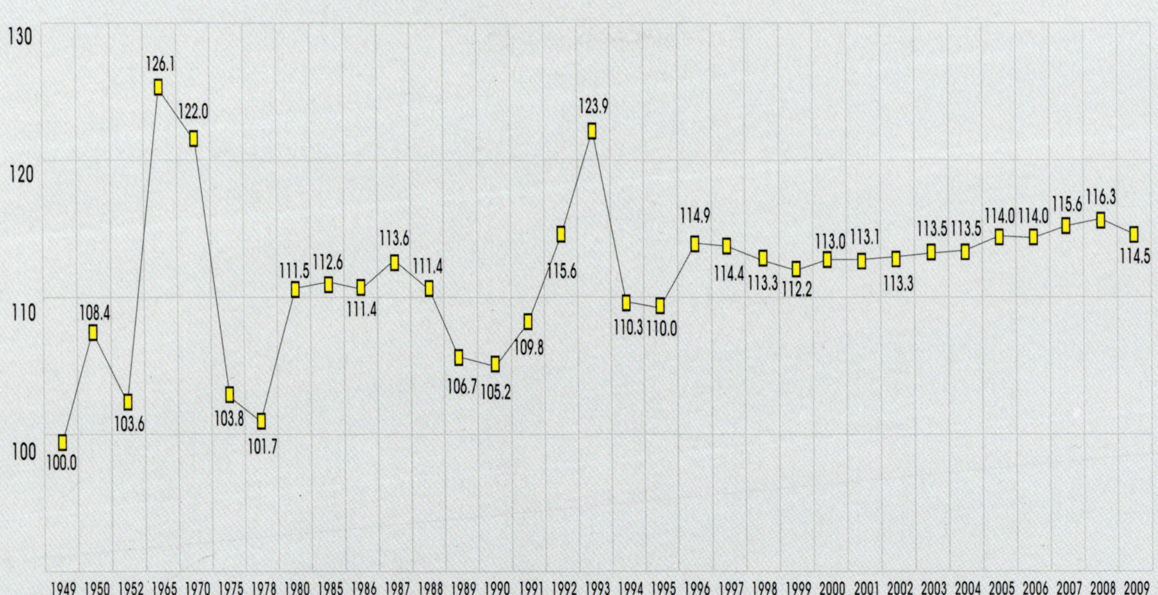

生产总值构成(%)

Composition of Gross Domestic Product(%)

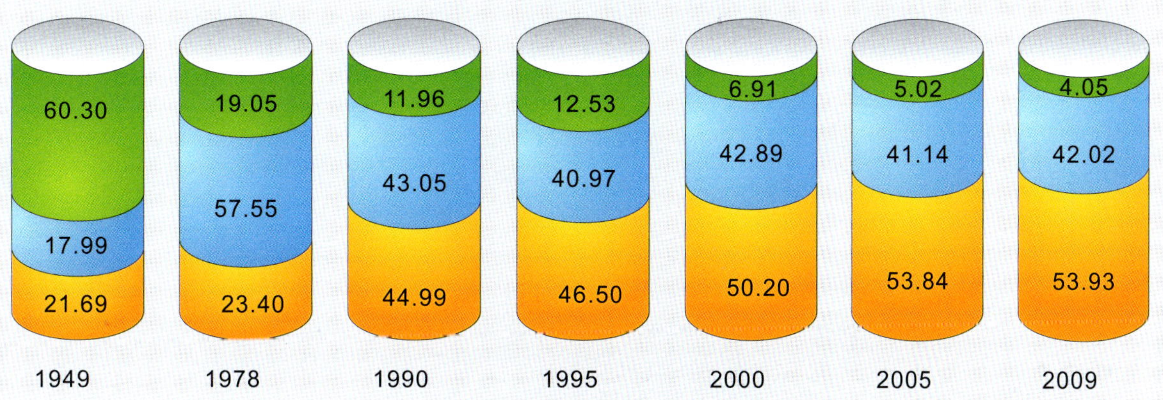

人均GDP(元/人)

Per Capita GDP (yuan/person)

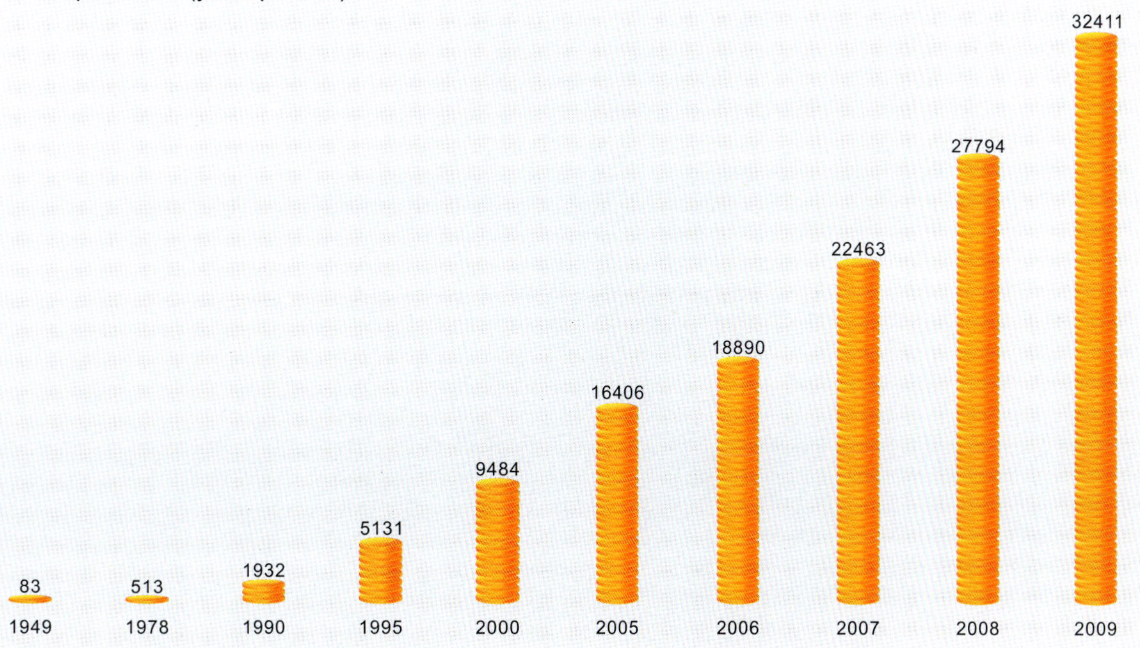

年末人口（万人）

The Resident Population of The year-end (10000 persons)

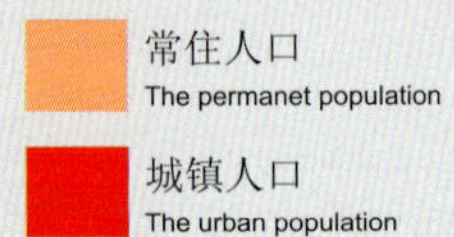

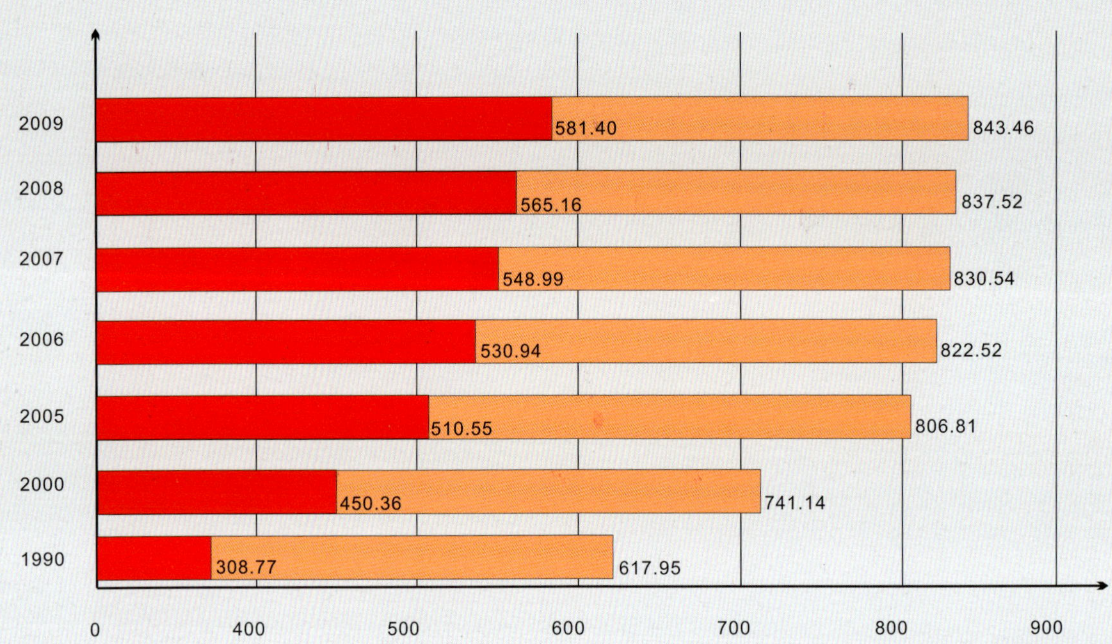

社会从业人员（万人）

Social Workers(10000 persons)

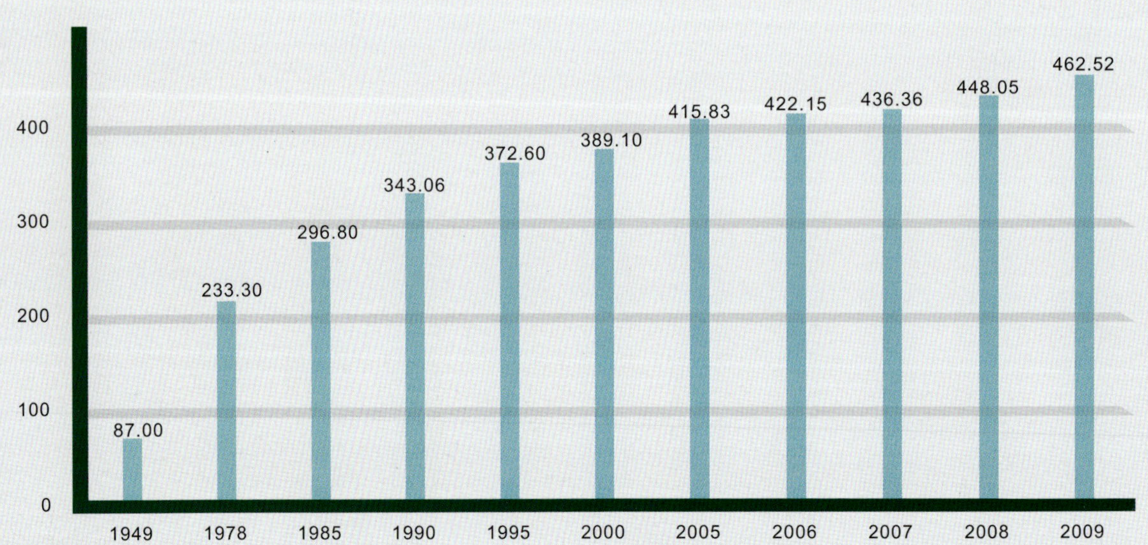

固定资产投资（亿元）

Investment In Fixed Assets(100 million yuan)

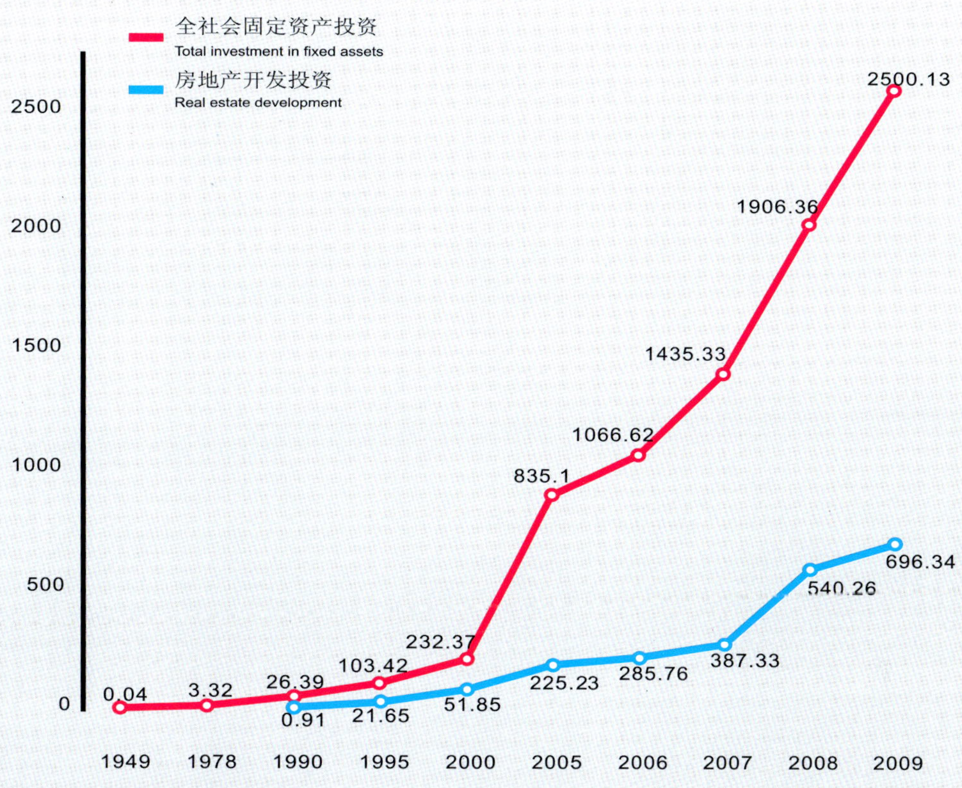

新增固定资产及住宅竣工面积

Newly Increased Fixed Assets and Residential Area of Completion

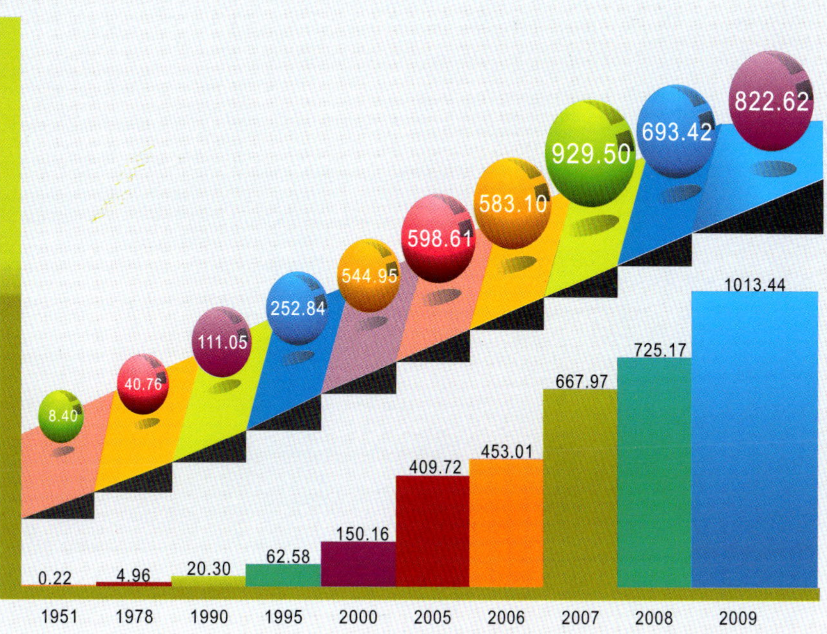

农林牧渔业总产值(亿元）
Output Value of Agricultural,Forestry,Animal Husbandry and Fishery (100 million yuan)

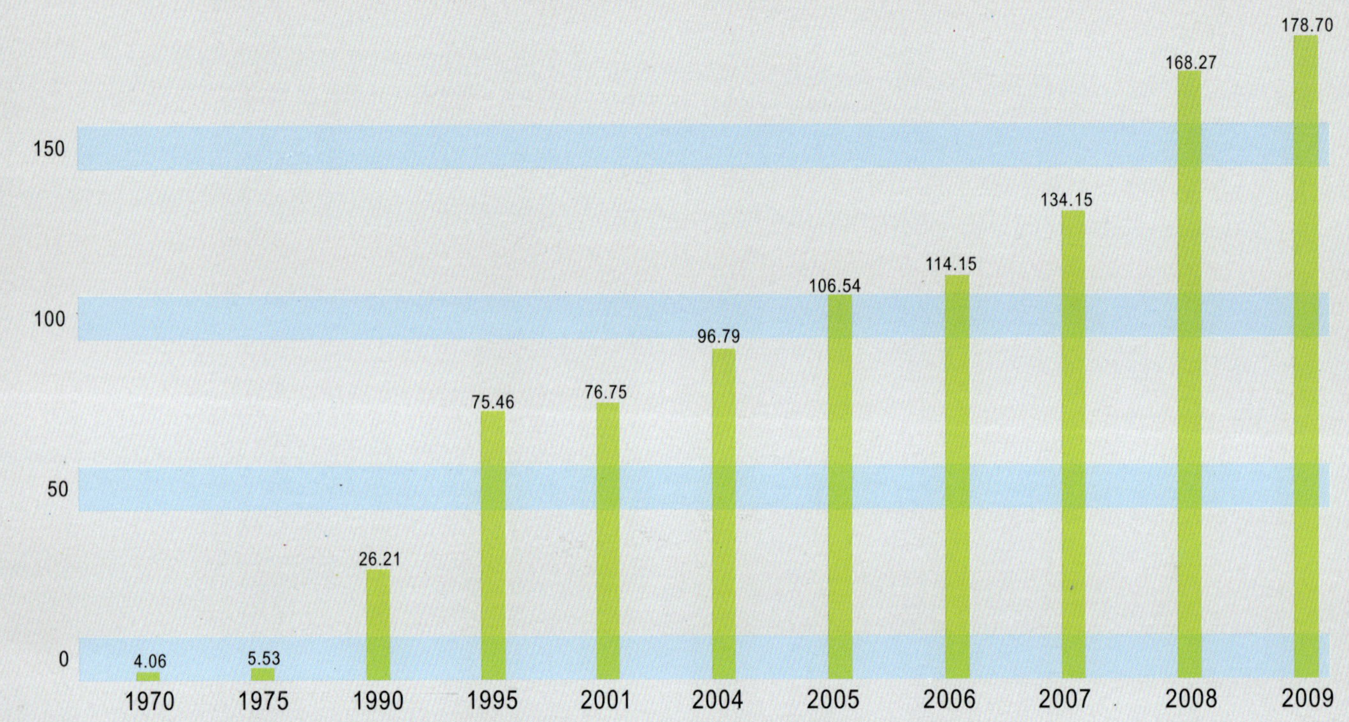

主要农产品产量（万吨）
Output of Major Agricultural Products (10000 tons)

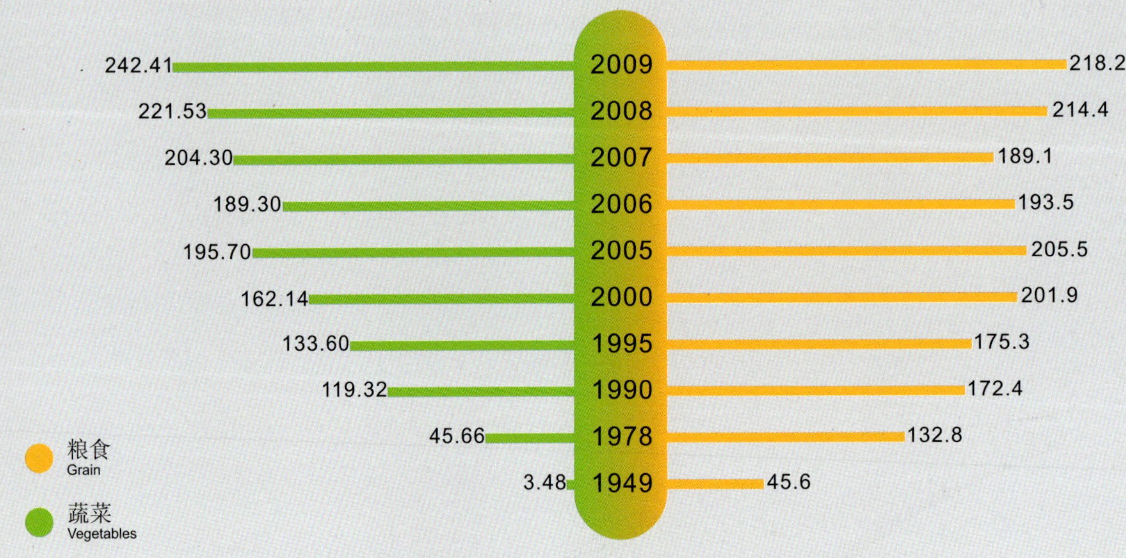

工业总产值（亿元）

Gross Industrial Output Valle (100 million yuan)

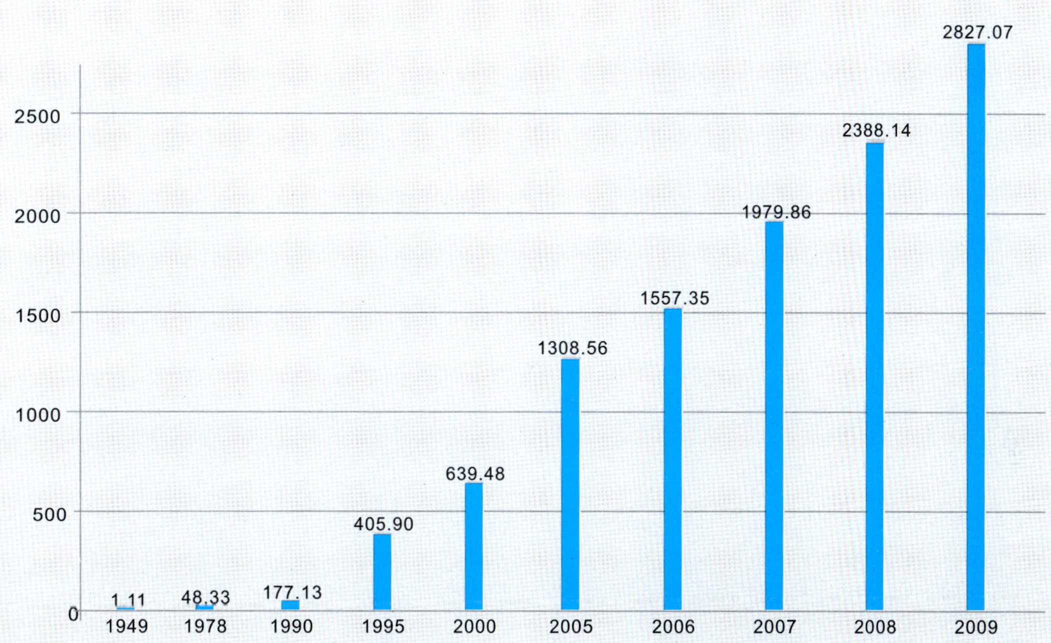

主要工业产品产量

Output of Major Industriat Products

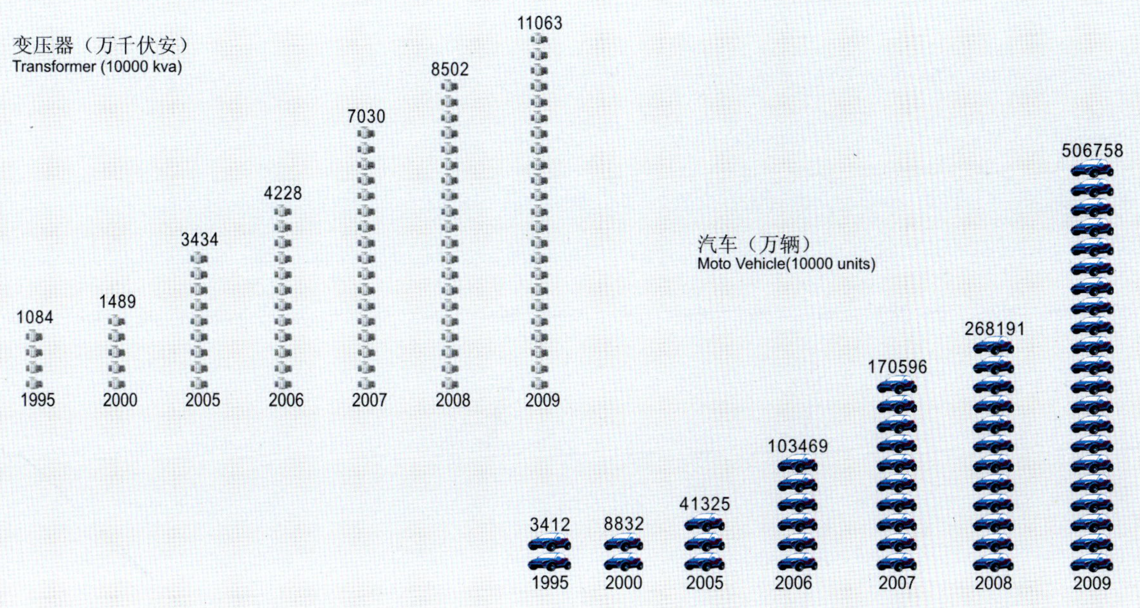

交通
Traffic

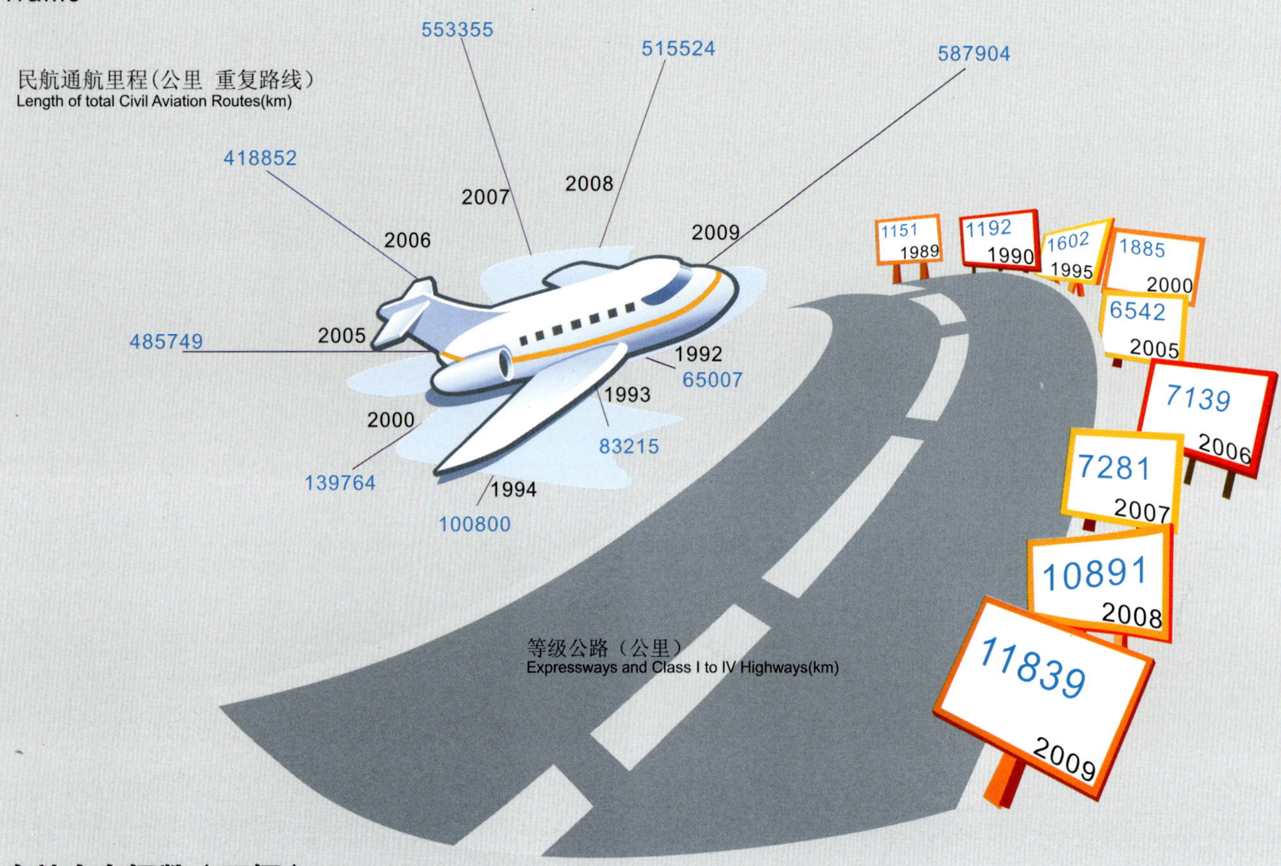

全社会车辆数（万辆）
Possession of Civil Vehicles (10000 units)

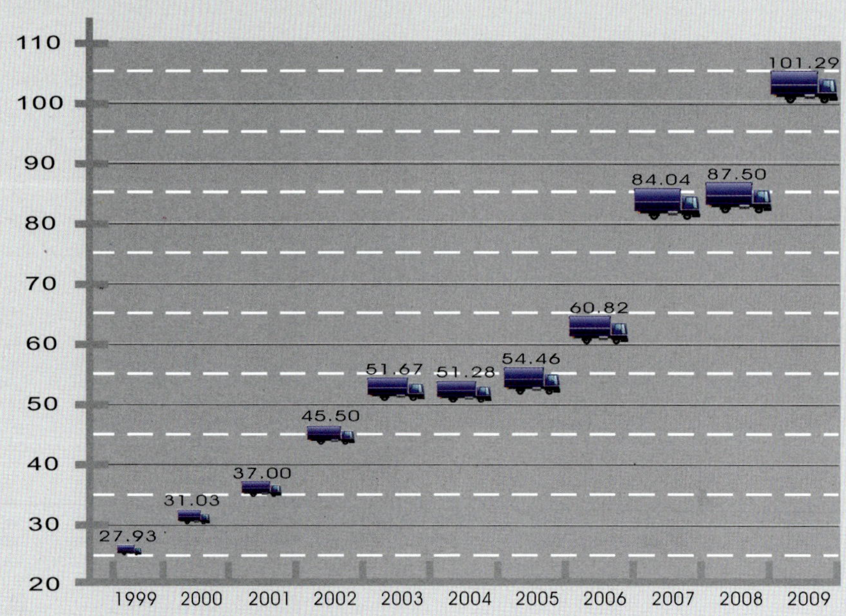

社会消费品零售总额(亿元)

Total Retail Sales of Consumer Goods (100 million yuan)

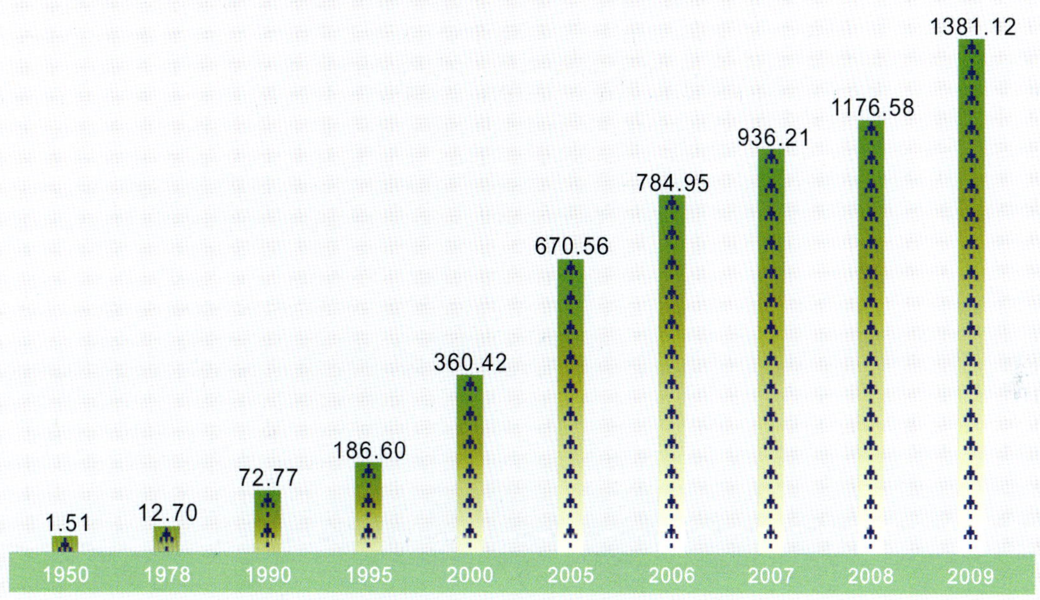

经营网点(个)

Business Network (unit)

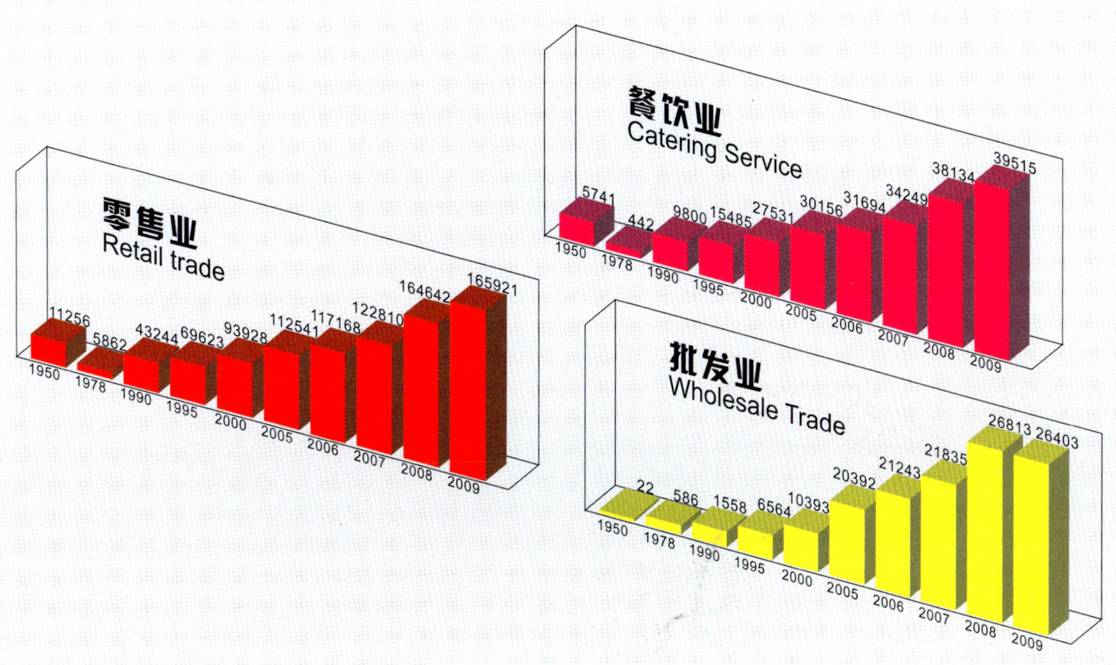

外商实际直接投资额（亿美元）
Value of Foreign Direct Investment (USD 100 million)

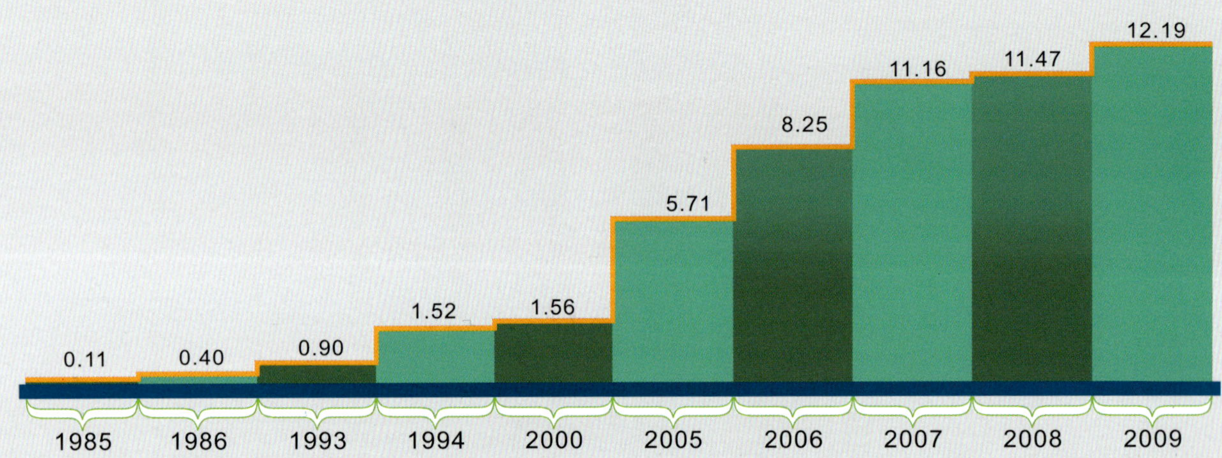

进出口总额（亿美元）
Total Value of Imports and Exports (USD 100 million)

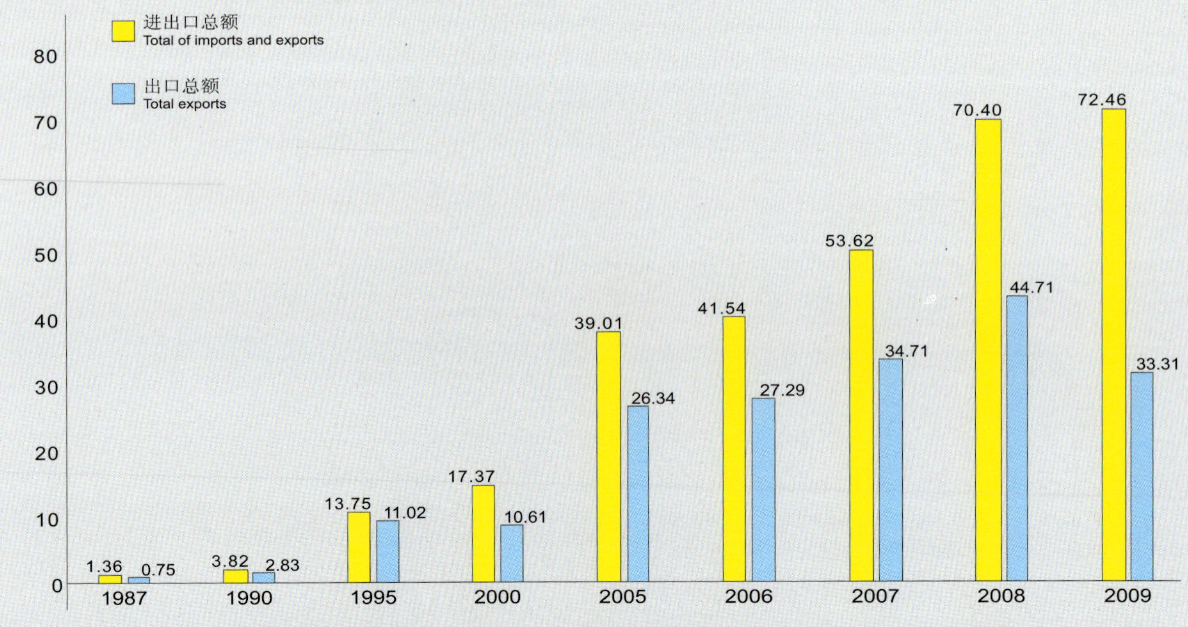

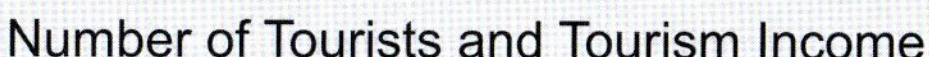

旅游人数及收入

Number of Tourists and Tourism Income

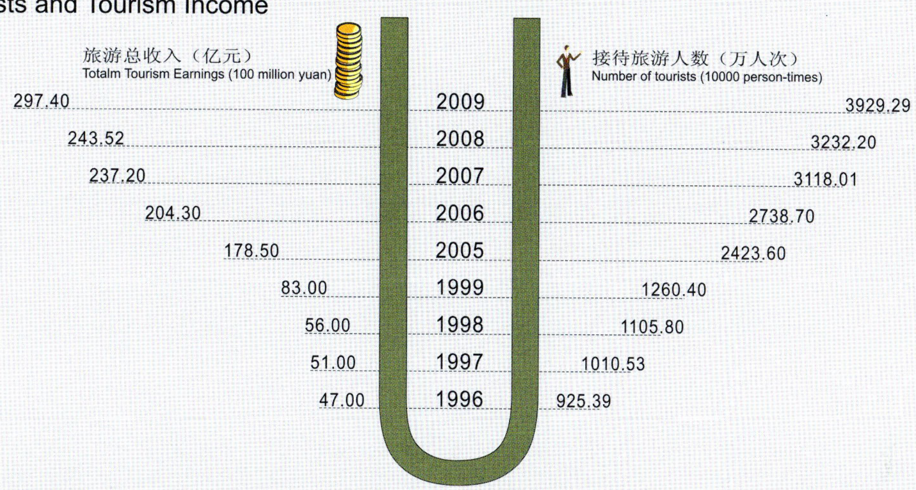

国际旅游人数及收入

Number of International Tourists and Tourism Income

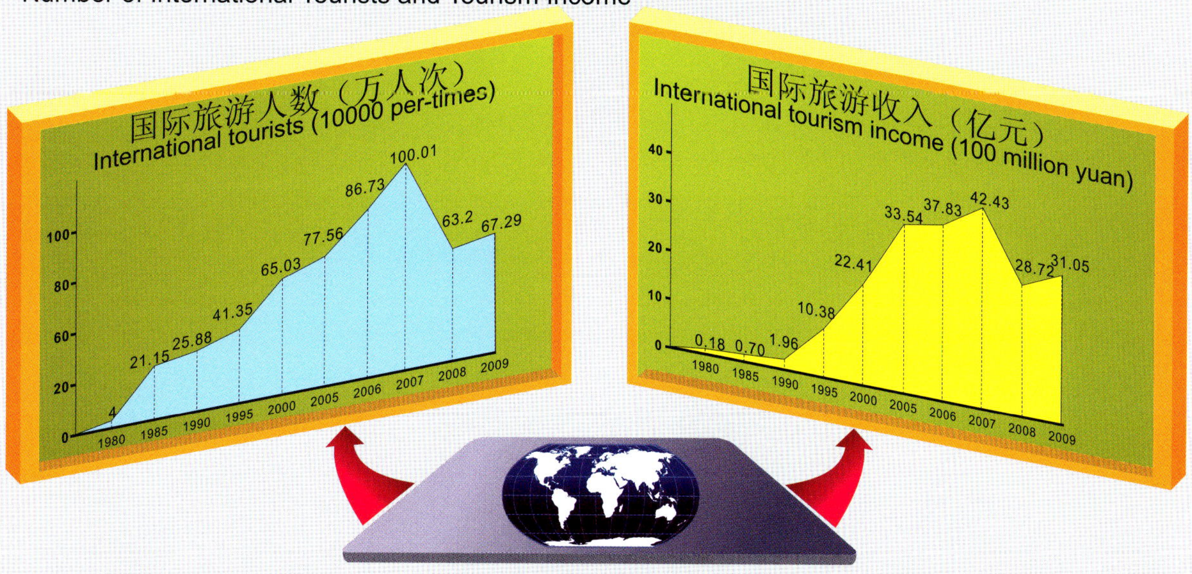

财政收支（亿元）

Government Revenue and Expenditure (100 million yuan)

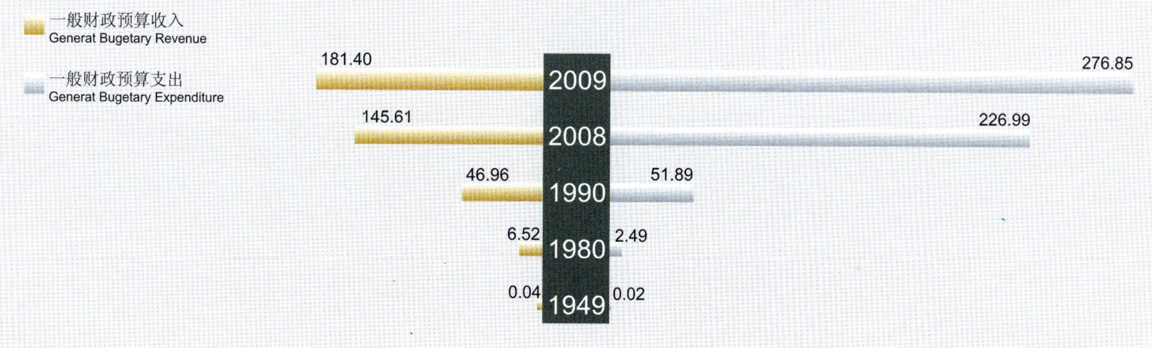

金融机构人民币存贷款余额（亿元）

Balance of Deposit and loans in Dmestic Funded Financial Institutions(100 million yuan)

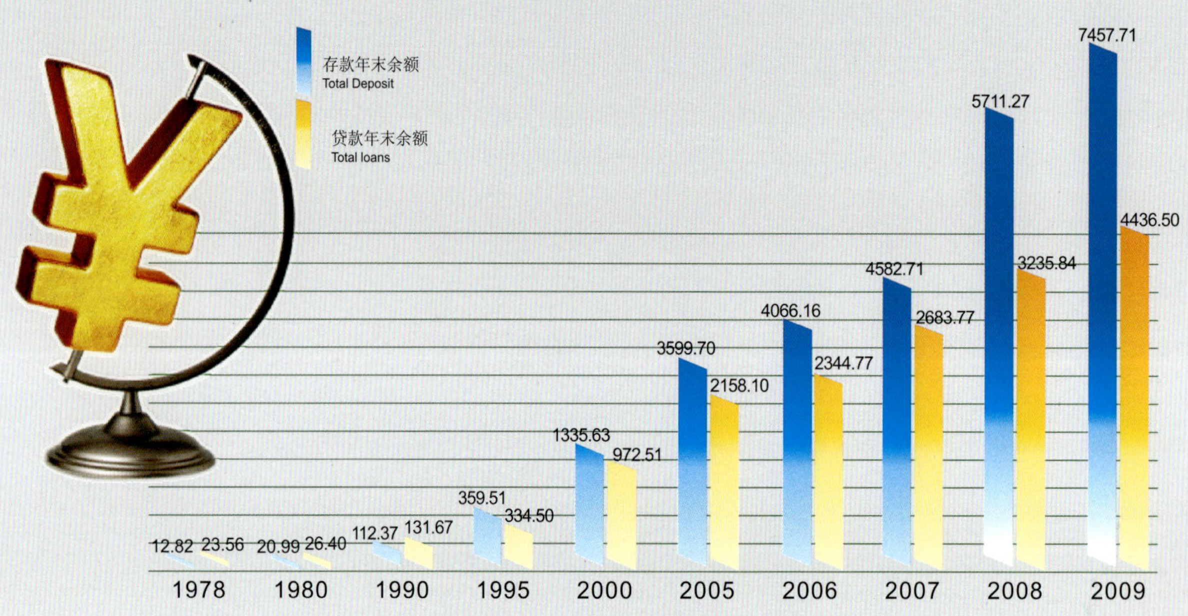

建成区面积（平方公里）

Area of the Regions Constructed(sq.km)

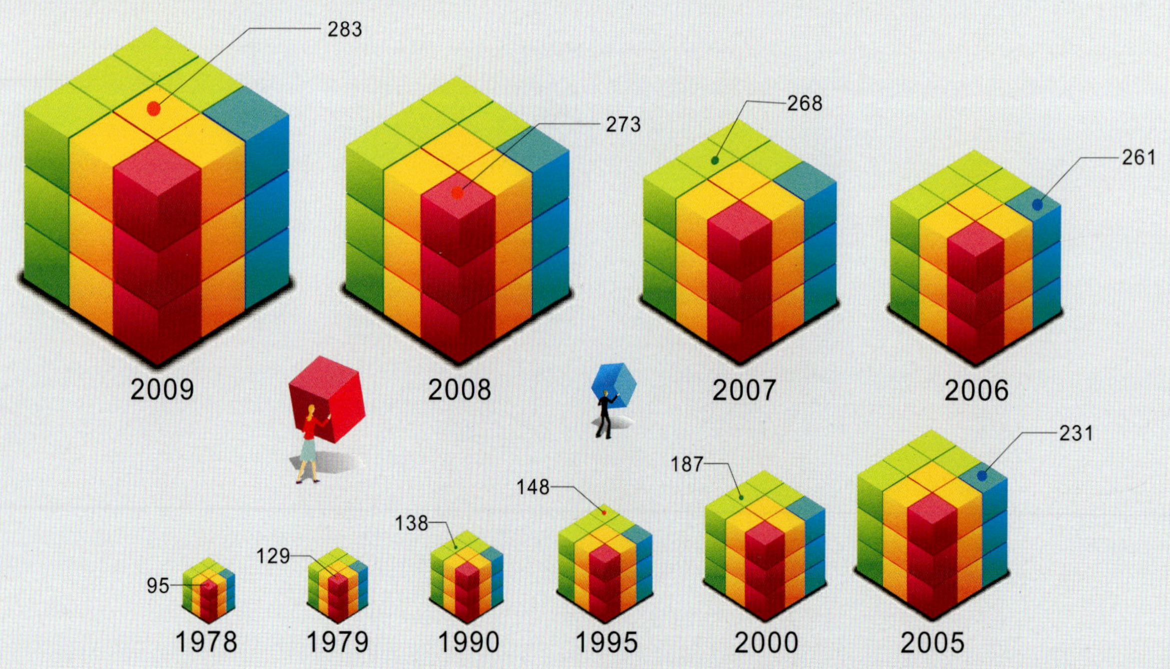

城市公共交通营运车辆（辆）

Operating Vehicles(unit)

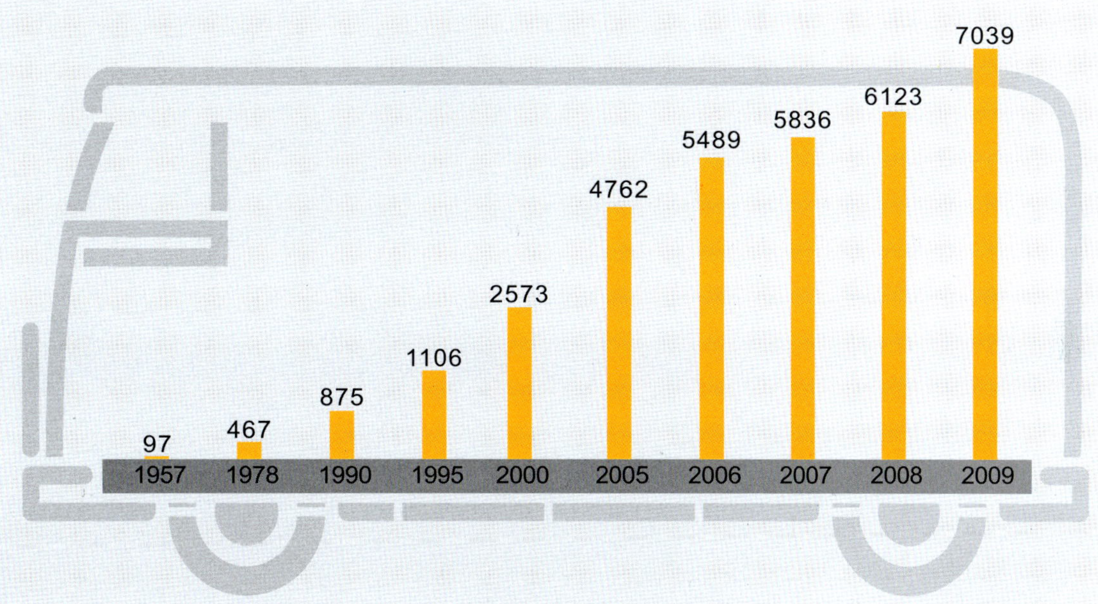

天然气供气总量（万立方米）

Total of Gas Supply (10000 cu.m)

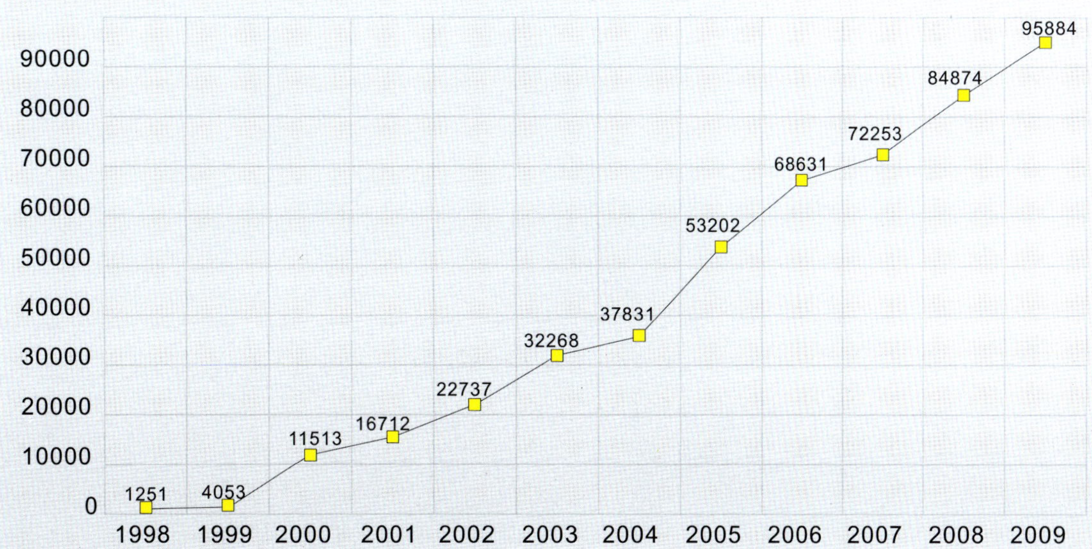

园林绿地总面积(公顷)
Total Area of Parks,Gardens and Green Area (hectare)

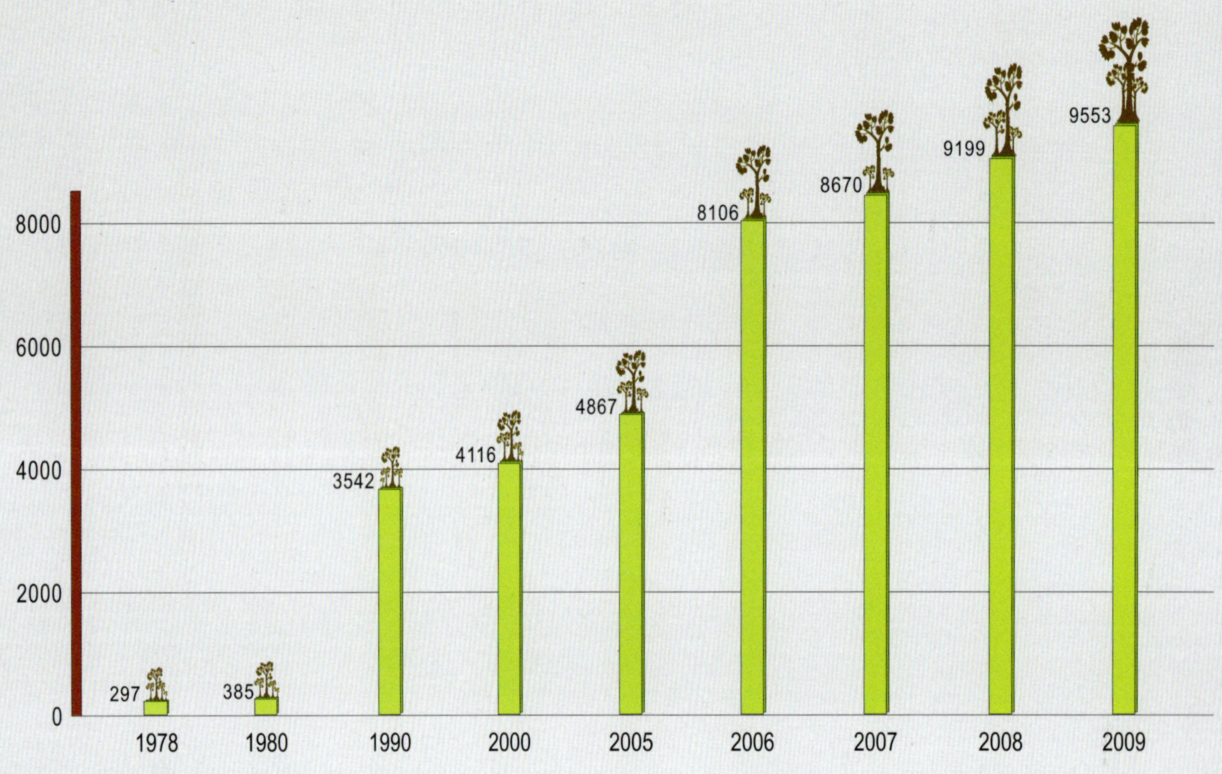

普通教育在校学生 (万人)
Total Enrollments (10000 persons)

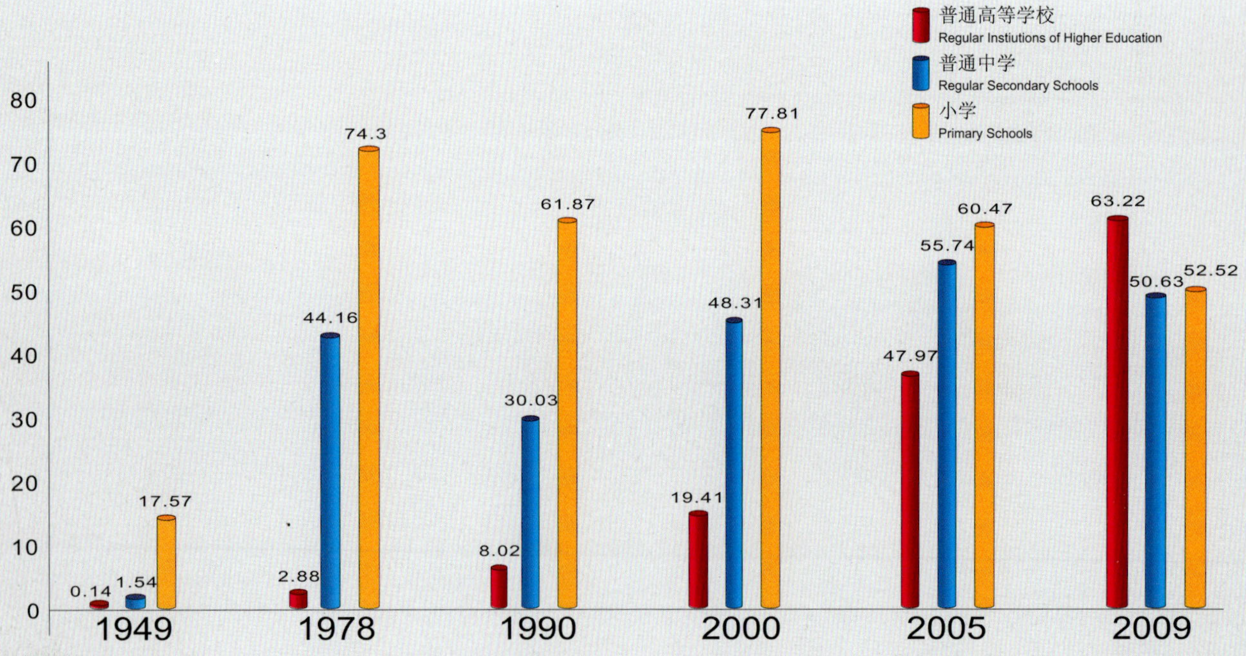

专任教师（万人）

Number of Full-time Teachers (10000 persons)

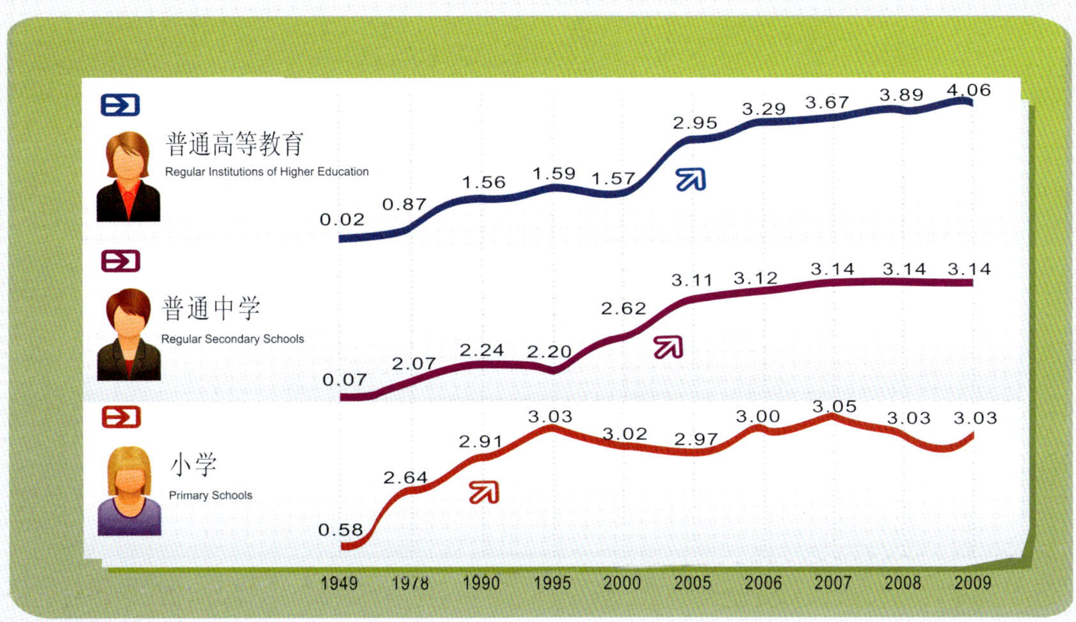

各种价格指数（以上年价格为100）

Various Price Indices (Price of Preceding year=100)

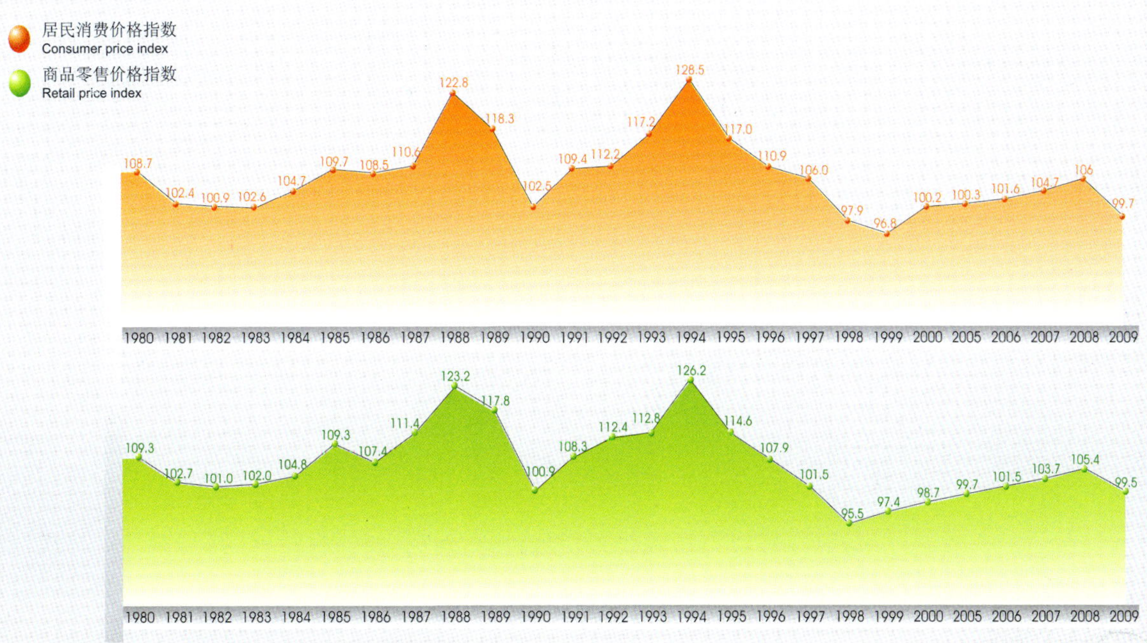

西安统计年鉴

2010

XI'AN STATISTICAL YEARBOOK

目　录

西安市2009年国民经济和社会发展统计公报……1

一、综　　合

1-1　行政区划（2009年）……1
1-2　土地面积和常住人口密度（2009年）……2
1-3　自然状况和资源（2009年）……3
1-4　气象情况（2009年）……3
1-5　国有土地使用权出让、划拨情况……4
1-6　各部门机构数……5
1-7　平均每天主要社会经济活动……8
1-8　国民经济和社会发展总量与速度指标……10
1-9　国民经济和社会发展结构指标……20
1-10　国民经济和社会发展比例和效益指标……24
主要统计指标解释……30

二、国民经济核算

2-1　主要年份生产总值……37
2-2　主要年份生产总值指数（上年=100）……38
2-3　主要年份生产总值指数（1952=100）……39
2-4　主要年份生产总值构成……40
2-5　全市分区县生产总值（2009年）……41
2-6　主要年份分行业增加值……42
2-7　主要年份分行业增加值指数（上年=100）……42
2-8　主要年份支出法生产总值……43
2-9　主要年份支出法生产总值指数（上年=100）……43
2-10　按支出法计算的生产总值及指数（2009年）……44
2-11　分行业资本形成总额（2009年）……44
2-12　最终消费（2009年）……45
2-13　居民总消费水平（2009年）……46
2-14　非公有制经济增加值（2009年）……46
主要统计指标解释……47

三、人口、从业人员与职工工资

3-1 主要年份人口、人口密度和人口发展情况……55
3-2 主要年份人口变动情况……56
3-3 分区县人口和户数（2009年）……57
3-4 分区县人口变动情况（2009年）……58
3-5 主要年份常住人口……58
3-6 城乡劳动力资源配置情况（2009年）……59
3-7 主要年份社会从业人数……60
3-8 分行业从业人数（2009年）……62
3-9 全部单位从业人员情况（2009年）……64
3-10 国有单位从业人员情况（2009年）……66
3-11 城镇集体单位从业人员情况（2009年）……68
3-12 其他经济类型单位从业人员情况（2009年）……70
3-13 全部单位从业人员劳动报酬（2009年）……72
3-14 国有单位从业人员劳动报酬（2009年）……73
3-15 城镇集体单位从业人员劳动报酬（2009年）……74
3-16 其他经济类型单位从业人员劳动报酬（2009年）……75
主要统计指标解释……76

四、固定资产投资

4-1 主要年份按城乡分全社会固定资产投资……81
4-2 主要年份按经济类型分全社会固定资产投资……82
4-3 主要年份按产业分全市固定资产投资……83
4-4 全市固定资产投资（2009年）……84
4-5 按行业分全市固定资产投资（2009年）……87
4-6 主要年份按资金来源及建设性质分全市固定资产投资……88
4-7 主要年份国有经济单位固定资产投资……90
4-8 农村集体固定资产投资（2009年）……92
4-9 主要年份农村集体固定资产投资……93
4-10 主要年份市属固定资产投资……96
4-11 市属固定资产投资（2009年）……98
4-12 按行业分市属固定资产投资（2009年）……100
4-13 按资金来源及建设性质分市属固定资产投资（2009年）……101
4-14 按登记注册类型及隶属关系分市区固定资产投资（2009年）……102
4-15 按行业分市区固定资产投资（2009年）……103
4-16 按资金来源及建设性质分市区固定资产投资（2009年）……104

4-17　全市固定资产投资资金来源（2009年）……105
4-18　市属固定资产投资资金来源（2009年）……105
4-19　全市固定资产投资效果（2009年）……106
4-20　市属固定资产投资效果（2009年）……106
4-21　分区县全社会固定资产投资额（2009年）……107
4-22　全市分行业房屋建筑面积（2009年）……108
4-23　市属分行业房屋建筑面积（2009年）……110
4-24　主要年份全市新增固定资产及房屋竣工面积……112
4-25　主要年份市属新增固定资产及房屋竣工面积……113
4-26　全市分行业施工项目（2009年）……114
4-27　市属分行业施工项目（2009年）……116
4-28　主要年份房地产开发投资主要指标……118
4-29　房地产开发投资主要指标（2009年）……120
4-30　商品房销售情况（2009年）……121
4-31　房地产开发投资资金来源（2009年）……122
4-32　房地产开发经营情况（2009年）……123
主要统计指标解释……124

五、财　政

5-1　财政收入（2009年）……129
5-2　财政支出（2009年）……130
5-3　分区县地方财政收入（2009年）……131
5-4　分区县地方财政支出（2009年）……134
主要统计指标解释……138

六、物价指数

6-1　主要年份各种价格指数……145
6-2　居民消费价格指数（2009年）……146
6-3　商品零售价格指数（2009年）……148
6-4　主要年份工业产品出厂价格指数……150
6-5　主要年份主要原材料、燃料、动力购进价格指数……152
6-6　土地交易价格指数（2009年）……153
6-7　房屋销售价格指数（2009年）……153
6-8　房屋租赁价格指数（2009年）……154
6-9　主要年份固定资产投资价格指数……154

6-10 主要年份建筑安装工程价格指数……154
主要统计指标解释……154

七、人民生活

7-1 主要年份城乡居民家庭人均收入及恩格尔系数……159
7-2 主要年份城乡居民人民币储蓄存款……160
7-3 主要年份城镇居民家庭基本情况……161
7-4 城镇居民家庭基本情况表（2009年）……164
7-5 城镇居民家庭年人均收入情况（2009年）……165
7-6 城镇居民家庭年人均支出情况（2009年）……166
7-7 城镇居民家庭年人均消费性支出情况（2009年）……167
7-8 主要年份城镇居民家庭年人均购买主要商品数量……170
7-9 主要年份城镇居民家庭平均每百户年末拥有主要耐用消费品数量……172
7-10 城镇居民家庭居住情况（2009年）……174
7-11 主要年份农民家庭基本情况……176
7-12 农村居民家庭基本情况……178
7-13 农村居民家庭平均每人总收入和纯收入（2009年）……180
7-14 农村居民家庭平均每人全年总支出（2009年）……180
7-15 农村居民家庭平均每人生活消费支出（2009年）……182
7-16 农村居民家庭人均生产情况……182
7-17 农村居民家庭人均出售产品情况……184
7-18 农村居民家庭人均粮食收支情况……184
7-19 农村居民家庭平均每人购买商品……186
7-20 农村居民家庭人均主要食品消费量……186
7-21 农村居民家庭每百户耐用消费品年末拥有量……188
7-22 农村居民家庭人均住房情况……188
主要统计指标解释……190

八、城市公用事业

8-1 城市供水……195
8-2 城市售电……195
8-3 城市供燃气……196
8-4 城市供热……196
8-5 城市公共交通……197
8-6 市政设施……197

8-7 城市设施水平……198
8-8 城市规模及用地情况……198
8-9 城市园林绿化……199
8-10 城市环境卫生……199
主要统计指标解释……200

九、环境保护

9-1 城市环境保护……205
9-2 主要年份工业“三废”排放及处理利用情况……206
9-3 工业污染排放及处理利用情况（2009年）……208
9-4 城市污水处理情况（2009年）……209
9-5 危险废物集中处置情况（2009年）……210
9-6 生活及其他污染情况（2009年）……210
9-7 工业污染治理项目建设情况（2009年）……211
主要统计指标解释……212

十、农　业

10-1 农村基层组织、乡村户数、人口及劳动力情况……217
10-2 各区县农村基层组织、乡村户数及人口（2009年）……218
10-3 各区县从业人员数（2009年）……218
10-4 主要年份耕地面积……219
10-5 各区县耕地面积（2009年）……220
10-6 主要年份农业机械拥有量（年末数）……222
10-7 主要年份农业机械、化肥、水利、水电情况……224
10-8 主要年份农林牧渔及服务业总产值及指数……226
10-9 各区县农林牧渔及服务业总产值（2009年）……227
10-10 各区县现价农林牧渔及服务业总产值指数及构成（2009年）……228
10-11 主要年份农林牧渔及服务业增加值……229
10-12 分区县农林牧渔及服务业增加值（2009年）……230
10-13 分区县农林牧渔及服务业增加值指数（2009年）……230
10-14 主要年份农作物播种面积……231
10-15 各区县主要农作物播种面积（2009年）……231
10-16 主要年份农作物产品产量……232
10-17 各区县主要农作物产品产量（2009年）……233
10-18 主要年份农作物单位面积产量……234

10-19 各区县主要农作物单位面积产量（2009年）……234
10-20 林业生产情况……235
10-21 各区县林业生产情况（2009年）……236
10-22 主要年份果业生产情况……236
10-23 各区县果业生产情况（2009年）……237
10-24 主要年份畜牧业生产情况……237
10-25 各区县畜牧业生产情况（2009年）……238
10-26 主要年份畜产品和水产品产量……239
10-27 各区县主要畜产品和水产品产量（2009年）……241
10-28 主要年份农产品人均占有量……242
10-29 主要年份农村经济效益主要指标……243
主要统计指标解释……244

十一、工业和能源

11-1 主要年份全部工业总产值……249
11-2 分区县规模以上工业总产值（2009年）……251
11-3 规模以上工业企业主要产品产量……253
11-4 主要年份规模以上工业企业主要经济指标……257
11-5 规模以上工业企业主要经济指标（2009年）……258
11-6 规模以上国有及国有控股工业企业主要经济指标（2009年）……270
11-7 规模以上股份制工业企业主要经济指标（2009年）……282
11-8 规模以上三资工业企业主要经济指标（2009年）……294
11-9 规模以上大中型工业企业主要经济指标（2009年）……306
11-10 规模以上工业高技术产业企业主要经济指标（2009年）……318
11-11 分区县规模以上工业企业主要经济指标（2009年）……324
11-12 规模以上工业企业能源购进、消费及库存（2009年）……328
11-13 主要能源按工业行业分组消费量（2009年）……330
11-14 规模以上工业分行业综合能源消费量（2009年）……332
主要统计指标解释……333

十二、建筑业

12-1 全市建筑施工企业基本情况（2009年）……343
12-2 施工总承包和专业承包建筑业企业生产情况（2009年）……344
12-3 施工总承包和专业承包建筑业企业财务状况（2009年）……348
12-4 劳务分包建筑业企业基本情况（2009年）……350

12-5 分区县建筑业主要经济指标（2009年）……351
主要统计指标解释……352

十三、运输和邮电

13-1 各种交通线路里程和桥梁数……357
13-2 全社会车辆数……358
13-3 交通运输量及运输周转量……359
13-4 邮政业务及服务网点……360
13-5 电信业务情况……360
主要统计指标解释……361

十四、国内贸易

14-1 主要年份社会消费品零售总额……367
14-2 社会消费品零售总额（2009年）……368
14-3 各区县社会消费品零售总额（2009年）……368
14-4 主要年份批发零售贸易业、餐饮业网点和人员……369
14-5 批发贸易业机构、网点、人员（2009年）……370
14-6 零售贸易业机构、网点、人员（2009年）……372
14-7 餐饮业机构、网点、人员（2009年）……374
14-8 限额以上批发零售贸易企业财务状况（2009年）……376
14-9 限额以上住宿和餐饮业企业主要财务状况（2009年）……388
14-10 限额以上批发和零售业商品购进、销售和库存总额（2009年）……396
14-11 限额以上住宿和餐饮业经营情况（2009年）……400
14-12 限额以上批发和零售业主要商品分类销售额（2009年）……402
14-13 亿元以上商品交易市场成交情况（2009年）……403
14-14 批发和零售业连锁经营情况（2009）……404
14-15 住宿和餐饮业连锁经营情况（2009）……405
14-16 成品油批发企业（单位）能源购进、销售与库存（2009）……406
14-17 成品油零售企业（单位）能源商品销售与库存（2009）……406
主要统计指标解释……407

十五、对外经济贸易和旅游

15-1 主要年份外资、外贸和国际旅游基本情况……413
15-2 主要年份利用外资情况……415

15-3 外国和港澳台地区在西安直接投资（2009年）……416
15-4 主要年份进出口总额……417
15-5 外贸商品进出口总额分国别和地区（2009年）……418
15-6 主要商品分大类出口金额……419
15-7 主要商品分大类进口金额……422
15-8 主要年份旅游人数及收入……423
15-9 主要年份国际旅游收入……424
15-10 主要涉外星级宾馆接待海外旅游者情况……425
主要统计指标解释……426

十六、金融和保险

16-1 西安银行系统机构、人员数……431
16-2 金融机构（含外资）本外币存贷款年末余额（2009年）……432
16-3 金融机构（不含外资）本外币存贷款年末余额（2009年）……433
16-4 金融机构（含外资）人民币存贷款年末余额（2009年）……434
16-5 金融机构（不含外资）人民币存贷款年末余额（2009年）……435
16-6 金融机构现金收入、支出（2009年）……436
16-7 保险业务情况……437
16-8 西安证券期货系统机构、人员数……438
16-9 证券期货市场基本情况……439
主要统计指标解释……440

十七、教育和科技

17-1 主要年份各类普通教育基本情况……445
17-2 各级普通教育基本情况（2009年）……446
17-3 主要年份普通高等教育基本情况……447
17-4 主要年份研究生情况……447
17-5 普通高等学校分学校研究生（2009年）……448
17-6 全市普通高等学校分学校情况（2009年）……449
17-7 主要年份博士后、博士、硕士流动站情况……451
17-8 主要年份普通中等专业学校基本情况……452
17-9 中等技术（中等专业）学校分学校基本情况（2009年）……453
17-10 主要年份普通中学基本情况……454
17-11 各区县普通中学基本情况（2009年）……454
17-12 主要年份职业中学基本情况……455

17-13 各区县职业中学基本情况（2009年）…………455
17-14 主要年份小学基本情况…………456
17-15 各区县小学基本情况（2009年）…………456
17-16 主要年份幼儿园基本情况…………457
17-17 主要年份特殊教育学校基本情况…………457
17-18 主要年份小学、初中升学率…………458
17-19 主要年份小学学龄儿童入学率…………459
17-20 主要年份平均每万人口在校学生数和大中小学生构成…………460
17-21 成人教育情况（2009年）…………461
主要统计指标解释…………463

十八、文化、体育、卫生、社会福利和其他

18-1 文化事业机构和人数（2009年）…………471
18-2 文化事业发展情况…………472
18-3 群众艺术馆、文化馆（站）活动情况…………472
18-4 文物保护业基本情况（2009年）…………473
18-5 广播电台及节目制作情况…………473
18-6 电视台及节目制作情况…………474
18-7 体育事业基本情况（市属）（2009年）…………474
18-8 少年儿童分项业余体校情况（市属）（2009年）…………475
18-9 卫生机构、床位及人员数（2009年）…………476
18-10 各区县卫生机构、床位及人员数（2009年）…………480
18-11 卫生机构各类人员数…………481
18-12 医院、卫生院诊疗人次及诊疗情况（2009年）…………482
18-13 医院、卫生院床位及病人治疗情况（2009年）…………484
18-14 县（区）村卫生室基本情况（2009年）…………486
18-15 社会福利事业单位基本情况（2009年）…………488
18-16 社会福利事业单位机构、人员数…………488
18-17 各区县优抚对象人员情况（2009年）…………489
18-18 计划生育和婚姻情况（2009年）…………490
18-19 律师、公证及调解基本情况…………491
18-20 共青团组织情况…………492
18-21 妇联组织状况…………492
18-22 妇联工作情况…………493
18-23 交通事故情况…………494
18-24 火灾情况…………494

18-25 安全生产情况……495
18-26 刑 事 案 件 情 况……496
18-27 治 安 案 件 情 况……496
18-28 分区县刑事、治安案件情况（2009年）……497
18-29 西安市人民检察院案件受理情况……498
18-30 西安市中级人民法院案件基本情况（2009年）……499
主要统计指标解释……502

十九、企业调查

19-1 企业景气指数（2009年）……509
19-2 企业家信心指数（2009年）……510
主要统计指标解释……511

CONTENTS

Statistic Communiqu on the 2009 National Economy and Social Development of the City of Xi'an 1

CHAPTER 1 GENERAL SURVEY

1-1 Administrative Division (2009) 1
1-2 Statistics on Land Area and Density of Permanent Population (2009) 2
1-3 Nature Conditions and Resources (2009) 3
1-4 Climate Condition (2009) 3
1-5 Basic Statistics on Lease and Administrative Allocation of Use Right of State-Owned Land 4
1-6 Grassroots Units in Various Sectors 5
1-7 Selected Indicators on Average Daily Social and Economic Activities 8
1-8 Principal Aggregate Indicators on National Economic and Social Development and Their Related Indices and Growth Rates 10
1-9 Structural Indicators on National Economic and Social Development 20
1-10 Indicators on Proportions and Efficiency in National Economic 24
Explanatory Notes on Main Statistical Indicators 30

CHAPTER 2 NATIONAL ACCOUNTS

2-1 Gross Domestic Product In Representative Years 37
2-2 Indices of Gross Domestic Product in Representative Years(preceding year = 100) 38
2-3 Indices of Gross Domestic Product in Representative Years(1952=100) 39
2-4 Composition of Gross Domestic Product in Respective Years 40
2-5 Gross Domestic Product by Region (2009) 41
2-6 Value-added by Ssctor in Respective Years 42
2-7 Indices of Value -addded by Sector In Representative Years(preceding year=100) 42
2-8 Gross Domestic Product by Expenditure Approach in Respective Years 43
2-9 Indices of Gross Domestic Product by Expenditure Approach in Years(preceding year = 100) 43
2-10 Gross Domestic Product and Indices by Expenditure Approach (2009) 44
2-11 Gross Capital Formation by Sector (2009) 44
2-12 Final Consumption Expenditures (2009) 45
2-13 Consumption of Residents (2009) 46
2-14 The Added Value of Non-public-owned Economic (2009) 46

Explanatory Notes on Main Statistical Indicator……47

CHAPTER 3 POPULATION ,EMPLOYMENT AND WAGES

3–1 Population, Population Density and Population Development in represontative……55
3–2 Population Changes in Representative Years……56
3–3 Population and Households by Region (2009) ……57
3–4 Population Changes by Region (2009) ……58
3–5 Permanent population in Representtative Years……58
3–6 Deployment of Urban and Rural Labor Resources (2009) ……59
3–7 Number of Social Laborers in Representative Years……60
3–8 Number of Employed Persons by Sector (2009) ……62
3–9 Basic Facts on All Employed Persons (2009) ……64
3–10 Basic Facts on Persons Employed by State–owned Units (2009) ……66
3–11 Basic Facts on Persons Employed by Urban Collective–owned Units (2009) ……68
3–12 Basic Facts on Persons Employed by Other Units (2009) ……70
3–13 Remuneration of All Employed Persons (2009) ……72
3–14 Remuneration of Persons Employed by State–owned Units (2009) ……73
3–15 Remuneration of Persons Employed by Urban Collective–owned Units in Towns and Cities (2009) ……74
3–16 Remuneration of Persons Employed by other Units (2009) ……75
Explanatory Notes on Main Statistical Indicator……76

CHAPTER 4 INVESTMENT IN FIXED ASSETS

4–1 Total Investment in Fixed Assets in the Whole Country by Rural and Urban Areas in Representative Years……81
4–2 Total Investment in Fixed Assets in the Whole Country by Registion Status in Representative Years……82
4–3 Total Investment in Fixed Assets in the Whole City by Three Strata of Industry in Representative Years……83
4–4 Total Investment in Fixed Assets in the Whole City (2009) ……84
4–5 Total Investment in Fixed Assets in the Whole City by Sector (2009) ……87
4–6 Total Investment in Fixed Assets in the Whole City by Sources of Funds and Type of Construction in Representative Years……88
4–7 Investment in Fixed Assets of State–owned Units in Representative Years……90
4–8 Investment in Fixed Assets of Rural Collective Owned Units (2009) ……92
4–9 Investment in Fixed Assels of Rural Collective Owned Units in Representative Years……93
4–10 Investment In Fixed Assets of Municipal Units in Representative Years……96
4–11 Investment in Fixed Assets of Municipal Units (2009) ……98
4–12 Investment in Fixed Assets of Municipal Units by Sector (2009) ……100

4-13 Investment in Fixed Assets of Municipal Units by Sources of Funds and Type of Construction (2009) ……101
4-14 Investments in Fixed Assets of Urban Districts by Registration Status……102
and Jurisdiction of Management (2009)
4-15 Investments in Fixed Assets of Urban Districts by Sector (2009) ……103
4-16 Investment in Fixed Assets of Urban Area by Sources of Funds and Type of Construction (2009) ……104
4-17 Source of Funds for Total Fixed Assets Investment of Whole City (2009) ……105
4-18 Source of Funds for Fixed Estate of Municipal Units (2009) ……105
4-19 Achievements of Total Assets Investment of Whole City (2009) ……106
4-20 Achievement of Fixed Assets Investment of Municipal Units (2009) ……106
4-21 Investment Fulfilled In Fixed Assets By Region (2009) ……107
4-22 Floor Space of Buildings Construction by Sector (2009) ……108
4-23 Floors Space of Buildings Construction of Municipal Units by Sector (2009) ……110
4-24 Value of Newly Added Fixed Assets and Floor Spaces Completed of Whole City……112
in Representative Years
4-25 Value of Newly Added Fixed Assets and Floor Spaces Completed of Municipal Units……113
in Representative Years
4-26 Construction Projects of Whole City by Sector (2009) ……114
4-27 Construction Projects of Municipal Units by Sector (2009) ……116
4-28 Main Indicators of Investment in Real Estate Development in Representative Years……118
4-29 Main Indicators of Investment in Real Estate Development (2009) ……120
4-30 Sales of Commercial Houses (2009) ……121
4-31 Source of Funds for Investment in Real Estate Development (2009) ……122
4-32 Running of Real Estate Development (2009) ……123
Explanatory Notes on Main Statistical Indicator……124

CHAPTER 5 GOVERNMENT FINANCE

5-1 Government Revenue (2009) ……129
5-2 Government Expenditures (2009) ……130
5-3 Financial Revenue of Local Government by Region (2009) ……131
5-4 Financial Expenditures of Local Government by Region (2009) ……134
Explanatory Notes on Main Statistical Indicator……138

CHAPTER 6 PRICE INDICES

6-1 Price Indices in Representative Years……145
6-2 Residents Consumer Price Indices (2009) ……146
6-3 Retail Price Indices (2009) ……148

6-4 Producer Price Index for Manufactured in Representative Years……150
6-5 Purchase Price Indices of Major Raw Materials,Fuels and Power in Representative Years……152
6-6 Transactions Price Indices of Land (2009)……153
6-7 Selling Price Indices of Real Estate (2009)……153
6-8 Renting Price Indices of Houses (2009)……154
6-9 Price Indices for Investment in Fixed Assets in Representative Years……154
6-10 Price Indecies of Construction and Installation in Representative Years……154
Explanatory Notes on Main Statistical Indicator……155

CHAPTER 7 PEOPLE'LIVELIHOOD

7-1 Per Capita Annual Income and Engel's Coefficient of Urban and Rural Households in Representative Years……159
7-2 Savings Deposit of Urban and Rural Household in Representative Years……160
7-3 Basic Conditions of Urban Households in Representative Years……161
7-4 Basic Conditions of Urban Households (2009)……164
7-5 Statistics on Per Capital Annual Income of Urban Residents (2009)……165
7-6 Statistics on Per Capital Annual Living Expenditure of Urban Households (2009)……166
7-7 Statistics on Per Capita Annual Consumption Expenditure of Urban Households (2009)……167
7-8 Per Capita Annual Purchases of Principal Goods in Urban Household in Representative Years……170
7-9 Number of Durable Consumer Goods Owned Every 100 Urban Households in Representative Years……172
7-10 Conditions of Dwellings of Urban Households (2009)……174
7-11 Basic Indicators of Rural Households In Representative Years……176
7-12 Basic Conditions of Rural Households (2009)……178
7-13 Per Capita Annual Total Revenue and Net Income of Rural Households (2009)……180
7-14 Per Capita Annual Total Expenditure of Rural Households (2009)……180
7-15 Per Capita Living Expenditure of Rural Households (2009)……182
7-16 Output of Major Farm Crops Per Capita by Rural Households (2009)……182
7-17 Per Capita Product Sold by Rural Households (2009)……184
7-18 Per Capita Annual Income and Expenditure of Grains of Rural Households (2009)……184
7-19 Per Capita Purchase of Commodities in Rural Households (2009)……186
7-20 Per Capita Average Food Consumption of Rural Households (2009)……186
7-21 Year-end Possession of Durable Consumer Goods Per 100 Rural Households (2009)……188
7-22 Per Capita Housing Conditions of Rural Households (2009)……188
Explanatory Notes on Main Statistical Indicator……190

CHAPTER 8 URBAN PUBLIC UTLITIES AND ENVIRONMENT PROTECTION

8-1 Urban Water Supply······195

8-2 Urban Consumption of Elecricity······195

8-3 Gas Supply in Urban Area······196

8-4 Heating in Urban Area······196

8-5 Urban Public Traffic······197

8-6 Manicipal Facilities······197

8-7 Urban Manicipal Facilities······198

8-8 City Scale and Land Use······198

8-9 Urban Park,Gardens and Green Areas in Cities ······199

8-10 Urban Environment Sanitation······199

Explanatory Notes on Main Statistical Indicator······200

CHAPTER 9 ENVIRONMENT PROTECTION

9-1 Urban Environmental Protection (2009) ······205

9-2 Discharge and Treatrment of Waste Gas Water & Solid Wastes in Repersentative Year······206

9-3 Discharge and Treatment of Industrial Pollution (2009) ······208

9-4 Urban Sewage Disposal (2009) ······209

9-5 Condition of Collected Dangerous Wastes Treated (2009) ······210

9-6 Domestic Pollution and Other conditions (2009) ······210

9-7 Condition of Anti-Industrial Pollution Projects (2009) ······211

Explanatory Notes on Main Statistical Indicator······212

CHAPTER 10 AGRICULTURE

10-1 Grass-root Organizations, Households, Population and Labor······217

10-2 Grass-root Organizations, Households and Population in Rural Area by Region (2009) ······218

10-3 Number of Labers in Families by Region (2009) ······218

10-4 Area of Cultivated Land in Representative Year······219

10-5 Area of Cultivated Land by Region (2009) ······220

10-6 Possession of Agricultural Machinery in Representative Year (Number of year-end) ······222

10-7 Agricultural Machinery,Chemical Fertilizers,Water Conservancy, ······224
Hydropower in Representative Year

10-8 Gross Output Value of Farming,Forestry,Animal Husbandry,Fishery,······226
Service and Related Indices in Representative Years

10-9 Gross Output Value of Farming, Forestry, Animal Husbandry, Fishery and Service Price by Region (2009) ……227
10-10 Gross Output Value and Its Composition of Farming, Forestry, Animal Husbandry,Fishery and Service at Current Price by Region (2009) ……228
10-11 Value Added of Farming, Forestry, Animal Husbandry, Fishery and Service in Representative Year ……229
10-12 Addition Value-Added of Farming, Forestry, Animal Husbandry, Fishery and Service by Region (2009) ……230
10-13 Proportion of Farming, Forestry, Animal Husbandry, Fishery and Service Value-Added to Total Output Value (2009) ……230
10-14 Sown Areas of Farm Crops In Representative Years ……231
10-15 Sown Areas of Major Farm Crops by Region (2009) ……231
10-16 Yeild of Major Farm Crops in Representative Year ……232
10-17 Yeild of Major Farm Crops by Region (2009) ……233
10-18 Field of Farm Crops Per Hectare in Representative Year ……234
10-19 The Output of Main Crops per Hectare by Region (2009) ……234
10-20 Statistcs on Forestry ……235
10-21 Statistics On Forestry by Region (2009) ……236
10-22 Statistics on Fruits in Representative Year ……236
10-23 Area and Output of Mulberry Yards and Orchards by Region (2009) ……237
10-24 Statistics on Livestock Husbandry in Representative Year ……237
10-25 Statistics On Livestock,Animal Husbandry by Region (2009) ……238
10-26 Output of Livestock Products and Aquatic Products in Representative Year ……239
10-27 Output of Major Livestock Products and Aquatic Products by Region (2009) ……241
10-28 Pre CapitaOutput of Major Farm Products in Representative Year ……242
10-29 Main Index of Rural Economic Benefit in Representative Year ……243
Explanatory Notes on Main Statistical Indicator ……244

CHAPTER 11 INDUSTRY AND ENERGY

11-1 Gross Output Value of Industry In Representative Years ……249
11-2 Gross Output Value of Industrial Enterpriese Above Designated Size by Region (2009) ……251
11-3 Output of Major Industrial Products Of Enterprises Above Designated size ……253
11-4 Main Economic Indicators of All Industrial Enterprises Above Designafed size in Representative Years ……257
11-5 Main Economic Indicators of All Industrial Enterprises Above Designafed size (2009) ……258
11-6 Economic Indicators of All State-owned and State-holding Share Industrial Enterprises Above Designafed size (2009) ……270

11-7 Main Indicators of Share-holding Corporation Industrial Enterprises Above Designafed size (2009) ……282
11-8 Economic Indicators of Foreign Fund Industrial Enterprises Above Designafed size (2009) ……294
11-9 Economic Indicators of Large and Medium-sizd Industrial Enterprises Above Designafed size (2009) ……306
11-10 Economic Indicators of High Technology Industry Industrial Enterprises Above Designafed size (2009) ……318
11-11 Economic Indicators of Industrial Enterprises Above Designated size by Region (2009) ……324
11-12 Energy Purchases Consumption and Inventory of Industrial Enterprises Above Designafed size (2009) ……328
11-13 Majar Energy Consumption by Sector (2009) ……330
11-14 Majar Energy Consumption by Sector Above Designated Size (2009) ……332
Explanatory Notes on Main Statistical Indicator……333

CHAPTER 12 CONSTRUCTION

12-1 Main Indicators on Construction Enterprise of Xi'an (2009) ……343
12-2 Main Indicators on Overall Constructing Contractors and Professional Contractors by Registration Status (2009) ……344
12-3 Financial Status of Overall Constructing Contractors and Professional Contractors (2009) ……348
12-4 Basic Statistic on Enterprises of Work Subcontractors……350
12-5 Main Indicators of Construction Enterprises by Region (2009) ……351
Explanatory Notes on Main Statistical Indicator……352

CHAPTER 13 TRANSPORTATION, POST AND TELECOMMUNICATION SERVICES

13-1 Length of Transportation Routes and Number of Bridges……357
13-2 Possession of Civil Vehicles……358
13-3 Passenger Traffic and Kilometers and Freight Traffic and Ton-kilometers……359
13-4 Postal service and branch post office……360
13-5 Telecommunication service……360
Explanatory Notes on Main Statistical Indicator……361

CHAPTER 14 DOMESTIC TRADE

14-1 Total Retail Sales of Consumer Goods in Representative Year……367

14-2 Total Retail Sales of Consumer Goods (2009) ······368
14-3 Total Retail Sales of Consumer Goods by Region (2009) ······368
14-4 Wholesale and retail trade, catering outlets and staff in Representative Years······369
14-5 Organizations, Establishments and Persons Engaged in Whole-sale Trade (2009) ······370
14-6 Organizations, Establishments and Persons Engaged in Retail Trade (2009) ······372
14-7 Organizations Staff and Branch Shopes of Catering Trade (2009) ······374
14-8 Financial Status of Enterprises Above Designated Size in Wholesale and Retail (2009) ······376
14-9 Finacial Status of Catering Enterprises Above Designated Size (2009) ······388
14-10 Total Sales of Enterprises Above Designated Size in Wholesale and Retail Trades Grouped by Category of Commodities (2009) ······396
14-11 Statistic on Hotel Services and Catering Services above Designed Size (2009) ······400
14-12 Sale Values of Enterprises above Designated Size of Wholesale and Retail Trades by Category of Main Commodities (2009) ······402
14-13 Basic Statistics on Commodity Exchange Markets of Transaction Value over 100 Million Yuan······403
14-14 Basic Statistics on Chain Business of Wholesale and Retail Trades······404
14-15 Basic Statistics on Chain Business of Hotels and Catering Services······405
14-16 Purchases,Sales and Stock of Refined Oil Wholesale Enterprises (2009) ······406
14-17 Purchases,Sales and Stock of Refined Oil Retail Enterprises (2009) ······406
Explanatory Notes on Main Statistical Indicator······407

CHAPTER 15 FOREIGN TRADE AND ECONOMIC COOPERATION,TOURISM

15-1 Main Indicators on Foreign Investments,International Trading and International Tourism in Representative Years······413
15-2 Utilization of Foreign Capital In Representative Years······415
15-3 Direct Investments from Foreign Countries and Hong Kong, Macao and Taiwan in Xi'an (2009) ······416
15-4 Total Imports and Exports In Representative Years······417
15-5 Total Value of Imports and Exports by Country and Region (2009) ······418
15-6 Export Value of Major Merchandise by Type ······419
15-7 Import Value of Major Merchandise by Type······422
15-8 Number of Tourists and Tourism Earnings In Representative Years······423
15-9 Earning of International Tourism In Representative Years······424
15-10 Mainly Concerning Oversea Tourists Reception in Star Hotels······425
Explanatory Notes on Main Statistical Indicator······426

CHAPTER 16 BANKING AND INSURANCE

16-1 Number of Institution and Employed Person in Finance System in Xi'an······431

16-2 Financial institution Including Foreign-funded balance of bisic currency ……432
and foreign currency at Year-end (2009)
16-3 Domestic Funded Financial institution balance of bisic currency……433
and foreign currency at Year-end (2009)
16-4 Year-end Balance of Deposit and Loans in Financial Institutions ……434
Including Foreign-funded (2009)
16-5 Year-end Balance of Deposit and Loans in Domestic Funded Financial Institutions (2009) ……435
16-6 Cash Income and Expenditure of Domestic Funded Financial Institutions (2009) ……436
16-7 Indicators of Insurance Business……437
16-8 Number of Institution and Employed Person in Securities and Futures System in Xi'an……438
16-9 Basic Facts on Securities and Futures Markets……439
Explanatory Notes on Main Statistical Indicator……440

CHAPTER 17 EDUCATION,SCIENCE AND TECHNOLOGY

17-1 Basic Statistics on Regular Eduction in Representative Years……445
17-2 Basic Facts on Regular Education by School Type (2009) ……446
17-3 Number of Schools by Level and Type of School in Representative Years……447
17-4 Basic Situation of the major Year on Post-graduates in Representative Years……447
17-5 Post-graduates in Regular Institutions of Higher Education (2009) ……448
17-6 Basic Facts on Regular Higher Education by Unit (2009) ……449
17-7 Mobile research centers for post-doctors, doctors and masters in Representative Years……451
17-8 Basic Statistics on Specialized Secondary Schools In Representative Years……452
17-9 Situation of every secondary technical and Specialized Secondary school (2009) ……453
17-10 Baisc Statistics on Regular Secondary Schools in Representative Years……454
17-11 Basic Statistics on Regular Secondary Schools by Region (2009) ……454
17-12 Basic Statistics on Vocational Secondary Schools in Representative Years……455
17-13 Basic Statistics on Vocational Secondary Schools by Region (2009) ……455
17-14 Basic Statistics on Primary Schools in Representative Years……456
17-15 Basic Statistics on Primary Schools by Region (2009) ……456
17-16 Basic Statistics on Kindergartens in Representative Years……457
17-17 Basic Statistics on Special Education Schools in Representative Years……457
17-18 Rate of Graduates from Junior Schools and Primary Schools Entering Higher Level Schools ……458
in Representative Years
17-19 Percentage of School-Age Children Enrolled in Representative Years……459
17-20 Student Enrollment Per 10000 Populations and Composition of Students Enrolled……460
in Representative Years
17-21 Adult Education (2009) ……461
Explanatory Notes on Main Statistical Indicator……463

CHAPTER 18 CULTURE,SPORTS,PUBLIC HEALTH, SOCIAL WELFARE INSTITUTIONS AND OTHER SOCIAL ACTIVITIES

18-1 Number of Institutions and Personnel in Culture and Art (2009) ······471
18-2 Basic Statistics on Culture Development······472
18-3 Basic Statistics on Activities of Mass Art Centers and Cultural Centers······472
18-4 Basic Statistics on Cultural Relics Protection (2009) ······473
18-5 Basic Statistics of Broadcasting Stations and Program Production······473
18-6 Basic Statistics of TV Stations and Production of TV Program······474
18-7 The Basic Situations of Sports (Under Municipality) (2009) ······474
18-8 Basic Statistics of Youth Part-time Physical Training School (2009) ······475
18-9 Number of Health Care Institutions , Beds and Employed Persons in Health Care Institutions (2009) ······476
18-10 Number of Health Care Institutions , Beds and Employed Persons in Health Care Institutions By Region (2009) ······480
18-11 Number of Employed Persons in Health Care Institutions······481
18-12 Number of Visits and Inpatients in Medical Institutions (2009) ······482
18-13 Beds and Patients Treated Conditions in Health Care Institutions (2009) ······484
18-14 The Market Circumstance of the Consumer Goods Wholesales (2009) ······486
18-15 Basic Statistics on Social Welfare Insititutions (2009) ······488
18-16 Number of Social Welfare Institutions and Employed Persons······488
18-17 Statistics on Persons Enjoying Favoured Treatment by Region (2009) ······489
18-18 Conditions of Birth Control and Marriage Registration (2009) ······490
18-19 Basic Statistics on Lawyers、Notaries and Mediation······491
18-20 Basic Facts on Communist Youth League······492
18-21 Women's Organizations Status······492
18-22 Basic Facts on Women's Federation······493
18-23 Statistics on Traffic Accidents······494
18-24 Statistics on Fires······494
18-25 Dato on Sasfety in Production······495
18-26 Data on Criminal Cases······496
18-27 Data on Public Order Cases······496
18-28 Data on criminal cases and public order cases grouped by districts and counties (2009) ······497
18-29 Data on Acceptance of Cases of Xi'an People's Procuratorate······498
18-30 Xi'an Intermediate People's Court Basic Data of the Law Cases (2009) ······499
Explanatory Notes on Main Statistical Indicator······502

CHAPTER 19 ENTERPRISES INVESTIGATION

19-1 Business Climate Index (2009) ······509
19-2 Entrepreneur Expectation Indicator (2009) ······510
Explanatory Notes on Main Statistical Indicator······511

西安市2009年国民经济和社会发展统计公报

西安市统计局　国家统计局西安调查队

2010年3月18日

2009年是新世纪以来我市经济发展最为困难的一年，面对金融危机的严峻挑战和复杂的国际国内形势，市委、市政府科学决策，果断出手，带领全市人民认真贯彻落实中央、陕西省的一揽子计划和政策措施，化危为机，砥砺奋进，较快扭转了经济增速下滑的势头，全市经济整体表现为生产较快回升、内需持续扩张、效益不断好转、物价总体稳定、民生加速改善，城市建设和各项社会事业取得新成绩。

一、综合

初步核算，全年实现生产总值（GDP）2719.10亿元，比上年增长14.5%。分产业看，第一产业增加值110.38亿元，增长6.3%；第二产业增加值1148.77亿元，增长14.4%；第三产业增加值1459.95亿元，增长15.1%。按常住人口计算，全市人均生产总值32351元，比上年增长13.6%。

全年居民消费价格比上年下降0.3%，商品零售价格下降0.5%，固定资产投资价格下降2.1%，工业品出厂价格下降0.1%，原材料、燃料、动力购进价格上涨0.7%。

2009年全市居民消费价格指数比上年涨跌幅度

单位：%

指　标	2009年
居民消费价格总水平	-0.3
食品	2.3
#粮食	2.9
烟酒及用品	1.6
衣着	1.3
家庭设备用品及维修服务	-0.6
医疗保健和个人用品	0.5
交通和通讯	-2.7
娱乐教育文化用品及服务	-2.2
居住	-5.0

二、农业

全年粮食播种面积628.69万亩，比上年减少1.62万亩；油料播种面积8.59万亩，与上年持平；蔬菜播种面积94.83万亩，增加1.82万亩；园林水果种植面积71.08万亩，增加6.77万亩。全年粮食产量218.20万吨，较上年增长1.8%，创历史最高水平，其中夏粮产量102.98万吨，下降2.8%，秋粮115.22万吨，增长6.2%。

2009年全市农业主要产品产量

产品名称	计量单位	绝对数	比上年增长（%）
油　料	万吨	1.12	-2.8
蔬　菜	万吨	242.41	9.4
园林水果	万吨	78.96	10.1
肉　类	万吨	12.62	9.4
奶　类	万吨	61.82	4.8
禽　蛋	万吨	11.67	7.5
水产品	万吨	1.30	4.0
大牲畜年末存栏数	万头	20.84	1.8
猪年末存栏数	万头	91.87	6.3
羊年末存栏数	万只	27.95	6.2
家禽年末存栏数	万只	980.83	6.6

全市农用机械总动力261.61万千瓦，比上年下降3.8%；农田有效灌溉面积273.18万亩；全年农用化肥施用量（实物量）77.6万吨，增长1.0%。

三、工业和建筑业

全年完成工业增加值820.94亿元，比上年增长12.2%。规模以上工业增加值725.33亿元，增长17.0%，其中轻工业增加值179.32亿元，增长12.9%，重工业增加值546.01亿元，增长18.4%；装备制造业增加值365.33亿元，增长20.7%；工业产品销售率97.5%。

2009年全市规模以上工业主要行业增加值

单位：亿元

指　　标	增加值	比上年增长（%）
电力热力的生产和供应业	36.93	12.0
装备制造业	365.33	20.7
医药制造业	43.74	16.3
通信设备、计算机及其他电子设备制造业	20.79	-9.3
农副食品加工业	26.41	19.8
石油和天然气开采业	28.89	19.4
非金属矿物制品业	30.21	35.8
石油加工、炼焦及核燃料加工业	18.53	39.0

2009年全市规模以上装备制造业分行业增加值

单位：亿元

指　　标	增加值	比上年增长（%）
金属制品业	11.73	36.2
通用设备制造业	33.64	-8.3
专用设备制造业	41.64	25.0
交通运输设备制造业	180.66	30.9
电气机械及器材制造业	82.86	16.6
仪器仪表及文化、办公用机械制造业	14.79	-2.5

2009年全市规模以上工业主要产品产量

产品名称	计量单位	绝对数	比上年增长（%）
发电量	亿千瓦小时	83.21	17.7
原油加工量	万吨	168.9	8.5
乳制品	万吨	78.6	10.4
软饮料	万吨	86.39	0.5
中成药	万吨	2.9	494.3
机制纸及纸板	万吨	47.63	27
缝纫机	万架	36.09	-6.4
饲料	万吨	42.56	3
合成洗涤剂	万吨	7.94	4.5
水泥	万吨	487.72	16
钢材	万吨	110.51	137.4
汽车	万辆	50.68	89
#轿车	万辆	42.77	121.7
交流电动机	万千瓦	618.06	-0.4
变压器	万千伏安	11063.72	29.7
电力电缆	千米	4357.98	4.9
通信及电子网络用电缆	对千米	3048	-48.5
彩色显象管	万只	763.26	-51.8

全市规模以上工业企业经济效益综合指数为215.43，比上年提高22.1个百分点。规模以上工业企业实现利税251.77亿元，增长46.2%；实现利润156.55亿元，增长46.7%；实现税金95.22亿元，增长45.2%。

全年建筑业实现增加值327.83亿元，比上年增长21.2%。全年具有资质等级的总承包和专业承包建筑企业337家。房屋建筑施工面积4173万平方米，比上年增长33.2%。按建筑业总产值计算，全员劳动生产率24.5万元/人。

四、固定资产投资

全年全社会固定资产投资2500.13亿元，比上年增长31.2%。其中，城镇投资2367.58亿元，增长32.5%；非公有制单位投资1277.31亿元，增长31.5%。

城镇投资中，第一产业投资24.46亿元，增长3.0%；第二产业投资482.30亿元，增长30.4%，其中工业投资441.57亿元，增长24.0%；第三产业投资1860.82亿元，增长33.6%。

2009年重点行业城镇固定资产投资及其增长速度

单位：亿元

指　标	绝对数	比上年增长（%）
农林牧渔业	24.46	3.0
制造业	378.08	24.9
交通运输、仓储及邮政业	150.25	33.7
信息传输、计算机服务和软件业	21.23	64.4
批发零售、住宿餐饮业	106.60	1.6
水利、环境和公共设施管理业	350.42	62.7
教　育	76.48	32.8
卫生、社会保障和社会福利业	16.56	11.2
公共管理和社会组织	222.62	1.5

全年房地产开发投资696.34亿元，增长28.9%；商品房销售面积1256.02万平方米，增长63.0%；商品房销售额488.55亿元，增长53.8%。

2009年房地产开发和销售主要指标

指　标	计量单位	绝对数	比上年增长（%）
房地产开发投资	亿元	696.34	28.9
#住宅	亿元	568.3	37.9
商品房施工面积	万平方米	5708.63	61.9
#住宅	万平方米	4901.59	64.6
新开工面积	万平方米	1693.38	88.1
#住宅	万平方米	1467.03	92.4
商品房竣工面积	万平方米	542.81	53.4
#住宅	万平方米	453.49	33.7
商品房销售面积	万平方米	1256.02	63
#住宅	万平方米	1202.12	69.2
商品房销售额	亿元	488.55	53.8
#住宅	亿元	450.71	56.4

全年“四区两基地”和国际港务区完成投资761.49亿元，比上年增长40.5%，占全社会固定资产投资总额的30.5%。

2009年“四区两基地”和国际港务务区固定资产投资及其增长速度

单位：亿元

指 标	绝对数	比上年增长（%）
高新技术产业开发区	264.3	28.4
经济技术开发区	206.02	41.8
曲江新区	181.76	48
浐灞生态区	50.87	61.5
航空高技术产业基地	25.56	36.3
民用航天产业基地	26.6	48.7
国际港务区	6.38	-

全年新增固定资产1013.32亿元，固定资产交付使用率42.8%。各类房屋竣工面积1527.91万平方米，竣工率16.3%。共有2071个城镇建设项目建成投产，项目建成投产率72.6%。

五、国内贸易

全年实现社会消费品零售总额1381.12亿元，比上年增长19.7%。分城乡看，城市消费品零售额1249.79亿元，增长19.7%；县及县以下消费品零售额131.33亿元，增长18.8%。分行业看，批发和零售业零售额1228.83亿元，增长20.3%；住宿和餐饮业零售额128.69亿元，增长14.6%；其他行业零售额23.60亿元，增长14.1%。

限额以上批发和零售业中，食品、饮料、烟酒类零售额比上年增长7.2%，服装鞋帽、针纺织品类增长19.7%，体育娱乐用品类增长31.8%，书报杂志类增长15.0%，日用品类增长13.9%，家用电器和音像器材类增长9.5%，通讯器材类下降9.3%，文化办公用品类增长16.9%，金银珠宝类增长21.2%，汽车类增长46.1%。

六、对外贸易

全年进出口总额72.55亿美元，比上年增长3.4%。其中，出口33.30亿美元，下降25.1%；进口39.25亿美元，增长52.8%。

分贸易方式看，一般贸易进出口47.7亿美元，下降8.3%；加工贸易进出口20.4亿美元，增长55.6%。分经营主体看，国有企业进出口31.6亿美元，下降7.3%；外商投资企业进出口21.6亿美元，增长22.7%；私营企业进出口19.2亿美元，增长5.3%。

主要进出口商品中，机电产品出口21.4亿美元，下降8.8%；进口24.8亿美元，增长45.2%。农产品出口2.8亿美元，下降24.9%，进口0.2亿美元，下降41.7%；矿产品出口2.5亿美元，下降69.1%，进口5.4亿美元，增长99.3%；纺织品出口1.7亿美元，下降11.1%；进口311万美元，增长27.6%。

全年批准外商直接投资项目65个，合同利用外商直接投资6.00亿美元，比上年下降49.2%；实际利用外商直接投资12.19亿美元，增长6.2%。

七、交通、邮电和旅游

全年交通运输、仓储和邮政业实现增加值110.60亿元，比上年增长5.0%。

全年交通运输总周转量477.12亿吨公里，比上年增长6.4%。其中，铁路213.79亿吨公里，增长2.8%；公路253.40亿吨公里，增长10.9%；民航9.93亿吨公里，增长1.9%。

全年铁路旅客发送量2585万人次，比上年下降3.5%，货物发送量614万吨，增长1.6%；公路客运量25271万人次，增长9.0%，货运量29986万吨，增长11.3%；民航旅客吞吐量1529万人次，增长28.3%，货物吞吐量12.69万吨，增长8.4%。

全年邮电业务总收入103.23亿元，比上年增长13.8%。其中，邮政业务收入8.10亿元，增长14.6%；电信业务收入95.13亿元，增长13.7%。

全年共接待国内游客3862万人次，比上年增长22.0%；国外游客67.29万人次，增长6.5%。全年实现旅游总收入297.40亿元，增长22.1%，其中外汇收入3.9亿美元，增长8.6%。

八、财政、金融、证券和保险

全年财政总收入398.84亿元，比上年增长22.9%。地方财政一般预算收入181.40亿元，增长24.6%，其中，营业税、增值税、企业所得税和个人所得税分别增长29.9%、20.5%、10.1%和11.0%。全年地方财政一般预算支出276.85亿元，比上年增长22.0%，其中，一般公共服务支出40.97亿元，增长19.0%；教育支出39.24亿元，增长19.3%；社会保障和就业支出454.24亿元，下降6.9%；城乡社区事务支出34.35亿元，增长39.0%；农林水事务支出

17.38亿元，增长56.3%；环境保护支出5.17亿元，增长60.2%。

年末全市金融机构本外币各项存款余额7622.93亿元，比上年末增长30.7%。其中，企事业存款余额3123.75亿元，增长39.1%；城乡居民储蓄存款余额3125.29亿元，增长22.5%。金融机构各项贷款余额（不含国家开发银行）4539.75亿元，比上年末增长36.9%，其中，短期贷款1168.25亿元，增长12.7%；中长期贷款2928.57亿元，增长52.4%。全年金融机构现金收入9121.40亿元，比上年增长12.4%；现金支出8842.75亿元，比上年增长12.7%；货币净回笼278.66亿元，比上年增长2.3%。

全年证券市场各类证券成交额13841.70亿元，比上年增长85.8%。其中股票成交额13096.47亿元，增长106.7%；基金成交额71.74亿元，下降4.2%；债券成交额11.58亿元，下降15.2%。年末全市有上市公司22家，上市总股本115.27亿元。年末股票市场累计开户数147.54万户，比上年末增长10.5%。

全市有各类保险公司36家，保险机构424家，保险专业中介机构88家。全年保费收入122.11亿元，比上年增长20.4%。其中，财产险保费收入25.90亿元，增长33.9%；人身险保费收入96.21亿元，增长17.2%。全年支付各类保险赔款及给付25.15亿元，比上年下降3.0%。其中财产险、人身险分别为12.61亿元和12.54亿元，分别比上年增长11.8%和下降14.3%。

九、科学技术和教育

全年实施市级科技计划项目270项，其中实施技术转移和科技成果转化项目114项，重点扶持高新技术企业125家，支持建设农业科技示范园11家，科技示范乡镇11个，实施重大区县工业科技引导项目11个。全年争取国家、省资金2.06亿元。全年技术市场交易额35.60亿元。全年申请专利量12772件，专利授权量4706件。

全市共有各级各类学校和办学机构6507所，在校学生306.20万人，教职工19.98万人。其中研究生培养单位46个，招收研究生2.49万人，在学研究生7.24万人；普通高校49所，招生18.84万人，在校学生63.22万人，毕业生15.04万人；高中阶段学校（包括普通中专、技工学校、成人中专、普通高中、职业高中等）429所，招生18.46万人，在校学生49.25万人；普通初中259所，招生10.14万人，在校学生32.27万人，毕业生11.56万人；小学1666所，招生7.84万人，在校学生52.52万人，毕业生9.96万人；各级各类民办学校（机构）835所（个），招生15.97万人，在校学生46.88万人。小学、初中学龄人口入学率分别为99.96%和99.61%。全市教育人口326.18万人，占全市户籍总人口的41.73%。

十、文化、卫生和体育

全市艺术表演团体11个，公共图书馆14个，文化馆15个，文化站182个，博物馆49个。全年组织开展各类群众文化活动569场次。全市拥有电视台2座、广播电台2座、广播电视台6座，电视人口覆盖率和广播人口覆盖率分别达98.41%、99.37%。

年末全市共有各类卫生机构5326个，其中医院、卫生院416个；各类卫生技术人员5.68万人，其中执业（助理）医师1.97万人；卫生机构床位3.49万张。

全年举办各类群众体育展示表演和竞赛活动250项次，参与群众达到200万人次。全年建成4个免费开放的全民健身广场。全市拥有体育场（馆、所）4830个，面积1664.37万平方米，人均占有体育场地面积1.8平方米。全市已有社会体育指导员6200名，全民健身路径440套，晨晚练点1600个，健身气功站点92个。成功举办了西安市第十四届运动会。我市输送的运动员在全国第十一届运动会上获得4.5枚金牌、4.5枚银牌。

十一、人口、人民生活和社会保障

年末常住人口843.46万人，其中男性人口435.77万人，占51.7%；女性人口407.69万人，占48.3%，性别比为107（以女性为100，男性对女性的比例）。全年出生人口8.47万人，出生率为10.08‰；死亡人口3.74万人，死亡率为5.63‰；全年净增人口5.94万人，自然增长率为4.45‰。城镇人口581.40万人，占68.93%；乡村人口262.06万人，占31.07%。年末全市户籍总人口781.67万人，比上年增长1.2%。

全市城镇居民人均可支配收入18963元，比上年增长24.7%；农民人均纯收入6275元，增长20.4%。城镇居民家庭食品消费支出占家庭消费总支出的比重为32.4%，农村为35.8%。城镇居民人均现住房总建筑面积28.4平方米，农村居民人均居住面积57.0平方米。

全市新增就业人数10.59万人，下岗失业人员再就业4.46万人，其中"4050"人员再就业1.30万人。城镇登记失业率4.3%。全市农村劳动力实现转移就业人员71.22万人。

全市城镇基本医疗保险参保人数352.42万人；城镇企业职工养老保险参保人数170.02万人；失业保险参保人数127.40万人；工伤保险参保人数104.11万人，职工生育保险参保人数81.95万人。参加农村新型合作医疗的农民人数达382.39万人，实际参合率96.77%，覆盖面为100%。

全市福利企业112家。全年共发行销售社会福利彩票18.02亿元。

十二、城市建设、环境保护和安全生产

全年完成城市基础设施投资354.77亿元，比上年增长45.3%。新增人行天桥6座，建设公交港湾98处。新增城区集中供热面积776万平方米。完成工程造林19.77万亩，新建改造绿地广场66个，新增城市园林绿化面积486万平方米。实施85个城中村和棚户区改造安置项目，安置房累计开工面积978万平方米，竣工面积87万平方米，安置回迁3209户、10799人。建成农村公路1351公里，农村公路总里程达到10850公里。乡镇、行政村、自然村通水泥（油）路率分别达到98.64%、92.68%、68.78%。

城市环境空气质量全年好于国家二级标准（良好）以上的天数304天，比上年增加3天，创有记录以来最高水平。全年建成并投入运行污水处理厂5家，全市污水管网总长度1054公里，污水处理能力达到95万吨/日，比上年增加25万吨/日；可吸入颗粒物年日均值与上年持平，环境空气中二氧化硫年均值比上年下降4%。全市饮用水源地的水质达标率为100%。区域环境噪声等效声级均值为55.1分贝，道路交通噪声等效声级均值为68分贝。

全年共发生各类安全生产事故4225起，比上年增加87起，上升2.1%；死亡586人，比上年减少5人，下降0.9%；受伤2264人，比上年减少208人，下降8.4%；经济损失3128.91万元，比上年增加326.92万元，上升11.7%。

注：

1.本公报数据为初步统计数。

2.本公报中增加值为现价，增加值增长速度均按可比价格计算。

Statistic Communiqu on the 2009 National Economy and Social Development of the City of Xi'an

Xi'an Municipal Bureau of Statistics and NBS Survey Office in xi'an

Mar.18st, 2010

The year of 2009 is the most difficult year during the new century for economic development of Xi'an. Confronting serve challenge of financial crisis and complex international and domestic situation, the municipal party committee and municipal government of Xi'an made decisions scientifically, took actions decisively, led the citizen to implement both central and provincial plans and policy thoroughly, turned crises into opportunities, forged ahead against difficulties, reversed the trend of slowdown in economic growth quickly. The economic tended to recover rapidly of production, expand continuously of domestic needs, improve constantly of efficiency, keep generally stable of price, improve rapidly of people's livelihood. The urban construction and other social projects obtained new achievements in 2009.

I. General Outlook

In 2009, the gross domestic product (GDP) preliminarily estimated was 271.910 billion Yuan, up by 14.5 percent over the previous year. View by different industries, the value-added of the primary industry was 11.038 billion Yuan, up by 6.3 percent; the value-added of the secondary industry was 114.877 billion Yuan, up by 14.4 percent; and the value-added of the tertiary industry was 145.995 billion Yuan, up by 15.1 percent. Calculated according to the permanent population, the per capita GDP in 2009 was 32,351 Yuan, up by 13.6 percent over the previous year.

The general level of consumer prices of Xi'an was down by 0.3 percent compared the previous year; the retail prices for commodities decreased by 0.5 percent; the investment prices in fixed assets was down by 2.1 percent; the ex-factory prices of industrial products was decreased by 0.1 percent; the purchasing price of raw materials, fuels and power went up by 0.7 percent.

*2.Agriculture*In 2009, the sown area of grain was 6286.9 thousand mu, a decrease of 16.2 thousand mu over the previous year; the sown area of oil-bearing crops was 85.9 thousand mu, maintaining the same level of the previous year; the sown area of vegetables was 948.3 thousand mu, an increase of 18.2 thousand mu; the sown area of garden fruits was 710.8 thousand mu, an increase of 67.7 thousand mu. The total output of grain in 2009 was 2.182 million tons, up by 1.8 percent over the previous year, creating the highest level in history. Of this, the output of summer grain crops was 1.0298 million tons, down by 2.8 percent, and the output of autumn grain crops was 1.1522 million tons, up by 6.2 percent.

Up and fall extent of Residents Consumer Price Indices with previous year (2009)

unit:%

Item	2009
General Level of Residents Consumer Price	-0.3
Food	2.3
#Grain	2.9
Tobaccos and Alcohols	1.6
Clothing	1.3
Household facilities and maintaining services	-0.6
Medical, Health and Personal Articles	0.5
Transportation and Communication	-2.7
Recreation, Education and Cultural articles and Services	-2.2
Residence	-5.0

Main agricultural products of Xi'an in 2009

Name of Products	Unit	Output	Increase over the last year (%)
Edible	10,000 ton	1.12	-2.8
Vegetable	10,000 ton	242.41	9.4
Fruit	10,000 ton	78.96	10.1
Meat	10,000 ton	12.62	9.4
Milk	10,000 ton	61.82	4.8
Egg	10,000 ton	11.67	7.5
Aquatic Product	10,000 head	1.30	4
Year-end Cattle on hand	10,000 head	20.84	1.8
Year-end Pig on hand	10,000 head	91.87	6.3
Year-end Sheep on hang	10,000 head	27.95	6.2
Year-end Fowl on hand	10,000 head	980.83	6.6

The total power of agricultural machinery was 2.6161 million kilowatts, down by 3.8 percent over the previous year; effective iirrigating farmland was 2731.8 thousand mu; the total of fertilizer utilized (physical quantity) was 776 thousand tons, up by 1.0 percent.

3. Industry and Construction

In 2009, the value-added by the industrial sector was 82.094 billion Yuan, up by 12.2 percent over the previous year. The value-added of industrial enterprises above the designated size was 72.533 billion Yuan, up by 17.0 percent. Of this, the value-added of the light industry was 17.932 billion Yuan, up by 12.9 percent; that of the value-added of the heavy industry was 54.601 billion Yuan, up by 18.4 percent; and the value-added of the equipment manufacturing industry was 36.533 billion Yuan, up by 20.7 percent. The sales ratio of industrial products was 97.5 percent.The comprehensive index of economic efficiency of enterprises above designated size was 215.43,up by 22.1 percent over the previous year; The profit and tax from industrial enterprises above the designated size in 2009 was 25.177 billion Yuan, up by 46.2 percent. Of this, the profit was 15.655 billion Yuan, up by 46.7 percent, and the tax was 9.522 billion Yuan, up by 45.2 percent.

value-added of the enterprises above designated size of Xi'an in 2009

Unit:100 million yuan

Item	Value-added	Increase over the last year (%)
Electric power,heating power generating and supplying industry	36.93	12.0
Equipment manufacturing industry	365.33	20.7
Medicine and Pharmaceutical Products	43.74	16.3
Communication equipment,computer and other electronic equipment manufacturing industry	20.79	-9.3
Agricultural products and non-stable food processing industry	26.41	19.8
Petroleum and Natural gas mining industry	28.89	19.4
Nonmetal Mineral Products	30.21	35.8
Petroleum refining,coke making and nuclear fuel processing industry	18.53	39

value-added of equipment manufacturing industry above designated size of Xi'an in 2009

Unit:100 million yuan

Item	Value-added	Increase over the last year (%)
Metal Products	11.73	36.2
General equipment manufacturing industy	33.64	-8.3
Special Purpose Equipment	41.64	25.0
Transport Equipment	180.66	30.9
Electric Equipment and Machinery	82.86	16.6
Instruments,Meters,Cultural and office Machinery	14.79	-2.5

Output of Major Industrial Products above designated size in Xi'an(2009)

Item	Unit	Output	Increase over the last year (%)
Electricity	10,000 kilowatt-hour	83.21	17.7
Crude Oil Processing	10,000 ton	168.90	8.5
Dairy	10,000 ton	78.60	10.4
Beverage Alcohol	10,000 ton	86.39	0.5
Chinese Medicine	10,000 ton	2.90	494.3
Machine Made Paper	10,000 ton	47.63	27.0
Sewing Machine	10,000 ton	36.09	-6.4
Feed	10,000 ton	42.56	3.0
Detergent	10,000 ton	7.94	4.5
Cement	10,000 ton	487.72	16.0
Steel	10,000 ton	110.51	137.4
Motor Vehicle	10,000 unit	50.68	89.0
#Car	10,000 unit	42.77	121.7
AC Motor	10,000 kilowatt-hour	618.06	-0.4
Transformer	10,000 kilovolt amperes	11063.72	29.7
Electric Cable	Km	4357.98	4.9
Communication Cable	Pair-Km	3048.00	-48.5
Color Kinescope	10,000pieces	763.26	-51.8

In 2009, the value-added by the construction enterprises in Xi'an was 32.783 billion Yuan, up by 21.2 percent over the previous year, and 337 construction enterprises qualified for general contracts and specialized contracts. The total floor space of buildings under construction was 41.73 million square meters, up by 33.2 percent. Calculated by the total output value of construction, the overall labor productivity was 245 thousand Yuan per person.

4.Investment in Fixed Assets

The completed investment in fixed assets of Xi'an in 2009 was 250.013 billion Yuan, up by 31.2 percent over the previous year. Of the total investment, in urban areas was 236.758 billon Yuan, up by 32.5 percent; and that in non-public sectors of the economy was 127.731 billon Yuan, up by 31.5 percent.

In urban areas, the investment in the primary

industry was 2.446 billion Yuan, up by 3.0 percent against the previous year; in the secondary industry, the investment was 48.230 billion Yuan, up by 30.4 percent, and the industrial investment was 44.157 billion Yuan, up by 24.0 percent; in the tertiary industry, the investment was 186.082 billion Yuan, up by 33.6 percent.

Investments in Fixed Assets and Growth Rate in important industries of Urban Districts (2009)

Unit:100 million yuan

Item	Investment	Increase over the last year （%）
Farming ,Forestry,Animal Husbandry and Fishery	24.46	3.0
Manufacturing	378.08	24.9
Transport,Storage and Postal Service	150.25	33.7
Information Transmission,Computer Service and Software Service	21.23	64.4
Wholesale,Retail,Accommodation and Catering Trade	106.60	1.6
Water conservancy,environment and public facilities administration industry	350.42	62.7
Education	76.48	32.8
Sanition,social insurance and social welfare industry	16.56	11.2
Public administration	222.62	1.5

In 2009, the real estate development investment was 69.634 billion Yuan, up by 28.9 percent; the sold area of commercial housing was 125.602 million square meters, up by 63.0 percent; the sales income of commercial housing was 48.855 billion Yuan, up by 53.8 percent.

Main Indicators of Real Estate Development and Sales in 2009

Item	Unit	Absolute Number	Increase over the last year （%）
Investment in Real Estate Deelopment	100 million yuan	696.34	28.9
#Residential Buildings	100 million yuan	568.30	37.9
Floor Spaces of Commercial Houses Under Construction	10,000 sq.m	5708.63	61.9
#Residential Buildings	10,000 sq.m	4901.59	64.6
Floor Spaces of Newly Constructed	10,000 sq.m	1693.38	88.1
#Residential Buildings	10,000 sq.m	1467.03	92.4
Floor Spaces of Commercial Houses Completed	10,000 sq.m	542.81	53.4
#Residential Buildings	10,000 sq.m	453.49	33.7
Floor Spaces of Commercial Houses Sold	10,000 sq.m	1256.02	63.0
#Residential Buildings		1202.12	69.2
Total Sales of Commercial Houses	100 million yuan	488.55	53.8
#Residential Buildings	100 million yuan	450.71	56.4

The completed investment in project of '4 zones and 2 bases' was 76.149 billion Yuan, up by 40.5 percent over the previous year, accounting for 30.5 percent of the total investment in fixed assets.

Investments in Fixed Assets and Growth Rate of '4 zones and 2 bases' and International Port District (2009)

Item	Investment	Increase over the last year （%）
Hi-tech zone	264.30	28.4
Economic-tech zone	206.02	41.8
New Qujiang zone	181.76	48.0
Chan-ba ecological zone	50.87	61.5
Hi-tech Aerospace base	25.56	36.3
Civil Aerospace base	26.60	48.7
International Port District	6.38	-

The value of fixed assets increased in 2009 was 101.332 billion Yuan, and the rate of projects delivered of fixed assets was 42.8 percent. The completed area of various kinds of buildings was 15.2791 million square meters, and the rate of completed area was 16.3 percent. 2071 projects of urban construction were completed and put into use this year, and the rate of construction projects completed and put into use was 72.6 percent.

5. Domestic Trade

In 2009, the total retail sales of consumer goods reached 138.112 billion Yuan, up by 19.7 percent over the previous year. In term of different areas , the total retail sales of consumer goods in urban areas was 124.979 billion Yuan, up by 19.7 percent;and that in rural areas was 13.133 billion Yuan, up by 18.8 percent. In term of different sectors, the sales of the wholesale and retail trade reached 122.883 billion Yuan, up 20.3 percent; the sales of the lodging and catering industry was 12.869 billion Yuan, up 14.6 percent, and the sales of other industries was 2.360 billion Yuan, up 14.1 percent.

Of the total retail sales by wholesale and retail enterprises above designated size, compared to the previous year, the sales of food, beverage, wine and cigarette was up by 7.2 percent; clothing, shoes, hats, and needle textiles was up by 19.7 percent; sports-recreation was up by 31.8 percent; books, newspapers and magazines was up by 15.0 percent; daily necessities was up by 13.9 percent; electric and electronic appliances for household use and audio-video equipment was up by 9.5 percent; telecommunication equipment was down by 9.3 percent; cultural and office goods was up by 16.9 percent; gold, silver and jewelry up by 21.2 percent and motor vehicles was up by 46.1 percent.

6. Foreign Trade

In 2009, the total value of imports and exports reached 7.255 billion US Dollars, up by 19.7 percent over the previous year. Of this, the value of exports was 3.330 billion US Dollars, down by 25.1 percent, and that of imports was 3.925 billion US Dollars, up by 52.8 percent.

In term of different trade patterns, the value of imports and exports of general trade was 4.77 billion Dollars, down by 8.3 percent; and that of processing trade was 2.04 billion Dollars, up by 55.6 percent. In term of different Management entities, the value of imports and exports of state-owned enterprises was 3.16 billion Dollars, down by 7.3 percent; the value of foreign-invested enterprises was 2.16 billion Dollars, up by 22.7 percent; and that of private enterprises was 1.92 billion Dollars, up by 5.3 percent.

Of the main import and export commodities, the value of exports of electromechanical products was 2.14 billion Dollars, down by 8.8 percent; that of imports of electromechanical products was 2.48 billion Dollars, up by 45.2 percent. The value of exports of agricultural product was 0.28 billion Dollars, down by 24.9 percent; that of imports of agricultural products was 0.02 billion Dollars, down by 41.7 percent. The value of exports of mineral products was 0.25 billion Dollars, down by 69.1 percent; that of imports of mineral products was 0.54 billion Dollars, up by 99.3 percent. The value of exports of textile products was 0.17 billion Dollars, down by 11.1 percent; that of imports of textile products was 3.11 million Dollars, up by 27.6 percent.

In 2009, there were 65 foreign direct investment projects approved in Xi'an; the contracted foreign direct investment was 0.6 billion US dollars, down by 49.2 percent over the pervious year; the foreign direct investment actually utilized was 1.219 billion dollars, up by 6.2 percent.

VII. Transportation, Post, Telecommunications and Tourism

The value-added of the transportation, storage, post and telecommunication sectors reached 11.060 billion Yuan in 2009, up by 5.0 percent over the previous year.

In 2009, the total volume of cargo transported was 47.712 billion ton-kilometers, up by 6.4 percent over the previous year. Of this , that transported by railway was 21.379 billion ton-kilometers, up by 2.8 percent; that by highway was 25.340 billion ton-kilometers, up by 10.9 percent; that by airway was 0.993 billion ton-kilometers, up by 1.9 percent.

The total passenger traffic dispatched by railway was 25.85 million person-times and freight traffic by railway was 6.14 million tons, down by 3.5 percent and up by 1.6 percent respectively as compared with previous year; passenger traffic by highway was 252.71 million person-times and freight traffic by highway was 299.86 million tons, increased by 9.0 percent and 11.3 percent respectively; passenger traffic dispatched by civil aviation was 15.29million person-times and freight traffic by civil aviation was 126.9 thousand tons, up by 28.3 percent and 8.4 percent respectively.

The revenue of post and telecommunication services totaled 10.323 billion Yuan, up by 13.8 percent over the previous year. Of this total, the post services was 0.810 billion Yuan, up by 14.6 percent; the telecommunication services was 9.513 billion Yuan, up by 13.7 percent.

The number of domestic tourists was 38.62 million person-times, up by 22.0 percent; that of oversea tourists was 672.9 thousand person-times, up by 6.5 percent. The total income from tourism reached 29.740 billion Yuan, up by 22.1 percent. Of this, the income from foreign exchange was 0.39 billion Yuan, up by 8.6 percent.

VIII. Finance, banking, securities and insurance

The financial revenue totaled 39.884 billion Yuan, up by 22.9 percent as compared with the previous year. The general budget revenue of regional finance reached 18.140 billion Yuan, up by 24.6 percent. Of this, business tax, value-added tax, income tax of enterprises and individual income tax were up by 29.9 percent, 20.5 percent, 10.1 percent and 11.0 percent respectively. The general budget expenditure of regional finance totaled 27.685 billion Yuan, up by 22.0 percent. Of this total, the expenditure on general public service was 4.097 billion Yuan, up by 19.0 percent; that on education was 3.924 billion Yuan, up by 19.3 percent; that on social security and employment was 45.424 billion Yuan, down by 6.9 percent; that on communities in urban and rural areas was 3.435 billion Yuan, up by 39.0 percent; that on agriculture, forestry and water affairs was 1.738 billion Yuan, up by 56.3 percent; that on environmental protection was 0.517 billion Yuan ,up by 60.2 percent.

Savings deposit in Renminbi and foreign currencies in all items of financial institutions totaled 762.293 billion Yuan at the end of 2009, an increase of 30.7 percent as compared with the end of the previous year. Of the total savings deposit, that of enterprises was 312.375 billion Yuan, up by 39.1 percent, and that of urban and rural residents was 312.529 billion Yuan, up by 22.5 percent. Loans in all items of financial institutions (without the National Development Bank) reached 453.975 billion Yuan, an increase of 36.9 percent as compared with the end of the previous year. Of this, short-term loans totaled 116.825 billion Yuan, up by 12.7 percent, and medium -and- long term loans reached 292.857 billion Yuan, up by 52.4 percent. Cash income in all items of financial institutions was 912.140 billion Yuan, up by 12.4 percent over the previous year; cash expenditure was 884.275 billion Yuan, up by 12.7 percent; net withdrawal of currency was 27.866 billion Yuan, up by 2.3 percent.

In 2009, the trading volume of stock exchange market was 1384.170 billion Yuan, an increase of 85.8 percent as compared with the previous year. Of the total trading volume, stock was 1309.647 billion Yuan, up by 106.7 percent; fund was 7.174 billion Yuan, down by 4.2 percent; bond was 1.158 billion Yuan, down by 15.2 percent. There were 22 listed companies in Xi'an at the end of 2009, of which the total capital stock was 11.527 billion Yuan. The were 14.754 million accounts in stock market at the end of 2009, an increase of 10.5 percent as compared with the end of the previous year.

By the end of 2009, there were36 insurance companies、 424 insurance institutiones and 88 insurance intermediary organes. Of this, the income from property insurance was 2.590 billion Yuan, up by 33.9 percent; that from life insurance was 9.621 billion Yuan, up by 17.2 percent. In total, insurance companies paid an indemnity worth of 2.515 billion Yuan, down by 3.0 percent over the previous year, of which the worth of property insurance and life insurance were 1.261 billion Yuan and 1.25 billion Yuan respectively, up by 11.8 percent and down by 14.3 percent respectively.

IX. Science and Technology and Education

In 2009, 270 science and technology projects were carried out. Of these, 114 projects were carried out for technology transfer and achievements transfer, 125 high-tech enterprises major were supported, 11 demonstration gardens of agricultural science and technology were supported for construction and 11 important direction projects of industrical science and technology in districts and counties were implemented. 0.206 billion Yuan was strived from the national and the province. The turnover in technology market reached 3.560 billion Yuan. 12,772 patents were applied and 4,706 were approved in 2009.

In 2009, there were 6,507 schools and educational institutions of various levels and kinds, 3.0620 million enrollments, and 199.8 thousand teachers and staff. Of this, there were 46 post-graduate training units, with 72.4 thousand post-graduate education enrollments, including 24.9 thousand new students; there were 49 general universities and colleges, with 632.2 thousand general tertiary education enrollments, including 188.4 thousand new students and 150.4 thousand graduates; there were 429 schools in the stage of senior high (including general secondary school, technical schools, adult secondary schools, general senior high school, vocational high schools, and so on), with 492.5 thousand senior high education enrollments, including 184.6 thousand new students; there were 259 general middle schools, with 322.7 thousand junior high education enrollments, including 101.4 thousand new students and 115.6 thousand graduates; there were 1,666 primary schools, with 525.2 thousand primary education enrollments, including 78.4 thousand new students and 99.6 thousand graduates; there were 835 private schools and institutions of various levels and kinds, with 468.8 thousand enrollments, including 159.7 thousand new students. The enrollment rates for school-age population of primary school and junior high school were 99.96 percent and 99.61 percent respectively. In total, the number of educated population was 3.2618 million, accounting for 41.73 percent of the city's total household registration.

X. Culture, Public Health and Sports

At the end of 2009, there were 11 art-performing groups, 14 public libraries, 15 culture centers, 182 culture stations, 49 museums. 569 various kinds of mass cultural activities were organized in 2009. There were 2 television stations, 2 radio broadcasting stations, and 6 radio broadcasting and television stations. The coverage rate of television broadcasting and radio broadcasting were 98.41 percent and 99.37 percent respectively.

At the end of 2009, there were 5.326 thousand health institutions in Xi'an, including 416 general hospitals and health centers. There were all 56.8 thousand health care workers, including 19.7 thousand practicing (assistant) doctors. General health centers in Xi'an possessed 34.9 thousand beds.

250 mass sports performances and competition activities were organized in 2009, with 2 million people taking part in per time. 4 national fitness squares were built in 2009 for free. There were 4830 stadiums (gyms, offices), of which the area was 16.6437 million square meters; per capita output of stadium area was 1.8 square meters. There were 6200 social sport instructors, 440 public health national fitness paths, 1600 sites for morning and evening exercise and 92 sites for Fitness Qigong. The 14th Sports Games of Xi'an was successfully held in 2009. Athletes from our city won 4.5 gold medals and 4.5 silver medals in the 11th National Games.

XI. Population, Living Conditions and Social Security

At the end of 2009, the total number of permanent residents in Xi'an reached 8.4346 million, among which there were 4.3577 million males, accounting for 51.7 percent , and 4.0769 million females, accounting for 48.3 percent .The sex ratio at birth was 107 (female=100). The year 2009 saw 84.7 thousand births, a crude birth rate of 10.08 per thousand, and 37.4 thousand deaths, a crude death rate of 5.63 per thousand; the net growth of population in 2009 was 59.4 thousand, and the natural growth rate was 4.45 per thousand. The number of people living in urban and rural were 5.8140 million and 2.6206 million respectively, accounting for 68.93 percent and 31.07 percent respectively. At the end of 2009, the registered population totaled 7.8167 million, up by 1.2 percent.

In 2009, the annual per capita disposable income of urban households was 18,963 Yuan, up by 24.7 percent over the previous year, and that of rural households was 6,275 Yuan, up by 20.4 percent. The proportion of expenditure on food to the total expenditure of households was 32.4 percent for urban households and 35.8 percent for rural households. The annual per capita building area of urban households was 28.4 square meters, and annual per capita living space of rural households was 57.0 square meters.

In 2009, 105.9 thousand residents were employed newly; 44.6 thousand laid-off workers were reemployed. Of this, the number of people between forty and fifty employed was 13 thousand. The rate of unemployment registered in urban reached 4.3 percent. The number of employment transfer of labor force in rural was 712.2 thousand.

By the end of 2009, a total of 3.5242 million people participated in urban basic health insurance program; a total of 1.7002 million people participated in basic pension program for staff and workers of enterprises; a total of 1.2740 million people participated in unemployment insurance programs; a total of 1.0411 million people participated in work accident insurance; a total of 819.5 thousand people participated in maternity insurance programs for staff and workers. The number of farmers taking part in the new cooperative medical care system in rural areas reached 3.8239 million, with a participation rate of 96.77 percent, 100% covered.

There were 112 social welfare enterprises in Xi'an and the number of social welfare lottery circulated and sold was 1.802 billion Yuan in 2009.

XII. Urban Construction, Environment Protection and Work Safety

The total investment in infrastructure in urban was 35.477 billion Yuan, up by 45.3 percent over the precious year .6 pedestrian bridges and 98 bus harbours were newly built. 7.76 million square meters area for centralized heating in urban areas was newly added. 13.18 thousand hectares area of afforestation was completed; 66 green squares were reformed and newly built; 4.86 million square meters area for landscaping in urban was newly added. 85 renovation of villages and the shanty settlement projects were carried out; the accumulative construction area of housing placement was 9.78 million square meters; the completed area was 0.87 million square meters; 3,209 households and 10,799 people were placed to move back. 1,351 kilometers of rural road were completed, and the total length of rural road reached 10.850 kilometers. The rate of villages and towns, administrative villages and natural villages accessed with cement (asphalts) roads reached 98.64 percent, 92.68 percent and 68.78 percent respectively.

In 2009, there were 304 days with air quality better than standard Grade II, an increase of 3 days, reaching a new high level in record. 5 sewage treatment plants were built and put into use in 2009; there were 1,054 kilometers sewage network; sewage treatment capacity reached 0.95 million tons per day, up by 0.25 million tons per day as compared with the previous year. The daily average value of inhaled particle matter annually in 2009, maintained the same level of the previous year; the .annual average value of sulfur dioxide in air was down by 4 percent. All of water quality of reference water source reached the state standard. The average value of sound level equivalent of regional environmental noises was 55.1 decibel, and the average value of sound level equivalent of transportation noises was 68 decibel.

In 2009, various kinds of work accidents amounted to 4,225, an increase of 87 as compared with the previous year, up by 2.1 percent. Of this, there ware 586 people dead, a decrease of 5, down by 0.9 percent; there were 2,264 people injured, a decrease of 208, down by 8.4 percent; the property losses was 31.2891 million Yuan, an increase of 3.2692 million Yuan, up by 11.7 percent.

Notes:

1.All figures in this communique were preliminary statistics.

2.Value-added in value terms as quoted in this communique are calculated at current prices, whereas their growth rates are calculated at comparable prices except for some with special notes.

1 综 合

GENERAL SURVEY

资料整理：栾立森　张小文

Data management:Luan Lisen Zhang Xiaowen

第一部分　综合

一、简要说明

本章资料主要包括西安市行政区划、自然地理、自然资源、气象、国民经济和社会发展等综合资料，由西安市统计局综合处根据局内各专业处及有关部门统计资料进行整理和编辑。

二、主要指标

生产总值（亿元）	2724.08	比上年增长	14.5%
工业增加值（亿元）	816.92	比上年增长	11.7%
农林牧渔业总产值（亿元）	178.70	比上年增长	6.5%
全社会固定资产投资额（亿元）	2500.13	比上年增长	31.1%
社会消费品零售总额（亿元）	1381.12	比上年增长	17.4%
地方财政收入（亿元）	331.42	可比增长	39.3%
地方财政支出（亿元）	420.08	可比增长	32.6%
外贸商品出口总额（亿美元）	72.46	比上年增长	2.9%
城镇居民人均可支配收入（元）	18963	比上年增长	24.7%
农村居民人均纯收入（元）	6275	比上年增长	20.4%

1 GENERAL SURVEY

Ⅰ.Brief Introduction

This chapter consists of mainly unified data of administrative divisions, natural geography, natural resources, meteorology, national economy and social development of Xi'an city. It is compiled by Integration Division of Xi'an Bureau of Statistics according to the reported data from other divisions of the Xi'an Bureau of Statistics and other departments of the municipal government.

Ⅱ.Major Indicators

		Increase over Preceding Year
Gross Domestic Product(100 mil. yuan)	2724.08	14.5%
Gross Industrial Added Value(100 mil. yuan)	816.92	11.7%
Gross Output Value of Farming, Forestry, Animal Husbandry and Fishery(100 mil. yuan)	178.70	6.5%
Investment Fulfilled In Fixed Assets(100 mil. yuan)	2500.13	31.1%
Total Retail Sales of Consumer Goods(100 mil. yuan)	1381.12	17.4%
Local Government Revenue(100 mil. yuan)	331.42	39.3%
Local Government Expenditures(100 mil. yuan)	420.08	32.6%
Total Value of Exports(USD 100 mil.)	72.46	2.9%
Per Capita Annual Disposable Income of Urban Households (yuan)	18963	24.7%
Per Capita Net Income of Rural Residents(yuan)	6275	20.4%

1-1 行政区划（2009年）

Administrative Division （2009）

单位:个 (unit)

区县名称	Name of District and County	乡镇及街道办 Township and Urban Subdistrict Office	镇数 Town	乡数 Township	街道办事处 Urban Subdistrict Office	村民委员会 Villagers' Committee	社区居委会 Neighbourhood Committee
西 安 市	**Xi'an**	**176**	**36**	**42**	**98**	**3114**	**621**
(一)市区	**Urban Districts**	**108**	**2**	**8**	**98**	**1613**	**577**
新城区	Xincheng	9			9	13	90
碑林区	Beilin	8			8	13	100
莲湖区	Lianhu	9			9	10	121
灞桥区	Baqiao	9			9	226	34
未央区	Weiyang	10			10	200	63
雁塔区	Yanta	8			8	115	93
阎良区	Yanliang	7	2		5	80	23
临潼区	Lintong	23		3	20	285	29
长安区	Chang'an	25		5	20	671	24
(二)四县	**Four Counties**	**68**	**34**	**34**		**1501**	**44**
蓝田县	Lantian	22	10	12		519	5
周至县	Zhouzhi	22	9	13		376	14
户　县	Huxian	16	11	5		518	21
高陵县	Gaoling	8	4	4		88	4

1-2 土地面积和常住人口密度（2009年）

Statistics on Land Area and Density of Permanent Population （2009）

区县名称	Name of District and County	土地面积 Area 绝对数（平方公里） Absolute Value (sq.km)	比 重(%) Proportion (%)	常住人口（万人） Total of Permanent Population (10 000 persons)	常住人口密度 (人/平方公里) Density of Permanent Population (person/ sq.km)
西 安 市	**Xi 'an**	**10108**	**100.0**	**843.46**	**834**
(一)市区	**Urban Districts**	**3582**	**35.4**	**647.28**	**1807**
新城区	Xincheng	30	0.3	62.80	20933
碑林区	Beilin	24	0.2	78.52	32717
莲湖区	Lianhu	43	0.4	73.82	17167
灞桥区	Baqiao	325	3.2	57.25	1762
未央区	Weiyang	262	2.6	62.96	2403
雁塔区	Yanta	149	1.5	113.67	7629
阎良区	Yanliang	244	2.4	26.27	1077
临潼区	Lintong	915	9.1	68.62	750
长安区	Chang'an	1590	15.7	103.37	650
(二)四县	**Four Counties**	**6526**	**64.6**	**196.18**	**301**
蓝田县	Lantian	2008	19.9	52.89	263
周至县	Zhouzhi	2949	29.2	55.72	189
户　县	Huxian	1282	12.7	56.77	443
高陵县	Gaoling	287	2.8	30.80	1073

1-3　自然状况和资源（2009年）

Nature Conditions and Resources（2009）

指　　　标	Item	2009
一、自然状况	**Nature Conditions**	
土地总面积(平方公里)	Total Land Area (sq.km)	10108
# 市区面积	Urban Area	3582
气候（市区）	Climate (Urban Area)	
平均气温(℃)	Average Annual Temperature (℃)	15.1
年降水量(毫米)	Total Annual Precipitation (mm)	660.3
日照时数(小时)	Total Sunshine Time (hour)	1729
平均风速(米/秒)	Average Wind-speed (m/sec.)	1.5
二、自然资源	**Natural Resources**	
年末实有耕地面积（万亩）	Cultivated Area Year-end (10 000 mu)	387.89
林业用地面积（千公顷）	Area of Forestry (1 000 hectare)	508.39
全市水面面积 (万亩)	Whole Water Area (10 000 mu)	4.20
# 可养殖面积	Area for Aquatics Breeding	3.00
水资源总量(亿立方米)	Total Water Resource (0.1 billion cu.m)	24.22
# 天然地表水资源总量	Total Savageness Surface Water Resource	20.36
地下水资源总量(亿立方米)	Total Ground Water Resource (0.1 billion cu.m)	14.78

注：全市水面面积包括湖泊、水库、鱼塘、城市段河流面积等。

Note:The whole water area of Xi'an includes the water area of lakes,reservoirs,fish ponds city sections of river,etc.

1-4　气 象 情 况（2009年）

Climate Condition （2009）

区县名称	Name of District and County	平均气温 (℃) Average Temperature (℃)	日照时数 (小时) Sunshine Time (hour)	降水天数 (天) Raining days (day)	年降水量 (毫米) Total Annual Precipitation (mm)	平均风速 (米/秒) Average Wind-speed (m/second)
市　区	Urban Districts	15.1	1729.0	111	660.3	1.5
临潼区	Lintong	14.3	1516.7	92	657.5	1.7
长安区	Chang'an	13.3	1698.4	118	801.2	1.2
蓝田县	Lantian	13.5	1726.3	129	846.9	1.5
周至县	Zhouzhi	13.6	1610.5	120	730.4	1.1
户　县	Huxian	14.7	1997.8	119	699.8	0.5
高陵县	Gaoling	14.2	1824.9	112	582.1	1.8

1-5 国有土地使用权出让、划拨情况

Basic Statistics on Lease and Administrative Allocation of Use Right of State-Owned Land

项　　目	Item	2000	2005	2006	2007	2008	2009
国有土地使用权出让	**Lease of the Use Right of State-owned Land**						
出让地块(宗)	Land leased (item)	202	312	316	333	278	297
协议	Agreement	200	241	225	171	119	100
招标	Invitation for Bid				1	3	
拍卖	Auction	2	8	7	3	5	1
挂牌交易	Listed Transaction		63	84	158	149	196
出让面积（公顷）	Area of Totally Leased Land (hectare)	3115	986	1208	843	809	1047
土地使用权出让总收入（万元）	**Total Revenue from Leasing of the Use Right (10 000 yuan)**	**38428**	**89039**	**156231**	**267666**	**309181**	**284405**
国有土地使用权划拨	**Administrative Allocation of the Use Right of State-owned Land**						
划拨地块（宗）	Land Allocated (item)	113	100	90	100	102	79
划拨面积（公顷）	Area of Land Allocated(hectare)	12543	835	259	388	455	1721

1-6 各部门机构数

Grassroots Units in Various Sectors

部　　门	Sector	机构数 Grassroots Units				
		2005	2006	2007	2008	2009
农村基层单位（个）	**Rural Grassroots Units（unit）**	**3264**	**3261**	**3251**	**3233**	**3192**
乡政府	Township Governments	52	52	47	47	42
镇政府	Town Governments	50	50	42	40	36
村民委员会	Village Committees	3162	3159	3162	3146	3114
国营农场(个)	**State-owned Farms (unit)**	**1**	**1**	**1**	**1**	**1**
规模以上工业企业(个)	**Industrial Enterprises Above Designated Size(unit)**	**902**	**904**	**937**	**934**	**1131**
内资企业	Domestic Funded Enterprises	798	787	809	808	989
国有企业	State-owned Industry	169	146	106	103	96
集体企业	Collective-owned Industry	77	72	73	68	65
股份合作企业	Cooperative Enterprises	24	22	20	19	16
联营经济企业	Joint Ownership Enterprises	8	6	4	3	3
有限责任公司	Limited Company	297	315	345	347	441
国有独资公司	State-owned appropriator ship corporation	14	15	16	18	22
其他有限责任公司	Limited Liability Corporations	283	300	329	329	419
股份有限公司	Share Holding Enterprises	45	46	51	54	63
私营企业	Private Enterprises	176	175	206	211	302
其他内资企业	Other Enterprises	2	5	4	3	3
港澳台商投资企业	Enterprises with Funds from Hong Kong, Macao and Taiwan	27	31	30	28	30
外商投资企业	Foreign Funded Enterprises	77	86	98	98	112

1-6 续表1 continued 1

部　门	Sector	机构数 Grassroots Units				
		2005	2006	2007	2008	2009
建筑业企业(个)	**Number of Construction Enterprise (unit)**	**235**	**212**	**279**	**329**	**326**
国有及国有控股	State-owned Or State Holding Majority Shares	69	59	50	76	79
集体企业	Collective-owned Enterprises	73	66	69	59	65
其他	Others	93	87	160	194	182
邮政营销网点(个)	**Establishments of Postal and Telecommunication Services (unit)**	**346**	**345**	**332**	**338**	**300**
卫生事业(个)	**Health Care (unit)**	**2769**	**2834**	**2546**	**2239**	**2162**
#医院、卫生院	Urban and Township Hospitals	479	475	459	432	415
疗养院	Sanatoriums	4	5	6	4	3
门诊部	Clinics	198	207	185	156	150
专科疾病防治院	Specialized Prevention & Treatment Stations	1	2	1	1	1
疾病控制预防中心	Sanitation and Antiepidemic Stations	17	17	17	17	17
妇幼保健院	Maternity and Childcare Centers	15	15	15	15	15
社会福利事业（个）	**Social Welfare Institutions (unit)**	**253**	**237**	**172**	**163**	**167**
社会福利机构	Social Welfare Establishments	42	36	37	42	55
#社会福利院	Social Welfare Institutions	5	5	3	4	5
社会福利企业	Social Welfare Enterprises	211	201	135	121	112
教育事业(所)	**Education (unit)**	**3414**	**3499**	**3398**	**3377**	**3296**
普通高等学校	Regular Institutions of Higher Education	44	47	48	48	49
普通中等学校	Secondary Schools	648	660	648	637	678
#普通中学	Regular Secondary Schools	460	457	453	442	439
小学	Primary Schools	1980	1929	1872	1781	1666

1-6 续表2 continued 2

部门	Sector	机构数 Grassroots Units				
		2005	2006	2007	2008	2009
幼儿园	Kindergartens	737	863	830	905	896
特殊教育	Special Schools	5			6	7
艺术事业(个)	**Art Institutions (unit)**	**39**	**39**	**36**	**36**	**36**
艺术表演团体	Art Performance Troupes	19	19	18	18	18
艺术表演场所	Art Show Centers	20	20	18	18	18
#剧场、影剧院	Theaters	13	13	13	13	13
公共图书馆(个)	**Public Libraries (unit)**	**15**	**15**	**15**	**15**	**15**
群众文化事业(个)	**Mass Cultural Establishments (unit)**	**192**	**192**	**196**	**197**	**197**
#文化馆	Cultural Centers	13	14	14	15	15
文物事业(个)	**Cultural Relic Carc (unit)**	**47**	**45**	**56**	**51**	**55**
#博物馆	Museum	14	14	16	15	19
文物科研机构	Cultural Relic Scientific Research Institutions	4	2	3	3	3
广播电视台站(座)	**Broadcasting and Television Stations (unit)**	**10**	**10**	**10**	**10**	**10**
广播电台	Radio Stations	2	2	2	2	2
电视台	Television Stations	2	2	2	2	2
县级广播电视台	Number of Wire Broadcasting and Television Stations in County Level	6	6	6	6	6
科学研究机构（个）	**Scientific Research Institutions（unit）**	**358**	**365**	**380**	**411**	
科研单位	Units of Scientific Research	103	101	96	94	
高等院校	Institutions of Higher Education	165	167	153	187	
大中型工业企业	Large-scale and Medium-scale Industrial Enterprises	90	97	131	130	

注：2009年因全国科技普查资料整理尚在进行，故无数。

Note:As the data of national science and technology census was sorting out ,there was no data in 2009.

1-7 平均每天主要社会经济活动

指　标	Item	1995	2000	2001
一、每天创造的财富	**Daily Production**			
生产总值(万元)	Gross Domestic Product(10 000 yuan)	9050.68	17702.19	20133.15
第一产业	Primary Industry	1134.25	1223.29	1256.71
第二产业	Secondary Industry	3707.67	7592.60	8572.60
#工业	Industry	3082.19	5984.66	6764.38
建筑业	Construction	625.48	1607.95	1808.22
第三产业	Tertiary Industry	4208.77	8886.30	10303.84
#交通运输、仓储及邮政业	Transport, Storage, Post & Telecommunication Services	673.97	1709.32	1808.22
批发和零售贸易餐饮业	Wholesale and Retail Trade & Catering Services	909.59	2164.38	2575.34
地方财政收入(万元)	Local Government Revenue(10 000 yuan)	498.79	1304.00	1534.16
地方财政支出(万元)	Local Government Expenditures(10 000 yuan)	504.66	1274.06	1565.47
粮食(吨)	Grain(ton)	4801.37	5532.05	5399.73
奶类(吨)	Milk(ton)	364.13	673.73	699.83
蔬菜(吨)	Vegetables(ton)	3660.27	4442.19	4186.30
肉类(吨)	Meat(ton)	350.18	404.30	430.90
水产品(吨)	Aquatic Products(ton)	23.33	31.19	34.19
布(万米)	Cloth(10 000 m)	83.00	77.00	70.00
发电量(万千瓦小时)	Electricity(10 000 kwh)	610.00	534.00	505.00
钢(吨)	Steel(ton)		85.10	88.41
水　泥(吨)	Cement(ton)	1898.90	3050.68	3399.73
二、每天消费量	**Daily National Consumption**			
最终消费(万元)	Final Consumption Expenditure(10 000 yuan)	6565.48	11326.85	12514.52
社会消费品零售总额(万元)	Total Retail Sales of Consumer Goods (10 000 yuan)	5112.33	9874.52	11129.04
三、每天其他经济活动	**Other Daily Economic Activities**			
资本形成总额(万元)	Gross Capital Formation(10 000 yuan)	4152.05	7885.48	9002.47
固定资本形成	Fixed Capital Formation			
存货增加	Changes in Stock			
城镇新建住宅面积(平方米)	Residential Buildings Completed in Urban Areas(sq.m)	6927	14930	13761
货运量(吨)	Freight Traffic(ton)	262734	191760	211736
客运量(人)	Passenger Traffic(person)	248466	221041	248753
邮电业务总量(万元)	Business Volume of Postal and Telecommunications Services(10 000 yuan)	209.60	1264.70	1007.20
进出口总额(万美元)	Total Value of Imports and Exports (USD 10 000)	110.19	475.88	465.52
出口总额	Total Exports	82.45	290.58	240.95
进口总额	Total Imports	27.74	185.30	224.56
外商实际直接投资额(万美元)	Foreign Capital Actually Used(USD 10 000)	51.11	42.83	48.46
国际旅游人数(人)	Number of Tourists from Abroad(person)	1133.82	1781.88	1841.14
城乡居民储蓄额(万元)	Outstanding Amount of Savings Deposit (10 000 yuan)	1546.29	2450.27	3425.65
四、每天人口变动和婚姻	**Daily Population Changes and Marriages**			
出　生(人)	Births(person)	211	247	140
死　亡(人)	Deaths(person)	88	113	79
结　婚(对)	Marriages(couple)	129	129	116
离　婚(对)	Divorces(couple)	12	14	15

Selected Indicators on Average Daily Social and Economic Activities

2002	2003	2004	2005	2006	2007	2008	2009
22648.77	25935.89	30202.47	34798.36	40374.79	48321.37	60001.10	74632.33
1308.77	1389.59	1649.59	1808.49	1938.90	2260.55	2834.25	3024.11
9687.12	11161.10	13066.30	14783.84	17503.56	21164.66	27060.27	31363.01
7676.71	8900.82	10505.75	11506.58	13530.41	16345.21	20346.58	22381.37
2010.41	2260.27	2560.55	3277.26	3973.15	4819.45	6713.70	8981.64
11652.88	13385.21	15486.58	18206.03	20932.33	24896.16	30106.58	40245.21
1917.53	2041.37	2189.59	2575.89	2941.37	3317.53	3744.38	3030.14
3008.77	3509.59	4110.96	4779.73	5476.44	6414.79	7912.33	10605.48
1646.60	1996.36	2357.89	2300.56	2638.63	3433.64	6517.81	9080.00
1884.90	2116.52	2452.23	2819.58	3689.04	4771.43	8679.18	11509.04
5271.50	4831.23	5363.01	5630.84	5831.38	5179.84	5873.97	5978.08
789.10	921.37	1052.93	1156.79	1291.61	1446.67	1615.62	1693.70
4650.40	4648.49	4957.81	5361.62	5709.33	5601.08	6069.32	6641.37
371.20	454.52	469.99	498.76	538.37	279.98	316.16	345.75
32.90	27.40	26.63	25.67	26.62	33.98	34.25	35.62
76.39	76.47	78.77	74.01	72.62	76.70	62.25	60.83
520.40	559.18	1308.97	1316.26	1830.14	1946.27	1964.11	2279.73
85.10	98.06	49.51	35.28	38.21	30.01	38.34	25.30
3677.50	3693.70	3809.59	3315.34	4349.17	7209.04	11089.32	13362.00
13851.23	14841.92	18883.29	21003.29	23861.10	27266.30	32400.27	38441.10
12596.16	13771.23	15852.05	18371.51	21505.48	25649.59	32235.07	37838.90
10560.27	13914.25	17806.30	22986.58	28637.53	39766.30	50352.33	62518.08
	12462.47	16161.64	20363.56	25967.12	34795.62	45315.34	58878.90
	1451.78	1644.66	1739.45	2232.60	4637.81	5036.99	3639.18
13319	15837	13906	16400	15975	25466	18998	22537
259836	257315	406712	431562	324164	414364	758137	838521
343206	312685	316027	310219	308082	341534	732740	786110
1411.70	2249.16	2814.84	3617.66	5116.66	6212.69	7256.44	8189.59
512.20	632.69	847.38	1068.89	1138.09	1468.94	1928.85	1985.25
308.20	384.46	557.64	721.76	747.57	951.05	1224.97	912.64
204.00	248.23	289.74	347.14	390.52	517.89	703.88	1072.61
55.60	70.02	75.60	156.47	225.93	305.66	314.35	333.90
2030.90	922.34	1781.71	2124.99	2376.09	2739.90	1731.51	1843.56
27069.63	33166.05	39256.55	47034.45	53439.13	54727.67	68613.97	84175.62
109	165	182	182	223	226	232	232
105	91	116	63	122	124	127	130
122	122	153	137	184	185	213	241
26	29	35	35	35	43	43	43

1-8 国民经济和社会发展总量与速度指标

指　　标	Item	总量指标				
		1995	2000	2004	2005	2006
人口与就业	**Population and Employment**					
人口(万人)	**Population(10 000 persons)**					
年底总人口	Population at the Year-end	648.21	688.01	725.01	741.73	753.11
非农业人口	Non-agricultural Population	255.71	285.79	318.50	333.14	343.78
农业人口	Agriculturral Population	392.50	402.22	406.51	408.59	409.33
男性人口	Male	334.75	355.18	374.16	382.02	387.37
女性人口	Female	313.46	332.83	350.85	359.71	365.74
就业(万人)	**Employment(10 000 persons)**					
就业人员数	Employment	372.60	389.10	409.57	415.83	422.15
#在岗职工人数	Number of Employed Staff and Workers	141.17	109.62	113.44	119.73	121.06
城镇登记失业人数	Registered Unemployed in Urban Areas	5.92	3.85	8.29	8.45	8.74
宏观经济	**Macroeconomic Indicator**					
国民经济核算(亿元)	**National Accounts(100 mil. yuan)**					
生产总值	Gross Domestic Product	330.35	646.13	1102.39	1313.93	1538.94
#第一产业	Primary Industry	41.40	44.65	60.21	66.01	70.44
第二产业	Secondary Industry	135.33	277.13	476.92	540.50	645.65
工业	Industry	112.50	218.44	383.46	420.00	494.22
第三产业	Tertiary Industry	153.62	324.35	565.26	707.42	822.85
#最终消费	Total Consumption	239.64	413.43	689.24	766.62	870.93
资本形成总额	Total Investment	151.55	287.82	649.93	839.01	1045.27
固定资产投资(亿元)	**Investment in Fixed Assets(100 mil. yuan)**					
全社会固定资产投资总额	Total Investment in Fixed Assets	103.42	232.37	646.69	835.10	1066.62
一、城镇	Urban Area	88.50	203.01	612.03	776.33	971.84
#房地产	Real Estate	21.65	51.85	169.67	225.23	285.76
二、农村	Rural Area	14.92	29.36	34.66	58.77	94.78
#国有单位	State-Owned Units	69.08	159.60	329.14	373.70	401.14
集体单位	Collective-Owned Units	9.78	14.65	40.06	59.23	110.68
个体经济	Individuals	11.13	24.40	48.95	79.04	107.33
财政(亿元)	**Public Finance(100 mil. yuan)**					
地方财政收入	Local Financial Revenue	18.21	46.96	86.06	83.97	96.31
地方财政支出	Local Financial Expenditure	18.42	51.89	89.51	102.91	134.65
物价总指数(上年=100)	**Price Indices(preceding year=100)**					
商品零售价格指数	Retail Price Index	114.6	98.7	101.9	99.7	101.5
居民消费价格指数	Consumer Price Index	117.0	100.2	102.3	100.3	101.6
工业品出厂价格指数	Ex-Factory Price Indices of Industrial Products	110.8	99.4	102.7	103.9	103.2

注：1.国民经济核算2004-2008年为全国第二次经济普查修订数据。

2.地方财政收支为一般预算收支与基金预算收支之和。

Principal Aggregate Indicators on National Economic and Social Development and Their Related Indices and Growth Rates

Aggregate Data			速度指标(%) Indices and Growth Rates						
2007	2008	2009	指数 Index (2009比以下各年) (2009 as percentage of the following years)			平均增长速度 Average Annual Growth Rate			
			2000	2005	2008	1996-2000	1996-2005	2001-2005	2006-2009
764.25	772.30	781.67	113.61	105.38	101.21	1.20	1.36	1.51	1.32
353.85	363.87	370.66	129.70	111.26	101.87	2.25	2.68	3.11	2.70
410.40	408.43	411.01	102.19	100.59	100.63	0.49	0.40	0.31	0.15
392.41	395.54	399.28	112.42	104.52	100.95	1.19	1.33	1.47	1.11
371.84	376.76	382.39	114.89	106.31	101.49	1.21	1.39	1.57	1.54
436.36	448.05	462.52	118.87	111.23	103.23	0.87	1.10	1.34	2.70
125.56	126.89	129.62	118.24	108.26	102.15	-4.93	-1.69	1.78	2.00
8.77	9.40	10.20	264.94	120.71	108.51	-8.25	3.62	17.03	4.80
1856.63	2318.14	2724.08	330.25	175.49	114.50	13.56	13.52	13.48	15.10
82.51	103.45	110.38	157.96	128.01	106.30	4.58	4.44	4.29	6.37
781.94	981.58	1144.75	353.98	174.56	114.00	16.75	15.97	15.18	14.94
594.95	721.40	816.92	332.74	166.76	111.70	15.47	15.32	14.29	13.64
992.18	1233.11	1468.95	332.80	180.58	115.50	10.89	11.94	13.00	15.92
995.22	1182.61	1403.10	279.05	165.81	118.40	9.88	9.38	8.90	13.47
1451.47	1837.86	2281.91	737.16	239.28	122.60	11.86	16.59	21.53	24.37
1435.33	1906.36	2500.13	1075.93	299.38	131.15	17.58	23.23	29.16	31.54
1340.59	1786.60	2367.58	1166.24	304.97	132.52	18.06	24.25	30.77	32.15
387.33	540.26	696.34	1342.99	309.17	128.89	19.09	26.39	34.15	32.60
94.74	119.76	132.55	451.46	225.54	110.68	14.50	14.69	14.89	22.55
476.78	694.89	932.91	584.53	249.64	134.25	18.23	18.39	18.55	25.70
207.08	246.89	289.91	1978.91	489.46	117.42	8.43	19.74	32.23	48.74
183.09	50.43	97.86	401.07	123.81	149.05	16.99	21.66	26.50	5.48
125.33	237.90	331.42	705.75	394.69	139.31	20.87	13.36	12.33	40.95
174.16	316.79	420.08	809.57	408.21	132.61	23.02	18.77	14.68	42.14
103.7	105.4	99.5							
104.7	106.0	99.7							
101.9	103.7	99.9							

1.The data of national account between 2004 and 2008 was from the second national economic census.

2.Local government revenue and expenditure was the sum of ordinary budgetary revenue and expenditure plus fund budgetary revenue and expenditure.

1-8　续表1

指　　标	Item	总量指标				
		1995	2000	2004	2005	2006
利用外资签订协议金额(万美元)	**Utilization of Foreign Capital(USD 10 000)**					
签订利用外资协议额	Amount of Foreign Capital for Utilization Through Signed Contracts or Agreements	28956.2	54123.0	78312.0	121499.0	182525.0
外商实际直接投资额	Amount of Foreign Capital Actually Utilized	18653.0	15633.0	27595.0	57113.0	82463.0
产　业	**Industry**					
农业	**Agriculture**					
耕地面积(万亩)	Cultivated Areas(1 000 hectares)	464.0	443.4	404.9	400.2	395.8
乡村劳动力资源总数（万人）	Total Number of Rural Labor Source (10 000 persons)	213.8	240.8	252.6	255.9	257.7
农林牧渔业总产值(亿元)	Gross Output Value of Farming Forestry, Animal Husbandry and Fishery(100 mil yuan)	75.46	74.37	96.79	106.54	114.15
主要农产品产量(万吨)	Output of Major Farm Products(10 000 tons)					
粮　食	Grain	175.3	201.9	195.8	205.5	193.5
奶　类	Milk	13.3	24.6	38.4	42.2	47.1
油　料	Oil-bearing Crops	2.2	1.3	1.1	1.2	1.1
蔬　菜	Vegetables	133.6	162.1	181.0	195.7	189.3
水　果	Fruits	24.1	34.4	46.3	51.3	55.3
肉　类	Meat	12.8	14.8	17.2	18.2	10.9
水产品	Aquatic Products	0.9	1.1	1.0	0.9	1.2
工业	**Industry**					
规模以上工业企业主要经济指标（亿元）	Principal Indicators of Industrial Enterprises of State Ownership and Non-state-owned Above Designated Size(100 mil. yuan)					
工业总产值	Gross industrial Output Value		417.97	830.06	981.02	1187.74
资产总计	Total Assets		958.05	1333.91	1503.85	1651.67
主营业务收入	Revenue from Principal Business		420.42	812.46	980.97	1183.51
利润总额	Profits		16.11	38.57	28.72	61.46
从业人员年平均人数（万人）	Annual Average Employers(10 000 persons)		43.25	38.08	37.92	37.94
主要工业产品产量	Output of Major Industrial Products					
布(万米)	Cloth(10 000 m)	30332	24818	28752	27012	26508
机制纸及纸板(吨)	Machine-Made Paper(tons)	364400	54711	407526	221865	325107
家用电冰箱(台)	Household Refrigerators(unit)	13000	5860	58254	25407	69199
发电量(亿千瓦时)	Electricity(100 million kwh)	22.00	19.00	48.00	48.00	67.00
成品钢材(吨)	Steel Products(ton)	314400	4320	67326	240182	715303
缝纫机(万架)	Sewing Machines (10 000 units)	16.80	41.40	55.80	48.20	61.50
汽车(万辆)	Motor Vehicle (10 000 units)	0.3	0.9	3.5	4.1	10.3
建筑业	**Construction**					
建筑业企业人数(人)	Number of Employed Persons(person)		136718	159134	158311	172179
建筑业总产值(亿元)	Gross Output Value(100 mil. yuan)	42.55	105.93	244.42	326.65	416.48
施工房屋面积(万平方米)	Floor Space of Buildings under Construction (10 000 sq.m)	601.7	793.3	1679.5	1801.2	2140.1

continued 1

Aggregate Data			速度指标(%)			Indices and Growth Rates			
2007	2008	2009	指数 Index (2009比以下各年) (2009 as percentage of the following years)			平均增长速度 Average Annual Growth Rate			
			2000	2005	2008	1996-2000	1996-2005	2001-2005	2006-2009
143978.3	118230.0	60027.0	110.91	49.41	50.77	13.33	15.42	17.55	-16.16
111567.0	114738.0	121872.0	779.58	213.39	106.22	-3.47	11.84	29.58	20.86
391.8	390.8	387.9	87.49	96.93	99.26	-0.90	-1.47	-2.03	-0.78
254.1	256.2	255.0	105.90	99.65	99.54	2.40	1.81	1.22	-0.09
134.15	168.27	178.70	162.00	129.60	106.20	4.92	4.78	4.04	6.70
189.1	214.4	218.2	108.07	106.18	101.77	2.87	1.61	0.35	1.51
52.8	59.0	61.8	251.30	146.49	104.83	13.10	12.25	11.40	10.01
1.0	1.2	1.1	86.15	93.33	97.39	-9.99	-5.88	-1.59	-1.71
204.3	221.5	242.4	149.54	123.87	109.43	3.95	3.89	3.84	5.50
60.5	71.7	79.0	229.53	153.92	110.14	7.32	7.83	8.32	11.38
10.2	11.5	12.6	85.26	69.33	109.34	2.95	3.60	4.22	-8.75
1.2	1.3	1.3	118.58	144.93	104.35	4.10	1.01	-3.93	9.72
1577.05	2007.85	2468.27	466.96	207.45	122.93			18.61	25.94
1940.52	2426.13	2913.56	304.11	193.74	120.09			9.44	17.98
1561.25	1928.05	2384.52	567.18	243.08	123.68			18.47	24.86
106.22	84.89	177.20	1099.94	616.99	208.74			12.26	57.60
38.55	40.17	43.42	100.39	114.50	108.09			-2.60	3.44
27995	22721	22202	89.46	82.19	97.71	-3.93	-1.15	1.71	-4.78
426520	442758	476258	870.50	214.66	107.57	-31.56	-4.84	32.31	21.04
94090	100854	92146	1572.46	362.68	91.37	-14.73	6.93	34.09	38.00
71.00	71.69	83.21	437.96	173.36	116.07	-2.87	7.99	20.36	14.75
787274	478819	1105074	25580.41	460.10	230.79	-57.58	-2.66	123.36	46.46
73.50	38.60	36.09	87.19	74.89	93.51	19.77	11.62	3.09	-6.98
17.1	26.8	50.7	5737.75	1226.27	188.95	20.95	28.33	36.15	87.13
296538	400740	461080	331.76	286.51	111.85			2.98	30.10
604.92	915.19	1296.58	1224.00	396.93	141.67	20.01	22.61	25.26	41.15
2802.0	3133.9	3947.0	497.54	219.13	125.95	5.68	11.59	17.82	21.67

1-8 续表2

指　　标	Item	总量指标				
		1995	2000	2004	2005	2006
竣工房屋面积(万平方米)	Floor Space of Buildings Completed(10 000 sq.m)	177.15	336.80	662.00	569.01	594.20
交通运输	**Transportation**					
货运量(万吨)	Freight Traffic(10 000 tons)	9590	6999	14845	12051	11832
铁 路	Railways	3317	3101	4126	540	573
公 路	Highways	6268	3890	10714	11505	11254
民用航空	Civil Aviation	5	8	5	6	5
客运量(万人次)	Passenger Traffic(10 000 persons-times)	9069	8068	10832	10479	11245
铁 路	Railways	2678	2130	2380	1796	2066
公 路	Highways	6128	5578	8128	8294	8682
民用航空	Civil Aviation	263	360	324	389	497
邮电通信业	**Post and Telecommunication Services**					
邮电业务总量(亿元)	Total Business Revenue(100 mil. yuan)	7.65	46.16	102.74	132.04	186.76
函 件(万件)	Number of Letters Delivered(10 000 pieces)	14647	8230	10961	9526	9328
本地电话局用交换机容量(万门)	Capacity of Local Office Telephone Exchanges (10 000 line)	58.3	204.8	418.1	457.3	474.7
本地电话年末用户(万户)	Number of Subscribers of Local Telephone at Year-end(10 000 subscribers)	30.79	141.28	293.44	321.48	315.96
城市电话用户	Urban Telephone Subscribers	29.95	124.26	245.41	271.40	269.21
乡村电话用户	Rural Telephone Subscribers	0.84	17.02	48.03	50.08	46.75
移动电话用户(万户)	Number of Mobile Telephone Subscribers (10 000 subscribers)		73.10	350.09	419.96	551.07
互联网年末宽带用户(万户)	Number of Subscribers of Internet Services (10 000 subscribers)			24.34	33.93	50.88
国内商业	**Domestic Trade**					
社会消费品零售总额(亿元)	Total Retail Sales of Consumer Goods (100 mil. yuan)	186.60	360.42	578.60	670.56	784.95
对外经济贸易	**Foreign Trade**					
进出口总额(万美元)	Total Exports and Imports(USD 10 000)	137510	173696	309295	390146	415403
出口额	Exports	110163	106062	203539	263441	272862
进口额	Imports	27347	67634	105756	126705	142541
国际旅游	**International Tourism**					
国际旅游人数(万人)	Number of International Tourists(10 000 persons)	41.35	65.03	65.03	77.56	86.73
旅游外汇收入(万元)	Foreign Exchange Earnings from Tourism (10 000 yuan)	103818	224100	273900	335380	378270
金融保险	**Finance and Insurance**					
金融机构人民币存款余额(亿元)（不含外资）	Balance of Deposits in Domestic Funded Financial Institutions (100 mil. yuan)	359.51	1335.63	3061.66	3599.70	4066.16
金融机构人民币贷款余额(亿元)（不含外资）	Balance of Loans in Domestic Funded Financial Institutions (100 mil. yuan)	334.50	972.52	2052.33	2158.10	2344.77

注：1.2006年铁路数据按新口径统计；

2.2006年国际互联网络用户改为互联网宽带用户。

continued 2

Aggregate Data			速度指标(%) Indices and Growth Rates						
			指数 Index (2009比以下各年) (2009 as percentage of the following years)			平均增长速度 Average Annual Growth Rate			
2007	2008	2009	2000	2005	2008	1996-2000	1996-2005	2001-2005	2006-2009
835.95	1046.41	1209.88	359.23	212.63	115.62	13.71	12.38	11.06	20.76
15124	27560	30606	437.29	253.97	111.05	-6.10	2.31	11.48	26.24
589	605	614	19.80	113.70	101.49	-1.34	-16.60	-29.50	3.26
14530	26949	29986	770.85	260.63	111.27	-9.10	6.26	24.22	27.06
5	6	6	75.00	100.00	100.00	9.86	1.84	-5.59	
12466	26501	28693	355.64	273.81	108.27	-2.31	1.46	5.37	28.64
2380	2680	2585	121.36	143.93	96.46	-4.48	-3.92	-3.35	9.53
9466	23175	25271	453.05	304.69	109.04	-1.86	3.07	8.26	32.12
620	646	837	232.50	215.17	129.57	6.48	3.99	1.56	21.11
226.76	264.67	298.92	647.58	226.39	112.94	43.26	32.95	23.39	22.66
5544	5638	6128	74.46	64.33	108.69	-10.89	-4.21	2.97	-10.44
479.7	462.5	441.1	215.38	96.46	95.37	28.57	22.87	17.43	-0.90
314.58	345.27	324.92	229.99	101.07	94.11	35.63	26.44	17.87	0.27
272.64	306.88	289.10	232.66	106.52	94.21	32.92	24.66	16.91	1.59
41.94	38.39	35.82	210.48	71.53	93.32	82.59	50.53	24.09	-8.03
664.59	737.76	1120.06	1532.23	266.71	151.82			41.86	27.79
58.62	81.40	116.79		344.21	143.48				36.21
936.21	1176.58	1381.12	383.20	205.97	117.38	14.07	13.58	13.22	19.80
536162	704029	724618	417.18	185.73	102.92	4.78	10.99	17.57	16.74
347133	447113	333114	314.07	126.45	74.50	-0.76	9.11	19.96	6.04
189029	256916	391504	578.86	308.99	152.39	19.85	16.57	13.38	32.58
100.01	63.20	67.29	103.48	86.76	106.47	9.48	6.49	3.59	-3.49
424263	287200	310500	138.55	92.58	108.11	16.64	12.44	8.40	-1.91
4582.71	5711.27	7457.71	558.37	207.18	128.84	30.02	25.91	21.93	19.97
2683.77	3235.84	4436.50	456.19	205.57	135.76	23.79	20.49	17.28	19.74

Note:1. The railway data is added up according to new aperture in 2006.

2. The number of broadband internet subscribers changed from Internet subscribers in 2006.

1-8 续表3

指　　标	Item	总量指标			
		1995	2000	2004	2005
保险公司保险金额(亿元)	Insurance Coverage of Insurance Companies (100 mil. yuan)	1155.01	1586.67	3381.56	3598.63
保险公司保费金额(亿元)	Insurance Premium of Insurance Companies (100 mil. yuan)	4.70	13.58	39.73	44.94
保险公司赔款及付给金额(亿元)	Indemnity Expenditure and Payment of Insurance Companies (100 mil. yuan)	1.70	1.39	7.98	9.50
教育、科技、文化	**Education, Science and Technology and Culture**				
教育	**Education**				
专任教师数(人)	Full-time Teachers(person)	74905	78817	94090	98561
普通高等学校	Institutions of Higher Education	15914	15679	26867	29498
中等学校	Secondary Schools	28721	32923	37856	39416
小 学	Primary Schools	30270	30215	29367	29647
在校学生数(万人)	Students Enrollment(10 000 person)	132.46	155.97	178.65	186.34
普通高等学校	Institutions of Higher Education	11.67	19.41	43.81	53.06
中等学校	Secondary Schools	41.43	58.75	71.09	72.81
小 学	Primary Schools	79.36	77.81	63.75	60.47
科技	**Science and Technology**				
各类专业技术人员(万人)	Different Kinds of Technical Personnel(10 000 person)	35.6	33.4	37.0	38.8
经认定的高新技术企业(个)	Identified Hitech Enterprises (unit)		632	951	1029
累计专利授权数（件）	Accumulated patents awarded	3164	6139	10390	11419
文化	**Culture**				
图书馆总藏量(千册件)	Total Collections in Library (1000 Volume-time)	2830	3214	3502	3671
文化馆、站（个)	Cultural Centers or Stations (unit)	201	251	190	190
电影放映单位数(个)	Film Projection Units (unit)	576	586	588	588
电视节目制作时间(小时)	Time for TV Programs Production(hours)	5738	11871	18643	27377
家庭、生活、环境	**Family, People's Livelihood and Environment**				
家庭	**Family**				
家庭总户数 (万户)	Total Number of Households(10 000 households)	171.25	187.08	199.33	203.04
城镇居民平均每户家庭人口(人)	Average Household Size in Urban Areas(person)	3.88	2.99	2.99	2.93
农村居民平均每户家庭人口(人)	Average Household Size in Rural Areas(person)	4.60	4.30	4.11	4.22
婚姻	**Marriages and Divorces**				
结婚登记总数(对)	Register Number of Marriages(couples)	47236	46415	55987	49962
离婚数(对)	Number of Divorces(couples)	4296	5161	12702	12747
居住	**Housing**				
城镇居民人均现住房总建筑面积(平方米)	Per capital total building area of urban residents' houses(sq.m)	13.05	14.82	15.53	16.38
农村居民人均居住面积(平方米)	Per Capita Net Floor Space of Rural Residents(sq.m)	21.77	28.31	34.66	36.73

注：1.2009年因全国科技普查资料整理尚在进行，故无数。
2.2008年及以前图书馆总藏量为图书馆藏书量。
3.2005年以前城镇居民人均现住房总建筑面积为城镇人均住房使用面积。

continued 3

Aggregate Data				速度指标(%) Indices and Growth Rates						
				指数 Index (2009比以下各年) (2009 as percentage of the following years)			平均增长速度 Average Annual Growth Rate			
2006	2007	2008	2009	2000	2005	2008	1996-2000	1996-2005	2001-2005	2006-2009
8152.93	10244.24	30224.55	18999.60	1197.45	527.97	62.86	6.56	12.04	17.80	51.58
52.51	72.33	101.45	122.11	899.19	271.73	120.37	22.17	24.58	27.04	28.39
11.80	19.91	25.92	25.16	1810.07	264.80	97.05	-3.95	18.78	46.87	27.56
100308	105863	110629	115076	158.20	126.37	112.58	1.02	2.78	4.57	6.03
32891	36717	38926	40605	258.98	137.65	104.31	-0.30	6.37	13.47	8.32
37399	38613	41321	44137	134.06	111.98	106.81	2.77	3.22	3.67	2.87
30018	30533	30382	30334	100.39	102.32	99.84	-0.04	-0.21	-0.38	0.57
193.13	196.34	199.73	203.49	130.47	109.20	101.88	3.32	3.47	3.62	2.23
57.10	62.31	66.68	70.31	362.24	132.51	105.45	10.71	16.35	22.28	7.29
76.70	77.2	78.39	80.66	137.29	110.78	102.89	7.24	5.80	4.38	2.59
59.33	56.83	54.66	52.52	67.50	86.85	96.08	-0.39	-2.68	-4.92	-3.46
39.1	41.8	43.7					-1.27	0.86	3.04	
1062	1311	1324							10.24	
13442	15971	19256					14.18	13.69	13.22	
3807	3893	4040	4324	134.54	117.79	107.03	2.58	2.64	2.69	4.18
192	196	197	197	78.49	103.68	100.00	4.54	-0.56	-5.42	0.91
588	588	588	588	100.34	100.00	100.00	0.34	0.02	0.07	
36337	25883	26897	27131	228.55	99.10	100.87	15.65	16.91	18.19	-0.23
207.04	211.12	216.52	221.51	118.40	109.10	102.30	1.78	1.72	1.65	2.20
2.90	2.91	2.82	2.84	94.98	96.93	100.71	-5.08	-2.77	-0.40	-0.78
4.19	4.48	4.03	4.07	94.71	96.50	100.99	-1.34	-0.86	-0.37	-0.89
67018	67637	77912	88138	189.89	176.41	113.13	-0.35	0.56	1.48	15.25
12708	15536	15722	15796	306.06	123.92	100.47	3.74	11.49	19.82	5.51
23.15	23.63	26.32	28.40	191.63	173.38	107.90	2.58	2.30	2.02	14.75
40.05	42.92	54.97	56.73	200.39	154.45	103.20	5.39	5.37	5.35	11.48

Note:1.As the data of national science and technology census was sorting out ,there was no data in 2009.

2.'Total collections in libraries' was the 'number of collections in libraries' in 2008 and before.

3.The per capital total building area of urban residents' houses was replaced as the per Capital dwelling area of urban residents before 2005.

1-8 续表4

指　　标	Item	总量指标			
		1995	2000	2004	2005
生活	**People's Livelihood**				
城镇居民人均可支配收入(元)	Per Capita Annual Disposable Income of Urban Households (yuan)	4153	6364	8544	9628
农村居民人均纯收入(元)	Per Capita Net Income of Rural Residents(yuan)	1353	2344	3143	3460
城乡储蓄存款余额(亿元)	Outstanding Amount of Saving Deposits in Urban and Rural Areas(100 mil yuan)	230.63	675.83	1432.86	1716.76
工资	**Wages and Welfare**				
在岗职工工资总额(亿元)	The gross salary of workers (100 mil yuan)	67.23	101.68	176.62	211.14
职工平均工资(元)	Average Wage of Staff and Workers(yuan)	4763	9179	15473	17728
卫生	**Health Care**				
医院、卫生院(个)	Number of Hospitals(unit)	368	426	495	479
医生（人)	Number of Doctors(person)	18846	18750	16749	17730
医院、卫生院床位数(张)	Number of Hospital Beds(unit)	28265	28697	30736	30087
市政建设	**City Construction**				
自来水供应量(万吨)	Volume of Tap Water Supply(10 000 tons)	35885	30273	36092	35776
供水管道总长度(公里)	Length of Water Supply Pipelines(km)	1066	2237	2279	2315
城市天然气供气量(万立方米)	Volume of and Natural Gas Supply in Urban Areas (10 000 cu.m)	8419	11513	38913	54115
公交运营汽(电)车总数(辆)	Total Number of Public Buses and Trolley Buses(unit)	977	2573	4288	4762
铺装道路长度(公里)	Length of Paved Roads(km)	835	975	1332	1382
绿地面积(公顷)	Areas of Green Land(hectare)	5603	4116	4502	4867
环境、灾害	**Environment and Disaster**				
工业废水排放量(万吨)	Volume of Waste Water up to the Standard for Discharge(10 000 tons)	12479	9145	12579	16969
工业废水排放达标量（万吨）	Volume of Waste Water up to the Standard for Discharge(10 000 tons)	8408	6130	11284	16215
火灾发生数(起)	Number of Fire Disasters(case)	426	1040	2218	2664
火灾事故损失额（万元）	Fire Loss(10 000 yuan)	742.1	472.4	421.0	1565.5
交通事故发生数（起）	Number of Traffic Accidents(case)	3065	4099	5226	4903
交通事故损失额（万元）	Loss of Traffic Accidents(10 000 yuan)	1103.2	1116.1	1986.0	2024.4

continued 4

Aggregate Data				速度指标(%)			Indices and Growth Rates			
2006	2007	2008	2009	指数 Index (2009比以下各年) (2009 as percentage of the following years)			平均增长速度 Average Annual Growth Rate			
				2000	2005	2008	1996-2000	1996-2005	2001-2005	2006-2009
10905	12662	15207	18963	297.98	196.96	124.7	8.91	8.77	8.63	18.47
3808	4399	5212	6275	267.71	181.36	120.4	11.61	9.84	8.1	16.05
1950.53	2002.38	2504.41	3072.41	454.61	178.97	122.68	18.32	19.40	20.50	15.66
246.43	313.40	373.24	439.74	432.48	208.27	117.82	8.63	12.13	15.74	20.13
20475	25012	29749	34032	370.76	191.97	114.40	14.02	14.05	14.07	17.71
475	459	432	415	97.42	86.64	96.06	2.97	2.67	2.37	-3.52
18007	17266	18066	19284	102.85	108.76	106.74	-0.10	-0.61	-1.11	2.12
30840	30823	32998	34904	121.63	116.01	105.78	0.30	0.63	0.95	3.78
28762	32959	36471	38307	126.54	107.07	105.03	-3.34	-0.03	3.40	1.72
1529	2424	2385	1985	88.73	85.75	83.23	15.98	8.06	0.69	-3.77
68631	72253	84874	95885	832.84	177.19	112.97	6.46	20.45	36.28	15.37
5489	5836	6123	7039	273.57	147.82	114.96	21.37	17.16	13.10	10.26
1480	1842	2115	2296	235.49	166.14	108.56	3.15	5.17	7.23	13.53
8106	8670	9199	9553	232.09	196.28	103.85	-5.98	-1.40	3.41	18.36
16389	19069	18304	13168	143.99	77.60	71.94	-6.03	3.12	13.16	-6.14
15267	18352	17862	12106	197.49	74.66	67.78	-6.12	6.79	21.48	-7.05
2310	2009	1537	1485	142.79	55.74	96.62	19.54	20.12	20.70	-13.59
1376.0	773.9	1907.7	1850.6	391.74	118.21	97.01	-8.64	7.75	27.08	4.27
3709	3647	2576	2702	65.92	55.11	104.89	5.99	4.81	3.65	-13.84
1328.3	1038.0	522.8	851.7	76.31	42.07	162.91	0.23	6.26	12.65	-19.46

1-9 国民经济和社会发展结构指标

Structural Indicators on National Economic and Social Development

单位: %　　　　(%)

指　　标	Item	1995	2000	2004	2005	2006	2007	2008	2009
人口与就业	**Population and Employment**								
人口	**Population**								
农业与非农业结构	Structure								
农业	Agriculture	60.55	58.46	56.07	55.09	54.40	53.70	52.88	52.58
非农业	Non-Agriculture	39.45	41.54	43.93	44.91	45.60	46.30	47.12	47.42
性别结构	Sexual Structure								
男	Male	51.64	51.62	51.61	51.50	51.40	51.35	51.22	51.08
女	Female	48.36	48.38	48.39	48.50	48.60	48.65	48.78	48.92
就业	**Employment**								
产业结构	Industrial Structure								
第一产业	Primary Industry	41.17	37.78	34.63	32.78	32.00	30.55	28.50	26.40
第二产业	Secondary Industry	29.43	27.57	27.27	27.46	27.50	28.66	29.10	28.45
第三产业	Tertiary Industry	29.40	34.65	38.10	39.76	40.50	40.79	42.40	45.15
宏观经济	**Macro Economy**								
国民经济核算	**National Accounting**								
生产总值产业结构	Industrial Structure								
第一产业	Primary Industry	12.53	6.91	5.46	5.02	4.58	4.44	4.46	4.05
第二产业	Secondary Industry	40.97	42.89	43.26	41.14	41.95	42.12	42.34	42.02
第三产业	Tertiary Industry	46.50	50.20	51.28	53.84	53.47	53.44	53.20	53.93
生产总值支出结构	Structure of Gross Domestic by Expenditures								
#最终消费	Total Consumption	72.54	63.99	55.29	58.35	56.59	53.60	51.02	51.51
资本形成总额	Total Investment	45.88	44.55	58.96	63.85	67.92	78.18	79.28	83.77
货物和服务净出口	Net Export of Goods and Services	-18.42	-8.54	-14.25	-22.20	-24.51	-31.78	-30.30	-35.28
投　资	**Investment**								
全社会固定资产投资结构	Structure of Total Investment in Fixed Assets								
国有单位	State-owned Enterprises Investment	66.78	68.68	50.90	44.75	37.61	33.22	36.45	37.31
集体单位	Collective-owned Enterprises Investment	9.45	6.31	6.20	7.09	10.38	14.43	12.95	11.60
其他单位投资	Other Investment	23.77	25.01	42.90	48.16	52.01	52.35	50.60	51.09

1-9 续表1 continued 1

单位:% (%)

指 标	Item	1995	2000	2004	2005	2006	2007	2008	2009
财 政	**Government Finance**								
财政收入结构	Structure of Government Revenue								
中 央	Central Government		31.94	47.68	58.30	59.40	60.40	26.65	16.90
地 方	Local Governments		68.06	52.32	41.70	40.60	39.60	73.35	83.10
产 业	**Industrial**								
农 业	**Agriculture**								
农林牧渔及服务业总产值	Structure of Gross Output Value of Farming,Forestry,Animal Husbandry, Fishery and Service								
农 业	Farming	68.03	69.23	60.00	61.69	60.93	59.50	56.85	59.42
林 业	Forestry	0.96	1.14	1.32	1.23	1.33	1.18	1.13	1.27
牧 业	Animal Husbandry	30.29	28.58	32.49	30.96	31.48	30.58	33.52	30.56
渔 业	Fishery	0.72	1.05	0.70	0.69	0.61	0.68	0.66	0.66
农林牧渔服务业	Farming,Forestry,Animal Husbandry and Fishery			5.49	5.43	5.65	8.06	7.84	8.09
工 业	**Industry**								
工业总产值经济类型结构	Structure of Gross Output Value of Industry by Registion Status								
国有经济	State-owned Enterprises	51.04	43.00	45.68	45.21	48.34	51.41	52.26	51.07
集体经济	Collective-owned Enterprises	40.98	32.76	7.39	5.16	3.31	1.85	1.85	1.38
其他经济类型	Others	7.98	24.24	46.93	49.63	48.35	46.74	45.89	47.55
工业总产值轻重结构	Structure of Gross Output Value of Industry by Ligth Industry and Heavy Industry								
轻工业	Light Industry	40.31	48.81	35.53	31.17	28.97	37.03	25.17	23.47
重工业	Heavy Industry	59.69	51.19	64.47	68.83	71.03	62.97	74.83	76.53
工业总产值规模结构	Structure of Gross Output Value of Industry by Size of Enterprises								
大型企业	Large Enterprises	38.80	36.29	30.33	35.46	38.34	42.18	43.85	43.54
中型企业	Medium-sized Enterprises	9.14	5.14	27.31	24.67	21.93	21.07	20.96	21.88
小型企业	Small Enterprises	52.06	58.57	42.36	39.87	39.73	36.75	35.19	34.58

1-9 续表2 continued 2

单位: % (%)

指　标	Item	1995	2000	2004	2005	2006	2007	2008	2009
建筑业	**Construction**								
建筑业总产值结构	Structure of Gross Output Value of Construction Industry								
土木工程建筑业	Civil Engineering Construction	86.27	88.50	52.24	56.59	57.81	57.78	58.88	67.14
房屋工程建筑	Building Construction	12.84	9.28	37.52	34.05	34.58	32.44	30.14	25.50
装修装饰业	Decoration	0.89	2.21	0.99	1.08	1.13	1.74	1.67	1.50
其　他	Others		0.01	9.25	8.28	6.48	8.04	9.31	5.86
交通运输业	**Transportation**								
货运量结构	Structure of Freight Traffic								
按运输方式分	By Means of Transportation								
铁 路	Railways	34.59	44.30	38.99	26.92	4.84	3.90	2.20	2.01
公 路	Highways	65.36	55.58	60.97	73.04	95.12	96.07	97.78	97.97
民 航	Civil Aviation	0.05	0.12	0.04	0.04	0.04	0.03	0.02	0.02
国内商业	**Domestic Trade**								
社会消费品零售总额结构	Composition of Retail Sales of Consumer Goods								
市	Cities	88.95	87.99	90.03	90.17	90.24	90.32	90.43	90.49
县及县以下	Counties and Below Counties	11.05	12.01	9.97	9.83	9.76	9.68	9.57	9.51
国际旅游	**International Tourism**								
国际旅游人数结构	Structure of Tourists								
外国人	Foreigners	89.76	84.03	81.11	84.91	84.63	85.09	84.78	87.81
华侨及港澳台同胞	Overseas Chinese and Compatriots form Hong Kong, Macao and Taiwan	10.24	15.97	18.89	15.09	15.37	14.91	15.22	12.19
教育文化、卫生、人民生活	**Education and Culture，Health Care，People's Livelihoo**								
教　育	**Education**								
在校学生结构	Structure of Student Enrollment								
大学生	College and University Students	8.81	12.44	24.53	28.48	29.57	31.74	33.38	34.55
中学生	Secondary School Students	31.28	37.67	39.79	39.07	39.71	39.32	39.25	39.64
小学生	Primary School Students	59.91	49.89	35.68	32.45	30.72	28.94	27.37	25.81

1-9 续表3 continued 3

单位: % (%)

指 标	Item	1995	2000	2004	2005	2006	2007	2008	2009
专任教师结构	Full-time Teachers by Type								
大 学	College and Universities	21.25	19.89	27.27	29.92	32.79	34.68	35.19	35.29
中 学	Secondary Schools	38.34	41.77	38.43	39.98	37.28	36.48	37.35	38.35
小 学	Primary Schools	40.41	38.34	34.30	30.10	29.93	28.84	27.46	26.36
人民生活	**People's Livelihood**								
城镇居民消费结构	Consumption Structure of Urban Residents								
食 品	Food	44.68	36.46	36.15	37.04	34.42	36.61	36.40	32.43
衣 着	Clothing	12.67	8.13	8.23	9.03	8.72	9.41	10.25	10.98
家庭设备用品及服务	Household facilities,Articles and Services	13.75	11.33	6.64	4.73	6.49	5.91	6.33	7.28
医疗保健	Health Care	3.27	7.23	8.64	9.45	7.73	8.40	9.67	9.65
交通和通讯	Transportation and Communication	5.58	6.93	9.27	9.67	10.27	11.35	10.37	11.33
娱乐教育和文化服务	Recreation,Education and Culture Articles	9.05	13.74	16.86	17.18	18.55	14.52	14.35	14.34
居 住	Residence	6.49	11.23	10.95	9.10	10.54	10.18	8.81	8.86
杂项商品和服务	Articles for Daily Use and Others	4.51	4.95	3.26	3.80	3.28	3.62	3.82	5.13
农村居民消费结构	Consumption Structure of Rural Residents								
食 品	Food	50.31	36.63	35.69	36.34	36.80	38.15	36.95	35.81
衣 着	Clothing	8.39	6.65	5.88	6.11	6.45	6.09	6.52	6.40
居 住	Residence	5.92	21.41	21.01	17.76	18.03	22.72	19.39	19.47
家庭设备用品及服务	Household facilities,Articles and Services	5.17	5.47	4.61	5.11	5.64	5.66	7.02	6.97
医疗保健	Health Care	1.78	6.93	7.64	8.19	8.00	7.61	8.05	8.50
交通和通讯	Transportation and Communication	8.09	4.21	8.43	8.19	8.75	7.58	7.84	9.83
文化娱乐用品及服务	Recreation,Education and Culture Articles	18.53	14.49	14.97	16.15	14.31	10.44	12.43	11.13
其它商品及服务	Articles for Daily Use and Others	1.81	4.21	1.77	2.15	2.02	1.75	1.80	1.89
卫 生	**Health Care**								
卫生技术人员结构	Medical Technical Personnel by Types								
执业（助理）医师	Licensed（Assistant） Doctors	45.42	44.82	41.57	41.96	41.05	39.51	38.09	37.34
注册护士	Registered Nurses	32.68	34.29	33.34	33.14	35.42	35.09	36.23	39.05
药 师	Junior Paramedics	8.78	8.31	7.39	7.30	6.81	6.19	5.74	5.45
技 师	Technicians	5.21	5.21	5.47	5.33	5.11	4.92	6.68	6.49
其 他	Others	7.91	7.37	12.23	12.27	11.61	14.29	13.26	11.67

1-10 国民经济和社会发展比例和效益指标

指　　标	Item	1995
人口与就业	**Population and Employment**	
人口	**Population**	
出生率(‰)	Birth Rate(‰)	11.95
死亡率(‰)	Death Rate(‰)	4.98
自然增长率(‰)	Natural Growth Rate(‰)	6.97
就业	**Employment**	
就业者负担人口	Dependency Ratio	1.74
三次产业就业者比例	Employment Ratio by Type of Industry	
(以第一产业为100)	(Employment in primary industry=100)	
第一产业	Primary Industry	100.00
第二产业	Secondary Industry	71.50
第三产业	Tertiary Industry	71.41
城镇登记失业率(%)	Unemployment Rate in Urban Areas(%)	3.10
宏观经济	**Macro Economy**	
国民核算	**National Accounting**	
三次产业增加值比例	Ratio of Value-added by Type of Industry	
(以第一产业为100)	(Employment in primary industry=100)	
第一产业	Primary Industry	100.00
第二产业	Secondary Industry	326.88
第三产业	Tertiary Industry	371.06
全社会劳动生产率(元／人)	Overall Labor Productivity(yuan/person)	8963
第一产业	Primary Industry	2698
第二产业	Secondary Industry	12404
第三产业	Tertiary Industry	14488
人均生产总值(元)	Per Capita GDP(yuan)	5131
固定资产投资	**Investment in Fixed Assets**	
全社会固定资产投资相当于生产总值比例(%)	Proportion of Investment in fixed Assets to GDP(%)	31.31
房屋建筑面积竣工率(%)	Rate of Floor Space of Buildings Completed in Construction(%)	33.41
固定资产交付使用率(%)	Rate of Fixed Assets Completed in Capital Construction and Put into Use(%)	70.71
建设项目建成投产率(%)	Rate of Projects Completed in Capital Construction and Put into Use(%)	43.73
财政	**Finance**	
地方财政收入相当于生产总值比例(%)	Proportion of Local Government Revenue to GDP(%)	5.51
地方财政支出相当于生产总值比例(%)	Proportion of Local Government Expenditures to GDP(%)	5.58
利用外资	**Utilization of Foreign Capital**	
外商实际直接投资额相当于利用外资协议金额比例(%)	Proportion of Foreign Capital Actually Used to Total Amount of Foreign Capital for Utilization by Signed Contracts or Agreements (%)	64.42

Indicators on Proportions and Efficiency in National Economic and Social Development

2000	2002	2003	2004	2005	2006	2007	2008	2009
13.07	7.64	8.48	9.19	9.58	9.98	10.00	10.15	10.08
5.96	4.41	4.68	5.87	5.16	5.46	5.48	5.57	5.63
7.11	3.23	3.80	3.32	4.42	4.52	4.52	4.58	4.45
1.77	1.77	1.77	1.77	1.78	1.78	1.89	1.89	1.85
100.00	100.00	100.00	100.00	100.00	100.00	100.00	100.00	100.00
72.95	78.03	74.38	78.77	83.78	85.93	93.80	101.85	107.73
91.69	99.62	101.70	110.05	121.28	126.54	133.48	148.55	170.98
3.40	3.70	4.50	4.30	4.30	4.30	4.30	4.20	4.30
100.00	100.00	100.00	100.00	100.00	100.00	100.00	100.00	100.00
620.67	740.17	803.19	792.09	818.82	916.60	947.69	948.84	1037.10
726.43	890.37	963.25	938.81	1071.69	1168.16	1202.50	1191.99	1330.81
16367	21023	23605	27069	31837	36730	43252	52422	59832
2960	3316	3501	4174	4747	5191	6148	7921	8830
25443	32059	36914	43199	47853	56073	64851	76899	87452
24024	30626	33502	37040	44024	48938	56870	67031	73674
9484	11831	13341	15294	16406	18890	22463	27794	32411
35.96	40.90	50.50	58.66	65.75	72.38	81.38	82.24	91.78
41.99	32.26	33.80	24.44	28.07	26.14	29.03	16.94	15.98
73.97	64.76	62.69	42.80	52.78	46.61	49.83	40.47	42.80
44.17	39.49	39.94	41.45	54.16	47.03	40.62	53.26	72.49
7.27	7.27	7.70	7.81	6.61	6.54	7.11	10.86	12.17
8.03	8.32	8.16	8.12	8.10	9.14	9.87	14.47	15.42
28.88	28.69	26.52	35.24	47.01	45.18	77.49	97.05	203.03

1-10 续表1

指　　标	Item	1995
产　业	**Industries**	
农业	**Agriculture**	
人均耕地面积(公顷)	Per Capita Cultivated Land(hectare)	0.08
农业从业者人均耕地面积(公顷)	Cultivated Land per Agricultural Laborer(hectare)	0.20
每公顷耕地农业机械总动力(千瓦)	Total Power of Agricultural Machinery per Hectare of Cultivated Land(kw)	5.23
每公顷耕地化肥施用量(公斤)	Chemical Fertilizer Consumption per Hectare of Cultivated Land(kg)	536
每公顷耕地生产的农业产值(元)	Agricultural Output Value per Hectare of Cultivated Land(yuan)	24396
每个农林牧渔及服务业劳动力农产品生产量(公斤)	Output of Farm Products per Farming,Forestry,Animal Husbandry,Fishery and Service Husbandry and Fishery Laborer (kg)	
粮食	Grain	1150
蔬菜	Vegetables	877
禽蛋	Poultry Eggs	93
肉类	Meat	84
水产品	Aquatic Products	6
每公顷播种面积农产品产量(公斤)	Output of Farm Crops per Hectare of Sown Area(kg)	
粮食	Grain	3806
油料	Oil-bearing Crops	1753
蔬菜	Vegetables	34800
建筑业	**Construction**	
机械装备率(元／人)	Value of Machinery per Laborer(yuan/person)	5990
产值利税率(%)	Ratio of Per-tax Profits to Gross Output Value (%)	3.50
全员劳动生产率(元／人)(按总产值计算)	Overall Labor Productivity(yuan/person)(in terms of gross output value per employee)	37689
邮电通信业	**Post and Communication Services**	
电话普及率(含移动电话）(部/百人)	Access to Telephones, National(include mobilphone)(set/100 persons)	7.92
移动电话普及率(部/百人)	Access to Mobilphones (set/100 persons)	0.48
国内商业	**Domestic Trade**	
人均批发零售和住宿餐饮业消费品零售额(元)	Per Capita Retail Sales of Wholesale,Retail Trade and Accommodation Catering Trade (yuan)	1979

continued 1

2000	2002	2003	2004	2005	2006	2007	2008	2009
0.07	0.07	0.07	0.07	0.07	0.06	0.06	0.06	0.06
0.20	0.20	0.19	0.19	0.22	0.23	0.25	0.21	0.21
6.78	7.25	7.54	7.93	8.39	8.63	8.99	10.41	10.12
664	709	725	780	794	819	843	867	891
25161	28181	30357	35862	39937	43261	51361	64593	69106
1382	1355	1213	1392	1493	1569	1433	1695	1792
1110	1196	1167	1287	1421	1536	1549	1752	1990
95	95	89	84	86	92	74	86	96
101	113	114	122	132	145	77	91	104
8	8	7	7	7	7	9	10	11
4342	4402	4182	4656	4796	5025	4452	5102	5206
1526	1603	1532	1758	1821	1880	1934	2008	1956
37797	37599	36657	35002	35231	35916	33677	35723	38344
6805	8904	9453	13240	13332	13502	9079	12025.77	11928.16
3.42	4.78	4.06	4.43	4.83	4.54	5.23	5.99	6.3
74347	80200	132981	163414	206337	241887	203994	226669	285854
31.16	57.78	69.09	88.76	99.96	111.1	117.9	124.69	167.07
10.62	27.96	33.67	48.29	56.62	66.99	80.02	88.09	132.79
4027	5163	6956	7859	8795	9437	10932	13840	16432

1-10 续表2

指　　标	Item	1995
对外经济贸易	**Foreign Trade**	
进出口总额相当于生产总值比例(%)	Proportion of Total Imports & Exports to GDP(%)	34.76
国际旅游	**International Tourism**	
每一来华游客花费(元)	Expenditure per International Tourist in China(yuan)	2510.83
金融保险	**Finance and Insurance**	
金融机构存款相当于生产总值比例(%)	Bank Deposits as Percentage of GDP(%)	108.83
金融机构贷款相当于生产总值比例(%)	Bank Loans as Percentage of GDP(%)	101.26
金融机构现金支出相当于收入比例(%)	Proportion of Cash Outlay to Cash Receipt in Bank(%)	88.84
教育、科技、文化	**Education, Science and Technology and Culture**	
教育	**Education**	
学龄儿童入学率(%)	Rate of School-age Children Enrollment(%)	99.69
小学升学率(%)	Rate of Graduates of Primary Schools Entering Junior Secondary Schools(%)	94.85
初中升学率(%)	Rate of Graduates of Junior Secondary Schools Entering Senior Secondary Schools(%)	72.35
学校教师负担系数	Student-teacher Ratio(in percentage)	
高等学校	Colleges and Universities	6.83
中等学校	Secondary Schools	14.42
小学	Primary Schools	26.22
文化(个)	**Culture (unit)**	
每百万人有艺术表演团体	Number of Troupes per Million Persons	3.39
每百万人有公共图书馆	Number of Public Libraries per Million Persons	2.31
家庭、生活、环境	**Family, People's Livelihood and Environment**	
家庭	**Family**	
城市居民家庭	Urban Households	
平均每户就业面（%）	Percentage of Employees Per Household (%)	55.90
每一就业者负担人数(人)	Persons Supported by Each Laborer (person)	1.79
农村居民家庭	Rural Households	
平均每一劳动力赡养人口（人）	Persons Supported by Each Laborer(person)	1.58
卫生	**Health Care**	
每千人医院数(个)	Number of Hospitals per 1000 Persons(unit)	0.06
每千人医生数(人)	Number of Doctors per 1000 Persons(person)	2.91
每千人医院床位数(张)	Number of Hospital Beds per 1000 Persons(unit)	4.36
市政建设	**City Construction**	
城市自来水普及率(%)	Percentage of Households with Access to Tap Water(%)	
城市用气普及率(%)	Percentage of Households with Access to Tap Gas (%)	
人均公共绿地面积(平方米)	Public Green Areas per 10 000 Persons(hectare)	3.80

continued 2

2000	2002	2003	2004	2005	2006	2007	2008	2009
22.25	18.72	20.19	23.29	24.79	22.01	22.21	21.97	18.17
3444.50	3507.29	3584.04	4212.00	4324.00	4353.00	4242.00	4544.30	4614.36
206.71	265.09	281.61	277.73	283.41	275.92	259.80	264.31	279.84
150.51	193.35	206.43	186.17	169.91	159.11	152.16	149.22	166.65
94.78	94.82	95.54	95.43	96.78	97.29	96.98	97.00	96.95
99.85	99.85	99.88	99.87	99.90	99.92	99.94	99.95	99.96
97.21	97.25	97.26	96.79	99.31	104.23	102.70	103.81	101.80
80.50	82.80	80.26	81.60	81.39	86.06	88.70	90.03	90.09
12.38	16.05	19.87	16.69	17.99	17.36	16.97	17.13	17.32
17.84	19.12	18.52	18.78	18.47	20.51	19.99	18.97	18.27
25.75	24.05	22.69	21.71	20.38	19.78	18.61	17.99	17.32
3.20	3.13	3.07	3.03	2.56	2.31	2.16	2.15	2.13
2.18	1.99	1.95	2.07	2.02	1.82	1.81	1.79	1.78
45.73	48.80	48.00	48.80	47.44	48.30	47.77	47.87	53.20
2.19	2.05	2.08	2.05	2.11	2.07	2.09	2.09	1.88
1.57	1.59	1.56	1.56	1.58	1.59	1.57	1.50	1.50
0.03	0.04	0.04	0.04	0.04	0.04	0.04	0.03	0.03
2.35	2.08	2.02	2.04	2.39	2.19	2.08	2.16	2.29
3.83	3.90	3.94	3.91	3.75	3.46	3.42	3.65	3.84
98.95	98.62	99.04	99.09	99.00	99.09	100.01	111.20	100.00
81.51	87.52	91.23	91.20	91.30	92.62	98.60	97.66	98.15
5.12	5.42	5.35	5.03	5.63	7.59	7.61	7.80	7.90

主 要 统 计 指 标 解 释

行政区划 指国家对行政区域的划分。根据宪法规定，我国的行政区域划分如下:⑴全国分为省、自治区、直辖市;⑵省、自治区分为自治州、县、自治县、市;⑶自治州分为县、自治县、市;⑷县、自治县分为乡、民族乡、镇;⑸直辖市和较大的市分为区、县;⑹国家在必要时设立的特别行政区。

自然资源 指人类可以直接从自然界获得，并用于生产和生活的物质资源。自然资源一般可以分成可再生资源和非再生资源两大类。可再生资源指在较短时间内可以再生、可以循环利用的资源，包括土地资源、水资源、气候资源、生物资源和海洋资源等。非再生资源指在使用后不能再生的资源，包括矿产资源和地热能源。

土地资源 土地指陆地的表层部分，它主要由岩石、岩石的风化物和土壤构成。土地资源按利用类型可以分为农用地、建筑用地和未利用地。农用地包括耕地、园地、林地、牧草地和水面。建筑用地包括居民点及工矿用地、交通用地和水利设施用地。未利用地指农用地和建筑用地以外的土地，包括滩涂、荒漠、戈壁、冰川和石山等。

耕地面积 指经过开垦用以种植农作物并经常进行耕耘的土地面积。包括种有作物的土地面积、休闲地、新开荒地和抛荒未满三年的土地面积。

林业用地面积 指生长乔木、竹类、灌木、沿海红树林等林木的土地面积，包括有林地、灌木林、疏林地、未成林造林地、迹地、苗圃等。

草地面积 指牧区和农区用于放牧牲畜或割草，植被盖度在5%以上的草原、草坡、草山等面积。包括天然的和人工种植或改良的草地面积。

水资源 水在自然界中以固体、液体和气态三种聚集状态存在，分布于海洋、陆地（包括土壤）以及大气之中，通过水循环形成水资源。水资源包括经人类控制并直接可供灌溉、发电、给水、航运、养殖等用途的地表水和地下水，以及江河、湖泊、井、泉、潮汐、港湾和养殖水域等。水资源是发展国民经济不可缺少的重要自然资源。

气温 指空气的温度，我国一般以摄氏度（℃）为单位表示。气象观测的温度表是放在离地面约1.5米处通风良好的百叶箱里测量的，因此，通常说的气温指的是离地面1.5米处百叶箱中的温度。其统计计算方法为:

月平均气温是将全月各日的平均气温相加，除以该月的天数而得。

年平均气温是将12个月的月平均气温累加后除以12而得。

降水量 指从天空降落到地面的液态或固态（经融化后）水，未经蒸发、渗透、流失而在地面上积聚的深度。其统计计算方法为:

月降水量是将全月各日的降水量累加而得。

年降水量是将12个月的月降水量累加而得。

日照时数 指太阳实际照射地面的时间。其统计方法与降水量相同。

现行价格 指计算各种总量指标所采用的价格，按报告期实际销售平均单价计算。

平均增长速度 我国计算平均增长速度有两种方法:一种是习惯上经常使用的“水平法”，又称几何平均法，是以间隔期最后一年的水平同基期水平对比来计算平均每年增长（或下降）速度;另一种是“累计法”，又称代数平均法或方程法，是以间隔期内各年水平的总和同基期水平对比来计算平均每年增长（或下降）速度。在一般正常情况下，两种方法计算的平均每年增长速度比较接近;但在经济发展不平衡、出现大起大落时，两种方法计算的结果差别较大。

企业（单位）登记注册类型 是以在工商行政管理机关登记注册的各类企业为划分对象，以工商行政管理部门对企业登记注册的类型为依据，将企业登记注册类型分为内资企业、港澳台商投资企业和外商投资企业三大类。内资企业包括国有企业、集体企业、股份合作企业、联营企业、有限责任公司、股份有限公司、私营公司和其他企业;港澳台商投资企业和外商投资企业分别包括合资经营企业、合作经营企业、独资经营企业和股份有限公司。对不在工商行政管理部门进行登记注册的行政机关、事业单位和社会团体，主要按其经费来源和管理方式进行划分。

国有企业 指企业全部资产归国家所有，并按《中华人民共和国企业法人登记管理条例》规定登记注册的非公司制的经济组织。不包括有限责任公司中的国有独资公司。

集体企业 指企业资产归集体所有，并按《中华人民共和国企业法人登记管理条例》规定登记注册的经济组织。

股份合作企业 指以合作制为基础，由企业职工共同出资入股，吸收一定比例的社会资产投资组建，实行自主经营，自负盈亏，共同劳动，民主管理，按劳分配与按股分红相结合的一种集体经济组织。

联营企业 指两个及两个以上相同或不同所有制性

质的企业法人或事业单位法人，按自愿、平等、互利的原则，共同投资组成的经济组织。联营企业包括国有联营企业、集体联营企业、国有与集体联营企业和其他联营企业。

有限责任公司 指根据《中华人民共和国公司登记管理条例》规定登记注册，由两个以上、五十个以下的股东共同出资，每个股东以其所认缴的出资额对公司承担有限责任，公司以其全部资产对其债务承担责任的经济组织。有限责任公司包括国有独资公司以及其他有限责任公司。

股份有限公司 指根据《中华人民共和国公司登记管理条例》规定登记注册，其全部注册资本由等额股份构成并通过发行股票筹集资本，股东以其认购的股份对公司承担有限责任，公司以其全部资产对其债务承担责任的经济组织。

私营企业 指由自然人投资设立或由自然人控股，以雇佣劳动为基础的营利性经济组织。包括按照《公司法》、《合伙企业法》、《私营企业暂行条例》规定登记注册的私营有限责任公司、私营股份有限公司、私营合伙企业和私营独资企业。

其他企业 指上述企业之外的其他内资经济组织。

中外合资经营企业 指外国企业或外国人与中国内地企业依照《中华人民共和国中外合资经营企业法》及有关法律的规定，按合同规定的比例投资设立、分享利润和分担风险的企业。

中外合作经营企业 指外国企业或外国人与中国内地企业依照《中华人民共和国中外合作经营企业法》及有关法律的规定，依照合作合同的约定进行投资或提供条件设立、分配利润和分担风险的企业。

外资企业 指依照《中华人民共和国外资企业法》及有关法律的规定，在中国内地由外国投资者全额投资设立的企业。

外商投资股份有限公司 指根据国家有关规定，经外经贸部依法批准设立，其中外资的股本占公司注册资本的比例达25%以上的股份有限公司。凡其中外资股本占公司注册资本的比例小于25%的，属于内资企业中的股份有限公司。

行政机关、事业单位和社会团体 参照企业登记注册类型，主要按其经费来源和管理方式划分。具体规定如下:

（1）行政机关:包括国家机关和政党机关，原则上均列为“国有”。但有特殊规定的，如供销社等，则列为“集体”。

（2）事业单位:包括经国家机构编制部门和有关业务主管部门批准成立的各类事业单位，不包括实行企业化管理的事业单位。事业单位的划分办法如下:

①由国家财政预算拨款或列入财政预算外资金管理以及经费主要来源于国有主管部门或国有上级单位的事业单位，列为“国有”。

②经费主要来源于集体单位的事业单位，列为“集体”。

③公民个人（或个人合伙）开办的事业单位，列为“私营”。

④上述以外的其他事业单位，如果其经费来源不明确，按管理方式进行归类。

（3）社会团体:包括经民政部门批准成立以及未纳入社会团体管理条例范围的工会、妇联等各类社会团体。社会团体的划分办法如下:

①未纳入民政部社会团体管理条例范围的工会、妇联、共青团、青联、工商联、科协、侨联等社会团体，国家拨款设立的基金会或基金管理组织以及经费主要来源于国有业务主管部门或国有上级单位的社会团体，列为“国有”。

②经费主要来源于集体单位的社会团体，列为“集体”。

③公民个人（或个人合伙）开办的社会团体，划为“私营”。

④上述以外的其他社会团体，如果其经费来源不明确，改按管理方式进行归类。

Explanatory Notes on Main Statistical Indicators

Administrative Division refers to the division of administrative areas by the state. The Constitution of the People's Republic of China stipulates that the administrative areas in China are divided as: 1) The whole country is divided into provinces, autonomous regions and municipalities directly under the central government; 2) Provinces and autonomous regions are divided into autonomous prefectures, counties, autonomous counties and cities; 3) Autonomous prefectures are divided into counties, autonomous counties and cities; 4) Counties and autonomous counties are divided into townships, nationality townships and towns; 5) Municipalities and large cities are divided into districts and counties, 6) The state shall, when necessary, establish special administrative regions.

Natural Resources refer to material resources that could be obtained from the nature by human being and used for production and living. Natural resources in general can be classified as renewable resources and non-renewable resources. Renewable resources refer to resources that could be renewed and recycled during a relatively short period of time, including land resource, water resource, climate resource, biology resource and marine resource. Non-renewable resources include resources that could not be renewed, such as minerals and geothermal resource.

Land Resource Land refers to the surface of the earth, consisting of mainly rocks and its whethering and earth. Land resource can be classified, by its utilization, as land for agriculture, land for construction and unused land. Land for agriculture includes cultivated land, plantation land, forestland, grassland and waters. Land for construction includes land for residential purpose, for manufacturing and mining, for transportation and for water-conservancy projects. Unused land refers to land other than land for agriculture and construction, including beaches, deserts, Gobi, glaciers and rock mountains.

Area of Cultivated Land refers to area of land reclaimed for the regular cultivation of various farm crops, including crop-cover land, fallow, newly reclaimed land and land laid idle for less than 3 years.

Area of Afforested Land refer to land for trees bamboo, bushes and mangrove, including forest-cover land, bush-covered land, sparse forest land, land planned for afforestation and nurseries of young trees.

Area of Grassland refers to areas of grassland, grass-slopes and grass-covered hills with a vegetation-covering rate of over 5% that are used for animal husbandry or harvesting of grass. It includes natural, cultivated and improved grassland areas.

Water Resource Water exists in the nature in solid, liquid and gaseous states, is distributed in the ocean, land (including earth) and air, and constitutes the water resource through the circulation of water. Water resource includes the surface water and underground water that is controlled by the human being for irrigation, power-generation, water supply, navigation and cultivation. It also includes rivers, lakes, wells, springs, tides, gulf and water area for cultivation. Water resource as an important natural resource is indispensable for the development of the national economy.

Temperature refers to the air temperature. China uses centigrade as the unit. The thermometry used for weather observation is put in a breezy shutter, which is 1.5 meters high from the ground. Therefore, the commonly used temperature refers to the temperature in the breezy shutter 1.5 meters away from the ground. The calculation method is as follows:

Monthly average temperature is the summation of average daily temperature of one month divided by the actual days of that particular month.

Annual average temperature is the summation of monthly average of a year divided by 12 months.

Volume of Precipitation refers to the deepness of liquid state or solid state (thawed) water falling from the sky to the ground that has not been evaporated, infiltrated or run off. The calculation method is as follows:

Monthly precipitation is the summation of daily precipitation of a month.

Annual precipitation is the summation of 12 months precipitation of a year.

Sunshine Hours refer to the actual hours of sunirradiating the earth. The calculation method is the same as that of the precipitation.

Current Prices refer to prices that used to caculate kinds of tatol amount indexes on the average unit prices of effective sale in report period.

Average Annual Growth Rate Two methods for calculating average annual growth rate are applied in China, one is often called level approach, or the method of calculating geometric average, which is derived by comparing the level of the last year of the interval with

uneven economic development occurred with striking fluctuations in growth.

Registration Status of Enterprises Enterprises are classified into 3 categories, namely domestic-funded enterprises, enterprises with investment from Hong Kong, Macau and Taiwan, and enterprises with foreign investment, in the light of the registration status of an enterprise in industrial and commercial administration agencies. Domestic-funded enterprises include state-owned enterprises, collective-owned enterprises, cooperative enterprises, joint ownership enterprises, limited liability corporations, share-holding corporations Ltd., private enterprises and other enterprises. Included in the enterprises with investment from Hong Kong, Macau and Taiwan and enterprises with foreign investment are joint-venture enterprises, cooperative enterprises, sole investment enterprises and share-holding corporations Ltd. For government agencies, institutions and social organizations which are not requested to be registered in industrial and commercial administration agencies, they are classified mainly by their sources of funds and way of management.

State-owned Enterprises refer to non-corporationeconomic units where the entire assets are owned by the state and which have registered in accordance with the *Regulation of the Peoples Republic of China on the Management of Registration of Corporate Enterprises*. Excluded from this category are sole state-funded corporations in the limited liability corporations.

Collective-owned Enterprises refer to economic units where the assets are owned collectively and which have registered in accordance with the *Regulation of the Peoples Republic of China on the Management of Registration of Corporate Enterprises*.

Cooperative Enterprises refer to a form of collective economic units (enterprises) where capitals come mainly from employees as their shares, with certain proportion of capital from the outside, where production is organized on the basis of independent operation, independent accounting for profits and losses, joint work, democratic management, and a distribution system that integrates remuneration according to work with dividend according to capital share.

Joint Ownership Enterprises refer to economic units established by two or more corporate enterprises or corporate institutions of the same or different ownership, through joint investment on the basis of equality, voluntary participation and mutual benefits. They include state jointownership enterprises, collective joint ownership enterprises, joint state-collective enterprises, other joint ownership enterprises.

Limited Liability Corporations refer to economic units established with investment from 2-50investors and registered in accordance with the *Regulation of the Peoples Republic of China on the Management of Registration of Corporations*, each investor bearing limited liability to the corporation depending on its share of investment, and the corporation bearing liability to its debt to the maximum of its total assets. Limited liability corporations include exclusive state-funded limited liability corporations and other limited liability corporations.

Share-holding Corporations Ltd. refer to economic units registered in accordance with the*Regulation of the Peoples Republic of China on the Management of Registration of Corporations*, with total registered capitals divided into equal shares and raised through issuing stocks. Each investor bears limited liability to the corporation depending on the holding of shares, and the corporation bears liability to its debt to the maximum of its total assets.

Private Enterprises refer to profit-making economic units invested and established by natural persons, or controlled by natural persons using employed labour. Included in this category are private limited liability corporations, private share-holding corporations Ltd., private partnership enterprises and private-fundedenterprises registered in accordance with the *Corporation Law*, *Partnership Enterprises Law* and *Interim Regulations on Private Enterprises* .

Other Domestic-funded Enterprises refer to domestic-funded economic units other than those mentioned above.

Joint-venture Enterprises with Foreign Investment refer to enterprises jointly established by foreign enterprises or foreigners with enterprises in the mainland of China in accordance with the *Law of the Peoples Republic of China on Sino-foreign Joint Venture Enterprises* and other relevant laws, where the share of investment, profits and risks is stipulated in the contract.

Cooperation Enterprises with Foreign Investment refer to enterprises jointly established by foreign enterprises or foreigners with enterprises in the mainland of China in accordance with the *Law of the Peoples Republic of China on Sino-foreign Cooperative Enterprises* and other relevant laws, where the investment or provision of facilities, and the share of profits and risks is stipulated in the cooperative contract.

Enterprises with Sole (exclusive) Foreign Investment refer to enterprises established in the mainland of China with exclusive investment from foreign investors in accordance with the *Law of the Peoples Republic of China on Foreign-Funded Enterprises* and other relevant laws.

Share-holding Corporations Ltd. with Foreign Investment refer to share-holding corporations Ltd. established with the approval from the Ministry of Foreign Trade and Economic Relations in line with relevant state regulations, where the share of investment from foreign investors exceeds 25% of the total registered capital of the corporation. In case the share of foreign investment is less than 25% of the total registered capital, the enterprise is to be classified as domestic-funded share-holding corporation Ltd.

Government Agencies, Institutions and Social Organizations are classified into following categories by source of funds and way of management taking reference of the registration status of enterprises:

(1) Government agencies: include state and party agencies, classified in principle as state-owned. There are exceptions, such as supply and marketing cooperatives which are classified as collective-owned.

(2) Institutions: include institutions of various types established with the approval by organization and staffing departments of the government, but excludeInstitutions where enterprise management system is introduced. Institutions are further classified as follows:

(a) Institutions whose main budget is listed in the government budget appropriations or extra-budget funds, or allocated from the budget of their competent government agencies. Such institutions are classified as state-owned.

(b) Institutions whose budget mainly comes from collective units. Such institutions are classified as collective-owned.

(c)Institutions established by individual or a group of citizens, which are classified as private.

(d) Institutions other than those mentioned above whose source of budget is not clear. Such institutions are classified by way of management.

(3) Social organizations: include social organizations established with the approval from the Ministry of Civil Affairs, and organizations that are not covered by social organization management regulations such as trade unions, womens federations etc.. Social organizations are further classified as follows:

(a) Social organizations that are not covered by social organization management regulations of the Ministry of Civil Affairs such as trade unions, womens federations, communist youth leagues, youth associations, industrial and commerce associations, scientists associations,overseas Chinese associations, etc., foundations and fund management organizations established with funds from the state, and social organizations whose funds mainly come from the budget of their competent government agencies. Such institutions are classified as state-owned.

(b) Social organizations whose budget mainly comes from collective units. Such institutions are classified as collective-owned.

(c)Social organizations established by individual or a group of citizens, which are classified as private.

(d) Social organizations established by individual or a group of citizens, which are classified as private.

2 国民经济核算

NATIONAL ECONOMIC ACCOUNTS

资料整理：王亚丽　马秋娟　吴　羽　连　鹏
Data management:Wang Yali　Ma Qiujuan　Wu Yu　Lian Peng

第二部分　国民经济核算

一、简要说明

本章资料包括西安生产总值、构成和指数，分区县生产总值等。根据国家统计局的统一要求，为保持GDP数据的历史可比性，根据国家统计局和陕西省统计局《年度GDP历史数据修订办法》，对2005—2007年度GDP历史数据进行了修订；人均GDP按户籍人口计算，2005年以后按常住人口计算。依据国家统计局《年度GDP核算方案》（试行）和各专业财务年报对西安市2009年生产总值进行了初步核实。资料由西安市统计局国民经济核算处提供。

二、主要指标

生产总值（亿元）	2724.08	比上年增长　14.5%
第一产业	110.38	比上年增长　6.3%
第二产业	1144.75	比上年增长　14.0%
第三产业	1468.95	比上年增长　15.5%
人均生产总值（元/人）	32411	比上年增加 4617元

2 NATIONAL ECONOMIC ACCOUNTS

Ⅰ.Brief Introduction

The data in this chapter consists of composition and indices of the GDP in Xi'an and GDP by region, etc. According to the request of National Bureau of Statistic, in order to keep the history GDP data comparable, the GDP of 2005 - 2007 had been adjusted based on Adjusting Method of yearly GDP released by National Bureau of Statistic and Shaan'xi Provincial Bureau of Statistic. Per capital GDP had been calculated on register population, and after 2005 was calculated on permanent population. The GDP of 2009 in Xi'an had been preliminary verified according to GDP yearly accounting scheme (for trial implementation) and financial annual report by professional department. Data in this chapter is provided by National Economic Accounting Division of the Xi'an Bureau of Statistics.

Ⅱ.Major Indicators

		Increase over Preceding Year
Gross Domestic Product(100 mil. yuan)	2724.08	14.5%
Primary Industry	110.38	6.3%
Secondary Industry	1144.75	14.0%
Tertiary Industry	1468.95	15.5%
Per Capita Gross Domestic Product（yuan/person)	32411	4617

2-1　主要年份生产总值

Gross Domestic Product In Representative Years

（本表按当年价格计算）　　(Data in the table are calculated at current prices)

单位：亿元　　(100 million yuan)

年　份 Year	生产总值 Gross Domestic Product	第一产业 Primary Industry	第二产业 Secondary Industry	第三产业 Tertiary Industry	人均GDP（元/人） Per Capita Gross Domestic Product (yuan/person)
1952	3.37	1.59	0.88	0.90	135
1965	12.76	2.62	7.22	2.92	323
1970	17.76	3.13	10.96	3.67	412
1975	21.33	4.14	12.63	4.56	448
1978	25.35	4.83	14.59	5.93	513
1980	31.66	4.73	18.69	8.24	623
1983	35.89	5.22	20.14	10.53	674
1984	44.14	7.45	24.17	12.52	817
1985	57.58	8.76	30.83	17.99	1049
1986	65.78	9.59	33.86	22.33	1178
1987	80.16	10.73	37.69	31.74	1409
1988	99.22	11.47	46.58	41.17	1711
1989	109.38	12.78	48.91	47.69	1861
1990	116.51	13.94	50.15	52.42	1932
1991	136.14	17.17	57.06	61.91	2224
1992	164.85	18.78	69.22	76.85	2662
1993	229.56	22.58	110.88	96.10	3661
1994	289.82	31.68	128.27	129.87	4563
1995	330.35	41.40	135.33	153.62	5131
1996	406.95	46.94	161.63	198.38	6246
1997	488.82	51.33	197.97	239.52	7424
1998	525.85	51.91	216.32	257.62	7906
1999	577.29	45.53	243.35	288.41	8599
2000	646.13	44.65	277.13	324.35	9484
2001	734.86	45.87	312.90	376.09	10628
2002	826.68	47.77	353.58	425.33	11831
2003	946.66	50.72	407.38	488.56	13341
2004	1102.39	60.21	476.92	565.26	15294
2005	1313.93	66.01	540.50	707.42	16406
2006	1538.94	70.44	645.65	822.85	18890
2007	1856.63	82.51	781.94	992.18	22463
2008	2318.14	103.45	981.58	1233.11	27794
2009	2724.08	110.38	1144.75	1468.95	32411

注：2005年以后人均GDP按常住人口计算。根据全国第二次经济普查结果，对2005-2007年生产总值及人均GDP进行了修订。

Note:Per capital GDP after 2005 was calculated on permanent population,according to the second national census,we made adjustments to the GDP , the value-added of the primary industry and per capital local GDP of 2005-2007.

2-2 主要年份生产总值指数（上年=100）

Indices of Gross Domestic Product in Representative Years(preceding year = 100)

（本表按可比价格计算） (Data in the table are calculated at constant prices)

年 份	Year	生产总值 Gross Domestic Product	第一产业 Primary Industry	第二产业 Secondary Industry	第三产业 Tertiary Industry
1952		103.6	92.2	137.5	123.7
1965		126.1	134.1	133.0	106.7
1970		122.0	109.4	140.0	100.1
1975		103.8	92.6	107.1	107.5
1978		101.7	101.6	99.4	108.2
1980		111.5	83.3	119.7	116.5
1985		112.6	107.5	111.8	116.9
1986		111.4	107.7	108.4	118.8
1987		113.6	100.8	109.1	126.6
1988		111.4	81.2	115.5	114.7
1989		106.7	103.0	104.5	110.8
1990		105.2	103.0	102.5	109.6
1991		109.8	118.6	108.6	108.6
1992		115.6	109.4	118.1	115.0
1993		123.9	112.5	142.7	108.4
1994		110.3	98.4	110.6	113.2
1995		110.0	104.5	112.1	108.6
1996		114.9	106.8	118.8	111.7
1997		114.4	109.1	116.7	112.4
1998		113.3	106.5	117.5	108.8
1999		112.2	97.4	115.7	110.1
2000		113.0	103.5	115.1	111.5
2001		113.1	102.5	115.3	112.6
2002		113.3	103.1	115.0	113.0
2003		113.5	101.8	117.5	111.2
2004		113.5	106.7	115.9	112.0
2005		114.0	107.5	112.3	116.3
2006		114.0	107.1	113.7	114.9
2007		115.6	104.5	115.7	116.4
2008		116.3	107.6	116.4	116.9
2009		114.5	106.3	114.0	115.5
平均每年增长	**Yearly Average Growth Rates**				
"一五"时期	**The First Five-Year Plan Period**	**15.8**	**5.9**	**37.7**	**16.9**
"二五"时期	**The Second Five-Year Plan Period**	**2.0**	**-3.7**	**2.4**	**8.4**
1963--1965年	**Readjust Period**	**14.2**	**16.2**	**23.3**	**0.3**
"三五"时期	**The Third Five-Year Plan Period**	**7.1**	**0.1**	**11.7**	**5.4**
"四五"时期	**The Fourth Five-Year Plan Period**	**5.0**	**4.0**	**5.3**	**5.0**
"五五"时期	**The Fiifth Five-Year Plan Period**	**6.0**	**-0.7**	**6.5**	**10.1**
"六五"时期	**The Sixth Five-Year Plan Period**	**10.7**	**7.9**	**10.4**	**12.9**
"七五"时期	**The Seventh Five-Year Plan Period**	**9.6**	**-1.3**	**7.9**	**16.0**
"八五"时期	**The Eighth Five-Year Plan Period**	**13.8**	**8.5**	**17.8**	**10.7**
"九五"时期	**The Ninth Five-Year Plan Period**	**13.5**	**4.6**	**16.8**	**10.9**
"十五"时期	**The Tenth Five-Year Plan Period**	**13.5**	**4.3**	**15.2**	**13.0**

注：根据全国第二次经济普查结果，对2005-2007年生产总值指数进行了修订。

Note:according to the second national census,we made the Indices to the GDP , the value-added of the primary industry and per capital local GDP of 2005-2007.

2-3 主要年份生产总值指数（1952年=100）

Indices of Gross Domestic Product in Representative Years(1952=100)

（本表按可比价格计算） (Data in the table are calculated at constant prices)

年份 Year	生产总值 Gross Domestic Product	第一产业 Primary Industry	第二产业 Secondary Industry	第三产业 Tertiary Industry
1952	100.0	100.0	100.0	100.0
1965	341.6	173.3	1048.3	329.2
1970	481.6	174.3	1821.0	428.6
1975	614.2	211.9	2362.5	547.9
1978	678.7	231.3	2560.8	643.8
1980	821.4	204.2	3237.2	885.2
1985	1366.8	299.1	5310.6	1632.4
1986	1523.1	322.3	5756.7	1928.9
1987	1730.0	324.9	6280.6	2441.6
1988	1926.3	263.7	7256.6	2801.2
1989	2054.8	271.6	7583.1	3104.6
1990	2162.5	279.7	7772.7	3403.6
1991	2374.4	331.7	8441.2	3696.3
1992	2744.8	362.9	9969.1	4250.7
1993	3400.8	408.2	14225.9	4607.8
1994	3751.1	401.8	15733.8	5216.0
1995	4126.2	419.9	17637.6	5664.6
1996	4741.0	448.5	20953.5	6327.4
1997	5423.7	489.3	24452.7	7112.0
1998	6145.1	521.1	28731.9	7737.9
1999	6894.8	507.6	33242.8	8519.4
2000	7791.1	525.4	38262.5	9499.1
2001	8811.7	538.5	44116.7	10696.0
2002	9983.7	555.2	50734.2	12086.5
2003	11331.5	265.2	59612.7	13440.2
2004	12861.3	603.1	69091.1	15053.0
2005	14661.9	648.3	77589.3	17506.6
2006	16714.6	694.3	88219.0	20115.1
2007	19322.1	725.5	102069.4	23414.0
2008	22471.6	780.6	118808.8	27371.0
2009	25730.0	829.8	135442.0	31613.5

2-4 主要年份生产总值构成

Composition of Gross Domestic Product in Respective Years

（本表按当年价格计算） (Data in the table are calculated at current prices)

单位：% (%)

年　份	Year	生产总值 Gross Domestic Product	第一产业 Primary Industry	第二产业 Secondary Industry	第三产业 Tertiary Industry
1952		100	47.18	26.11	26.71
1965		100	20.53	56.58	22.89
1970		100	17.62	61.71	20.67
1975		100	19.41	59.21	21.38
1978		100	19.05	57.55	23.40
1980		100	14.94	59.03	26.03
1985		100	15.22	53.54	31.24
1986		100	14.58	51.47	33.95
1987		100	13.38	47.02	39.60
1988		100	11.56	46.95	41.49
1989		100	11.68	44.72	43.60
1990		100	11.96	43.05	44.99
1991		100	12.61	41.91	45.48
1992		100	11.39	41.99	46.62
1993		100	9.84	48.30	41.86
1994		100	10.93	44.26	44.81
1995		100	12.53	40.97	46.50
1996		100	11.53	39.72	48.75
1997		100	10.50	40.50	49.00
1998		100	9.87	41.14	48.99
1999		100	7.89	42.15	49.96
2000		100	6.91	42.89	50.20
2001		100	6.24	42.58	51.18
2002		100	5.78	42.77	51.45
2003		100	5.36	43.03	51.61
2004		100	5.46	43.26	51.28
2005		100	5.02	41.14	53.84
2006		100	4.58	41.95	53.47
2007		100	4.44	42.12	53.44
2008		100	4.46	42.34	53.20
2009		100	4.05	42.02	53.93
"一五"时期	**The First Five-Year Plan Period**	**100**	**32.88**	**43.92**	**23.20**
"二五"时期	**The Second Five-Year Plan Period**	**100**	**18.08**	**58.63**	**23.29**
1963-1965年	**Readjust Period**	**100**	**19.36**	**55.37**	**25.27**
"三五"时期	**The Third Five-Year Plan Period**	**100**	**18.60**	**57.33**	**24.07**
"四五"时期	**The Fourth Five-Year Plan Period**	**100**	**20.46**	**59.59**	**19.95**
"五五"时期	**The Fiifth Five-Year Plan Period**	**100**	**18.40**	**57.69**	**23.91**
"六五"时期	**The Sixth Five-Year Plan Period**	**100**	**16.03**	**55.01**	**28.96**
"七五"时期	**The Seventh Five-Year Plan Period**	**100**	**12.42**	**46.11**	**41.47**
"八五"时期	**The Eighth Five-Year Plan Period**	**100**	**11.44**	**43.52**	**45.04**
"九五"时期	**The Ninth Five-Year Plan Period**	**100**	**9.09**	**41.45**	**49.46**
"十五"时期	**The Tenth Five-Year Plan Period**	**100**	**5.49**	**42.47**	**52.04**

2-5 全市分区县生产总值（2009年）

Gross Domestic Product by Region（2009）

单位：亿元 (100 million yuan)

区县名称	Name of District and County	生产总值 Gross Domestic Product	第一产业 Primary Industry	第二产业 Secondary Industry	第三产业 Tertiary Industry	生产总值比上年增长(%) Increase Rate Preceding Year
新城区	Xincheng	276.97		105.56	171.41	14.6
碑林区	Beilin	300.24		60.72	239.52	15.0
莲湖区	Lianhu	330.38		150.28	180.10	14.0
灞桥区	Baqiao	137.65	8.79	74.89	53.97	15.4
未央区	Weiyang	340.93	2.42	179.88	158.63	15.8
雁塔区	Yanta	500.74	2.19	180.39	318.16	15.5
阎良区	Yanliang	78.45	11.29	39.98	27.18	13.1
临潼区	Lintong	122.64	20.72	63.74	38.18	14.4
长安区	Chang'an	227.09	19.21	108.84	99.04	15.9
蓝田县	Lantian	57.06	13.03	20.24	23.79	13.4
周至县	Zhouzhi	43.70	11.11	11.83	20.76	10.5
户　县	Huxian	90.27	12.44	49.29	28.54	12.4
高陵县	Gaoling	118.37	9.20	94.14	15.03	27.1

2–6　主要年份分行业增加值

Value-added by Ssctor in Respective Years

单位：亿元　　(100 million yuan)

指　标	Item	2004	2005	2006	2007	2008	2009
生产总值	**Gross Domestic Product**	**1102.39**	**1313.93**	**1538.94**	**1856.63**	**2318.14**	**2724.08**
第一产业	Primary Industry	60.21	66.01	70.44	82.51	103.45	110.38
第二产业	Secondary Industry	476.92	540.50	645.65	781.94	981.58	1144.75
工业	Industry	383.46	420.00	494.22	594.95	721.40	816.92
建筑业	Construction	93.46	120.50	151.43	186.99	260.18	327.83
第三产业	Tertiary Industry	565.26	707.42	822.85	992.18	1233.11	1468.95
交通运输、仓储及邮政业	Transportation,Storage,Post and Telecommunications	55.10	66.30	74.08	84.21	99.16	110.60
批发和零售业	Wholesale and Retail Trades	125.12	147.20	166.72	195.51	242.91	293.05
住宿和餐饮业	Accommodation and Catering Trade	35.89	50.44	52.23	70.09	85.65	94.05
金融保险业	Banking and Insurance	61.49	75.00	96.50	128.50	160.84	198.47
房地产业	Real Estate	39.05	52.48	62.32	75.26	92.97	124.98
其他服务业	Others Services	248.61	316.00	371.00	438.61	551.58	647.80

2–7　主要年份分行业增加值指数（上年=100）

Indices of Value -addded by Sector In Representative Years(preceding year=100)

（本表按可比价格计算）　　(Data in the table are calculated at constant prices)

指　标	Item	2005	2006	2007	2008	2009
生产总值	**Gross Domestic Product**	**114.0**	**114.0**	**115.6**	**116.3**	**114.5**
第一产业	Primary Industry	107.5	107.1	104.5	107.6	106.3
第二产业	Secondary Industry	112.3	113.7	115.7	116.4	114.0
工业	Industry	110.3	112.3	114.9	115.7	111.7
建筑业	Construction	120.0	118.7	118.4	118.9	121.2
第三产业	Tertiary Industry	116.3	114.9	116.4	116.9	115.5
交通运输、仓储及邮政业	Transportation,Storage,Post and Telecommunications	113.2	112.3	110.3	108.4	105.0
批发和零售业	Wholesale and Retail Trades	112.7	112.5	112.9	115.0	119.7
住宿和餐饮业	Hotels and Catering Services	136.1	116.6	117.3	111.6	106.6
金融保险业	Banking and Insurance	109.3	107.3	126.7	113.6	121.4
房地产业	Real Estate	112.9	117.5	119.7	107.6	131.6
其他服务业	Others Services	117.7	117.7	116.3	122.5	113.2

2-8 主要年份支出法生产总值

Gross Domestic Product by Expenditure Approach in Respective Years

（本表按当年价格计算） (Data in the table are calculated at current prices)

单位：亿元 (100 million yuan)

年 份 Year	生产总值 Gross Domestic Product	最终消费 Final Consumption Expenditures	资本形成总额 Total Investment	货物和服务净出口 Net Export of Goods and Services
1992	164.85	148.09	68.61	-51.85
1993	229.56	172.60	113.48	-56.52
1994	289.82	200.88	131.97	-43.03
1995	330.35	239.64	151.55	-60.84
1996	406.95	272.46	170.35	-35.86
1997	488.82	317.61	182.30	-11.09
1998	525.85	343.15	200.96	-18.26
1999	577.29	377.89	257.65	-58.25
2000	646.13	413.43	287.82	-55.12
2001	734.86	456.78	328.59	-50.51
2002	826.68	505.57	385.45	-64.34
2003	946.66	541.73	507.87	-102.94
2004	1102.39	689.24	649.93	-236.78
2005	1313.93	766.62	839.01	-291.70
2006	1538.94	870.93	1045.27	-377.26
2007	1856.63	995.22	1451.47	-590.06
2008	2318.14	1182.61	1837.86	-702.33
2009	2724.08	1403.10	2281.91	-960.93

2-9 主要年份支出法生产总值指数（上年=100）

Indices of Gross Domestic Product by Expenditure Approach in Years(preceding year = 100)

年 份 Year	生产总值 Gross Domestic Product	最终消费 Final Consumption Expenditures	资本形成总额 Total Investment
1992	115.6	114.4	116.0
1993	123.9	103.1	124.9
1994	110.3	104.9	116.4
1995	110.0	110.0	114.6
1996	114.9	102.1	105.8
1997	114.4	108.2	106.6
1998	113.3	114.9	108.1
1999	112.2	114.8	123.6
2000	113.0	109.9	116.2
2001	113.1	108.5	111.2
2002	113.3	109.7	117.1
2003	113.5	108.8	129.6
2004	113.5	109.8	123.7
2005	114.0	107.7	127.0
2006	114.0	109.4	120.1
2007	115.6	109.5	135.2
2008	116.3	116.9	120.2
2009	114.5	118.4	122.6

2-10 按支出法计算的生产总值及指数（2009年）

Gross Domestic Product and Indices by Expenditure Approach（2009）

单位：亿元 (100 million yuan)

指　标	Item	2009	指数（以上年为100）Indices (preceding year=100)
生产总值	**Gross Domestic Product**	**2724.08**	**114.5**
（一）最终消费支出	Final Consumption Expenditures	1403.10	118.4
1.居民消费支出	Resident Consumption Expenditures	1017.47	119.8
农村居民	Village Residents	135.95	115.4
城镇居民	Urban Residents	881.52	120.4
2.政府消费支出	Government Consumption Expenditures	385.63	115.0
（二）资本形成总额	Gross Total Capital Formation	2281.91	122.6
1.固定资本形成总额	Fixed Capital	2149.08	127.4
2.存货增加	chang of Goods in Stock	132.83	76.7
（三）货物和服务净出口	Net Export of Goods and Services	-960.93	

2-11 分行业资本形成总额（2009年）

Gross Capital Formation by Sector（2009）

单位：亿元 (100 million yuan)

指　标	Item	2009
资本形成总额	**Total Investment**	**2281.91**
固定资本形成总额	**Gross Fixed Capital Formation**	**2149.08**
第一产业	Primary Industry	23.38
农林牧渔业	Farming,Forestry,Animal Husbandry and Fishery	23.38
第二产业	Secondary Industy	422.82
工　业	Industry	388.12
建筑业	Construction	34.70
第三产业	Tertiary Industry	1702.88
交通运输、仓储及邮政业	Transportation,Storage,Post and Telecommunications	130.17
信息传输、计算机服务和软件业	Information Transmission,Computer Service and Software Service	17.88
批发和零售业	Wholesale, Retail and Catering Businesses	54.05
住宿和餐饮业	Hotels and Catering Services	39.11
金融业	Banking and Insurance	0.90
房地产业	Real Estate	686.00
其他行业	Others	774.77
存货增加	**Change of Goods in Stock**	**132.83**
第一产业	Primary Industry	0.16
农林牧渔业	Farming,Forestry,Animal Husbandry and Fishery	0.16
第二产业	Secondary Industy	64.22
工　业	Industry	76.56
建筑业	Construction	-12.34
第三产业	Tertiary Industry	68.45
交通运输、仓储及邮政业	Transportation,Storage,Post and Telecommunications	3.56
批发和零售业	Wholesale, Retail and Catering Businesses	-4.68
住宿和餐饮业	Hotels and Catering Services	0.16
其他行业	Others	69.41

2-12 最 终 消 费（2009年）

Final Consumption Expenditures（2009）

单位：亿元 (100 million yuan)

指 标	Item	2009
最终消费支出	**Final Consumption Expenditures**	**1403.10**
一、居民消费支出	**Resident Consumption Expenditures**	**1017.47**
（一）农村居民	Rural Residents	135.95
1.食品类支出	Food Expenditures	46.65
2.衣着类支出	Clothing Expenditures	8.16
3.居住类支出	Residence Expenditures	10.71
4.家庭设备、用品及服务类支出	Household Facilities、Articles and Services Expenditures	8.89
5.医疗保健类支出	Medical Care Expenditures	10.84
6.公共医疗消费支出	Public Medical Consumption Expenditures	1.00
7.交通和通信类支出	Transportion and Communication Expenditures	12.53
8.文教娱乐用品及服务类支出	Culture、Education and Entertainment Expenditures	14.20
9.间接计算的金融中介服务支出	Indirect Calculated Expenditures of Financial Intermediation Services	5.70
10.直接付费的金融机构实际服务消费支出	Directly Paid Expenditures of Financial Institution Services	0.30
11.保险服务消费支出	Insurance Services Consumption Expenditures	0.33
12.自有住房服务虚拟类支出	Virtual Expenditures of Private Housing Services	14.24
13.其它商品和服务类支出	Other goods and services Expenditures	2.40
（二）城镇居民	Urban Residents	881.52
1.食品类支出	Food Expenditures	264.93
2.衣着类支出	Clothing Expenditures	89.69
3.居住类支出	Residence Expenditures	72.39
4.家庭设备、用品及服务类支出	Household Facilities、Articles and Services Expenditures	59.50
5.医疗保健类支出	Medical Care Expenditures	78.86
6.公共医疗消费支出	Public Medical Consumption Expenditures	15.20
7.交通和通信类支出	Transportion and Communication Expenditures	92.57
8.文教娱乐用品及服务类支出	Culture、Education and Entertainment Expenditures	117.15
9.间接计算的金融中介服务支出	Indirect Calculated Expenditures of Financial Intermediation Services	21.15
10.直接付费的金融机构服务支出	Directly Paid Expenditures of Financial Institution Services	3.79
11.保险服务消费支出	Insurance Services Consumption Expenditures	3.21
12.自有住房服务虚拟类支出	Virtual Expenditures of Private Housing Services	19.80
13.实物消费支出	Physical goods Consumption Expenditures	1.41
14.其它商品和服务类支出	Other goods and services Expenditures	41.87
二、政府消费支出	**Government Consumption Expenditures**	**385.63**

2-13 居民总消费水平（2009年）

Consumption of Residents （2009）

指　　标	Item	2009	指数（%）(上年=100) Indices (preceding year=100)
一、按当年价格计算 (元/人)	**Calculated at Current Prices (yuan/person)**		
全体居民消费水平	Per Capita Consumption of All Residents	12106	119.3
农村居民	Farmer	5088	120.7
城镇居民	Non-Farmer	15377	117.4
二、按可比价格计算 (元/人)	**Calculated at Comparable Prices (yuan/person)**		
全体居民消费水平	Per Capita Consumption of All Residents	11059	118.8
农村居民	Farmer	4547	119.6
城镇居民	Non-Farmer	14094	117.0
三、常住居民年平均人口(万人)	**Average Annual Population of Residents (10 000 persons)**	**840.00**	**100.80**

2-14 非公有制经济增加值（2009年）

The Added Value of Non-public-owned Economic （2009）

单位：亿元　　(100 million yuan)

产　业	Industry	生产总值 Gross Domestic Product	非公有制经济增加值 the Added Value of Non-public-owned Economic	非公有制经济增加值占GDP比重(%) the Added Value of Non-public-owned Economic Percentage to GDP
总　计	**Gross Domestic Product**	**2724.08**	**1327.49**	**48.7**
第一产业	Primary Industry	110.38	36.32	32.9
第二产业	Secondary Industry	1114.75	542.37	47.4
第三产业	Tertiary Industry	1468.95	748.80	51.0

主要统计指标解释

生产总值（GDP） 是按市场价格计算的一个地区（或国家）所有常住单位在一定时期内生产活动的最终成果。生产总值有三种表现形态，即价值形态、收入形态和产品形态。从价值形态看，它是所有常住单位在一定时期内生产的全部货物和服务价值超过同期中间投入的全部非固定资产货物和服务价值的差额，即所有常住单位的增加值之和;从收入形态看，它是所有常住单位在一定时期内创造并分配给常住单位和非常住单位的初次收入分配之和;从产品形态看，它是所有常住单位在一定时期内最终使用的货物和服务价值与货物和服务净出口价值之和。在实际核算中，生产总值有三种计算方法，即生产法、收入法和支出法。三种方法分别从不同的方面反映生产总值及其构成。

三次产业 是根据社会生产活动历史发展的顺序对产业结构的划分，产品直接取自自然界的部门称为第一产业，对初级产品进行再加工的部门称为第二产业，为生产和消费提供各种服务的部门称为第三产业。它是世界上较为通用的产业结构分类，但各国的划分不尽一致。

我国的三次产业划分是:

第一产业:农业（包括农业、林业、畜牧业、渔业和农林牧渔服务业）。

第二产业:工业（包括采矿业，制造业，电力、燃气及水的生产和供应业）和建筑业。

第三产业:除第一、第二产业以外的其他各业。

支出法生产总值 指一个地区（或国家）所有常住单位在一定时期内用于最终消费、资本形成总额，以及货物和服务的净出口总额，它反映本期生产的生产总值的使用及构成。

最终消费 指常住单位在一定时期内对于货物和服务的全部最终消费支出，也就是常住单位为满足物质、文化和精神生活的需要，从本国经济领土和国外购买的货物和服务的支出;不包括非常住单位在本国经济领土内的消费支出。最终消费分为居民消费和政府消费。

居民消费 指常住住户对货物和服务的全部最终消费支出。居民消费按市场价格计算，即按居民支付的购买者价格计算。购买者价格是购买者取得货物所支付的价格，包括购买者支付的运输和商业费用。居民消费除了直接以货币形式购买货物和服务的消费之外，还包括以其他方式获得的货物和服务的消费支出，即所谓的虚拟消费支出。居民虚拟消费支出包括以下几种类型：单位以实物报酬及实物转移的形式提供给劳动者的货物和服务；住户生产并由本住户消费了的货物和服务，其中的服务仅指住户的自有住房服务；金融机构提供的金融媒介服务；保险公司提供的保险服务。

政府消费 指政府部门为全社会提供公共服务的消费支出和免费或以较低价格向住户提供的货物和服务的净支出。前者等于政府服务的产出价值减去政府单位所获得的经营收入的价值，政府服务的产出价值等于它的经常性业务支出加上固定资产折旧;后者等于政府部门免费或以较低价格向住户提供的货物和服务的市场价值减去向住户收取的价值。

资本形成总额 指常住单位在一定时期内获得的减去处置的固定资产加存货的变动，包括固定资本形成总额和存货增加。

固定资本形成总额 指常住单位购置、转入和自产自用的固定资产，扣除固定资产的销售和转出后的价值，分有形固定资产形成总额和无形固定资产形成总额。有形固定资产形成总额包括一定时期内完成的建筑工程、安装工程和设备工器具购置（减处置）价值，以及土地改良、新增役、种、奶、毛、娱乐用牲畜和新增经济林木价值。无形固定资产形成总额包括矿藏的勘探、计算机软件、娱乐和文学艺术品原件等获得减处置。

存货增加 指常住单位存货实物量变动的市场价值，即期末价值减期初价值的差额。存货增加可以是正值，也可以是负值；正值表示存货上升，负值表示存货下降。它包括生产单位购进的原材料、燃料和储备物资等存货，以及生产单位生产的产成品、在制品等存货等。

货物和服务净出口 指货物和服务出口减货物和服务进口的差额。出口包括常住单位向非常住单位出售或无偿转让的各种货物和服务的价值；进口包括常住单位从非常住单位购买或无偿得到的各种货物和服务的价值。由于服务活动的提供与使用同时发生，因此服务的进出口业务并不发生出入境现象，一般把常住单位从国外得到的服务作为进口，非常住单位从本国得到的服务作为出口。货物的出口和进口都按离岸价格计算。

劳动者报酬 指劳动者因从事生产活动所获得的全部报酬。包括劳动者获得的各种形式的工资、奖金和津贴，既包括货币形式的，也包括实物形式的；还包括劳动者所享受的公费医疗和医药卫生费、上下班交通补贴和单位支付的社会保险费等。对于个体经济来说，其所有者所获得的劳动报酬和经营利润不易区分，这两部分统一作为劳动者报酬处理。

生产税净额 指生产税减生产补贴后的余额。生产税指政府对生产单位生产、销售和从事经营活动以及因从事生产活动使用某些生产要素（如固定资产、土地、劳动力）所征收的各种税、附加费和规费。生产补贴与生产税相反，指政府对生产单位的单方面收入转移，因此视为负生产税，包括政策亏损补贴、粮食系统价格补贴、外贸企业出口退税收入等。

固定资产折旧 指一定时期内为弥补固定资产损耗按照核定的固定资产折旧率提取的固定资产折旧，或按国民经济核算统一规定的折旧率虚拟计算的固定资产折旧。它反映了固定资产在当期生产中的转移价值。各类企业和企业化管理的事业单位的固定资产折旧是指实际计提并计入成本费中的折旧费；不计提折旧的政府机关、非企业化管理的事业单位和居民住房的固定资产折旧是按照统一规定的折旧率和固定资产原值计算的虚拟折旧。原则上，固定资产折旧应按固定资产的重置价值计算，但是目前我国尚不具备对全社会固定资产进行重估价的基础，所以暂时只能采用上述办法。

营业盈余 指常住单位创造的增加值扣除劳动者报酬、生产税净额和固定资产折旧后的余额。它相当于企业的营业利润加上生产补贴，但要扣除从利润中开支的工资和福利等。

Explanatory Notes on Main Statistical Indicators

Gross Domestic Product (GDP) refers to the final products of all resident units in a oregin (or a country) during a certain period at market price. Gross domestic product is expressed in three different forms, i.e. value, income, and products respectively. The form of value refers to the total value of all products and services produced by all resident units during a certain period of time minus total value of intimidate input of materials and services of the nature of non-fixed assets or the summation of the value-added of all resident units; the form of income includes all the income created by all resident units and distributed primarily to all resident and non-resident units; the form of products refers to the value of all final goods and services for final use by all resident units plus the value of net exports of goods and services during a given period of time. In the practice of national accounting, gross domestic product is calculated with three approaches, i.e. production approach, income approach, and expenditure approach, which reflect gross domestic product and its composition from different aspects.

Three Industries Industry structure has been classified according to the historical sequence of development. Primary industry refers to extraction of natural resources; secondary industry involves processing of primary products; and tertiary industry provides services of various kinds for production and consumption. The above classification is universal although it varies to some extent form country to country.

Industry in China comprises:

Primary industry: agriculture (including farming, forestry, animal husbandry and fishery).

Secondary industry: industry (including mining and quarrying, manufacturing, production and supply of electricity, water and gas) and construction.

Tertiary industry: all other industries not included in primary or secondary industry.

GDP Calculated with Expenditure Approach refers to total expenditure on final consumption, total capital formation and net export of goods and services by resident units of a country in a certain period of time. It reflects the composition of GDP by its use.

Final Consumption refers to the total expenditure of resident units on final consumption of goods and services in a certain period, namely the expenditure of the resident units for purchases of goods and services from domestic economic territory and abroad to meet the requirements of material, cultural and spiritual life. It excludes the expenditure of non-resident units on consumption in the economic territory of the country. The final consumption is classified into household consumption and government consumption.

Households Consumption refers to the total expenditure of resident households on the final consumption of goods and services. The households consumption is calculated at market prices, namely the purchasers prices which the households pay; the purchasers prices of goods are the prices the households pay when they obtain the goods, including the transport and commercial expenses paid by the households. In addition to the consumption of goods and services bought by the households directly with money, the expenditure on goods and services obtained by the households in other ways, i.e. the so-called imputed expenditure on consumption, is also included in the households consumption. The imputation expenditure of the households on consumption includes the following types: (a) the goods and services provided to the households by the units in the form of payment in kind and transfer in kind; (b) the goods and services produced and consumed by the households themselves, in which the services refer only to the services provided by the residential buildings owned by the households; (c) the services of financial intermediary provided by the financial institutions; (d) theinsurance services provided by the insurance companies.

Government Consumption refers to the expenditure on the consumption of the public services provided by the government to the whole society and the net expenditure on the goods and services provided by the government to the households at free charge or lower prices. The former equals to the output value of the government services minus the value of operating income obtained by the government departments. (The output Value of the government services equals to its current operating expenditure plus depreciation of fixed assets).

The latter equals to the market value of the goods and services provided by the government free of charge or at low prices to the households minus the value received by the government from the households.

Total Capital Formation refers to the fixed assets acquired minus those disposed and the change in inventory, including the total fixed assets formation and the increase in inventory.

Total Fixed Capital Formation refers to the value of fixed assets purchased, transferred in by the resident units and those produced and used by themselves deducting the value of fixed assets sold and transferred out. It can be classified into total tangible assets formation and total intangible assets formation. The total tangible assets Formation include the value of the construction projects, installation projects completed and the equipment, apparatus and instruments purchased as well as the value of land improved, the value of draught animals, breeding stock, milk, wool and recreational animals and the newly increased economic forest in a certain period. The total intangible assets formation includes the prospecting of minerals, the acquisition of computer software, theoriginals of recreational works and works of literature and arts minus the disposal of them.

Increase in Inventory refers to the market value of the change in inventory, i.e. the difference of value between the beginning and the end of the period. The increase in inventory can be positive or negative. A positive value indicates the increase in inventory while a negative value indicates the decrease in stock. The inventory includes the raw materials, fuels and reserve materials purchased by the production units as well as the inventory of finished products, semi-finished products, work-in-progress, etc.

Net Export of Goods and Services refers to the difference of the exports of goods and services minus the imports of goods and services. The imports include the value of various goods and services sold or gratuitously transferred by the resident units to the non-resident units. The imports include the value of various goods and services purchased or gratuitously acquired by the resident units from the non-resident units. Because the provision of services and the use of them happen simultaneously, the import and export of services do not appear to have the phenomena of crossing the border of the country. The acquisition of services by the resident units from abroad is usually treated as import while the acquisition of services by non-resident units in this country is usually treated as export. The export and import of goods are calculated at FOB.

Labourers Remuneration refers to the whole payment of various forms earned by the labourers from the productive activities they are engaged in. It includes wages, bonuses and allowances the labourers earned in monetary form and in kind. It also includes the free medical services provided to the labourers and the medicine expenses, traffic subsidies and social insurance fee paid by the labourers working units for them. As the individual economy is concerned, since the labourers remuneration is not easily distinguished from the operating profit, both are treated as labourers remuneration.

Net Taxes on Production refers to the residual of the taxes on production minus the subsidies on production. The taxes on production refers to the various taxes, extra charges and fees levied on the production units on theirproduction, sale and business activities as well as on some factors of production, such as fixed assets, land and labour force, used in the production activities they are engaged in. In contrast to the taxes on production, the subsidies on production refer to the unilateral transfer of part of the governments revenue to the production units and is therefore regarded as negative taxes on production. They include subsidies on the loss due to implementation of government policies, price subsidies to the grain institutions, foreign trade corporations receipts from drawback, etc.

Depreciation of Fixed Assets refers to the depreciation of fixed assets of a given period, drawn in accordance with the stipulated depreciation rate for the purpose of compensating the wear loss of the fixed assets or the depreciation of fixed assets calculated in a fictitious way in accordance with the stipulated unified depreciation rate in the national economic accounting system. It reflects the value of transfer of the fixed assets in the production of the current period. The depreciation of fixed assets in various enterprises and institutions managed as enterprisesrefers to the depreciation expenses actually drawn and calculated as part of the cost. In government agencies and institutions not managed as enterprises which do not draw the depreciation expenses, as well as for the houses of residents, the depreciation of Fixed assets is the imputed depreciation, which is calculated in accordance with the stipulated unified depreciation rate. In principle, the depreciation of fixedassets should be calculated on the basis of the repurchased value of the fixed assets. However, there is no actual condition to re-evaluate all the fixed assets in China. Therefore, the above-mentioned methods are temporarily adopted at present.

Operating Surplus refers to the balance of the value added created by the resident units deducting the labourers remuneration, net taxes on production and the depreciation of fixed assets. It is equivalent to the business profit of the enterprises plus subsidies on production, but the wages and welfare expenses paid from the profits should be deducted.

3 人口、从业人员与职工工资

POPULATION，EMPLOYMENT AND WAGES

资料整理：王义龙　张　静
Data management:Wang Yilong　Zhang Jing

第三部分　人口、从业人员与职工工资

一、简要说明

本章资料包括主要年份人口、分区县户籍和常住人口及变动、从业人员及劳动报酬等。户籍人口数为公安年报数，1991年以前年份市区数未包括临潼、长安。主要数据由西安市统计局人口就业处提供。

二、主要指标

年末户籍人口（万人）	781.67	比上年增长	1.2%
人口自然增长率（‰）	4.45	比上年下降	0.13‰
常住人口（万人）	843.46	比上年增长	0.7%
男女性别比（以女性为100）	106.89	比上年下降	0.11%
户籍人口密度（人/平方公里）	773	比上年增加	9人
城镇非私营单位在岗职工年均工资（元）	34032	比上年增长	14.4%

3 POPULATION,EMPLOYMENT AND WAGES

Ⅰ.Brief Introduction

This chapter consists of the data about the population of consequent years, population of all the districts and counties and the correspondent changes, the employed and their wages. The population data are from the annual report of the Xi'an Bureau of Public Security, with Lintong, Chang'an not included before 1991. The population data is provided primarily by Population & Employment Division of the Xi'an Bureau of Statistics.

Ⅱ.Major Indicators

		Increase over Preceding Year
Total Population of Year-end(10 000 persons)	781.67	1.2%
Natural Gorwth Rate(‰)	4.45	-0.13‰
Permanent Population(10 000 persons)	843.46	0.7%
Sex Ratio (female = 100)	106.89	-0.11%
Density of Population (person/sq.km)	773	9
Aunual Average Wage of Stuff and Workers in Urban Non-privite Enterprises(yuan)	34032	14.4%

3-1 主要年份人口、人口密度和人口发展情况

Population, Population Density and Population Development in represontative

单位：万人

(10 000 persons)

年 份 Year	总人口 Total population	市区 Urban Area	女性人口数 Number of Female	非农业人口数 Non-Agricultural Population	人口密度（人/平方公里） Density of Population (person/sq.km)	总人口指数(上年为100) Total Population Index (100 for preceding year) 全市 Whole City	市区 Urban Area
1952	252.92	92.42	118.81	57.61	254	102.6	103.1
1965	400.05	179.88	190.72	136.39	401	102.5	103.4
1970	435.12	188.12	210.47	139.12	436	101.9	101.4
1978	498.10	210.15	241.82	159.98	499	101.7	102.7
1980	511.91	221.19	249.26	172.85	513	101.4	102.6
1985	553.11	245.76	268.40	201.90	554	101.6	102.2
1986	563.97	251.80	273.30	205.92	565	102.0	102.5
1987	574.46	257.69	278.12	210.25	575	101.9	102.3
1988	585.85	264.94	283.68	216.99	587	102.0	102.8
1989	597.36	270.80	289.44	222.54	598	102.0	102.2
1990	608.89	275.69	295.29	226.98	610	101.9	101.8
1991	615.48	419.29	298.13	230.85	617	101.1	152.1
1992	623.20	429.54	301.92	236.45	624	101.3	102.4
1993	630.91	435.41	305.30	240.85	632	101.2	101.4
1994	639.45	442.30	309.17	248.35	641	101.4	101.6
1995	648.21	448.65	313.46	255.71	645	101.4	101.4
1996	654.87	454.68	316.60	261.28	653	101.0	101.3
1997	662.06	461.17	320.18	267.52	663	101.1	101.4
1998	668.22	466.31	323.20	271.75	669	100.9	101.1
1999	674.50	463.56	326.12	276.14	676	100.9	99.4
2000	688.01	483.10	332.83	285.79	689	102.0	104.2
2001	694.84	489.88	336.04	292.62	696	101.0	101.4
2002	702.59	497.38	339.51	300.05	704	101.1	101.5
2003	716.58	510.26	346.26	312.88	718	102.0	102.6
2004	725.01	516.30	350.85	318.50	717	101.2	101.2
2005	741.73	533.21	359.71	333.14	734	102.3	103.3
2006	753.11	540.97	365.74	343.78	745	101.5	101.5
2007	764.25	549.19	371.84	353.85	756	101.5	101.5
2008	772.30	554.73	376.76	363.87	764	101.1	101.0
2009	781.67	561.58	382.39	370.66	773	101.2	101.2

注:人口部分均为公安年报数据。1991年以前年份，市区数未包括临潼、长安。

Note: The population data are taken from annual reports of public recurity.The population of urban area before 1991 doesn't include Lintong and Chang'an.

3-2 主要年份人口变动情况

Population Changes in Representative Years

单位：万人 (10 000 persons)

年 份 Year	出生 Birth 人数 Population	出生率(‰) Birth Rate (‰)	死亡 Death 人数 Population	死亡率(‰) Death Rate (‰)	自然增长率(‰) Natural Gorwth Rate (‰)	迁入人口 Immigrant population	迁出人口 Emigrant population
1952	7.68	30.74	2.21	8.86	21.88		
1965	11.53	29.19	3.36	8.50	20.69	13.11	10.83
1970	12.05	27.96	2.34	5.44	22.52	6.88	8.39
1978	7.81	19.04	3.17	6.66	12.38	8.98	9.16
1980	6.59	12.96	3.19	6.28	6.68	13.36	9.64
1985	8.95	16.30	3.01	5.48	10.82	11.60	8.74
1986	10.14	18.15	2.78	4.97	13.18	11.79	8.39
1987	9.76	17.14	2.83	4.97	12.17	12.58	9.26
1988	9.42	16.24	2.89	4.98	11.26	13.54	8.97
1989	11.78	19.92	3.04	5.13	14.79	12.73	10.15
1990	12.40	20.55	3.45	5.72	14.83	11.82	9.86
1991	8.73	14.25	3.26	5.33	8.92	8.98	6.09
1992	8.98	14.49	3.39	5.48	9.01	13.94	9.54
1993	9.25	14.75	3.37	5.38	9.37	11.50	8.33
1994	8.08	12.71	3.16	4.97	7.74	13.40	8.59
1995	7.69	11.95	3.21	4.98	6.97	14.41	8.85
1996	7.26	11.15	3.41	5.24	5.91	11.94	8.88
1997	6.84	10.38	3.12	4.75	5.63	12.58	8.62
1998	6.40	9.62	3.10	4.66	4.96	10.89	8.36
1999	6.19	9.22	3.88	5.78	3.44	12.58	9.23
2000	8.90	13.07	4.06	5.96	7.11	17.12	9.23
2001	5.11	7.39	2.89	4.19	3.20	15.16	10.83
2002	5.34	7.64	3.08	4.41	3.23	13.90	9.41
2003	6.02	8.48	3.32	4.68	3.80	20.60	9.15
2004	6.63	9.19	4.23	5.87	3.32	15.56	10.19
2005	7.67	9.58	4.13	5.16	4.42	22.61	9.46
2006	8.13	9.98	4.45	5.46	4.52	17.23	11.75
2007	8.27	10.00	4.53	5.48	4.52	19.90	14.01
2008	8.47	10.15	4.65	5.57	4.58	18.49	15.04
2009	8.47	10.08	4.73	5.63	4.45	16.84	13.14

注：2004年以前为公安年报数据。2005年以后出生、死亡、自然增长率为人口变动抽样调查数据。

Note:Before 2004, the data were taken from annual reports of public security. After 2005,the data of birthrate、death rate and the natural population growth rate were taken from the statistics from spot check on population changes.

3-3 分区县人口和户数（2009年）

Population and Households by Region（2009）

单位：万人 (10 000 person)

区 县 District and County		总户数(户) Number of Households (household)	总人口 Total Population	非农业人口 Non-agriculture	按性别分 Grouped by Sex 男 Male	女 Female	常住人口 Permanent population 2000	2009
合 计	**Total**	**221.51**	**781.67**	**370.66**	**399.28**	**382.39**	**741.14**	**843.46**
新城区	Xincheng	16.40	50.33	50.33	25.65	24.68	53.63	62.80
碑林区	Beilin	20.03	74.84	74.84	39.25	35.59	71.16	78.52
莲湖区	Lianhu	21.05	63.85	63.85	32.44	31.41	64.32	73.82
灞桥区	Baqiao	15.77	50.53	23.03	25.22	25.31	50.38	57.25
未央区	Weiyang	15.33	50.04	31.72	25.10	24.94	46.91	62.96
雁塔区	Yanta	20.29	78.94	62.78	39.90	39.04	81.00	113.67
阎良区	Yanliang	7.07	25.23	8.80	12.79	12.44	24.01	26.27
临潼区	Lintong	18.68	70.25	11.78	35.53	34.72	65.14	68.62
长安区	Chang'an	26.02	97.56	13.89	49.05	48.51	87.99	103.37
蓝田县	Lantian	17.65	64.34	5.79	33.33	31.01	57.07	52.89
周至县	Zhouzhi	17.00	67.11	6.10	35.42	31.69	60.87	55.72
户 县	Huxian	17.87	59.85	10.98	31.18	28.67	56.01	56.77
高陵县	Gaoling	8.35	28.80	6.77	14.42	14.38	22.65	30.80

注：2009年常住人口为人口变动抽样调查数据。

Note:The permanent population of 2009 were taken from sample survey on population changing.

3-4 分区县人口变动情况（2009年）

Population Changes by Region（2009）

区 县	District and County	出生率(‰) Birth Rate (‰)	死亡率(‰) Death Rate (‰)	自然增长率(‰) Natural Gorwth Rate (‰)	迁入人口(人) Immigrant population (person)	迁出人口(人) Emigrant population (person)
合 计	**Total**	**10.08**	**5.63**	**4.45**	**168446**	**131385**
新城区	Xincheng	7.46	4.01	3.45	5489	2688
碑林区	Beilin	7.40	4.20	3.20	28679	30590
莲湖区	Lianhu	8.48	5.02	3.46	10628	6828
灞桥区	Baqiao	10.06	5.72	4.34	10122	5019
未央区	Weiyang	10.58	5.48	5.10	21364	5489
雁塔区	Yanta	9.78	5.44	4.34	44221	45707
阎良区	Yanliang	9.60	5.82	3.78	3167	2607
临潼区	Lintong	11.39	5.97	5.42	3702	2790
长安区	Chang'an	10.65	6.20	4.45	12822	9283
蓝田县	Lantian	13.00	7.53	5.47	5462	5362
周至县	Zhouzhi	12.58	7.17	5.41	6373	5613
户 县	Huxian	10.90	5.44	5.46	8613	7263
高陵县	Gaoling	10.79	6.31	4.48	7804	2146

注：出生率、死亡率、自然增长率为人口变动抽样调查数据。

Note:Birth rate, death rate, and natural growth rate were taken from sample survey on population changing.

3-5 主要年份常住人口

Permanent population in Representtative Years

单位：万人 (10 000 persons)

年 份 Year	年末常住人口 Permanent population (year-end)	城镇 Urban	农村 Rural
2000	741.14	450.36	290.78
2005	806.81	510.55	296.26
2006	822.52	530.94	291.58
2007	830.54	548.99	281.55
2008	837.52	565.16	272.36
2009	843.46	581.40	262.06

注：2000年常住人口为人口普查数据；其他年份常住人口为人口变动抽样调查数据。

Note:Data in 2000 were taken from population census, The permanent population of other were taken from sample survey on population changing.

3-6 城乡劳动力资源配置情况（2009年）

Deployment of Urban and Rural Labor Resources（2009）

单位：万人 (10 000 persons)

分组	Classify	城乡合计 Total	城镇 Urban Area	乡村 Rural
一、经济活动人口	**Economically Active Population**	**472.72**	**249.59**	**223.13**
（一）从业人员	Total Employed Persons	462.52	239.39	223.13
1.按就业身份分组	Grouped by Employees' Status			
（1）全部职工	Total	142.70	142.70	
（2）再就业的离退休人员	Retirees Reemployed	0.94	0.94	
（3）私营业主	Private Owners	17.53	15.55	1.98
（4）个体户主	Self-employed Persons	32.54	20.95	11.59
（5）私营企业和个体从业人员	Employees in Private and Individual Enterprises	104.71	59.25	45.46
（6）农村劳动力	Rural Labor Resources	164.10		164.10
（7）其他	Others			
2.按国民经济类型分组	Grouped by Type			
（1）国有经济	State-owned Enterprises	90.83	90.83	
（2）集体经济	Collective-owned Enterprises	171.73	7.63	164.10
（3）私营经济	Private Enterprises	92.87	63.57	29.30
（4）个体经济	Individual Enterprises	61.91	32.18	29.73
（5）股份合作经济	Share-Holding Cooperatiive Enterprises	0.63	0.63	
（6）联营经济	Joint -owned Enterprises	0.33	0.33	
（7）有限责任公司	Limited Liability Corporations	26.55	26.55	
（8）股份有限公司	Share-holding Corporation Ltd.	8.50	8.50	
（9）外商投资经济	Foreign-funded Enterprises	6.24	6.24	
（10）港、澳、台投资经济	Enterprises with Funds from Hong Kong, Macao and Taiwan	1.69	1.69	
（11）其他经济	Others	1.24	1.24	
3.按国民经济行业分组	Grouped by Sector			
（1）农、林、牧、渔业	Agriculture,Forestry,Animal Husbandry and Fishery	122.13	0.36	121.77
（2）采矿业	Mining	0.23	0.23	
（3）制造业	Manufacturing	86.45	63.78	22.67
（4）电力、燃气及水的生产和供应业	Production and Distribution of Electricity,Gas and Water	3.23	3.23	
（5）建筑业	Construction	41.66	15.43	26.23
（6）交通运输、仓储和邮政业	Traffic,Transport,Storage and Post	32.04	21.12	10.92
（7）信息传输、计算机服务和软件业	Information Transmission,Computer Service and Software	6.22	5.06	1.16
（8）批发和零售业	Wholesale and Retail Trades	51.94	41.98	9.96
（9）住宿和餐饮业	Hotels and Catering Services	24.39	16.27	8.12
（10）金融业	Financial Intermediation	6.07	5.47	0.60
（11）房地产业	Real Estate	3.36	3.36	
（12）租赁和商务服务业	Leasing and Business Services	10.16	7.28	2.88
（13）科学研究、技术服务和地质勘察业	Scientific Research,Technical Service and Geologic Prospecting	13.04	9.19	3.85
（14）水利、环境和公共设施管理业	Management of Water Conservancy, Environment and Public Facilities	2.06	2.06	
（15）居民服务和其他服务业	Services to Households and Other Services	13.94	8.05	5.89
（16）教育	Education	20.42	18.28	2.14
（17）卫生、社会保障和社会福利业	Health,Social Security and Social Welfare	11.69	6.71	4.98
（18）文化、体育和娱乐业	Culture, Sports and Entertainment	2.41	2.41	
（19）公共管理和社会组织	Public Management and Social Organization	11.08	9.12	1.96
（二）失业人员	Unemployed	10.20	10.20	
二、非经济活动人口	**Non-economical Activity Population**	**154.00**		
#16岁以上在校学生	Students Aged 16 and Over	119.00		

3-7 主要年份社会从业人数

单位：万人

年份 Year	合计 Total	一、按城乡分 Grouped by Urban area and Rural area 1.城镇 Urban	国有经济 State-owned Enterprises	集体经济 Collective-owned Enterprises	其他经济 Others	2.乡村 Village
1985	296.80	129.07	96.80	29.07	3.20	167.73
1986	299.45	132.82	101.28	28.43	3.11	166.63
1987	312.16	138.56	104.58	30.72	3.26	173.60
1988	327.76	142.24	106.46	30.73	5.05	185.52
1989	332.65	145.65	108.80	30.44	6.41	187.00
1990	343.06	147.93	110.95	29.78	7.20	195.13
1991	347.65	149.48	111.87	29.80	7.81	198.17
1992	357.51	151.67	113.19	29.97	8.51	205.84
1993	363.70	155.72	112.98	29.77	12.97	207.98
1994	364.56	154.88	113.39	27.97	13.52	209.68
1995	372.60	158.80	113.79	25.58	19.43	213.80
1996	379.29	164.54	113.29	24.82	26.43	214.75
1997	385.14	169.52	112.44	23.52	33.56	215.62
1998	393.95	177.20	106.06	21.50	49.64	216.75
1999	400.43	180.27	105.08	20.50	54.69	220.16
2000	389.10	176.45	103.46	18.40	54.59	212.65
2001	389.30	177.94	100.47	17.10	60.37	211.36
2002	397.16	181.85	100.54	16.90	64.41	215.31
2003	404.92	183.23	94.51	16.78	71.94	221.69
2004	409.57	187.53	93.43	15.41	78.69	222.04
2005	415.83	192.53	93.27	14.47	84.79	223.30
2006	422.15	196.16	84.46	14.41	97.29	225.99
2007	436.36	214.27	90.58	11.88	111.81	222.09
2008	448.05	224.20	90.17	10.60	123.43	223.85
2009	462.52	239.39	90.83	7.63	140.93	223.13

Number of Social Laborers in Representative Years

(10 000 persons)

二、按三次产业分		Grouped by Industry
第一产业 Primary Industry	第二产业 Secondary Indusyry	第三产业 Tertiary Industry
135.89	98.61	62.30
127.46	100.61	71.38
130.36	107.75	74.05
138.87	108.12	80.77
142.21	106.40	84.04
149.64	106.74	86.68
152.24	108.19	87.22
154.75	110.22	92.54
154.02	114.02	95.66
153.51	108.53	102.52
153.39	109.67	109.54
153.43	109.17	116.69
153.23	109.46	122.45
153.00	110.45	130.50
154.64	110.58	135.21
147.03	107.26	134.81
145.09	108.96	135.25
143.04	111.62	142.50
146.67	109.09	149.16
141.81	111.70	156.06
136.31	114.20	165.32
135.10	116.09	170.96
133.33	125.06	177.97
127.87	130.23	189.95
122.13	131.57	208.82

3-8　分行业从业人数（2009年）

单位：万人

行　　业	Sector	合 计 Total
总　计	**Total**	**462.52**
一、按国民经济行业分组	**Grouped by Sector**	
（一）农、林、牧、渔业	Agriculture ,Forestry,Animal Husbandry and Fishery	122.13
（二）采矿业	Mining	0.23
（三）制造业	Manufacturing	86.45
（四）电力、燃气及水的生产和供应业	Production and Distribution of Electricity,Gas and Water	3.23
（五）建筑业	Construction	41.66
（六）交通运输、仓储和邮政业	Traffic,Transport,Storage and Post	32.04
（七）信息传输、计算机服务和软件业	Information Transmission,Computer Service and Software	6.22
（八）批发和零售业	Wholesale and Retail Trades	51.94
（九）住宿和餐饮业	Hotels and Catering Services	24.39
（十）金融业	Financial Intermediation	6.07
（十一）房地产业	Real Estate	3.36
（十二）租赁和商务服务业	Leasing and Business Services	10.16
（十三）科学研究、技术服务和地质勘察业	Scientific Research,Technical Service and Geologic Prospecting	13.04
（十四）水利、环境和公共设施管理业	Management of Water Conservancy, Environment	2.06
	and Public Facilities	13.94
（十五）居民服务和其他服务业	Services to Households and Other Services	20.42
（十六）教育	Education	11.69
（十七）卫生、社会保障和社会福利业	Health,Social Security and Social Welfare	2.41
（十八）文化、体育和娱乐业	Culture, Sports and Entertainment	11.08
（十九）公共管理和社会组织	Public Management and Social Organization	
二、按三次产业分	**Guroped by Industry**	
第一产业	Primary Industry	122.13
第二产业	Secondary Industry	131.57
第三产业	Tertiary Industry	208.82

Number of Employed Persons by Sector（2009）

(10 000 persons)

国有经济 State-owned Enterprises	集体经济 Collective-owned Enterprises	城镇其他经济 Urban Other Enterprises	城镇私营经济及个体劳动者 Urban Private Enterprises and Individual Labors	乡镇劳动者 Rural and Urban Labourer
90.83	**7.63**	**45.18**	**95.75**	**223.13**
0.36				121.77
0.06		0.17		
23.17	2.68	19.94	17.99	22.67
2.81	0.02	0.40		
6.65	1.89	4.42	2.47	26.23
9.27	0.26	1.36	10.23	10.92
2.09		2.05	0.92	1.16
2.18	1.18	3.59	35.03	9.96
1.10	0.25	2.25	12.67	8.12
1.84		3.63		0.60
0.76	0.27	2.33		
1.02	0.20	0.38	5.68	2.88
8.31	0.10	0.78		3.85
1.02	0.08	0.96		
0.49	0.49	0.41	6.66	5.89
14.34	0.03	1.46	2.45	2.14
4.66	0.15	0.25	1.65	4.98
1.58	0.03	0.80		
9.12				1.96
0.36				121.77
32.69	4.59	24.93	20.46	48.90
57.78	3.04	20.25	75.29	52.46

3-9 全部单位从业人员情况（2009年）

单位：人

分组	Classify	单位从业人员 Employed Persons	女性 Female
总　计	**Total**	**1356418**	**498022**
一、按企业、事业、机关分组	**Groped by Enterprises,Insitutions and Agencies**		
1.企业	Enterprises	1024687	352817
2.事业	Institutions	229105	115405
3.机关	Agencies and Organizations	93157	25120
4.民间非盈利组织	Non-profit NGO	2183	1098
5.其他	Others	7286	3582
二、按国民经济行业分组	**Grouped by Sector**		
（一）农、林、牧、渔业	Agriculture ,Forestry,Animal Husbandry and Fishery	3272	912
（二）采矿业	Mining	2282	656
（三）制造业	Manufacturing	427749	133600
（四）电力、燃气及水的生产和供应业	Production and Distribution of Electricity,Gas and Water	31295	9688
（五）建筑业	Construction	113413	22374
（六）交通运输、仓储和邮政业	Traffic,Transport,Storage and Post	102600	27831
（七）信息传输、计算机服务和软件业	Information Transmission,Computer Service and Software	41072	20131
（八）批发和零售业	Wholesale and Retail Trades	60480	30258
（九）住宿和餐饮业	Hotels and Catering Services	35508	20189
（十）金融业	Financial Intermediation	51616	26157
（十一）房地产业	Real Estate	29519	11877
（十二）租赁和商务服务业	Leasing and Business Services	13474	5178
（十三）科学研究、技术服务和地质勘察业	Scientific Research,Technical Services and Geological Prospecting	88296	28892
（十四）水利、环境和公共设施管理业	Management of Water Conservancy, Environment and Public Facilities	20082	8834
（十五）居民服务和其他服务业	Services to Households and Other Services	13664	5972
（十六）教育	Education	157906	80532
（十七）卫生、社会保障和社会福利业	Health,Social Security and Social Welfare	49885	30493
（十八）文化、体育和娱乐业	Culture, Sports and Entertainment	23413	10091
（十九）公共管理和社会组织	Public Management and Social Organization	90892	24357

Basic Facts on All Employed Persons（2009）

(person)

在岗职工合计 Total Fully Employed Staff and Workers	专业技术人员 Scientific and Technical Personnel	女性 Female	其他从业人员 Other Employed Persons	单位从业人员平均人数 Average Employment	在岗职工 Fully Employed Staff and Workers	其他从业人员 Other Employed Persons
1296157	**456651**	**170515**	**60261**	**1345710**	**1292192**	**53518**
980862	305516	88039	43825	1037793	996767	41026
219370	139371	77460	9735	213635	206924	6711
87249	7445	2741	5908	84857	79851	5006
2005	1146	560	178	2258	2102	156
6671	3173	1715	615	7167	6548	619
3206	932	372	66	3266	3200	66
2276	999	149	6	1894	1888	6
413983	131201	30761	13766	454611	441381	13230
30823	9497	2475	472	31105	30637	468
108883	41827	8635	4530	111665	107296	4369
94219	9738	3598	8381	101778	93626	8152
41006	13411	4077	66	37905	37843	62
57477	8621	2673	3003	59642	57330	2312
34781	3157	1238	727	35219	34452	767
45897	21123	10448	5719	47120	42260	4860
28544	8089	4293	975	27538	26923	615
12766	1952	893	708	13512	12817	695
84846	45074	14607	3450	88715	84999	3716
18202	7413	788	1880	19407	17933	1474
13443	1571	796	221	13311	13161	150
150512	105897	58420	7394	147045	142064	4981
47370	31465	20410	2515	46242	44229	2013
22682	7818	3634	731	23126	22524	602
85241	6866	2248	5651	82609	77629	4980

3-10 国有单位从业人员情况（2009年）

单位：人

分 组	Classify	单位从业人员 Employed Persons	女性 Female
合 计	**Total**	**854208**	**313202**
一、按隶属关系分组	**Grouped by Administrative Relationship**		
1.中央	Central	361177	115804
2.省	Province,Autonomous Region and Municipalities	134681	52742
3.市	District	167099	58221
4.县及县以下	County and Below	167461	74911
5.其他	Others	23790	11524
二、按企业业、事业、机关分组	**Groped by Enterprises,Insitutions and Agencies**		
1.企业	Enterprises	540544	176260
2.事业	Institutions	218185	110739
3.机关	Agencies and Organizations	93157	25120
4.民间非盈利组织	Non-profit NGO		
5.其他	Others	2322	1083
三、按国民经济行业分组	**Grouped by Economic Sector**		
(一)农、林、牧、渔业	Agriculture ,Forestry,Animal Husbandry and Fishery	3222	899
(二)采矿业	Mining	626	138
(三)制造业	Manufacturing	211395	65676
(四)电力、燃气及水的生产和供应业	Production and Distribution of Electricity,Gas and Water	27011	8260
(五)建筑业	Construction	54176	12062
(六)交通运输、仓储和邮政业	Traffic,Transport,Storage and Post	87679	23432
(七)信息传输、计算机服务和软件业	Information Transmission,Computer Service and Software	20560	11245
(八)批发和零售业	Wholesale and Retail Trades	16515	6019
(九)住宿和餐饮业	Hotels and Catering Services	10673	6090
(十)金融业	Financial Intermediation	18311	8109
(十一)房地产业	Real Estate	5892	2081
(十二)租赁和商务服务业	Leasing and Business Services	9004	3663
(十三)科学研究、技术服务和地质勘察业	Scientific Research,Technical Service and Geologic Prospecting	79540	26302
(十四)水利、环境和公共设施管理业	Management of Water Conservancy, Environment and Public Facilities	9956	4979
(十五)居民服务和其他服务业	Services to Households and Other Services	4829	2320
(十六)教育	Education	143009	74087
(十七)卫生、社会保障和社会福利业	Health,Social Security and Social Welfare	45872	27852
(十八)文化、体育和娱乐业	Culture, Sports and Entertainment	15046	5631
(十九)公共管理和社会组织	Public Management and Social Organization	90892	24357

Basic Facts on Persons Employed by State-owned Units (2009)

(person)

在岗职工合计 Total Fully Employed Staff	其他从业人员 Other Employed Persons	单位从业人员平均人数 Average Employment	在岗职工 Fully Employed Staff and Workers	其他从业人员 Other Employed Persons
813995	**40213**	**882911**	**847258**	**35653**
345738	15439	412535	397162	15373
129187	5494	135388	130059	5329
158019	9080	152436	145853	6583
158113	9348	157688	150064	7624
22938	852	24864	24120	744
514522	26022	594021	569222	24799
209939	8246	201789	195976	5813
87249	5908	84857	79851	5006
2285	37	2244	2209	35
3156	66	3216	3150	66
626		626	626	0
202934	8461	268582	261148	7434
26539	472	27412	26944	468
51208	2968	53007	50283	2724
79948	7731	86866	79298	7568
20534	26	20055	20033	22
16260	255	16044	15784	260
10616	57	10664	10578	86
17325	986	17859	17008	851
5720	172	5936	5744	192
8349	655	8966	8324	642
76219	3321	79136	75529	3607
8674	1282	9660	8626	1034
4780	49	4782	4733	49
137771	5238	132041	128643	3398
43449	2423	41295	39340	1955
14646	400	14155	13838	317
85241	5651	82609	77629	4980

3-11 城镇集体单位从业人员情况（2009年）

单位：人

分组	Classify	单位从业人员 Employed Persons	女性 Female
总 计	**Total**	**64093**	**23976**
一、按企业、事业、机关分组	**Groped by Enterprises,Insitutions and Agencies**		
1.企业	Enterprises	61963	22903
2.事业	Institutions	1925	967
3.机关	Agencies and Organizations		
4.民间非盈利组织	Non-profit NGO	46	32
5.其他	Others	159	74
二、按国民经济行业分组	**Grouped by Sector**		
(一)农、林、牧、渔业	Agriculture ,Forestry,Animal Husbandry and Fishery		
(二)采矿业	Mining		
(三)制造业	Manufacturing	23371	7950
(四)电力、燃气及水的生产和供应业	Production and Distribution of Electricity,Gas and Water	246	63
(五)建筑业	Construction	15219	3706
(六)交通运输、仓储和邮政业	Traffic,Transport,Storage and Post	1695	560
(七)信息传输、计算机服务和软件业	Information Transmission,Computer Service and Software	18	6
(八)批发和零售业	Wholesale and Retail Trades	9516	6041
(九)住宿和餐饮业	Hotels and Catering Services	2428	1340
(十)金融业	Financial Intermediation		
(十一)房地产业	Real Estate	1500	556
(十二)租赁和商务服务业	Leasing and Business Services	1413	321
(十三)科学研究、技术服务和地质勘察业	Scientific Research,Technical Service and Geologic Prospecting	958	317
(十四)水利、环境和公共设施管理业	Management of Water Conservancy, Environment and Public Facilities	758	362
(十五)居民服务和其他服务业	Services to Households and Other Services	4879	1577
(十六)教育	Education	319	169
(十七)卫生、社会保障和社会福利业	Health,Social Security and Social Welfare	1453	895
(十八)文化、体育和娱乐业	Culture, Sports and Entertainment	320	113
(十九)公共管理和社会组织	Public Management and Social Organization		

Basic Facts on Persons Employed by Urban Collective-owned Units（2009）

(person)

在岗职工合计 Total Fully Employed Staff and Workers	其他从业人员 Other Employed Persons	单位从业人员平均人数 Average Employment	在岗职工 Fully Employed Staff and Workers	其他从业人员 Other Employed Persons
62672	**1421**	**77497**	**76051**	**1446**
60652	1311	74318	72948	1370
1827	98	2918	2854	64
34	12	92	80	12
159		169	169	
22996	375	30449	30080	369
246		245	245	
14789	430	17137	16609	528
1693	2	1674	1672	2
18		18	18	
9104	412	10159	9756	403
2428		2443	2443	
1488	12	2346	2334	12
1413		1554	1554	
930	28	2065	2037	28
758		808	806	2
4879		4792	4792	
300	19	595	576	19
1361	92	2235	2177	58
269	51	977	952	25

3-12 其他经济类型单位从业人员情况（2009年）

单位：人

分组	Classify	单位从业人员 Employed Persons	女性 Female
合计	**Total**	**438117**	**160844**
一、按登记注册类型分组	**Grouped by Registion Status**		
（一）内资	Domestic Investment	358762	132463
1.股份合作	Share-holding Cooperative	6384	2617
2.联营	Joint Ownership	3250	499
3.有限责任公司	Limited Liability Corporations	253270	91556
#国有独资	Sole State-funded	33312	2413
4.股份有限公司	Share-holding Corperation Ltd.	85016	32912
5.其他	Others	10842	4879
（二）港、澳、台商投资	Enterprises with Funds from Hong Kong, Macao and Taiwan	16916	7653
（三）外商投资	Enterprises with Foreign Funded	62439	20728
二、按企业、事业分组	**Grouped by Enterprise and Instilution**		
1.企业	Enterprises	422180	153654
2.事业	Institutions	8995	3699
3.民间非盈利组织	Non-profit NGO	2137	1066
4.其他	Others	4805	2425
三、按国民经济行业分组	**Grouped by Sector**		
（一）农、林、牧、渔业	Agriculture,Forestry,Animal Husbandry and Fishery	50	13
（二）采矿业	Mining	1656	518
（三）制造业	Manufacturing	192983	59974
（四）电力、燃气及水的生产和供应业	Production and Distribution of Electricity,Gas and Water	4038	1365
（五）建筑业	Construction	44018	6606
（六）交通运输、仓储和邮政业	Traffic,Transport,Storage and Post	13226	3839
（七）信息传输、计算机服务和软件业	Information Transmission,Computer Service and Software	20494	8880
（八）批发和零售业	Wholesale and Retail Trades	34449	18198
（九）住宿和餐饮业	Hotels and Catering Services	22407	12759
（十）金融业	Financial Intermediation	33305	18048
（十一）房地产业	Real Estate	22127	9240
（十二）租赁和商务服务业	Leasing and Business Services	3057	1194
（十三）科学研究、技术服务和地质勘察业	Scientific Research,Technical Service and Geologic Prospecting	7798	2273
（十四）水利、环境和公共设施管理业	Management of Water Conservancy, Environment and Public Facilities	9368	3493
（十五）居民服务和其他服务业	Services to Households and Other Services	3956	2075
（十六）教育	Education	14578	6276
（十七）卫生、社会保障和社会福利业	Health,Social Security and Social Welfare	2560	1746
（十八）文化、体育和娱乐业	Culture, Sports and Entertainment	8047	4347
（十九）公共管理和社会组织	Public Management and Social Organization		

Basic Facts on Persons Employed by Other Units（2009）

(person)

在岗职工合计 Fully Employed Staff and Workers	其他从业人员 Other Employed Persons	单位从业人员平均人数 Average Employment	在岗职工 Fully Employed Staff and Workers	其他从业人员 Other Employed Persons
419490	**18627**	**385302**	**368883**	**16419**
340704	18058	329465	313573	15892
6255	129	5732	5625	107
2610	640	3095	2473	622
243851	9419	235622	226726	8896
33007	305	33310	33020	290
78561	6455	73882	68657	5225
9427	1415	11134	10092	1042
16655	261	15621	15362	259
62131	308	40216	39948	268
405688	16492	369454	354597	14857
7604	1391	8928	8094	834
1971	166	2166	2022	144
4227	578	4754	4170	584
50		50	50	
1650	6	1268	1262	6
188053	4930	155580	150153	5427
4038		3448	3448	
42886	1132	41521	40404	1117
12578	648	13238	12656	582
20454	40	17832	17792	40
32113	2336	33439	31790	1649
21737	670	22112	21431	681
28572	4733	29261	25252	4009
21336	791	19256	18845	411
3004	53	2992	2939	53
7697	101	7514	7433	81
8770	598	8939	8501	438
3784	172	3737	3636	101
12441	2137	14409	12845	1564
2560		2712	2712	
7767	280	7994	7734	260

3-13 全部单位从业人员劳动报酬（2009年）

Remuneration of All Employed Persons（2009）

单位:千元 (1 000yuan)

分　　组	Classify	单位从业人员劳动报酬 Remuneration of Employment	在岗职工工资总额 Total Wages of Employed Staff and Workers	其他从业人员劳动报酬 Remuneration of Other Employed Persons
总　计	**Total**	**45048362**	**43974313**	**1074049**
一、按企业、事业、机关分组	**Groped by Character of Unit**			
1.企业	Enterprises	32123649	31262695	860954
2.事业	Institutions	9310540	9177256	133284
3.机关	Agencies and Organizations	3290574	3227506	63068
4.民间非盈利组织	Non-profit NGO	55461	51162	4299
5.其他	Others	268138	255694	12444
二、按国民经济行业分组	**Grouped by Sector**			
（一）农、林、牧、渔业	Agriculture ,Forestry,Animal Husbandry and Fishery	75748	75192	556
（二）采矿业	Mining	28528	28442	86
（三）制造业	Manufacturing	11259294	10972120	287174
（四）电力、燃气及水的生产和供应业	Production and Distribution of Electricity, Gas and Water	1138174	1130918	7256
（五）建筑业	Construction	2883073	2786888	96185
（六）交通运输、仓储和邮政业	Traffic,Transport,Storage and Post	3770339	3636201	134138
（七）信息传输、计算机服务和软件业	Information Transmission,Computer Service and Software	1627104	1626183	921
（八）批发和零售业	Wholesale and Retail Trades	1239405	1184000	55405
（九）住宿和餐饮业	Hotels and Catering Services	637588	629680	7908
（十）金融业	Financial Intermediation	3160776	3022374	138402
（十一）房地产业	Real Estate	1101474	1091050	10424
（十二）租赁和商务服务业	Leasing and Business Services	465695	457611	8084
（十三）科学研究、技术服务和地质勘察业	Scientific Research,Technical Service and Geologic Prospecting	3989121	3905750	83371
（十四）水利、环境和公共设施管理业	Management of Water Conservancy, Environment and Public Facilities	472779	456887	15892
（十五）居民服务和其他服务业	Services to Households and Other Services	320507	319178	1329
（十六）教育	Education	7033376	6945488	87888
（十七）卫生、社会保障和社会福利业	Health,Social Security and Social Welfare	1963224	1893051	70173
（十八）文化、体育和娱乐业	Culture, Sports and Entertainment	683216	677105	6111
（十九）公共管理和社会组织	Public Management and Social Organization	3198941	3136195	62746

3–14 国有单位从业人员劳动报酬（2009年）

Remuneration of Persons Employed by State-owned Units （2009）

单位:千元 (1 000yuan)

分组	Classify	单位从业人员劳动报酬 Remuneration of Employment	在岗职工工资总额 Total Wages of Employed Staff and Workers	其他从业人员劳动报酬 Remuneration of Other Employed Persons
总计	**Total**	**30019297**	**29324704**	**694593**
一、按隶属关系分组	**Grouped by Administrative Relationship**			
1.中央	Central	13381823	13092051	289772
2.省、自治区、直辖市	Provincial	5165086	5045814	119272
3.地区	District	5409713	5236318	173395
4.县及县以下	County and Below	5044716	4951487	93229
5.其他	Others	1017959	999034	18925
二、按企业、事业、机关分组	**Groped by Character of Unit**			
1.企业	Enterprises	17737005	17223538	513467
2.事业	Institutions	8893071	8775523	117548
3.机关	Agencies and Organizations	3290574	3227506	63068
4.民间非盈利组织	Non-profit NGO			
5.其他	Others	98647	98137	510
三、按国民经济行业分组	**Grouped by Sector**			
（一）农、林、牧、渔业	Agriculture ,Forestry,Animal Husbandry and Fishery	75172	74616	556
（二）采矿业	Mining	10452	10452	
（三）制造业	Manufacturing	5327382	5142634	184748
（四）电力、燃气及水的生产和供应业	Production and Distribution of Electricity, Gas and Water	947598	940342	7256
（五）建筑业	Construction	1646551	1575622	70929
（六）交通运输、仓储和邮政业	Traffic,Transport,Storage and Post	3129276	3007840	121436
（七）信息传输、计算机服务和软件业	Information Transmission,Computer Service and Software	877445	877249	196
（八）批发和零售业	Wholesale and Retail Trades	414052	411130	2922
（九）住宿和餐饮业	Hotels and Catering Services	180648	179726	922
（十）金融业	Financial Intermediation	1071055	1058301	12754
（十一）房地产业	Real Estate	187405	185087	2318
（十二）租赁和商务服务业	Leasing and Business Services	377200	369932	7268
（十三）科学研究、技术服务和地质勘察业	Scientific Research,Technical Service and Geologic Prospecting	3460053	3378879	81174
（十四）水利、环境和公共设施管理业	Management of Water Conservancy, Environment and Public Facilities	228660	219591	9069
（十五）居民服务和其他服务业	Services to Households and Other Services	157091	156804	287
（十六）教育	Education	6436531	6379572	56959
（十七）卫生、社会保障和社会福利业	Health,Social Security and Social Welfare	1867878	1798676	69202
（十八）文化、体育和娱乐业	Culture, Sports and Entertainment	425907	422056	3851
（十九）公共管理和社会组织	Public Management and Social Organization	3198941	3136195	62746

3-15 城镇集体单位从业人员劳动报酬（2009年）

Remuneration of Persons Employed by Urban Collective-owned Units in Towns and Cities（2009）

单位:千元 (1 000yuan)

分 组	Classify	单位从业人员劳动报酬 Remuneration of Employment	在岗职工工资总额 Total Wages of Employed Staff and Workers	其他从业人员劳动报酬 Remuneration of Other Employed Persons
总 计	**Total**	**906828**	**887638**	**19190**
一、按企业、事业、机关分组	**Groped by Character of Unit**			
1.企业	Enterprises	865573	847664	17909
2.事业	Institutions	36529	35378	1151
3.机关	Agencies and Organizations			
4.民间非盈利组织	Non-profit NGO	1095	965	130
5.其他	Others	3631	3631	
二、按国民经济行业分组	**Grouped by Sector**			
（一）农、林、牧、渔业	Agriculture ,Forestry,Animal Husbandry and Fishery			
（二）采矿业	Mining			
（三）制造业	Manufacturing	361741	356456	5285
（四）电力、燃气及水的生产和供应业	Production and Distribution of Electricity, Gas and Water	4092	4092	
（五）建筑业	Construction	160269	152566	7703
（六）交通运输、仓储和邮政业	Traffic,Transport,Storage and Post	22895	22878	17
（七）信息传输、计算机服务和软件业	Information Transmission,Computer Service and Software	253	253	
（八）批发和零售业	Wholesale and Retail Trades	112865	109524	3341
（九）住宿和餐饮业	Hotels and Catering Services	39736	39736	
（十）金融业	Financial Intermediation			
（十一）房地产业	Real Estate	40917	40797	120
（十二）租赁和商务服务业	Leasing and Business Services	20510	20510	
（十三）科学研究、技术服务和地质勘察业	Scientific Research,Technical Service and Geologic Prospecting	24270	23552	718
（十四）水利、环境和公共设施管理业	Management of Water Conservancy, Environment and Public Facilities	13818	13818	
（十五）居民服务和其他服务业	Services to Households and Other Services	64224	64224	
（十六）教育	Education	7577	7382	195
（十七）卫生、社会保障和社会福利业	Health,Social Security and Social Welfare	24446	23475	971
（十八）文化、体育和娱乐业	Culture, Sports and Entertainment	9215	8375	840
（十九）公共管理和社会组织	Public Management and Social Organization			

3-16 其他经济类型单位从业人员劳动报酬（2009年）

Remuneration of Persons Employed by other Units（2009）

单位: 千元 (1 000 yuan)

分组	Classify	单位从业人员劳动报酬 Remuneration of Employment	在岗职工工资总额 Total Wages of Employed Staff and Workers	其他从业人员劳动报酬 Remuneration of Other Employed Persons
合计	**Total**	**14122237**	**13761971**	**360266**
一、按登记注册类型分组	**Grouped by Registion Status**			
（一）内资	Domestic Investment	12086617	11732790	353827
1.股份合作	Share-holding Cooperative	171903	170674	1229
2.联营	Joint Ownership	116485	104721	11764
3.有限责任公司	Limited Liability Corporations	7856760	7687119	169641
4.股份有限公司	Share-holding Corperation Ltd.	3500070	3354120	145950
5.其他	Others	441399	416156	25243
（二）港、澳、台商投资	Enterprises with Funds from Hong Kong, Macao and Taiwan	480931	479377	1554
（三）外商投资	Enterprises with Foreign Funded	1554689	1549804	4885
二、按企业、事业分组	**Grouped by Enterprise and Instilution**			
1.企业	Enterprises	13521071	13191493	329578
2.事业	Institutions	380940	366355	14585
3.民间非盈利组织	Non-profit NGO	54366	50197	4169
4.其他	Others	165860	153926	11934
三、按国民经济行业分组	**Grouped by Sector**			
（一）农、林、牧、渔业	Agriculture,Forestry,Animal Husbandry and Fishery	576	576	
（二）采矿业	Mining	18076	17990	86
（三）制造业	Manufacturing	5570171	5473030	97141
（四）电力、燃气及水的生产和供应业	Production and Distribution of Electricity, Gas and Water	186484	186484	
（五）建筑业	Construction	1076253	1058700	17553
（六）交通运输、仓储和邮政业	Traffic,Transport,Storage and Post	618168	605483	12685
（七）信息传输、计算机服务和软件业	Information Transmission,Computer Service and Software	749406	748681	725
（八）批发和零售业	Wholesale and Retail Trades	712488	663346	49142
（九）住宿和餐饮业	Hotels and Catering Services	417204	410218	6986
（十）金融业	Financial Intermediation	2089721	1964073	125648
（十一）房地产业	Real Estate	873152	865166	7986
（十二）租赁和商务服务业	Leasing and Business Services	67985	67169	816
（十三）科学研究、技术服务和地质勘察业	Scientific Research,Technical Service and Geologic Prospecting	504798	503319	1479
（十四）水利、环境和公共设施管理业	Management of Water Conservancy, Environment and Public Facilities	230301	223478	6823
（十五）居民服务和其他服务业	Services to Households and Other Services	99192	98150	1042
（十六）教育	Education	589268	558534	30734
（十七）卫生、社会保障和社会福利业	Health,Social Security and Social Welfare	70900	70900	
（十八）文化、体育和娱乐业	Culture, Sports and Entertainment	248094	246674	1420
（十九）公共管理和社会组织	Public Management and Social Organization			

主 要 统 计 指 标 解 释

人口数 指一定时点、一定地区范围内的有生命的个人的总和。年度统计的年末人口数，指每年12月31日24时的人口数。

出生率（又称粗出生率） 指在一定时期内（通常为一年）平均每千人所出生的人数的比率，一般用千分率表示。其计算公式为:

出生率=年出生人数/年平均人数*1000‰

式中：出生人数指活产婴儿，即胎儿脱离母体时（不管怀孕月数），有过呼吸或其他生命现象。年平均人数指年初、年底人口数的平均数，也可用年中人口数代替。

死亡率（又称粗死亡率） 指在一定时期内（通常为一年）一定地区的死亡人数与同期内平均人数（或期中人数）之比，一般用千分率表示。本资料中的死亡率指年死亡率，其计算公式为:

死亡率=年死亡人数/年平均人数*1000‰

人口自然增长率 指在一定时期内（通常为一年）人口自然增加数（出生人数减死亡人数）与该时期内平均人数（或期中人数）之比，一般用千分率表示。计算公式为:

人口自然增长率=（本年出生人数-本年死亡人数）/年平均人数*1000‰

经济活动人口 指在16岁以上，有劳动能力，参加或要求参加社会经济活动的人口； 包括就业人员和失业人员。

就业人员 指从事一定社会劳动并取得劳动报酬或经营收入的人员，包括在岗职工、再就业的离退休人员、私营业主、个体户主、私营和个体就业人员、乡镇企业就业人员、农村就业人员、其他就业人员（包括民办教师、宗教职业者、现役军人等）。这一指标反映了一定时期内全部劳动力资源的实际利用情况，是研究我国基本国情国力的重要指标。

单位从业人员 指在各级国家机关、政党机关、社会团体及企业、事业单位中工作，取得工资或其他形式的劳动报酬的全部人员。包括在岗职工、再就业的离退休人员、民办教师以及在各单位中工作的外方人员和港澳台方人员、兼职人员、借用的外单位人员和第二职业者。不包括离开本单位仍保留劳动关系的职工。各单位的就业人员反映了各单位实际参加生产或工作的全部劳动力。

城镇私营和个体就业人员 城镇私营就业人员指在工商管理部门注册登记，其经营地址设在县城关镇（含城关镇）以上的私营企业就业人员; 包括私营企业投资者和雇工。城镇个体就业人员指在工商管理部门注册登记，并持有城镇户口或在城镇长期居住，经批准从事个体工商经营的就业人员; 包括个体经营者和在个体工商户劳动的家庭帮工和雇工。

城镇登记失业人员 指有非农业户口，在一定的劳动年龄内，有劳动能力，无业而要求就业，并在当地就业服务机构进行求职登记的人员。

城镇登记失业率 指城镇登记失业人数同城镇从业人数与城镇从业人数与城镇登记失业人数之和的比。计算公式为:

城镇登记失业率=城镇登记失业人数/（城镇单位就业人数+城镇私营企业及个体就业人数+城镇登记失业人数）*100%

职工 指在国有经济、城镇集体经济、联营经济、股份制经济、外商和港、澳、台投资经济、其他经济单位及其附属机构工作，并由其支付工资的各类人员，不包括返聘的离退休人员、民办教师、在国有经济单位工作的外方人员和港、澳、台人员。

(1998年以后的的职工数据均为在岗职工，其他相关指标如职工工资总额，职工平均工资等指标也从1998年按此口径进行了相应调整。)

国有单位职工 指在国有经济单位及其附属机构工作，并由其支付工资的各类人员。

城镇集体单位职工 指在城镇集体经济单位及其管理部门工作，并由其支付工资的各类人员。

其他单位职工 指在联营经济、股份制经济、外商投资经济、港、澳、台投资经济单位工作，并由其支付工资的各类人员。

在岗职工 指在本单位工作并由单位支付工资的人员，以及有工作岗位，但由于学习、病伤产假等原因暂未工作，仍由单位支付工资的人员。

职工工资总额 指各单位在一定时期内直接支付给本单位全部职工的劳动报酬总额。工资总额的计算原则应以直接支付给职工的全部劳动报酬为根据。各单位支付给职工的劳动报酬以及其他根据有关规定支付的工资，不论是计入成本的还是不计入成本的，不论是按国家规定列入计征奖金税项目的，还是未列入计征奖金税项目的，不论是以货币形式支付的还是以实物形式支付的，均包括在工资总额内。

职工平均工资 指企业、事业、机关单位的职工在一定时期内平均每人所得的货币工资额。它表明一定时期职工工资收入的高低程度，是反映职工工资水平的主要指标。计算公式为:

职工平均工资=报告期实际支付的全部职工工资总额/报告期全部职工平均人数

Explanatory Notes on Main Statistical Indicators

Total Population refers to the total number of people alive at a certain point of time within a given area.Annual statistics on the total population is taken at midnight, the 31st of December.

Birth Rate or (Crude Birth Rate) refers to the ratio of the number of births to the average population (or mid-period population) during a certain period of time (usually a year) which is often expressed in ‰. Birth rate in the chapter refers to annual birth rate. The following formula is used:

Birth Rate = Number of Births/Average Number of Population×1000‰

Number of births refers to live births i.e. the births when babies had showed any vital phenomena regardless of the length of pregnancy.Annual Average Number of Population is the average of the number of population at the beginning of the year and that at the end of the year. Sometimes it is substituted for with the mid year population.

Death Rate (or Crude Death Rate) refers to the ratio of the number of deaths to the average population (or mid-period population) during a certain period of time (usually a year) which is often expressed in ‰. Death rate in the chapter refers to annual death rate. The following formula is used:

Death Rate= Number of Deaths/Annual Average Number of Population×1000‰

Natural Growth Rate of Population refers to the ratio of natural increase in population (number of births minus number of deaths) in a certain period of time (usually a year) to the average population (or mid-period population) of the same period which is often expressed in ‰. The following formulas are applied:

Natural Growth of Population = (Number of Births-Number of Deaths)/Average Number of Population× 1000‰

Economically Active Population refers to the population aged 16 and over who are capable to work, are participating in or willing to participate in economic activities, including employed persons and unemployed persons.

Employed Persons refer to the persons who are engaged in social working and receive remuneration payment or earn business income, including total staff and workers, re-employed retirees, employers of private enterprises, self-employed workers, employees in private enterprises and individual economy, employees in township enterprises, employed persons in the rural areas, and other employed persons (including teachers in the schools run by the local people, people engaged in religious profession and the servicemen, etc.). This indicator reflects the actual utilization of total labour force during a certain period of time and is often used for the research on China's economic situation and national power.

Persons Employed in Various Units refer to all the persons working in government agencies of various levels, political and party organizations, social organizations, enterprises and institutions, and receiving wages or other forms of payment. They include fully-employed staff and workers, re-employed retirees, teachers in schools run by the local people, foreigners and Chinese compatriots from Hong Kong, Macao, and Taiwan working in various units, part-time employees, employees of other units working temporarily at current posts, and employees holding the second job, but exclude staff and workers who have left their working units while keeping their labour contract (employment relation) unchanged. This indicator reflects the total number of laborers actually engaged in production or other operations in various units.

Persons Employed in Private Enterprises and Self-Employed Individuals in Urban Areas Persons employed in private enterprises refer to the persons employed in the private enterprises which have been registered at the departments of industrial and commercial administration and are situated at a county town (i.e. a town where the county government is located) for business operation or at urban areas with the level higher than a county town. The self-employed individuals in urban areas refer to persons who hold the certificates of residence in urban areas or have resided in the urban areas for a long time and have been registered at the departments of industrial and commercial administration and approved to be engaged in individual industrial or commercial business, including self-employed persons as well as helpers and hired labourers who work in the individual households engaged in industrial or commercial business.

Registered Urban Unemployed Persons The registered unemployed persons in urban areas refer to the persons who are registered as permanent residents in the urban areas engaged in non-agricultural activities, aged within the range of working age, capable to labour, unemployed but desirous to be employed and have been registered at the local employment service agencies to apply for a job.

Registered Urban Unemployment Rate Registered unemployment rate in urban areas refers to the ratio of the number of the registered unemployed persons to the sum of the number of persons employed in various units and in private enterprises in urban areas, urban self-employed individuals and the registered urban unemployed persons . The formula is as follows:

Registered urban unemployment rate = number of registered urban unemployed persons÷ (number of persons employed in urban units + number of persons employed in urban private enterprises + and self-employed individuals in urban Areas + number of registered urban unemployed persons) × 100%.

Staff and Workers refer to the persons who work in (and receive payment therefrom) enterprises and institutions of state ownership, collective ownership, joint ownership, share holding, foreign ownership, and ownership by entrepreneurs from Hong Kong, Macao, and Taiwan, and other types of ownership and their affiliated units, excluding the retired persons invited to work in the units again, teachers in the schools run by the local people and foreigners and persons coming from Hong Kong, Macao and Taiwan and working in the state-owned economic units.

(Number of staff and workers in this yearbook include only fully employed staff and workers, excluding those who have left their working units while keeping their labour contract/employment relation unchanged).

Staff and Workers in State-owned Economic Units refer to the persons who work in the state-owned economic units or their attached units and are listed in their payrolls.

Staff and Workers of Collective Owned Units in Urban Areas refer to the persons who work in collective owned units in urban areas and their administration departments and receive payment therefrom.

Staff and Workers in Units of Other types of Ownership refer to those who work in (and receivepayment therefrom) enterprises and institutions of joint ownership, share holding, foreign ownership, and ownership by entrepreneurs from Hong Kong, Macao, and Taiwan.

Fully Employed Staff and Workers refer to persons who work in, and receive wages from their working units, as well as persons who have their work posts, but are temporarily absent from work for reasons of study or on sick, injury or maternal leave and still receive wages from their working units.

Total Wages of Staff and Workers refer to the total remuneration payment to staff and workers in various units during a certain period of time. The calculation of total wages is based on the total remuneration payment to the staff and workers. Therefore, all the wages and salaries and other payments to staff and workers are included in the total wages regardless of their sources, category, and forms (in kind or cash). (Total wages of staff and workers in this yearbook include only total wages of fully employed staff and workers, excluding the living allowances distributed to those who have left their working units while keeping their labour contract/employment relation unchanged).

Average Wage of Staff and Workers refers to the average wage in money terms per person during a certain period of time for staff and workers in enterprises, institutions, and government agencies, which reflects the general level of wage income during a certain period of time and is calculated as follows:

Average Wage of Staff and Workers = Total Wages of Staff and Workers at the Report/Average Number of Staff and Workers at the Report Period.

4 固定资产投资

INVESTMENT IN FIXED ASSETS

资料整理：张利民　令润翠　康　敏
Data management:Zhang Limin　Ling Runcui　Kang Min

第四部分　固定资产投资

一、简要说明

本章资料主要包括全社会固定资产投资、城镇投资、房地产开发投资、城乡集体固定资产投资和城乡私人建房投资以及分区县情况，由西安市统计局固定资产投资处提供。

二、主要指标

全社会固定资产投资（亿元）	2500.13	比上年增长 31.1%
#国有经济单位	932.91	比上年增长 34.3%
集体经济单位	289.91	比上年增长 17.4%
#城镇投资	2367.58	比上年增长 32.5%
房地产开发	696.34	比上年增长 28.9%
全市新增固定资产（亿元）	1013.44	比上年增长 39.8%
全市竣工住宅面积（万平方米）	822.62	比上年下降 18.6%

4　INVESTMENT IN FIXED ASSETS

Ⅰ.Brief Introduction

This chapter consists of primarily the data on fixed asset investment, Investment of Urban Units, real estate development investment, urban and rural area collective fixed asset investment, urban and rural area private housing investment and the classified Data of the districts and the counties on real estate development investment, provided by Fixed Asset Investment Division of the Xi'an Bureau of Statistics.

Ⅱ.Major Indicators

		Increase over Preceding Year
Investment Fulfilled In Fixed Assets(100 mil. yuan)	2500.13	31.1%
State-owned Enterprises	932.91	34.3%
Collective-owned Enterprises	289.91	17.4%
Investment of Urban Units	2367.58	32.5%
Real Estate Development	696.34	28.9%
Investment Fulfilled Newly Increased Fixed Assets(100 mil. yuan)	1013.44	39.8%
Total Floor Space of Building Completed(10 000 sq.m)	822.62	18.6%

4-1 主要年份按城乡分全社会固定资产投资

Total Investment in Fixed Assets in the Whole Country by Rural and Urban Areas in Representative Years

单位：亿元 (100 million yuan)

年 份 Year	合 计 Total	城镇 Urban Area	房地产开发 Real Estate	农村 Rural Area
1979	4.08	3.01		1.07
1980	6.12	4.48		1.64
1981	5.59	4.56		1.03
1982	9.49	8.02		1.47
1983	10.46	9.17		1.29
1984	12.89	10.69		2.20
1985	18.44	14.44		4.00
1986	22.15	18.54		3.61
1987	27.05	23.15		3.90
1988	29.14	24.43		4.71
1989	28.30	23.85		4.45
1990	26.39	23.10	0.91	3.29
1991	30.76	25.55	2.01	5.21
1992	38.48	32.85	3.32	5.63
1993	75.06	66.65	7.39	8.41
1994	85.57	73.47	12.02	12.10
1995	103.42	88.50	21.65	14.92
1996	114.38	96.98	24.66	17.40
1997	116.90	95.17	24.68	21.73
1998	154.80	138.68	38.21	16.12
1999	197.31	172.64	44.30	24.67
2000	232.37	203.01	51.85	29.36
2001	287.72	256.95	67.42	30.77
2002	338.15	307.24	79.37	30.91
2003	478.10	445.74	124.82	32.36
2004	646.69	612.03	169.67	34.66
2005	835.10	776.33	225.23	58.77
2006	1066.62	971.84	285.76	94.78
2007	1435.33	1340.59	387.33	94.74
2008	1906.36	1786.60	540.26	119.76
2009	2500.13	2367.58	696.34	132.55

4–2 主要年份按经济类型分全社会固定资产投资

Total Investment in Fixed Assets in the Whole Country by Registion Status in Representative Years

单位：亿元 (100 million yuan)

年 份 Year	合 计 Total	国有经济 State-owned	集体经济 Collective-owned	个体经济 Self-employed Individual	其他经济 Others
1985	18.44	13.96	1.36	3.12	
1986	22.15	18.05	0.97	3.13	
1987	27.05	22.18	1.50	3.37	
1988	29.14	23.72	1.86	3.56	
1989	28.30	23.22	1.46	3.62	
1990	26.39	22.21	1.44	2.74	
1991	30.76	24.42	2.26	4.08	
1992	38.48	32.04	1.45	4.99	
1993	75.06	59.66	3.03	6.55	5.82
1994	85.57	64.71	4.14	10.09	6.63
1995	103.42	69.08	9.78	11.13	13.43
1996	114.38	80.66	8.73	12.50	12.49
1997	116.90	77.46	10.21	15.11	14.12
1998	154.80	113.07	7.89	10.59	23.25
1999	197.31	136.50	13.62	16.22	30.97
2000	232.37	159.60	14.65	24.40	33.72
2001	287.72	175.58	14.67	38.57	58.90
2002	338.15	200.06	13.70	44.68	79.71
2003	478.10	264.83	22.33	73.43	117.51
2004	646.69	329.14	40.06	48.95	228.54
2005	835.10	373.70	59.23	79.04	323.13
2006	1066.62	401.14	110.68	107.33	447.47
2007	1435.33	476.78	207.08	183.09	568.38
2008	1906.36	694.89	246.89	50.43	914.15
2009	2500.13	932.91	289.91	97.86	1179.45

注：集体经济：包括城镇集体和农村集体。

个体经济：包括私营个体投资及城镇工矿区私人建房和农村私人建房。

Note: Collective-owned: Including Urban Collective-owned and Rural Collective-owned.

Individual: Including Individual Investment Private Building Construction in Urban Industrial and Mining Regions and Rural Areas.

4-3 主要年份按产业分全市固定资产投资

Total Investment in Fixed Assets in the Whole City by Three Strata of Industry in Representative Years

单位：亿元 (100 million yuan)

年 份 Year	合 计 Total	第一产业 Primary Industry	第二产业 Secondary Industry	工业 Industry	第三产业 Tertiary Industry
1979	3.01	0.06	1.24	1.20	1.71
1980	4.48	0.06	2.09	1.99	2.33
1981	4.56	0.11	2.10	1.83	2.35
1982	8.02	0.04	4.07	3.63	3.91
1983	9.17	0.11	4.97	4.41	4.09
1984	10.69	0.19	4.56	3.99	5.94
1985	14.44	0.18	7.22	6.45	7.04
1986	18.54	0.16	8.98	8.37	9.40
1987	23.15	0.19	11.81	11.26	11.15
1988	24.43	0.15	11.95	11.20	12.33
1989	23.85	0.13	11.94	11.50	11.78
1990	23.10	0.25	11.03	10.59	11.82
1991	25.55	0.27	12.48	11.95	12.80
1992	32.85	0.10	15.60	14.73	17.15
1993	66.65	0.07	24.50	22.44	42.08
1994	73.47	0.03	27.04	25.85	46.40
1995	88.50	0.14	28.80	27.71	59.56
1996	96.98	0.13	25.96	24.24	70.89
1997	95.17	0.24	23.65	21.66	71.28
1998	138.68	0.48	35.33	29.86	102.87
1999	172.64	0.94	39.88	36.40	131.82
2000	203.01	0.76	57.21	54.37	145.04
2001	256.95	0.86	63.31	61.28	192.78
2002	307.24	4.29	74.34	68.45	228.61
2003	445.74	3.34	83.25	78.41	359.15
2004	612.03	3.38	97.69	95.67	510.96
2005	776.33	5.26	144.25	140.44	626.82
2006	971.84	10.04	213.43	206.48	748.37
2007	1340.59	10.20	297.53	286.61	1032.86
2008	1786.60	23.75	369.74	356.12	1393.11
2009	2367.58	24.46	458.44	442.70	1884.68

4-4 全市固定资产投资（2009年）

Total Investment in Fixed Assets in the Whole City（2009）

单位：万元 (10 000 yuan)

分组	Classify	合计 Total	房地产开发 Real Estate
一、本年完成投资	**Investment Completed This Year**	**23675759**	**6963350**
按登记注册类型分	**Grouped by Registion Status**		
内资	Domestic Funded	22699789	6319383
国有	State-owned Enterprises	9117432	396138
集体	Collective-owned Enterprises	1464386	131375
股份合作	Share-holding Corperative	371265	99535
国有联营	State Joint Ownership Enterprises	1841	
集体联营	Collective Joint Ownership Enterprises	201644	
国有与集体联营	Joint State-collective Enterprises	8732	2000
其他联营	Other Joint Ownership Enterprises	41387	19000
国有独资公司	State Sole-funded Corporations	209798	116925
其他有限责任公司	Other Limited Liability Corporations	6808237	3207359
股份有限公司	Share-holding Corperation Ltd.	499332	107996
私营及个体	Private and Individual	3434969	2215763
其他	Others	540766	23292
港澳台商投资	Enterprises with Funds from Hong Kong,Macao and Taiwan	459424	279720
合资经营企业(港或澳、台资)	Joint Venture	208438	54598
合作经营企业(港或澳、台资)	Cooperation	38591	38591
独资企业	Sole-funded	210364	186531
股份有限公司	Share-Holding Corporations Ltd.	2031	
外商投资	Enterprises with Foreign Investment	516546	364247
合资经营企业(港或澳、台资)	Joint Venture	290556	222769
合作经营企业(港或澳、台资)	Cooperation	93723	93523
独资企业	Sole-Funded	128729	47955
股份有限公司	Share-Holding Corporations Ltd.	3538	
按隶属关系分	**Grouped by Jurisdiction of Management**		
中央	Central	2208996	40237
省属	Provincial	2403688	347587
市属	Municipal	19063075	6575526

4–4 续表1 continued 1

单位：万元 (10 000 yuan)

指标	Item	合计 Total	房地产开发 Real Estate
按建设性质分	**Grouped by Type of Construction**		
#新建	New Construction	8567540	
扩建	Expansion	3054929	
改建和技术改造	Reconstruction	2738799	
按构成分	**Grouped by Composition**		
1.建筑工程	Construction Projects	14971817	5194019
2.安装工程	Installment Projects	1365649	724354
3.设备、工器具购置	Purchasing of Equipment and Instruments	2619783	125305
4.其他费用	Others	4718510	919672
按工程用途分	**Grouped by Purpose of Project**		
#住宅	Residential Buildings	7194206	5683026
按国民经济行业分	**Grouped by Sector (10 000 yuan)**		
农、林、牧、渔业	Agriculture,Forestry,Animal Husbandry and Fishery	244605	
采矿业	Mining	124845	
制造业	Manufacturing	3785001	
电力、燃气及水的生产和供应业	Production & Supply of Electricity,Gas & Water	517149	
建筑业	Construction	157365	
交通运输、仓储和邮政业	Transport,Storage and Post	1505375	
信息传输、计算机服务和软件业	Information Transmission,Computer Service and Software	212287	
批发和零售业	Wholesale and Retail Trades	630216	
住宿和餐饮业	Hotels and Catering Services	445102	
金融业	Financial Intermediation	10730	
房地产业	Real Estate	8016677	6963350
租赁和商务服务业	Leasing and Business Services	551354	
科学研究、技术服务和地质勘察业	Scientific Research,Technical Service and Geologic Prospecting	305797	
水利、环境和公共设施管理业	Management of Water Conservancy, Environment and Public	3616972	
居民服务和其他服务业	Services to Households and Other Services	63999	
教育	Education	764845	
卫生、社会保障和社会福利业	Health,Social Security and Social Welfare	165639	
文化、体育和娱乐业	Culture, Sports education and Entertainment	326143	
公共管理和社会组织	Public Management and Social Organization	2231658	

4-4 续表2 continued 2

指　　标	Item	合 计 Total	房地产开发 Real Estate
二、构成（%）	**Proportion (%)**		
按登记注册类型分	**Grouped by Status**		
#国有经济	State-owned	39.40	7.37
集体经济	Collective-owned	8.60	3.32
按隶属关系分	**Grouped by Jurisdiction of Management**		
中央	Central	9.33	0.58
省属	Provincial	10.15	4.99
市属	Municipal	80.52	94.43
按建设性质分	**Grouped by Type of Construction**		
#新建	New Construction	36.19	
扩建	Expansion	12.90	
改建和技术改造	Reconstruction	11.57	
按构成分	**Grouped by Composition of Funds**		
1.建筑工程	Construction Projects	63.24	74.59
2.安装工程	Installation Projects	5.77	10.40
3.设备工器具购置	Purchasing of the Equipment and Instruments	11.07	1.80
4.其他费用	Others	19.92	13.21
按工程用途分	**Grouped by Purpose of Project**		
#住宅	Residential Buildings	30.39	81.61
三、房屋面积(平方米)	**Floor Space (sq.m)**		
本年施工房屋面积	Floor Space of Buildings Under Construction This Year	95712549	57086279
#住宅	Residential Buildings	62848991	49015888
本年竣工房屋面积	Floor Space of Buildings Completed This Year	15291263	5428145
#住宅	Residential Buildings	8226162	4534926
四、本年新增固定资产(万元）	**Newly Increase in Fixed Assets(10 000 yuan)**	**10134370**	**1957125**

4-5 按行业分全市固定资产投资（2009年）

Total Investment in Fixed Assets in the Whole City by Sector （2009）

指 标	Item	2009
本年完成投资（万元）	**Grouped by Sector (10 000 yuan)**	**23675759**
（一）农、林、牧、渔业	Agriculture,Forestry,Animal Husbandry and Fishery	244605
（二）采矿业	Mining	124845
（三）制造业	Manufacturing	3785001
农副食品加工业	Processing of Food from Agricultural Products	75602
食品制造业	Manufacture of Foods	58245
饮料制造业	Manufacture of Beverages	
石油加工、炼焦及核燃料加工业	Processing of Petroleum, Coking,Processing of Nuclear Fuel	23960
化学原料及化学制品制造业	Manufacture of Raw Chemical Materials and Chemical Products	70330
医药制造业	Manufacture of Medicines	88348
金属制品业	Manufacture of Metal Products	139521
通用设备制造业	Manufacture of General Purpose Machinery	574901
专用设备制造业	Manufacture of Special Purpose Machinery	371236
交通运输设备制造业	Manufacture of Transport Equipment	585419
电气机械及器材制造业	Manufacture of Electrical Machinery and Equipment	339615
通信设备、计算机及其他电子设备制造业	Manufacture of Communication Equipment, Computers and Other Electronic Equipment	656228
仪器仪表及文化办公用机械制造业	Manufacture of Measuring Instruments and Machinery for Cultural Activity and Office Work	63071
（四）电力、燃气及水的生产 和供应业	Production & Supply of Electricity,Gas & Water	517149
（五）建筑业	Construction	157365
（六）交通运输、仓储和邮政业	Transport,Storage and Post	1505375
（七）信息传输、计算机服务和软件业	Information Transmission,Computer Service and Software	212287
（八）批发和零售业	Wholesale and Retail Trades	630216
（九）住宿和餐饮业	Hotels and Catering Services	445102
（十）金融业	Financial Intermediation	10730
（十一）房地产业	Real Estate	8016677
（十二）租赁和商务服务业	Leasing and Business Services	551354
（十三）科学研究、技术服务和地质勘察业	Scientific Research,Technical Service and Geologic Prospecting	305797
（十四） 水利、环境和公共设施管理业	Management of Water Conservancy, Environment and Public Facilities	3616972
（十五）居民服务和其他服务业	Services to Households and Other Services	63999
（十六）教育	Education	764845
（十七）卫生、社会保障和社会福利业	Health,Social Security and Social Welfare	165639
（十八）文化、体育和娱乐业	Culture, Sports and Entertainment	326143
（十九）公共管理和社会组织	Public Management and Social Organization	2231658

4-6 主要年份按资金来源及建设性质分全市固定资产投资

指　　标	Item	1995	2000
一、投资总额(万元)	**Total Investment (10 000 yuan)**	**884994**	**2030122**
（一）按资金来源分	Grouped by Funds SourceS		
1.国家预算内资金	State Budgetary Funds	69185	160982
2.国内贷款	Domestic Loans	216565	432282
3.债券	Bonds	873	32460
4.利用外资	Utilization of Foreign Funds	80792	31622
5.自筹资金	Self-raising Funds	385047	875352
6.其他资金	Others	132532	497424
（二）按构成分	Grouped by Composition of Funds		
1.建筑安装工程	Construction and Installation Projects	527220	1404184
2.设备、工器具购置	Purchasing of Equipment and Instruments	233730	382495
3.其它费用	Others	124044	243443
（三）按建设性质分	Grouped by Type of Construction		
#新　建	New Construction	210926	533058
扩　建	Expansion	180210	542510
改　建	Reconstruction	157457	263657
二、房屋施工面积(平方米)	**Floor Space Under Construction**	**10705800**	**17025783**

Total Investment in Fixed Assets in the Whole City
by Sources of Funds and Type of Construction in Representative Years

2001	2002	2003	2004	2005	2006	2007	2008	2009
2569496	**3072442**	**4457381**	**6120324**	**7763283**	**9718418**	**13405920**	**17865977**	**23675759**
256403	355960	365263	436496	728885	677145	670592	1555809	2562756
672379	666146	1219234	1565246	1257175	1631689	1619218	2162957	3301919
6753	766	3278						
54907	15192	47509	47401	40583	165390	183422	261325	144124
1121502	1392915	1733132	2629720	4001700	5538393	8565573	12771844	15776565
457552	641463	1088965	1441461	1734940	1705801	2367115	1114042	1890395
1698777	2119151	3067309	4127677	5086664	6486233	9165668	12864657	16337466
452602	552251	577240	708988	1021079	1409589	1858720	2024631	2619783
418117	401040	812832	1283659	1655540	1822596	2381532	2976689	4718510
723957	874392	1294032	1874116	2907551	3511432	5123975	6356716	8567540
581138	868603	1102914	1169537	1208430	1101740	994841	2118013	3054929
344879	343184	447944	670229	782953	1099304	1548130	1921664	2738799
17671256	23968913	27161785	31773643	40303828	45893855	57592754	65709447	95712549

4–7 主要年份国有经济单位固定资产投资

指　　标	Item	1985	1990	1995
一、投资总额(万元)	**Total Investment (10 000 yuan)**	**139567**	**222084**	**690806**
1.按资金来源分	Grouped by Funds Source			
国家预算内投资	State Budgetary Funds	45815	48770	67426
国内贷款	Domestic Loans	27102	58602	145108
债 券	Bonds			
利用外资	Utilization of Foreign Funds	2244	9970	46811
自筹资金	Self-raising Funds	56758	91527	330333
其它资金	Others	7648	13215	101128
2.按构成分	Grouped by Composition of Funds			
建筑安装工程	Construction and Installation Projects	83542	130615	405057
设备、工具、器具购置	Purchasing of Equipment and Instruments	36328	72043	209351
其它费用	Others	19697	19426	76398
3.按建设性质分	Grouped by Type of Construction			
#新　建	New Construction	33366	55242	165793
扩　建	Expansion	55370	60641	162796
改　建	Reconstruction	33505	63253	145783
4.按国民经济行业分	Grouped by Sector			
#农林牧渔业	Agriculture,Forestry,Animal Husbandry and Fishery	1736	1888	1127
工业建筑业	Industry and Construction	61634	101407	240665
运输邮电业	Transportation,Post and Telecommunications	4949	28180	
二、新增固定资产(万元)	**Newly Increased in Fixed Assets (10 000 yuan)**	**83030**	**195429**	**509328**
三、房屋建筑面积(万平方米)	**Floor Space of Buildings (10 000 sq.m)**			
施工面积	Floor Space Under Construction	586	509	841
竣工面积	Floor Space Completed	214	203	304
#住 宅	Residential Building	125	108	214

Investment in Fixed Assets of State-owned Units in Representative Years

2000	2001	2002	2003	2004	2005	2006	2007	2008	2009
1596002	**1755787**	**2000636**	**2648283**	**3291356**	**3736992**	**4011446**	**4767827**	**6948899**	**9329071**
165304	255860	351540	268537	361654	722673	699765	655259	1034930	1367405
280585	471506	453958	823374	858396	850554	882295	664703	1175473	1766395
32886	6865		2310						
15276	20815	6617	4846	10851	9900	73830	58711	65209	29033
689732	715351	840082	803648	779205	1405167	1968662	2830256	4055904	5047734
412219	285390	348439	745568	1281250	748698	386894	558898	617383	1118504
1102548	1177790	1449583	1897323	2197052	2394409	2532743	2925696	4973312	5596104
328432	334174	347647	335454	333272	384157	536340	865951	728554	1131474
165022	243823	203406	415506	761032	958426	942363	976180	1247033	2601493
390119	486585	537537	883859	1157470	1740071	1737828	1893488	2881551	4358755
460381	436404	672297	726753	965832	907723	884083	658048	1617290	1670225
254860	328685	272499	377060	514870	617680	642848	950958	1005897	1484559
4077	3666	24087	25034	14908	26132	66279	67049	6422942	8694113
408234	361954	358027	427632	410907	571954	572491	989275	1565134	1541388
360779	472278	375131	312306	407674	147961	317144	292019	4795642	7114717
1220632	**1120240**	**1134623**	**1732895**	**1733550**	**1988546**	**1799515**	**2651549**	**1963274**	**3743856**
1342	1155	1590	1331	1041	1397	1331	1546	1367	2384
577	492	452	514	255	518	390	552	266	312
475	392	311	343	162	234	219	350	151	226

4-8 农村集体固定资产投资（2009年）

Investment in Fixed Assets of Rural Collective Owned Units（2009）

单位：万元 (10 000 yuan)

指　　标	Item	2009
一、本年完成投资	**Investment Completed This Year**	**861851**
建筑工程	Constrution Projects	719680
安装工程	Installment Projects	17786
设备购置	Purchasing of Equipment	54654
其他	Others	69731
二、本年新增固定资产	**Newly Inceased Fixed in Assets This Year**	**792448**
三、本年资金来源合计	**Subtotal of Sources of Funds This Year**	**854997**
上年末结余资金	**Balance of Last Year**	**600**
本年资金来源小计	**Total Funds This Year**	**854397**
国家资金	State Funds	52944
国内贷款	Domestic Loans	31150
利用外资	Utilization of Foreign Funds	
自筹资金	Self-raising Funds	760147
其他资金	Others	10156
四、房屋建筑面积(平方米)	**Floor Space of Buildings(sq.m)**	
施工面积	Floor Space Under Construction	2734243
#住宅	Residential Buildings	519953
竣工面积	Floor Space Completed	2076921
#住宅	Residential Buildings	110803

4-9 主要年份农村集体固定资产投资

Investment in Fixed Assets of Rural Collective Owned Units in Representative Years

指　标	Item	1995	2000	2001	2002
一、投资总额(万元)	**Total Investment (10 000 yuan)**	**37892**	**89626**	**82623**	**68610**
1.按资金来源分	Grouped by Founds Source				
国家资金	State Funds	1442	9388	994	2369
国内贷款	Domestic Loans	10925	2977	5596	1818
利用外资	Utilization of Foreign Funds	5021	5394	70	8973
自筹资金	Self-raising Funds	12220	53338	58911	41183
群众集资	Mass Fund-raising	3732	7413	8248	10647
其他资金	Others	4552	11116	8804	3620
2.按行业划分	Grouped by Sector				
农林牧渔业	Ariculture, Forestry, Animal Husbandry, Fishery	170	9075	4452	4358
工业	Industry	20286	32437	21155	16998
建筑业	Construction	2475	12309	8523	5243
交通运输、仓储和邮政业	Transport,Storage,and Post	668	2444	1023	1057
信息传输、计算机服务和软件业	Information Transmission,Computer Service and Software				
批发和零售贸易业	Wholesale and Retail Trade,Catering Services and Storage	3749	8444	26611	9273
住宿和餐饮业	Hotels and Catering Services				
金融业	Financial Intermediation		10	700	
房地产业	Real Estate	2338	12519	8260	10286
租赁和商务服务业	Leasing and Business Services				
居民服务和其他服务	Services to Households and Other Services				
卫生体育社会福利业	Health Care,Sports and Social Welfare	3054	126	107	281
教育文化艺术及广播电影电视业	Education,Culture and Arts,Radio, Film and Television	4642	6110	7973	9713
科学研究和综合技术服务业	Scientific Research and Polytechnical Services		500	790	
水利、环境和公共设施管理业	Management of Water Conservancy, Environment and Public Facilities	350	5017	1170	8747
国家机关政党机关和社会团体	Governmental and Party Agencies and Social Organizations	160	635	1859	2654
二、竣工房屋建筑面积(万平方米)	**Floor Space of the Building Completed (10 000 sq.m)**	**16.08**	**83.96**	**41.1**	**43.31**
#住宅	Residential Buildings	0.92	21.33	10.82	8.35
三、本年新增固定资产(万元)	**Newly Increase Fixed Assets This Year (10 000 yuan)**	**32405**	**89626**	**75732**	**55215**

4–9 续表1 continued 1

指 标	Item	2003	2004	2005	2006
一、投资总额(万元)	**Total Investment (10 000 yuan)**	**79216**	**132614**	**324932**	**704576**
1.按资金来源分	Grouped by Founds Source				
国家资金	State Funds	3198	3388	4295	14889
国内贷款	Domestic Loans	742	981	10994	19415
利用外资	Utilization of Foreign Funds	3887	41		21
自筹资金	Self-raising Funds	52946	95820	212297	576709
群众集资	Mass Fund-raising	6256			
其他资金	Others	12187	32384	97346	93542
2.按行业划分	Grouped by Sector				
农林牧渔业	Ariculture, Forestry, Animal Husbandry, Fishery	3632	3174	17663	11684
工业	Industry	5228	19382	21023	72083
建筑业	Construction	10248	17442	1591	2437
交通运输、仓储和邮政业	Transport,Storage,and Post	220	3188	21479	17576
信息传输、计算机服务和软件业	Information Transmission,Computer Service and Software			390	905
批发和零售贸易业	Wholesale and Retail Trade,Catering Services and Storage	2760	6819	12528	33516
住宿和餐饮业	Hotels and Catering Services			15182	15160
金融业	Financial Intermediation	25			
房地产业	Real Estate	19315	1400		70
租赁和商务服务业	Leasing and Business Services			300	
居民服务和其他服务	Services to Households and Other Services			1049	1760
卫生体育社会福利业	Health Care,Sports and Social Welfare	326	150	55	3595
教育文化艺术及广播电影电视业	Education,Culture and Arts,Radio, Film and Television	4831	6160	10054	21602
科学研究和综合技术服务业	Scientific Research and Polytechnical Services			10571	641
水利、环境和公共设施管理业	Management of Water Conservancy, Environment and Public Facilities	20001	62016	212007	61173
国家机关政党机关和社会团体	Governmental and Party Agencies and Social Organizations	12630	12883	1040	462374
二、竣工房屋建筑面积(万平方米)	**Floor Space of the Building Completed (10 000 sq.m)**	**48.26**	**55.62**	**46.04**	**215.98**
#住宅	Residential Buildings	23.2	34.46	25.89	86.45
三、本年新增固定资产(万元)	**Newly Increase Fixed Assets This Year (10 000 yuan)**	**72862**	**87865**	**148210**	**432586**

4-9 续表2 continued 2

指　　标	Item	2007	2008	2009
一、投资总额(万元)	**Total Investment (10 000 yuan)**	**666887**	**785921**	**861851**
1.按资金来源分	Grouped by Founds Source			
国家资金	State Funds	26924	35800	53406
国内贷款	Domestic Loans	42216	79031	31422
利用外资	Utilization of Foreign Funds	2029	3058	
自筹资金	Self-raising Funds	528735	590202	766778
群众集资	Mass Fund-raising			
其他资金	Others	66983	77830	10245
2.按行业划分	Grouped by Sector			
农林牧渔业	Ariculture, Forestry, Animal Husbandry, Fishery	27578	30115	69950
工业	Industry	136203	184342	142060
建筑业	Construction	1200	5400	
交通运输、仓储和邮政业	Transport,Storage,and Post	55138	42731	30990
信息传输、计算机服务和软件业	Information Transmission,Computer Service and Software	670	650	
批发和零售贸易业	Wholesale and Retail Trade,Catering Services and Storage	62206	19691	10740
住宿和餐饮业	Hotels and Catering Services	5631	19178	27580
金融业	Financial Intermediation			1600
房地产业	Real Estate	900	7256	8330
租赁和商务服务业	Leasing and Business Services	1300	1000	250
居民服务和其他服务	Services to Households and Other Services	5390	500	3630
卫生体育社会福利业	Health Care,Sports and Social Welfare	200	795	7613
教育文化艺术及广播电影电视业	Education,Culture and Arts,Radio, Film and Television	32247	12294	21622
科学研究和综合技术服务业	Scientific Research and Polytechnical Services	930		900
水利、环境和公共设施管理业	Management of Water Conservancy, Environment and Public Facilities	49418	133369	218661
国家机关政党机关和社会团体	Governmental and Party Agencies and Social Organizations	287876	328600	317925
二、竣工房屋建筑面积(万平方米)	**Floor Space of the Building Completed (10 000 sq.m)**	**192.01**	**46.89**	**207.69**
#住宅	Residential Buildings	37.06	11.8	11.08
三、本年新增固定资产(万元)	**Newly Increase Fixed Assets This Year (10 000 yuan)**	**586012**	**376378**	**792448**

4-10 主要年份市属固定资产投资

单位：万元

指　　标	Item	1985	1990	1995	2000	2001
一、投资总额	**Total Investment**	**38896**	**80958**	**432451**	**1263023**	**1539717**
1.按经济类型分	Grouped by Type of Enterprises					
国有经济	State-owned Enterprises	34313	72078	258545	890546	894700
集体经济	Collective-owned Enterprises	4583	8880	5720	52893	62895
其他经济	Others			168186	319584	582122
2.按管理渠道分	Grouped by Management					
城镇投资	Investment of Urban Units	38896	80958	432451	1263023	1539717
房地产开发	Real Estate		5485	171291	473787	566557
二、新增固定资产	**Newly Increased Fixed Assets**	**27872**	**69434**	**273324**	**953173**	**1159980**
三、房屋竣工面积	**Floor Space of the**	**986197**	**950215**	**2025223**	**5094751**	**5359752**
(平方米)	**Building Completed(sq.m)**					
#住 宅	Residential Buildings	451128	501234	1433005	3735111	3960060

Investment In Fixed Assets of Municipal Units in Representative Years

(10 000 yuan)

2002	2003	2004	2005	2006	2007	2008	2009
1848833	**2978747**	**4355271**	**5788693**	**7835681**	**10555849**	**14648360**	**19063075**
1006245	1586057	1884624	2198836	2591184	2972840	4480627	6527566
63877	142849	257226	258327	363909	1366567	1646111	1614290
778711	1249841	2213421	3331530	4880588	6216442	8521622	10921219
1848833	2978747	4355271	5788693	7835681	10555849	14648360	19063075
702233	1114809	1492693	2062940	2641871	3515719	4938202	6575526
1295389	**1812099**	**1962795**	**3011104**	**3495179**	**5279938**	**6488364**	**8380033**
5374374	**6318902**	**6062317**	**7677031**	**9147989**	**13438785**	**9870482**	**13594584**
3314467	3878178	3887867	4364275	4324291	7340515	6026891	7274105

4-11 市属固定资产投资（2009年）

Investment in Fixed Assets of Municipal Units（2009）

单位：万元 (10 000 yuan)

分类	Classify	城镇 Urban Area	房地产开发 Real Estate
一、本年完成投资	**Accomplished Invstment This Year**	**19063075**	**6575526**
区县属	District and County	**13730601**	**5430469**
按登记注册类型分	**Grouped by Registion Status**		
内资	Domestic Funded	18045098	5931559
国有	State-owned Enterprises	6413843	320041
集体	Collective-owned Enterprises	1459048	131004
股份合作	Share-holding Corperative	148742	79325
国有联营	State Joint Ownership Enterprises	1841	
集体联营	Collective Joint Ownership Enterprises	6500	
国有与集体联营	State-owned and Collective-owned Joint Enterprises	3132	2000
其他联营	Other Joint Ownership Enterprises	41387	19000
国有独资公司	Sole State-funded Corporations	111882	92462
其他有限责任公司	Other Limited Liability Corporations	5555001	2940676
股份有限公司	Share-holding Corperation Ltd.	459256	107996
私营及个体	Private and Individual	3383700	2215763
其他	Others	460766	23292
港澳台商投资	Enterprises with Investment from Hong Kong, Macao and Taiwan	452288	279720
合资经营企业(港或澳、台资)	Joint Venture	201302	54598
合作经营企业(港或澳、台资)	Cooperation	38591	38591
独资企业	Sole-Funded	210364	186531
股份有限公司	Share-Holding Corporations Ltd.	2031	
外商投资	Enterprises with Foreign Investment	514420	364247
合资经营企业(港或澳、台资)	Joint Venture	289430	222769
合作经营企业(港或澳、台资)	Cooperation	93723	93523
独资企业	Sole-Funded	127729	47955
股份有限公司	Share-Holding Corporations Ltd.	3538	
按建设性质分	**Grouped by Type of Construction**		
#新建	New Construction	7252255	
扩建	Expansion	1716423	
改建和技术改造	Reconstruction	2152216	
按构成分	**Grouped by Composition**		
1.建筑工程	Construction Projects	12457691	4904088
2.安装工程	Installment Projects	1230299	692346
3.设备工器具购置	Purchasing of Equipment and Instruments	1586022	119262
4.其他费用	Others	3789063	859830
按工程用途分	**Grouped by Purpose of Project**		
#住宅	Residential Buildings	6506340	5355273

4-11 续表 continued

指　　标	Item	城镇 Urban Area	房地产开发 Real Estate
按国民经济行业分（万元）	**Grouped by Sector (10 000 yuan)**		
农、林、牧、渔业	Agriculture,Forestry,Animal Husbandry and Fishery	244605	
采矿业	Mining	41935	
制造业	Manufacturing	2359925	
电力、燃气及水的生产和供应业	Production & Supply of Electricity,Gas & Water	257464	
建筑业	Construction	61702	
交通运输、仓储和邮政业	Transport,Storage and Post	672535	
信息传输、计算机服务和软件业	Information Transmission,Computer Service and Software	78572	
批发和零售业	Wholesale and Retail Trades	553507	
住宿和餐饮业	Hotels and Catering Services	341994	
金融业	Financial Intermediation	4830	
房地产业	Real Estate	7569868	6575526
租赁和商务服务业	Leasing and Business Services	468731	
科学研究、技术服务和地质勘察业	Scientific Research,Technical Service and Geologic Prospecting	95572	
水利、环境和公共设施管理业	Management of Water Conservancy, Environment and Public	3395695	
居民服务和其他服务业	Services to Households and Other Services	61059	
教育	Education	309544	
卫生、社会保障和社会福利业	Health,Social Security and Social Welfare	123270	
文化、体育和娱乐业	Culture, Sports education and Entertainment	250149	
公共管理和社会组织	Public Management and Social Organization	2172118	
二、构成（%）	**Proportion (%)**		
区县属	District and County	72.03	82.59
按登记注册类型分	**Grouped by Status**		
#国有经济	State-owned	34.24	6.27
集体经济	Collective-owned	8.47	3.20
按建设性质分	**Grouped by Type of Construction**		
#新建	New Construction	38.04	
扩建	Expansion	9.00	
改建和技术改造	Reconstruction	11.29	
按构成分	**Grouped by Composition of Funds**		
1.建筑工程	Construction Projects	65.35	74.58
2.安装工程	Installation Projects	6.45	10.53
3.设备工器具购置	Purchasing of the Equipment and Instruments	8.32	1.81
4.其他费用	Others	19.88	13.08
按工程用途分	**Grouped by Purpose of Project**		
#住宅	Residential Buildings	34.13	81.44
三、房屋面积(平方米)	**Floor Space (sq.m)**		
本年施工房屋面积	Floor Space of Buildings Under Construction This Year	83596364	53195495
#住宅	Residential Buildings	56797313	45661407
本年竣工房屋面积	Floor Space of Buildings Completed This Year	13594584	5202812
#住宅	Residential Buildings	7274105	4364340
四、本年新增固定资产(万元）	**Newly Increase in Fixed Assets(10 000 yuan)**	**8380033**	**1803655**

4-12 按行业分市属固定资产投资（2009年）

Investment in Fixed Assets of Municipal Units by Sector（2009）

指　标	Item	2009
本年完成投资（万元）	**Grouped by Sector (10 000 yuan)**	**19063075**
（一）农、林、牧、渔业	Agriculture,Forestry,Animal Husbandry and Fishery	244605
（二）采矿业	Mining	41935
（三）制造业	Manufacturing	2359925
#农副食品加工业	Processing of Food from Agricultural Products	75602
食品制造业	Manufacture of Foods	58245
饮料制造业	Manufacture of Beverages	63551
石油加工、炼焦及核燃料加工业	Processing of Petroleum, Coking,Processing of Nuclear Fuel	6800
化学原料及化学制品制造业	Manufacture of Raw Chemical Materials and Chemical Products	55801
医药制造业	Manufacture of Medicines	83052
金属制品业	Manufacture of Metal Products	139001
通用设备制造业	Manufacture of General Purpose Machinery	226497
专用设备制造业	Manufacture of Special Purpose Machinery	191965
交通运输设备制造业	Manufacture of Transport Equipment	229054
电气机械及器材制造业	Manufacture of Electrical Machinery and Equipment	282834
通信设备、计算机及其他电子设备制造业	Manufacture of Communication Equipment, Computers and Other Electronic Equipment	347992
仪器仪表及文化办公用机械制造业	Manufacture of Measuring Instruments and Machinery for Cultural Activity and Office Work	43151
（四）电力、燃气及水的生产 和供应业	Production & Supply of Electricity,Gas & Water	257464
（五）建筑业	Construction	61702
（六）交通运输、仓储和邮政业	Transport,Storage and Post	672535
（七）信息传输、计算机服务和软件业	Information Transmission,Computer Service and Software	78572
（八）批发和零售业	Wholesale and Retail Trades	553507
（九）住宿和餐饮业	Hotels and Catering Services	341994
（十）金融业	Financial Intermediation	4830
（十一）房地产业	Real Estate	7569868
（十二）租赁和商务服务业	Leasing and Business Services	468731
（十三）科学研究、技术服务和地质勘察业	Scientific Research,Technical Service and Geologic Prospecting	95572
（十四） 水利、环境和公共设施管理业	Management of Water Conservancy, Environment and Public Facilities	3395695
（十五）居民服务和其他服务业	Services to Households and Other Services	61059
（十六）教育	Education	309544
（十七）卫生、社会保障和社会福利业	Health,Social Security and Social Welfare	123270
（十八）文化、体育和娱乐业	Culture, Sports and Entertainment	250149
（十九）公共管理和社会组织	Public Management and Social Organization	2172118

4-13 按资金来源及建设性质分市属固定资产投资（2009年）

Investment in Fixed Assets of Municipal Units by Sources of Funds and Type of Construction（2009）

指 标	Item	2009
投资总额(万元)	**Total Investment (10 000 yuan)**	**19063075**
一、按资金来源分	**Grouped by Funds Sources**	
1.国家预算内资金	State Budgetary Funds	1241337
2.国内贷款	Domestic Loans	3062055
3.债 券	Bonds	
4.利用外资	Utilization of Foreign Funds	129150
5.自筹资金	Self-raising Funds	10516637
6.其他资金	Others	4113896
二、按建设性质分	**Grouped by Type of Construction**	
#新 建	New Construction	7252255
扩 建	Expansion	1716423
改 建	Reconstruction	2152216
三、按构成分	**Grouped by Composition of Funds**	
1.建筑工程	Construction Project	12457691
2.安装工程	Installation Projects	1230299
3.设备、工器具购置	Purchasing of Equipment and Instruments	1586022
4.其它费用	Others	3789063

4-14 按登记注册类型及隶属关系分市区固定资产投资（2009年）

Investments in Fixed Assets of Urban Districts by Registration Status and Jurisdiction of Management（2009）

分 组	Classify	2009
本年完成投资（万元）	**Investment Completed This Year (10 000yuan)**	**21202852**
一、按登记注册类型分	**Grouped by Registion Status**	
内资	Domestic Funded	20242948
国有	State-owned Enterprises	7986118
集体	Collective-owned Enterprises	1314215
股份合作	Share-holding Corperative	353555
国有联营	State Joint Ownership Enterprises	1841
集体联营	Collective Joint Ownership Enterprises	195944
国有与集体联营	Joint State-collective Enterprises	8732
其他联营	Other Joint Ownership Enterprises	37481
国有独资公司	State Sole-funded Corporations	209798
其他有限责任公司	Other Limited Liability Corporations	6338288
股份有限公司	Share-holding Corperation Ltd.	380535
私营及个体	Private and Individual	2956629
其他	Others	459812
港澳台商投资	Enterprises with Funds from Hong Kong,Macao and Taiwan	445178
合资经营企业(港或澳、台资)	Joint Venture	194192
合作经营企业(港或澳、台资)	Cooperation	38591
独资企业	Sole-funded	210364
股份有限公司	Share-Holding Corporations Ltd.	2031
外商投资	Enterprises with Foreign Investment	514726
合资经营企业(港或澳、台资)	Joint Venture	290556
合作经营企业(港或澳、台资)	Cooperation	93723
独资企业	Sole-Funded	126909
股份有限公司	Share-Holding Corporations Ltd.	3538
二、按隶属关系分	**Grouped by Jurisdiction of Management**	
中央	Central	2175658
省属	Provincial	2266876
市属	Municipal	16760318

4-15 按行业分市区固定资产投资（2009年）

Investments in Fixed Assets of Urban Districts by Sector（2009）

指　标	Item	2009
本年完成投资（万元）	**Grouped by Sector (10 000 yuan)**	**21202852**
（一）农、林、牧、渔业	Agriculture,Forestry,Animal Husbandry and Fishery	98067
（二）采矿业	Mining	113261
（三）制造业	Manufacturing	3081321
农副食品加工业	Processing of Food from Agricultural Products	30515
食品制造业	Manufacture of Foods	48285
饮料制造业	Manufacture of Beverages	38064
石油加工、炼焦及核燃料加工业	Processing of Petroleum, Coking,Processing of Nuclear Fuel	23960
化学原料及化学制品制造业	Manufacture of Raw Chemical Materials and Chemical Products	50095
医药制造业	Manufacture of Medicines	48987
金属制品业	Manufacture of Metal Products	84803
通用设备制造业	Manufacture of General Purpose Machinery	528772
专用设备制造业	Manufacture of Special Purpose Machinery	303943
交通运输设备制造业	Manufacture of Transport Equipment	462931
电气机械及器材制造业	Manufacture of Electrical Machinery and Equipment	263084
通信设备、计算机及其他电子设备制造业	Manufacture of Communication Equipment, Computers and Other Electronic Equipment	637068
仪器仪表及文化办公用机械制造业	Manufacture of Measuring Instruments and Machinery for Cultural Activity and Office Work	42615
（四）电力、燃气及水的生产和供应业	Production & Supply of Electricity,Gas & Water	451466
（五）建筑业	Construction	143235
（六）交通运输、仓储和邮政业	Transport,Storage and Post	1389591
（七）信息传输、计算机服务和软件业	Information Transmission,Computer Service and Software	201847
（八）批发和零售业	Wholesale and Retail Trades	561057
（九）住宿和餐饮业	Hotels and Catering Services	366703
（十）金融业	Financial Intermediation	7830
（十一）房地产业	Real Estate	7754540
（十二）租赁和商务服务业	Leasing and Business Services	548554
（十三）科学研究、技术服务和地质勘察业	Scientific Research,Technical Service and Geologic Prospecting	287392
（十四）水利、环境和公共设施管理业	Management of Water Conservancy, Environment and Public Facilities	2954121
（十五）居民服务和其他服务业	Services to Households and Other Services	37791
（十六）教育	Education	684869
（十七）卫生、社会保障和社会福利业	Health,Social Security and Social Welfare	128007
（十八）文化、体育和娱乐业	Culture, Sports and Entertainment	281433
（十九）公共管理和社会组织	Public Management and Social Organization	2111767

4-16 按资金来源及建设性质分市区固定资产投资（2009年）

Investment in Fixed Assets of Urban Area by Sources of Funds and Type of Construction（2009）

指 标	Item	2009
投资总额(万元)	**Total Investment (10 000 yuan)**	**21202852**
一、按资金来源分	**Grouped by Funds Sources**	
1.国家预算内资金	State Budgetary Funds	1339104
2.国内贷款	Domestic Loans	3258917
3.债 券	Bonds	
4.利用外资	Utilization of Foreign Funds	133296
5.自筹资金	Self-raising Funds	12050704
6.其他资金	Others	4420831
二、按建设性质分	**Grouped by Type of Construction**	
#新 建	New Construction	7007550
扩 建	Expansion	2687773
改 建	Reconstruction	2542342
三、按构成分	**Grouped by Composition of Funds**	
1.建筑工程	Construction Project	13581660
2.安装工程	Installation Projects	1232095
3.设备、工器具购置	Purchasing of Equipment and Instruments	2236634
4.其它费用	Others	4152463

4-17 全市固定资产投资资金来源（2009年）

Source of Funds for Total Fixed Assets Investment of Whole City（2009）

单位：万元 (10 000 yuan)

指 标	Item	城镇 Urban Area	房地产开发 Real Estate
一、本年资金来源合计	**Subtotal of Sources of Funds This Year**	**27181902**	**11145329**
1.上年末结余资金	Balance of Last Year	1736693	1236438
2.本年资金来源小计	Total Funds This Year	25445209	9908891
(1) 国家预算内资金	State Budgetary Funds	1681711	
(2) 国内贷款	Domestic Loans	3990245	1823486
(3) 债券	Bonds		
(4) 利用外资	Utilization of Foreign Funds	146240	51664
(5) 自筹资金	Self-raising Funds	14507790	4155018
(6) 其他资金	Others	5119223	3878723
二、本年各项应付款合计	**Total Sums of Money to be Paid This Year**	**2814720**	**550382**

4-18 市属固定资产投资资金来源（2009年）

Source of Funds for Fixed Estate of Municipal Units（2009）

单位：万元 (10 000 yuan)

指 标	Item	城镇 Urban Area	房地产开发 Real Estate
一、本年资金来源合计	**Subtotal of Sources of Funds This Year**	**23046904**	**10318759**
1.上年末结余资金	Balance of Last Year	1461344	1071496
2.本年资金来源小计	Total Funds This Year	21585560	9247263
(1) 国家预算内资金	State Budgetary Funds	1405595	
(2) 国内贷款	Domestic Loans	3467236	1641306
(3) 债券	Bonds		
(4) 利用外资	Utilization of Foreign Funds	146240	51664
(5) 自筹资金	Self-raising Funds	11908231	3911400
(6) 其他资金来源	Others	4658258	3642893
二、本年各项应付款合计	**Total Sums of Money to be Paid This Year**	**1332836**	**499584**

4-19 全市固定资产投资效果（2009年）

Achievements of Total Assets Investment of Whole City（2009）

指　　标	Item	城镇 Urban Area	房地产开发 Real Estate
一、建设项目投产率(%)	**Rate of Projects Put Into use(%)**	**72.49**	
施工项目个数（个）	Number of Constructing Projects (unit)	2868	
本年投产项目个数（个）	Number of Projects Put into Use (unit)	2079	
二、固定资产交付使用率(%)	**Rate Tate of Fixed Assets Put into Use(%)**	**42.80**	**28.11**
本年新增固定资产（万元）	Newly Increased Fixed Assets This Year (10000.yuan)	10134370	1957125
本年完成投资（万元）	Investment Completed This Year (10000.yuan)	23675759	6963350
三、建设周期(年)	**Construction Period (year)**	**3.16**	**5.00**
计划总投资（万元）	Total Planned Investment (10000.yuan)	74760349	34833803
本年完成投资（万元）	Investment Completed This Year (10000.yuan)	23675759	6963350
四、房屋建筑面积竣工率(%)	**Completion Rate of Buildings (%)**	**15.98**	**9.51**
本年施工房屋面积（平方米）	Floor Space of the Constructing Buildings This Year (sq.m)	95712549	57086279
本年竣工房屋面积（平方米）	Floor Space of the Building Completed This Year (sq.m)	15291263	5428145

4-20 市属固定资产投资效果（2009年）

Achievement of Fixed Assets Investment of Municipal Units（2009）

指　　标	Item	城镇 Urban Area	房地产开发 Real Estate
一、建设项目投产率(%)	**Rate of Projects Put Into use(%)**	**74.58**	
施工项目个数(个)	Number of Constructing Projects (unit)	2585	
本年投产项目个数(个)	Number of Projects Put into Use (unit)	1928	
二、固定资产交付使用率(%)	**Rate Tate of Fixed Assets Put into Use(%)**	**43.96**	**27.43**
本年新增固定资产（万元）	Newly Increased Fixed Assets This Year (10000.yuan)	8380033	1803655
本年完成投资（万元）	Investment Completed This Year (10000.yuan)	19063075	6575526
三、建设周期(年)	**Construction Period (year)**	**3.36**	**5.07**
计划总投资（万元）	Total Planned Investment (10000.yuan)	64021744	33368547
本年完成投资（万元）	Investment Completed This Year (10000.yuan)	19063075	6575526
四、房屋建筑面积竣工率(%)	**Completion Rate of Buildings (%)**	**16.26**	**9.78**
本年施工房屋面积（平方米）	Floor Space of the Constructing Buildings This Year (sq.m)	83596364	53195459
本年竣工房屋面积（平方米）	Floor Space of the Building Completed This Year (sq.m)	13594584	5202812

4-21 分区县全社会固定资产投资额（2009年）

Investment Fulfilled In Fixed Assets By Region （2009）

单位：万元 (10 000 yuan)

区县名称	Name of District and County	全社会固定资产投资 Investment Fulfilled In Fixed Assets	城镇 Urban Area	房地产 Real Estate	农村集体 Rural Collective-owned Units	农村私人建房 Private Housing in Country
新城区	Xincheng	2036572	2036572	621141		
碑林区	Beilin	2153761	2153761	975911		
莲湖区	Lianhu	2680534	2680534	501678		
灞桥区	Baqiao	1198689	1147202	162853	18876	32611
未央区	Weiyang	3233584	3161572	1016134	46930	25081
雁塔区	Yanta	6518640	6338405	3172314	161683	18552
阎良区	Yanliang	885243	806508	45966	60400	18335
临潼区	Lintong	822243	724042	12366	34195	64006
长安区	Chang'an	2264095	2052791	323448	117545	93759
蓝田县	Lantian	515382	322542	22770	128227	64613
周至县	Zhouzhi	506898	263113	15765	175657	68128
户　县	Huxian	841986	668847	25843	118338	54801
高陵县	Gaoling	1343651	1319869	67161		23782

4-21 续表 continued

区县名称	Name of District and County	商品房销售面积（平方米）Floor Space of Houses Sales(sq.m)	商品房销售额（万元）Sales Income of Commercial Houses(10 000 yuan)
新城区	Xincheng	843670	338025
碑林区	Beilin	597601	232785
莲湖区	Lianhu	1170712	455155
灞桥区	Baqiao	440027	155168
未央区	Weiyang	2768857	974380
雁塔区	Yanta	5037739	2255101
阎良区	Yanliang	217316	44851
临潼区	Lintong	44569	9263
长安区	Chang'an	1010416	333343
蓝田县	Lantian	81014	15680
周至县	Zhouzhi	81525	15128
户　县	Huxian	117703	24099
高陵县	Gaoling	149063	32480

4-22 全市分行业房屋建筑面积（2009年）

单位：平方米

行　业	Item	本年施工房屋面积 Floor Space of Buildings Under Construction This Year	住宅 Residenctial Buildings
合　计	**Total**	**95712549**	**62848991**
（一）农、林、牧、渔业	Agriculture, Forestry, Animal Husbandry and Fishery	247778	156515
（二）采矿业	Mining	157490	420
（三）制造业	Manufacturing	5663987	1465787
（四）电力、燃气及水的生产和供应业	Generation and supply of Electricity, production and supply of gas and water	397244	144500
（五）建筑业	Construction	693647	494552
（六）交通运输、仓储和邮政业	Transportation, storage and post	560546	118231
（七）信息传输、计算机服务和软件业	Information transmission, computer service and software	196018	
（八）批发和零售业	Wholesale and Retail Trades	2305919	220531
（九）住宿和餐饮业	Hotels and Catering Services	797691	213183
（十）金融业	Financial Intermediation	38240	
（十一）房地产业	Real Estate	62335600	50712291
（十二）租赁和商务服务业	Leasing and Business Services	1444094	141086
（十三）科学研究、技术服务和地质勘查业	Scientific research, technical service and Geologic Prospecting	1187957	214230
（十四）水利、环境和公共设施管理业	Management of Water Conservancy, Environment and Public Facilities	2628343	1701458
（十五）居民服务和其他服务业	Services to Households and Other Services	156518	68398
（十六）教育	Education	4461655	1058287
（十七）卫生、社会保障和社会福利业	Health,Social Security and Social Welfare	931529	404236
（十八）文化、体育和娱乐业	Culture, Sports and Entertainment	997970	154570
（十九）公共管理和社会组织	Public Management and Social Organization	10510323	5580716

Floor Space of Buildings Construction by Sector（2009）

(sq.m)

本年竣工房屋面积 Floor Space of Buildings Completed This Year	住宅 Residential Buildings	竣工房屋价值（万元） Value of Buildings Completed(10 000yuan)	住宅 Residential Buildings
15291263	**8226162**	**3744437**	**2106360**
81095	20015	13285	4500
480	420	79	70
1858570	442335	347951	105107
23550	7500	8475	1800
7200	7200	3000	3000
134126	20000	20975	8500
10259		944	
1217307	78920	193131	19430
228613	36033	50646	11222
7500		2614	
6273477	5350058	1839424	1529004
187962	92270	36659	24000
210890	15000	58878	6673
642350	467970	112908	77582
80698	67398	24285	21500
1034364	234081	238464	38200
400004	239928	61220	35730
212514	95610	39484	19876
2680304	1051424	692015	200166

4-23 市属分行业房屋建筑面积（2009年）

单位：平方米

行　业	Item	本年施工房屋面积 Floor Space of Buildings Under Construction This Year	住　宅 Residenctial Residence
合　计	**Total**	**83596364**	**56797313**
（一）农、林、牧、渔业	Agriculture, Forestry, Animal Husbandry and Fishery	247778	156515
（二）采矿业	Mining	147980	420
（三）制造业	Manufacturing	4460431	722502
（四）电力、燃气及水的生产和供应业	Generation and supply of Electricity, production and supply of gas and water	117994	22500
（五）建筑业	Construction	283510	243550
（六）交通运输、仓储和邮政业	Transportation, storage and post	350009	57831
（七）信息传输、计算机服务和软件业	Information transmission, computer service and software	120754	
（八）批发和零售业	Wholesale and Retail Trades	1848894	196921
（九）住宿和餐饮业	Hotels and Catering Services	608742	143963
（十）金融业	Financial Intermediation	3500	
（十一）房地产业	Real Estate	57896038	47239337
（十二）租赁和商务服务业	Leasing and Business Services	1362174	141066
（十三）科学研究、技术服务和地质勘查业	Scientific research, technical service and Geologic Prospecting	375240	187000
（十四）水利、环境和公共设施管理业	Management of Water Conservancy, Environment and Public Facilities	2597195	1675806
（十五）居民服务和其他服务业	Services to Households and Other Services	145518	68398
（十六）教育	Education	1375741	143971
（十七）卫生、社会保障和社会福利业	Health,Social Security and Social Welfare	678844	234151
（十八）文化、体育和娱乐业	Culture, Sports and Entertainment	705770	42408
（十九）公共管理和社会组织	Public Management and Social Organization	10270252	5520974

Floors Space of Buildings Construction of Municipal Units by Sector（2009）

(sq.m)

本年竣工房屋面积 Floor Space of Buildings Completed This Year	住　宅 Residential Residence	竣工房屋价值(万元) Value of Buildings Completed (10 000 yuan)	住　宅 Residential Residence
13594584	**7274105**	**3289502**	**1887278**
81095	20015	13285	4500
480	420	79	70
1433871	130074	252671	25335
19450	7500	6475	1800
7200	7200	3000	3000
82126		9675	
2000		520	
1186406	78920	184737	19430
219713	27133	48724	9300
3500		1350	
5989771	5121099	1756629	1470219
187962	92270	36659	24000
69190		11505	
633800	459720	111868	76582
80698	67398	24285	21500
586215	45833	119324	7500
286927	150451	45220	21330
115016	14648	12106	2546
2609164	1051424	651390	200166

4-24 主要年份全市新增固定资产及房屋竣工面积

Value of Newly Added Fixed Assets and Floor Spaces Completed of Whole City in Representative Years

年份 Year	新增固定资产(万元) Newly Increased Fixed Assets (10 000 yuan)	房屋竣工面积(平方米) Floor Space of Buildings Completed (sq.m)	住宅 Residential Residence
1978	49582	990996	407554
1980	46377	1648691	1001544
1985	86174	2224195	1290728
1986	134037	2729528	1559067
1987	167160	2414751	1192115
1988	168152	2118312	1024255
1989	165811	1784546	877691
1990	203000	2118777	1110535
1991	178572	1853384	958364
1992	223270	2047478	1126628
1993	416963	2578987	1448829
1994	553714	2829057	1844859
1995	625803	3576699	2528435
1996	600353	3321838	2495208
1997	628819	3744631	2865398
1998	802337	3828026	2756265
1999	1189176	6810370	5508336
2000	1501585	7148313	5449502
2001	1677665	6925619	5022617
2002	1989689	7732772	4861279
2003	2794439	9179629	5780646
2004	2619467	7765905	4983286
2005	4097225	11314125	5986051
2006	4530136	11994519	5830981
2007	6679699	16721647	9295019
2008	7251721	11133098	6934222
2009	10134370	15291263	8226162

4-25 主要年份市属新增固定资产及房屋竣工面积

Value of Newly Added Fixed Assets and Floor Spaces Completed of Municipal Units in Representative Years

年 份 Year	新增固定资产 (万元) Newly Increased Fixed Assets (10 000 yuan)	房屋竣工面积 (平方米) Floor Space of Buildings Completed (sq.m)	住 宅 Residential Buildings
1978	7529	249793	103060
1980	10664	497472	284022
1985	27872	986197	451128
1986	47827	1077660	690965
1987	56953	937402	417050
1988	50175	717169	351330
1989	69817	713432	315937
1990	69434	950215	501234
1991	67392	788184	377550
1992	108469	981637	417800
1993	181449	1384411	689602
1994	314996	1351075	894704
1995	273324	2025223	1433005
1996	296898	1984330	1487837
1997	374318	2264862	1666509
1998	521350	2383041	1691699
1999	859070	5012547	4074889
2000	953173	5094751	3735111
2001	1159980	5359752	3960060
2002	1295389	5374374	3314467
2003	1812099	6318902	3878178
2004	1962795	6062317	3887867
2005	3011104	7677031	4364275
2006	3495179	9147989	4324291
2007	5279938	13438785	7340515
2008	6488361	9870482	6026891
2009	8380033	13594584	7274105

4-26 全市分行业施工项目（2009年）

行业	Item	本年新增固定资产（万元） Increased Fixed Assets This Year(10 000 yuan)
合计	**Total**	**10134370**
（一）农、林、牧、渔业	Agriculture, Forestry, Animal Husbandry and Fishery	179976
（二）采矿业	Mining	32566
（三）制造业	Manufacturing	1933150
（四）电力、燃气及水的生产和供应业	Generation and supply of Electricity, production and supply of gas and water	432066
（五）建筑业	Construction	43312
（六）交通运输、仓储和邮政业	Transportation, storage and post	295864
（七）信息传输、计算机服务和软件业	Information transmission, computer service and software	50145
（八）批发和零售业	Wholesale and Retail Trades	520182
（九）住宿和餐饮业	Hotels and Catering Services	330028
（十）金融业	Financial Intermediation	26894
（十一）房地产业	Real Estate	2264144
（十二）租赁和商务服务业	Leasing and Business Services	142461
（十三）科学研究、技术服务和地质勘查业	Scientific research, technical service and Geologic Prospecting	152686
（十四）水利、环境和公共设施管理业	Management of Water Conservancy, Environment and Public Facilities	1379017
（十五）居民服务和其他服务业	Services to Households and Other Services	99623
（十六）教育	Education	435944
（十七）卫生、社会保障和社会福利业	Health,Social Security and Social Welfare	125751
（十八）文化、体育和娱乐业	Culture, Sports and Entertainment	200465
（十九）公共管理和社会组织	Public Management and Social Organization	1490096

Construction Projects of Whole City by Sector（2009）

施工项目个数（个） Number of Constructing Projects（unit）	本年新开工 Newly Started This Year	投产项目个数（个） Projects put into Use (unit)
2868	**2189**	**2079**
116	109	104
9	7	5
697	471	465
122	60	83
26	16	12
107	79	74
21	11	9
176	160	147
124	107	103
6	5	5
99	83	67
62	35	35
61	36	36
490	412	386
57	53	19
159	123	122
67	51	57
75	53	48
394	318	302

4-27 市属分行业施工项目（2009年）

行　业	Item	本年新增固定资产（万元） Increased Fixed Assets This Year(10 000 yuan)
合　计	**Total**	**8380033**
（一）农、林、牧、渔业	Agriculture, Forestry, Animal Husbandry and Fishery	179976
（二）采矿业	Mining	29656
（三）制造业	Manufacturing	1466887
（四）电力、燃气及水的生产和供应业	Generation and supply of Electricity, production and supply of gas and water	148929
（五）建筑业	Construction	37012
（六）交通运输、仓储和邮政业	Transportation, storage and post	214505
（七）信息传输、计算机服务和软件业	Information transmission, computer service and software	32821
（八）批发和零售业	Wholesale and Retail Trades	466171
（九）住宿和餐饮业	Hotels and Catering Services	243874
（十）金融业	Financial Intermediation	4830
（十一）房地产业	Real Estate	2069758
（十二）租赁和商务服务业	Leasing and Business Services	137402
（十三）科学研究、技术服务和地质勘查业	Scientific research, technical service and Geologic Prospecting	50864
（十四）水利、环境和公共设施管理业	Management of Water Conservancy, Environment and Public Facilities	1268876
（十五）居民服务和其他服务业	Services to Households and Other Services	96683
（十六）教育	Education	254485
（十七）卫生、社会保障和社会福利业	Health,Social Security and Social Welfare	103651
（十八）文化、体育和娱乐业	Culture, Sports and Entertainment	138547
（十九）公共管理和社会组织	Public Management and Social Organization	1435106

Construction Projects of Municipal Units by Sector（2009）

施工项目个数（个） Number of Constructing Projects（unit）	本年新开工 Newly Started This Year	投产项目个数（个） Projects put into Use (unit)
2585	**2034**	**1928**
116	109	104
7	6	4
631	445	436
113	55	78
17	11	11
82	65	59
13	6	4
159	145	135
112	98	95
3	3	3
92	78	64
55	30	33
35	27	25
477	402	376
56	52	18
117	104	98
61	49	53
57	38	36
382	311	296

4-28 主要年份房地产开发投资主要指标

单位：万元

指标	Item	1997	1998	1999	2000
本年完成投资额	Investment Completed This Year	246817	382142	442982	518460
本年施工面积（平方米）	Floor Space of Buildings Under Construction This Year(sq.m)	4514661	6788737	7934602	7631791
#住宅	Residential Buildings	3311624	5523667	6495345	6198502
本年竣工面积（平方米）	Floor Space of Buildings Completed This Year(sq.m)	1356154	1561710	3777862	3210975
#住宅	Residential Buildings	1203270	1333330	3522764	2955463
竣工价值	Value of Floor Space of Buildings Completed	119557	143620	382245	269408
#住宅	Residential Buildings	96347	109982	330190	229708
商品房销售面积（平方米）	Floor Space of Commercialized Buildings sold(sq.m)	784514	1171051	2969705	2129156
#住宅	Residential Buildings	726872	1086108	2849545	2007741
商品房销售额	Total Sales of Commercialized Buildings	128058	177389	351861	325193
#住宅	Residential Buildings	113917	154614	323482	294562
商品房预售面积（平方米）	Floor Space of Commercialized Buildings Presold(sq.m)	263531	2520176	302513	2530349
#住宅	Residential Buildings	232660	2467716	273431	2530349
商品房空置面积（平方米）	Floor Space of Vacant Commercialized Buildings(sq.m)	587064	325156	623796	364097
#住宅	Residential Buildings	502608	228149	523181	240212
商品房出租面积（平方米）	Floor Space of Commercialized Buildings Recenting(sq.m)	256918	10365	18780	11673
#住宅	Residential Buildings	228672	120	1461	200
本年新增固定资产	Newly Increased in Fixed Assets This Year	143616	199261	430985	383811

Main Indicators of Investment in Real Estate Development in Representative Years

(10 000 yuan)

2001	2002	2003	2004	2005	2006	2007	2008	2009
674211	793689	1248177	1696685	2252303	2857605	3873342	5402617	6963350
7437846	11725803	13431222	16336814	21742931	23835612	29159540	36328733	57086279
5804332	9646770	9436123	12040107	17833558	18902667	23768164	30791305	49015888
3162449	3297069	3396721	3808406	3616231	3996417	4832987	4439585	5428145
2696055	2902965	2895565	3080577	3165164	3421533	4224701	4124612	4534926
372040	369347	547322	737507	805820	820227	1011283	1064984	1680809
286154	304553	440117	555753	681123	657982	771267	960167	1374229
2253468	2528958	2527368	3054710	4973421	6215019	8339198	7607224	12560212
1921961	2370397	2302824	2799011	4763928	5840605	7829108	7157617	12021163
472204	513468	542851	813529	1712897	2061450	2817880	2964440	4885458
355310	454597	442468	712650	1580322	1794716	2517411	2689174	4507051
674407	610198	523516	1764049	3000743	4282029	4910694	5692237	11254387
651990	557343	491159	1590960	2871309	4081064	4575415	5411982	10951690
508233	571417	638528	1085214	1235881	1124943	454242	554012	406750
341836	446968	523449	727633	991685	858896	386193	354024	287267
91889	157455	105608	111812	173178	85334	108370	349432	382331
970	11326	54250	57799	40863	37400	53554	45294	65549
507658	484349	621336	833564	927832	1002244	1431710	1240156	1957125

4-29 房地产开发投资主要指标（2009年）

Main Indicators of Investment in Real Estate Development（2009）

单位：万元 (10 000 yuan)

指　　标	Item	全市合计 Total	国有 State-owned	市区 Urban Area	市属 Municipal
企业(单位)个数(个)	Number of Enterprises(unit)	494	31	468	460
本年完成投资	Investment Completed This Year	6963350	513063	6831811	6575526
#土地开发投资额	Investments in Land Development	303811	118512	302683	269512
按工程用途分	Grouped by Function				
住宅	Residential Buildings	5683026	424388	5568749	5355273
#别墅、高档公寓	Villas and Top-Grade Apartments	223421		222257	220901
经济适用房	Econornically Affordable Housing	272778	62508	272778	266482
办公楼	Office Buildings	233406	7095	224370	219684
商业营业用房	Houses for Business Use	661127	44527	655907	638151
其他	Others	385791	37053	382785	362418
本年新增固定资产	Incressed Fixed Assets This Year	1957125	204340	1901533	1803655
房屋建筑面积及竣工价值	Floor Space of Buildings and Value of Buildings Completed				
施工房屋面积(平方米)	Floor Space of Buildings Under Construction (sq.m)	57086279	6579064	55890413	53195495
#住宅	Residential Buildings	49015888	6063347	47902563	45661407
经济适用房	Econornically Affordable Housing	2371155	466954	2371155	2303452
竣工房屋面积(平方米)	Floor Space of Buildings Completed (sq.m)	5428145	589289	5092371	5202812
#住宅	Residential Buildings	4534926	412814	4234534	4364340
经济适用房	Econornically Affordable Housing	1127066		98327	98327
竣工房屋价值	Value of Buildings Completed	1680809	190744	1633853	1605602
#住宅	Residential Buildings	1374229	103220	4234534	1323032
经济适用房	Econornically Affordable Housing	23079		98327	23079
商品房销售面积(平方米)	Floor Space of Commercialized Buildings Sold(sq.m)	12560212	841226	12130907	12007950
商品房销售额(万元)	Sales Income of Commercialized Buildings	4885458	285149	4798071	4673086
年平均从业人员数(人)	Annual Average Number of Employed Persons(person)	26530	4158	21826	24876
本年应付工资总额	Total Income of Working Staff Engaged	73072	7351	66303	68163
本年应付福利费总额	Total Welfare Expense payable	7683	1563	7457	7226

4-30 商品房销售情况（2009年）

Sales of Commercial Houses（2009）

指　　标	Item	全市合计 Total	国有 State Owned	市区 Urban Area	市属 municipal
商品房销售面积(平方米)	**Floor Space of Commercialized Buildings Sold(sq.m)**	**12560212**	**841226**	**12130907**	**12007950**
现房销售面积	**Floor space of completed apartment sales**	**1305825**	**225623**	**1165747**	**1251420**
期房销售面积	**Floor space of forward delivery housing sales**	**11254387**	**615603**	**10965160**	**10756530**
住宅	Residential Buildings	12021163	735921	11591858	11488123
#别墅、高档公寓	Villas and High-grade Apartments	221365	1425	219769	191075
经济适用房	Economically Affordable Housing	672650	204622	672650	657852
办公楼	Office Buildings	182271		182271	167562
商业营业用房	Houses for Business Use	330144	105305	330144	325653
其他	Others	26634		26634	26612
商品房销售额(万元)	**Sales Income of Commercialized Buildings (10 000 yuan)**	**4885458**	**285149**	**4798071**	**4673086**
现房销售额(万元)	**Floor Space of Completed Apartment Sales**	**537246**	**99729**	**509428**	**514159**
期房销售额(万元)	**Floor Space of Forward Delivery Housing Sales**	**4348212**	**185420**	**4288643**	**4158927**
住宅	Residential Buildings	4507051	219468	4419664	4311936
#别墅、高档公寓	Villas and High-grade Apartments	122439	850	121864	110497
经济适用房	Economically Affordable Housing	192632	53119	192632	188154
办公楼	Office Buildings	96185		96185	83726
商业营业用房	Houses for Business Use	270725	65681	270725	265979
其他	Others	11497		11497	11445
商品房空置面积(平方米)	**Vacancy of Commercialized Buildings(sq.m)**	**406750**	**16912**	**389198**	**393544**
#空置一年以上	Being Idle for One Year	209273	12293	203611	199758
空置三年以上(含三年)	Being Idie for One Year	7456		7456	7456
住宅	Residence	287267	10410	269715	281955
#别墅、高档公寓	Villas and High-grade Apartments	24418	459	24418	20727
经济适用房	Economically Affordable Housing	12946		12946	12946
办公楼	Office Buildings	15400		15400	12400
商业营业用房	Houses for Business Use	83050	6502	83050	78156
其他	Others	21033		21033	21033
商品房出租面积(平方米)	**Floor Space of Commercialized Leased Buildings(sq.m)**	**382331**	**90845**	**375184**	**354999**
住宅	Residential Buildings	65549	60289	65549	40847
办公楼	Office Buildings	214378	17610	214378	214378
商业营业用房	Houses for Business Use	100368	12946	93221	97738
其他	Others	2036		2036	2036

4-31 房地产开发投资资金来源（2009年）

Source of Funds for Investment in Real Estate Development（2009）

单位：万元 (10 000 yuan)

指　标	Item	全市合计 Total	国有 State-owned	市区 Urban Area	市属 Municipal
一、本年资金来源合计	**Total**	**11145329**	**915983**	**10965991**	**10318759**
1.上年末结余资金	Balance of Last Year	1236438	90726	1200408	1071496
2.本年资金来源小计	Total Funds This Year	9908891	825257	9765583	9247263
(1) 国内贷款	Domestic Loans	1823486	265626	1823006	1641306
#银行贷款	Bank Loan	1674747	234686	1674267	1515467
非银行金融机构贷款	Loans from financial Institutions except bank	148739	30940	148739	125839
(2) 利用外资	Utilization of Foreign Funds	51664		49664	51664
#外商直接投资	Foreign Direct Investment	51664		49664	51664
(3) 自筹资金	Self-raising Funds	4155018	216606	4090051	3911400
#企事业单位自有资金	Funds at the disposal of enterprises	1915251	106413	1894126	1709762
(4) 其他资金	Others	3878723	343025	3802862	3642893
#定金及预付款	Earnest Money and Advance payment	2480465	242394	2456345	2362521
个人按揭贷款	Personal Mortgage loan	1074240	27143	1062373	1013449
二、本年各项应付款合计	**Total Sums of Money to be Paid This Year**	**550382**	**58104**	**538700**	**499584**
#工程款	Project Fund	355681	42019	344119	327426

4-32 房地产开发经营情况（2009年）

Running of Real Estate Development（2009）

单位：万元 (10 000 yuan)

指 标	Item	全市合计 Total	国有 State-owned	市区 Urban Area	市属 Municipal
一、资产总计	**Total Assets**	**15691700**	**1545035**	**15518592**	**14900981**
负债总计	Total Liabilities	12173638	1274815	12028743	11579427
所有者权益合计	Total Creditor's Equity	3518061	270220	3489849	3321554
#实收资本	Held Capital	2947236	246074	2936145	2798284
国家资本	State Capital	204623	172358	204540	197688
集体资本	Collectively Owned Capital	24889	37	24852	23583
法人资本	Corporation Capital	1565859	73415	1562894	1513115
个人资本	Individual Capital	700311	264	692304	612343
港澳台资本	Capital from Hong Kong,Maocao and Taiwan	137009		137009	137009
外商资本	Foreign Capital	314545		314546	314546
二、损益情况	**Total Revenue**				
1.主营业务收入	Revenue from Principal Business	3958101	209423	3881568	3661410
土地转让收入	Revenue of land Transferred	25456		23656	25456
商品房屋销售收入	Revenue of Commercial Houses Sold	3782150	201368	3707979	3490742
房屋出租收入	Revenue of Houses Leased	1884	60	1884	1824
其他收入	Other Revenue	148611	7994	148050	143388
2.主营业务成本	Cost of Principal Business	3155475	155001	3095272	2922803
3.主营业务税金及附加	Taxes and Other Charges on Principal Business	261544	13129	256115	241921
4.主营业务利润	Principal Business Profit	486177	37128	478643	442840
5.其他业务收入	Other Business Revenue	21961	2348	21941	21713
6.其他业务利润	Other Business Profit	16982	1797	16974	16741
7.销售费用	Sales Expenditures	139951	7368	136048	132902
8.管理费用	Management Cost	173899	14014	169870	163823
#税金	Tax	16551	331	15841	15745
差旅费	Travel Expense	3989	180	3891	3865
工会经费	Labor Union Expenditure	505	55	482	467
9.财务费用	Fiscal Expenditure	39228	3916	38550	36031
#利息支出	Interest Exchange	24949	2774	24513	22876
10.营业利润	Operating Profit	213039	21586	210740	189537
投资收益	Investment Revenue	9508	3891	9507	9496
营业外收入	Non-business Revenue	3901	593	3862	3654
营业外支出	Non-business Expenditures	11841	1386	11347	11630
11.利润总额	Total Profit	273121	24224	269925	246039

主要统计指标解释

全社会固定资产投资 即固定资产投资额是以货币表现的建造和购置固定资产活动的工作量，它是反映固定资产投资规模、速度、比例关系和使用方向的综合性指标。全社会固定资产投资按登记注册类型可分为国有、集体、个体、联营、股份制、外商、港澳台商、其他等。按照报表种类，全社会固定资产投资总额分为城镇固定资产投资、房地产开发投资和农村农户和非农户投资等。

房地产开发投资 指房地产开发公司、商品房建设公司及其他房地产开发法人单位和附属于其他法人单位实际从事房地产开发或经营的活动单位统一开发的包括统代建、拆迁还建的住宅、厂房、仓库、饭店、宾馆、度假村、写字楼、办公楼等房屋建筑物和配套的服务设施，土地开发工程（如道路、给水、排水、供电、供热、通讯、平整场地等基础设施工程）的投资;不包括单纯的土地交易活动。

施工项目 指报告期内曾进行建筑或安装工程施工活动的建设项目，包括报告期内新开工项目、报告期以前开工跨入报告期继续施工的项目以及报告期施过工并在报告期内全部建成投产或停缓建的项目。

全部建成投产项目 工业项目是指设计文件规定形成生产能力的主体工程及其相应配套的辅助设施全部建成，经负荷试运转，证明具备生产设计规定合格产品的条件，并经过验收鉴定合格或达到竣工验收标准，与生产性工程配套的生活福利设施可以满足近期正常生产的需要，正式移交生产的建设项目。非工业项目是指设计文件规定的主体工程和相应的配套工程全部建成，能够发挥设计规定的全部效益，经验收鉴定合格或达到竣工验收标准，正式移交使用的建设项目。

新增生产能力 指通过固定资产投资活动而增加的设计能力或工程效益，它是用实物形态表示的固定资产投资的成果。新增生产能力的计算，是以能独立发挥生产能力或工程效益的单项工程（或项目）为对象。当单项工程（或项目）建成，经有关部门鉴定合格，正式移交投入生产，即可计算新增生产能力。

新增生产能力或工程效益有以下几种表现形式:

（1）以建设项目或单项工程建成后的年产能力表示，如煤炭开采、石油开采等。

（2）以建设项目或单项工程建成后处理原料的能力表示，如选矿工程的年处理矿石能力、洗煤厂年洗原煤能力等。

（3）以新增的主要设备数量或容量表示，如棉纺锭锭数、发电机组容量等。

（4）以建筑物容积、容量、面积或长度表示，如水库容量、铁路公路里程等。

新增生产能力的数量一般按设计能力计算。设计能力是指设计文件中规定的在正常情况下能够达到的生产能力，而不论投产后的实际产量如何。以设备数量、建筑物容积、面积、长度等表示生产能力或工程效益，则按建成的实际数量计算。

房屋建筑面积 指从房屋外墙线算起的各层平面面积的总和，包括可供使用的有效面积和房屋结构（如柱、墙）占用的面积。多层建筑按各层（包括地下室）面积总和计算。

住宅建筑面积 指施工和竣工房屋建筑面积中供居住用的施工和竣工房屋建筑面积。

施工面积 指报告期内施工的全部房屋建筑面积。包括本期新开工的面积、上期跨入本期继续施工的房屋面积、上期停缓建在本期恢复施工的房屋面积、本期竣工的房屋面积及本期施工后又停缓建的房屋面积。

竣工面积 指在报告期内房屋建筑按照设计要求已全部完工，达到住人和使用条件，经验收鉴定合格，正式移交使用单位的建筑面积。

房屋建筑面积竣工率 指一定时期内房屋竣工面积占同期房屋施工面积的比率。它是从房屋建筑施工速度的角度反映投资效果和建筑业经济效益的指标。

新增固定资产 指通过投资活动所形成的新的固定资产价值，包括已经建成投入生产或交付使用的工程价值和达到固定资产标准的设备、工具、器具的价值及有关应摊入的费用。它是以价值形式表示的固定资产投资成果的综合性指标，可以综合反映不同时期、不同部门、不同地区的固定资产投资成果。

建设项目投产率 指一定时期内全部建成投入生产项目个数与同期正式施工项目个数的比率。它是从项目建设速度的角度反映投资效果的指标。

固定资产交付使用率 指一定时期新增固定资产与同期完成投资额的比率。它是反映各个时期固定资产动用速度，衡量建设过程中投资效果的一个综合性指标。

Explanatory Notes on Main Statistical Indicators

Total Investment in Fixed Assets in the Whole Country Total investment in fixed assets refers to the volume of activities in construction and purchases of fixed assets in monetary terms. It is a comprehensive indicator which shows the size, pace, proportional relations and use orientation of the investment in fixed assets. Total investment in fixed assets in the whole country includes, by registration type of ownership, the investment by the state-owned units, collective units, individuals, joint ownership units, share-holding units, as well as investment by businessmen from foreign countries and from Hong Kong, Macau and Taiwan, and by other units. According to category of report form, total investment in Fixed Assets in whole country includes urban investment in fixed Assets, investment in real estate development, rural households and non-rural households investment, etc.

Investment in Real Estate Development It includes the investment by the real estate development companies, commercial buildings construction companies and other real estate development units of various types of ownership in the construction of house buildings, such as residential buildings, factory buildings, warehouses, hotels, guesthouses, holiday villages, office buildings, and the complementary service facilities and land development projects, such as roads, water supply, water drainage, power supply, heating, telecommunications, land leveling and other projects of infrastructure. It excludes the activities in simple land transactions.

Projects under Construction refer to projects having construction and installation activities undertaken in the reference period, including projects started in the reference period, or continued from the previous period, or completed and put into production or suspended in the reference period.

Projects Completed and Put into Use Industrial projects refer to the major projects and accessory facilities completed which result in forming production capacity and have been checked and accepted while the living and welfare facilities have been completed and can ensure normal production and formally put into production. Non-industrial projects refer to the major projects and accessory facilities completed which possess the designed capacity and have been checked, accepted and formally put into production.

Newly Increased Production Capacity refers to the increase of designed capacity and project efficiency through investment in fixed assets, which reflects the accomplishment of investment in fixed assets in kind. The calculation of newly increased production capacity is based on individual project which operates independently and efficiently. When an individual project is completed and checked and accepted and put into production, it is counted as newly increased production capacity.

The newly increased production capacity and project efficiency are usually expressed in one of the following forms:

(1)annual production capacity, such as extraction of coal and petroleum;

(2)raw material processing capacity, such as ore dressing capacity of ore dressing projects, the dressing capacity of a coal washery;

(3)number or capacity of major equipment increased, such as the number of cotton spindles increased and the capacity of generating sets increased;

(4)physical measures of construction, such as volume, capacity, area, and length, for instance, the capacity of reservoirs, the length of railways or highways.

Newly increased production capacity in terms of quantity is calculated in designed capacity in general, which refers to the production capacity of a project under normal conditions designed in construction documents regardless of the actual output.

Floor Space of Buildings under Construction andCompleted refers to total floor space in each story of buildings calculated from the outside line of building walls, including both usable space and the space occupied by constructions like pillars or walls. The floor space of multi-story buildings includes the total floor space of each story (including basement).

Floor Space of Residential Buildings refers to the floor space of the residential buildings under construction and completed among the total space of buildings under construction and completed.

Floor Space under Construction refers to total floor space of all buildings under construction during the reference period, including floor space of newly started buildings during the reference period, floor space of construction extended from the previous period to the current period, floor space of construction suspended during the previous period and resumed in the current period, floor space of construction completed in the current period, and floor space of construction started and then suspended in the current period.

Floor Space of Buildings Completed refers to the floor space of buildings completed in the reference period, which have come up to the designed standards and have been put into use.

Completion Rate of Floor Space of Buildings refers to the ratio of the floor space of buildings completed in certain period of time to the floor space of buildings under construction in the same period which reflects the investment result and economic efficiency of the construction industry from the angle of the speed of project construction.

Newly Increased Fixed Assets refer to the newly increased value of fixed assets through investment, including the value of projects completed and put into production, the value of equipment, tools, and vessels considered as fixed assets, as well as the relevant expenses as investment in fixed assets. This is a comprehensive indicator of investment in fixed assets, reflecting the achievements of investment in fixed assets in different periods, different sectors, and different regions.

Rate of Construction Projects Completed and Put into Use refers to the ratio of the number of construction projects completed and put into use in certain period of time to the number of projects under construction in the same period. this reflects the investment efficiency from the angle of the speed of projects construction.

Rate of Projects of Fixed Assets Completed and Put into Operation refers to the ratio of the newly increased fixed assets to the total investment made in the same period. This is a comprehensive indicator, reflecting the speed of the employment of fixed assets and the investment efficiency.

5 财 政

GOVERNMENT FINANCE

资料整理：刘　婷
Data management:Liu Ting

第五部分　财政

一、简要说明

本章资料主要包括地方财政收入、支出总额构成及分区县情况，由西安市统计局综合处根据西安市财政局提供资料整理。

二、主要指标

财政总收入（亿元）	398.84	比上年同口径增长 22.9%
一般预算收入（亿元）	181.40	比上年同口径增长 24.6%
一般预算支出（亿元）	276.85	比上年同口径增长 22.0%

5 GOVERNMENT FINANCE

Ⅰ.Brief Introduction

This chapter consists primarily of data on regional revenue, expenditure of the municipal government, regional revenue and expenditure of the districts and the counties. The data are provided by the Xi'an Bureau of Finance and are compiled by Integration division of the Xi'an Bureau of Statistics.

Ⅱ.Major Indicators

		Increase over Preceding Year
Total Government Revenue(100 mil. Yuan)	398.84	22.9%
General Budgetary Revenue(100 mil. Yuan)	181.40	24.6%
Ordinary Budgetary Expenditures(100 mil. Yuan)	276.85	22.0%

5-1 财政收入（2009年）

Government Revenue（2009）

单位：万元　　（10 000 yuan）

指　　标	Item	2009
财政总收入	**Total Government Revenue**	**3988396**
#基金预算	**Fund Bugetary**	**1500189**
一般预算	**General Bugetary**	**1813992**
一、税收收入	**Total Tax Revenue**	**1491384**
1.增值税	Value Added Tax	191539
2.营业税	Business Tax	615641
3.企业所得税	Corporate Income Tax	138646
4.企业所得税退税	Return for corporate Income Tax	-232
5.个人所得税	Individual Income Tax	63191
6.资源税	Resource Tax	320
7.固定资产投资方向调节税	Tax on Adjustment of the Orientation of Investment in Fixed Assets	
8.城市维护建设税	City Maintenance and Construction Tax	115249
9.房产税	House Property Tax	59075
10.印花税	Stamp Tax	41165
11.城镇土地使用税	Urban Land Use Tax	60072
12.土地增值税	Land Appreciation Tax	50743
13.车船使用和牌照税	Tax on the Use of Vehicles and Ships	21527
14.耕地占用税	Farm Land Occupatian Tax	44640
15.契税	Deed Tax	89808
16.烟叶税	Tobacco Leaf Tax	
17.其他税收收入	Other Tax Revenue	
二、非税收收入	**Total Non-tax Revenue**	**322608**
1.专项收入	Special Program Receipts	53370
2.行政事业性收费收入	Charge of Adminnistrative and Institutional Units	112751
3.罚没收入	Penalty Receipts	59095
4.国有资本经营收入	State-downed Assets Profit	36307
5.国有资源（资产）有偿使用收入	Revenue for the use of State-owned Assets（Resources）	56299
6.其他收入	Other Revenue	4786

5-2 财政支出（2009年）

Government Expenditures（2009）

单位:万元 (10 000 yuan)

指　　标	Item	2009
一、基金预算	**Fund Bugetary**	**1432342**
二、一般预算	**General Bugetary**	**2768502**
1.一般公共服务	Expenditure for General Public Services	409683
2.外交支出	Expenditure for Foreign Affairs	
3.国防支出	Expenditure for National Defense	3537
4.公共安全支出	Expenditure for Public Security	212906
5.教育支出	Expenditure for Education	392412
6.科学技术支出	Expenditure for Science and Technology	38080
7.文化体育与传媒支出	Expenditure for Cultural, sports and the media	49365
8.社会保障和就业支出	Expenditure for Social Safety Net and Employment Effort	452354
9.医疗卫生支出	Expenditure for Medical and Health Care	181050
10.环境保护支出	Expenditure for Environment Protection	51692
11.城乡社区事务支出	Expenditure for Urban and Rural Community Affairs	343542
12.农林水事务支出	Expenditure for Agriculture, Forestry and Water Conservancy	173755
13.交通运输支出	Expenditure for Transportation	94342
14.采掘电力信息等事务	Expenditure for Mining ,Electricity and Information	146549
15.粮油物资储备管理等事务	Material Reserves Management Affairs Spending	41784
16.金融监管支出	Expenditure for Financial Supervision	39471
17.地震灾后恢复重建支出	Expenditure for Post-earthquake Recovery and Reconstruction	4336
18.预备费	Budget	
19.国债还本付息支出	Expenditure for National Debt and Interest(10 000yuan)	328
20.其它支出	Other Expenditure	133316

5-3 分区县地方财政收入（2009年）

Financial Revenue of Local Government by Region（2009）

单位：万元 （10 000 yuan）

区　县	Region	一般预算收入 General Budgetary Revenue	税收收入 Tax Revenue	增值税 Value Added Tax	营业税 Business Revenue	企业所得税 Corporate Income Tax
全市	**Total**	**1813992**	**1491384**	**191539**	**615641**	**138646**
市本级	**Sum of city level**	**736506**	**570428**	**76666**	**174048**	**72286**
市区县合计	**Region**	**1077486**	**920956**	**114873**	**441593**	**66360**
新城区	Xincheng	130002	107190	10333	50475	15388
碑林区	Beilin	179401	160253	16406	77522	17304
莲湖区	Lianhu	182161	153579	28502	71207	10274
雁塔区	Yanta	155260	144042	11295	90592	6798
灞桥区	Baqiao	70281	66197	5067	35782	2188
未央区	Weiyang	108301	94686	16205	40967	6950
阎良区	Yanliang	39024	31419	1888	9775	2235
临潼区	Lintong	35086	27508	6037	7040	1581
长安区	Chang'an	95124	69085	8855	33003	2267
蓝田县	Lantian	10587	7796	1186	4689	128
周至县	Zhouzhi	6038	4052	323	2754	40
户　县	Huxian	26083	20727	3588	8644	383
高陵县	Gaoling	40138	34422	5188	9143	824

5-3 续表1 continued 1

单位：万元 （10 000 yuan）

区　县	Region	税收收入 Tax Revenue 个人所得税 Individual Income Tax	资源税 Resource Tax	城市维护建设税 City Maintenance and Construction Tax	耕地占用税 Farm Land Occupation Tax	契税 Deed Tax	其他各项税收收入 Other Tax Revenue
全市	**Total**	**63191**	**320**	**115249**	**44640**	**89808**	**232350**
市本级	**Sum of city level**	**25952**	**1**	**30490**		**75647**	**115338**
市区县合计	**Region**	**37239**	**319**	**84759**	**44640**	**14161**	**117012**
新城区	Xincheng	5347		10998			14649
碑林区	Beilin	13788		12953			22280
莲湖区	Lianhu	4975	11	17414			21196
雁塔区	Yanta	5833		12851	1934		14739
灞桥区	Baqiao	663	1	5233	10900		6363
未央区	Weiyang	2225	2	10716	5179		12442
阎良区	Yanliang	1634		1590	5296	4090	4911
临潼区	Lintong	728		3498	3526	2150	2948
长安区	Chang'an	1172	2	3696	6100	4997	8993
蓝田县	Lantian	85	270	463	235	229	511
周至县	Zhouzhi	39	30	244	79	154	389
户　县	Huxian	301	3	1663	2308	1003	2834
高陵县	Gaoling	449		3440	9083	1538	4757

5-3 续表2

单位：万元

区　县	Region	非税收入 Non-tax Revenue	专项 收入 Special Program Receipts	行政事业性收费收入 Charge of Adiministrative and Institutional Units
全市	**Total**	**322608**	**53370**	**112751**
市本级	**Sum of city level**	**166078**	**17600**	**65998**
市区县合计	**Region**	**156530**	**35770**	**46753**
新城区	Xincheng	22812	4312	5673
碑林区	Beilin	19148	5397	6650
莲湖区	Lianhu	28582	7364	3992
雁塔区	Yanta	11218	5408	1756
灞桥区	Baqiao	4084	2241	745
未央区	Weiyang	13615	4628	1187
阎良区	Yanliang	7605	668	5074
临潼区	Lintong	7578	823	2809
长安区	Chang'an	26039	1574	15180
蓝田县	Lantian	2791	218	381
周至县	Zhouzhi	1986	159	1023
户　县	Huxian	5356	994	1480
高陵县	Gaoling	5716	1984	803

continued 2

（10 000 yuan）

罚没收入 Penalty Receipts	国有资本经营收入 State-owned Assets Profit	国有资源(资产)有偿使用收入 The Revenues of the Compensation for the Use of State-owned Resoures(Assants)	其他收入 Other Income	基金收入 Fund Revenue
59095	**36307**	**56299**	**4786**	**1500189**
31540	**33838**	**13839**	**3263**	**1440370**
27555	**2469**	**42460**	**1523**	**59819**
3989		8838		
4088		3013		
3108		12681	1437	
3994		60		
1075		23		
1691		6109		
820	1013	30		1493
1430		2516		9965
2118		7167		10228
1928	60	204		4081
454		300	50	1021
1574		1300	8	4720
1286	1396	219	28	28311

5-4 分区县地方财政支出（2009年）

单位:万元

区 县	Region	一般预算支出 Ordinary Budgetary Expenditures	一般公共服务 General Public Services	国防支出 Expenditure for National Defense	公共安全 Public Safety
合 计	**Total**	**2768502**	**409683**	**3537**	**212906**
市级合计	**Sum of city level**	**1475623**	**187168**	**2229**	**102986**
区、县合计	**Region**	**1292879**	**222515**	**1308**	**109920**
新城区	Xincheng	107883	23212	301	13440
碑林区	Beilin	100956	16203	264	13580
莲湖区	Lianhu	110360	19666	123	15477
雁塔区	Yanta	101301	19154	114	12874
灞桥区	Baqiao	73026	12423	111	6496
未央区	Weiyang	98167	25285	57	9150
阎良区	Yanliang	66758	10105		4643
临潼区	Lintong	108894	13840		6737
长安区	Chang'an	157795	31840	143	8043
蓝田县	Lantian	96725	10628	58	4840
周至县	Zhouzhi	98075	10751	46	4389
户 县	Huxian	92851	12600	41	5832
高陵县	Gaoling	80088	16808	50	4419

Financial Expenditures of Local Government by Region（2009）

(10 000 yuan)

教育支出 Expenditure for Education	科学技术支出 Expenditure for Science and Technology	文化体育与传媒支出 Expenditure for Culture,Sport and Media	社会保障和就业支出 Expenditure for Social Safety Net and Employment Effort	医疗卫生支出 Expenditure for Medical and Health Care	环境保护支出 Expenditure for Environment Protection
392412	**38080**	**49365**	**452354**	**181050**	**51692**
72883	**29599**	**36978**	**250398**	**75655**	**38956**
319529	**8481**	**12387**	**201956**	**105395**	**12736**
21104	713	310	20796	5309	
21492	856	738	23825	7874	337
22656	886	528	27292	8607	
22870	1137	600	14920	7879	71
24241	587	499	12052	7615	10
23634	873	528	10468	8031	624
15747	430	923	8947	4636	137
31512	528	1283	15144	10748	1913
44270	994	2142	23987	10534	822
25934	204	952	13014	10462	4317
24763	187	1416	12895	10201	3917
24479	493	1189	9244	7779	545
16827	593	1279	9372	5720	43[illegible]

5-4 续表

单位:万元

区　县	Region	一般预算 Ordinary Budgetary 城乡社区事务支出 Expenditure for Urban and Rural Community Affairs	农林水事务支出 Expenditure for Agriculture,Foresty Water Conservancy	交通运输支出 Expenditure for Industry,Commerce and Banking	采掘电力信息等事务支出 Expenditure for Mining,Electricity and Information
合　计	**Total**	**343542**	**173755**	**94342**	**146549**
市级合计	**Sum of city level**	**230874**	**74431**	**56518**	**135540**
区、县合计	**Region**	**112668**	**99324**	**37824**	**11009**
新城区	Xincheng	18854	296	830	244
碑林区	Beilin	11506		420	240
莲湖区	Lianhu	12730	111	451	119
雁塔区	Yanta	11965	4379	901	321
灞桥区	Baqiao	1709	3607	2009	172
未央区	Weiyang	11552	5021	1538	435
阎良区	Yanliang	8128	6435	1687	3605
临潼区	Lintong	6144	12942	4196	399
长安区	Chang'an	8712	17616	4178	358
蓝田县	Lantian	3730	12867	5341	1497
周至县	Zhouzhi	5074	12412	7137	332
户　县	Huxian	6425	12425	5352	2854
高陵县	Gaoling	6139	11213	3784	433

continued

(10 000 yuan)

粮油物资储备管理等事务支出 Material Reserves Management Affairs Spending	金融监管支出 Expenditure for Financial Supervision	地震灾后恢复重建支出 Expenditure for Post-earthquake Reconstruction	国债还本付息支出 Expenditure for National Debt and Interst	其他支出 Other Expenditure	基金支出 Fund expenditure
41784	**39471**	**4336**	**328**	**133316**	**1432342**
26325	**39447**	**2839**	**328**	**112469**	**1352577**
15459	**24**	**1497**		**20847**	**79765**
359				2115	281
377				3244	130
258		18		1438	792
470				3646	1067
904				591	3585
786				185	41
969		10		356	3855
2356				1152	12043
3058				1098	15109
1671	24			1186	6209
1332		70		3153	2201
1459		1359		775	3569
1460		40		1908	30883

主要统计指标解释

财政收入 指国家财政参与社会产品分配所取得的收入，是实现国家职能的财力保证。财政收入所包括的内容几经变化，目前主要包括:

（1）各项税收:包括增值税、营业税、消费税、土地增值税、城市维护建设税、资源税、城市土地使用税、印花税、个人所得税、企业所得税、关税、农牧业税和耕地占用税等。

（2）专项收入:包括征收排污费收入、征收城市水资源费收入、教育费附加收入等。

（3）其他收入:包括基本建设贷款归还收入、基本建设收入、捐赠收入等。

（4）国有企业亏损补贴:这项为负收入，冲减财政收入。

财政支出 国家财政将筹集起来的资金进行分配使用，以满足经济建设和各项事业的需要，主要包括:

（1）基本建设支出:指按国家有关规定，属于基本建设范围内的基本建设有偿使用、拨款、资本金支出以及经国家批准对专项和政策性基建投资贷款，在部门的基建投资额中统筹支付的贴息支出。

（2）企业挖潜改造资金:指国家预算内拨给的用于企业挖潜、革新和改造方面的资金。包括各部门企业挖潜改造资金和企业挖潜改造贷款资金，为农业服务的县办“五小”企业技术改造补助，挖潜改造贷款利息支出。

（3）地质勘探费用:指国家预算用于地质勘探单位的勘探工作费用，包括地质勘探管理机构及其事业单位经费、地质勘探经费。

（4）科技三项费用:指国家预算用于科技支出的费用，包括新产品试制费、中间试验费、重要科学研究补助费。

（5）支援农村生产支出:指国家财政支援农村集体（户）各项生产的支出。包括对农村举办的小型农田水利和打井、喷灌等的补助费，对农村水土保持措施的补助费，对农村举办的小水电站的补助费，特大抗旱的补助费，农村开荒补助费，扶持乡镇企业资金，农村农技推广和植保补助费，农村草场和畜禽保护补助费，农村造林和林木保护补助费，农村水产补助费，发展粮食生产专项资金。

（6）农林水利气象等部门的事业费用:指国家财政用于农垦、农场、农业、畜牧、农机、林业、森工、水利、水产、气象、乡镇企业的技术推广、良种推广（示范）、动植物（畜禽、森林）保护、水质监测、勘探设计、资源调查、干部训练等项费用，园艺特产场补助费，中等专业学校经费，飞播牧草试验补助费，营林机构、气象机构经费，渔政费以及农业管理事业费等。

（7）工业交通商业等部门的事业费:指国家预算支付给工交商各部门用于事业发展的经费，包括勘探设计费、中等专业学校经费、技术学校经费、干部训练费。

（8）文教科学卫生事业费:指国家预算用于文化、出版、文物、教育、卫生、中医、公费医疗、体育、档案、地震、海洋、通讯、电影电视、计划生育、党政群干部训练、自然科学、社会科学、科协等项事业的经费支出和高技术研究专项经费。主要包括工资、补助工资、福利费、离退休费、助学金、公务费、设备购置费、修缮费、业务费、差额补助费。

（9）抚恤和社会福利救济费:指国家预算用于抚恤和社会福利救济事业的经费。包括由民政部门开支的烈士家属和牺牲病残人员家属的一次性、定期抚恤金，革命伤残人员的抚恤金，各种伤残补助费，烈军属、复员退伍军人生活补助费，退伍军人安置费，优抚事业单位经费，烈士纪念建筑物管理、维修费，自然灾害救济事业费和特大自然灾害灾后重建补助费等。

（10）国防支出:指国家预算用于国防建设和保卫国家安全的支出，包括国防费、国防科研事业费、民兵建设以及专项工程支出等。

（11）行政管理费:包括行政管理支出，党派团体补助支出，外交支出，公安安全支出，司法支出，法院支出，检察院支出和公检法办案费用补助。

（12）价格补贴支出:指经国家批准，由国家财政拨给的政策性补贴支出。主要包括粮食加价款，粮、棉、油差价补贴，棉花收购价外奖励款，副食品风险基金，市镇居民的肉食价格补贴，平抑市价肉食、蔬菜差价补贴等以及经国家批准的教材课本、报刊新闻纸等价格补贴。

中央财政收入和地方财政收入 指按财政体制划分的中央本级收入和地方本级收入。1994年分税制财政体制以后，属于中央财政的收入包括关税、海关代征消费税和增值税，消费税，中央企业所得税，地方银行和外资银行及非银行金融企业所得税，铁道、银行总行、保险总公司等集中缴纳的营业税、所得税、利润和城市维护建设税，增值税的75%部分，证券交易税（印花税）50%部分和海洋石油资源税。属于地方财政的收入包括营业税，地方企业所得税，个人所得税，城镇土地使用税，固定资产投资方向调节税，城镇维护建设税，房产税，车船使用税，印花税，屠宰税，农牧业税，农业特产税，耕地占用税，契税，增值税25%部分，证券交易税（印花税）50%部分和除海洋石油资源税以外的其他资源税。

中央财政支出和地方财政支出 指根据政府在经济和社会活动中的不同职责，划分中央和地方政府的责权，按照政府的责权划分确定的支出。中央财政支出包括国防支出，武装警察部队支出，中央级行政管理费和各项事业费，重点建设支出以及中央政府调整国民经济结构、协调地区发展、实施宏观调控的支出。地方财政支出主要包括地方行政管理和各项事业费，地方统筹的基本建设、技术改造支出，支援农村生产支出，城市维护和建设经费，价格补贴支出等。

Explanatory Notes on Main Statistical Indicators

Government Revenue refers to the revenue of the government finance by means of participating in the distribution of the social products, which is the financial resources for ensuring the government to function. The contents of government revenue have been changed several times. Now it includes the following main items:

(1) Various tax revenues, including value added tax, business tax, consumption tax, land value added tax, tax on city maintenance and construction, resources tax, tax on use of urban land, stamp tax, personal income tax, enterprise income tax, tariff, tax on agriculture and animal husbandry and tax on occupancy of cultivated land, etc.

(2) Special revenues, including revenue collected from imposing fee on sewage treatment, revenue collected from imposing fee on urban water resources, and extra-charges for education, etc.

(3) Other revenues, including revenue from the repayment of capital construction loan, revenue from capital construction projects, and donations and grants.

(4) Planned subsidies for the losses of the state-owned enterprises. This is an item of negative revenue, used to eat up part of the government revenue.

Government Expenditure refers to the distribution and use of the funds the government finance has raised, so as to meet the needs of economic construction and various causes. It includes the following main items:

(1) Expenditure for capital construction: It refers to the non-gratuitous use and appropriation of funds for capital construction in the range of capital construction, outlay of capital as well as the loans on capital construction approved by the government for special purpose or policy purpose and the expenditure with discount paid in an overall way within the amount of the funds appropriated to the departments for capital construction.

(2) Innovation funds of the enterprises: They refer to the funds appropriated from the government budget for the enterprises to tap the latent power, upgrade the technology and carry out innovation, including the innovation fund of the departments, loan of the enterprises for innovation, subsidies on the innovation of the small fertilizer plant, small cement plant, small coal mines, small machinery plant and small steel plant, the expenditure of interest for the loan for innovation.

(3) Geological prospecting expenses: They refer to the expenses appropriated from the government budget to the geological prospecting units for the expenditure of the prospecting work, including the expenditures of the administrative agencies for geological prospecting and their institutional units as well as the geological prospecting expenditure.

(4) expenditures for science and technology promotion: They refer to the expenses appropriated from the government budget for the scientific and technological expenditure, including new products development expenditure, expenditure for intermediate trial and subsidies on important scientific researches.

(5) Expenditure for supporting rural production: It refers to the expenditures appropriated from the government budget for supporting the various expenditures of the rural collective units or households for production, including the subsidies to the small water conservancy projects and well drilling, sprinkling irrigation projects run by the villages; subsidies on the rural water and soil conserving measures; subsidies to the small power stations run by the villages; subsidies to the expenditure for fighting against particularly severe draughts; subsidies on the rural waste land exclamation; fund for supporting the township enterprises; subsidies to the expenditure for popularization of the agricultural technologies and plant protection in the rural areas; subsidies to the expenditure for the protection of grasslands and cattle and fowls; subsidies on afforestation and forest protection in rural areas; subsidies on the rural aquatic products industry; special fund for developing grain production.

(6) Operating expenses of the departments of farming, forestry, water conservancy and meteorology etc.: They refer to the expenses appropriated from the government budget for the expenditures of agricultural exclamation, farms, agriculture, animal husbandry, agricultural machinery, forestry, timber industry, water conservancy, aquatic products industry, meteorology, technology popularization in township enterprises, popularization (demonstration) of improved varieties, plant (cattle and fowls, forest) protection, water quality monitoring, prospecting and designing, resources investigation, cadres training, subsidies to horticulture gardens, expenditure of specialized secondary schools, subsidies on the experiments of sowing herbage seeds by flights, expenditures of afforestation agencies and

meteorology agencies, expenses for fishery administration and operating expenses for agricultural administration, etc.

(7) Operating expenses of the departments of industry, transport and commerce: They refer to the expenses appropriated from the government budget to the departments of industry, transport and commerce for the expenditure of business development, including expenses for prospecting and designing, expenditures of specialized secondary schools, expenditures of the technical training schools and expenditures for cadres training, etc.

(8) Operating expenses of the departments of culture, education, science and public health: They refer to the expenses appropriated from the government budget for the expenditures of the causes of culture, publication, cultural relics, education, public health, traditional Chinese medical science, free medical services, sports, archives, earthquake, ocean, communications, broadcasting, film and television, family planning; expenditure for training of cadres of government, party and mass organization; expenditures for natural sciences, social sciences, associations for science and technology and the special expenditure for the high-tech researches. They include mainly wages, extra wages, welfare funds, pension for the retirees, stipend, expenses for official business, expenses for equipment purchases, expenses for repairs, business expenses and subsidies to the units which are unable to support their expenditures by their own earnings.

(9) Pension for the disabled or for the families of the bereaved and relief funds for social welfare: They refer to the funds appropriated from the government budget for the expenditures of pension for the disabled or for the families of the bereaved and relief funds for social welfare, including the lump-sum or regular pension paid by the departments of civil affairs to the members of martyrs families and families of those who died for the public interest, pension to the revolutionary disabled, subsidies for permanent disability of various kinds, subsidies to the military martyrs dependents and the demobilized servicemen, expenditure for settling down the demobilized servicemen, operating expenses of the consoling institutions, expenses for management and repair of the commemorative buildings for the martyrs, the expenses managed by the departments of civil affairs for the retirees and those who have quitted their work, expenses for social relief in rural and urban areas, operating expenses for providing relief to the areas of natural calamity and subsidies on the reconstruction after the particularly severe natural calamities, etc.

(10) Expenditures for national defence: They refer to the funds appropriated from the government budget for the expenditures for building up national defence and safeguarding national security, including expenses of national defence, expenses of scientific researches on national defence, expenses for building up peoples militia and expenditure for special projects, etc.

(11) Administrative expenses: They include expenditure for administration, subsidies to the parties and mass organizations, diplomatic expenditure, expenditure for public security, judicial expenditure, law court expenditure, procuratorial expenditure and subsidies to the expenses for treating the cases by the public security departments, procuratorial organs and law courts.

(12) Expenditure for price subsidies: It refers to the expenditure appropriated, with the approval of the government, from the government budget for the policy subsidies to price adjustment, including the fund for the increase of grain prices, the subsidies to the difference between the selling prices and purchasing prices of grains, cotton and edible oil, awards in addition to the purchasing prices of cotton, risk fund for non-staple food, subsidies on the prices of meat and meat products, subsidies on the price difference for curbing the high market prices of meat, meat products and vegetables and the subsidies approved by the government on the prices of textbooks and newsprint of newspapers and periodicals.

Revenue of the central government and revenue of the local governments: In accordance with the classification of the structure of the government finance in 1994 on the basis of the classification of channels for collection of tax revenues, the revenue of the central government and the revenue of the local governments have different coverage. The revenue of the central government includes tariff, consumption tax and value added tax levied by the customs, consumption tax, income tax of the enterprises subordinate to the central government, income taxes of the local banks, foreign-funded banks and non-bank financial institutions, business tax, income tax and profits of railways, head offices of banks, head office of insurance company , which are handed over to the government in a centralized way, tax on city maintenance and construction, 75% of the value added tax, tax on ocean petroleum resources, 50% of the tax on stock dealing (stamp tax). The revenue of the local governments includes business tax, income tax of the enterprises subordinate to the local government, personal income tax, tax on the use of urban land, tax on the adjustment of the investment in fixed assets, tax on town maintenance and construction, tax on real estates, tax on the use of vehicles and ships, stamp tax, slaughter tax, tax on agriculture and animalhusbandry, tax on special agricultural products, tax on the occupancy of cultivated land, contract tax, 25% of the husbandry, tax on special agricultural products, tax on the occupancy of cultivated land, contract tax, 25% of the value added tax, 50% of the tax on stock dealing (stamp tax) and tax on resources other than the ocean petroleum resources.

Expenditure of the central government and expenditure of the local governments: according to the different functions of the central government and local governments in the economic and social activities, the rights of affairs administration are classified between the central government and local governments; and the classification of the expenditure between the central government and local governments are made on the basis of the classification of the rights of affairs administration between them. The expenditure of the central government includes the expenditure for national defence, expenditure for armed police forces, the administrative expenses and various operating expenses at the level of central government, expenditure for key projects and the expenditure of the central government for adjusting the national economic structure, coordinating the development among different regions and exercising the macro-economic regulation and control. The expenditure of the local governments includes mainly the administrative expenses and various operating expenses at the level of local governments, the expenditure for capital construction and technological innovation with the funds raised by the local government, expenditure for supporting rural production, expenditure for city maintenance and construction and expenditure for price subsidies, etc.

6 物价指数

PRICE INDICES

资料整理：高小琴　张元振　周　文　陈续慧　胡旭鹏　陆　兴
Data management:Gao Xiaoqin　Zhang Yuanzhen　Zhou Wen　Chen Xuhui　Hu Xupeng　Lu Xing

第六部分　物价指数

一、简要说明

本章资料主要包括居民消费、零售、工业产品出厂、主要原材料购进、土地交易、房地产销售、租赁以及固定资产投资和建筑安装工程等价格指数，由国家统计局西安调查队提供。

二、主要指标

商品零售价格总指数（上年=100）	99.5	比上年下降 5.9个百分点
居民消费价格总指数（上年=100）	99.7	比上年下降 6.3个百分点

6 PRICE INDICES

Ⅰ.Brief Introduction

This chapter consists primarily of data on price indices of residents consumption, retail, industrial products dispatching sales, primary raw material purchasing, land deal, real estate selling, leasing, fixed asset investment and construction installation projects, provided by Fixed Asset Investment Division of the NBS Survey Office in Xi'an.

Ⅱ.Major Indicators

		Increase over Preceding Year
Retail Price Index(the price Preceding year=100)	99.5	-5.9 percentage points
Consumer Price Index(the price Preceding year=100)	99.7	-6.3 percentage points

6-1 主要年份各种价格指数

Price Indices in Representative Years

(以上年价格为100) (the price of Preceding year=100)

年 份 Year	居民消费价格指数 Consumer Price Index	商品零售价格指数 Retail Price Index	工业品出厂价格指数 Producer Price Index for Manufactured Goods	原材料，燃料，动力购进价格指数 Purchasing Price Index for Raw Material, Fuel and Power	固定资产投资价格指数 Price Index for Investment in Fixed Assets
1980	108.7	109.3			
1981	102.4	102.7			
1982	100.9	101.0			
1983	102.6	102.0			
1984	104.7	104.8			
1985	109.7	109.3			
1986	108.5	107.4			
1987	110.6	111.4			
1988	122.8	123.2			
1989	118.3	117.8			
1990	102.5	100.9			
1991	109.4	108.3			
1992	112.2	112.4			
1993	117.2	112.8	102.5	104.3	
1994	128.5	126.2	132.2	115.0	
1995	117.0	114.6	110.8	113.1	
1996	110.9	107.9	100.7	103.8	
1997	106.0	101.5	98.6	102.5	
1998	97.9	95.5	94.4	97.5	
1999	96.8	97.4	97.5	96.9	100.8
2000	100.2	98.7	99.4	102.4	102.1
2001	99.9	98.9	99.3	101.0	101.3
2002	98.6	98.5	98.2	98.4	101.2
2003	100.5	100.0	101.5	105.3	102.4
2004	102.3	101.9	102.7	110.4	103.3
2005	100.3	99.7	103.9	109.6	102.4
2006	101.6	101.5	103.2	106.1	102.0
2007	104.7	103.7	101.9	106.2	103.5
2008	106.0	105.4	103.7	108.5	110.5
2009	99.7	99.5	99.9	100.7	97.9

6-2 居民消费价格指数（2009年）

Residents Consumer Price Indices（2009）

(以上年价格为100) (the price of Preceding year=100)

类　　别	Item	2009
居民消费价格总指数	**Consumer Price Index**	**99.7**
非食品价格指数	Non-foodstuff Price Index	98.4
服务项目价格指数	Price Index of Service	97.1
工业品价格指数	Ex-factory Price Indices of Industrial Products	99.3
扣除食品和能源价格指数	Price Index with Food and Energy Excluded	98.5
扣除鲜菜鲜果总指数	Price Index With Fresh Vegetables and Fruits Excluded	98.5
消费品价格指数	Price Index of Consumer Goods	100.6
一、食品	**Food**	**102.3**
1.粮食	Grain	102.9
2.淀粉	Starches and Tubers	103.4
3.干豆类及豆制品	Beans and Bean Products	101.9
4.油脂	Oil or Fat	76.5
5.肉禽及其制品	Meat,Poultry and Processed Products	90.2
6.蛋	Eggs	104.7
7.水产品	Aquatic Products	104.5
8.菜	Vegetables	121.1
9.调味品	Flavouring	102.9
10.糖	Carbohydrate	105.4
11.茶及饮料	Tea and Beverages	100.3
12.干鲜瓜果	Dried and Fresh Melons and Fruits	112.6
13.糕点饼干面包	Cake,Biscuit and Bread	101.7
14.液体乳及乳制品	Milk and Its Product	97.1
15.在外用膳食品	Dining Out	102.8
16.其他食品及食品加工服务	Other Food and Manufacturing Services	100.8
二、烟酒及用品	**Tobacco,Liquor and Articles**	**101.6**
1.烟草	Tobacco	101.1
2.酒	Liquor	102.5
3.吸烟、饮酒用品	Articles for Smoking and Drinking	100.0
三、衣着	**Clothing**	**101.3**
1.服装	Garments	98.1
2.衣着材料	Clothing Material	103.5
3.鞋袜帽	Footgear and Hats	109.9
4.衣着加工服务费	Clothing Manufacturing Services	101.2

6-2 续表 continued

(以上年价格为100) (the price of Preceding year=100)

类别	Item	2009
四、家庭设备用品及维修服务	**Household facilities,Articles and Services**	**99.4**
1.耐用消费品	Durable Consumer Goods	96.2
2.室内装饰品	Interior Decorations	95.3
3.床上用品	Bed Articles	97.8
4.家庭日用杂品	Daily Use Household Articles	104.6
5.家庭服务及加工维修服务	Household Service and Maintenance Renovation	103.6
五、医疗保健和个人用品	**Health Care and Personal Articles**	**100.5**
1.医疗保健	Health Care	101.3
（1）医疗器具及用品	Medical Instrument Articles	100.8
（2）中药材及中成药	Traditional Chinese Medicine	102.8
（3）西药	Western Medicine	102.0
（4）保健器具及用品	Health Care Appliances and Articles	100.3
（5）医疗保健服务	Health Care Services	100.0
2.个人用品及服务	Personal Articles and Services	98.5
六、交通和通信	**Transportation and Communication**	**97.3**
1.交通	Transportation	98.3
（1）交通工具	Transportation Facility	97.8
（2）车用燃料及零配件	Fuels and Parts	88.4
（3）车辆使用及维修费	Fees for Vehicles Use and Maintenance	103.8
（4）市区公共交通费	Incity Traffic Fare	100.0
（5）城市间交通费	Intercity Traffic Fare	100.2
2.通信	Communication	96.2
（1）通信工具	Telecommunication Facility	73.6
（2）通信服务	Telecommunication Service	100.0
七、娱乐教育文化用品及服务	**Recreation,Education and Culture Articles**	**97.8**
1.文娱用耐用消费品及服务	Durable Consumer Goods for Cultural and Recreational Use and Services	88.6
2.教育	Education	98.4
3.文化娱乐	Cultural and Recreational Articles	103.0
4.旅游及外出	Touring and Outing	95.3
八、居住	**Residence**	**95.0**
1.建房及装修材料	Building and Building Decoration Materials	100.7
2.租房	Renting	101.7
3.自有住房	Private Housing	80.8
4.水、电、燃料	Water, Electricity and Fuels	99.0

6-3 商品零售价格指数（2009年）

Retail Price Indices（2009）

(以上年价格为100) (the price of Preceding year=100)

类 别	Item	2009
商品零售价格总指数	**Retail Price Indices**	**99.5**
一、食品类	**Food**	**102.7**
1.粮食及薯类	Grain	102.8
2.淀粉	Starches and Tubers	103.4
3.干豆类及豆制品	Beans and Bean Products	100.8
4.油 脂	Oil or Fat	76.6
5.肉禽及其制品	Meat,Poultry and Processed Products	91.2
6.蛋	Eggs	104.7
7.水产品	Aquatic Products	104.6
8.菜	Vegetables	120.6
9.调味品	Flavouring	102.7
10.糖	Carbohydrate	105.1
11.干鲜瓜果	Dried and Fresh Melons and Fruits	112.0
12.糕点饼干面包	Cake,Biscuit and Bread	101.6
13.奶及奶制品	Milk and Its Product	97.5
14.在外用膳食品	Dining Out	102.8
15.其它食品	Other Food and Manufacturing Services	100.8
二、饮料、烟酒	**Beverages,Tobacco and Liquor**	**101.1**
1.茶及饮料	Tea and Beverages	101.2
2.烟草	Tobacco	100.4
3.酒	Liquor	102.2
三、服装、鞋帽类	**Garments,Shoes and Hats**	**101.3**
1.服装	Garments	98.4
2.鞋袜帽	Footgear and Hats	109.5
四、纺织品类	**Textiles**	**97.2**
1.衣着材料	Cotton Cloth	103.5
2.床上用品	Blend Cloth	96.9
五、家用电器及音像器材	**Household Appliances,Music and Video Equipment**	**90.4**
1.家庭设备	Household facility	96.6
2.文娱用耐用消费品	Durable Consumer Goods on Cultural and Recreational Use	84.5
3.音像器材	Music and Video Equipment	99.3
六、文化办公用品	**Cultural and Office Appliances**	**98.5**

6-3 续表 continued

（以上年价格为100） (the price of Preceding year=100)

类　　别	Item	2009
七、日用品	**Articles for Daily Use**	**105.6**
1.日用百货	General Merchandise for Daily Use	99.8
2.日用杂品	Miscellaneous for Daily Use	101.6
3.洗涤用品	Daily Use Articles For Washing	117.7
4.其它日用品	Other Daily Articles	100.8
八、体育娱乐用品	**Sports and Recreation Articles**	**91.8**
1.体育用品	Sports Goods	102.5
2.娱乐用品	Receration Goods	87.4
九、交通、通信用品	**Transportation and Communication Goods**	**94.3**
1.交通运输机械	Transportation Machinery	97.9
2.通讯器材	Communication Machinery	77.7
十、家具	**Furniture**	**95.9**
十一、化妆品类	**Cosmetics**	**101.8**
十二、金银珠宝类	**Gold,Silver and Jewelry**	**85.1**
十三、中西药品及医疗保健用品类	**Traditional Chinese and Western Medicines And Health Care Articles**	**101.8**
1.医疗器具及用品	Medical Apparatus and Article	100.8
2.中药材及中成药	Traditional Chinese Medicinal Materials and Medicines Western Medicines	102.8
3.西药	Western Medicine	102.0
4.保健器具及用品	Health Care Apparatus and Article	100.3
十四、书报杂志及电子出版物	**Books,Newspapers,Magazines and Electronic Publications**	**105.8**
1.教材及参考书	Teaching Materials and Reference Books	104.8
2.书报杂志	Books, Newspapers and Magazines	110.2
3.电子音像制品	Electronic Audio-video Products	100.0
十五、燃料类	**Fuel**	**94.3**
1.煤炭及制品类	Coal and Its Products	118.0
2.石油及制品类	Oil and Its Products	91.5
十六、建筑材料及五金电料	**Building Materials and Hardware**	**99.9**
1.建筑装潢材料	Building Decoration Materials	100.1
2.五金电料	Hardware	99.6

6-4 主要年份工业产品出厂价格指数

（上年价格=100）

类　别	Classify	1996	1997	1998	1999
全部工业品	**Total Industry Products**	**100.71**	**98.63**	**94.37**	**97.49**
按轻重工业分	Grouped by Light Industry and Heavy Industry				
轻工业	Light Industry	100.93	98.17	91.11	95.87
以农产品为原料	Using Farm Products as Raw Materials	101.60	99.21	89.47	95.19
以非农产品为原料	Using Non-farm Products as Raw Materials	98.11	96.79	93.41	96.97
重工业	Heavy Industry	100.20	98.98	97.30	98.92
采掘工业	Mining and Quarrying Industry			104.14	101.52
原料工业	Raw Materials Industry	99.44	100.96	100.70	102.27
加工工业	Processing Industry	101.49	97.86	95.63	98.00
按用途分	Grouped by Use				
生产资料	Means of Production	100.35	99.58	96.57	98.28
采掘工业	Mining & Quarrying Industry			104.14	101.52
原料工业	Raw Materials Industry	99.41	100.89	100.57	100.20
加工工业	Processing Industry	101.94	98.87	94.67	97.59
生活资料	Consumer Goods	100.89	97.03	91.36	96.46
（1）食品	Food	107.95	108.21	97.75	95.79
（2）衣着	Clothing	98.57	92.96	83.88	95.19
（3）一般日用品	Articles for Daily Use	97.29	91.63	95.06	97.62
（4）耐用消费品	Durable Consumer Goods	92.59	99.65	95.41	98.02
按工业部门分	Grouped by Industrial Sector				
1.冶金工业	Metallurgical Industry	98.63	99.17	97.50	91.20
2.电力工业	Power Industry		111.29	111.23	109.33
3.煤炭及炼焦工业	Coal and Coking Industry	102.09	98.87	98.48	96.30
4.石油工业	Petroleum Industry				107.09
5.化学工业	Chemical Industry	101.46	91.77	92.93	96.61
6.机械工业	Machine Manufacturing Industry	99.47	98.76	94.59	98.09
7.建筑材料工业	Building Materials Industry	94.49	98.19	99.30	96.71
8.森林工业	Timber Industry	98.94	107.55	104.47	97.94
9.食品工业	Food Industry	108.47	106.80	95.27	95.45
10.纺织工业	Textiles Industry	95.68	94.32	82.58	93.65
11.缝纫工业	Tailoring Industry		100.14	97.29	99.10
12.皮革工业	Leather Industry	133.81	91.18	96.78	98.00
13.造纸工业	Paper Industry	98.82			95.33
14.文教艺术用品工业	Cultural,Educational & Handicrafts Articles	100.87			96.65
15.其他工业	Other Industry	100.00	109.51	109.22	98.89

Producer Price Index for Manufactured in Representative Years

(the price of Preceding year=100)

2000	2001	2002	2003	2004	2005	2006	2007	2008	2009
99.43	**99.30**	**98.20**	**101.45**	**102.67**	**103.89**	**103.22**	**101.90**	**103.72**	**99.85**
97.82	99.60	98.40	101.27	103.40	99.93	100.16	101.80	103.68	100.64
99.18	99.00	98.40	104.45	108.67	97.30	100.06	103.32	106.02	98.91
95.45	100.60	98.60	99.89	100.80	101.19	100.22	100.81	102.12	101.79
100.75	99.20	98.20	101.64	101.92	107.86	105.52	101.92	103.77	99.32
97.48	94.80	101.30	103.38	140.50	107.88	100.63	111.56	122.27	89.99
107.74	101.10	101.30	111.18	108.95	114.23	111.77	104.88	110.75	99.52
98.36	98.50	97.70	100.09	100.56	106.66	104.19	101.19	101.94	99.35
100.50	99.10	98.00	101.84	102.74	105.34	104.19	101.27	103.38	99.33
97.48	94.80	101.30	103.38	140.50	107.88	100.63	111.56	122.27	89.99
106.38	101.10	101.00	108.13	106.62	111.27	111.56	104.76	110.17	99.73
98.67	98.50	97.40	100.89	102.03	104.34	102.98	100.62	102.00	99.31
97.27	99.90	99.10	100.50	102.54	100.36	100.36	103.54	104.74	101.43
94.40	99.60	101.20	101.02	103.55	100.31	100.43	105.31	106.57	100.26
101.56	99.40	100.80	99.43	102.68	101.97	103.34	104.56	105.05	102.68
96.89	101.90	97.90	101.22	101.17	101.29	100.79	100.09	102.67	102.64
95.93	97.00	98.10	97.18	98.30	99.07	99.39	100.73	100.74	103.89
98.20	97.20	98.70	103.77	107.12	103.91	106.47	103.20	104.77	91.98
109.63	102.40	100.00	103.19	104.05	110.55	107.85	105.53	109.95	108.97
100.54	110.30	106.70	136.75	131.38	97.06	95.36	106.83	104.80	101.69
134.24	96.60	100.70	118.63	110.52	121.74	117.61	104.82	115.64	96.73
96.69	100.50	99.20	100.16	100.80	103.23	100.77	101.10	104.11	102.60
98.02	98.30	97.60	99.83	100.61	104.94	103.43	100.98	101.65	99.93
98.51	100.60	99.60	99.69	99.95	98.61	98.88	98.85	101.75	101.91
98.90	98.10	98.90	100.08	100.21	101.63	101.61	101.10	101.10	101.10
94.32	99.80	101.10	102.78	107.52	98.27	99.00	106.10	109.29	98.33
103.35	97.50	94.90	117.34	119.08	89.92	102.42	98.38	99.66	97.51
103.50	100.00	101.10	100.22	103.57	100.84	103.52	104.64	105.10	102.61
99.20	101.00	101.80	98.68	99.59	101.16	100.00	99.04	99.57	99.68
96.68	102.30	95.00	96.91	100.15	101.16	100.04	100.13	104.46	98.43
96.36	101.10	103.40	97.52	96.47	98.10	100.08	99.08	99.15	102.24
104.84	107.10	99.40	103.26	105.02	103.42	105.65	111.37	104.31	99.66

6-5 主要年份主要原材料、燃料、动力购进价格指数

Purchase Price Indices of Major Raw Materials,Fuels and Power in Representative Years

(上年价格=100) (the price of Preceding year=100)

类别	Item	2000	2001	2002	2003	2004
全部原材料	**Total of Raw Materials**	**102.38**	**101.00**	**98.40**	**105.29**	**110.39**
(一)燃料、动力类	Fuel and Power	105.01	101.80	100.90	105.65	109.36
(二)黑色金属材料类	Ferrous Metals	102.69	102.10	98.50	107.43	117.38
#钢材	Steel	103.35	102.40	97.90	105.97	114.76
(三)有色金属材料和电线类	NonFerrous Metals and Electric Wires	105.17	95.50	96.80	105.80	114.08
(四)化工原料类	Raw Chemical Materials	104.55	102.50	97.90	102.43	106.30
(五)木材及纸浆类	Timber and Paper Pulp	101.21	102.80	99.40	101.19	100.27
(六)建筑材料及非金属矿类	Building Materials and Non-metal ores	100.28	99.70	98.60	99.62	110.42
(七)其它工业原材料及半成品类	Other Industrial Raw Materials and Semi-Products	98.75	100.80	98.90	102.50	111.17
(八)农副产品类	Agricultural Products	100.42	102.80	98.20	113.72	112.74
(九)纺织原料类	Textile Materials	98.03	96.80	90.60	103.44	103.88

6-5 续表 continued

(上年价格=100) (the price of Preceding year=100)

类别	Item	2005	2006	2007	2008	2009
全部原材料	**Total of Raw Materials**	**109.62**	**106.08**	**106.17**	**108.50**	**100.74**
(一)燃料、动力类	Fuels and Power	123.50	112.55	106.96	109.83	105.08
(二)黑色金属材料类	Ferrous Metals	107.56	99.17	104.78	111.27	99.17
#钢材	Steel	107.46	98.48	104.90	111.65	98.71
(三)有色金属材料和电线类	Non-Ferrous Metals and Electric Wires	107.82	116.46	110.71	99.13	93.86
(四)化工原料类	Raw Chemical Materials	106.06	101.57	105.59	111.36	94.96
(五)木材及纸浆类	Timber and Paper Pulp	108.18	111.66	105.90	106.50	102.60
(六)建筑材料及非金属矿类	Building Materials and Non-metal ores	99.27	100.69	104.01	104.82	106.84
(七)其它工业原材料及半成品类	Other Industrial Raw Materials and Semi-Products	106.09	104.34	108.84	110.62	101.41
(八)农副产品类	Agricultural and Sideline Products	100.89	107.19	107.17	108.87	99.57
(九)纺织原料类	Textile Raw Materials	97.62	101.53	100.52	99.81	97.58

6-6 土地交易价格指数（2009年）

Transactions Price Indices of Land（2009）

(上年价格=100) (the price of Preceding year=100)

项　　目	Item	2009
土地交易总计	**Transactions Price Indices of Land**	**101.2**
一、居住用地	**Land for Residential Building Use**	**101.5**
（一）经济适用房用地	Economically Affordable Housing	
（二）商品住宅用地	Commercialized Housing	101.5
1.普通住宅用地	Luxury Residential Buildings	101.5
2.高档住宅用地	General Residential Buildings	100.1
二、工业用地	**Land for Industry and Storage Use**	**100.6**
三、商业用地	**Land for Business,Tourism and Entertainment**	**100.9**
四、其他用地	**Land for Other Uses**	**101.4**

6-7 房屋销售价格指数（2009年）

Selling Price Indices of Real Estate（2009）

(上年价格=100) (the price of Preceding year=100)

项　　目	Item	2009
房屋销售总计	**Selling Price Indices of Houses**	**100.5**
一、商品房	**Newly Commercial Houses**	**100.3**
（一）住宅	Residential Buildings	99.9
按房屋类型分	By Type of Housing	
1.经济适用房	Economically Affordable Housing	100.4
2.商品住宅	Commercialized Houses	99.8
（1）普通住宅	General Residential Buildings	99.8
①多层住宅	Multi-storey Buildings	100.9
②高层住宅	High-layer Buildings	99.9
③其他住宅	Others Buildings	
（2）高档住宅	Luxury Residential Buildings	99.8
①别墅	Villas	100.5
②高档公寓	High-grade Apartment	100.1
按套型分	By Dwelling Size Classification	
#90平方米以下	#90 Square Meters Below	104.0
（二）非住宅	Non-Residential Buildings	103.0
1.办公楼	Office Buildings	102.3
2.商业营业用房	Houses for Business Use	104.4
3.其他用房	Others	101.0
二、二手房	**Second-hand Houses**	**101.6**
（一）住宅	Residential Buildings	101.9
1.普通住宅	General Residential Buildings	102.0
（1）多层住宅	Multi-storey Buildings	100.6
（2）高层住宅	High-layer Buildings	102.8
（3）其他住宅	Others Buildings	103.9
2.高档住宅	High-Rise Buildings	101.3
（1）别墅	Villas	
（2）)高档公寓	High-grade Apartment	101.3
（二）非住宅	Non-Residential Buildings	100.3

6-8 房屋租赁价格指数（2009年）

Renting Price Indices of Houses（2009）

(上年价格=100) (the price of Preceding year=100)

项　　目	Item	2009
房屋租赁价格指数	**Renting Price Indices of Houses**	**100.3**
一、住　宅	**Residential Buildings**	**102.1**
（一）经济适用房	Economical Affordable Housing	100.0
（二）廉租房	Tenement House	100.0
（三）商品住宅	Commercialized Residential Buildings	102.1
1.普通住宅	General Residential Buildings	102.2
2.高档住宅	Luxury Residential Buildings	101.8
（1）别墅	Villas	
（2）高档公寓	High-grade Apartment	**101.8**
二、非住宅	**Non-residential Buildings**	98.9
（一）办公楼	Office Buildings	99.7
（二）商业营业用房	Commercial Business Buildings	98.5
（三）其他	Others Buildings	100.0

6-9 主要年份固定资产投资价格指数

Price Indices for Investment in Fixed Assets in Representative Years

(上年价格=100) (the price of Preceding year=100)

项　　目	Item	2000	2003	2004	2005	2006	2007	2008	2009
固定资产投资价格指数	**Price Indices for Investment in Fixed Assets**	**102.1**	**102.4**	**103.3**	**102.4**	**102.0**	**103.5**	**110.5**	**97.9**
建筑安装、装饰工程	Construction,Installation and decoration	103.9	103.3	104.6	102.3	102.6	104.9	114.9	97.1
设备、工器具购置	Purchase of Equipment and Instruments	97.9	99.9	100.5	104.5	100.8	100.7	101.0	98.6
其他费用	Others	100.0	101.5	100.6	100.5	100.5	100.6	101.9	100.9

6-10 主要年份建筑安装工程价格指数

Price Indecies of Construction and Installation in Representative Years

(上年价格=100) (the price of Preceding year=100)

项　　目	Item	2000	2003	2004	2005	2006	2007	2008	2009
建筑安装工程价格指数	**Expenditure of Construction and Installation**	**103.9**	**103.3**	**104.6**	**102.3**	**102.6**	**104.9**	**114.9**	**97.1**
#人工费	Labor-hour Expense	103.6	105.8	105.2	106.9	108.3	109.1	114.5	110.6
材料费	Material Expense	104.4	103.6	105.1	101.4	101.1	104.3	117.6	94.1
机械使用费	Machinery use Expense	103.9	100.8	102.8	102.5	104.5	104.5	106.5	99.3

主要统计指标解释

商品零售价格指数 是反映一定时期内城乡商品零售价格变动趋势的一种经济指数。零售物价的调整变动直接影响到城乡居民的生活支出和国家的财政收入，影响居民购买力和市场供需平衡，影响消费与积累的比例。因此，计算零售价格指数，可以从一个侧面对上述经济活动进行观察和分析。

居民消费价格指数 是反映一定时期内城乡居民所购买的生活消费品价格和服务项目价格变动趋势和程度的相对数，是对城市居民消费价格指数和农村居民消费价格指数进行综合汇总计算的结果。利用居民消费价格指数，可以观察和分析消费品的零售价格和服务价格变动对城乡居民实际生活费用支出的影响程度。

城市居民消费价格指数 是反映城市居民家庭所购买的生活消费品价格和服务项目价格变动趋势和程度的相对数。城市居民消费价格指数可以观察和分析消费品的零售价格和服务项目价格变动对职工货币工资的影响，作为研究职工生活和确定工资政策的依据。

工业品出厂价格指数 是反映全部工业产品出厂价格总水平的变动趋势和程度的相对数，包括工业企业售给本企业以外所有单位的各种产品和直接售给居民用于生活消费的产品。通过工业品出厂价格指数能观察出厂价格变动对工业总产值的影响。

固定资产投资价格指数 是反映固定资产投资价格变动趋势和程度的相对数。固定资产投资额是由建筑安装工程投资完成额、设备、工器具购置投资完成额和其他费用投资完成额三部分组成的。编制固定资产投资价格指数应首先分别编制上述三部分投资的价格指数，然后采用加权算术平均法求出固定资产投资价格总指数。

编制固定资产投资价格指数可以准确地反映固定资产投资中涉及的各类商品和取费项目价格变动趋势和变动幅度，消除按现价计算的固定资产投资指标中的价格变动因素，真实地反映固定资产投资的规模、速度、结构和效益，为国家科学地制定、检查固定资产投资计划并提高宏观调控水平，为完善国民经济核算体系提供科学的、可靠的依据。

房地产价格指数 包括房屋销售价格指数、房屋租赁价格指数和土地交易价格指数。这三套指数的计算方法相似，均采用由下到上逐级汇总的方法。即由细项到小类，由小类到中类，再由中类到大类，最后由大类汇出总指数。对没有细项或小类的部分，其起始类就是小类或中类。中类以下（含中类）指数采用样本资料作权数的加权调和平均公式计算，大类和总指数采用固定权数加权的算术平均公式计算。

Explanatory Notes on Main Statistical Indicators

Retail Price Index it is an economic index which reflects the trend of commodity retail price changes of urban and rural area in an period of time. The change and adjustment in retail prices directly affect the living expenditure of urban and rural residents, government revenue, purchasing power of residents and the equilibrium of market supply and demand, and the ratio of consumption to accumulation. Therefore, the calculation of retail price index is useful to analyze the changes of the above economic activities.

Consumer Price Index reflects the trend and degree of changes in prices of consumer goods and services purchased by urban and rural residents, and is a composite index derived from the urban consumer price index and the rural consumer price index. Consumer price index can be used to analyze the impact of consumer price change on actual expenditure for living cost of urban and rural residents.

Urban Consumer Price Index reflects the trend and degree of changes in prices of consumer goods and services purchased by urban households. It can be used to observe and analyze the impact of price changes in consumer goods and services on money wages of staff and workers, and provide basis for policy making concerning the living cost and wages of staff and workers.

Ex-factory Price Index of Industrial Products reflects the trend and degree of changes in general ex-factory prices of all industrial products, including sales of industrial products by an industrial enterprise to all units outside the enterprise, as well as sales of consumer goods to residents. It can be used to analyze the impact of ex-factory prices on gross industrial output value.

Price Index of Investment in Fixed Assets reflects the trend and degree of changes in prices of investment in fixed assets. The investment in fixed assets consists of three components, namely the investment in construction and installation, the investment in purchases of equipment and instrument, and the investment in other items. Price index of investment in fixed assets is calculated as the weighted arithmetic mean of the price indices of the three components of investment in fixed assets. Removing the factor of price change in the aggregates of investment at current prices, this indicator shows the changes in the prices of commodities and fees involved in the investment of fixed assets, and can be used to observe the actual size, growth, structure, and efficiency of investment in fixed assets and provides reliable and scientific data for government planning, management, decision making, and further improving the current national accounting system.

Price Indices for Real Estate include price index for selling houses and buildings, price index for leasing houses and buildings and price index for land transaction. The methods for the compilation of the three sets of indices are similar in that they all use bottom-up approach, under which indices for the item groups are compiled first, and then indices for the major groups, categories, major categories and finally the overall indices are compiles. The indices for item groups, major groups and categories are calculated using the formulae of weighted harmonic mean with sample data as the weights, and the indices for the major categories and the overall indices are calculated using the arithmetic mean with fixed weights.

7 人民生活

PEOPLE'S LIVELIHOOD

资料整理：赵兰莉　贾薪蓉
Data management:Zhao Lanli Jia Xinrong

第七部分　人民生活

一、简要说明

本章资料主要内容包括城乡居民家庭基本情况、主要商品购买数量、耐用消费品拥有数量等，由西安市统计局人口就业处提供。

二、主要指标

城镇居民人均可支配收入（元）	18963	比上年增长 24.7%
城镇居民人均消费性支出（元）	14251	比上年增长 18.6%
农村居民人均纯收入（元）	6275	比上年增长 20.4%
农村居民人均生活消费支出（元）	4771	比上年增长 21.1%

7 PEOPLE'S LIVELIHOOD

Ⅰ.Brief Introduction

Data in this chapter reflects situation of the people's daily life of Xi'an city. It consists of mainly basic condition of urban and rural households, volume of primary commodity purchasing, possession of endurable goods, etc. The data come from Population & Employment Division of the Xi'an Bureau of Statistics.

Ⅱ.Major Indicators

		Increase over Preceding Year
Per Capita Annual Disposable Income of Urban Households (yuan)	18963	24.7%
Per Capita Annual Consumption Expenditure of Urban Households (yuan)	14251	18.6%
Per Capita Living Expenditure Built(yuan)	6275	20.4%
Per Capita Net Income of Rural Residents(yuan)	4771	21.1%

7-1 主要年份城乡居民家庭人均收入及恩格尔系数

Per Capita Annual Income and Engel's Coefficient of Urban and Rural Households in Representative Years

年 份 Year	城镇居民家庭人均可支配收入 Per Capita Annual Disposable Income of Urban Households		农村居民家庭人均纯收入 Per Capita Annual Net Income of Rural Households		城镇居民家庭恩格尔系数（%） Engel's Coefficient of Urban Households	农村居民家庭恩格尔系数（%） Engel's Coefficient of Rural Households
	绝对数（元） Value(yuan)	指数（1980年=100） Indax (preceding year=100)	绝对数（元） Value(yuan)	指数（1980年=100） Indax (preceding year=100)		
1978			140	100.0		
1979						
1980	414		190	135.7	53.3	53.3
1981	446	107.7	207	147.9	52.9	53.7
1982	479	115.6	254	181.4	55.1	56.7
1983	509	122.9	245	175.0	55.1	58.4
1984	540	130.3	299	213.6	54.9	51.7
1985	719	173.5	351	250.7	49.5	48.5
1986	911	219.8	390	278.6	49.9	47.9
1987	1034	249.7	434	310.0	50.6	50.3
1988	1142	275.6	482	344.3	44.9	47.5
1989	1344	324.3	530	378.6	51.7	48.2
1990	1518	366.5	610	435.7	53.1	49.5
1991	1619	390.9	707	505.0	51.6	46.7
1992	1992	481.0	783	559.3	52.5	50.9
1993	2661	642.5	870	621.4	46.4	46.0
1994	3517	849.1	1078	770.0	45.2	50.1
1995	4153	1002.5	1353	966.4	44.7	50.3
1996	5023	1212.6	1586	1132.9	42.6	49.9
1997	5344	1290.1	1846	1318.6	40.7	49.2
1998	5670	1368.7	2052	1465.7	39.8	42.4
1999	5999	1448.3	2203	1573.6	36.3	39.1
2000	6364	1536.5	2344	1674.3	36.5	36.6
2001	6705	1618.8	2490	1778.6	34.8	33.9
2002	7184	1734.3	2641	1886.4	34.4	31.1
2003	7748	1870.7	2838	2027.1	34.8	37.6
2004	8544	2062.8	3143	2245.0	36.1	35.7
2005	9628	2324.5	3460	2471.4	37.0	36.3
2006	10905	2632.9	3808	2720.0	34.4	36.8
2007	12662	3057.0	4399	3142.1	36.6	38.2
2008	15207	3671.4	5212	3722.9	36.4	37.0
2009	18963	4578.2	6275	4482.3	32.4	35.8

7–2 主要年份城乡居民人民币储蓄存款

Savings Deposit of Urban and Rural Household in Representative Years

单位：亿元 (100 million yuan)

年 份 Year	年末余额 Balance at Year-end
1978	3.72
1979	4.85
1980	5.48
1981	6.36
1982	7.76
1983	10.02
1984	14.70
1985	16.70
1986	23.10
1987	32.13
1988	32.51
1989	45.78
1990	62.23
1991	78.64
1992	96.09
1993	124.61
1994	174.19
1995	230.63
1996	394.02
1997	358.78
1998	499.68
1999	586.40
2000	675.83
2001	800.86
2002	988.04
2003	1210.56
2004	1432.86
2005	1716.76
2006	1950.53
2007	2002.38
2008	2504.41
2009	3084.20

7-3 主要年份城镇居民家庭基本情况

Basic Conditions of Urban Households in Representative Years

指　　标	Item	2001	2002	2003
一、调查户数(户)	**Number of Households Surveyed (household)**	**300**	**300**	**350**
二、平均每户家庭人口(人)	**Average Household Size(person)**	**3.03**	**3.01**	**3.04**
三、平均每户就业人口(人)	**Average Number of Employed Persons Per Housedhold (person)**	**1.38**	**1.47**	**1.46**
四、平均每户就业面(%)	**Proportion Percentage of Employment Per Housedhold (%)**	**45.6**	**48.8**	**48.0**
五、平均每一就业者负担人数(人)	**Number of Dependents per Emplyee(person)**	**2.19**	**2.05**	**2.08**
六、年人均家庭总收入(元)	**Per Capita Annual Income(yuan)**	**6743.12**	**7670.67**	**8315.13**
#可支配收入	Disposable Income	6704.86	7183.54	7748.38
(一)工资性收入	Income from Wages and Salaries	4288.09	5075.62	5443.21
(二)经营性收入	Net Business Income	135.27	159.03	111.82
(三)财产性收入	Income from Propeties	49.35	60.90	194.17
(四)转移性收入	Income from Transfer	2270.41	2375.12	2565.92
七、年人均家庭总支出(元)	**Annual Actual Expenditure Per Capita (yuan)**	**6678.56**	**7819.74**	**8610.43**
1.消费性支出	Consumption Expenditure	5815.66	6419.21	6805.30
(1)食品	Food	2023.91	2205.38	2371.02
(2)衣着	Clothing	485.93	540.52	574.56
(3)设备用品及服务	Facilities,Articles and Services	628.91	467.36	403.24
(4)医疗保健	Health Care and Medical Services	406.13	535.52	602.31
(5)交通和通讯	Transport and Communication Services	453.12	567.96	630.48
(6)娱乐教育和文化服务	Recreation,Education and Cultural Services	908.07	1126.68	1230.60
(7)居住	Residence	531.45	783.56	779.33
(8)杂项商品和服务	Miscellaneous Goods and Services	378.14	192.23	213.77
2.购房与建房支出	Purchase and Construction Expenditure of Houses	289.23	415.08	532.19
3.转移性支出	Transfer Expenditure	573.59	567.81	786.70
4.财产性支出	Property Expenditure			
5.社会保障支出	Social Services Expenditure		417.64	486.24
八、人均期末手存现金(元)	**Cash Reserves at Hand at the end of Year Per Capita (yuan)**	**550.39**	**587.82**	**810.60**

7-3 续表1 continued 1

指　　标	Item	2004	2005	2006
一、调查户数(户)	**Number of Households Surveyed (household)**	**350**	**350**	**350**
二、平均每户家庭人口(人)	**Average Household Size(person)**	**2.99**	**2.93**	**2.90**
三、平均每户就业人口(人)	**Average Number of Employed Persons Per Housedhold (person)**	**1.46**	**1.39**	**1.40**
四、平均每户就业面(%)	**Proportion Percentage of Employment Per Housedhold (%)**	**48.8**	**47.4**	**48.3**
五、平均每一就业者负担人数(人)	**Number of Dependents per Emplyee(person)**	**2.05**	**2.11**	**2.07**
六、年人均家庭总收入(元)	**Per Capita Annual Income(yuan)**	**9150.65**	**10387.44**	**11708.43**
#可支配收入	Disposable Income	8544.03	9627.89	10905.39
（一）工资性收入	Income from Wages and Salaries	6050.38	6926.28	7622.92
（二）经营性收入	Net Business Income	251.36	163.66	345.70
（三）财产性收入	Income from Propeties	186.95	193.20	317.87
（四）转移性收入	Income from Transfer	2661.95	3104.30	3421.93
七、年人均家庭总支出(元)	**Annual Actual Expenditure Per Capita (yuan)**	**9312.05**	**10030.64**	**12033.94**
1.消费性支出	Consumption Expenditure	7427.82	7899.81	8986.87
(1)食品	Food	2685.10	2926.32	3093.12
(2)衣着	Clothing	611.03	712.98	783.93
(3)设备用品及服务	Facilities,Articles and Services	493.33	373.36	582.84
(4)医疗保健	Health Care and Medical Services	641.77	746.67	695.09
(5)交通和通讯	Transport and Communication Services	688.22	763.55	922.99
(6)娱乐教育和文化服务	Recreation,Education and Cultural Services	1252.55	1357.50	1666.93
(7)居住	Residence	813.14	719.00	946.87
(8)杂项商品和服务	Miscellaneous Goods and Services	242.68	300.42	295.09
2.购房与建房支出	Purchase and Construction Expenditure of Houses	590.33	722.35	1273.52
3.转移性支出	Transfer Expenditure	768.01	745.23	1043.44
4.财产性支出	Property Expenditure			1.89
5.社会保障支出	Social Services Expenditure	525.89	663.24	728.23
八、人均期末手存现金(元)	**Cash Reserves at Hand at the end of Year Per Capita (yuan)**	**882.65**	**1121.29**	**15251.31**

7-3 续表2 continued 2

指　　标	Item	2007	2008	2009
一、调查户数(户)	**Number of Households Surveyed (household)**	**350**	**1500**	**1500**
二、平均每户家庭人口(人)	**Average Household Size(person)**	**2.91**	**2.82**	**2.84**
三、平均每户就业人口(人)	**Average Number of Employed Persons Per Housedhold (person)**	**1.39**	**1.35**	**1.51**
四、平均每户就业面(%)	**Proportion Percentage of Employment Per Housedhold (%)**	**47.8**	**47.9**	**53.2**
五、平均每一就业者负担人数(人)	**Number of Dependents per Emplyee(person)**	**2.09**	**2.09**	**1.88**
六、年人均家庭总收入(元)	**Per Capita Annual Income(yuan)**	**13421.45**	**16365.67**	**20299.12**
#可支配收入	Disposable Income	12662.03	15206.89	18963.31
（一）工资性收入	Income from Wages and Salaries	8595.84	10944.90	13562.24
（二）经营性收入	Net Business Income	375.68	410.70	715.99
（三）财产性收入	Income from Propeties	208.83	241.24	357.26
（四）转移性收入	Income from Transfer	3939.67	4768.83	5663.63
七、年人均家庭总支出(元)	**Annual Actual Expenditure Per Capita (yuan)**	**12257.69**	**14380.69**	**17619.36**
1.消费性支出	Consumption Expenditure	10097.95	12015.81	14250.78
(1)食品	Food	3696.57	4374.24	4621.40
(2)衣着	Clothing	950.50	1232.12	1564.44
(3)设备用品及服务	Facilities,Articles and Services	597.11	761.01	1037.98
(4)医疗保健	Health Care and Medical Services	847.80	1161.86	1375.57
(5)交通和通讯	Transport and Communication Services	1145.90	1246.34	1614.68
(6)娱乐教育和文化服务	Recreation,Education and Cultural Services	1466.55	1724.63	2043.52
(7)居住	Residence	1027.90	1058.11	1262.81
(8)杂项商品和服务	Miscellaneous Goods and Services	365.62	457.49	730.36
2.购房与建房支出	Purchase and Construction Expenditure of Houses	524.62	262.31	606.42
3.转移性支出	Transfer Expenditure	933.52	1042.50	1517.15
4.财产性支出	Property Expenditure	9.33	23.30	23.09
5.社会保障支出	Social Services Expenditure	692.27	1036.78	1221.92
八、人均期末手存现金(元)	**Cash Reserves at Hand at the end of Year Per Capita (yuan)**	**1563.41**	**1296.10**	**2553.73**

注：2007年因统计制度变化，部分数据有调整。

Note:As statistical system was changed in 2007, some data was adjusted.

7-4 城镇居民家庭基本情况表（2009年）

Basic Conditions of Urban Households（2009）

指　　标	Item	合计 Total
一、调查户数(户)	**Number of Households Surveyed (Household)**	**1500**
二、可支配收入(新算法)(元)	**Disposable Income (New Algorithm)(yuan)**	**18963.31**
三、家庭人口数(人/户)	**Number of Family Members (Person/Household)**	**2.84**
（一）有收入者人数	Family Members Earning Income	2.13
1.就业人口数	Family Members Employed	1.51
（1）国有经济单位职工人数	Employed by State-Owned Enterprises	0.90
（2）城镇集体经济单位职工人数	Employed by Urban Collective Enterprises	0.05
（3）其他各种经济类型单位职工	Employed by Other Units	0.10
（4）城镇个体经营者人员数	Personnel of Urban Individual Business	0.06
（5）城镇个体被雇人员数	Employed by Self-Employers	0.25
（6）离退休再就业人员数	Re-Employed Resigned and Retired Personnel	0.05
（7）其他就业人员数	Others	0.09
2.离退休人数	Resigned and Retired	0.59
3.其他有收入者人数	Others	0.03
（二）无收入者人数	Family Members Without No Income	0.71
四、非家庭人口在家用餐人次数	**None-Family Members Eating At Home**	**3.34**
(人次/户)	**(Person-Times/Household)**	
五、家庭人口在外用餐人次数	**Family Members Eating Outside**	**10.30**
(人次/户)	**(Person-Times/Household)**	

7-5 城镇居民家庭年人均收入情况（2009年）

Statistics on Per Capital Annual Income of Urban Residents （2009）

单位：元 (yuan)

项　目	Item	总平均 Total
一、家庭总收入	**Total Family Income**	**20299.12**
#可支配收入	Disposable Income	18963.31
（一）工薪收入	Income from Wages and Salaries	13562.24
1.工资及补贴收入	Wages and Subsidies	13382.99
2.其他劳动收入	Other Payments to Labor	179.25
（二）经营性收入	Net Income from Business	715.99
（三）财产性收入	Income from Properties	357.26
1.利息收入	Interest Income	65.73
2.股息与红利收入	Dividend and Bonus	83.13
3.保险收益	Interests Of Insurance	13.89
4.其他投资收入	Income from Other Investments	47.17
5.出租房屋收入	House Rents	123.40
6.知识产权收入	Income from Intellectual Property Rights	
7.其他财产性收入	Other Property Income	23.95
（四）转移性收入	Transfer Income	5663.63
1.养老金或离退休金	Pensions	4751.74
2.社会救济收入	Social Relieve	33.07
3.辞退金	Severance Pay	0.31
4.赔偿收入	Compensation	0.59
5.保险收入	Insurance Proceeds	20.55
#失业保险金	Unemployment Insurance	16.95
6.赡养收入	Support Money from Offsprings	373.94
7.捐赠收入	Donations	297.81
8.亲友搭伙费	Payment For Boarding By Relatives and Friends	
9.提取住房公积金	Withdrawal of Housing Funds	12.73
10.记账补贴	Book-Keeping Allowances	93.18
11.其他转移性收入	Others	79.70
二、出售财物收入	**Income from Sales Of Property**	**2.99**
1.出售住房收入	Sales of Housing	0.02
2.出售其他物品收入	Sales of Other Properties	2.97
三、借贷收入	**Income For Savings and Credit**	**3193.03**
1.提取储蓄存款	Withdrawal of Deposits	2901.40
2.借入款	Borrow Money	129.95
3.收回借出款	Funds Lent out Refunded	56.64
4.收回储蓄性保险本金	Corpus of Insurance Withdrawn	2.09
5.兑售有价证券	En-Cash/Sell Securities	
6.收回投资本金	Corpus of Investments Withdrawn	4.02
7.住房贷款	Housing Credit	5.89
8.汽车贷款	Automobile Credit	0.30
9.教育贷款	Education Credit	
10.其他贷款	Other Credit	28.41
11.其他借贷收入	Other Income from Savings and Credit	64.34

7-6 城镇居民家庭年人均支出情况（2009年）

Statistics on Per Capital Annual Living Expenditure of Urban Households（2009）

单位:元 (yuan)

项　　目	Item	总平均 Total
一、家庭总支出	**Total Expenditures**	**17619.36**
（一）消费支出	Consumption Expenditures	14250.78
#服务性消费支出	Consumption on Service	4321.94
1.食品	Food	4621.40
2.衣着	Clothing	1564.44
3.家庭设备用品及服务	Household Facilities,Articles and Service	1037.98
4.医疗保健	Health Care and Medical Service	1375.57
5.交通和通信	Transport and Communications	1614.68
6.教育文化娱乐服务	Education,Receration and Cultural Services	2043.52
7.居住	Residence	1262.81
8.杂项商品和服务	Miscellaneous Goods and Services	730.36
（二）购房与建房支出	Expenditures on House Purchasing/Construction	606.42
1.购房	House Purchasing	606.31
2.建房	House Construction	0.12
（三）转移性支出	Transfer Expenditures	1517.15
1.缴纳的个人收入税	Personal income Taxes	20.70
2.捐赠支出	Expenditures on Donations	701.73
3.购买彩票	Expenditures on Lottery	11.42
4.赡养支出	Expenditures for Maintenance	414.62
#在外就学子女费用	Expendrtures for Children Studying Away From Home	102.19
5.各种非储蓄性保险支出	Expenditures on Non-saving insurances	132.13
#车辆保险支出	Expenditures on Vehicles insurance	15.90
6.其他转移性支出	Other Transfer Expenditures	236.55
（四）财产性支出	Property Expenditures	23.09
1.非生产性利息支出	Non-Productive interest Payments	10.91
2.其他	Others	12.17
（五）社会保障支出	Expenditures on Social Security	1221.93
1.个人交纳的养老基金	Retirement Funds Raised by individuals	638.88
2.个人交纳的住房公积金	Housing Funds Raised by individuals	327.83
3.个人交纳的医疗基金	Medical Funds Raised by individuals	181.29
4.个人交纳的失业基金	Unemployment Funds Raised by individuals	37.76
5.其他社会保障支出	Others	36.17
二、借贷支出	**Expenditures on Loans and Debts**	**4855.34**
1.存入储蓄款	Depositting to Bank	4497.47
2.借出款	Amout of Money Lent	35.95
3.归还借款	Paying off Debts	102.25
4.储蓄性保险支出	Expenditures for Savings Premium	62.23
5.购买有价证券	Purchasing Securities	29.66
6.其它投资支出	Other investments	11.63
7.归还住房贷款	Refund Housing Loans	82.75
8.归还汽车贷款	Refund Automobile Loans	7.35
9.归还教育贷款	Refund Education Loans	
10.归还其他贷款	Refund Other Loans	5.22
11.其他借贷支出	Others	20.83

7-7 城镇居民家庭年人均消费性支出情况（2009年）

Statistics on Per Capita Annual Consumption Expenditure of Urban Households（2009）

单位:元 (yuan)

项　　目	Item	总平均 Total
消费支出	**Consumption Expenditures**	**14250.78**
#服务性消费支出	Consumption on services	4321.94
食品	**Food**	**4621.40**
（一）粮油类	Grains and oil	595.44
1.粮食	Grain	346.34
2.淀粉及薯类	Starches and Tubers	30.54
3.干豆类及豆制品	Bean and Bean Products	72.24
4.油脂类	Oil or Fats	146.32
（二）肉禽蛋水产品类	Meat,Poultry,Egg and Aquatic Products	791.78
1.肉类	Meat	465.65
2.禽类	Poultry	114.03
3.蛋类	Egg	82.33
4.水产品类	Aquatic Products	129.77
（三）蔬菜类	Vegetables	436.95
1.鲜菜	Fresh Vegetables	391.93
2.干菜	Dried Vegetables	30.65
3.菜制品	Vegetable Products	14.36
（四）调味品	Flavouring	91.05
（五）糖烟酒饮料类	Sugar,Tobacco,Liquor and Beverage	623.62
1.糖类	Sugar	39.86
2.烟草类	Tobacco	293.99
3.酒类	Liquor	159.33
4.饮料	Beverage	130.44
（六）干鲜瓜果类	Dried and Fresh Melons &Fruits	385.90
（七）糕点、奶及奶制品	Cakes, Milk and Processed Products	365.16
1.糕点	Cakes	129.23
2.奶及奶制品	Milk and Its Products	235.94
（八）其他食品	Other Food	147.80
（九）饮食服务	Catering Services	1183.71
1.食品加工服务费	Charge for Food Processing Services	1.24
2.在外饮食	Foods Consumed outside	1182.46

7-7 续表1 continued 1

单位:元 (yuan)

项　目	Item	总平均 Total
非食品类	**Non-food**	
一、衣着	**Clothing**	**1564.44**
（一）服装	Garments	1051.73
（二）衣着材料	Cloth Materials	13.68
（三）鞋类	Shoes	421.84
（四）其他衣着用品	Others	69.43
（五）衣着加工服务费	Tailoring and Laundering	7.76
二、家庭设备用品及服务	**Household Facilities,Articles and Services**	**1037.98**
（一）耐用消费品	Durable Consumer Goods	415.76
1.家具	Furniture	115.06
2.家庭设备	Household Facilities	300.70
（二）室内装饰品	Interior Decorations	16.43
（三）床上用品	Bed Articles	95.23
（四）家庭日用杂品	Daily Use Household Articles	427.81
（五）家具材料	Furniture Materials	43.55
（六）家庭服务	Household Services	39.20
三、医疗保健	**Medicine and Medical Services**	**1375.57**
（一）医疗器具	Medical Appliances and Articles	16.34
（二）保健器具	Health Care Articles	20.49
（三）药品费	Medicines	559.91
（四）滋补保健品	Tonic	168.47
（五）医疗费	Medical Care Services	555.99
（六）其他	Others	54.37
四、交通和通讯	**Transportation ,Post and Telecommumication Services**	**1614.68**
（一）交通	Trasportation	947.46
1.家庭交通工具	Family Vehicles	328.73
2.车辆用燃料及零配件	Fuel and Accessories	98.88
3.交通工具服务支出	Expenditure on Maintenance of Vehicles	99.10
4.交通费	Transport Servi	420.74
（二）通信	Telecommumication	667.22
1.通信工具	Telecommunication Tools	124.62
2.通信服务	Telecommunication Services	542.60

7-7 续表2 continued 2

单位:元 (yuan)

项目	Item	总平均 Total
五、教育文化娱乐服务	**Recreation,Culture and Education Services**	**2043.52**
（一）文化娱乐用品	Recreating Goods	392.95
（二）文化娱乐服务	Recreation and Culture Services	672.69
1.参观游览	Travel	220.15
2.健身活动	Health Care Activities	37.47
3.团体旅游	Traveling in a Group	281.38
4.其他文娱活动	Others	126.99
5.文娱用品修理服务费	Repair and Maintenance of Entertainment Tools	6.70
（三）教育	Education	977.88
1.教材	Textbook	50.46
2.教育费用	Fee of Education	927.42
六、居住	**Residence**	**1262.81**
（一）住房	Housing	379.25
1.租赁房房租	House Renting	78.68
2.住房装潢支出	Home Decorate Expenditure	198.15
3.维修用建筑材料	Building Material for Repair	65.87
4.其他	Others	36.55
（二）水电燃料及其他	Water,Electricity,Fuel and Others	711.16
1.水	Water	74.75
2.电	Electricity	278.37
3.燃料	Fuel	147.03
4.其他	Others	31.67
（三）居住服务费	Cost on Housing Service	172.41
1.物业管理费	Housing Management	105.47
2.维修服务费	Expenditures on House Maintenance	19.15
3.其他	Others	47.79
七、杂项商品和服务	**Miscellaneous Commodities and Services**	**730.36**
（一）杂项商品	Miscellaneous Commodities	460.74
1.金银珠宝饰品	Jewel	64.58
2.手表	Watches	11.90
3.理发美容用具	Hair-care	8.76
4.化妆品	Cosmetics	157.92
5.其他杂品	Others	217.59
（二）服务	Services	269.62
1.旅馆住宿费	Rent for Hotels	11.54
2.理发洗澡费	Hair-cutting and Bathing	56.43
3.美容费	Cosmetic	70.09
4.其他服务	Others	131.56

7-8　主要年份城镇居民家庭年人均购买主要商品数量

商品名称	Name of Commodities	2000	2001	2002
植物油（市斤）	Vegetable Oil(500g)	10.0	9.1	9.9
猪　肉（市斤）	Pork (500g)	13.7	12.0	12.9
牛　肉（市斤）	Beef(500g)	1.7	1.6	1.4
羊　肉（市斤）	Mutton (500g)	0.7	0.5	0.8
鸡　（市斤）	Chicken (500g)	4.4	3.6	3.7
鲜　蛋（市斤）	Eggs (500g)	12.3	10.8	11.4
鱼（市斤）	Fish(500g)	3.7	3.8	4.5
鲜　菜（市斤）	Fresh Vegetables (500g)	107.0	104.5	112.3
白　酒（市斤）	Liquor(500g)	0.9	1.0	1.0
果　酒（市斤）	Fruit Wine (500g)	0.2	0.3	0.3
啤　酒（市斤）	Beer (500g)	3.0	3.6	4.7
糕　点（市斤）	Cake(500g)	4.6	4.2	4.8
鲜乳品（市斤）	Fresh Dairy Products (500g)	12.0	12.8	18.9
奶　粉（市斤）	Milk Powder (500g)	0.6	0.6	0.6
服装（件）	Clothes(unit)	5.1	5.6	6.6
鞋（双）	Shoes(pair)	2.4	2.5	2.6
水（吨）	Water(ton)	25.7	24.5	28.6
电（度）	Electricity (degree)	307.5	309.7	390.8
煤炭（公斤）	Coal (kg)	62.0	61.7	51.8
液化石油气（公斤）	Liquified Petroleum Gas (kg)	17.9	14.5	13.3
管道煤气（立方米）	Piping Gas (cu.m)	26.1	26.4	35.1

Per Capita Annual Purchases of Principal Goods in Urban Household in Representative Years

2003	2004	2005	2006	2007	2008	2009
9.4	9.4	12.3	10.1	10.2	11.5	10.2
13.6	12.5	15.0	13.6	12.8	19.0	12.6
1.5	2.0	2.6	2.4	1.9	2.1	2.7
1.0	1.1	1.1	0.8	0.8	0.7	1.0
4.0	3.5	5.0	3.8	4.1	6.3	4.2
11.9	10.4	14.1	11.8	11.1	13.2	10.7
5.2	4.3	5.6	4.6	5.3	6.1	5.0
109.7	113.4	132.5	110.9	113.9	126.5	111.7
1.0	1.4	1.3	1.3	1.5	0.9	1.1
0.2	0.2	0.2	0.3	0.2	0.2	0.3
4.0	4.0	6.5	6.3	4.6	3.8	5.2
5.3	5.4	6.6	5.9	6.5	11.3	8.1
21.8	20.4	28.0	25.0	25.3	16.9	19.6
0.7	0.7	0.6	0.5	0.7	0.9	0.6
6.5	6.8	6.9	7.1	9.0	6.9	8.7
2.7	2.8	2.8	2.8	2.8	3.2	4.2
28.8	26.5	26.1	22.9	22.8	22.2	27.1
385.3	435.6	449.5	444.9	460.6	439.3	523.1
45.1	51.4	33.9	46.0	66.5	70.4	34.3
12.2	12.7	9.8	7.5	6.9	8.1	7.5
39.0	38.4	58.2	46.4	38.8	33.4	45.2

7-9 主要年份城镇居民家庭平均每百户年末拥有主要耐用消费品数量

商品名称	Commodity Names	2000	2001	2002
摩托车（辆）	Motorcycle (unit)	5.0	6.0	8.7
家用汽车（辆）	Car (unit)			0.3
洗衣机（台）	Washing Machine (unit)	96.7	97.7	97.3
电冰箱（台）	Refrigerator (unit)	91.0	91.3	95.7
彩色电视机（台）	Color TV Set (unit)	124.0	123.7	128.3
家用电脑（台）	Computer (unit)	11.7	15.7	19.0
组合音响（套）	Hi-Fi System (set)	16.7	19.3	23.0
摄像机（台）	Pick-up Camera (unit)	1.0	0.3	1.0
照相机（架）	Camera (set)	46.3	47.3	48.0
钢琴（架）	Piano (set)	1.3	0.3	1.7
其它中高档乐器（件）	Other High-Grade Musical Instruments (unit)	2.3	3.7	6.7
微波炉（台）	Oven (unit)	18.0	27.7	39.3
空调器（台）	Air Conditioner (unit)	51.3	54.3	75.0
淋浴热水器（台）	Shower(unit)	52.3	52.3	63.7
健身器材（件）	Health Care Equipment (unit)	3.3	3.0	1.7
消毒碗柜（台）	Disinfecting Cupboard(unit)			1.7
洗碗机（台）	Dishwasher (unit)			
普通电话（部）	Telephone (unit)	81.3	86.0	88.0
移动电话（部）	Hand Telephone (unit)	7.6	19.3	48.3

Number of Durable Consumer Goods Owned Every 100 Urban Households in Representative Years

2003	2004	2005	2006	2007	2008	2009
10.2	9.1	8.6	8.9	5.4	7.9	7.6
0.3	0.3	0.6	0.9	2.0	4.0	9.0
95.7	98.3	101.1	101.1	98.9	95.3	98.8
91.8	91.2	90.9	94.4	95.7	89.2	95.0
127.0	134.0	134.0	136.0	134.5	119.9	126.7
23.9	31.7	20.3	37.1	45.6	54.0	68.8
22.9	20.0	34.0	20.6	24.8	19.0	25.2
1.7	1.1	3.1	4.3	4.8	7.7	9.7
48.3	44.3	49.7	47.7	50.1	39.9	52.1
2.0	2.0	1.4	1.7	1.1	2.4	2.4
5.9	7.1	11.4	12.9	6.0	4.7	5.3
42.2	47.1	52.0	52.9	56.4	52.7	62.1
82.4	92.6	99.7	102.9	116.0	104.0	119.7
70.0	74.9	110.3	71.4	74.1	70.9	79.9
2.6	2.9	6.9	3.4	4.0	4.3	4.8
4.7	7.1	29.4	6.0	7.4	5.5	7.8
				0.6	0.6	0.3
87.1	85.7	88.0	79.1	75.2	67.4	72.8
74.4	102.0	119.7	144.3	162.3	162.1	185.3

7-10 城镇居民家庭居住情况（2009年）

Conditions of Dwellings of Urban Households （2009）

住房情况	Accommodation data	2009
一、家庭居住人口（人/户）	**Number of Persons Per Household(person/household)**	**2.84**
二、现住房总建筑面积（平方米/人）	**Building Area of Living Houses(sq.m/person)**	**28.40**
三、房屋产权(合计)（%）	**Proportion of Property Right of Houses(%)**	
租赁公房	Public Houses Rent	8.87
租赁私房	Private Houses Rent	4.76
原有私房	Originally Self-owned Houses	4.68
房改私房	Present Self-owned Houses	51.31
商品房	Commercial Houses	13.96
其 他	Others	16.42
四、住宅建筑式样(合计)（%）	**Proportion of Patterns of Residential Building(%)**	
单栋住宅	Flats With Complete Facilities (%)	1.15
四居室	4 Rooms	1.23
三居室	3 Rooms	25.45
二居室	2 Rooms	62.81
一居室	1 Rooms	4.19
普通楼房	Ordinary Storeyed Building	3.53
平房及其他	Single-storey Houses and Others	1.64
五、装修状况(合计)（%）	**Proportion of Decoration Condition(%)**	
有装修	Decorated	63.14
未装修	Undecorated	36.86
如果装修过,最近一次装修花费（元/户）	Expenditure of Latest Decoration(yuan/household)	16495.34
六、现有住房按市场价估计值（元/户）	**Estimated Market Price of Present Houses(yuan/household)**	**174232.90**
七、租赁房房租（元/户）	**Expenditure of Rent Houses(yuan/household)**	**363.68**
八、自有房房租折算（元/户）	**Rent of Self-owned Houses(yuan/household)**	**3016.22**
九、购房总金额（元/户）	**Total Expenditure on Purchase of Houses(yuan/household)**	**60076.01**
购房实际支出金额	Expenditure on Purchase Practice of Houses	57472.78
十、饮水情况(合计)（%）	**Proportion of Water Drinking(%)**	
自来水	Tap Water	89.41
矿泉水	Mineral Water	5.75
纯净水	Pure Water	4.76
井、河水	Well Water and River Water	0.08
其 他	Others	

7-10 续表 continued

住房情况	Accommodation data	2009
十一、用水情况(合计)(%)	**Proportion of Water Use Condition(%)**	
独用自来水	Moloply Use of Tap Water	97.95
公用自来水	Public Tap Water	2.05
井、河水	Well Water and River Water	
其 他	Others	
十二、卫生设备(合计)(%)	**Proportion of Sanitary Facilities(%)**	
无卫生设备	Without Sanitary Facilities	0.16
有厕所浴室	With Bathroom and Lavatory	78.82
有厕所无浴室	With Lavatory but without Bathroom	16.75
公 用	Common-used Sanitary Facilities	4.27
十三、取暖设备(合计)(%)	**Proportion of Heating Facilities(%)**	
无取暖设备	Without Heating Facilities (%)	10.34
空调设备	Air-conditioner	9.36
暖 气	Central Heating	63.46
其 他	Others	16.83
十四、炊用燃料使用情况(合计)(%)	**Proportion of Cooking Fuels(%)**	
管道煤气	Pipeline Gas	61.33
液化石油气	Liquefied Gas	33.58
煤	Coal	1.40
其 他	Others	3.69
十五、除了现住房，还有几处其他住房（套/户）	**Other Living Houses besides Present Living House(unit/household)**	0.09
①出租房（套/户）	Houses for Rent(unit/household)	0.06
②偶尔居住房（套/户）	Houses Seldom Living in (unit/household)	0.03
③其它用途房（套/户）	Houses for other Purposes(unit/household)	0.01

7-11 主要年份农民家庭基本情况

项　　目	Item	1998	1999
一、调查户数（户）	**Households Surveyed(household)**	**460**	**460**
二、调查人口（人）	**Residents Sueveyed(person)**		
1.常住人口	Average Number of Permanent Residents	2028	2024
2.整半劳动力	Average Number Able-bodied and Semi-able-bodied Laborers Per Households	1279	1296
3.平均每个劳动力负担人口	Persons Supported by Each Laborers	1.59	1.56
三、平均每人全年收入(元)	**Per Capita Annual Income(yuan)**		
1.总收入	Total Revenue	2597.24	2711.55
2.纯收入	Net Income	2052.07	2202.73
3.现金收入	Cash Income	2087.96	2288.00
4.可支配收入	Disposable Income		
四、按人均纯收入分组（%）	**Grouped by Per Capita Annual Net Income(%)**		
户数占总户数比重	Percentage of Households		
1000元以下	Below 1000 yuan		
1000-2000元	1000-2000 yuan		
2000-3000元	2000-3000 yuan		
3000-4000元	3000-4000 yuan		
4000-5000元	4000-5000 yuan		
5000元以上	Over 5000 yuan		
五、农民家庭房屋情况	**Rural Household Housing Condition**		
1.年末人均住房价值(元)	Average Value of Living House Per Capita of Year-end(yuan)	4813.50	4850.32
2.年末人均住房面积(m^2)	Average Floor Space of Living House Per Capita at Year-end(sq.m)	27.32	26.80
3.年内人均新建房屋面积(m^2)	Percapita Space of Building Newly Built Within the year (sq.m)	1.33	2.03
4.年内人均新建房屋价值(元)	Percapita Value of Building Newly Built Within the Year(yuan)	308.01	304.40
六、生活消费支出总计（元）	**Living Expenditure Built(yuan)**	**1564.81**	**1492.43**
食品	Food	663.75	584.18
衣着	Clothing	120.76	112.83
居住	Residence	327.56	247.45
家庭设备用品及服务	Household Facilities,Articles and Services	87.43	97.79
医疗保健	Health Care and Health Care Services	72.72	94.60
交通通讯	Transport and Communications	51.99	62.45
文化娱乐用品及服务	Culture,Educational and Recreational Articles and Services	196.96	230.09
其它商品及服务	Miscellaneous Goods and Services	43.64	63.04

Basic Indicators of Rural Households In Representative Years

2000	2001	2002	2003	2004	2005	2006	2007	2008	2009
500	**770**	**770**	**750**	**710**	**720**	**700**	**700**	**900**	**940**
2147	3214	3212	3102	2920	3040	2935	2924	3628	3828
1371	2008	2017	1993	1873	1904	1841	1863	2422	2557
1.57	1.60	1.59	1.56	1.56	1.60	1.59	1.57	1.50	1.50
2929.23	3185.54	3370.82	3571.71	3889.12	4495.44	4968.93	5605.12	6746.04	7961.26
2343.76	2490.27	2641.44	2837.83	3142.78	3459.60	3808.38	4398.64	5212.14	6275.22
2513.14	2747.00	2965.92	3042.02	3299.16	3940.24	4466.49	4969.58	6249.34	7297.58
2225.13	2357.30	2560.58	2729.88	3021.25	3353.43	3562.80	4167.18	4983.23	6008.41
		11.69	10.00	5.49	5.14	3.57	2.57	1.89	1.70
		28.57	26.67	22.40	18.33	14.57	7.57	7.33	3.83
		27.92	26.00	28.45	25.00	22.43	15.14	13.78	7.98
		15.45	16.13	19.30	20.70	19.43	21.00	13.00	12.55
		5.97	10.00	9.01	11.94	13.57	17.72	14.00	12.87
		10.40	11.20	15.35	18.89	26.43	36.00	50.00	61.07
5398.21	6286.53	6883.06	7354.40	7780.97	9052.30	10878.22	13145.27	20476.11	24500.32
28.31	29.72	32.54	33.90	34.66	36.73	40.05	42.92	54.97	56.73
1.58	1.81	2.20	0.98	1.13	1.13	1.82	2.03	1.80	2.62
408.07	475.33	484.18	239.47	309.07	365.97	746.64	787.03	784.68	1349.27
1605.36	**1676.42**	**1782.14**	**1802.75**	**2276.65**	**2602.68**	**2708.87**	**3380.80**	**3938.09**	**4771.06**
587.97	567.62	553.78	677.03	812.47	945.76	996.75	1289.61	1455.22	1708.35
106.80	105.53	115.02	113.15	133.97	159.09	174.81	205.85	256.92	305.46
343.71	409.90	444.92	314.04	478.37	462.21	488.47	768.16	763.44	928.87
87.89	74.29	83.64	98.59	104.93	133.11	152.83	191.26	276.61	332.52
111.25	115.92	136.18	128.47	173.89	213.04	216.67	257.14	316.95	405.62
67.51	88.83	115.14	143.45	191.89	213.12	236.97	256.27	308.85	469.06
232.61	241.31	275.38	296.80	340.88	420.45	387.51	352.98	489.68	531.23
67.62	73.02	58.08	31.22	40.25	55.90	54.86	59.53	70.42	89.95

7-12 农村居民家庭基本情况（2009年）

项 目	Item	西安市 Xi'an	灞桥区 Baqiao	未央区 Weiyang
一、调查户数（户）	**Number of Households Surveyed (household)**	**940**	**100**	**80**
二、常住人口（人）	**Permanent Residents(person)**	**3828**	**405**	**336**
6岁及以下	6 Year-old and Below	195	21	20
7-15岁人口	7-15 Year-old	360	32	27
16-60岁人口	16-60 Year-old	2791	306	241
61岁以上人口	61 Year-old and Above	482	46	48
三、整半劳动力（人）	**Able-bodied and Semi-able-bodied Labourer(person)**	**2557**	**289**	**226**
四、常住人口外出从业人数（人）	**Permanent Residents Employed in Other Places Outside(person)**	**503**	**63**	**53**
五、劳动力文化程度（人）	**Labourer Literacy(person)**			
1.不识字或识字很少	Illiterates or Semi-illiterates	15	1	
2.小学文化程度	Primary Schools	194	6	5
3. 初中文化程度	Junior Secondary Schools	1468	185	157
4. 高中程度	Senior Secondary Schools	663	71	38
5.中专程度	Specialized Secondary Schools	93	6	15
6. 大专及以上	Universities and Colleges and Above	122	20	11
六、人均耕地经营面积（亩）	**Area of Cultivated Land Managed per Capita(mu)**	**0.99**	**0.44**	**0.24**

Basic Conditions of Rural Households（2009）

(yuan)

雁塔区 Yanta	阎良区 Yanliang	临潼区 Lintong	长安区 Chang'an	蓝田县 Lantian	周至县 Zhouzhi	户 县 Huxian	高陵县 Gaoling
80	**80**	**100**	**120**	**90**	**90**	**100**	**100**
327	**299**	**403**	**487**	**362**	**399**	**436**	**374**
17	6	20	22	18	23	28	20
23	20	41	45	50	46	49	27
265	230	290	341	252	278	303	285
22	43	52	79	42	52	56	42
248	**226**	**247**	**297**	**250**	**244**	**279**	**251**
2	**37**	**70**	**57**	**61**	**41**	**68**	**51**
1		4		3	3	3	
7	8	24	15	41	40	25	23
104	83	143	208	166	118	140	164
86	112	66	49	34	63	94	50
13	18	3	17	3	6	5	7
37	5	5	8	3	14	12	7
0.11	**0.89**	**1.34**	**0.86**	**2.12**	**1.35**	**1.14**	**1.27**

7-13 农村居民家庭平均每人总收入和纯收入（2009年）

单位：元

项　　目	Item	西安市 Xi'an	灞桥区 Baqiao	未央区 Weiyang
一、全年总收入	**Annual Total Revenue**	**7961.26**	**8056.35**	**9066.79**
（一）工资性收入	Income from Wages and Salaries	2587.25	3336.81	4035.31
1.在非企业组织中劳动得到的	Get from Non-enterprise Organizition	207.09	237.17	369.44
2.在本乡地域内劳动得到的	Income from Labor Providing Inside Administrative Region	1505.06	2193.87	3504.80
3.常住人口外出从业得到的	Get from Permanent Residents	875.10	905.77	161.07
（二）家庭经营收入	Income from Household Operations	4109.86	2931.26	2172.99
#农业收入	Farming	1966.41	821.58	471.60
牧业收入	Animal Husbandry	646.04	117.96	457.99
（三）财产性收入	Income from Properties	738.95	1172.61	2239.63
（四）转移性收入	Income from Transfers	525.20	615.67	618.86
二、全年纯收入	**Annual Net Income**	**6275.22**	**7136.00**	**7826.08**
三、可支配收入	**Disposable Income**	**6008.41**	**6796.41**	**7653.21**

7-14 农村居民家庭平均每人全年总支出（2009年）

单位：元

项　　目	Item	西安市 Xi'an	灞桥区 Baqiao	未央区 Weiyang
全年总支出	**Annual Total Expenditure**	**6721.19**	**6751.11**	**7983.73**
一、家庭经营费用支出	**Expenditure for Household Business**	**1441.49**	**709.20**	**1010.66**
#农业支出	Farming	709.79	256.09	59.02
牧业支出	Animal Husbandry	408.73	80.66	666.89
二、购置生产用固定资产支出	**Purchasing Productive Fixed Assets**	**177.99**	**386.40**	
三、建造生产性固定资产雇工支出	**Expenditure on labor hiring on building of productive fixed assets**	**8.21**	**51.41**	
四、税费支出	**Expenditure for Tax and Fee**	**9.63**	**3.33**	
五、生活消费支出	**Expenditure for Living Consumption**	**4771.06**	**5255.01**	**6736.03**
六、财产性支出	**Expenditure for Property**	**4.51**	**6.93**	
七、转移性支出	**Expenditure for Transfer**	**308.31**	**338.83**	**237.04**

Per Capita Annual Total Revenue and Net Income of Rural Households（2009）

（yuan)

雁塔区 Yanta	阎良区 Yanliang	临潼区 Lintong	长安区 Chang'an	蓝田县 Lantian	周至县 Zhouzhi	户 县 Huxian	高陵县 Gaoling
8491.50	**11823.80**	**7964.64**	**7111.26**	**5233.18**	**5715.74**	**7838.09**	**7496.46**
3233.11	1842.46	2232.39	2608.10	1810.80	1620.77	2649.64	2302.97
434.89	265.56	218.31	88.01	88.28	196.34	40.92	245.85
1510.28	1005.50	1049.13	1612.29	563.21	611.20	1567.26	1234.38
1287.94	571.40	964.95	907.80	1159.31	813.23	1041.46	822.74
1868.67	8812.51	4871.33	3669.02	2998.90	3721.18	4785.72	4275.46
7.98	6534.17	1847.76	1015.72	1639.85	2421.89	2137.73	2258.27
	518.57	2027.75	34.72	164.44	401.62	1468.30	970.39
3122.38	513.50	134.50	251.23	5.64	132.77	20.51	497.94
267.34	655.33	726.42	582.91	417.84	241.02	382.22	420.09
7948.31	**7233.27**	**5793.66**	**5964.92**	**4315.22**	**4248.11**	**5307.00**	**5735.10**
7815.18	**6976.67**	**5571.74**	**5630.29**	**4088.63**	**3825.35**	**5132.54**	**5400.28**

Per Capita Annual Total Expenditure of Rural Households（2009）

(yuan)

雁塔区 Yanta	阎良区 Yanliang	临潼区 Lintong	长安区 Chang'an	蓝田县 Lantian	周至县 Zhouzhi	户 县 Huxian	高陵县 Gaoling
6249.23	**9345.01**	**7758.55**	**5824.61**	**4516.89**	**6117.15**	**6928.31**	**5378.82**
373.87	**4294.61**	**1782.53**	**1004.16**	**733.97**	**1142.08**	**2271.39**	**1510.14**
3.60	4228.74	597.41	320.77	299.23	646.92	695.77	695.69
	7.44	975.87	12.24	116.31	295.87	1112.90	697.99
4.39	**57.82**	**564.25**	**116.63**	**51.02**	**360.92**	**127.60**	**10.23**
						7.08	**20.08**
16.65	**0.54**	**23.76**	**29.40**	**7.95**		**5.18**	**2.31**
5674.52	**4691.46**	**5108.55**	**4315.62**	**3430.43**	**4152.43**	**4256.32**	**3471.03**
	29.93	**0.82**	**9.20**			**0.93**	**0.80**
179.80	**270.65**	**278.64**	**349.60**	**293.52**	**461.72**	**259.81**	**364.23**

7-15　农村居民家庭平均每人生活消费支出（2009年）

单位：元

项　目	Item	西安市 Xi'an	灞桥区 Baqiao	未央区 Weiyang
生活消费支出总计	**Living Expenditure**	**4771.06**	**5255.00**	**6736.04**
一、食品消费支出	**Food**	**1708.35**	**1924.96**	**1460.97**
二、衣着	**Clothing**	**305.46**	**411.04**	**352.09**
三、居住	**Residence**	**928.87**	**716.61**	**2359.47**
四、家庭设备用品及服务	**Household Facilities,Articles and Service**	**332.52**	**364.71**	**383.34**
五、医疗保健	**Medical and Health Care Services**	**405.62**	**613.59**	**464.63**
六、交通通讯	**Transport,Post and Telecommunication Services**	**469.06**	**534.23**	**1142.98**
七、文化娱乐用品及服务	**Cultural,Education and Recreation and Services**	**531.23**	**585.68**	**519.40**
八、其它商品及服务	**Other Commodities and Services**	**89.95**	**104.18**	**53.16**
附：人均生活消费现金支出	Per Capita Cash Expenditure for Living Consumption	4429.35	5128.15	6710.22

7-16　农村居民家庭人均生产情况（2009年）

单位：公斤

项　目	Item	西安市 Xi'an	灞桥区 Baqiao	未央区 Weiyang
粮食产量	Output of Grain	561.78	202.81	123.38
#1.小麦	Wheat	272.45	138.40	46.09
2.玉米	Corn	282.83	63.46	33.78
3.大豆	Soybean	4.24	0.21	37.50
棉花产量	Output of Cotton	2.40	0.19	
油料产量	Output of Oil-bearing Crops	0.57	0.94	
蔬菜产量	Output of Vegetables	293.46	56.27	76.49
水果产量	Output of Fruits	132.56	74.24	

Per Capita Living Expenditure of Rural Households（2009）

（yuan）

雁塔区 Yanta	阎良区 Yanliang	临潼区 Lintong	长安区 Chang'an	蓝田县 Lantian	周至县 Zhouzhi	户 县 Huxian	高陵县 Gaoling
5674.52	**469.44**	**5108.55**	**4315.63**	**3430.43**	**4152.43**	**4256.32**	**3471.04**
2216.49	**1676.02**	**1503.63**	**1457.96**	**1286.31**	**1210.91**	**1795.26**	**1590.79**
395.54	**326.83**	**311.96**	**277.74**	**223.76**	**278.64**	**301.33**	**194.96**
855.55	**568.91**	**867.66**	**1106.27**	**765.29**	**963.21**	**582.58**	**585.70**
399.23	**621.50**	**525.40**	**269.54**	**215.47**	**249.90**	**198.66**	**194.26**
438.27	**332.04**	**554.22**	**404.38**	**263.46**	**315.83**	**379.97**	**262.42**
549.99	**480.68**	**712.46**	**257.18**	**226.56**	**290.82**	**402.06**	**229.56**
754.89	**656.98**	**571.25**	**457.21**	**386.80**	**633.72**	**510.40**	**294.86**
64.56	**28.48**	**61.97**	**85.35**	**62.78**	**209.40**	**86.06**	**118.49**
5674.52	4362.78	4905.85	4146.48	2945.48	3922.63	3707.92	3260.62

Output of Major Farm Crops Per Capita by Rural Households（2009）

（kg）

雁塔区 Yanta	阎良区 Yanliang	临潼区 Lintong	长安区 Chang'an	蓝田县 Lantian	周至县 Zhouzhi	户 县 Huxian	高陵县 Gaoling
	918.74	865.94	480.30	718.73	324.78	935.40	993.87
	334.22	423.36	258.39	447.69	85.96	441.84	497.36
	583.17	442.58	221.09	253.51	233.19	493.39	495.46
			0.82	8.01	0.13	0.06	0.45
	30.41						
					4.52		
	1765.13	93.24	193.02	254.51	120.59	233.64	463.63
	40.78	64.32	0.28	77.87	951.39	58.11	16.00

7-17 农村居民家庭人均出售产品情况（2009年）

单位：公斤

项　目	Item	西安市 Xi'an	灞桥区 Baqiao	未央区 Weiyang
粮食	Grain	367.26	61.05	57.41
棉花	Cotton	0.76		
油料	Oil-bearing Corps	0.16		
蔬菜	Vegetables	212.90	53.84	75.02
水果	Fruits	93.02	60.90	
肉猪及猪肉	Fattened Hogs & Pork	17.54	5.82	
菜牛及牛肉	Beef Cattle & Beef	0.81		2.17
菜羊及羊肉	Mutton Sheep & Mutton	0.18		
蛋类	Poultry Eggs	5.92		
奶类	Milks	63.31	1.48	35.09

7-18 农村居民家庭人均粮食收支情况（2009年）

单位：公斤

项　目	Item	西安市 Xi'an	灞桥区 Baqiao	未央区 Weiyang
一、粮食收入合计	**Total Grain Income**	**802.56**	**278.71**	**1777.86**
1.家庭经营生产	Self-produced	561.78	202.81	123.38
2.购入	Purchased	237.88	75.90	1654.48
3.借入	Borrowed	0.46		
4.收回借出粮	Grains Taken Back	2.16		
5.其它粮食收入	Other Grain Income	0.28		
二、粮食支出合计	**Total Grain Expenditure**	**770.20**	**214.37**	**1728.05**
1.主食用粮	Staple Food	186.33	150.72	88.52
2.其它生活用粮	Other Living Uses			
3.出售	Sold Out	367.25	61.05	57.41
4.种籽	Seeds	12.29	2.44	1.25
5.饲料	Fodder	204.02	0.16	1580.87
6.借出	Lent Out			
7.归还借粮	Grains Returned			
8.其它粮食支出	Other Grain Expenditure	0.31		
三、年末粮食结存调查数	**Year-end Grain Deposite Balance**	**327.99**	**91.99**	**17.98**

Per Capita Product Sold by Rural Households（2009）

（kg)

雁塔区 Yanta	阎良区 Yanliang	临潼区 Lintong	长安区 Chang'an	蓝田县 Lantian	周至县 Zhouzhi	户 县 Huxian	高陵县 Gaoling
4.28	598.49	823.05	440.38	341.77	85.76	424.50	781.52
	9.77						
				1.67	0.03		
	1461.76	113.41	91.42	15.07	105.39	219.90	260.13
	23.41	60.41	0.28	45.14	635.71	56.67	14.03
	4.87	25.16	0.68	2.30	7.16	76.38	42.40
		1.81		4.56			
	0.23	0.09		1.28	0.19	0.10	
				0.88	0.04	35.14	18.79
	172.94	307.47		3.61			141.83

Per Capita Annual Income and Expenditure of Grains of Rural Households（2009）

（kg)

雁塔区 Yanta	阎良区 Yanliang	临潼区 Lintong	长安区 Chang'an	蓝田县 Lantian	周至县 Zhouzhi	户 县 Huxian	高陵县 Gaoling
68.10	**972.53**	**1081.50**	**529.57**	**782.06**	**394.63**	**1101.00**	**1161.81**
	918.74	865.93	480.30	718.73	324.78	935.40	993.88
68.10	53.79	190.99	47.83	63.33	68.71	165.59	167.88
		4.34					0.05
		20.24	0.21				
			1.23		1.14	0.01	
72.38	**852.29**	**1230.66**	**594.38**	**668.57**	**305.21**	**947.48**	**1176.60**
68.10	248.77	151.65	143.54	292.07	188.87	350.77	162.50
4.28	598.49	823.05	440.39	341.77	85.76	424.50	781.52
0.00	3.30	17.72	10.45	10.31	11.70	28.93	30.49
	1.73	235.26		24.42	18.88	143.28	202.09
		2.98					
	191.64	**569.95**	**530.69**	**538.71**	**275.83**	**411.98**	**486.93**

7-19 农村居民家庭平均每人购买商品（2009年）

单位：元

商品名称	Commodity Names	西安市 Xi'an	灞桥区 Baqiao	未央区 Weiyang
一、食品类	Food	1089.58	1459.19	1232.84
二、衣着类	Clothing	303.90	410.19	350.94
三、居住类	Residence	598.64	436.06	1637.19
四、家用设备和日用品	Household Facilities and Articles	321.32	358.58	376.57
五、交通、通讯类	Transport,post and Telecommunication	294.58	306.04	977.11
六、文教类	Cultural and Edueation	149.29	83.52	131.92
七、医疗保健类	Health Care and Medical Services	144.67	122.13	198.92
八、其他杂项商品	Other Commodities and Services	66.69	82.86	16.39

7-20 农村居民家庭人均主要食品消费量（2009年）

单位：公斤

食品名称	Food Names	西安市 Xi'an	灞桥区 Baqiao	未央区 Weiyang
一、粮食	Grain	186.33	150.72	88.52
#小麦	Wheet	139.37	99.54	52.19
二、油脂类	Oil or Fat	10.00	10.46	7.13
三、蔬菜及菜制品	Vegetable and Its Products	65.58	81.37	68.52
四、瓜果类	Melons and Fruits	8.39	12.36	9.23
五、水果类	Fruits	15.50	20.37	15.99
六、肉禽及制品	Meat,Poultry and Their Products	10.19	15.32	10.18
七、蛋类及蛋制品	Eggs and Its Products	6.22	7.22	5.74
八、奶和奶制品	Milk and Processed Products	8.88	13.61	12.14
九、酒	Liquor	4.42	5.14	3.13

Per Capita Purchase of Commodities in Rural Households（2009）

（yuan)

雁塔区 Yanta	阎良区 Yanliang	临潼区 Lintong	长安区 Chang'an	蓝田县 Lantian	周至县 Zhouzhi	户 县 Huxian	高陵县 Gaoling
1842.03	**1268.58**	**936.97**	**854.71**	**625.73**	**701.89**	**1024.49**	**1168.34**
392.82	**326.58**	**309.52**	**275.11**	**223.08**	**278.03**	**299.26**	**193.33**
251.44	**500.12**	**561.70**	**693.20**	**563.82**	**737.78**	**361.32**	**302.56**
368.46	**608.43**	**516.47**	**263.12**	**202.95**	**235.21**	**191.34**	**184.06**
274.97	**362.24**	**520.13**	**103.74**	**89.74**	**135.73**	**200.27**	**115.21**
331.84	**450.89**	**169.02**	**92.27**	**74.79**	**88.21**	**111.54**	**69.66**
153.29	**144.76**	**173.76**	**212.60**	**90.46**	**107.12**	**173.24**	**52.16**
37.15	**16.17**	**42.84**	**66.24**	**49.85**	**185.92**	**59.25**	**84.67**

Per Capita Average Food Consumption of Rural Households（2009）

（kg)

雁塔区 Yanta	阎良区 Yanliang	临潼区 Lintong	长安区 Chang'an	蓝田县 Lantian	周至县 Zhouzhi	户 县 Huxian	高陵县 Gaoling
68.10	**248.77**	**151.65**	**143.54**	**292.07**	**188.87**	**350.77**	**162.50**
42.92	226.00	129.60	114.16	238.58	118.23	257.28	108.30
13.99	**13.42**	**8.70**	**8.29**	**5.68**	**8.34**	**14.21**	**10.58**
92.38	**70.20**	**63.91**	**59.99**	**49.03**	**32.92**	**51.43**	**95.19**
4.68	**11.68**	**9.01**	**5.62**	**4.25**	**6.81**	**7.11**	**14.02**
12.08	**21.72**	**19.61**	**13.97**	**9.21**	**12.40**	**13.97**	**16.53**
15.70	**17.15**	**5.82**	**7.43**	**5.56**	**9.00**	**11.42**	**6.89**
10.89	**8.75**	**5.22**	**5.14**	**5.96**	**3.31**	**5.59**	**6.01**
7.29	**7.36**	**8.65**	**9.94**	**6.17**	**8.92**	**5.85**	**8.47**
1.94	**6.14**	**7.50**	**4.53**	**4.71**	**3.37**	**2.08**	**5.74**

7-21 农村居民家庭每百户耐用消费品年末拥有量（2009年）

品　　名	Item	西安市 Xi'an	灞桥区 Baqiao	未央区 Weiyang
大型家具(件)	Large Furnitures (unit)			
洗衣机(台)	Washing Machine(unit)	98	103	103
电风扇(台)	Electric Fan(unit)			
电冰箱(台)	Refrigerator(unit)	55	75	95
自行车(辆)	Bicycle (unit)	132	128	123
摩托车(辆)	Motorcycle(unit)	38	27	9
电话机(部)	Telephone (unit)	63	52	48
彩色电视机(台)	Color TV Set(unit)	134	158	135
黑白电视机(台)	Black-white TV Set(unit)	3		
影碟机(台)	Video Disc Player (unit)	59	83	19
照相机(架)	Camera(set)	17	33	15
家用计算机(台)	Computer(unit)	16	18	21

7-22 农村居民家庭人均住房情况（2009年）

指　　标	Item	西安市 Xi'an	灞桥区 Baqiao	未央区 Weiyang
一、年末住房面积 (平方米)	**Floor Space of Houses at the End of Year (sq.m)**	**56.73**	**69.95**	**89.41**
二、住房类型 (平方米)	**Pattern of Houses(sq.m)**			
1. 楼房面积	Floor Space of Storied Building	41.99	61.68	81.44
2. 砖瓦平房面积	Floor Space of Single-storey Building	13.68	8.10	7.98
3. 其他	Others	1.06	0.17	
三、年末住房价值(元)	**Value of Houses at the End of Year (yuan)**	**24500.32**	**29183.95**	**49915.51**
四、年内新建（购）房屋面积(平方米)	**Floor Space Of Newly-Built Purchased Houses (sq.m)**	**2.62**	**2.98**	**0.18**
年内新建（购）房屋价值(元)	Value of Houses of Newly-Built Purchased (yuan)	1349.27	1392.59	74.40

Year-end Possession of Durable Consumer Goods Per 100 Rural Households（2009）

雁塔区 Yanta	阎良区 Yanliang	临潼区 Lintong	长安区 Chang'an	蓝田县 Lantian	周至县 Zhouzhi	户 县 Huxian	高陵县 Gaoling
103	100	107	94	74	94	92	106
101	93	42	39	21	22	22	61
80	159	160	123	69	136	182	153
6	48	65	21	52	71	24	53
76	58	77	71	68	40	78	62
179	121	133	116	112	129	130	130
		5	13		4	1	
98	68	65	53	60	49	40	55
79	13	3	11	6	11	3	11
68	15	10	3	8	8	4	21

Per Capita Housing Conditions of Rural Households（2009）

雁塔区 Yanta	阎良区 Yanliang	临潼区 Lintong	长安区 Chang'an	蓝田县 Lantian	周至县 Zhouzhi	户 县 Huxian	高陵县 Gaoling
136.01	**14.65**	**40.59**	**40.55**	**37.08**	**44.11**	**47.27**	**59.33**
136.01	9.20	9.62	26.51	27.06	28.02	41.07	14.72
	5.45	28.66	13.55	6.84	15.21	5.10	42.44
		2.31	0.49	3.18	0.88	1.10	2.17
69171.25	**12304.35**	**13614.96**	**11326.69**	**14948.90**	**19127.82**	**19770.87**	**16662.03**
8.56		**1.19**	**1.39**	**3.18**	**4.09**	**1.96**	**3.10**
4678.90		610.42	790.55	1795.58	2130.33	876.15	1425.13

主要统计指标解释

城镇居民家庭全部收入 指被调查城市居民家庭全部的实际收入，包括经常或固定得到的收入和一次性收入。不包括周转性收入，如提取银行存款、向亲友借款、收回借出款以及其他各种暂收款。

城镇居民家庭可支配收入 指被调查的城市居民家庭在支付所得税、记帐补贴、个人交纳的社会保障费后所余下的实际收入。

城镇居民家庭消费性支出 指被调查的城市居民家庭用于日常生活的全部支出，包括购买商品支出和文化生活、服务等非商品性支出。不包括罚没、丢失款和缴纳的各种税款（如个人所得税、牌照税、房产税等），也不包括个体劳动者生产经营过程中发生的各项费用。

农村居民家庭纯收入 指农村常住户当年从各个来源得到的总收入相应地扣除所发生的费用后的收入总和。

农村居民家庭生活消费支出 指农村住户用于物质生活和精神生活方面的支出。

Explanatory Notes on Main Statistical Indicators

Total Income of Urban Households refers to the total actual income of the sample households, including regular or fixed income and occasional income. The income of a circulating nature such as withdrawal from bank deposits, loans borrowed from relatives or friends, repayment of loans received and various temporary collection of money is excluded.

Disposable Income of Urban Households refers to the actual income of the sample households which can be used for daily expenses, i.e., total income minus income tax, sample household subsidy and personal social security.

Expenditure for Consumption of Urban Households refers to total expenditure of the sample households for consumption in daily life, including expenditure for various commodities and expenses for non-commodity items such as culture and service, etc. ,but excluding fines and confiscation, loss, tax payments (such as income tax, license tax, real estates tax, etc.) and various expenses by individual laborers for business purposes.

Net income of country household: it refers to sum of income of country households after taking out of the expenditures from all sides of resources of the year.

Living consuming expenditure of country household: it refers to expenditures used for material life and culture life of the country households.

8 城市公用事业

URBAN PUBLIC UTILITIES

资料整理：陈超毅

Data management:Chen Chaoyi

第八部分　城市公用事业

一、简要说明

本章资料主要包括城市供水、售电、供燃气、供热、公共交通、市政设施、城市设施水平、城市规模及用地状况、园林绿地、环境卫生等情况，由西安市统计局社会科技处根据有关部门提供的数据资料整理。

二、主要指标

人均公园绿地面积（平方米）	7.90	比上年增长 1.3%
人均拥有道路面积（平方米）	14.80	比上年增长 5.4%
用水普及率（%）	100.00	与上年持平
燃气普及率（%）	98.15	比上年增加 0.5个百分点
每万人拥有公共交通车辆（标台）	22.92	比上年增长 20.2%

8 URBAN PUBLIC UTILITIES

Ⅰ.Brief Introduction

Data in this chapter reflects basic condition of urban public utilities of Xi'an city. Data on public utilities are consist of primarily urban water supply, electricity sales, gas sales, urban heating, public transportation, municipal facilities, condition of city utilities, scale of the city, condition of land utilization, parks, greenbelt and environmental sanitation. Data in this chapter is compiled by Social & Science and Technology Division of the Xi'an Bureau of Statistics according to the data provided by department concerned of the municipal government.

Ⅱ.Major Indicators

		Increase over Preceding Year
Per Capita Public Green Areas (sq.m)	7.90	1.3%
Per Captia Area of Roads (sq.m)	14.80	5.4%
Water-Consuming Popularization (%)	100.00	(increase as last year)
Gas-Consuming Popularization (%)	98.15	0.5 percentage points
Number of Public Transport Vehicles Per 10 000 Population (unit)	22.92	20.2%

8-1 城市供水

Urban Water Supply

指　　标	Item	2000	2006	2007	2008	2009
年末水厂个数（个）	Number of Water Factory at Year-end (unit)	8	9	9	9	9
供水综合生产能力（万立方米/日）	Total Volume of Water Supply (10 000 cu.m/day)	139.9	163.5	180.7	180.5	190.0
#地下水	Groundwater	73.9	41.5	53.7	52.4	55.3
年末供水管道总长度（公里）	Length of Water Supply Pipelines at Year-end (km)	2237	1529	2424	2385	1985
全年供水总量（万立方米）	Total Annual Volume of Water Supply (10 000 cu.m)	30273	28762	32959	36471	38307
#生产运营用水	For Productive Use	6486	4573	5570	6292	6414
居民家庭用水	For Residential Use	10949	11084	13931	17510	18513
用水人口（万人）	Population with Access to Tap Water (10 000 persons)	257.0	311.5	331.3	374.1	357.6

注：2009年部门统计制度变化，年末供水管道总长度和用水人口数调整。

Note:Departmental statistical system was changed in 2009,length of water supply pipelines at year-end and population with access to tap water were adjusted.

8-2 城市售电

Urban Consumption of Elecricity

单位:万千瓦时　　(10 000kwh)

分　　类	Classify	2000	2006	2007	2008	2009
总　　计	**Total**	**732373**	**1378864**	**1482896**	**1605089**	**1724067**
#行业用电合计	Total Electricity Consumed	599855	1110876	1215799	1293574	1358483
1.第一产业	Primary Industry	77579	118635	120134	127054	99083
2.第二产业	Secondary Industry	354245	637641	700026	724852	766029
3.第三产业	Tertiary Industry	168031	354600	395639	441668	493371
一、农、林、牧、渔业	**Farming,Forestry,Animal Husbandry and Fishery**	**77579**	**118635**	**120134**	**127054**	**99083**
二、工业	**Industry**	**345175**	**615476**	**674990**	**696291**	**724920**
1.轻工业用电	Light Industrial	152125	175538	187323	182176	167144
2.重工业用电	Heavy Industrial	193050	439938	487667	514115	557776
三、信息传输、计算机服务和软件业	**Information Transmission,Computer Service and Software Service**		**17281**	**21938**	**26680**	**29328**
四、建筑业	**Construction**	**9070**	**22166**	**25036**	**28561**	**41108**
五、交通运输、仓储和邮政业	**Transport,Storage and Postal Service**	**22904**	**50003**	**53825**	**56614**	**62031**
六、公共事业及管理组织	**Public administration non-profit institution**		**130728**	**144859**	**165024**	**177409**
七、商业、住宿和餐饮业	**Accommodation and Catering Trade**		**97352**	**107343**	**111676**	**122203**
八、金融、房地产、商务及居民服务业	**Banking,Real Estate Trade and Resident Services**		**59235**	**67674**	**81674**	**102400**
九、城乡居民生活用电	**Residential Electricity Consumption**	**132518**	**267987**	**267097**	**311515**	**365585**
1.乡村	In Rural Areas	31281	36901	38395	63072	265644
2.城市	In Urban Areas	101237	231086	228702	248443	99941

8-3 城市供燃气

Gas Supply in Urban Area

指　　标	Item	2000	2006	2007	2008	2009
一、天然气	**Natural Gas**					
管道长度（公里）	Total Length of Gas Pipelines (km)	480	905	3121	3540	3932
供气总量（万立方米）	Total Gas Supply(10 000 cu.m)	11513	68631	72253	84874	95884
#家庭用量	Residential Households	2808	13294	9854	13767	15473
用气人口（万人）	Population with Access to Gas (10 000 persons)	79.5	212.05	233.6	246.7	285.0
二、液化石油气	**Liquefied Petroeum Gas**					
供气总量（吨）	Total Gas Supply (ton)	43304	75700	73081	74164	
#家庭用量	Residential Households	43303	48400	46051	46342	
用气人口（万人）	Population with Access to Gas (10 000 persons)	101.6	90.2	93.0	81.9	

注：2009年部门统计制度变化，取消液化石油气相关统计指标。

Note:Departmental statistical system was changed in 2009,statistical indicators about liquefied petroeum gas were canceled.

8-4 城市供热

Heating in Urban Area

指　　标	Item	2000	2006	2007	2008	2009
供热能力	Heating Capacity					
蒸气（吨/小时）	Steam (ton/hour)	766	1671	1680	1063	2118
热水（兆瓦）	Hot Water (1 billion kw)	405	1030	1627	11085	11467
供热总量	Volume Supplied					
蒸气（万吉焦）	Steam (10 000 gigajoules)	126	1433	1510	1192	1541
热水（万吉焦）	Hot Water (10 000 gigajoules)	202	724	1075	896	1220
管道长度（公里）	Length of Pipelines (km)					
蒸气	Steam	221	280	296	97	209
热水	Hot Water	133	173	263	179	289
供热面积（万平方米）	Heated Area (10 000sq.m)	854	2134	2811	3179	5178
#住宅	Residential Buildings	536	1849	2098	2616	4325

注：2008年及以后年份热水供热能力统计口径发生变化，故与以前年份不可比。

Note:Statistical caliber of hot water heating capacity has changed since 2008,so it couldn't be compared with that of former years.

8-5 城市公共交通

Urban Public Traffic

指　　标	Item	2000	2006	2007	2008	2009
运营车辆(辆)	Operating Vehicles (unit)	2573	5489	5836	6123	7039
1.汽车	Bus	2488	5414	5772	6059	7004
2.电车	Trolley	85	75	64	64	35
标准运营车辆（标台）	Standard Vehicles (unit)	2509	5270	5969	6416	7833
运营线路网长度（公里）	Length of Routes (km)	434	571	734	856	940
客运总量(万人次)	Number of Passengers carried (10 000 persons)	44570	97078	114859	139924	161782
出租汽车数（辆）	Number of Taxis (unit)	10277	11177	11879	11879	12786

8-6 市政设施

Manicipal Facilities

指　　标	Item	2000	2006	2007	2008	2009
一、道路长度（公里）	**Length of Roads (km)**	**975**	**1480**	**1842**	**2115**	**2296**
二、道路面积（万平方米）	**Area of Roads (10 000 sq.m)**	**1263**	**3219**	**4190**	**4722**	**5057**
三、人行道面积（万平方米）	**Area of Sidewalks (10 000 sq.m)**	**636**	**1006**	**1337**	**1470**	**1517**
四、桥梁数（座）	**Number of Bridges (unit)**	**79**	**194**	**259**	**305**	**314**
#立交桥	Crossroads	22	37	48	71	71
五、路灯盏数（盏）	**Number of Street Lights (unit)**	**27516**	**141000**	**260000**	**266442**	**271444**
六、排水管道长度（公里）	**Length of Drainage Pipelines (km)**	**835**	**1610**	**1964**	**2562**	**2848**
七、污水年排放量（万立方米）	**Annual Discharge Volume of Sewage (10 000 cu.m)**	**23543**	**23618**	**24719**	**21886**	**31394**
八、污水处理厂处理能力（万立方米/日）	**Daily Disposal Capacity of Sewage (10 000 cu.m/day)**	**29**	**41**	**43.5**	**77.5**	**80**
九、污水处理厂年处理量（万立方米）	**Yearly Disposal Capacity of Sewage Disposal Plant (10 000 cu.m)**	**5441**	**11315**	**12338**	**13003**	**20386**
十、防洪堤长度（公里）	**Length of Flood control Dikes (km)**	**1.60**	**19.00**	**39.00**	**119.00**	**119.00**

8-7 城市设施水平

Urban Manicipal Facilities

指　　标	Item	2000	2006	2007	2008	2009
一、人均日生活用水量（升）	**Per Capita Daily Consumption of Tap Water For Residential Use (liter)**	**241.54**	**126.50**	**187.01**	**179.74**	**198.36**
二、用水普及率（%）	**Water-Consuming Popularization (%)**	**98.95**	**99.09**	**100.01**	**111.22**	**100.00**
三、每万人拥有公共交通车辆（标台）	**Number of Public Transport Vehicles Per 10 000 Population (unit)**	**10.17**	**16.15**	**18.02**	**19.07**	**22.92**
四、燃气普及率（%）	**Gas-Consuming Popularization (%)**	**81.51**	**92.62**	**98.60**	**97.66**	**98.15**
五、人均拥有道路面积（平方米）	**Per Captia Area of Roads (sq.m)**	**5.12**	**9.86**	**12.65**	**14.04**	**14.80**
六、排水管道密度（公里/平方公里）	**Density of Drainage Pipelines (km/sq.km)**	**4.47**	**5.13**	**6.26**	**8.04**	**10.06**
七、污水处理率（%）	**Rate of Sewerage Disposal (%)**	**23.11**	**60.10**	**61.56**	**65.12**	**80.97**
八、园林绿化	**Afforestation and Parks and Gardens**					
#人均公园绿地面积（平方米）	Per Capita Public Green Areas (sq.m)	5.12	7.59	7.61	7.80	7.90
建城区绿地率（%）	Rate of Green Areas in Developed Areas (%)	19.67	31.01	31.11	31.89	40.42
九、垃圾无害化处理率（%）	**Rate of No Harm Disposal of Garbage (%)**	**90.89**	**81.57**	**81.23**	**90.35**	**90.30**

注：由于用水人口包括不在城市辖区内但已经使用城市供水的人口，故有些年份用水普及率有大于100%。

Note:As population with access to tap water contained the people who were out of urban area but had used tap water, water-consuming popularization was over 100% in some year.

8-8 城市规模及用地情况

City Scale and Land Use

指　　标	Item	2000	2006	2007	2008	2009
建成区面积（平方公里）	Area of the Constructed Regions (sq.km)	187	261	268	273	283
城市建设用地（平方公里）	Land use for Construction (sq.km)	175	277	277	370	277
#工业用地	Industrial	35	61	61	64	61
仓储用地	Storage	8	12	12	4	12
对外交通用地	External Transportation	10	8	8	8	8
生活居住用地	Residential Area	73	66	66	122	122

8-9 城市园林绿化

Urban Park,Gardens and Green Areas in Cities

指　　标	Item	2000	2006	2007	2008	2009
一、公园个数（个）	**Number of Parks (unit)**	**47**	**49**	**50**	**54**	**55**
二、公园面积（公顷）	**Area of Parks (hectare)**	**880**	**999**	**1129**	**1233**	**1241**
三、园林绿地总面积（公顷）	**Total Area of Parks,Gardens and Green Areas (hectare)**	**4116**	**8106**	**8670**	**9199**	**9553**
#公园绿地面积	Public Green Areas	1263	2476	2520	2625	2700
四、年末绿化覆盖面积（公顷）	**Coverage Space of Green Areas at year-end (hectare)**	**6542**	**10737**	**11087**	**11616**	**12059**
五、建成区绿化覆盖率（%）	**Coverage of Green Areas in Developed Areas (%)**	**33.29**	**39.82**	**39.71**	**40.33**	**40.42**

注：2006年国家绿化统计重新规范，故口径发生变化，原“公共绿地面积”改为“公园绿地面积”。

Note:As national greening regulations of 2006 were changed, 'public green area' was replaced by 'park green area'.

8-10 城市环境卫生

Urban Environment Sanitation

指　　标	Item	2000	2006	2007	2008	2009
清扫面积(万平方米)	Area Under Cleaning Program (10 000 sq.m)	1739	3238	3646	4218	5285
清运生活垃圾（万吨）	Volume of Residential Garbage Disposal (10 000 tons)	98	119	147	152	179
清运粪便（万吨）	Volume of Excrement and Urine Disposal (10 000 tons)	5	6	4	4	3
公共厕所（座）	Number of Public Lavatories (unit)	430	891	962	1131	1131
市容环卫专用车辆（台）	Special Vehicles of Environmental Sanitation (unit)	330	790	768	716	939

主要统计指标解释

标准运营车数 指不同类型的运营车辆按统一的标准当量折合成的运营车数。计算公式：

标准运营车数=∑（每类型车辆数×相应换算系数）

每万人拥有公共交通车辆 指按城市人口计算的每万人平均拥有的公共交通车辆标台数。计算公式：

每万人拥有公共交通车辆（标台）=全市公共交通运营车标台数/城市人口数（万人）

运营线路总长度 指全部运营线路长度之和。计算公式：

运营线路长度=∑各条运营线路长度

=∑[1/2（上行起点至终点里程+下行起点至终点里程+上下行终点掉头里程）]

单向行驶的环行线路长度等于起点至终点里程与终点下客站至起点里程之和的一半。不包括折返、试车、联络线等非运营线路。

运营线路网长度 指全部固定运营线路所经过的道路长度。计算公式：

运营线路网长度=运营线路总长度-∑重复线路长度

道路长度 指道路长度和道路相通的桥梁、隧道的长度，按车行道中心线计算。

道路面积 指道路面积和与道路相通的广场、桥梁、隧道的面积（统计时，将人行道面积单独统计）。

人行道面积按道路两侧面积相加计算。包括步行街和广场，含人车混行的道路。

人均拥有道路面积 指平均每个城市人口拥有的道路面积。计算公式：

人均拥有道路面积=道路面积/城市人口数

排水管道长度 指所有排水总管、干管、支管、检查井及连续井进出口等长度之和。计算时应按单管计算，即在同一条街道上如有两条或两条以上并排的排水管道时，应按每条排水管道的长度相加计算。

路灯盏数 指城市道路照明用灯盏数，一根电杆上有几盏即计算几盏。也可分别统计各类路灯盏数。

绿地面积 指报告期末用作园林和绿化的各种绿地面积。包括公园绿地、防护绿地、附属绿地和其他绿地的面积。

公园绿地面积 指城市中向公众开放的、以游憩为主要功能，有一定的游憩设施和服务设施，同时兼有健全生态、美化景观、防灾减灾等综合作用的绿化用地。

公园面积 指报告期末综合公园、专类公园和带状公园的全部占地总面积。即公园内的园路及铺装场地，管理建筑用地，游览、休憩、服务公用建筑用地，绿化用地及水域面积的总和。

生活垃圾无害化处理率 指报告期生活垃圾无害化处理量与生活垃圾产生量的比率。计算公式：

生活垃圾无害化处理率=生活垃圾无害化处理量/生活垃圾产生量×100%

在统计时，由于生活垃圾产生量不易取得，可用清运量代替。

Explanatory Notes on Main Statistical Indicators

Number of standard vehicles under operating refers to equivalent of number of vehicles under operating which was converted by number of different kinds of vehicles with related standard equivalent.

The formula is as following:

Number of standard vehicles = Σ (number of each kind of vehicle × related reduction coefficient)

Number of public transportation vehicles per 10,000 persons refers to number of public transportation vehicles per 10,000 persons based on urban population.

The formula is as following:

Number of public transportation vehicles per 10,000 persons = total number of public transportation vehicles / urban population (10,000 person)

Total length of lines under operating refers to sum of every line under operating.The formula is as following:

Total length of lines under operating = Σ length of every line under operating

Σ [1/2 (mileage from start to end in upline + mileage from start to end in downline + mileage of turning around between ends of upline and downline)

Length of unidirection loop line equals to half of sum of mileage from start to end and mileage from end-station to start, which excludes line without operating such as line of turning back, test-drive, communication and so on..

Length of line network under operating refers to length of paved roads which were passed by total fixed line under operating.

The formula is as following:

Length of line network under operating = total length of line under operating - Σ length of lines repeated

Length of paved road refers to length of paved surface including bridge and tunnel connecting with the paved road, it was measured by central line in carriageway.

Area of paved road refers to area of paved road and square or bridge or tunnel connecting to paved road. (area of pavement was accounted separately)

Area of sidewalks equals area of both side of road which includes road for man and car, including pedestrian street and square.

Per capita area of paved road refers to Per capita area of paved road of urban residents

The formula is as following:

Per capita area of paved road = area of paved road / urban population

Length of sewer pipelines refers to sum of length of header sewer pipelines, main sewer pipeline, branch sewer pipeline, inspection pit , entrance and exit of continuous well, etc. it was calculated on single pipeline, which was equal to sum of length of every pipe while two and more pipelines in same street

Number of street lights refers to number of lights for road lighting, it was calculated on the number of lights on electric poles or accounted by each kind of street lights respectively.

Greening land area refers to the various greenbelt area used as gardens and afforestation at the end of reference time, including green parks, green space protection, subsidiary green space and other area.

Park green area refers to the green space open to the public and take strolling and having a rest as main function , which have a certain recreational facilities and services facilities, have the comprehensive functions of perfect ecological, beautify landscapes and disaster prevention and reduction.

Park area refers to total park floor area of synthetical parks, ribbon categories parks and tape parks at the end of reference time ,including alley and paved ground in park, administrative building plot, public building plot used for visit, rest and service, sum of green space and water area.

Innocent treatment rate of household garbage refers to ratio of volume of household garbage under innocent treatment in reference time to volume of household garbage produced.The formula is as following:

Innocent treatment rate of household garbage = volume of household garbage under innocent treatment / volume of household garbage produced ×100%

In practical statistic, volume of household garbage produced is replaced by volume of household garbage transported, as it is difficult to estimate.

9 环境保护

ENVIRONMENT PROTECTION

资料整理：陈超毅
Data management:Chen Chaoyi

第九部分　环境保护

一、简要说明

本章资料反映环境保护、工业污染排放及处理利用情况、危险废物集中处置情况、生活及其他污染情况和工业污染治理项目建设情况，由西安市统计局社会科技处根据西安市环保局提供的数据资料整理。

二、主要指标

工业废水排放达标率（%）	93.51	比上年下降 4.07个百分点
工业用水重复利用率（%）	79.24	比上年上升 8.30个百分点
工业固体废物综合利用率（%）	97.83	比上年上升 0.05个百分点
污水处理厂处理能力（万吨/日）	80.00	比上年增长 0.6%
污水处理量（万吨）	18078	比上年增长 34.1%

9　ENVIRONMENT PROTECTION

Ⅰ.Brief Introduction

This chapter contain information that reflect environment protection, discharge and treatment of industrial pollutant, centralized treatment of dangerous wastes, domestic pollution and other pollution, construction of projects of industrial pollution treatment. Data in this chapter is compiled by Social & Science and Technology Division of the Xi'an Bureau of Statistics according to the reported data from Environment Protection Administration department of the municipal government.

Ⅱ.Major Indicators

		Increase over Preceding Year
Percentage of Industrial Waste Water up to the Standards for Discharge (%)	93.51	-4.07 percentage points
Percentage of Industrial Water Recycled (%)	79.24	8.30 percentage points
Percentage of Industrial Solid Waste Utilized (%)	97.83	0.05 percentage points
Daily Disposal Capacity of Sewage(10 000 tons/day)	80.00	0.6%
Volume of Sewgae Disposal(10 000 tons)	18078	34.1%

9-1 城市环境保护（2009年）

Urban Environmental Protection（2009）

指　　标	Item	2009
一、饮用水环境	**Potable Water**	
1.水资源总量(万立方米)	Total Amount of Water Resources(10 000cu.m)	33458.7
#地表水资源量	Surface Water Resources	27125.9
地下水资源量	Groundwater Resources	6332.8
2.全市饮用水水质达标率(%)	Percentage of Urban Potable Water Quality up to the Standards(%)	100.0
二、大气环境	**Air**	
1.可吸入颗粒物浓度年平均值(毫克/立方米)	Annual Average Concentration of Particulate Matters(mg/cu.m)	0.113
二氧化硫浓度年平均值	Annual Average concentration of Sulphur Dioxide	0.048
二氧化氮浓度年平均值	Annual Average concentration of Nitrogen Dioxide	0.046
2.全年环境空气质量达标天数(天)	Days of Air Quality up to the Standards(day)	304
全年环境空气质量达标率(%)	Percentage of Air Quality up to the Standards(%)	83.3
三、声环境	**Voice**	
1.功能区噪声平均值(Db(A))	Average Noise Value of Functional Districts(Db(A))	
0类区	Class 0	51.0
1类区	Class 1	56.5
2类区	Class 2	59.3
3类区	Class 3	67.8
4类区	Class 4	73.1
2.道路交通噪声平均值(Db(A))	Average Noise Value of Road Traffic(Db(A))	68.0
3.区域噪声平均值(Db(A))	Average Noise Value of Region(Db(A))	55.1
四、环境污染治理	**Treatment of Environment Pollution**	
1.环境保护投资(亿元)	Investment in Environment Protection(100 million yuan)	53.19
#城市环境基础设施建设投资	Investment in Urban Environment Infrastructure	21.91
2.环境保护投资占地区生产总值比重(%)	Investment in Environment Protection as percent of regional GDP(%)	1.96

9-2 主要年份工业“三废”排放及处理利用情况

Discharge and Treatrment of Waste Gas Water & Solid Wastes in Repersentative Year

指　　标	Item	2000	2006
一、工业废水排放量（万吨）	**Volume of Waste Water Discharge (10 000 tons)**	**9145**	**16389**
工业废水排放达标量	Industrial Waste Wster Meeting Discharge Standards	6130	15267
工业废水排放达标率(%)	Percentage of Industrial Waste Wster Meeting Discharge Standards(%)	67.03	93.15
二、工业废气排放量（万标立方米）	**Total Volume of Industrial Waste Gas** Emission (10 000 cu.m)	**2759719**	**6425076**
#燃料燃烧过程中排放量	Volume of Waste Gas in the Process of Fuel Burning	1942884	3885611
生产工艺过程中排放量	Volume of Waste Gas from the Process of Production	816835	2539465
废气治理设施数（套）	Number of Facilities for Treatment of Waste Gas(set)		466
三、工业固体废物产生量（万吨）	**Volume of Industrial Solid Wastes Produced (10 000 tons)**	**107**	**161**
工业固体废物处置量	Volume of Industrial Solid Wastes Treated	20	5
工业固体废物综合利用量	Volume of Industrial Solid Waste Utilized in a Comprehensive Way	63	143
工业固体废物综合利用率（%）	Percentage of Volume of Industrial Solid Waste Utilized in a Comprehensive Way(%)	58.88	89.07
四、工业锅炉（台/蒸吨）	**Industrial Boilers (unit/ton)**	**691/6258**	**447/5679**
#烟尘排放达标的	Up to the Standards	662/6107	441/5655

9-2 续表 continued

指　　标	Item	2007	2008	2009
一、工业废水排放量（万吨）	**Volume of Waste Water Discharge (10 000 tons)**	**19069**	**18304**	**13168**
工业废水排放达标量	Industrial Waste Wster Meeting Discharge Standards	18352	17862	12106
工业废水排放达标率(%)	Percentage of Industrial Waste Wster Meeting Discharge Standards(%)	96.24	97.58	93.51
二、工业废气排放量（万标立方米）	**Total Volume of Industrial Waste Gas** Emission (10 000 cu.m)	**11494114**	**15191799**	**7372387**
#燃料燃烧过程中排放量	Volume of Waste Gas in the Process of Fuel Burning	3731610	8980681	4275975
生产工艺过程中排放量	Volume of Waste Gas from the Process of Production	7762504	6211118	3096412
废气治理设施数（套）	Number of Facilities for Treatment of Waste Gas(set)	846	920	852
三、工业固体废物产生量（万吨）	**Volume of Industrial Solid Wastes Produced (10 000 tons)**	**193**	**220**	**246**
工业固体废物处置量	Volume of Industrial Solid Wastes Treated	6.00	5.00	4.85
工业固体废物综合利用量	Volume of Industrial Solid Waste Utilized in a Comprehensive Way	171	215	241
工业固体废物综合利用率（%）	Percentage of Volume of Industrial Solid Waste Utilized in a Comprehensive Way(%)	88.48	97.78	97.83
四、工业锅炉（台/蒸吨）	**Industrial Boilers (unit/ton)**	**560/10198**	**617/11438**	**569/11987**
#烟尘排放达标的	Up to the Standards	538/9662	607/11274	561/11665

9–3 工业污染排放及处理利用情况（2009年）

Discharge and Treatment of Industrial Pollution（2009）

指 标	Item	2009
一、被调查企业基本情况	**Basic condition of Enterprises investigated**	
1.企业数（个）	Number of Enterprises (unit)	376
2.工业总产值（万元）	Gross Industry Output Value (10 000 yuan)	16394017.4
3.企业专职环保人员（人）	Number of professional staff of Environmental Protection(person)	3393
4."三废"综合利用产品产值（万元）	Output Value of Produsts Made from Waste Gas, Waste Water and Solid Wastes (10 000 yuan)	9067.0
5.工业锅炉数（台/蒸吨）	Number of Industrial Boilers (unit/ton)	569/11986.6
#烟尘排放达标的	Soot Emission up to the Discharge Standards	561/11664.6
二氧化硫排放达标的	Sulphur Dioxide Emission up to the Discharge Standards	541/11224.1
6.工业炉窑数（座）	Number of Industrial Grates (item)	189
#烟尘排放达标的	Soot Emission up to the Discharge Standards	184
二氧化硫排放达标的	Sulphur Dioxide Emission up to the Discharge Standards	184
二、工业废水	**Industrial Waste Water**	
1.工业用水总量（万吨）	Total Volume of Industrial Water (10 000 tons)	116491.96
#新鲜水量	Volume of Fresh Water	24182.81
重复用水量	Volume of Water Recycled	92309.17
2.工业用水重复利用率（%）	Percentage of Industrial Water Recycled (%)	79.24
3.废水治理设施数（套）	Number of Facilities for Treatment of Waste Water (set)	383
4.废水治理设施处理能力（万吨/日）	Disposal Capacity of Facilities for Treatment of Waste Water (10 000 tons/day)	45.48
5.废水治理设施运行费用（万元）	Operating Expense of Facilities for Treatment of Waste Water (10 000 yuan)	13360.2
6.工业废水排放量（万吨）	Volume of Industrial Waste Water Discharged (10 000 tons)	13168
7.工业废水排放达标量（万吨）	Volume of Industrial Waste Water up to the Standards for Discharge (10 000 tons)	12105.83
8.工业废水排放达标率（%）	Percentage of Industrial Waste Water up to the Standards for Discharge (%)	93.51
三、工业废气	**Industrial Waste Gas**	
1.煤炭消费总量（万吨）	Total Coal Consumption (10 000 tons)	732.9
2.燃料油消费量（万吨）	Fuel Oil Consumption (10 000 tons)	1.82
3.洁净燃气消费量（万标立方米）	Natural Gas Consumption (10 000 cu.m.)	9397
4.工业废气排放总量（万标立方米）	Total Volume of Industrial Waste Gas Emission (10 000 cu.m.)	7372387
5.废气治理设施数（套）	Number of Facilities for Treatment of Waste Gas (set)	852
6.废气治理设施处理能力（万标立方米/时）	Disposal Capacity of Facilities for Treatment of Waste Gas (10 000 cu.m./h)	3179.93
7.废气治理设施设备运行费用（万元）	Operating Expense of Facilities for Treatment of Waste gas(10 000 yuan)	19463.9
8.二氧化硫去除量（吨）	Volume of Sulphur Dioxide Removed (ton)	48879.85
9.二氧化硫排放量（吨）	Volume of Sulphur Dioxide Emission (ton)	82864.22
#燃料燃烧过程中排放量	Volume of Emission from the Burning Process of Fuels	82031.43
#排放达标量	Volume of Emission up to the Standards for Discharge	74476.45
生产工艺过程中排放量	Volume of Emission from the Process of Production	835.77
#排放达标量	Volume of Emission up to the Standards for Discharge	832.17
10.烟尘去除量（吨）	Volume of Soot Removed (ton)	780445.92
11.烟尘排放量（吨）	Volume of Soot Emission (ton)	20409.64
#排放达标量	Volume of Emission up to the Standards for Discharge	20063.72
12.工业粉尘去除量（吨）	Volume of Industrial Dust Removed (ton)	133130.14
13.工业粉尘排放量（吨）	Volume of Industrial Dust Emission (ton)	4235.23
#排放达标量	Volume of Emission up to the Standards for Discharge	3789.97
四、工业固体废物	**Industrial Solid Waste**	
1.工业固体废物产生量（万吨）	Volume of Industrial Solid Waste Produced (10 000tons)	246.33
2.工业固体废物综合利用量（万吨）	Volume of Industrial Solid Waste Utilized (10 000tons)	240.98
3.工业固体废物综合利用率（%）	Percentage of Industrial Solid Waste Utilized (%)	97.83
4.工业固体废物贮存量（万吨）	Volume of Industrial Solid Waste Accumulated (10 000tons)	0.10
5.工业固体废物处置量（万吨）	Volume of Industrial Solid Waste Treated (10 000tons)	4.85
6.工业固体废物排放量（万吨）	Volume of Industrial Solid Waste Discharged (10 000tons)	0.40

9-4 城市污水处理情况（2009年）

Urban Sewage Disposal（2009）

指　　标	Item	2009
一、污水处理厂数（座）	**Number of Sewage Treatment works(unit)**	**8**
污水处理厂处理能力（万吨/日）	Daily Disposal Capacity of Sewage(10 000 tons/day)	80
二、污水处理量（万吨）	**Volume of Sewgae Disposal(10 000 tons)**	**18078.0**
#处理生活污水量	Volume of Domestic Sewgae Disposal	16314.5
处理工业废水量	Volume of Industrial Sewage Disposal	1763.5
三、污水再生利用量（万吨）	**Volume of Sewage Recycled(10 000 tons)**	**837**
四、化学需氧量去除量（吨）	**Volume of COD Removed (ton)**	**85301**
五、氨氮去除量（吨）	**Volume of Ammonia and Nitrogen Removed(ton)**	**6343.6**
六、总磷去除量（吨）	**Volume of Total Phosphorus Removed(ton)**	**828**
七、污泥产生量（吨）	**Volume of Sludge pruduced(ton)**	**295701**
八、污泥处置量（吨）	**Volume of Sludge Disposal(ton)**	**295527**
九、污泥利用量（吨）	**Volume of Sludge Utilized(ton)**	**174**
十、污泥排放量（吨）	**Volume of Sludge Discharged(ton)**	
十一、本年运行费用（万元）	**Operating Expense(10 000 yuan)**	**11632.3**

注：污水处理厂数及污水处理能力为市建委部门统计数据。

Note:The number of sewage disposal plant and the disposal capacity of sewage were statistics from Municipal Construction Commission.

9-5 危险废物集中处置情况（2009年）

Condition of Collected Dangerous Wastes Treated（2009）

指　　标	Item	2009
一、危险废物集中处置厂数（座）	**Number of Colleted Dangerous Wastes Treated Plants(item)**	**3**
#当年新增	Newly Increased in Current year	
二、危险废物实际处置能力（吨/日）	**Actual Disposal Capacity of Dangerous Wastes (ton/day)**	**50.0**
#当年新增	Newly Increased in Current year	
三、危险废物处置量（吨）	**Volume of Dangerous Wastes Treated (ton)**	**9890.0**
四、危险废物综合利用量（吨）	**Volume of Dangerous Wastes Utilized in a Comprehensive Way (ton)**	**409.0**
五、焚烧残渣流向（吨）	**Flow Direction of Residuum after Burning (ton)**	
（1）焚烧残渣量	Volume of Residuum after Burning	553.0
（2）焚烧残渣利用量	Volume of Residuum after Burning Utilized	
（3）焚烧残渣填埋量	Volume of Residuum after Burning Landfilled	
六、当年运行费用（万元）	**Operating Expenses in Current year(10 000 yuan)**	**2839.0**

9-6 生活及其他污染情况（2009年）

Domestic Pollution and Other conditions（2009）

指　　标	Item	2009
一、基本情况	**Basic Condition**	
1.煤炭消费总量（万吨）	Total Coal Consumption (10 000 tons)	785.60
#工业煤炭消费量	Industrial Coal Consumption	733.20
生活及其他煤炭消费量	Domestic and Other Coal Consumption	52.38
2.生活及其他煤炭含硫量（%）	Percentage of Sulphur Content in Domestic and Other Coal (%)	0.75
3.生活及其他煤炭灰份（%）	Percentage of Ash Content in Domestic and Other Coal (%)	14.03
二、污染排放情况	**Discharge of Pollutant**	
1.城镇生活污水排放量（万吨）	Volume of Urban Domestic Sewage Discharged(10 000 tons)	28200.7
2.城镇生活污水中CDD去除量（吨）	Volume of CDD in Urban Domestic Sewage Removed (ton)	63646.9
3.城镇生活污水中氨氮产生量（吨）	Volume of Ammonia and Nitrogen in Urban Domestic Sewage Produced (ton)	13096.4
4.城镇生活污水中氨氮排放量（吨）	Volume of Ammonia and Nitrogen in Urban Domestic Sewage Discharged (ton)	8638.5
5.污水处理厂去除生活污水中氨氮量（吨）	Sewage disposal plant removing the amount of ammonia nitrogen in wastewater.(ton)	4457.8
6.生活及其他二氧化硫排放量（吨）	Volume of Domestic and Other Sulphur Dioxide Emission (ton)	3438.0
7.生活及其他烟尘排放量（吨）	Volume of Domestic and Other Soot Emission (ton)	9134.0

9-7 工业污染治理项目建设情况（2009年）

Condition of Anti-Industrial Pollution Projects（2009）

指　　标	Item	2009
一、工业企业数（个）	**Number of Industrial Enterprises (unit)**	**35**
二、本年施工项目总数（个）	**Total Number of Projects Under Construction (unit)**	**37**
#废水治理项目	Treatment of Waste Water	14
废气治理项目	Treatment of Waste Gas	19
固体废物治理项目	Treatment of Solid Wastes	
三、施工项目本年完成投资额（万元）	**Investment Completed in Anti-pollution Projects** Under Construction (10 000 yuan)	**6647.8**
#废水治理项目	Treatment of Waste Water	2290.2
废气治理项目	Treatment of Waste Gas	2691.0
固体废物治理项目	Treatment of Solid Wastes	
四、施工项目本年投资来源合计（万元）	**Investment Sources of Projects Under Construction (10 000 yuan)**	**6647.8**
#排污费补助	Pollution Charges Subsidies	188.0
政府其他补助	Other Government Subsidies	1903.8
企业自筹	Self-raising Funds	4556.0
#银行贷款	Loans	
五、本年竣工项目数（个）	**Number of Projects Completed(unit)**	27
#废水治理项目	Treatment of Waste Water	11
废气治理项目	Treatment of Waste Gas	13
噪声治理项目	Treatment of Noise Pollution	
六、本年竣工项目新增设计处理能力	**Newly Increased Disposal Capacity of Projects Completed**	
#治理废水（吨/日）	Treatment of Waste Water (ton/day)	9584
治理废气（万标立方米/时）	Treatment of Waste Gas (10 000 cu.m./h)	78.92
治理固体废物（吨/日）	Treatment of Solid Wastes (ton/day)	

主要统计指标解释

工业废水排放量 指经过企业厂区所有排放口排到企业外部的工业废水量。包括生产废水、外排的直接冷却水、超标排放的矿井地下水和与工业废水混排的厂区生活污水，不包括外排的间接冷却水（清污不分流的间接冷却水应计算在内）。

工业废水排放达标量 指各项指标都达到国家或地方排放标准的外排工业废水量，包括未经处理外排达标和经过处理后外排达标两部分。

工业废水处理量 指报告期内各种水治理设施实际处理的工业废水量，包括处理后外排和处理后回用的工业废水量和虽经处理但未达到国家或地方排放标准的废水量。如车间和厂排放口均有治理设施，并对同一废水分级处理时，不应重复计算工业废水处理量。

工业废气排放量 指企业厂区内燃料燃烧和生产工艺过程中产生的各种排入空气的含有污染物的气体总量，按标准状态〔273K，101325Pa〕计算。

工业二氧化硫排放量 指企业在燃料燃烧和生产工艺过程中排入大气的二氧化硫数量。

烟尘排放量 指企业厂区内燃料燃烧产生的烟气中夹带的颗粒物数量。

工业粉尘排放量 指企业在生产工艺过程中排放的颗粒物重量，如钢铁企业的耐火材料粉尘、焦化企业的筛焦系统粉尘、烧结机的粉尘、石灰窑的粉尘、建材企业的水泥粉尘等。不包括电厂排入大气的烟尘。

工业固体废物产生量 指企业在生产过程中产生的固体状、半固体状和高浓度液体状废弃物的总量，包括危险废物、冶炼废渣、粉煤灰、炉渣、煤矸石、尾矿、放射性废物和其他废物等;不包括矿山开采的剥离废石和掘进废石（煤矸石和呈酸性或碱性的废石除外）。酸性或碱性废石指采掘的废石其流经水、雨淋水的pH值小于4或pH值大于10.5者。

工业固体废物处置量 指将固体废物焚烧或者最终置于符合环境保护规定要求的场所，并不再回取的工业固体废物量（包括当年处置往年的工业固体废物累计贮存量）。处置方法有填埋（其中危险废物应安全填埋）、焚烧、专业贮存场（库）封场处理、深层灌注、回填矿井等。

工业固体废物排放量 指将所产生的固体废物排到固体废物污染防治设施、场所以外的数量，不包括矿山开采的剥离废石和掘进废石（煤矸石和呈酸性或碱性的废石除外）。

"三废"综合利用产品产值 指利用"三废"（废液、废气、废渣）作为主要原料生产的产品价值（现行价）；已经销售或准备销售的应计算产品价值，留作生产自用的不应计算产品价值。

"三废"综合利用产品利润 指利用"三废"（废液、废气、废渣）生产的产品，销售后所得到的利润。

Explanatory Notes on Main Statistical Indicators

Volume of Industrial Waste Water Discharged refers to the volume of industrial waste water discharged, through all outlets, to the outside of industrial enterprises, including waste water produced, direct-cooling water, underground water from mines that does not meet the standard of discharge, and the domestic sewage mixed up with industrial waste water when discharged, but excluding discharged indirect-cooling water.

Volume of Waste Water up to the Standard for Discharge refers to the volume of discharged industrial waste water that, with or without treatment, has come up to the national or local standards for discharge.

Volume of Treated Industrial Waste Water refers to the volume of industrial waste water after being treated and purified through various water treatment facilities in the reference period, including the volume discharged or recovered after being treated. The volume of waste water that fails to meet the national or local standards after treatment is also included. If there are treatment facilities both at the outlets of workshops and at the outlets of the factory, and the same volume of waste water has been treated twice, duplication should be avoided in the calculation of the volume of treated industrial waste water.

Volume of Waste Industrial Gas Emission refers to waste gas emitted from burning of fuels and from production process in the area of the factory, and is measured by 10000 standard cubic meters each year under normal condition.

Volume of Industrial Sulphur Dioxide Discharged refers to the volume of sulphur dioxide discharged to the air in the process of fuel burning or in the production process.

Volume of Industrial Soot Discharged refers to the volume of solid soot in the smoke discharged in the process of fuel burning in the area of the factory.

Industrial Dust Discharged refers to the total weight of solid dust discharged by industrial enterprises in the production process, such as dust of refractory materials from iron plants, dust from coke-screening system or from sintering machines of coking plants, dust from lime kilns, cement dust from building material enterprises, etc., but excluding smoke and dust discharged by power plants.

Volume of Industrial Solid Wastes Produced refers to the total volume of solid, semi-solid or high concentration liquid residue produced by industrial enterprises in their production process, including dangerous wastes, residues from melting, slag, powdered coal ash, gangue, chemical residues, tailings, radioactive residues and other residues, but excluding stripped or dug stones in mining (except gangue and acid or alkali stones which are stones washed or soaked by water with a pH value smaller than 4 or larger than 10.5)

Volume of Industrial Solid Wastes Treated refers to solid wastes disposed of in a non-recoverable place that meet the requirement of environmental protection, such as burying (The dangerous wastes should be buried safely), burning, piling in designated sites, pouring water into the deep strata, filling of old mines, etc. (including treatment of solid wastes piled up in the previous years).

Volume of Industrial Solid Wastes Discharged refers to the volume of industrial solid wastes produced and discharged at the places outside the special facilities or special sites for preventing against pollution, excluding stripped or dug stones in mining (except gangue and acid or alkali waste stones).

Output Value of Products Made from Utilization of Waste Gas, Waste Water and Industrial Solid Wastes refers to the value of products (calculated at current prices) made by industrial enterprises using recovered waste water, waste gas or solid wastes as main raw materials. Only the value of the products which have been sold or are ready to be sold should be included. The value of the products which will be used in the production of the enterprises should not be included.

Profit Obtained from Utilization of Waste Gas, Waste Water and Industrial Solid Wastes refers to profit obtained from selling or own-consumption of products made by industrial enterprises using recovered waste water, waste gas or solid wastes as main raw materials.

10 农业

AGRICULTURE

资料整理：张喜兰　刘栋婷　薛　丰　王子明
Data management:Zhang Xilan　Liu Dongting　Xue Feng　Wang Ziming

第十部分 农业

一、简要说明

本章资料主要包括农村基本情况、农业生产条件与生产情况、耕地、农林牧渔及服务业产值、主要农产品产量以及各区县农业生产和农村经济效益主要指标，由西安市统计局农村处提供，其中除10-1、10-2、10-3、10-4、10-5、10-6、10-13、10-14、10-20、10-21、10-22表外，其余表2006年和2007年数据为第二次农业普查衔接数。

二、主要指标

年末耕地面积（万亩）	387.89	占全市土地面积	25.6%
农林牧渔及服务业总产值（亿元）	178.70	比上年增长	6.5%
农作物播种面积（万亩）	757.11	比上年下降	0.1%
粮食产量（万吨）	218.20	比上年下降	1.8 %

10 AGRICULTURE

Ⅰ.Brief Introduction

Data in this chapter reflects basic condition of agriculture production of Xi'an city. It is primarily consist of basic condition of rural area, condition of agriculture production, plow land, production value of farming, forestry, animal husbandry and fishery, gross yield of primary produce and primary Indicators of agriculture production and rural area economic performance. The data are provided and compiled by Rural Area Division of the Xi'an Bureau of Statistics.The data in this chapter in 2006 and 2007 is conformity with the second national agriculture census, except table of 10-1、10-2、10-3、10-4、10-5、10-6、10-13、10-14、10-20、10-21、10-22.

Ⅱ.Major Indicators

		Increase over Preceding Year
Cultivated Area Year-end(10 000 mu)	387.89	25.6% (percentage to total land area)
Gross Output Value of Farming, Forestry, Animal Husbandry,Fishery and Service(100 mil. yuan)	178.70	6.5%
Sown Area of Crops(10 000 mu)	757.11	0.1%
Grain Output(10 000 tons)	218.20	1.8%

10–1 农村基层组织、乡村户数、人口及劳动力情况

Grass-root Organizations, Households, Population and Labor Resources in Rural Area

指　　标	Item	2000	2005	2006	2007	2008	2009
一、农村基层组织情况	**Village Units**						
1.乡镇个数（个）	Number of Township and Town(unit)	168	102	97	84	82	73
#镇个数	Number of Town	52	50	45	37	35	31
2.村民委员会个数（个）	Number of Villagers' Committees(unit)	3165	3162	3161	3161	3145	3104
3.村民小组个数（个）	Number of Village Group(unit)	16294	16281	16275	16260	16272	16068
二、乡村户数（万户）	**Number of Households (10 000 households）**	**98.77**	**101.5**	**102.35**	**100.85**	**101.02**	**101**
三、农村人口和从业人员情况	**Rural Population and Employment**						
1.乡村人口数（万人）	Rural Population(10 000 persons)	401.64	408.9	409.77	403.02	404.18	404.17
2.乡村劳动力资源总数（万人）	Total Number of Rural Labor Source (10 000 persons)	240.76	255.93	257.66	254.06	256.17	255
#劳动年龄内人口	Population at Labor Age	232.43	229.74	234.12	230.28	231.96	231.04
3.乡村从业人员数（万人）	Rural Laborers(10 000 persons)	212.65	223.3	225.99	222.09	223.85	223.13
#劳动年龄内人口	Population at Labor Age		205.97	208.36	201.29	202.51	201.79
#女性	Female	99.07	103.22	103.87	101.83	103.11	102.76
(1)农业	Laborers of Farming	146.07	137.69	135.64	131.96	126.46	121.78
(2)工业	Laborers of Industry	15.43	18.41	19.92	20.6	22.29	22.67
(3)建筑业	Laborers of Construction	16.45	21.73	22.37	23.28	25.27	26.24
(4)交通仓储邮电业	Laborers of Transportation,Postal and Telecommunications Services	7.64	8.74	9.26	9.22	10.45	10.92
(5)批零贸易、餐饮业	Laborers of Trade and Catering	8.14	12.7	14.14	14.18	16.61	18.09
(6)金融、保险业	Laborers of Banking and Insurance	0.45					
(7)其他	Laborers of Others	18.47	24.03	24.66	22.85	22.77	23.43
四、国有农林牧渔业从业人员数（万人）	**Number of staff and Workers in State-owned farms(10 000 persons)**	**0.29**	**0.11**	**0.11**	**0.08**	**0.07**	**0.07**
五、自来水受益村数（个）	**Number of Villages Benefited from the Tap Water System (unit)**	**1527**	**1756**	**1794**	**1881**	**1934**	**2058**
六、通汽车村数（个）	**Number of Villages Accessible by motor Vehicles (unit)**	**2785**	**2952**	**2923**	**2973**	**2996**	**2989**
七、通电话村数（个）	**Number of Villages Accessible by Telephone (unit)**	**2885**	**3101**	**3113**	**3129**	**3086**	**3071**

10-2 各区县农村基层组织、乡村户数及人口（2009年）

Grass-root Organizations, Households and Population in Rural Area by Region（2009）

区 县	Region	乡镇个数（个）Number of Township and Town (unit)	镇个数 Number of Town	村民委员会个数（个）Number of Villagers' Committees (unit)	村民小组个数（个）Number of Village Group (unit)	乡村户数（户）Number of Households (household)	乡村人数（人）Number Rural Population (person)
合 计	**Total**	**73**	**31**	**3104**	**16068**	**1010000**	**4041673**
新城区	Xincheng			11	9		
碑林区	Beilin						
莲湖区	Lianhu			11	23		
灞桥区	Baqiao			228	847	71374	284257
未央区	Weiyang			200	614	60319	218620
雁塔区	Yanta			117	445	49584	161717
阎良区	Yanliang	2	2	80	592	41399	159820
临潼区	Lintong	3		285	2084	134122	557920
长安区	Chang'an	5		671	3228	204791	817286
蓝田县	Lantian	21	9	519	2479	138025	563215
周至县	Zhouzhi	21	8	376	2535	138623	593850
户 县	Huxian	14	9	518	2472	118953	477687
高陵县	Gaoling	7	3	88	740	52810	207301

10-3 各区县从业人员数（2009年）

Number of Labers in Families by Region（2009）

单位：万人 (10 000 persons)

区 县	Region	乡村从业人员数合计 Rural Laborers Total	女性 Female	农林牧渔业 Farming,Forestry Animal Husbandry and Fishery	工业 Industry	建筑业 Laborers of Construction
合 计	**Total**	**223.13**	**102.76**	**121.78**	**22.67**	**26.24**
新城区	Xincheng					
碑林区	Beilin					
莲湖区	Lianhu					
灞桥区	Baqiao	15.81	6.99	7.02	1.75	1.80
未央区	Weiyang	12.00	5.40	3.14	2.54	0.97
雁塔区	Yanta	7.85	3.87	1.45	0.79	0.60
阎良区	Yanliang	8.78	3.74	5.27	0.55	1.24
临潼区	Lintong	29.57	14.44	19.62	1.63	3.72
长安区	Chang'an	42.56	18.45	20.70	4.81	6.91
蓝田县	Lantian	32.05	15.50	19.62	1.69	2.61
周至县	Zhouzhi	34.60	15.58	21.83	3.52	3.59
户 县	Huxian	28.30	13.27	17.18	4.26	2.83
高陵县	Gaoling	11.61	5.52	5.95	1.13	1.97

10-3 续表 continued

单位：万人 (10 000 persons)

区 县	Region	交通运输、仓储及邮政业 Transportation,Postal and Telecommunication Services	批零贸易餐饮业 Trade and Catering	金融、保险业 Banking and Insurance	其 他 Others
合 计	**Total**	**10.92**	**18.09**		**23.43**
新城区	Xincheng				
碑林区	Beilin				
莲湖区	Lianhu				
灞桥区	Baqiao	1.24	1.08		2.92
未央区	Weiyang	0.82	1.89		2.64
雁塔区	Yanta	0.70	1.88		2.43
阎良区	Yanliang	0.41	0.50		0.81
临潼区	Lintong	0.93	1.53		2.14
长安区	Chang'an	2.67	3.61		3.86
蓝田县	Lantian	1.31	3.08		3.74
周至县	Zhouzhi	1.04	2.24		2.38
户 县	Huxian	1.00	1.33		1.70
高陵县	Gaoling	0.80	0.95		0.81

10-4 主要年份耕地面积

Area of Cultivated Land in Representative Year

单位：万亩 (10 000 mu)

年 份 Year	年末实有耕地面积 Cultivated Area Year-end	#水 田 Paddy Field	水浇地 Irrigable Land
1970	554.09	18.20	297.05
1975	538.35	20.34	349.13
1978	530.96	16.70	370.46
1980	526.29	17.45	372.96
1985	508.88	17.63	328.10
1990	495.32	17.97	311.91
1991	492.09	17.03	309.17
1992	485.30	16.44	298.19
1993	479.04	14.36	304.49
1994	471.44	13.98	299.58
1995	463.97	17.04	278.01
1996	451.50	14.21	283.76
1997	456.62	11.90	290.49
1998	455.15	11.18	282.23
1999	450.74	11.31	281.96
2000	443.37	10.26	284.04
2001	431.69	9.00	274.73
2002	424.46	7.98	275.96
2003	413.84	6.65	263.75
2004	404.87	6.59	254.04
2005	400.17	5.55	254.04
2006	395.79	5.33	263.75
2007	391.77	4.80	255.95
2008	390.77	4.64	255.36
2009	387.89	4.39	260.71

10-5 各区县耕地面积（2009年）

单位：亩

区　县	Region	年末实有耕地面积 Cultivated Area Year-end	水田 Paddy Field	旱地 Dry Land	水浇地 Irrigable Land	当年增加的耕地面积 Area of Newly Increased Cultivated Land	新开荒地面积 Area of Newly Reclamation of Wasteland
合　计	**Total**	**3878857**	**43889**	**3834968**	**2607110**	**18524**	**3515**
新城区	Xincheng						
碑林区	Beilin						
莲湖区	Lianhu						
灞桥区	Baqiao	177360	699	176661	100360	716	
未央区	Weiyang	62231	300	61931	61931		
雁塔区	Yanta	25375		25375	25375	140	
阎良区	Yanliang	240138		240138	236464	344	
临潼区	Lintong	743785	1021	742764	567201	591	
长安区	Chang'an	697529	25924	671605	339543	5391	945
蓝田县	Lantian	614735	10921	603814	176750	3542	921
周至县	Zhouzhi	502776	3203	499573	367675	4966	1629
户　县	Huxian	576147	1821	574326	493030	492	20
高陵县	Gaoling	238781		238781	238781	2342	

Area of Cultivated Land by Region（2009）

(mu)

当年减少的耕地面积 Decrease in Cultivated Area in the Year	国家基建占地 Capital Construction	乡村集体基建占地 Village Collective Construction	农民个人建房占地 Peasant Housing Construction	退耕改果、茶、桑面积 Area for Change into Fruit, Tea and Mulberry	退耕造林面积 Area for Change into Woods
136861	**31155**	**1477**	**2810**	**46446**	**3507**
21729	6128	18		15583	
8184	5622	30	6		
4058	1743	255	21	296	744
349	257		58		
4218	2189	41	351	1350	
8703	4877	294	464	1646	414
5986	2013	521	801	2651	
71781	179	64	330	23071	2349
3473	2989	45	33	406	
8380	5158	209	746	1443	

10-6 主要年份农业机械拥有量（年末数）

Possession of Agricultural Machinery in Representative Year（Number of year-end）

指　标	Item	2004	2005	2006
农业机械总动力(千瓦)	**Total Power of Agricultural Machinery(kw)**	**2140737**	**2239001**	**2277584**
主要农业机械与设备	**Major Agricultural Machinery and Equipment**			
大中型拖拉机(台)	Large and Medium Tractors(unit)	7500	8415	8963
(千瓦)	(kw)	246978	290638	312325
小型拖拉机(台)	Mini-tractors(unit)	27225	26326	23437
(千瓦)	(kw)	307382	303831	263565
大中型拖拉机配套农具（部）	Number of Large and Medium Tractor Towing Farm Machinery(unit)	18446	19334	18724
小型拖拉机配套农具（部）	Mini-Tractor Towing Farm Machinery (unit)	47260	47883	30439
#柴 油 机(台)	Diesel Engines(unit)	2522	2219	3547
(千瓦)	(kw)	21865	22993	29112
电 动 机(台)	Motors(unit)	78542	79666	76614
(千瓦)	(kw)	343230	369843	360684
农用水泵（台）	Agricultural Water Pump(unit)	74701	77567	73039
节水灌溉类机械（套）	Equipment in Water-saving Irrigation(set)	1141	1290	2656
联合收割机（台）	Combine Harvesters(unit)	4053	4802	5026
(千瓦)	(kw)	150982	173183	183313
自走式机动割晒机（台）	Self-propelled Motorized Swather(unit)	3147	4226	1342
(千瓦)	(kw)	150982	173183	52740
机动脱粒机（台）	Motorized Huller (unit)	13060	13870	5806
农用运输车（辆）	Agricultucal Transporter(unit)	42247	47348	50395
#三轮运输车	Three-wheel Transporter	34736	36436	41907

10–6 续表 continued

指 标	Item	2007	2008	2009
农业机械总动力(千瓦)	**Total Power of Agricultural Machinery(kw)**	**2348856**	**2712616**	**2616053**
主要农业机械与设备	**Major Agricultural Machinery and Equipment**			
大中型拖拉机(台)	Large and Medium Tractors(unit)	10431	11092	11479
(千瓦)	(kw)	387962	421581	474115
小型拖拉机(台)	Mini-tractors(unit)	21555	19036	18406
(千瓦)	(kw)	237550	213806	204965
大中型拖拉机配套农具（部）	Number of Large and Medium Tractor Towing Farm Machinery(unit)	23487	25125	26575
小型拖拉机配套农具（部）	Mini-Tractor Towing Farm Machinery (unit)	28780	26984	29039
#柴 油 机(台)	Diesel Engines(unit)	2709	2670	2691
(千瓦)	(kw)	24445	23546	23008
电 动 机(台)	Motors(unit)	84416	85349	83243
(千瓦)	(kw)	387042	421435	400534
农用水泵（台）	Agricultural Water Pump(unit)	80722	80462	80174
节水灌溉类机械（套）	Equipment in Water-saving Irrigation(set)	1991	1728	1799
联合收割机（台）	Combine Harvesters(unit)	5294	5390	6155
(千瓦)	(kw)	211490	220185	252976
自走式机动割晒机（台）	Self-propelled Motorized Swather(unit)	4918	2174	1220
(千瓦)	(kw)	211388	90899	52129
机动脱粒机（台）	Motorized Huller (unit)	11585	23781	11960
农用运输车（辆）	Agricultucal Transporter(unit)	49576	54860	50671
#三轮运输车	Three-wheel Transporter	40373	44953	41899

10-7 主要年份农业机械、化肥、水利、水电情况

Agricultural Machinery,Chemical Fertilizers,Water Conservancy, Hydropower in Representative Year

指　　标	Item	2000	2005	2006
一、农业机械化情况(万亩)	**Statistics on Agricultural Machinery (10 000 mu)**			
当年实际机耕地面积	Area Ploughed by Tractors	366.81	360.68	354.05
当年实际机播面积	Seeded Area by Tractors	482.74	485.62	519.00
当年实际机械收获面积	Harvest Area by Tractors	272.83	271.77	280.88
二、农用化肥施用量(吨)	**Use of Agricultural Fertilizers and Insecticides(Ton)**			
1.按实物量计算	Practicality Consumption	697243	749802	759882
氮 肥	Nitrogenous Fertilizer	392366	411161	413514
磷 肥	Phosphate Fertilizer	155480	161444	164781
钾 肥	Potash Fertilizer	31841	34114	31414
复合肥	Compound Fertilizer	78620	115458	121124
2.按折纯量计算	Standard Consumption	196343	211790	216093
氮 肥	Nitrogenous Fertilizer	102982	107645	110137
磷 肥	Phosphate Fertilizer	18658	19368	19772
钾 肥	Potash Fertilizer	15921	17055	15709
复合肥	Compound Fertilizer	39313	57009	59731
三、农用塑料薄膜使用量（公斤）	**Plastic Sheet for Agricultural Use(kg)**	**1622198**	**1855383**	**1931527**
四、农用柴油（吨）	**Diesel Oil for Agricultural Use (ton)**	**52706**	**50832**	**49686**
五、农药使用量（公斤）	**Pesticide (kg)**	**1559333**	**1427879**	**1471672**
六、农村办沼气池（个）	**Number of Mash Gas Pond Managed by Village Government(unit)**	**10199**	**12445**	**16211**
七、农村水利化情况（万亩）	**Irrigation and Water Conservancy (10 000 mu)**			
有效灌溉面积	Effective Irrigation Area	335.97	280.10	276.58
旱涝保收面积	Stable-Harvesting Arable Land	294.06	255.37	253.66
机电排灌面积	Electrical Irrigation Area	249.11	223.74	214.03
八、农村电气化情况	**Rural electrization**			
乡村及村以下办水电站（个）	Hydropower Station in Rural Areas(unit)	67	79	79
装机容量（千瓦）	Installed Power Generation Capacity(kw)	7236	13775	14252
发 电 量（万千瓦小时）	Generating Capacity (10 000 kwh)	1138	2239	2253
已配套机电井（眼）	Electricity Powered Well(unit)	50289	46505	46112

10-7 续表 continued

指　　标	Item	2007	2008	2009
一、农业机械化情况(万亩)	**Statistics on Agricultural Machinery (10 000 mu)**			
当年实际机耕地面积	Area Ploughed by Tractors	361.62	404.42	413.70
当年实际机播面积	Seeded Area by Tractors	521.36	539.81	544.86
当年实际机械收获面积	Harvest Area by Tractors	296.06	313.11	342.82
二、农用化肥施用量(吨)	**Use of Agricultural Fertilizers and Insecticides(Ton)**			
1.按实物量计算	Practicality Consumption	762401	767980	776319
氮 肥	Nitrogenous Fertilizer	408847	413397	414481
磷 肥	Phosphate Fertilizer	160932	157145	153825
钾 肥	Potash Fertilizer	34284	34149	33069
复合肥	Compound Fertilizer	124784	132481	142137
2.按折纯量计算	Standard Consumption	220251	225949	230299
氮 肥	Nitrogenous Fertilizer	109484	112000	112275
磷 肥	Phosphate Fertilizer	19311	18855	18457
钾 肥	Potash Fertilizer	17141	17077	16534
复合肥	Compound Fertilizer	62398	66247	71042
三、农用塑料薄膜使用量（公斤）	**Plastic Sheet for Agricultural Use(kg)**	**2096169**	**2122310**	**2141969**
四、农用柴油（吨）	**Diesel Oil for Agricultural Use (ton)**	**50137**	**51097**	**51346**
五、农药使用量（公斤）	**Pesticide (kg)**	**1444867**	**1465819**	**1325459**
六、农村办沼气池（个）	**Number of Mash Gas Pond Managed by Village Government(unit)**	**26448**	**36540**	**46737**
七、农村水利化情况（万亩）	**Irrigation and Water Conservancy (10 000 mu)**			
有效灌溉面积	Effective Irrigation Area	276.28	274.48	273.17
旱涝保收面积	Stable-Harvesting Arable Land	247.99	249.31	247.60
机电排灌面积	Electrical Irrigation Area	210.51	211.01	213.42
八、农村电气化情况	**Rural electrization**			
乡村及村以下办水电站（个）	Hydropower Station in Rural Areas(unit)	76	76	75
装机容量（千瓦）	Installed Power Generation Capacity(kw)	24827	24827	25047
发 电 量（万千瓦小时）	Generating Capacity (10 000 kwh)	10085	10477	10678
已配套机电井（眼）	Electricity Powered Well(unit)	45783	47032	46790

10-8 主要年份农林牧渔及服务业总产值及指数

Gross Output Value of Farming,Forestry,Animal Husbandry,Fishery,Service and Related Indices in Representative Years

单位：万元 (10 000yuan)

年份 Year	总产值（现价） Gross Output Value (At current prices)	农业 Farming	林业 Forestry	牧业 Animal Husbandry	渔业 Fishery	农林牧渔服务业 Service of Farming, Forestry, Animal Husbandry and Fishery	指数（上年=100）（可比价） Indices(preceding year=100) (At constant prices)
1970	40617	35965	713	3896	43		111.2
1975	55322	47378	1509	6403	32		93.9
1978	65423	56519	1444	7427	33		104.7
1980	65322	54004	1177	10106	35		85.0
1985	134933	105888	2559	26186	300		106.4
1990	262073	191088	3134	65840	2011		102.5
1991	295620	208324	3362	81070	2864		108.6
1992	321155	219160	4225	94045	3725		108.6
1993	387068	261959	5031	115810	4268		112.8
1994	565056	359609	7819	192140	5488		102.4
1995	754597	513348	7185	228598	5466		106.8
1996	786003	552726	7573	219214	6490		102.1
1997	836201	585973	9226	233623	7379		110.3
1998	853279	625465	8146	212045	7623		107.5
1999	739905	530029	8883	194552	6441		100.7
2000	743712	514845	8482	212612	7773		104.3
2001	767511	527160	8427	223861	8063		102.8
2002	797444	539978	11378	238761	7327		103.0
2003	837857	551398	10550	269610	6299		101.5
2004	967946	580798	12773	314517	6728	53130	108.4
2005	1065437	657262	13086	329856	7340	57893	107.7
2006	1141484	686748	15188	346626	7017	85905	107.2
2007	1341450	798163	15845	410213	9051	108178	105.3
2008	1682725	956549	19031	564095	11084	131966	107.8
2009	1787032	1061756	22663	546191	11830	144592	106.5

10-9 各区县农林牧渔及服务业总产值（2009年）

Gross Output Value of Farming, Forestry, Animal Husbandry, Fishery and Service Price by Region（2009）

单位：万元 （10 000yuan)

区　县	Region	总产值 Gross Output Value	农业产值 Gross Output Value of Farming	林业产值 Gross Output Value of Forestry	牧业产值 Gross Output Value of Animal Husbandry	渔业产值 Gross Output Value of Fishery	农林牧渔服务业 Service of Farming, Forestry, Animal Husbandry and Fishery
全　市	**Total**	**1787032**	**1061756**	**22663**	**546191**	**11830**	**144592**
新城区	Xincheng						
碑林区	Beilin						
莲湖区	Lianhu						
灞桥区	Baqiao	136095	98337	444	25365	1716	10233
未央区	Weiyang	39860	19853	16	14690	2001	3300
雁塔区	Yanta	31094	20005	154	8135		2800
阎良区	Yanliang	169394	117522	496	37484	226	13666
临潼区	Lintong	333229	160451	2078	142004	1696	27000
长安区	Chang'an	304864	191560	1750	85921	2035	23598
蓝田县	Lantian	223567	132262	11413	60430	1850	17612
周至县	Zhouzhi	185796	116278	4910	49092	691	14825
户　县	Huxian	208089	130432	933	57416	850	18458
高陵县	Gaoling	155044	75056	469	65654	765	13100

10-10 各区县现价农林牧渔及服务业总产值指数及构成（2009年）

Gross Output Value and Its Composition of Farming, Forestry, Animal Husbandry,Fishery and Service at Current Price by Region（2009）

单位：%　　(%)

区　县	Region	总产值 Gross Output Value	农业产值 Gross Output Value of Farming	林业产值 Gross Output Value of Forestry	牧业产值 Gross Output Value of Animal Husbandry	渔业产值 Gross Output Value of Fishery	农林牧渔服务业 Service of Farming, Forestry, Animal Husbandry and Fishery
全市指数	**Total**	**106.5**	**105.4**	**121.3**	**106.8**	**107.4**	**110.2**
（可比价）	**（At constant prices）**						
新城区	Xincheng						
碑林区	Beilin						
莲湖区	Lianhu						
灞桥区	Baqiao	106.7	105.8	116.9	108.8	108.1	108.3
未央区	Weiyang	104.9	99.0	69.6	109.7	112.2	114.3
雁塔区	Yanta	101.9	99.8	93.3	102.2		117.9
阎良区	Yanliang	106.7	105.1	102.8	110.8	100.6	108.9
临潼区	Lintong	106.5	106.5	142.8	105.7	113.8	108.2
长安区	Chang'an	106.8	108.0	95.3	104.7	107.0	107.8
蓝田县	Lantian	106.2	103.2	126.6	107.9	101.2	112.1
周至县	Zhouzhi	106.6	106.4	121.7	104.3	104.9	112.8
户　县	Huxian	106.8	105.3	106.4	109.2	101.7	109.9
高陵县	Gaoling	106.6	103.7	111.8	108.2	109.1	114.6
全市构成	**Total**	**100.0**	**59.4**	**1.3**	**30.6**	**0.7**	**8.1**
新城区	Xincheng						
碑林区	Beilin						
莲湖区	Lianhu						
灞桥区	Baqiao	100.0	72.3	0.3	18.6	1.3	7.5
未央区	Weiyang	100.0	49.8		36.9	5.0	8.3
雁塔区	Yanta	100.0	64.3	0.5	26.2		9.0
阎良区	Yanliang	100.0	69.4	0.3	22.1	0.1	8.1
临潼区	Lintong	100.0	48.2	0.6	42.6	0.5	8.1
长安区	Chang'an	100.0	62.8	0.6	28.2	0.7	7.7
蓝田县	Lantian	100.0	59.2	5.1	27.0	0.8	7.9
周至县	Zhouzhi	100.0	62.6	2.6	26.4	0.4	8.0
户　县	Huxian	100.0	62.7	0.4	27.6	0.4	8.9
高陵县	Gaoling	100.0	48.4	0.3	42.3	0.5	8.5

10-11 主要年份农林牧渔及服务业增加值

Value Added of Farming，Forestry，Animal Husbandry, Fishery and Service in Representative Year

单位:万元 (10 000 yuan)

年 份 Year	农林牧渔及服务业业增加值 Farming,Forestry, Animal Husbandry, Fishery and Service	农 业 Farming	林 业 Forestry	牧 业 Animal Husbandry	渔 业 Fishery	农林牧渔服务业 Service of Farming, Forestry, Animal Husbandry and Fishery
1995	413981	329662	4413	76746	3160	
2000	446481	336777	4323	101353	4028	
2001	458720	342427	4258	108096	3939	
2002	477691	351358	6419	116591	3323	
2003	458378	312849	5473	137236	2820	
2004	582009	393349	6811	164572	2919	14358
2005	660148	444320	6888	169701	3373	35866
2006	704427	465823	8556	177431	3227	49390
2007	825053	538794	8420	210930	4467	62442
2008	1034471	639071	10592	301305	5598	77905
2009	1103793	698043	11958	303594	5913	84285

10-12 分区县农林牧渔及服务业增加值（2009年）

Addition Value-Added of Farming, Forestry, Animal Husbandry, Fishery and Service by Region（2009）

单位:万元 (10 000yuan)

区县	Region	农林牧渔及服务业增加值 Farming,Forestry, Animal Husbandry, Fishery and Service	农业 Farming	林业 Forestry	牧业 Animal Husbandry	渔业 Fishery	农林牧渔服务业 Service of Farming, Forestry, Animal Husbandry and Fishery
全市	**Total**	**1103793**	**698043**	**11958**	**303594**	**5913**	**84285**
新城区	Xincheng						
碑林区	Beilin						
莲湖区	Lianhu						
灞桥区	Baqiao	87876	66279	266	15016	686	5629
未央区	Weiyang	24153	12448	3	8757	800	2145
雁塔区	Yanta	21920	14204	108	5369		2239
阎良区	Yanliang	112873	79210	248	24927	111	8377
临潼区	Lintong	207229	105256	1143	83072	1018	16740
长安区	Chang'an	192059	142521	875	33552	1425	13686
蓝田县	Lantian	130309	76844	6334	36210	833	10088
周至县	Zhouzhi	111070	75581	2210	25479	359	7441
户县	Huxian	124357	79916	513	34249	451	9228
高陵县	Gaoling	91947	45784	258	36963	230	8712

10-13 分区县农林牧渔及服务业增加值指数（2009年）

Proportion of Farming, Forestry, Animal Husbandry, Fishery and Service Value-Added to Total Output Value（2009）

（上年=100）（可比价） (preceding year = 100)（At constant prices）

区县	Region	农林牧渔及服务业 Farming,Forestry, Animal Husbandry, Fishery and Service	农业 Farming	林业 Forestry	牧业 Animal Husbandry	渔业 Fishery	农林牧渔服务业 Service of Farming, Forestry, Animal Husbandry and Fishery
全市	**Total**	**106.3**	**103.6**	**114.6**	**111.2**	**106.3**	**108.8**
新城区	Xincheng						
碑林区	Beilin						
莲湖区	Lianhu						
灞桥区	Baqiao	106.6	103.9	103.3	114.7	108.1	115.3
未央区	Weiyang	104.1	86.9	69.4	126.7	132.1	125.5
雁塔区	Yanta	100.9	94.4	100.1	103.7		145.1
阎良区	Yanliang	106.6	105.2	102.9	107.5	101.3	117.6
临潼区	Lintong	106.3	105.3	121.1	112.3	100.7	85.5
长安区	Chang'an	106.7	105.9	96.5	110.0	115.2	106.0
蓝田县	Lantian	106.0	103.4	122.1	108.1	81.1	112.0
周至县	Zhouzhi	106.5	102.0	105.4	114.3	109.3	128.3
户县	Huxian	106.7	101.8	106.8	112.5	101.7	131.9
高陵县	Gaoling	106.5	103.8	116.9	108.6	138.3	110.4

10-14　主要年份农作物播种面积

Sown Areas of Farm Crops In Representative Years

单位：万亩 (10 000 mu)

年　份 Year	总播种面积 Total Sown Area	粮　食 Grain Crops	小　麦 Wheat	玉　米 Corn	棉　花 Cotton	油　料 Oil-bearing Crops	蔬　菜 Vegetables
1980	835.43	706.35	324.17	273.14	81.23	10.01	24.02
1985	795.41	704.36	378.20	271.14	21.02	8.01	45.03
1990	816.41	731.42	387.20	282.14	15.02	12.00	51.03
1991	820.41	731.37	389.19	283.14	19.01	13.01	47.03
1992	820.65	715.50	384.60	273.60	26.70	16.20	54.60
1993	821.63	713.49	380.40	273.69	17.66	14.84	63.90
1994	821.10	719.00	375.90	272.40	19.70	13.80	59.90
1995	784.74	690.63	370.41	259.55	11.07	18.57	57.59
1996	797.40	709.00	366.30	286.80	7.70	18.80	55.50
1997	755.78	670.83	367.71	248.79	4.50	15.53	59.36
1998	789.99	705.03	370.17	285.45	3.56	14.69	60.95
1999	793.08	709.95	371.94	294.00	2.85	12.74	60.68
2000	784.94	697.55	369.89	283.70	2.48	13.46	64.35
2001	763.16	678.05	359.19	278.57	2.91	11.87	61.77
2002	751.10	655.59	350.64	271.95	2.63	11.40	67.71
2003	737.06	632.55	336.05	261.89	3.38	11.04	69.44
2004	753.83	630.63	311.52	286.50	4.94	9.74	77.55
2005	757.91	642.75	325.10	287.87	5.40	9.51	83.33
2006	769.49	648.00	313.23	307.89	6.09	8.58	87.03
2007	762.38	637.05	306.98	304.13	6.93	7.41	91.07
2008	756.06	630.31	319.39	286.69	6.35	8.59	93.02
2009	757.11	628.69	318.36	285.20	6.45	8.59	94.83

10-15　各区县主要农作物播种面积（2009年）

Sown Areas of Major Farm Crops by Region（2009）

单位：万亩 (10 000 mu)

区　县	Region	总播种面积 Total Sown Area	粮　食 Grain Crops	夏　粮 Summer Grain	小　麦 Wheat	秋　粮 Autumn Grain	稻　谷 Rice	玉　米 Corn
合　计	**Total**	**757.11**	**628.69**	**321.52**	**318.36**	**307.17**	**1.85**	**285.20**
新城区	Xincheng							
碑林区	Beilin							
莲湖区	Lianhu							
灞桥区	Baqiao	33.87	24.44	13.88	13.84	10.56		9.58
未央区	Weiyang	11.26	8.12	4.29	4.29	3.83		3.81
雁塔区	Yanta	2.14	0.60	0.40	0.40	0.20		0.20
阎良区	Yanliang	48.61	23.09	11.97	11.97	11.12		11.05
临潼区	Lintong	138.92	118.44	63.06	62.78	55.38		52.14
长安区	Chang'an	148.77	122.05	62.13	62.09	59.92	0.92	57.97
蓝田县	Lantian	119.34	104.18	51.93	50.90	52.25	0.51	38.71
周至县	Zhouzhi	99.13	89.71	44.56	43.45	45.15	0.42	43.74
户　县	Huxian	104.36	93.52	46.99	46.33	46.53		46.19
高陵县	Gaoling	50.71	44.54	22.31	22.31	22.23		21.81

10-16 主要年份农作物产品产量

Yeild of Major Farm Crops in Representative Year

单位：万吨 (10 000 ton)

年 份 Year	粮食作物 Grain Crops	夏 粮 Summer Grain	小麦 Wheat	秋 粮 Autumn Grain	稻谷 Rice	玉米 Corn	棉 花 Cotton	油 料 Oil-bearing Crops	油菜籽 Rapeseeds	蔬 菜 Vegetables
1978	132.8	64.2	58.2	68.7	5.1	55.8	2.85	0.09	0.07	45.66
1979	145.7	81.8	74.2	63.9	4.5	53.4	2.63	0.33	0.29	49.11
1980	114.4	56.6	52.2	57.8	4.7	47.7	1.97	0.54	0.50	40.13
1981	116.1	78.7	74.3	37.4	3.4	31.5	1.36	0.76	0.75	34.06
1982	148.9	85.6	82.2	63.3	4.9	55.5	2.88	0.51	0.49	53.71
1983	148.1	81.8	79.6	66.3	4.8	58.5	0.85	0.36	0.34	46.99
1984	157.6	82.4	81.0	75.2	5.0	66.5	1.49	0.46	0.29	75.47
1985	150.1	76.1	74.8	74.0	5.1	65.1	0.49	0.75	0.39	86.44
1986	162.4	91.7	90.1	70.7	4.8	61.8	0.44	1.25	0.82	85.84
1987	171.2	87.0	85.2	84.2	5.0	74.3	0.47	1.57	1.22	95.16
1988	158.0	86.8	84.6	71.1	3.8	61.4	0.42	0.89	0.51	113.50
1989	173.6	93.5	91.2	80.2	4.7	70.4	0.55	1.33	0.94	129.32
1990	172.4	91.7	89.7	80.8	5.5	70.4	0.70	1.35	0.94	119.32
1991	178.8	91.1	89.2	87.7	5.0	77.5	0.97	1.20	0.74	117.41
1992	183.4	101.7	99.6	81.7	4.7	72.3	0.74	1.49	0.87	128.12
1993	190.0	101.1	99.0	88.9	4.9	78.6	0.75	1.40	1.00	145.80
1994	157.4	86.9	84.9	70.5	4.5	61.4	0.65	1.08	0.78	135.26
1995	175.3	99.8	97.4	75.5	3.4	67.8	0.29	2.17	1.90	133.60
1996	187.5	80.1	78.4	107.4	3.4	95.6	0.24	1.83	1.55	138.01
1997	190.5	114.3	112.3	76.3	3.5	69.4	0.17	1.86	1.65	142.11
1998	212.7	104.4	104.0	108.3	3.2	99.1	0.14	1.67	1.36	148.87
1999	204.4	95.5	94.4	108.9	2.9	99.7	0.15	1.30	1.00	153.24
2000	201.9	92.6	91.6	109.3	3.1	100.5	0.14	1.34	0.95	162.14
2001	197.1	98.1	97.2	98.9	2.7	91.3	0.17	1.23	0.90	152.80
2002	192.4	94.5	93.5	97.9	2.1	91.6	0.18	1.22	0.84	169.74
2003	176.3	98.2	96.7	78.2	1.6	72.3	0.22	1.13	0.70	169.67
2004	195.8	97.8	96.0	98.0	1.7	91.6	0.40	1.14	0.84	180.96
2005	205.5	100.0	99.1	105.5	1.6	99.3	0.45	1.16	0.89	195.70
2006	193.5	86.0	85.4	107.4	1.4	101.2	0.48	1.08	0.87	189.30
2007	189.1	77.3	76.7	111.8	1.5	105.6	0.59	0.96	0.77	204.30
2008	214.4	105.9	105.6	108.5	0.9	103.0	0.62	1.15	0.95	221.53
2009	218.2	103.0	102.1	115.2	0.9	109.5	0.63	1.12	0.93	242.41

10-17 各区县主要农作物产品产量（2009年）

Yeild of Major Farm Crops by Region（2009）

单位：万吨 (10 000 tons)

区 县	Region	粮食总产量 Total Yield of Grain Crops	夏 粮 Summer Grain	小 麦 Wheat	秋 粮 Autumn Grain	玉 米 Corn
合 计	**Total**	**218.20**	**102.97**	**102.05**	**115.23**	**109.47**
新城区	Xincheng					
碑林区	Beilin					
莲湖区	Lianhu					
灞桥区	Baqiao	7.20	3.74	3.74	3.46	3.23
未央区	Weiyang	2.90	1.42	1.42	1.48	1.48
雁塔区	Yanta	0.18	0.11	0.11	0.07	0.07
阎良区	Yanliang	9.60	4.98	4.98	4.62	4.60
临潼区	Lintong	38.56	19.43	19.27	19.13	18.04
长安区	Chang'an	41.57	19.28	19.27	22.29	21.56
蓝田县	Lantian	33.11	14.03	13.80	19.08	16.23
周至县	Zhouzhi	28.22	13.43	13.09	14.79	14.33
户 县	Huxian	35.78	16.89	16.72	18.89	18.76
高陵县	Gaoling	21.08	9.66	9.65	11.42	11.17

10-17 续表 continued

单位：万吨 (10 000 tons)

区 县	Region	棉 花 Cotton	油 料 Oil-bearing Crops	油菜籽 Rapeseeds	蔬 菜 Vegetables
合 计	**Total**	**0.63**	**1.12**	**0.93**	**242.41**
新城区	Xincheng				
碑林区	Beilin				
莲湖区	Lianhu				
灞桥区	Baqiao	0.01	0.05	0.04	29.07
未央区	Weiyang		0.01	0.01	6.48
雁塔区	Yanta				5
阎良区	Yanliang	0.46	0.01	0.01	46.67
临潼区	Lintong	0.13	0.23	0.16	36.95
长安区	Chang'an		0.22	0.22	47.74
蓝田县	Lantian	0.03	0.33	0.27	14.8
周至县	Zhouzhi		0.19	0.16	14.38
户 县	Huxian		0.08	0.06	24.2
高陵县	Gaoling				17.12

10-18 主要年份农作物单位面积产量

Field of Farm Crops Per Hectare in Representative Year

单位：公斤/亩 (kg/mu)

年 份 Year	粮食作物 Grain Crops	夏 粮 Summer Grain	小麦 Wheat	秋 粮 Autumn Grain	玉米 Corn	棉 花 Cotton	油 料 Oil-bearing Crops	油菜籽 Rapeseeds	蔬 菜 Vegetables
1990	236	232	232	241	249	46	103	101	2349
1991	245	229	229	264	274	51	94	89	2332
1992	256	259	259	253	264	28	92	101	2344
1993	266	260	260	274	287	42	94	107	2282
1994	219	226	226	211	225	33	79	84	2260
1995	254	263	263	243	261	27	117	128	2320
1996	265	214	214	321	333	32	86	100	2489
1997	284	305	306	257	279	38	76	129	2395
1998	302	278	279	328	347	40	114	121	2443
1999	288	253	254	327	339	52	102	106	2526
2000	289	247	248	338	354	55	102	112	2520
2001	291	270	271	314	328	60	104	113	2474
2002	293	266	267	326	337	70	107	115	2507
2003	279	287	288	269	276	67	102	110	2444
2004	310	308	308	313	320	81	117	129	2333
2005	320	304	305	336	345	84	121	132	2349
2006	299	273	273	323	329	80	125	135	2175
2007	297	250	250	341	347	85	129	132	2245
2008	340	330	331	350	359	97	134	137	2382
2009	347	320	321	375	384	97	131	131	2556

10-19 各区县主要农作物单位面积产量（2009年）

The Output of Main Crops per Hectare by Region（2009）

单位：公斤/亩 (kg/mu)

区 县	Region	粮食作物 Grain Crops	夏 粮 Summer Grain	小 麦 Wheat	秋 粮 Autumn Grain	玉 米 Corn
合 计	**Total**	**347.07**	**320.28**	**320.53**	**375.11**	**383.83**
新城区	Xincheng					
碑林区	Beilin					
莲湖区	Lianhu					
灞桥区	Baqiao	294.65	269.50	270.02	327.70	336.64
未央区	Weiyang	364.97	330.19	330.19	387.81	388.51
雁塔区	Yanta	295.69	272.16	272.16	343.91	338.83
阎良区	Yanliang	415.57	416.00	416.00	415.10	416.04
临潼区	Lintong	325.54	308.10	306.93	345.40	346.03
长安区	Chang'an	340.64	310.40	310.40	372.00	371.98
蓝田县	Lantian	317.85	270.20	271.19	365.20	419.27
周至县	Zhouzhi	314.64	301.50	301.17	327.60	327.60
户 县	Huxian	382.66	359.50	360.80	406.05	406.20
高陵县	Gaoling	472.89	432.80	432.80	513.11	512.19

10–19 续表 continued

单位：公斤/亩 (kg/mu)

区 县	Region	棉 花 Cotton	油 料 Oil-bearing Crops	油菜籽 Rapeseeds	蔬 菜 Vegetables
合 计	**Total**	**96.92**	**130.54**	**131.17**	**2556.17**
新城区	Xincheng				
碑林区	Beilin				
莲湖区	Lianhu				
灞桥区	Baqiao	53.17	123.06	126.38	3458.67
未央区	Weiyang		212.92	172.41	2396.58
雁塔区	Yanta				3282.11
阎良区	Yanliang	98.63	120.96	118.39	3132.43
临潼区	Lintong	96.62	94.01	92.84	2620.85
长安区	Chang'an	80.00	176.55	178.30	2111.04
蓝田县	Lantian	90.08	122.20	118.00	1826.81
周至县	Zhouzhi	230.77	157.57	151.98	1858.23
户 县	Huxian	93.33	182.14	189.12	2757.19
高陵县	Gaoling				2866.15

10–20 林业生产情况

Statistcs on Forestry

指 标	Item	2000	2005	2006	2007	2008	2009
一、营林情况	**Afforestation**						
当年造林面积合计（万亩）	Build Forestry Areas(10 000 mu)	27.47	16.56	12.95	6.17	8.76	15.60
更新造林面积（万亩）	Reforestation Areas(10 000 mu)	1.08	0.62	0.63	0.65	0.45	0.48
封山育林面积（万亩）	Hill-closeure for Afforestation Areas (10 000 mu)	18.78	18.65	20.71	23.97	30.19	37.40
零星四旁植树（万株）	Planting(10 000 plants)	731	1064	1096	1176	952	931
育苗面积（万亩）	Raise Seedlings Areas(10 000 mu)	2	6	5	6	5	3
#本年新育	New Seedling of Current Year	2	3	3	3	2	2
二、主要林产品产量（吨）	**Main Forestry Product(ton)**						
生漆	Lacquer	11	2	4	5	6	508
核桃	Walnuts	997	3351	3120	3349	4589	4306
板栗	Chinese Chestnut	744	2076	1944	2153	2728	3122
花椒	Pepper	140	525	507	575	842	689
三、村及村以下采伐木材（万立方米）	**Timber Harvested at or below Village Level（10 000 cu.m)**	**1.62**	**1.87**	**1.41**	**0.96**	**1.23**	**0.97**

注：2009年迹地更新面积改为更新造林面积。

Note:Slash updating areas in 2009 were reforestation areas.

10-21 各区县林业生产情况（2009年）

Statistics On Forestry by Region（2009）

区 县	Region	当年造林面积（亩）Build Forestry Areas in The Year (mu)	零星植树（万株）Planting (10 000 plants)	育苗面积（亩）Raise Seedlings Areas (mu)	核桃产量（吨）Output of Walnuts (ton)	板栗产量（吨）Output of Chinese Chestnut (ton)	村及村以下木材采伐量（万立方米）Timber Harvesting at\under Vallage level (10 000 cu.m)
全 市	**Total**	**156023**	**930.56**	**34113**	**4306**	**3122**	**0.97**
新城区	Xincheng						
碑林区	Beilin						
莲湖区	Lianhu						
灞桥区	Baqiao	3315	17.88	360	79	55	
未央区	Weiyang		3.63				
雁塔区	Yanta	2620	1.00	3200			
阎良区	Yanliang	6800	52.37	814			0.44
临潼区	Lintong	30285	82.98	900	298	10	
长安区	Chang'an	19950	145.00	5875	303	182	0.20
蓝田县	Lantian	27236	434.00	3609	3126	2513	
周至县	Zhouzhi	42000	85.00	10680	435	342	0.03
户 县	Huxian	20617	78.70	8175	65	20	0.22
高陵县	Gaoling	3200	30.00	500			0.08

10-22 主要年份果业生产情况

Statistics on Fruits in Representative Year

指 标	Item	2000	2005	2006	2007	2008	2009
果园面积(万亩)	**Areas of Orchards (10 000 mu)**	**47.86**	**55.55**	**57.68**	**60.86**	**64.31**	**71.08**
苹果园	Apple Orchards	12.15	5.96	5.95	5.94	5.82	5.66
梨 园	Pears Orchards	5.79	3.01	2.76	2.90	2.82	2.66
葡萄园	Grapes Orchards	1.89	3.02	3.20	3.18	3.55	4.59
桃 园	Peach Orchards	3.47	8.66	9.01	8.87	8.75	8.48
猕猴桃园	Chinese Goosebeery Orchards	16.83	4.33	18.39	21.04	23.61	29.01
杏 园	Apricot Orchards	0.62	2.50	2.54	2.65	2.78	2.97
柿子园	Presimmons Orchards	1.96	2.69	2.73	2.97	3.28	3.26
石榴园						3.94	3.61
水果产量（吨）	**Output of Fruits (ton)**	**343551**	**512869**	**553433**	**605075**	**716902**	**789587**
苹 果	Apple	89416	53387	51809	52180	53194	53023
梨	Pears	65459	57059	51517	52869	55945	57929
葡 萄	Grapes	16647	30951	35504	43621	50185	56731
桃	Peach	27010	89755	103142	124393	139058	146651
猕猴桃	Chinese Goosebeery	96640	137853	153678	146301	210393	233296
杏	Apricot					39690	55535
柿 子	Persimmon					28540	34780
石 榴	Pomegranate					43701	42122

10-23 各区县果业生产情况（2009年）

Area and Output of Mulberry Yards and Orchards by Region（2009）

区　县	Region	果园（万亩） Area of Orchards(10 000 mu)	水果产量（吨） Output of Fruits(ton)
全　市	**Total**	**71.08**	**789587**
新城区	Xincheng		
碑林区	Beilin		
莲湖区	Lianhu		
灞桥区	Baqiao	7.09	82409
未央区	Weiyang	1.87	24538
雁塔区	Yanta	0.85	12675
阎良区	Yanliang	2.4	47385
临潼区	Lintong	5.44	63402
长安区	Chang'an	5.47	59161
蓝田县	Lantian	10.46	135456
周至县	Zhouzhi	29.32	235806
户　县	Huxian	4.65	80050
高陵县	Gaoling	3.53	48705

10-24 主要年份畜牧业生产情况

Statistics on Livestock Husbandry in Representative Year

指　标	Item	2000	2005	2006	2007	2008	2009
一、大牲畜年末总头数(头）	**Large Animals In Stock at Year-end (head)**	**260742**	**322521**	**175435**	**181353**	**204723**	**208358**
#能繁殖母畜	Female Animals of Reprductive Ability	137087	176682	105042	110451	132772	136276
#役 畜	Draught Animals	98130	90717	44416	39968	36069	42670
1.牛	Cattle	256073	320773	173834	180200	203596	207237
#能繁殖母畜	Female Animals of Reprductive Ability	136626	176445	104391	109970	132657	136143
当年生仔畜	Newborn Livestock in the Year	69015	72163	39836	43313	41457	39403
肉 牛	Farm Cattle					60490	63804
奶 牛	Dairy Cattle	48164	96498	78056	96400	108164	112071
2.马（匹）	Horses	736	559	527	477	499	515
3.驴	Donkeys	476	175	97	108	83	87
4.骡	Mutes	3457	1014	977	568	545	519
二、猪年末头数（头）	**Hogs in Stock Year-end (head)**	**1284592**	**1472869**	**764579**	**774534**	**864083**	**918734**
#能繁殖母猪	Female Hogs of Reprductive Ability	93775	123543	65313	71600	85419	96522
三、羊年末只数（只）	**Sheeps and Goats in Stock at Year-end(head)**	**421103**	**532471**	**221809**	**234900**	**263164**	**279463**
1.山 羊	Goats	397121	520354	213981	226810	258287	274359
#奶山羊	Milch Goats	266525	358733	156429	177547	201007	229301
2.绵 羊	Sheeps	23982	12117	7828	8090	4877	5104
四、家禽年末存栏数（万只）	**Poultry in Stock at Year-end (10 000 heads)**	**1623.81**	**1372.56**	**831.25**	**849.12**	**919.91**	**980.83**
五、年末养蜂箱数（箱）	**Honey (box)**	**20408**	**24287**	**18871**	**18371**	**22124**	**22779**

10-25 各区县畜牧业生产情况（2009年）

Statistics On Livestock,Animal Husbandry by Region（2009）

区 县	Region	大牲畜年末头数（头）Large Animals In Stock at Year-end (head)	#能繁殖母畜 Female Animals of Reprductive Ability	#役畜 Draught Animals	牛（头）Cattle (head)	奶牛 Dairy Cattle	马（匹）Horses (head)	驴（头）Donkeys (head)
全 市	**Total**	**208358**	**136276**	**42670**	**207237**	**112071**	**515**	**87**
新城区	Xincheng							
碑林区	Beilin							
莲湖区	Lianhu							
灞桥区	Baqiao	14254	8601	887	14240	12839	14	
未央区	Weiyang	6906	4504		6906	6696		
雁塔区	Yanta	380	231		380	294		
阎良区	Yanliang	11575	7915	104	11575	9800		
临潼区	Lintong	70858	54172	7721	70847	63126	11	
长安区	Chang'an	7222	3019	1020	6582	3415	293	
蓝田县	Lantian	44810	28252	20574	44654	2108	55	45
周至县	Zhouzhi	33967	17666	12154	33911	2804	29	
户 县	Huxian	11863	6862	30	11778	6510	30	5
高陵县	Gaoling	6523	5054	180	6364	4479	83	37

10-25 续表 continued

区 县	Region	骡（头）Mutes (head)	猪（头）Hogs (head)	能繁殖母猪 Female Hogs of Reprductive Ability	羊（只）Sheeps and Goats (head)	山羊 Goats	奶山羊 Milch Goats	家禽（万只）Poultry (10 000 head)	蜂（箱）Honey (box)
全 市	**Total**	**519**	**918734**	**96522**	**279463**	**274359**	**229301**	**980.83**	**22779**
新城区	Xincheng								
碑林区	Beilin								
莲湖区	Lianhu								
灞桥区	Baqiao		48337	4266	10216	10100	9141	47.62	329
未央区	Weiyang		40507	3723	988	988	783	8.03	
雁塔区	Yanta		35840	2186	240	240	220	2.60	
阎良区	Yanliang		27145	3486	36800	36696	33696	42.20	610
临潼区	Lintong		248396	21024	117362	117362	117362	259.00	3743
长安区	Chang'an	347	87686	9379	13972	11302	4598	260.00	3177
蓝田县	Lantian	56	84037	11025	72575	72575	47925	79.42	3125
周至县	Zhouzhi	27	187337	23033	10996	10996	2120	78.31	7653
户 县	Huxian	50	122153	13552	6270	6270	6130	121.65	4100
高陵县	Gaoling	39	37296	4848	10044	7830	7326	82.00	42

10-26 主要年份畜产品和水产品产量

Output of Livestock Products and Aquatic Products in Representative Year

单位：吨 (ton)

年份 Year	肉类总产量 Output of Meat	猪肉 Pork	牛肉 Beef	羊肉 Mutton	禽肉 Poultry
1990	63273	50646	4667	1931	5885
1991	72268	55086	5623	2162	9062
1992	88994	68134	6468	2460	11290
1993	93420	71274	7249	2220	12174
1994	106691	79433	8298	2350	15681
1995	127815	86513	11251	3731	23948
1996	91468	63750	5402	2578	19324
1997	106597	75381	6672	3468	20596
1998	134152	98974	8788	4710	21424
1999	130124	93859	9827	4147	21963
2000	147571	106137	12066	4766	23760
2001	157277	113353	11900	5153	20540
2002	161092	118634	11516	5394	20515
2003	165860	122759	13241	5180	19682
2004	171545	126404	13641	5874	18493
2005	182046	136503	14031	6106	18803
2006	108634	81199	8267	2841	13417
2007	102191	73254	8589	3111	14075
2008	115352	84654	9840	3335	16060
2009	126182	94490	10142	3677	17190

10-26 续表 continued

单位：吨 (ton)

年 份 Year	奶类总产量 Output of Milk	牛 奶 Cow Milk	禽蛋 Poultry Eggs	蜂蜜（公斤） Honey(kg)	水产品 Output of Aquatic Products	养殖面积（万亩） Water Raise Areas (10 000 mu)
1990	82017	50528	55938	1035392	4259	2.55
1991	91006	57700	90558	1022797	4949	2.63
1992	100080	63586	104970	739275	6015	2.80
1993	111070	73897	125244	662049	7132	2.97
1994	145412	99025	146503	547808	7900	3.10
1995	132909	85753	141227	535891	8517	3.21
1996	133372	86103	138044	613290	8910	3.51
1997	150964	98078	156066	713918	10054	3.46
1998	174099	119719	142519	537304	10480	3.40
1999	209144	145191	135981	541613	11061	3.38
2000	245913	176155	138305	460598	11384	3.35
2001	255437	179977	132303	479839	12480	3.17
2002	288009	202826	134336	497530	12017	3.31
2003	336296	245407	128833	537805	9967	2.48
2004	384319	289564	117597	449765	9721	2.46
2005	422229	327961	118115	421052	9370	2.38
2006	471438	374813	97816	414271	11937	1.60
2007	528037	428462	98140	401761	12402	1.38
2008	589697	475681	108515	503031	12487	1.40
2009	618186	498394	116685	528731	13044	1.52

10-27 各区县主要畜产品和水产品产量（2009年）

Output of Major Livestock Products and Aquatic Products by Region（2009）

单位：吨 (ton)

区 县	Region	肉类总产量 Output of Meat	猪肉 Pork	牛肉 Beef	羊肉 Mutton	禽肉 Poultry
全 市	**Total**	**126182**	**94490**	**10142**	**3677**	**17190**
新城区	Xincheng					
碑林区	Beilin					
莲湖区	Lianhu					
灞桥区	Baqiao	6509	4894	734	120	753
未央区	Weiyang	3632	3364	150	14	104
雁塔区	Yanta	3266	3217	8	3	38
阎良区	Yanliang	4119	2774	315	350	582
临潼区	Lintong	34128	25696	2439	1622	4332
长安区	Chang'an	16025	9835	402	213	5321
蓝田县	Lantian	15516	9717	3308	1042	1297
周至县	Zhouzhi	23370	20097	1904	153	1201
户 县	Huxian	14429	11572	651	65	2120
高陵县	Gaoling	5188	3324	231	95	1442

10-27 续表 continued

单位：吨 (ton)

区 县	Region	奶类总产量 Output of Milk	牛奶 Cow Milk	禽蛋 Poultry Eggs	蜂 蜜（公斤） Honey(kg)	水产品 Output of Aquatic Products	养殖面积（亩） Water Raise Areas(mu)
全 市	**Total**	**618186**	**498394**	**116685**	**528731**	**13044**	**15225**
新城区	Xincheng						
碑林区	Beilin						
莲湖区	Lianhu						
灞桥区	Baqiao	63075	57133	5714	8220	1955	1800
未央区	Weiyang	29625	29285	693		2223	1680
雁塔区	Yanta	1384	1264	312			
阎良区	Yanliang	62665	43728	5060	34480	238	255
临潼区	Lintong	338729	282583	30186	129215	2060	3000
长安区	Chang'an	17601	15026	31900	57172	2274	2915
蓝田县	Lantian	36098	9275	9265	47521	1624	2310
周至县	Zhouzhi	12435	11434	8988	72604	945	1230
户 县	Huxian	33626	30326	14466	179101	825	790
高陵县	Gaoling	22948	18340	10101	418	900	1245

10-28 主要年份农产品人均占有量

Pre CapitaOutput of Major Farm Products in Representative Year

单位：公斤/人 (kg/person)

年 份 Year	粮 食 Grain	棉 花 Cotton	油 料 Oil-bearing Crops	猪牛羊肉 Pork Beef and Mutton	禽 蛋 Poultry Eggs	奶 类 Milk	水 果 Fruits	蔬 菜 Vegetables
1978	266.7	5.7	0.2	5.4	0.9	3.3	6.8	91.7
1979	288.6	5.2	0.6	6.7	1.0	4.0	5.1	97.3
1980	223.5	3.8	1.1	5.9	1.2	4.1	6.9	78.4
1981	222.9	2.6	1.5	6.6	1.7	4.7	5.8	65.4
1982	281.5	5.5	1.0	4.9	2.7	5.6	5.9	101.6
1983	276.6	1.6	0.7	4.9	3.2	6.5	5.0	87.8
1984	289.4	2.7	0.8	4.8	6.2	8.7	4.8	138.6
1985	271.4	0.9	1.4	6.8	5.7	10.2	7.6	156.3
1986	288.0	0.8	2.2	7.8	6.4	12.1	9.6	152.2
1987	298.0	0.8	2.7	7.3	6.8	13.8	10.6	165.6
1988	269.7	0.7	1.5	8.0	8.9	15.6	11.1	193.7
1989	290.7	0.9	2.2	8.4	7.6	13.1	10.2	216.5
1990	298.7	1.2	2.1	9.4	9.2	14.2	11.5	196.0
1991	290.6	1.6	2.0	10.2	14.7	14.8	11.7	190.8
1992	294.3	1.2	2.4	12.4	16.8	16.2	17.3	205.6
1993	301.2	1.2	2.2	12.8	19.9	17.6	25.9	231.1
1994	246.1	1.0	1.7	14.1	22.9	22.7	28.0	211.5
1995	270.4	0.5	3.4	15.7	21.8	20.5	37.5	206.1
1996	286.3	0.4	3.2	11.0	21.1	20.4	43.9	210.8
1997	287.8	0.3	2.8	12.9	23.6	22.8	43.3	214.7
1998	318.3	0.2	2.5	16.8	21.3	26.1	50.0	222.8
1999	303.0	0.2	1.9	16.0	20.2	31.0	52.7	227.2
2000	293.5	0.2	1.9	17.9	20.1	35.7	49.9	235.7
2001	283.7	0.2	1.8	18.8	19.0	36.8	48.8	219.9
2002	273.8	0.3	1.7	19.3	19.1	41.0	53.5	241.6
2003	246.0	0.3	1.6	19.7	18.0	46.9	53.6	236.8
2004	270.1	0.6	1.6	20.1	16.2	53.0	63.9	249.6
2005	277.1	0.6	1.6	21.1	15.9	56.9	69.1	263.8
2006	256.9	0.6	1.4	12.3	13.0	62.6	73.5	251.4
2007	247.4	0.8	1.3	11.1	12.8	69.1	79.2	267.3
2008	256.0	0.7	1.4	11.7	13.0	70.4	85.6	264.5
2009	258.7	0.7	1.3	12.8	13.8	73.3	93.6	287.4

10-29 主要年份农村经济效益主要指标

Main Index of Rural Economic Benefit in Representative Year

年 份 Year	每一农业劳动力创造的 Average Labor Force Production 农林牧渔及服务业总产值（元） Gross Output Value of Farming,Forestry，Animal Husbandry, Fishery and Service (yuan)	粮食（公斤） Grain Crops(kg)	棉花（公斤） Cotton (kg)	油料（公斤） Oil-bearing Crops(kg)	每亩耕地种植业产值（元） Output of Each Unit of Area Planting(yuan)	每百元物耗生产的总产值（元） Output per 100-Yuan of Material Consumed(yuan)
1978	504.7	1024.6	22.0	0.7	104.3	
1979	549.0	1096.5	19.8	2.3	116.0	
1980	483.1	846.1	14.5	4.0	99.2	
1981	502.8	840.5	9.9	5.5	105.4	
1982	631.5	1058.9	20.5	3.6	139.3	
1983	606.5	1053.2	6.1	2.6	124.1	
1984	850.7	1154.2	10.9	3.4	163.6	
1985	1020.1	1134.6	3.7	5.6	183.1	
1986	1132.2	1236.4	3.4	9.5	204.6	
1987	1280.3	1277.2	3.5	11.7	231.5	
1988	1558.4	1148.0	3.0	6.5	273.2	
1989	1605.3	1231.9	3.9	9.5	295.0	
1990	1766.3	1279.1	5.2	10.0	343.4	233.3
1991	1958.8	1326.6	7.2	8.9	380.4	238.4
1992	2093.7	1360.7	5.5	11.1	451.6	241.8
1993	2528.9	1409.7	5.6	10.4	546.8	240.1
1994	3705.0	1167.8	4.8	8.0	762.8	227.6
1995	4953.0	1300.6	2.2	16.1	1106.5	225.9
1996	5154.8	1391.2	1.8	13.6	1224.2	234.5
1997	5493.0	1413.4	1.3	13.8	1283.3	239.2
1998	5615.9	1578.1	1.0	12.4	1374.3	247.0
1999	4826.5	1516.6	1.1	9.7	1175.9	251.7
2000	5091.5	1498.0	1.0	9.9	1161.1	250.2
2001	5328.5	1462.4	1.3	9.1	1221.1	248.6
2002	5617.4	1427.5	1.3	9.1	1272.0	265.9
2003	5761.2	1308.1	1.6	8.4	1332.4	254.3
2004	6885.4	1452.7	3.0	8.5	1434.6	261.7
2005	7737.9	1524.7	3.3	8.6	1642.3	262.9
2006	8415.5	1435.7	3.6	8.0	1756.9	263.1
2007	10165.6	1403.0	4.4	7.1	2037.3	259.8
2008	13306.4	1695.4	4.9	9.1	2447.9	259.6
2009	14674.3	1791.7	5.1	9.2	2737.9	261.6

主要统计指标解释

农林牧渔及服务业产值 指以货币表现的农、林、牧、渔业全部产品和服务业收入的总量，它反映一定时期内农林牧渔及服务业生产总规模和总成果。农林牧渔及服务业总产值的计算方法通常是按农、林、牧、渔业产品加上服务业产值。

粮食产量 指全社会的产量。包括国有经济经营的、集体统一经营的和农民家庭经营的粮食产量，还包括工矿企业办的农场和其他生产单位的产量。粮食除包括稻谷、小麦、玉米、高粱、谷子及其他杂粮外，还包括薯类和豆类。其产量计算方法，豆类按去豆荚后的干豆计算；薯类（包括甘薯和马铃薯，不包括芋头和木薯）按5公斤鲜薯折1公斤粮食计算。城市郊区作为蔬菜的薯类（如马铃薯等）按鲜品计算，并且不作粮食统计。其他粮食一律按脱粒后的原粮计算。

棉花产量 指全社会的产量。包括春播棉和夏播棉。产量按皮棉计算。

油料产量 指全部油料作物的生产量。包括花生、油菜籽、芝麻、向日葵籽、胡麻籽（亚麻籽）和其他油料。不包括大豆、木本油料和野生油料。花生以带壳干花生计算。

水产品产量 指人工养殖的水产品和天然生长的水产品的捕捞量。包括海水的鱼类、虾蟹类、贝类和藻类以及内陆水域的鱼类、虾蟹类和贝类，不包括淡水生植物。

猪、牛、羊肉产量 指当年出栏并已屠宰、除去头蹄下水后带骨肉（即胴体重）的重量。

期初（末）畜禽存栏头（只）数 指报告期初（末）农村各种合作经济组织和国营农场、农民个人、机关、团体、学校、工矿企业、部队等单位以及城镇居民饲养的大牲畜、猪、羊、家禽等畜禽的存栏数。

常用耕地 是指耕地总资源中专门种植农作物并经常进行耕种、能够正常收获的土地。包括当年实际耕种的熟地；弃耕、休闲不满三年，随时可以复耕的地；开荒利用三年以上的地。不包括临时种植农作物的坡度在25度以上的陡坡地；在河套、湖畔、库区临时开发的成片或零星土地；也不包括已列为国家和省（区、市）退耕计划但临时耕种的土地。

农作物播种面积 指实际播种或种植有农作物的面积。凡是实际种植有农作物的面积，不论种植在耕地上还是种植在非耕地上，均包括在农作物播种面积中。在播种季节基本结束后，因遭灾而重新改种和补种的农作物面积，也包括在内。

有效灌溉面积 指具有一定的水源，地块比较平整，灌溉工程或设备已经配套，在一般年景下当年能够进行正常灌溉的耕地面积。在一般情况下，有效灌溉面积应等于灌溉工程或设备已经配备，能够进行正常灌溉的水田和水浇地面积之和。

农用化肥施用量 指本年内实际用于农业生产的化肥数量，包括氮肥、磷肥、钾肥和复合肥。化肥施用量要求按折纯量计算数量。折纯量是指把氮肥、磷肥、钾肥分别按含氮、含五氧化二磷、含氧化钾的百分之一百成份进行折算后的数量。复合肥按其所含主要成分折算。

农业机械总动力 指主要用于农、林、牧、渔业的各种动力机械的动力总和。包括耕作机械、排灌机械、收获机械、农用运输机械、植物保护机械、牧业机械、林业机械、渔业机械、农产品加工机械和其他农业机械〔内燃机按引擎马力折成瓦（特）计算、电动机按功率折成瓦（特）计算〕。不包括专门用于乡、镇、村、组办工业、基本建设、非农业运输、科学试验和教学等非农业生产方面用的动力机械与作业机械。

农林牧渔业劳动力 指全社会直接参加农林牧渔业生产活动的劳动力。

Explanatory Notes on Main Statistical Indicators

Gross Output Value of Farming, Forestry, Animal Husbandry, Fishery and Service refers to the total value of products of farming, forestry, animal husbandry, fishery and service, which reflects the total scale and result of agricultural production during a given period. The calculation method of gross output value of agriculture generally obtained value of product and its service of farming, forestry, animal husbandry and fishery.

Grain Output refers to the grain production in the whole country including grains produced by state farms, collective units, industrial enterprises and mines. Grain includes rice, wheat, corn, sorghum, millet and other miscellaneous grains as well as tubers and beans. Output of beans refers to dry beans without pods. The output of tubers (sweet potatoes and potatoes, not including taros and cassava) was converted into that of grain at the ratio 5:1. Tubers supplied as vegetables (such as potatoes) in cities and suburbs are calculated as fresh vegetables and their output is not included in the output of grain. Output of all other grains refers to husked grain.

Cotton Output refers to the cotton production in the whole country including cotton sown in spring and in autumn. Output is measured as the weight of ginned cotton.

Output of Oil-bearing Crops refers to the total production of oil bearing crops of various kinds, including peanuts, (dry, in shell) rapeseeds, sesame, sunflower seeds, flax seeds, and other oil bearing crops. Soybeans, oil-bearing woody plants, and wild oil-bearing crops are not included.

Output of Aquatic Products refers to catches of both artificially cultured and naturally grown aquatic products, including fish, shrimps, crabs and shellfish in sea and inland water as well as seaweed. Freshwater plants are not included.

Output of Pork, Beef, and Mutton refers to the meat of slaughtered hogs, cattle, sheep and goats with head, feet, and offal taken away.

Number of Livestock or Poultry in Stock at Beginning (or End) refers to the total number of large animals, pigs, sheep, fowls, etc. raised by rural cooperative organizations, state farms, rural individuals, government agencies, schools, industrial and mining enterprises, army, and urban residents at the beginning (or end) of the reference period.

Regularly Cultivated Land refers to farmland among the total land resources which is exclusively used for farming and is under regular cultivation with harvest in normal years. Included are currently cultivated land, land that has been abandoned or put in idle for less than 3 years and could be re-used for cultivation at any time, and new-claimed land that has been put into cultivation for more than 3 years. Excluded under this category are steep slope land over 25 degrees under temporary cultivation, land (large or small plots) that is claimed along river bends, lake sides or banks of reservoirs, as well as land that has been designated under the "Green for Grain" programmes of the state and provincial governments but is still temporarily under cultivation.

Sown Area of Crops refers to area of land sown or transplanted with crops regardless of being in cultivated area or non cultivated area. Area of land re-sown due to natural disasters is also included.

Irrigated Area refers to areas that are effectively irrigated, i.e. level land which has water source and complete sets of irrigation facilities to lift and move adequate water for irrigation purpose under normal conditions. Under normal conditions, irrigated area is the sum of watered fields and irrigated fields where irrigation systems or equipment have been installed for regular irrigation purpose.

Consumption of Chemical Fertilizers in Agriculture refers to the quantity of chemical fertilizers applied in agriculture in the year, including nitrogenous fertilizer, phosphate fertilizer, potash fertilizer, and compound fertilizer. The consumption of chemical fertilizers is required in calculation to convert the gross weight into weight containing 100% effective component (e.g. 100% nitrogen content in nitrogenous fertilizer, 100% phosphorous pentoxide contents in phosphate fertilizer, 100% potassium oxide contents in potash fertilizer). Compound fertilizer is converted with its major component.

Total Power of Farm Machinery refers to total mechanical power of machinery used in farming, forestry, animal husbandry, and fishery, including ploughing,irrigation and drainage, harvesting, transport, plant protection, stock breeding, forestry and fishery. The power of internal combustion engines is required to convert horsepower into watts and the power of electric motors is required to be converted into watts. Machinery employed for non agricultural purposes, such as the machines used in township run and village-run industry, construction, non agricultural transport, scientific experiments and teaching, is excluded.

Labour Force Engaged in Farming, Forestry, Animal Husbandry and Fishery refers to the total laborers who are directly engaged in production of farming, forestry, animal husbandry and fishery.

11 工业和能源

INDUSTRY AND ENERGY

资料整理：赵　晖　王风玲　赵　博　陈小兵　李　玫　王　玥
张　育　雷稳强　于元英
Data management:Zhao Hui　Wang Fengling　Zhao Bo　Chen Xiaobing　Li Mei　Wang Yue
Zhang Yu　Lei Wenqiang　Yu Yuanying

第十一部分　工业和能源

一、简要说明

本章资料包括全部工业总产值，规模以上工业企业单位数、总产值、主要经济指标以及能源购销存情况等，由西安市统计局工业处和能源处提供。

二、主要指标

规模以上工业企业单位数（个）	1131	比上年增加 99个
#大中型工业企业	190	比上年增加 15个
全部工业增加值（亿元）	816.92	比上年增长 11.7%
#规模以上工业增加值	700.31	比上年增长 13.3%
单位GDP能耗（吨标准煤/万元）	0.820	比上年下降 5.56%
单位GDP电耗（千瓦时/万元）	754.45	比上年下降 5.33%
规模以上工业单位增加值能耗（吨标准煤/万元）	0.8000	比上年下降 10.48%

11　INDUSTRY AND ENERGY

Ⅰ.Brief Introduction

Data in this chapter reflects Gross Industrial Output Value, number of industrial enterprises above designated size, gross product, primary economic and performance indicators for industrial enterprises,Energy Purchases Consumption and Inventory of Industrial Enterprises Above Designafed size. Data in this chapter are provided and compiled by Industry & Transportation Division of the Xi'an Bureau of Statistics.

Ⅱ.Major Indicators

		Increase over Preceding Year
Number of Industrial Enterprises Above Designated Size(item)	1131	99
Large-size and Medium-size Industrial Enterprises	190	15
Value Added of Industry(100 mil. yuan)	816.92	11.7%
Value Added of Industry Above Designated Size	700.31	13.3%
Energy Consumption of GDP per Unit (Tons of Standard Coal /10,000yuan)	0.820	-5.56%
Power Consumption of GDP per Unit (kilowatt-hour/10,000yuan)	754.45	-5.33%
Energy Consumption of value added per Unit of Industrial Enterprises Above Designated Size (Tons of Standard Coal /10,000yuan)	0.8000	-10.48%

11-1 主要年份全部工业总产值

Gross Output Value of Industry In Representative Years

单位：万元 （10 000 yuan）

年 份 Year	全部工业总产值 Gross Industrial Output Value	工业总产值指数 (上年=100) Index of Gross Industry Output Value (Preceding Year=100)	国有经济 State-owned Enterprises	集体经济 Collective-owned Enterprises	其他经济类型 Enterprises of Other Ownership
1952	23512.0	139.6	9917.0	464.0	13131.0
1962	120833.0	86.8	102103.0	17599.0	1131.0
1965	200416.0	132.1	183164.0	17252.0	
1970	333386.0	143.5	305303.0	28083.0	
1975	385509.0	106.1	332982.0	52527.0	
1978	483262.0	116.9	405376.0	77886.0	
1979	517483.0	106.6	438850.0	78633.0	
1980	531755.0	101.8	440139.0	91577.0	39.0
1981	524587.0	98.6	433740.0	90675.0	172.0
1982	549200.0	107.1	450308.0	98516.0	456.0
1983	603507.0	112.2	493773.0	108923.0	811.0
1984	674963.0	112.8	520593.0	153056.0	1314.0
1985	853196.0	120.4	632702.0	218893.0	1601.0
1986	976326.0	112.1	706380.0	267282.0	2664.0
1987	1142220.0	114.2	809186.0	328701.0	4341.0
1988	1429811.0	116.0	1012268.0	416217.0	1326.0
1989	1653472.0	106.1	1160877.0	486754.0	5814.0
1990	1771310.0	107.4	1196777.0	548605.0	25928.0
1991	2002727.0	110.0	1325242.0	604495.0	72990.0
1992	2300472.0	112.5	1488541.0	561369.0	250562.0
1993	3045988.0	121.7	1748145.0	1071122.0	226721.0
1994	3891584.0	120.6	1960533.0	1581321.0	349730.0
1995	4058952.0	108.7	2071755.0	1663536.0	323661.0
1996	5338510.0	133.4	2132140.0	2836176.0	370194.0
1997	5794532.0	121.8	1915536.0	2005610.0	1873386.0
1998	6738224.0	117.3	2593405.0	2077273.0	2067546.0
1999	7151528.0	117.1	2128243.0	2174220.0	2849065.0
2000	6394812.0	115.3	2749778.0	2094680.0	1550354.0
2001	7361510.0	116.4	3098431.0	2380910.0	1882169.0
2002	8379363.0	115.8	3472067.0	2312923.0	2594373.0
2003	9750800.0	115.1	4149015.0	1501372.0	4100413.0
2004	11853224.0	118.4	5414952.0	875412.0	5562860.0
2005	13085580.0	106.3	5916553.0	674900.0	6494127.0
2006	15573515.9	119.0	7527606.7	514810.4	7531098.8
2007	19798592.6	122.1	10179302.9	365328.6	9253961.1
2008	23881446.2	120.6	12479652.4	441987.2	10959806.6
2009	28270651.8	118.3	14440320.8	388777.4	13441553.6

11-1 续表 continued

单位：万元 （10 000 yuan）

年 份 Year	轻工业 Ligth Industry	重工业 Heavy Industry	大型工业 Large-size Industry Enterprises	中型工业 Medium-size Industry Enterprlses	小型工业 Small-size Industry Enterprises
1952	20800.0	2712.0			
1962	68221.0	52618.0			
1965	98631.0	101785.0			
1970	124467.0	208919.0			
1975	167285.0	218224.0	145262.0	130592.0	109655.0
1978	220480.0	262782.0	168397.0	121813.0	193052.0
1979	243043.0	274440.0	189877.0	133759.0	193847.0
1980	283475.0	248280.0	193092.0	130053.0	208610.0
1981	309199.0	215388.0	178130.0	140810.0	205639.0
1982	303249.0	246031.0	213015.0	128597.0	207668.0
1983	315785.0	287722.0	245053.0	127164.0	231290.0
1984	321678.0	353285.0	241842.0	143165.0	289956.0
1985	401748.0	451448.0	333820.0	147488.0	371888.0
1986	458270.0	518056.0	401037.0	150644.0	424609.0
1987	516776.0	625452.0	472958.0	171698.0	497572.0
1988	699593.0	730210.0	615946.0	210089.0	603776.0
1989	712743.0	940729.0	696368.0	258414.0	698690.0
1990	787857.0	983453.0	716421.0	279098.0	775791.0
1991	897676.0	1105051.0	888052.0	303151.0	811524.0
1992	967104.0	1333368.0			
1993	1121957.0	1924031.0	1258137.0	384255.0	1403596.0
1994	1578875.0	2312709.0	1479613.0	390233.0	2021738.0
1995	1626219.0	2432733.0	1575030.0	371156.0	2112766.0
1996	2347887.0	2990623.0	1693985.0	358913.0	3285612.0
1997	2700085.0	3094447.0	1675521.0	274888.0	3844123.0
1998	3232681.0	3505543.0	1821556.0	308424.0	4608244.0
1999	3488547.0	3662981.0	1744637.0	337795.0	5069096.0
2000	3121419.0	3273393.0	2320973.0	328494.0	3745345.0
2001	3518054.0	3843456.0	2656010.0	368497.0	4337003.0
2002	3935764.0	4443599.0	3038828.0	398834.0	4941701.0
2003	4028859.0	5721941.0	2662073.0	2027256.0	5061471.0
2004	4211592.0	7641632.0	3595150.0	3237701.0	5020373.0
2005	4078417.0	9007163.0	4640325.0	3228553.0	5216702.0
2006	4510970.1	11062545.8	5970535.3	3414468.1	6188512.5
2007	7331719.0	12466873.6	8351303.0	4171131.3	7276158.3
2008	6010865.1	17870581.1	10472685.9	5005676.2	8403084.1
2009	6636464.3	21634187.5	12309192.0	6186394.5	9775065.3

11-2 分区县规模以上工业总产值（2009年）

Gross Output Value of Industrial Enterpriese Above Designated Size by Region（2009）

单位：亿元　　　　(100 million yuan)

区县名称	Name of District and County	单位数（个）Name of Enterprises (unit)	全部工业总产值 Gross Industrial Output Value	国有经济 State-owned Enterprises	集体经济 Collective-owned Enterprises	其他经济类型 Enterprises of Other Ownership
新城区	Xingcheng	38	195.45	61.03	0.25	134.17
区属	Under District	30	128.63	58.51	0.25	69.87
碑林区	Beilin	41	58.60	39.76	2.84	16.00
区属	Under District	31	49.60	39.69	2.84	7.07
莲湖区	Lianhu	64	399.83	213.13	0.84	185.86
区属	Under District	58	368.43	209.29	0.84	158.30
灞桥区	Baqiao	149	178.82	21.60	8.16	149.06
区属	Under District	144	161.01	14.02	8.16	138.83
未央区	Weiyang	187	393.22	89.20	7.91	296.11
区属	Under District	83	161.64	86.04	7.91	67.69
雁塔区	Yanta	188	249.69	65.24	1.37	183.08
区属	Under District	56	39.71	8.48	1.37	29.86
阎良区	Yanliang	54	128.99	3.79	0.70	124.50
区属	Under District	50	26.79	3.15	0.70	22.94
临潼区	Lintong	51	165.77	40.72	0.12	124.93
区属	Under District	51	165.77	40.72	0.12	124.93
长安区	Chang'an	105	277.98	16.19	3.24	258.55
区属	Under District	60	25.84	0.75	3.24	21.85
蓝田县	Lantian	38	23.40	2.15	0.53	20.72
县属	Under County	37	22.65	1.40	0.53	20.72
周至县	Zhouzhi	27	9.03		0.51	8.52
县属	Under County	27	9.03		0.51	8.52
户县	Huxian	91	81.54	12.95	4.78	63.81
县属	Under County	90	66.43	12.95	4.78	48.70
高陵县	Gaoling	98	305.94	0.52		305.42
县属	Under County	78	47.88	0.52		47.36

11-2 续表 continued

单位：亿元 （100 million yuan）

区县名称	Name of District and County	轻工业 Ligth Industry	重工业 Heavy Industry	大型工业 Large-size Industry Enterprises	中型工业 Medium-size Industry Enterprlses	小型工业 Small-size Industry Enterprises
新城区	Xingcheng	52.64	142.81	165.81	20.30	9.34
区属	Under District	51.29	77.33	105.52	13.70	9.42
碑林区	Beilin	12.27	46.33		45.52	13.08
区属	Under District	7.44	42.15		41.61	7.98
莲湖区	Lianhu	53.04	346.80	315.98	50.04	33.81
区属	Under District	53.18	315.25	295.63	43.52	29.28
灞桥区	Baqiao	32.26	146.56	13.84	23.62	141.36
区属	Under District	32.06	128.96	4.38	16.25	140.39
未央区	Weiyang	91.71	301.50	85.68	193.08	114.45
区属	Under District	20.89	140.75	20.36	107.97	33.32
雁塔区	Yanta	52.77	196.91	50.49	124.99	74.20
区属	Under District	8.62	31.09		15.94	23.77
阎良区	Yanliang	17.20	111.79	101.20	0.64	27.16
区属	Under District	16.90	9.89			26.79
临潼区	Lintong	70.57	95.21	46.60	64.83	54.34
区属	Under District	70.57	95.21	46.60	64.83	54.34
长安区	Chang'an	21.04	256.94	210.38	27.75	39.86
区属	Under District	13.93	11.91		3.16	22.68
蓝田县	Lantian	6.39	17.02		8.13	15.28
县属	Under County	6.39	16.26		8.13	14.52
周至县	Zhouzhi	5.44	3.59		0.86	8.17
县属	Under County	5.44	3.59		0.86	8.17
户县	Huxian	37.02	44.52	15.11	25.70	40.73
县属	Under County	37.20	29.40		25.70	40.73
高陵县	Gaoling	14.13	291.80	225.82	33.19	46.92
县属	Under County	14.13	33.74		14.27	33.61

11-3 规模以上工业企业主要产品产量

Output of Major Industrial Products Of Enterprises Above Designated size

产品名称	Name of Products	2009	比上年增长（%） Increase over Preceding Year (%)
铁矿石成品矿（吨）	Iron Ore(ton)	7190	-64.1
发电量（万千瓦小时）	Electricity Generation Volume(10 000 kw.h)	832126.4	17.7
#火电	Thermal Power	832126.4	17.7
自来水生产量（万吨）	Tap Water Production (10 000 tons)	1456	147.2
大米（吨）	Rice (ton)	35210	-18.8
小麦粉（万吨）	Wheat Flour (10 000 tons)	88.42	22.0
精制食用植物油（吨）	Edible Vegetable Oil (ton)	211806	13.0
鲜冷藏冻肉(吨)	Fresh/Frozen Meat(ton)	15361.7	27.9
浓缩饲料（吨）	Concentrated Feed(ton)		
配混合饲料（吨）	Mixed Feed(ton)	425586.2	3.0
糕点（吨）	Cake (ton)	5975	-3.0
方便面（吨）	Instant Noodle	67731	35.9
乳制品（吨）	Dairy Products (ton)	786028.7	10.4
液体乳	Milk	736981	7.8
罐头（吨）	Canned Food (ton)	2195	-6.3
饮料酒（千升）	Beverage Wine (kiloliter)	407473	14.3
白酒	Liquor	410	2.0
啤酒	Beer	407063	14.3
软饮料（吨）	Soft Beverage (ton)	863899.85	0.5
碳酸饮料	Carbonated Beverage	326831	8.3
果汁及果汁饮料	Juice and Fruit Beverage	335082	-34.5
包装饮用水类	Canned Drinking Water	201986.85	336.4
纱（吨）	Yarn (ton)	46758.56	-15.9
棉纱	Cotton Yarn	26686.27	-29.9
混纺纱	Blend Fabric	7404.65	2.7
纯化纤纱	Pure Chemical-Fibre Yarn	12667.64	22.5
布（万米）	Cloth (10 000 m)	22201.61	-7.3
棉布	Cotton Cloth	12550.68	-22.2
混纺交织布	Blend Fabric	4992.25	20.1
纯化纤布	Pure Chemical-Fibre Cloth	4658.68	27.0
无纺织布（无纺织物）（吨）	Non-textile fabrics(Non-extile stuff) (ton)	1947	142.8
服装（万件）	Garment (10 000 units)	783.5	26.8
梭织服装	Shuttle-Woven Garment	780.36	27.0
皮鞋（万双）	Leather Shoes (10 000 pairs)	77.18	-31.7

11-3 续表1 continued 1

产品名称	Name of Products	2009	比上年增长（%） Increase over Preceding Year (%)
人造板（立方米）	Artificial Board (cu.m)	310978.43	55.3
纤维板	Fibre Board	310978.43	55.3
家具（件）	Furniture (unit)	415392	10.5
木质家具	Wooden Furniture	316937	8.4
软体家具（包括床垫、沙发）	Soft Furniture (inc.: Sofa ,Mattress etc.)	98455	17.9
机制纸及纸板（吨）	Machine Made Paper(ton)	476258.41	27.0
新闻纸	Newsprint Paper	4001	-63.7
纸制品（吨）	Paper-Made Products (ton)	117617	-7.8
纸箱	Carton	78155	-13.2
多色印刷品（万对开色令）	Colored Printed products(10000 reams)	5077508.08	-5.6
本册(万本）	book（10000 book)	755.9	96.8
原油加工量（吨）	Crude Oil Processing (ton)	1688953	8.5
汽油	Petrol	225043	28.4
石油沥青（吨）	Petroleum pitch (ton)	598788	70.0
液化石油气（吨）	Liquefied Petroleum Gas (ton)	46338	-18.8
盐酸（含量31%以上）（吨）	Salt Acid (Content over31%) (ton)	45411	-21.7
氢氧化钠（烧碱）（折100%）（吨）	Caustic Soda (100%)(ton)	64036	-29.2
碳化钙（电石）（折 300升/千克)（吨）	Calcium Carbide Lonverted into(ton)	52307	-22.6
合成复合肥（吨）	Synthetic Compound Fertilizer(ton)		
化学农药原料药(折有效成分100%)（吨）	Chemical Pesticide(100% effective content)(ton)	1525.83	-32.1
涂料（吨）	Construction Paint(ton)	10706	3.1
初级形态的塑料（塑料树脂及共聚物）（吨）	Plastic,Resin and Copolymer (ton)	32636	-32.1
聚氯乙烯树酯	PVC	32636	-32.1
合成洗涤剂（吨）	Synthetic Detergents (ton)	79360	4.5
合成洗衣粉	Washing Power	21576	-12.5
化学原料药（吨）	Chemical Medicine (ton)	608.14	-7.9
中成药（吨）	Traditional Chinese Medicine (ton)	28952.04	494.3
塑料制品（吨）	Plastic Product (ton)	110534.16	22.7
1.塑料薄膜	Plastic Sheet	5428.2	58.7
农用薄膜	Agricultural Sheet	3433	66.1
3.塑料管及其附件	Plastic Pipe and Accessories	7740	55.5
4.塑料条、棒、型材	Plastic Wicker,Rod and Section Bar	49403	14.2
5.塑料丝、绳及编织品	Plastic Silk,Rope and Knit	3112	181.6
6.泡沫塑料	Plastic Foam	1873.17	84.5
8.塑料包装箱及容器	Plastic Package and Container	7305	27.4

11-3 续表2 continued 2

产品名称	Name of Products	2009	比上年增长（%）Increase over Preceding Year (%)
水泥熟料（万吨）	Cement Clinker (10 000 tons)	216.68	14.6
水泥（万吨）	Cement (10 000 tons)	487.72	16.0
水泥电杆（根）	Cement Pole(unit)	63093	75.7
商品混凝土（万立方米）	Ready-mixed Concrete（10 000 cu.m）	1183.08	91.6
沥青和改性沥青防水卷材（平方米）	Asphalt and Modified Bitumen Membrane(sq.m)	198929	-46.5
平板玻璃（重量箱）	Plate Glass (wt.cases)	832202	83.3
钢化玻璃(平方米)	Toughened Glass(sq.m)	642882	15.0
日用玻璃制品（吨）	Glassware(ton)	4099	8.7
生铁（吨）	Csat iron(ton)	54937	53.6
粗钢（吨）	Thick Steel (ton)	9233:5	-32.1
成品钢材（吨）	Rolled-steel Final Products (ton)	1105074	137.4
中小型型钢	Rolled-steel Medium and Small	8790	33.2
钢筋	Corrugated Steel Bar	591769	60.9
（盘条）线材	Wire Rod	476998	531.9
冷轧薄板	Non-hot-roll Thin Steel	2790	212.4
无缝钢管	Seamless Steel Pipe	15494	49.9
焊接钢管	Welded Steel Pipes	9233	109.7
铁合金	Ferroalloy	11384	152.0
铝材（吨）	Aluminum Material (ton)	42041	12.9
工业锅炉（蒸发量吨）	Industrial Boiler steam(ton)	988.2	-15.4
金属切削机床（台）	Metal-cutting Machines (unit)	681	72.8
泵（液体泵）（台）	Pump (Liquid pump)(unit)	1537	-25.7
风机（台）	Fan(unit)	713	-45.9
气体压缩机（台）	Gas Compressor(unit)	1996734	-46.4
滚动轴承（万套）	Bearing (10 000 sets)		
阀门（吨）	Valves (ton)	876	-4.8
粉末冶金制品（吨）	Powder Melallurgy Products(ton)	380.8	28.6
采矿设备（吨）	Mining Equipment (ton)	8038	18.6
粮食加工机械（台）	Food Processing Machine(unit)	117	15.8
烟草加工机械（台、条、组）	Tobacco Processing Machine(unit)		
缝纫机（架）	Sewing Machines (unit)	360946	-6.4
造纸机械（台）	Paper Making Machine(unit)		
炼油、化工专用设备（吨）	Oil Refining and Chemical Industry Machine(ton)	3525	10.7
水泥专用设备（吨）	Cement Producing Equipment(ton)		

11-3 续表3 continued 3

产品名称	Name of Products	2009	比上年增长（%）Increase over Preceding Year (%)
金属冶炼设备（吨）	Metal Smelting Equipments(ton)	24138.8	18.7
金属轧制设备（吨）	Metal-rolling Machine(ton)	2892.2	-66.7
铲土运输机械（台）	Earth-moving Machine(unit)	604	153.8
混凝土机械（台）	Concrete Machinery(unit)	164	-5.7
环境保护专用设备（台、套）	Special Equipment for Environment Protection	160	-7.5
大气污染防治设备	Equipment for Preventing Atmospheric Pollution	133	
铁路货车（辆）	Freight(unit)	2658	-12.5
汽车（辆）	Motor Vehicle (unit)	506758	89.0
载货汽车	Trucks	77519	5.5
公路客车	Buses	1507	-12.1
大型（40座及以上）	Large(40seats and above)	1507	-12.1
轿车	Cars	427732	121.7
排气量1.0升及以下	1.0L and Below Gas Displacement	102068	291.7
排气量1.0-1.6升（含1.6升）	1.0L-1.6L Gas Displacement(1.6L included)	273510	76.5
排气量1.6-2.0升（含2.0升）	1.6L-2.0L Gas Displacement(2.0L included)	49332	394.6
排气量2.0-2.5升（含2.5升）	2.0L-2.5L Gas Displacement(2.5L included)	2822	44.5
改装汽车（辆）	Refit Trucks (unit)	2619	6.3
摩托车（辆）	Motorcycles(unit)	9404	-37.7
两轮自行车（非助动）（辆）	Bicycle (unit)	10696	-13.3
交流电动机（千瓦）	Alternating Current Motor (kw)	6180614	-0.4
变压器（千伏安）	Transformer (kwa)	110637185	29.7
高压开关板（面）	High-voltage Switch Panel(unit)	3448	5.9
低压开关板（面）	Low-voltage Switch Panel(unit)	15103	101.9
电力电缆（千米）	Electric Power Cables(km)	4357.98	4.9
通讯及电子网络用电缆（对千米）	Communication Cables(pair km)	3048	-48.5
光缆（光纤通迅电缆）（芯千米）	Cable (Optical Communication Cable) (Core.km)	2257552	7.1
绝缘制品（吨）	Insulating Products(ton)	4245	-10.6
家用电冰箱（台）	Household refrigerator(unit)	92146	-8.6
电子计算机整机（台）	Air-conditioner Compressor(unit)	38990	27.3
微型计算机设备	Micro-computers	38990	27.3
#笔记本计算机	Notebooks PCs	13802	26.4
显示器（台）	Display(unit)	38281	20.2
#平板显示器	Flat Plate Display	38281	20.2
彩色显象管（只）	Color kinescope (unit)	7632608	-51.8
半导体分立器件（万只）	Semiconductor Discrete Device(10 000units)	27.15	-13.8
电子元件（万只）	Electronic Components(10 000units)	44403.76	-3.9
自动化仪表及系统（台、套）	Automatization meter and system (unit)	1749	-24.3
电工仪器仪表（台）	Electronic Instruments and Meters(unit)	284514	61.5

11-4 主要年份规模以上工业企业主要经济指标

Main Economic Indicators of All Industrial Enterprises Above Designafed size In Representative Years

单位：亿元　　　　(100 million yuan)

年　份 Year	企业单位数（个） Number of Enterprises (unit)	工业总产值（现价） Gross Industrial Output Value	工业增加值（现价） Value-added of Industry	从业人员年平均人数（万人） Annual Average Employed Persons (10 000 persons)
1998	793	350.38	99.20	51.71
1999	770	366.59	106.56	45.64
2000	816	417.97	130.18	43.25
2001	785	482.61	149.06	40.12
2002	771	544.78	170.39	38.48
2003	735	638.66	202.74	36.55
2004	1066	830.06	254.17	38.08
2005	902	981.02	314.01	37.92
2006	904	1187.74	370.11	37.94
2007	937	1577.05	499.96	38.55
2008	1032	2007.85	605.25	40.17
2009	1131	2468.27	700.13	43.42

11-4 续表 continued

单位：亿元　　　　(100 million yuan)

年　份 Year	资产合计 Total Assets	负债合计 Total Liabilities	所有者权益 Owners' Equities	主营业务收入 Revenue from Principal Business	利润总额 Total Profits	利税总额 Total Pre-tax Profits
1998	810.56	548.68	261.88	346.84	-1.26	14.82
1999	853.90	577.94	275.96	346.26	8.26	27.30
2000	958.05	622.46	323.72	420.42	16.11	36.29
2001	1054.36	657.88	384.65	451.62	17.97	40.84
2002	1065.76	643.78	412.27	541.64	25.43	51.31
2003	1195.69	733.04	460.97	645.53	33.82	64.99
2004	1333.91	869.30	464.60	812.46	38.57	74.23
2005	1503.85	977.42	508.82	980.97	28.72	67.25
2006	1651.67	1062.11	578.33	1183.51	61.46	110.23
2007	1940.52	1254.01	686.51	1561.25	106.22	168.54
2008	2426.13	1518.86	907.27	1928.05	84.89	168.63
2009	2913.56	1779.38	1130.76	2384.52	177.20	280.68

11-5 规模以上工业企业主要经济指标（2009年）

单位：万元

分　组	Item	企业单位数（个） Number of Enterprises (unit)	亏损企业 Loss Making Enterprises	工业总产值（当年价） Gross Industrial Output Value (At Current Prices)
总　计	**Total**	**1131**	**258**	**24682651.8**
#市　区	Urban Area	877	174	20483533.5
按隶属关系分	Grouped by Jurisdiction of Management			
中央企业	Central Enterprises	65	6	7610466.0
省属企业	Provincial Enterprises	79	26	4474606.3
市属企业	Municipal Enterprises	987	226	12597579.5
按登记注册类型分组	Grouped by Registion Status			
内资企业	Domestic Investment Enterprises	989	219	19371646.4
国有经济	State-owned Enterprises	96	30	5662712.7
集体经济	Collective-owned Enterprises	65	17	312565.7
股份合作	Share-holding Corperative	16	3	135338.0
联营企业	Joint Ownership Enterprises	3	2	8416.3
有限责任公司	Limited company	441	94	10035487.3
国有独资公司	State-owned appropriator ship corporation	22	5	1946975.6
其他有限责任公司	Other limited corporation	419	89	8088511.7
股份有限公司	Share-holding Corperation Ltd.	63	17	1241637.0
私营企业	Private Enterprises	302	55	1970813.2
其他内资企业	Other Domestic Funded Enterprises	3	1	4676.2
港、澳、台商投资企业	Enterprises with Funds from Hong Kong,Macao and Taiwan	30	5	271815.9
外商投资企业	Enterprises with Foreign Investment	112	34	5039189.5
在总计中:亏损企业	Deficit Enterprises	258	258	1683573.4
按轻重工业分	Grouped by Ligth Industry and Heavy Industry			
轻工业	Light Industry	344	87	4665016.0
重工业	Heavy Industry	787	171	20017635.8
按企业规模分	Grouped by Size of Enterprises			
大型工业	Large-size	31	3	12309192.0
中型工业	Medium-size	159	29	6186394.5
小型工业	Small-size	941	226	6187065.3
按经济组织类型分	Grouped by Economic Type of Orgnization			
独资企业	Appropratorship	245	62	7064283.2
合作、合伙企业	Partnership	33	7	192147.4
股份有限公司	Corporaton	91	22	1655126.1
有限责任公司	Limited company	762	167	15771095.1
按工业行业大类分	Grouped by Sector			
煤炭开采和洗选业	Mining and Washing of Coal			
石油和天然气开采业	Extraction of Petroleum and Natural Gas	3		101639.3
黑色金属矿采选业	Mining and Processing of Ferrous Metal Ores	1	1	1006.0
有色金属矿采选业	Mining and Processing of Non-ferroous Metal Ores	1		25518.7
非金属矿采选业	Mining and Processing of Nonmetal Ores			
其他采矿业	Mining of other Ores			

Main Economic Indicators of All Industrial Enterprises Above Designafed size（2009）

（10 000 yuan）

工业销售产值（当年价）Value of Industry Products Sales (At Current Prices)	从业人员年平均人数（人）Annual Average Employers (person)	资产合计 Total Assets	流动资产小计 Total Working Capitals	固定资产小计 Total Fixed Assets	固定资产原价合计 Origing Value of Fixed Assets	累计折旧 Accumulative Total Depreciation
24080509.5	**434158**	**29135595.0**	**17155053.1**	**9865236.4**	**12766040.2**	**4500484.4**
3022946.6	367230	24926456.0	14718576.2	8426727.6	11080304.9	4039350.4
7420153.4	137944	12842714.6	7014054.4	5295164.1	6538699.8	2313901.6
4431129.0	63825	4386172.0	2995946.8	1091588.6	1321700.5	390361.9
12229227.1	232389	11906708.4	7145051.9	3478483.7	4905639.9	1796220.9
18836172.8	373379	25233913.0	14819239.6	8616749.9	11024550.9	3909621.3
5546816.2	83234	8730771.2	4283176.8	4005579.7	4961090.5	1654647.9
285924.2	9768	148927.4	96549.6	43137.0	59298.5	20358.2
135596.2	2467	86922.3	40624.9	25777.6	43676.3	19191.2
7537.3	257	5553.6	3831.8	1687.8	1428.0	751.6
9863118.6	206736	13034082.3	8618224.6	3550772.9	4636786.5	1700778.6
1876856.7	58610	3311485.4	1910669.5	1193717.1	1656528.9	643726.6
7986261.9	148126	9722596.9	6707555.1	2357055.8	2980257.6	1057052.0
1190254.8	29366	1964099.0	977861.2	634082.2	854711.3	364550.8
1802594.8	41282	1255352.7	793497.3	353594.6	464153.3	147672.1
4330.7	269	8204.5	5473.4	2118.1	3406.5	1670.9
249096.0	6305	326612.9	169045.4	71535.3	142113.5	70580.3
4995240.7	54474	3575069.1	2166768.1	1176951.2	1599375.8	520282.8
1624628.4	57239	3283718.3	1317450.0	1596742.4	2179496.0	783231.2
4553771.6	96838	3723753.8	1812330.6	1399662.3	2113379.7	842651.5
19526737.9	337320	25411841.2	15342722.5	8465574.1	10652660.5	3657832.9
12179893.9	203304	15892806.4	10121256.2	4944725.4	6298271.9	2476267.5
5985928.2	125856	8065890.3	3885998.7	3385792.4	4320656.4	1319619.1
5914687.4	104998	5176898.3	3147798.2	1534718.6	2147111.9	704597.8
6883312.2	109452	9742084.6	4838461.5	4369702.4	5498192.5	1856995.7
188190.6	3917	117443.9	59588.2	34314.0	54611.0	23923.7
1596276.9	35093	2428096.6	1229430.7	821994.5	1078336.4	414386.1
15412729.8	285696	16847969.9	11027572.7	4639225.5	6134900.3	2205178.9
81666.5	2419	104998.9	75697.6	17067.4	43706.9	14461.9
843.5	130	2430.4	1518.0	725.2	1188.6	463.4
25518.7	430	22560.9	8925.9	8287.9	13267.8	4979.9

11-5 续表1

单位：万元

分　组	Item	负债合计 Total Liabilites	流动负债小计 Total Working Liabilities	长期负债小计 Long-term Liabilities
总　计	**Total**	**17793819.0**	**14098749.8**	**3126667.7**
#市　区	Urban Area	14917907.8	11747866.0	2652007.9
按隶属关系分	Grouped by Jurisdiction of Management			
中央企业	Central Enterprises	8573864.3	6222372.7	2127901.5
省属企业	Provincial Enterprises	2825050.7	2497164.3	310552.1
市属企业	Municipal Enterprises	6394904.0	5379212.8	688214.1
按登记注册类型分组	Grouped by Registion Status			
内资企业	Domestic Investment Enterprises	15834958.7	12339013.9	2947897.8
国有经济	State-owned Enterprises	6291921.6	4226629.5	1801124.2
集体经济	Collective-owned Enterprises	94752.3	85392.5	8796.0
股份合作	Share-holding Corperative	48239.9	41900.7	6120.3
联营企业	Joint Ownership Enterprises	4393.3	4393.3	0.0
有限责任公司	Limited company	7763557.9	6588244.7	906435.3
国有独资公司	State-owned appropriator ship corporation	1541996.2	1246195.3	205599.9
其他有限责任公司	Other limited corporation	6221561.7	5342049.4	700835.4
股份有限公司	Share-holding Corperation Ltd.	920184.5	755730.0	158898.4
私营企业	Private Enterprises	707549.1	632710.9	66175.8
其他内资企业	Other Domestic Funded Enterprises	4360.1	4012.3	347.8
港、澳、台商投资企业	Enterprises with Funds from Hong Kong,Macao and Taiwan	164793.2	157137.6	6453.5
外商投资企业	Enterprises with Foreign Investment	1794067.1	1602598.3	172316.4
在总计中:亏损企业	Deficit Enterprises	2263123.0	1411304.2	725479.2
按轻重工业分	Grouped by Ligth Industry and Heavy Industry			
轻工业	Light Industry	1897627.1	1620080.3	234704.1
重工业	Heavy Industry	15896191.9	12478669.5	2891963.6
按企业规模分	Grouped by Size of Enterprises			
大型工业	Large-size	9891014.9	7904521.8	1710558.5
中型工业	Medium-size	4848509.2	3753586.9	1004548.7
小型工业	Small-size	3054294.9	2440641.1	411560.5
按经济组织类型分	Grouped by Economic Type of Orgnization			
独资企业	Appropratorship	6713007.1	4599032.0	1845764.5
合作、合伙企业	Partnership	64440.8	57341.9	6880.0
股份有限公司	Corporaton	1188837.8	949778.5	232797.5
有限责任公司	Limited company	9827533.3	8492597.4	1041225.7
按工业行业大类分	Grouped by Sector			
煤炭开采和洗选业	Mining and Washing of Coal			
石油和天然气开采业	Extraction of Petroleum and Natural Gas	54083.3	54083.3	
黑色金属矿采选业	Mining and Processing of Ferrous Metal Ores	3239.8	1154.3	2085.5
有色金属矿采选业	Mining and Processing of Non-ferrous Metal Ores	13528.9	13399.9	129.0
非金属矿采选业	Mining and Processing of Nonmetal Ores			
其他采矿业	Mining of other Ores			

continued 1

(10 000 yuan)

所有者权益合计 Total Owners' Equities	实收资本 Total Capital Hold	主营业务收入 Revenue from Principal Business	主营业务成本 Cost of Principal Business	主营业务税金及附加 Taxes and Other Charges on Principal Business
11307575.6	**5144650.8**	**23845157.5**	**19414868.6**	**253962.6**
9985716.3	4211016.3	19930711.1	15954176.0	244802.5
4268819.3	1444387.3	7545234.5	5929559.8	126714.4
1559507.2	714303.3	4362399.8	3681346.5	9717.7
5479249.1	2985960.2	11937523.2	9803962.3	117530.5
9373981.3	4074753.2	18703949.9	15451355.8	180904.3
2434413.3	993073.1	5364315.9	4059755.0	127251.9
54176.6	29310.6	285147.7	255064.6	1386.2
38669.1	15106.6	133013.6	113204.6	580.5
1160.3	2126.0	6322.6	5695.8	12.5
5263729.1	2182954.9	9967759.8	8567176.5	35017.8
1769489.1	374728.7	1957236.4	1654117.0	5916.0
3494240.0	1808226.2	8010523.4	6913059.5	29101.8
1033165.8	495192.7	1170666.2	955644.9	6281.9
544825.7	351852.0	1772148.2	1490470.3	10362.1
3841.4	5137.3	4575.9	4344.1	11.4
161819.7	122656.7	250407.8	185805.8	41.6
1771774.6	947240.9	4890799.8	3777707.0	73016.7
1011985.8	924268.2	1535415.2	1409342.5	6768.0
1816475.7	1075115.1	4433286.1	3397166.3	19858.4
9491099.9	4069535.7	19411871.4	16017702.3	234104.2
5996518.9	1919736.0	12111274.4	9668478.3	101196.9
3209650.8	1726472.4	5896716.3	4795226.6	127425.6
2101405.9	1498442.4	5837166.8	4951163.7	25340.1
3019303.1	1334738.2	6673164.5	5080251.0	131555.7
52986.4	30751.4	184144.6	156761.6	707.8
1228519.7	563210.9	1573352.7	1290354.6	7732.5
7006766.4	3215950.3	15414495.7	12887501.4	113966.6
50915.6	17708.6	79256.0	63689.9	1477.3
-809.4	300.0	840.0	627.6	
9031.9	4900.0	25518.7	23036.0	64.3

11-5 续表2

单位：万元

分　　组	Item	营业费用 Expenses for Operation	管理费用 Expenses for Management
总　　计	**Total**	**1042742.0**	**1294742.1**
#市　区	Urban Area	923164.4	1136239.9
按隶属关系分	Grouped by Jurisdiction of Management		
中央企业	Central Enterprises	182930.7	485137.2
省属企业	Provincial Enterprises	287211.3	188987.8
市属企业	Municipal Enterprises	572600.0	620617.1
按登记注册类型分组	Grouped by Registion Status		
内资企业	Domestic Investment Enterprises	622307.3	1131687.5
国有经济	State-owned Enterprises	156769.7	356761.2
集体经济	Collective-owned Enterprises	8290.8	14274.3
股份合作	Share-holding Corperative	2987.7	5731.3
联营企业	Joint Ownership Enterprises	284.2	341.6
有限责任公司	Limited company	307478.4	581132.9
国有独资公司	State-owned appropriator ship corporation	45471.3	167977.6
其他有限责任公司	Other limited corporation	262007.1	413155.3
股份有限公司	Share-holding Corperation Ltd.	72791.2	95370.1
私营企业	Private Enterprises	73546.4	77663.9
其他内资企业	Other Domestic Funded Enterprises	158.9	412.2
港、澳、台商投资企业	Enterprises with Funds from Hong Kong,Macao and Taiwan	28216.1	16586.1
外商投资企业	Enterprises with Foreign Investment	392218.6	146468.5
在总计中:亏损企业	Deficit Enterprises	61008.2	144699.7
按轻重工业分	Grouped by Ligth Industry and Heavy Industry		
轻工业	Light Industry	495521.7	222779.1
重工业	Heavy Industry	547220.3	1071963.0
按企业规模分	Grouped by Size of Enterprises		
大型工业	Large-size	508016.8	672151.2
中型工业	Medium-size	329138.1	331617.3
小型工业	Small-size	205587.1	290973.6
按经济组织类型分	Grouped by Economic Type of Orgnization		
独资企业	Appropratorship	285418.7	421781.6
合作、合伙企业	Partnership	5925.1	9476.3
股份有限公司	Corporaton	88664.2	113769.3
有限责任公司	Limited company	662734.0	749714.9
按工业行业大类分	Grouped by Sector		
煤炭开采和洗选业	Mining and Washing of Coal		
石油和天然气开采业	Extraction of Petroleum and Natural Gas	1013.0	4795.8
黑色金属矿采选业	Mining and Processing of Ferrous Metal Ores	18.0	349.8
有色金属矿采选业	Mining and Processing of Non-ferroous Metal Ores	1172.8	694.7
非金属矿采选业	Mining and Processing of Nonmetal Ores		
其他采矿业	Mining of other Ores		

continued 2

(10 000 yuan)

财务费用 Financial cost	营业利润 Operating Profit	利润总额 Total Profits	亏损企业亏损总额 Total Loss of Deficit Enterprises	利税总额 Total Pre-tax Profits	本年应交增值税 Value Added Tax Payable
233795.9	**1963744.5**	**1771959.9**	**179265.5**	**2806811.0**	**780888.5**
186267.4	1850533.6	1659911.6	146189.7	2599969.0	695254.9
115206.5	741616.7	788970.4	17252.0	1089398.6	173713.8
27044.9	142177.0	166083.0	15428.3	324167.0	148366.3
91544.5	1079950.8	816906.5	146585.2	1393245.4	458808.4
203993.2	1331153.4	1206541.3	156305.9	1872965.3	485519.7
69796.8	686205.8	697524.0	22606.1	1013520.9	188745.0
1361.9	11150.2	7020.2	1552.7	15736.0	7329.6
1456.9	10220.8	6603.8	1561.2	11477.5	4293.2
27.3	-38.7	-0.1	68.5	131.3	118.9
81441.4	474800.1	422253.4	40471.1	654957.8	197686.6
11597.2	87051.4	97209.4	6436.0	149836.7	46711.3
69844.2	387748.7	325044.0	34035.1	505121.1	150975.3
23971.5	-4878.4	-6333.2	82565.8	43993.7	44045.0
25902.4	154079.4	79875.4	7030.0	133432.2	43194.7
35.0	-385.8	-402.2	450.5	-284.1	106.7
501.0	20456.1	21173.5	1586.0	32072.7	10857.6
29301.7	612135.0	544245.1	21373.6	901773.0	284511.2
60916.9	-181919.8	-179265.5	179265.5	-120402.3	52095.2
47829.1	444376.8	278354.5	27114.6	513691.3	215478.4
185966.8	1519367.7	1493605.4	152150.9	2293119.7	565410.1
86937.2	1078701.0	1113998.3	74194.7	1634093.5	418898.3
86958.2	474616.2	359904.4	44611.8	679236.7	191906.7
59900.5	410427.3	298057.2	60459.0	493480.8	170083.5
73926.4	842936.1	807637.6	33887.1	1186328.7	247135.4
1795.0	11863.8	7489.9	2094.4	13362.1	5164.4
33439.6	53263.5	17927.1	84365.7	86007.0	60347.4
124634.9	1055681.1	938905.3	58918.3	1521113.2	468241.3
181.4	8862.8	8669.9		19588.6	9441.4
194.6	-590.2	-590.5	590.5	-536.5	54.0
271.3	265.0	920.0		1633.0	648.7

11-5 续表3

单位：万元

分　　组	Item	企业单位数(个) Number of Enterprises (unit)	亏损企业 Loss Making Enterprises	工业总产值（当年价） Gross Industrial Output Value (At Current Prices)
农副食品加工业	Processing of Food from Agricultural Porducts	63	5	971191.5
食品制造业	Manufacture of Foods	30	3	604806.2
饮料制造业	Manufacture of Beverages	17	5	525885.7
烟草加工业	Manufacture of Tobacco	1		3473.6
纺织业	Manufacture of Textile	22	11	189902.6
纺织服装、鞋、帽制造业	Manufacture of Textile Wearing Apparel,Footwear and Caps	10	1	87436.6
皮革、毛皮、羽毛(绒)及其制品业	Manufacture of Leather, Fur, Feather (eiderdown) and Related Products	1		12428.1
木材加工及竹、藤、棕、草制品业	Processing of Timber,Manufacture of Wood,Plam and Straw Products	10	3	83936.0
家具制造业	Manufacture of Furniture	6		27904.2
造纸及纸制品业	Manufacture of Paper and Paper Products	28	8	226195.8
印刷业、记录媒介的复制	Printing,Reproduction of Recording Media	32	8	365434.5
文教体育用品制造业	Manufacture of Articles For Cultural,Educational and Sports Activities	2		13267.0
石油加工、炼焦及核燃料加工业	Processing of Petroleum, Cokeing,Processing of Nuclear and Nuclear Fuel	7	2	990828.5
化学原料及化学制品制造业	Manufacture of Raw Chemical Materials and Chemical Products	48	11	653117.8
医药制造业	Manufacture of Medicines	54	16	950925.8
化学纤维制造业	Manufacture of Chemical Fibers	3	2	83694.7
橡胶制品业	Manufacture of Rubber	6	1	17593.6
塑料制品业	Manufacture of Plastics	37	11	289700.2
非金属矿物制品业	Manufacture of Non-metallic Mineral Products	88	19	914420.1
黑色金属冶炼及压延加工业	Smelting and Pressing of Ferrous Metals	17	6	215365.4
有色金属冶炼及压延加工业	Smelting and Pressing of Non-ferrou Metals	31	5	414468.5
金属制品业	Manufacture of Metal Products	69	11	287907.2
通用设备制造业	Manufacture of General Purpose Machinery	113	19	1081758.8
专用设备制造业	Manufacture of Special Equipment	113	33	1882736.5
交通运输设备制造业	Manufacture of Transport Equipment	62	9	7830056.5
电气机械及器材制造业	Manufacture of Electric Equipment and Machinery	123	31	2939215.3
通信设备、计算机及其他电子设备制造业	Manufacture of Communication Equipment, Computers and other Electronic Equipment	48	13	770544.2
仪器仪表及文化办公用	Manufacture of Measuring Instruments and Machinery for Cultural Activity and Office Work	47	6	631027.6
工艺品及其他制造业	Manufacture of Artwork and Other Manufacturing	8	3	55901.9
废弃资源和废旧材料回收加工业	Recycling and Disposal of Waste	1		4211.3
电力、热力的生产和供应业	Production and Supply of Electric Power and Heat Power	16	11	1215570.8
燃气生产和供应业	Gas mining and supplying industry	4		155145.5
水的生产和供应业	Production and Supply of Water	9	4	58435.8

continued 3

(10 000 yuan)

工业销售产值（当年价）Value of Industry Products Sales (At Current Prices)	从业人员年平均人数（人）Annual Average Employers (person)	资产合计 Total Assets	流动资产小计 Total Working Capitals	固定资产小计 Total Fixed Assets	固定资产原价合计 Origing Value of Fixed Assets	累计折旧 Accumulative Total Depreciation
902585.5	9355	447471.4	270861.1	118662.5	176561.9	66304.8
576410.7	8690	263118.2	128578.5	88349.8	141991.9	62107.0
619784.3	7507	683773.3	269052.4	308716.2	436713.1	130419.9
3285.9	212	5800.0	2825.6	2196.2	3177.4	981.2
191438.9	16916	193070.3	93339.6	54781.7	94158.6	43326.5
91950.3	2340	66593.1	56570.1	7318.5	11273.4	4774.2
12500.0	1053	35220.0	12043.1	23176.9	4042.2	1160.2
59607.2	1402	93006.4	53668.0	25287.1	33568.8	10168.1
26583.5	1613	11476.0	7690.0	2794.3	6524.6	3733.6
210344.9	11018	132502.4	45185.4	85481.5	98760.4	16523.0
356668.3	9033	470122.9	197600.7	212797.4	324095.1	152316.7
13083.0	171	4674.1	2971.4	1702.7	2160.0	457.3
989422.5	1657	309231.5	188687.2	113319.1	142181.8	47340.4
641431.4	20289	929236.2	401225.4	387437.0	542653.3	210698.5
923917.5	15326	851380.5	437684.9	248314.9	361884.5	138621.2
88415.8	301	51749.3	25223.1	26381.1	56463.2	30165.0
15542.3	637	12568.8	7995.3	3380.9	4930.2	1549.3
269777.2	5931	316915.5	191363.2	107986.0	121083.3	38257.2
881798.9	13110	734713.6	379268.9	282477.9	328161.8	95937.1
262062.9	2055	121013.1	73892.6	44055.2	53864.1	11504.0
386707.6	6497	622870.5	339478.9	143988.2	184735.6	49507.2
273866.1	7697	243676.5	173463.2	54365.3	81778.5	30945.0
1063695.6	21892	1564476.8	1216127.6	223997.5	335516.2	135150.7
1745870.6	47016	2900607.4	1887613.7	849079.6	1040983.7	397279.2
7792031.3	122496	8929032.0	6196644.4	2239338.4	2705938.0	948439.4
2754880.8	36873	3366957.7	2385457.7	921745.6	862097.2	302705.2
757751.0	22581	1379780.3	870311.6	393317.7	602828.5	289504.5
581626.0	19003	1010589.7	618176.3	287471.5	427133.3	187410.9
50475.2	1385	29983.6	12685.6	11815.8	13242.9	5271.0
4191.3	70	1630.0	300.0	1152.0	1200.0	548.0
1215661.0	10752	2781679.5	381120.1	2323950.1	3118955.9	916782.1
151990.5	2406	302380.9	111275.2	139028.6	165025.4	26669.4
57122.8	3895	138303.3	30530.8	105288.7	224192.1	124021.4

11-5 续表4

单位：万元

分 组	Item	负债合计 Total Liabilites	流动负债小计 Total Working Liabilities	长期负债小计 Long-term Liabilities
农副食品加工业	Processing of Food from Agricultural Porducts	269719.1	245685.5	15181.0
食品制造业	Manufacture of Foods	124043.5	120542.8	2687.7
饮料制造业	Manufacture of Beverages	369122.3	285742.4	83379.9
烟草加工业	Manufacture of Tobacco	1016.6	1016.6	
纺织业	Manufacture of Textile	100882.7	94441.1	5267.7
纺织服装、鞋、帽制造业	Manufacture of Textile Wearing Apparel,Footwear and Caps	45518.0	45515.1	2.9
皮革、毛皮、羽毛(绒)及其制品业	Manufacture of Leather, Fur, Feather (eiderdown) and Related Products	21933.0	14213.3	7719.7
木材加工及竹、藤、棕、草制品业	Processing of Timber,Manufacture of Wood,Plam and Straw Products	49055.0	31850.3	17204.7
家具制造业	Manufacture of Furniture	5242.6	5241.0	1.6
造纸及纸制品业	Manufacture of Paper and Paper Products	66414.6	47628.7	18701.7
印刷业、记录媒介的复制	Printing,Reproduction of Recording Media	169812.7	141478.0	28330.6
文教体育用品制造业	Manufacture of Articles For Cultural,Educational and Sports Activities	2568.5	2568.5	
石油加工、炼焦及核燃料加工业	Processing of Petroleum, Cokeing,Processing of Nuclear and Nuclear Fuel	245326.8	136739.6	45.4
化学原料及化学制品制造业	Manufacture of Raw Chemical Materials and Chemical Products	470777.6	369965.5	54243.4
医药制造业	Manufacture of Medicines	420193.9	379772.2	27159.5
化学纤维制造业	Manufacture of Chemical Fibers	11302.8	11302.8	
橡胶制品业	Manufacture of Rubber	6609.8	6333.6	276.2
塑料制品业	Manufacture of Plastics	187059.4	148837.1	35165.2
非金属矿物制品业	Manufacture of Non-metallic Mineral Products	414215.0	359556.1	50137.4
黑色金属冶炼及压延加工业	Smelting and Pressing of Ferrous Metals	91948.0	87725.3	4077.7
有色金属冶炼及压延加工业	Smelting and Pressing of Non-ferrou Metals	342948.9	276034.6	64374.4
金属制品业	Manufacture of Metal Products	163434.3	128677.3	21793.2
通用设备制造业	Manufacture of General Purpose Machinery	938703.3	879488.7	48437.4
专用设备制造业	Manufacture of Special Equipment	1540110.5	1355430.5	172977.2
交通运输设备制造业	Manufacture of Transport Equipment	5394891.5	4698892.3	664265.6
电气机械及器材制造业	Manufacture of Electric Equipment and Machinery	2326801.5	1936688.5	225710.9
通信设备、计算机及其他电子设备制造业	Manufacture of Communication Equipment, Computers and other Electronic Equipment	805435.2	666689.2	133680.2
仪器仪表及文化办公用	Manufacture of Measuring Instruments and Machinery for Cultural Activity and Office Work	512834.2	409659.4	34619.7
工艺品及其他制造业	Manufacture of Artwork and Other Manufacturing	22699.4	14535.1	8081.5
废弃资源和废旧材料回收加工业	Recycling and Disposal of Waste	885.0	330.0	555.0
电力、热力的生产和供应业	Production and Supply of Electric Power and Heat Power	2391168.6	975052.5	1356073.5
燃气生产和供应业	Gas mining and supplying industry	149919.3	114269.8	35649.5
水的生产和供应业	Production and Supply of Water	60373.4	38208.9	8652.8

continued 4

(10 000 yuan)

所有者权益合计 Total Owners' Equities	实收资本 Total Capital Hold	主营业务收入 Revenue from Principal Business	主营业务成本 Cost of Principal Business	主营业务税金及附加 Taxes and Other Charges on Principal Business
177271.1	93801.4	888365.5	787337.4	1955.4
137745.9	89140.6	543148.7	418230.7	674.1
310940.4	159489.2	617379.5	465002.8	9385.6
4783.4	1514.7	4083.6	2317.9	35.9
91990.1	46730.1	190071.6	166867.8	989.8
20589.3	12610.0	99793.3	83163.5	638.5
13287.0	6000.0	13838.3	11999.1	23.8
43951.4	16559.2	36678.1	30949.2	246.7
6003.2	4786.1	26199.9	20677.3	99.8
66035.9	44327.9	198365.4	173494.7	358.0
299943.4	167052.1	355644.9	264724.2	2721.2
2105.6	1260.0	13083.0	9078.3	161.1
63904.7	39123.8	1021389.2	883765.0	98630.8
448574.6	178621.5	649557.7	544097.8	2667.8
431186.0	241656.9	858904.0	463511.5	1428.1
40446.4	25400.0	88486.2	74502.0	4.1
5602.6	3215.4	14127.6	10763.8	53.5
129824.4	83914.0	277780.0	228212.6	1089.9
317778.9	165183.7	897439.1	743876.8	7202.5
28605.4	27866.0	253022.4	219272.4	820.5
279731.0	121200.0	374745.4	305427.2	1782.2
79934.5	56030.5	259510.5	221063.1	1357.4
622356.5	175840.3	1015968.7	819753.8	4032.4
1357663.9	625743.6	1748857.2	1455875.1	8672.9
3533955.1	1172535.0	7873155.3	6747541.5	78192.3
1037171.1	436871.5	2454593.5	1895090.2	15969.5
573027.4	370863.6	748855.1	635010.6	4446.4
497687.1	275269.2	581022.1	471272.3	3354.5
7284.1	7682.2	56836.5	47846.8	65.1
745.0	400.0	3720.0	3315.0	110.0
390510.8	281711.3	1364048.4	945850.3	3461.4
152461.6	133780.0	153146.6	127530.3	1365.8
75339.7	55562.4	57725.5	50094.1	424.0

11-5 续表5

单位：万元

分　　组	Item	营业费用 Expenses for Operation	管理费用 Expenses for Management
农副食品加工业	Processing of Food from Agricultural Porducts	34274.1	21483.4
食品制造业	Manufacture of Foods	75604.9	15467.5
饮料制造业	Manufacture of Beverages	89298.2	22567.6
烟草加工业	Manufacture of Tobacco	146.2	894.8
纺织业	Manufacture of Textile	5884.2	16161.4
纺织服装、鞋、帽制造业	Manufacture of Textile Wearing Apparel,Footwear and Caps	5939.1	6859.4
皮革、毛皮、羽毛(绒)及其制品业	Manufacture of Leather, Fur, Feather (eiderdown) and Related Products	438.8	1135.9
木材加工及竹、藤、棕、草制品业	Processing of Timber,Manufacture of Wood,Plam and Straw Products	1266.1	1496.0
家具制造业	Manufacture of Furniture	1735.5	1746.3
造纸及纸制品业	Manufacture of Paper and Paper Products	3462.0	5189.4
印刷业、记录媒介的复制	Printing,Reproduction of Recording Media	10436.4	40719.4
文教体育用品制造业	Manufacture of Articles For Cultural,Educational and Sports Activities	538.0	1028.4
石油加工、炼焦及核燃料加工业	Processing of Petroleum, Cokeing,Processing of Nuclear and Nuclear Fuel	9062.8	13509.3
化学原料及化学制品制造业	Manufacture of Raw Chemical Materials and Chemical Products	28819.6	66312.1
医药制造业	Manufacture of Medicines	244238.0	57581.1
化学纤维制造业	Manufacture of Chemical Fibers	267.8	2002.6
橡胶制品业	Manufacture of Rubber	585.1	1659.7
塑料制品业	Manufacture of Plastics	12967.1	15263.5
非金属矿物制品业	Manufacture of Non-metallic Mineral Products	20769.7	24196.0
黑色金属冶炼及压延加工业	Smelting and Pressing of Ferrous Metals	2459.4	4805.2
有色金属冶炼及压延加工业	Smelting and Pressing of Non-ferrou Metals	7976.0	17121.5
金属制品业	Manufacture of Metal Products	9759.5	15962.5
通用设备制造业	Manufacture of General Purpose Machinery	38106.1	96943.3
专用设备制造业	Manufacture of Special Equipment	58084.0	162769.3
交通运输设备制造业	Manufacture of Transport Equipment	167961.2	322079.4
电气机械及器材制造业	Manufacture of Electric Equipment and Machinery	143499.4	172592.0
通信设备、计算机及其他电子设备制造业	Manufacture of Communication Equipment, Computers and other Electronic Equipment	32590.5	79920.2
仪器仪表及文化办公用	Manufacture of Measuring Instruments and Machinery for Cultural Activity and Office Work	16523.6	70023.9
工艺品及其他制造业	Manufacture of Artwork and Other Manufacturing	2313.8	3872.5
废弃资源和废旧材料回收加工业	Recycling and Disposal of Waste	443.9	117.6
电力、热力的生产和供应业	Production and Supply of Electric Power and Heat Power	929.4	9264.6
燃气生产和供应业	Gas mining and supplying industry	11392.9	13348.0
水的生产和供应业	Production and Supply of Water	2764.9	4808.0

continued 5

(10 000 yuan)

财务费用 Financial cost	营业利润 Operating Profit	利润总额 Total Profits	亏损企业亏损总额 Total Loss of Deficit Enterprises	利税总额 Total Pre-tax Profits	本年应交增值税 Value Added Tax Payable
6154.1	100619.7	33549.6	452.5	43255.2	7750.2
664.5	122623.4	32256.7	215.6	57761.5	24830.7
6642.0	41123.9	41728.0	4671.0	81073.8	29960.2
-9.3	682.5	700.8		1095.8	359.1
875.5	2193.4	1480.0	2968.1	8131.8	5662.0
262.1	2892.6	2622.1	106.3	5872.8	2612.2
93.7	354.2	651.2		675.0	
844.9	2034.3	3244.0	119.1	6718.0	3227.3
330.0	1954.2	1956.2		3526.9	1470.9
3144.0	14661.7	5464.8	2760.8	12395.2	6572.4
1204.0	47009.3	46961.0	1860.2	67059.6	17377.4
350.3	2050.0	1969.0		2745.6	615.5
3955.9	91586.0	13407.6	376.9	128072.9	16034.5
8478.8	4660.2	5184.0	16113.0	29859.3	22007.5
22688.7	79597.0	78631.7	8598.9	180862.1	100802.3
197.2	12526.9	12428.7	12.6	16326.7	3893.9
259.9	737.3	737.5	2.7	1570.1	779.1
2984.2	11450.8	11292.6	648.9	21086.0	8703.5
5371.0	101982.7	94785.6	2625.3	139566.5	37578.4
1122.6	9791.4	8706.4	1645.5	13487.2	3960.3
16732.5	29751.2	31498.1	1237.1	40572.8	7292.5
1734.3	18104.2	11729.8	453.7	21794.9	8707.7
-4142.4	93056.7	72696.9	2625.5	112790.9	36061.6
13040.5	104078.8	102074.7	14253.8	160213.3	49465.7
54553.6	474797.5	526456.3	6878.9	789834.3	185185.7
26335.1	217302.3	229812.5	3308.3	337708.2	91926.2
7021.7	-43086.9	-22474.1	76246.7	3110.0	21137.7
4165.5	28363.5	31760.5	4732.1	70328.5	35213.5
182.7	1649.7	1493.7	901.9	2468.7	909.9
9.1	395.0	150.0		280.4	20.4
47789.4	368538.8	368589.2	23882.5	404892.9	32842.3
-674.1	11489.5	11187.2		17104.6	4551.6
786.6	235.1	228.2	977.1	3884.4	3232.2

11-6 规模以上国有及国有控股工业企业主要经济指标（2009年）

单位：万元

分　组	Item	企业单位数（个）Number of Enterprises (unit)	亏损企业 Loss Making Enterprises	工业总产值（当年价）Gross Industrial Output Value (At Current Prices)
总　计	**Total**	**231**	**61**	**14271687.6**
按隶属关系分	Grouped by Jurisdiction of Management			
中央企业	Central Enterprises	63	6	7588089.7
省属企业	Provincial Enterprises	41	16	3504124.0
市属企业	Municipal Enterprises	127	39	3179473.9
在总计中:亏损企业	Deficit Enterprises	61	61	903996.2
按轻重工业分	Grouped by Ligth Industry and Heavy Industry			
轻工业	Light Industry	52	16	852333.4
重工业	Heavy Industry	179	45	13419354.2
按企业规模分	Grouped by Size of Enterprises			
大型工业	Large-size	27	3	9601128.5
中型工业	Medium-size	76	15	3171725.0
小型工业	Small-size	128	43	1498834.1
按工业行业大类分	Grouped by Sector			
煤炭开采和洗选业	Mining and Washing of Coal			
石油和天然气开采业	Extraction of Petroleum and Natural Gas	1		4804.3
黑色金属矿采选业	Mining and Processing of Ferrous Metal Ores			
有色金属矿采选业	Mining and Processing of Non-ferroous Metal Ores			
非金属矿采选业	Mining and Processing of Nonmetal Ores			
其他采矿业	Mining of Other Ores			
农副食品加工业	Processing of Food from Agricultural Porducts	5	2	35920.0
食品制造业	Manufacture of Foods	4		121782.9
饮料制造业	Manufacture of Beverages	2	1	81819.9
烟草加工业	Manufacture of Tobacco	1		3473.6
纺织业	Manufacture of Textile	8	3	98655.8
纺织服装、鞋、帽制造业	Manufacture of Textile Wearing Apparel, Footwear and Caps	2	1	3494.1
皮革、毛皮、羽毛(绒)及其制品业	Manufacture of Leather, Fur, Feather (eiderdown) and Related Products	1		12428.1
木材加工及竹、藤、棕、草制品业	Processing of Timber,Manufacture of Wood,Plam and Straw Products	1	1	347.6

Economic Indicators of All State-owned and State-holding Share Industrial Enterprises Above Designafed size（2009）

（10 000 yuan）

工业销售产值（当年价）Value of Industry Products Sales (At Current Prices)	从业人员年平均人数（人）Annual Average Employers (person)	资产合计 Total Assets	流动资产小计 Total Working Capitals	固定资产小计 Total Fixed Assets	固定资产原价合计 Origing Value of Fixed Assets	累计折旧 Accumulative Total Depreciation
14038209.3	**258651**	**21354195.9**	**12492086.4**	**7556038.7**	**9674656.7**	**3478397.4**
7397543.5	136843	12814093.4	6993275.8	5288935.7	6526118.1	2305722.6
3485496.3	51663	3785463.8	2577778.2	966084.7	1110707.6	308159.7
3155169.5	70145	4754638.7	2921032.4	1301018.3	2037831.0	864515.1
902727.0	30147	2122470.6	745784.6	1192691.1	1643869.9	601848.7
952214.9	31268	882656.7	374785.0	390219.1	736160.7	384038.4
13085994.4	227383	20471539.2	12117301.4	7165819.6	8938496.0	3094359.0
9391133.5	173827	14606400.4	9268837.4	4591381.4	5835888.6	2322456.6
3169173.2	66465	5128231.8	2322381.8	2370718.5	3032496.2	926140.4
1477902.6	18359	1619563.7	900867.2	593938.8	806271.9	229800.4
3480.2	95	4641.7	3438.8	1202.9	1545.1	342.2
35539.5	873	45207.3	17638.8	25814.0	32011.2	6358.6
121394.3	1607	26683.8	11708.1	13544.6	24056.7	10814.0
186307.8	1294	111417.9	47309.1	24005.0	52433.4	28826.9
3285.9	212	5800.0	2825.6	2196.2	3177.4	981.2
103257.7	14150	141003.8	62498.3	35212.6	69117.2	37734.0
3203.7	120	3251.5	2879.4	209.1	412.9	203.8
12500.0	1053	35220.0	12043.1	23176.9	4042.2	1160.2
471.2	98	4881.9	746.8	4135.1	4917.9	835.2

11-6 续表1

单位：万元

分组	Item	负债合计 Total Liabilites	流动负债 小计 Total Working Liabilities	长期负债 小计 Long-term Liabilities
总 计	**Total**	**13733412.2**	**10484788.4**	**2765616.2**
按隶属关系分	Grouped by Jurisdiction of Management			
中央企业	Central Enterprises	8560087.0	6209260.2	2127901.5
省属企业	Provincial Enterprises	2445118.7	2136533.8	294437.1
市属企业	Municipal Enterprises	2728206.5	2138994.4	343277.6
在总计中:亏损企业	Deficit Enterprises	1542359.1	812626.4	628053.6
按轻重工业分	Grouped by Ligth Industry and Heavy Industry			
轻工业	Light Industry	372015.9	330037.0	35707.0
重工业	Heavy Industry	13361396.3	10154751.4	2729909.2
按企业规模分	Grouped by Size of Enterprises			
大型工业	Large-size	9180667.9	7201923.2	1702810.1
中型工业	Medium-size	3344219.8	2431972.6	836888.4
小型工业	Small-size	1208524.5	850892.6	225917.7
按工业行业大类分	Grouped by Sector			
煤炭开采和洗选业	Mining and Washing of Coal			
石油和天然气开采业	Extraction of Petroleum and Natural Gas	2575.4	2575.4	
黑色金属矿采选业	Mining and Processing of Ferrous Metal Ores			
有色金属矿采选业	Mining and Processing of Non-ferroous Metal Ores			
非金属矿采选业	Mining and Processing of Nonmetal Ores			
其他采矿业	Mining of Other Ores			
农副食品加工业	Processing of Food from Agricultural Porducts	22762.9	18086.5	71.0
食品制造业	Manufacture of Foods	13012.6	12837.6	175.0
饮料制造业	Manufacture of Beverages	47498.9	47376.6	122.3
烟草加工业	Manufacture of Tobacco	1016.6	1016.6	
纺织业	Manufacture of Textile	67732.2	61381.1	5177.2
纺织服装、鞋、帽制造业	Manufacture of Textile Wearing Apparel, Footwear and Caps	1497.7	1497.7	
皮革、毛皮、羽毛(绒)及其制品业	Manufacture of Leather, Fur, Feather (eiderdown) and Related Products	21933.0	14213.3	7719.7
木材加工及竹、藤、棕、草制品业	Processing of Timber,Manufacture of Wood,Plam and Straw Products	4054.3	2646.5	1407.8

continued 1

(10 000 yuan)

所有者权益合计 Total Owners' Equities	实收资本 Total Capital Hold	主营业务收入 Revenue from Principal Business	主营业务成本 Cost of Principal Business	主营业务税金及附加 Taxes and Other Charges on Principal Business
7605833.2	**3101627.9**	**14072233.4**	**11599792.0**	**155936.0**
4253975.4	1438450.9	7522595.2	5910716.7	126680.6
1338721.7	591754.6	3435829.9	3045831.0	8108.6
2013136.1	1071422.4	3113808.3	2643244.3	21146.8
578607.4	486278.1	857671.7	805568.8	3279.1
509957.5	320545.2	939673.5	736075.0	11469.7
7095875.7	2781082.7	13132559.9	10863717.0	144466.3
5423046.6	1716877.3	9443348.4	7658010.4	35389.2
1782100.4	1035156.2	3138830.3	2598621.6	117278.1
400686.2	349594.4	1490054.7	1343160.0	3268.7
2066.3	1800.0	3480.2	1368.0	32.4
22444.4	12263.5	36882.5	29946.1	132.8
13185.8	15105.1	117333.1	94853.7	88.6
63919.0	31481.5	188116.2	149309.8	7686.9
4783.4	1514.7	4083.6	2317.9	35.9
73074.2	28869.1	102768.3	90090.3	492.0
1753.8	1537.0	4827.6	4131.8	14.6
13287.0	6000.0	13838.3	11999.1	23.8
827.6	867.0	695.5	586.2	8.2

11-6 续表2

单位：万元

分　组	Item	营业费用 Expenses for Operation	管理费用 Expenses for Management
总　　计	**Total**	**432938.0**	**881336.9**
按隶属关系分	Grouped by Jurisdiction of Management		
中央企业	Central Enterprises	182210.7	482782.0
省属企业	Provincial Enterprises	107678.9	159504.2
市属企业	Municipal Enterprises	143048.4	239050.7
在总计中:亏损企业	Deficit Enterprises	23921.4	84625.3
按轻重工业分	Grouped by Ligth Industry and Heavy Industry		
轻工业	Light Industry	58622.8	66356.3
重工业	Heavy Industry	374315.2	814980.6
按企业规模分	Grouped by Size of Enterprises		
大型工业	Large-size	287946.5	617142.3
中型工业	Medium-size	103390.9	202468.0
小型工业	Small-size	41600.6	61726.6
按工业行业大类分	Grouped by Sector		
煤炭开采和洗选业	Mining and Washing of Coal		
石油和天然气开采业	Extraction of Petroleum and Natural Gas	22.8	522.0
黑色金属矿采选业	Mining and Processing of Ferrous Metal Ores		
有色金属矿采选业	Mining and Processing of Non-ferroous Metal Ores		
非金属矿采选业	Mining and Processing of Nonmetal Ores		
其他采矿业	Mining of Other Ores		
农副食品加工业	Processing of Food from Agricultural Porducts	2011.7	2154.9
食品制造业	Manufacture of Foods	17408.5	4150.7
饮料制造业	Manufacture of Beverages	13897.7	3953.4
烟草加工业	Manufacture of Tobacco	146.2	894.8
纺织业	Manufacture of Textile	1993.4	9453.1
纺织服装、鞋、帽制造业	Manufacture of Textile Wearing Apparel, Footwear and Caps	169.2	572.1
皮革、毛皮、羽毛(绒)及其制品业	Manufacture of Leather, Fur, Feather (eiderdown) and Related Products	438.8	1135.9
木材加工及竹、藤、棕、草制品业	Processing of Timber,Manufacture of Wood,Plam and Straw Products	58.5	169.8

continued 2

(10 000 yuan)

财务费用 Financial cost	营业利润 Operating Profit	利润总额 Total Profits	亏损企业亏损总额 Total Loss of Deficit Enterprises	利税总额 Total Pre-tax Profits	本年应交增值税 Value Added Tax Payable
144293.0	**1034838.8**	**986733.5**	**130014.0**	**1485959.4**	**343289.9**
115259.3	740875.0	788166.1	17252.0	1086926.9	172080.2
15268.2	74872.2	99418.1	12401.3	165864.3	58337.6
13765.5	219091.6	99149.3	100360.7	233168.2	112872.1
43293.0	-137782.1	-130014.0	130014.0	-98233.3	28501.6
4700.2	99878.1	80169.4	4120.3	132295.5	40656.4
139592.8	934960.7	906564.1	125893.7	1353663.9	302633.5
69820.6	759275.4	791893.7	74194.7	1055379.5	228096.6
54904.8	151254.6	143271.3	27255.2	342223.2	81673.8
19567.6	124308.8	51568.5	28564.1	88356.7	33519.5
-0.4	1535.3	1535.3		1973.8	406.1
1437.3	1578.8	1605.6	172.4	2099.1	360.7
126.2	25857.2	579.6		4471.5	3803.3
-295.7	14490.2	14778.9	17.2	31530.0	9064.2
-9.3	682.5	700.8		1095.8	359.1
400.0	969.5	1941.1	1338.0	5471.5	3038.4
-0.8	4.7	20.7	106.3	189.9	154.6
93.7	354.2	651.2		675.0	
-0.6	-126.6	-102.1	102.1	-12.0	81.9

11-6 续表3

单位：万元

分组	Item	企业单位数（个） Number of Enterprises (unit)	亏损企业 Loss Making Enterprises	工业总产值（当年价） Gross Industrial Output Value (At Current Prices)
家具制造业	Manufacture of Furniture			
造纸及纸制品业	Manufacture of Paper and Paper Products			
印刷业、记录媒介的复制	Printing,Reproduction of Recording Media	7	1	226924.0
文教体育用品制造业	Manufacture of Articles For Cultural,Educational and Sports Activities			
石油加工、炼焦及核燃料加工业	Processing of Petroleum, Cokeing,Processing of Nuclear and Nuclear Fuel	2		959556.2
化学原料及化学制品制造业	Manufacture of Raw Chemical Materials and Chemical Products	12	5	377466.8
医药制造业	Manufacture of Medicines	5		71437.8
化学纤维制造业	Manufacture of Chemical Fibers	1		82238.9
橡胶制品业	Manufacture of Rubber			
塑料制品业	Manufacture of Plastics	3		108507.6
非金属矿物制品业	Manufacture of Non-metallic Mineral Products	14	4	66661.8
黑色金属冶炼及压延加工业	Smelting and Pressing of Ferrous Metals	3	1	17178.8
有色金属冶炼及压延加工业	Smelting and Pressing of Non-ferrou Metals	10	1	187092.7
金属制品业	Manufacture of Metal Products	10	2	48964.3
通用设备制造业	Manufacture of General Purpose Machinery	11	2	567453.5
专用设备制造业	Manufacture of Special Equipment	34	10	1396609.4
交通运输设备制造业	Manufacture of Transport Equipment	26	2	5435708.0
电气机械及器材制造业	Manufacture of Electric Equipment and Machinery	16	5	2027696.0
通信设备、计算机及其他电子设备制造业	Manufacture of Communication Equipment, Computers and other Electronic Equipment	20	7	497562.0
仪器仪表及文化办公用	Manufacture of Measuring Instruments and Machinery for Cultural Activity and Office Work	13	1	462471.4
工艺品及其他制造业	Manufacture of Artwork and Other Manufacturing	1	1	7865.0
废弃资源和废旧材料回收加工业	Recycling and Disposal of Waste			
电力、热力的生产和供应业	Production and Supply of Electric Power and Heat Power	11	8	1183817.4
燃气生产和供应业	Gas mining and supplying industry	1		129526.3
水的生产和供应业	Production and Supply of Water	6	3	54223.4

continued 3

（10 000 yuan）

工业销售产值（当年价）Value of Industry Products Sales (At Current Prices)	从业人员年平均人数（人）Annual Average Employers (person)	资产合计 Total Assets	流动资产小计 Total Working Capitals	固定资产小计 Total Fixed Assets	固定资产原价合计 Origing Value of Fixed Assets	累计折旧 Accumulative Total Depreciation
221071.8	4457	238793.9	113908.1	103312.9	202230.1	103918.4
958782.2	1426	288497.3	173672.2	108380.2	134711.9	44545.2
376055.9	15661	745927.4	270037.9	348188.7	485022.3	189531.0
70514.1	1677	42162.9	22667.0	17342.6	25184.2	9445.6
86995.2	230	50540.2	24393.4	26001.7	56034.5	30068.0
106968.5	2549	199388.7	118249.1	69574.8	68265.2	19083.0
66289.6	2436	103027.7	59544.5	36242.6	43374.6	14743.5
69996.1	783	49814.4	38327.0	11364.6	11113.3	916.8
173766.7	3110	385144.5	181192.0	93332.4	105067.0	20016.1
44813.0	1633	52485.6	37510.7	11496.2	16052.9	5102.9
575011.4	9262	1182666.6	952014.3	142638.8	207538.9	82722.6
1293883.4	34604	2319950.1	1468349.2	732798.5	869549.8	325905.5
5317456.0	94181	7781806.4	5421427.6	1929959.6	2348637.6	853681.4
1932663.5	21523	2587298.0	1819461.7	756866.0	639061.4	237170.1
488087.1	15291	1027768.6	667598.2	273347.1	443430.7	226800.8
417909.4	14983	831119.2	486130.0	254826.2	385993.3	172079.8
5506.0	115	1407.8	217.3	563.3	682.2	153.0
1183817.4	9682	2735772.5	357853.2	2304181.1	3097109.7	912639.5
126271.3	1974	238518.5	90384.5	120915.4	140205.5	19290.1
52910.4	3572	113997.7	28060.5	85209.6	203677.6	123328.0

11-6 续表4

单位：万元

分　组	Item	负债合计 Total Liabilites	流动负债 小计 Total Working Liabilities	长期负债 小计 Long-term Liabilities
家具制造业	Manufacture of Furniture			
造纸及纸制品业	Manufacture of Paper and Paper Products			
印刷业、记录媒介的复制	Printing,Reproduction of Recording Media	64005.9	55779.9	8226.0
文教体育用品制造业	Manufacture of Articles For Cultural,Educational and Sports Activities			
石油加工、炼焦及核燃料加工业	Processing of Petroleum, Cokeing,Processing of Nuclear and Nuclear Fuel	235966.5	127859.3	45.4
化学原料及化学制品制造业	Manufacture of Raw Chemical Materials and Chemical Products	379213.8	297101.3	38714.1
医药制造业	Manufacture of Medicines	25812.5	25531.0	281.5
化学纤维制造业	Manufacture of Chemical Fibers	10677.4	10677.4	
橡胶制品业	Manufacture of Rubber			
塑料制品业	Manufacture of Plastics	128015.9	97385.9	29811.0
非金属矿物制品业	Manufacture of Non-metallic Mineral Products	82198.9	69013.9	13183.8
黑色金属冶炼及压延加工业	Smelting and Pressing of Ferrous Metals	39651.8	39151.8	500.0
有色金属冶炼及压延加工业	Smelting and Pressing of Non-ferrou Metals	223099.6	167178.0	53391.9
金属制品业	Manufacture of Metal Products	39757.9	27764.7	11993.2
通用设备制造业	Manufacture of General Purpose Machinery	748413.3	713764.7	34648.6
专用设备制造业	Manufacture of Special Equipment	1269335.4	1109545.9	159079.3
交通运输设备制造业	Manufacture of Transport Equipment	4734357.6	4050626.9	658389.0
电气机械及器材制造业	Manufacture of Electric Equipment and Machinery	1915180.4	1548359.6	204227.4
通信设备、计算机及其他电子设备制造业	Manufacture of Communication Equipment, Computers and other Electronic Equipment	690611.3	563949.8	121870.9
仪器仪表及文化办公用	Manufacture of Measuring Instruments and Machinery for Cultural Activity and Office Work	432155.7	331081.8	32626.8
工艺品及其他制造业	Manufacture of Artwork and Other Manufacturing	994.9	994.9	
废弃资源和废旧材料回收加工业	Recycling and Disposal of Waste			
电力、热力的生产和供应业	Production and Supply of Electric Power and Heat Power	2358337.3	954849.2	1343445.5
燃气生产和供应业	Gas mining and supplying industry	126634.3	94778.3	31856.0
水的生产和供应业	Production and Supply of Water	46908.2	37762.8	8652.8

continued 4

(10 000 yuan)

所有者权益合计 Total Owners' Equities	实收资本 Total Capital Hold	主营业务收入 Revenue from Principal Business	主营业务成本 Cost of Principal Business	主营业务税金及附加 Taxes and Other Charges on Principal Business
174787.9	82986.0	219506.6	155125.6	2194.9
52530.8	28083.2	989779.7	857130.7	98606.0
356913.5	135300.3	386798.9	326454.5	1547.0
16350.4	21393.6	59270.9	38003.8	144.7
39862.8	24800.0	86995.2	73193.6	
71372.8	28565.1	111759.6	93323.5	585.7
20542.2	19004.2	57687.1	48970.6	543.8
10162.6	10600.0	69871.4	67462.0	113.5
162044.7	70731.4	169935.5	140478.4	235.9
12727.5	10233.0	39566.6	32069.4	215.1
431598.0	52725.6	533873.1	413592.1	1928.9
1049158.2	470965.3	1311944.9	1111563.6	5537.7
3047448.7	992684.7	5487930.8	4782078.8	11879.4
672117.5	206508.4	1655269.0	1239653.2	13173.2
337157.1	215348.0	490825.9	412661.8	2903.1
398895.4	226103.4	410895.9	347120.2	2703.6
412.8	512.6	6457.2	3146.0	0.1
377435.2	256082.8	1332045.2	917428.7	3417.3
111884.2	100000.0	126281.5	109191.2	1294.5
67089.4	49562.4	53513.1	46541.4	396.4

11-6 续表5

单位：万元

分　组	Item	营业费用 Expenses for Operation	管理费用 Expenses for Management
家具制造业	Manufacture of Furniture		
造纸及纸制品业	Manufacture of Paper and Paper Products		
印刷业、记录媒介的复制	Printing,Reproduction of Recording Media	6506.6	28893.1
文教体育用品制造业	Manufacture of Articles For Cultural,Educational and Sports Activities		
石油加工、炼焦及核燃料加工业	Processing of Petroleum, Cokeing,Processing of Nuclear and Nuclear Fuel	8528.8	11110.5
化学原料及化学制品制造业	Manufacture of Raw Chemical Materials and Chemical Products	12516.8	52284.8
医药制造业	Manufacture of Medicines	11445.2	3991.7
化学纤维制造业	Manufacture of Chemical Fibers	153.5	1894.3
橡胶制品业	Manufacture of Rubber		
塑料制品业	Manufacture of Plastics	7284.3	7620.2
非金属矿物制品业	Manufacture of Non-metallic Mineral Products	2919.0	3428.8
黑色金属冶炼及压延加工业	Smelting and Pressing of Ferrous Metals	400.4	1792.1
有色金属冶炼及压延加工业	Smelting and Pressing of Non-ferrou Metals	1942.2	11227.6
金属制品业	Manufacture of Metal Products	2488.4	3341.9
通用设备制造业	Manufacture of General Purpose Machinery	16429.4	66625.7
专用设备制造业	Manufacture of Special Equipment	38120.8	126389.7
交通运输设备制造业	Manufacture of Transport Equipment	136184.1	284135.9
电气机械及器材制造业	Manufacture of Electric Equipment and Machinery	114578.4	118204.8
通信设备、计算机及其他电子设备制造业	Manufacture of Communication Equipment, Computers and other Electronic Equipment	22996.1	63006.5
仪器仪表及文化办公用	Manufacture of Measuring Instruments and Machinery for Cultural Activity and Office Work	5401.1	51958.7
工艺品及其他制造业	Manufacture of Artwork and Other Manufacturing		28.6
废弃资源和废旧材料回收加工业	Recycling and Disposal of Waste		
电力、热力的生产和供应业	Production and Supply of Electric Power and Heat Power	0.4	7734.8
燃气生产和供应业	Gas mining and supplying industry	6922.3	10483.7
水的生产和供应业	Production and Supply of Water	1973.4	4176.8

continued 5

(10 000 yuan)

财务费用 Financial cost	营业利润 Operating Profit	利润总额 Total Profits	亏损企业亏损总额 Total Loss of Deficit Enterprises	利税总额 Total Pre-tax Profits	本年应交增值税 Value Added Tax Payable
-71.9	36465.5	36449.8	7.3	51358.5	12713.8
3687.1	89518.7	11667.3		124878.8	14605.5
5859.0	-6811.6	-2850.0	15540.4	13860.2	15163.2
925.4	5542.5	4819.4		7195.4	2231.3
197.2	12557.7	12441.3		16297.7	3856.4
1492.5	5159.8	5285.0		9868.7	3998.0
523.2	580.9	517.4	785.3	3343.0	2281.8
278.3	-179.8	312.0	626.5	967.1	541.6
4401.0	22108.8	24401.6	107.4	28231.7	3594.2
416.5	6796.9	1104.9	99.2	2210.8	890.8
-6887.4	65640.1	50232.9	410.6	74690.7	22528.9
8931.2	73137.8	69922.4	8931.4	107388.1	31928.0
48471.8	186206.5	235569.6	4684.6	311759.5	64310.5
18746.1	155596.0	168662.5	426.4	246803.3	64967.6
4660.3	-52962.6	-46179.2	72290.1	-28061.1	15215.0
3960.4	11528.7	14183.4	394.5	45659.7	28772.7
	-11.4	-14.1	14.1	-13.0	1.0
47400.0	368152.4	368167.0	23211.6	402661.5	31077.2
-1111.2	10269.6	10143.3		15732.7	4294.9
663.1	196.5	185.9	748.6	3631.5	3049.2

11-7 规模以上股份制工业企业主要经济指标（2009年）

单位：万元

分　组	Item	企业单位数（个） Number of Enterprises (unit)	亏损企业 Loss Making Enterprises	工业总产值（当年价） Gross Industrial Output Value (At Current Prices)
总　计	**Total**	**853**	**189**	**17426221.2**
#市　区	Urban Area	667	124	13571050.7
按隶属关系分	Grouped by Jurisdiction of Management			
中央企业	Central Enterprises	28	2	3085532.7
省属企业	Provincial Enterprises	54	11	4220934.6
市属企业	Municipal Enterprises	771	176	10119753.9
在总计中:亏损企业	Deficit Enterprises	189	189	1212161.2
按轻重工业分	Grouped by Ligth Industry and Heavy Industry			
轻工业	Light Industry	261	62	3593491.4
重工业	Heavy Industry	592	127	13832729.8
按企业规模分	Grouped by Size of Enterprises			
大型工业	Large-size	21	3	8514544.0
中型工业	Medium-size	111	17	3818566.3
小型工业	Small-size	721	169	5093110.9
按工业行业大类分	Grouped by Sector			
煤炭开采和洗选业	Mining and Washing of Coal			
石油和天然气开采业	Extraction of Petroleum and Natural Gas	3		101639.3
黑色金属矿采选业	Mining and Processing of Ferrous Metal Ores	1	1	1006.0
有色金属矿采选业	Mining and Processing of Non-ferroous Metal Ores	1		25518.7
非金属矿采选业	Mining and Processing of Nonmetal Ores			
其他采矿业	Mining of Other Ores			
农副食品加工业	Processing of Food from Agricultural Porducts	51	3	925696.0
食品制造业	Manufacture of Foods	23	3	237971.7
饮料制造业	Manufacture of Beverages	11	2	401934.7
烟草加工业	Manufacture of Tobacco			
纺织业	Manufacture of Textile	16	8	138770.9
纺织服装、鞋、帽制造业	Manufacture of Textile Wearing Apparel, Footwearand Caps	5		69056.2
皮革、毛皮、羽毛(绒)及其制品业	Manufacture of Leather, Fur, Feather (eiderdown) and Related Products			
木材加工及竹、藤、棕、草制品业	Processing of Timber,Manufacture of Wood,Plam and Straw Products	7	2	79795.8

Main Indicators of Share-holding Corporation Industrial Enterprises Above Designafed size（2009）

（10 000 yuan）

工业销售产值（当年价）Value of Industry Products Sales (At Current Prices)	从业人员年平均人数（人）Annual Average Employers (person)	资产合计 Total Assets	流动资产小计 Total Working Capitals	固定资产小计 Total Fixed Assets	固定资产原价合计 Origing Value of Fixed Assets	累计折旧 Accumulative Total Depreciation
17009006.7	**320789**	**19276066.5**	**12257003.4**	**5461220.0**	**7213236.7**	**2619565.0**
1968213.3	261192	15508219.8	9948590.8	4314989.4	5905568.6	2255207.3
2956541.2	84436	6501013.8	4294131.5	1833657.5	2311124.8	927700.0
4182673.5	52805	3892817.0	2714638.5	974073.0	1196732.7	345489.5
9869792.0	183548	8882235.7	5248233.4	2653489.5	3705379.2	1346375.5
1170151.4	43682	2248421.4	1074496.5	872458.3	1221650.8	526513.2
3524444.3	73903	2921929.4	1429768.4	1086872.2	1618675.6	617386.5
13484562.4	246886	16354137.1	10827235.0	4374347.8	5594561.1	2002178.5
8488549.8	151842	10451921.0	6867911.5	3034913.6	3907605.1	1498734.7
3701912.8	88679	4699820.2	2756974.6	1333787.3	1767845.4	611731.9
4818544.1	80268	4124325.3	2632117.3	1092519.1	1537786.2	509098.4
81666.5	2419	104998.9	75697.6	17067.4	43706.9	14461.9
843.5	130	2430.4	1518.0	725.2	1188.6	463.4
25518.7	430	22560.9	8925.9	8287.9	13267.8	4979.9
854036.5	8003	402216.2	248696.9	108191.5	161642.4	60915.2
234373.3	4717	113130.3	35806.7	42128.3	64170.0	24959.0
500807.2	5153	541917.5	223462.1	245601.7	338333.1	94894.9
140523.1	15136	168255.1	82575.8	52505.6	88155.4	39599.4
73893.1	1889	59780.9	51271.1	6571.3	9845.5	4093.5
55389.3	1178	86497.9	51610.8	20835.8	28135.6	9133.8

11-7 续表1

单位：万元

分　组	Item	负债合计 Total Liabilites	流动负债 小计 Total Working Liabilities	长期负债 小计 Long-term Liabilities
总　计	**Total**	**11016371.1**	**9442375.9**	**1274023.2**
#市　区	Urban Area	8442968.9	7225021.0	968201.8
按隶属关系分	Grouped by Jurisdiction of Management			
中央企业	Central Enterprises	3770241.8	3233756.3	495733.0
省属企业	Provincial Enterprises	2452554.0	2187722.0	256831.1
市属企业	Municipal Enterprises	4793575.3	4020897.6	521459.1
在总计中:亏损企业	Deficit Enterprises	1370992.4	1056223.7	193553.7
按轻重工业分	Grouped by Ligth Industry and Heavy Industry			
轻工业	Light Industry	1563301.5	1345692.4	180188.9
重工业	Heavy Industry	9453069.6	8096683.5	1093834.3
按企业规模分	Grouped by Size of Enterprises			
大型工业	Large-size	6052632.8	5256486.8	751340.3
中型工业	Medium-size	2618191.6	2245540.6	307866.9
小型工业	Small-size	2345546.7	1940348.5	214816.0
按工业行业大类分	Grouped by Sector			
煤炭开采和洗选业	Mining and Washing of Coal			
石油和天然气开采业	Extraction of Petroleum and Natural Gas	54083.3	54083.3	
黑色金属矿采选业	Mining and Processing of Ferrous Metal Ores	3239.8	1154.3	2085.5
有色金属矿采选业	Mining and Processing of Non-ferroous Metal Ores	13528.9	13399.9	129.0
非金属矿采选业	Mining and Processing of Nonmetal Ores			
其他采矿业	Mining of Other Ores			
农副食品加工业	Processing of Food from Agricultural Porducts	240044.1	221092.6	14704.3
食品制造业	Manufacture of Foods	51475.0	49280.0	2195.0
饮料制造业	Manufacture of Beverages	311841.8	254455.1	57386.7
烟草加工业	Manufacture of Tobacco			
纺织业	Manufacture of Textile	84969.8	83705.4	90.5
纺织服装、鞋、帽制造业	Manufacture of Textile Wearing Apparel, Footwearand Caps	42705.5	42705.5	
皮革、毛皮、羽毛(绒)及其制品业	Manufacture of Leather, Fur, Feather (eiderdown) and Related Products			
木材加工及竹、藤、棕、草制品业	Processing of Timber,Manufacture of Wood,Plam and Straw Products	42986.6	27920.0	15066.6

continued 1

(10 000 yuan)

所有者权益合计 Total Owners' Equities	实收资本 Total Capital Hold	主营业务收入 Revenue from Principal Business	主营业务成本 Cost of Principal Business	主营业务税金及附加 Taxes and Other Charges on Principal Business
8235286.1	**3779161.2**	**16987848.4**	**14177856.0**	**121699.1**
7052139.4	2937199.7	13366271.6	10955425.0	113807.9
2730741.3	845045.5	3234269.9	2709191.8	9198.9
1440074.8	616035.7	4110362.9	3470268.7	7381.2
4064470.0	2318080.0	9643215.6	7998395.5	105119.0
874006.9	702039.7	1092068.2	1000396.3	4062.3
1353545.3	812550.8	3420781.3	2646586.5	15172.0
6881740.8	2966610.4	13567067.1	11531269.5	106527.1
4396670.9	1393632.7	8592156.6	7202165.9	79387.1
2080658.8	1160554.6	3623606.4	2952195.1	21179.3
1757956.4	1224973.9	4772085.4	4023495.0	21132.7
50915.6	17708.6	79256.0	63689.9	1477.3
-809.4	300.0	840.0	627.6	
9031.9	4900.0	25518.7	23036.0	64.3
161691.0	86236.3	840375.8	743288.2	1568.7
61169.8	54309.1	224537.4	185076.8	643.1
230075.7	89978.4	502895.8	382883.8	7813.0
83087.8	43411.8	137825.1	122019.6	885.1
16589.6	10200.0	80733.0	68488.8	554.1
43511.3	15098.0	32190.0	26731.8	211.7

11–7 续表2

单位：万元

分　组	Item	营业费用 Expenses for Operation	管理费用 Expenses for Management
总　计	**Total**	**751398.2**	**863484.2**
#市　区	Urban Area	636069.7	714506.1
按隶属关系分	Grouped by Jurisdiction of Management		
中央企业	Central Enterprises	58950.5	268342.0
省属企业	Provincial Enterprises	278546.0	148382.5
市属企业	Municipal Enterprises	413901.7	446759.7
在总计中:亏损企业	Deficit Enterprises	48243.3	115282.1
按轻重工业分	Grouped by Ligth Industry and Heavy Industry		
轻工业	Light Industry	374935.5	154306.6
重工业	Heavy Industry	376462.7	709177.6
按企业规模分	Grouped by Size of Enterprises		
大型工业	Large-size	346009.0	415125.7
中型工业	Medium-size	234557.1	221917.6
小型工业	Small-size	170832.1	226440.9
按工业行业大类分	Grouped by Sector		
煤炭开采和洗选业	Mining and Washing of Coal		
石油和天然气开采业	Extraction of Petroleum and Natural Gas	1013.0	4795.8
黑色金属矿采选业	Mining and Processing of Ferrous Metal Ores	18.0	349.8
有色金属矿采选业	Mining and Processing of Non-ferroous Metal Ores	1172.8	694.7
非金属矿采选业	Mining and Processing of Nonmetal Ores		
其他采矿业	Mining of Other Ores		
农副食品加工业	Processing of Food from Agricultural Porducts	32696.8	19390.7
食品制造业	Manufacture of Foods	24058.8	7697.4
饮料制造业	Manufacture of Beverages	65379.6	15430.9
烟草加工业	Manufacture of Tobacco		
纺织业	Manufacture of Textile	3161.8	13426.0
纺织服装、鞋、帽制造业	Manufacture of Textile Wearing Apparel, Footwearand Caps	4102.2	4745.6
皮革、毛皮、羽毛(绒)及其制品业	Manufacture of Leather, Fur, Feather (eiderdown) and Related Products		
木材加工及竹、藤、棕、草制品业	Processing of Timber,Manufacture of Wood,Plam and Straw Products	1180.5	1279.6

continued 2

（10 000 yuan）

财务费用 Financial cost	营业利润 Operating Profit	利润总额 Total Profits	亏损企业亏损总额 Total Loss of Deficit Enterprises	利税总额 Total Pre-tax Profits	本年应交增值税 Value Added Tax Payable
158074.5	**1108944.6**	**956832.4**	**143284.0**	**1607120.2**	**528588.7**
122498.8	1020175.9	872978.8	120989.3	1446371.7	459585.0
45401.0	141194.3	173488.6	3761.4	227473.2	44785.7
24391.3	141034.9	155276.5	10843.4	301016.1	138358.4
88282.2	826715.4	628067.3	128679.2	1078630.9	345444.6
31086.5	-143755.4	-143284.0	143284.0	-102747.5	36474.2
45190.5	306734.8	200934.2	20997.5	383511.4	167405.2
112884.0	802209.8	755898.2	122286.5	1223608.8	361183.5
72118.5	432170.6	470214.0	74194.7	813649.3	264048.2
43255.7	300816.7	218442.3	29993.8	368665.5	129043.9
42700.3	375957.3	268176.1	39095.5	424805.4	135496.6
181.4	8862.8	8669.9		19588.6	9441.4
194.6	-590.2	-590.5	590.5	-536.5	54.0
271.3	265.0	920.0		1633.0	648.7
5977.7	100497.0	33084.6	280.1	42290.6	7637.3
860.0	36073.6	5232.0	215.6	12768.8	6893.7
6839.3	41015.1	41252.8	1632.3	73743.8	24678.0
654.5	337.4	1231.7	2689.8	7195.5	5078.7
242.5	2749.4	2336.7		5099.1	2208.3
827.2	2132.3	3317.5	17.0	6674.6	3145.4

11-7 续表3

单位：万元

分　　组	Item	企业单位数（个）Number of Enterprises (unit)	亏损企业 Loss Making Enterprises	工业总产值（当年价）Gross Industrial Output Value (At Current Prices)
家具制造业	Manufacture of Furniture	4		22782.1
造纸及纸制品业	Manufacture of Paper and Paper Products	22	7	173073.3
印刷业、记录媒介的复制	Printing,Reproduction of Recording Media	23	5	171964.0
文教体育用品制造业	Manufacture of Articles For Cultural, Educational and Sports Activities	1		9200.0
石油加工、炼焦及核燃料加工业	Processing of Petroleum, Cokeing,Processing of Nuclear and Nuclear Fuel	4	2	356573.4
化学原料及化学制品制造业	Manufacture of Raw Chemical Materials and Chemical Products	38	9	616153.3
医药制造业	Manufacture of Medicines	48	15	842139.0
化学纤维制造业	Manufacture of Chemical Fibers	2	1	83025.5
橡胶制品业	Manufacture of Rubber	5	1	11033.6
塑料制品业	Manufacture of Plastics	26	8	164329.6
非金属矿物制品业	Manufacture of Non-metallic Mineral Products	67	14	710864.1
黑色金属冶炼及压延加工业	Smelting and Pressing of Ferrous Metals	12	5	190507.7
有色金属冶炼及压延加工业	Smelting and Pressing of Non-ferrou Metals	26	3	367251.3
金属制品业	Manufacture of Metal Products	52	9	232950.0
通用设备制造业	Manufacture of General Purpose Machinery	82	16	535356.1
专用设备制造业	Manufacture of Special Equipment	92	23	1555173.1
交通运输设备制造业	Manufacture of Transport Equipment	41	6	7252929.5
电气机械及器材制造业	Manufacture of Electric Equipment and Machinery	99	24	970874.2
通信设备、计算机及其他电子设备制造业	Manufacture of Communication Equipment, Computers and other Electronic Equipment	37	11	547644.2
仪器仪表及文化办公用	Manufacture of Measuring Instruments and Machinery for Cultural Activity and Office Work	33	3	374929.4
工艺品及其他制造业	Manufacture of Artwork and Other Manufacturing	5	1	17695.3
废弃资源和废旧材料回收加工业	Recycling and Disposal of Waste	1		4211.3
电力、热力的生产和供应业	Production and Supply of Electric Power and Heat Power	6	5	28597.1
燃气生产和供应业	Gas mining and supplying industry	4		155145.5
水的生产和供应业	Production and Supply of Water	5	2	50429.3

continued 3

(10 000 yuan)

工业销售产值（当年价）Value of Industry Products Sales (At Current Prices)	从业人员年平均人数（人）Annual Average Employers (person)	资产合计 Total Assets				
			流动资产小计 Total Working Capitals	固定资产小计 Total Fixed Assets	固定资产原价合计 Origing Value of Fixed Assets	
						累计折旧 Accumulative Total Depreciation
22225.7	1323	8185.3	5857.9	2263.0	5694.6	3434.9
162921.1	9078	103465.3	33300.3	68832.3	80074.8	14203.4
169582.5	5165	280622.1	106688.7	129303.4	151076.2	57724.2
9016.0	125	3084.6	1646.3	1438.3	1800.0	361.7
356573.4	291	139054.1	117670.9	14505.6	16061.6	2009.5
606716.4	18066	857294.7	357308.5	368631.4	522066.8	204712.7
811393.7	12344	742234.4	379283.7	213357.4	299463.2	107705.4
87774.5	265	50918.8	24674.3	26099.4	56136.6	30104.1
9113.5	562	11210.6	7010.1	3007.9	4387.2	1379.3
146103.7	2970	120179.2	74618.7	39844.9	52269.6	17523.9
685162.3	10108	565788.2	315156.8	189965.2	224531.2	72063.1
184728.6	1773	72299.5	36177.3	33484.1	43483.0	10525.9
339301.8	6149	594815.7	319504.4	139260.6	174436.4	43935.6
225357.8	5900	190581.0	134326.1	44200.9	64252.9	23529.5
510967.5	12463	505089.6	359568.0	102735.6	147531.6	57145.4
1459307.7	39519	2397371.0	1553666.4	710530.0	851254.4	331095.8
7234890.9	105650	8103664.1	5751994.3	1923419.7	2331385.6	792331.4
865630.3	15592	835515.2	607979.6	172439.1	241947.9	75845.8
535606.0	16526	984957.4	674607.3	281510.3	475978.2	241907.9
367939.1	10518	539097.2	337322.5	178465.1	232452.0	100222.7
16344.6	820	17943.8	7741.8	7468.7	10385.4	3394.6
4191.3	70	1630.0	300.0	1152.0	1200.0	548.0
28687.3	895	222453.1	134923.1	70893.9	97600.4	27950.6
151990.5	2406	302380.9	111275.2	139028.6	165025.4	26669.4
50429.3	3156	124442.6	24836.3	97467.9	214296.4	119739.2

11-7　续表4

单位：万元

分　　组	Item	负债合计 Total Liabilites	流动负债小计 Total Working Liabilities	长期负债小计 Long-term Liabilities
家具制造业	Manufacture of Furniture	3773.8	3773.8	
造纸及纸制品业	Manufacture of Paper and Paper Products	56954.5	38773.8	18096.5
印刷业、记录媒介的复制	Printing,Reproduction of Recording Media	126552.2	108327.1	18225.1
文教体育用品制造业	Manufacture of Articles For Cultural, Educational and Sports Activities	2007.6	2007.6	
石油加工、炼焦及核燃料加工业	Processing of Petroleum, Cokeing,Processing of Nuclear and Nuclear Fuel	115191.1	6649.4	
化学原料及化学制品制造业	Manufacture of Raw Chemical Materials and Chemical Products	419025.9	329060.9	47889.8
医药制造业	Manufacture of Medicines	378897.2	338881.6	26753.4
化学纤维制造业	Manufacture of Chemical Fibers	10803.1	10803.1	
橡胶制品业	Manufacture of Rubber	6009.8	5733.6	276.2
塑料制品业	Manufacture of Plastics	60277.3	52117.5	5102.7
非金属矿物制品业	Manufacture of Non-metallic Mineral Products	337880.3	300275.9	33169.8
黑色金属冶炼及压延加工业	Smelting and Pressing of Ferrous Metals	55296.0	51093.3	4057.7
有色金属冶炼及压延加工业	Smelting and Pressing of Non-ferrou Metals	324499.5	261689.6	60270.1
金属制品业	Manufacture of Metal Products	122740.7	95165.8	14712.8
通用设备制造业	Manufacture of General Purpose Machinery	268714.5	220017.6	38480.1
专用设备制造业	Manufacture of Special Equipment	1278398.8	1138978.8	128364.1
交通运输设备制造业	Manufacture of Transport Equipment	4941456.9	4360632.5	571590.4
电气机械及器材制造业	Manufacture of Electric Equipment and Machinery	444061.9	422297.4	19673.4
通信设备、计算机及其他电子设备制造业	Manufacture of Communication Equipment, Computers and other Electronic Equipment	558521.2	459971.0	93794.3
仪器仪表及文化办公用	Manufacture of Measuring Instruments and Machinery for Cultural Activity and Office Work	288165.2	258163.3	29893.7
工艺品及其他制造业	Manufacture of Artwork and Other Manufacturing	11893.9	3762.1	8049.0
废弃资源和废旧材料回收加工业	Recycling and Disposal of Waste	885.0	330.0	555.0
电力、热力的生产和供应业	Production and Supply of Electric Power and Heat Power	155345.9	79232.8	19620.5
燃气生产和供应业	Gas mining and supplying industry	149919.3	114269.8	35649.5
水的生产和供应业	Production and Supply of Water	54224.7	32571.5	8141.5

continued 4

(10 000 yuan)

所有者权益合计 Total Owners' Equities	实收资本 Total Capital Hold	主营业务收入 Revenue from Principal Business	主营业务成本 Cost of Principal Business	主营业务税金及附加 Taxes and Other Charges on Principal Business
4181.4	3236.1	21788.9	16950.0	78.3
46458.9	32987.9	145409.6	127561.4	311.0
153719.3	94185.8	168322.3	129269.3	692.3
1077.0	760.0	9016.0	6191.8	53.1
23863.0	6700.0	389441.6	376689.1	72.9
428389.6	168844.2	610275.6	516045.9	2542.2
363336.6	210087.5	745466.9	403522.8	1397.7
40115.6	25100.0	87844.9	73975.0	1.5
4844.4	3115.4	7698.8	6235.6	17.2
59870.4	52095.2	147727.3	117566.6	514.7
225474.7	140583.8	704147.3	603813.5	5760.0
16544.7	17133.0	175688.1	145948.2	706.2
270125.7	110825.1	332514.0	269405.0	1553.0
67532.7	49011.1	211116.7	179297.7	1201.6
235613.3	134455.3	502633.0	425948.9	1657.0
1117565.1	523397.1	1467990.5	1225565.1	6469.4
3162022.0	1056845.6	7335358.9	6298644.1	76243.5
388465.9	263446.0	842000.5	683277.1	3245.4
425899.1	251670.3	534731.9	447220.6	2521.8
250931.8	92431.1	365061.3	283553.5	1254.0
6049.9	5812.3	19683.1	14628.7	46.0
745.0	400.0	3720.0	3315.0	110.0
67107.3	33076.2	30184.2	33688.5	288.2
152461.6	133780.0	153146.6	127530.3	1365.8
67627.8	47040.0	52708.6	46169.8	379.0

11-7 续表5

单位：万元

分　组	Item	营业费用 Expenses for Operation	管理费用 Expenses for Management
家具制造业	Manufacture of Furniture	1642.7	1428.0
造纸及纸制品业	Manufacture of Paper and Paper Products	2330.2	4185.0
印刷业、记录媒介的复制	Printing,Reproduction of Recording Media	5868.3	16051.8
文教体育用品制造业	Manufacture of Articles For Cultural, Educational and Sports Activities	470.5	940.4
石油加工、炼焦及核燃料加工业	Processing of Petroleum, Cokeing,Processing of Nuclear and Nuclear Fuel	7565.8	1692.1
化学原料及化学制品制造业	Manufacture of Raw Chemical Materials and Chemical Products	27803.3	56761.9
医药制造业	Manufacture of Medicines	214006.2	46188.8
化学纤维制造业	Manufacture of Chemical Fibers	190.9	1953.0
橡胶制品业	Manufacture of Rubber	266.1	1021.2
塑料制品业	Manufacture of Plastics	5443.5	6875.9
非金属矿物制品业	Manufacture of Non-metallic Mineral Products	18523.5	17803.1
黑色金属冶炼及压延加工业	Smelting and Pressing of Ferrous Metals	1663.8	3557.2
有色金属冶炼及压延加工业	Smelting and Pressing of Non-ferrou Metals	4984.3	15503.9
金属制品业	Manufacture of Metal Products	7895.5	11765.5
通用设备制造业	Manufacture of General Purpose Machinery	22015.9	33217.3
专用设备制造业	Manufacture of Special Equipment	49880.2	135802.3
交通运输设备制造业	Manufacture of Transport Equipment	162469.8	262954.6
电气机械及器材制造业	Manufacture of Electric Equipment and Machinery	31586.6	55456.2
通信设备、计算机及其他电子设备制造业	Manufacture of Communication Equipment, Computers and other Electronic Equipment	26381.6	55557.4
仪器仪表及文化办公用	Manufacture of Measuring Instruments and Machinery for Cultural Activity and Office Work	11068.7	44774.3
工艺品及其他制造业	Manufacture of Artwork and Other Manufacturing	1170.9	1569.2
废弃资源和废旧材料回收加工业	Recycling and Disposal of Waste	443.9	117.6
电力、热力的生产和供应业	Production and Supply of Electric Power and Heat Power	926.0	3463.6
燃气生产和供应业	Gas mining and supplying industry	11392.9	13348.0
水的生产和供应业	Production and Supply of Water	2623.6	3685.4

continued 5

(10 000 yuan)

财务费用 Financial cost	营业利润 Operating Profit	利润总额 Total Profits	亏损企业亏损总额 Total Loss of Deficit Enterprises	利税总额 Total Pre-tax Profits	本年应交增值税 Value Added Tax Payable
241.0	1813.5	1814.7		3221.3	1328.3
2953.3	8892.7	-669.7	2723.9	2613.6	2972.3
1398.2	16671.2	17030.3	1397.6	25819.4	8096.8
282.3	1201.0	1201.0		1786.8	532.7
316.8	81028.4	3028.4	376.9	3812.5	711.2
7677.1	3794.2	2583.5	15375.0	25438.4	20312.7
20648.3	69356.8	68474.6	8590.9	162060.1	92187.8
197.2	12528.4	12430.2	11.1	16293.3	3861.6
68.7	36.0	36.2	2.7	472.2	418.8
1604.6	5835.0	5524.3	536.5	11440.0	5401.0
3744.8	59555.8	52777.6	1834.2	84167.9	25630.3
672.1	8934.1	7317.2	1635.1	11562.9	3539.5
16022.1	29087.2	31111.9	941.1	39296.4	6631.5
1503.0	16948.4	10574.5	325.3	19156.2	7380.1
3000.4	21784.3	20726.8	2164.9	34907.2	12523.4
9597.6	83296.8	74963.7	8958.6	122958.5	41525.4
51962.6	440818.6	484459.5	5834.4	732870.4	172167.4
8255.5	70528.7	75473.8	3103.0	106038.8	27319.6
5766.2	-47856.1	-44223.4	75566.7	-26088.1	15613.5
2205.9	26113.1	29406.3	102.5	42346.1	11685.8
84.5	2434.0	2280.7	92.8	3009.5	682.8
9.1	395.0	150.0		280.4	20.4
3758.0	-7277.7	-6476.4	7533.3	-5574.6	613.6
-674.1	11489.5	11187.2		17104.6	4551.6
730.8	193.3	194.8	752.2	3668.9	3095.1

11-8 规模以上三资工业企业主要经济指标（2009年）

单位：万元

分组	Item	企业单位数（个） Number of Enterprises (unit)	亏损企业 Loss Making Enterprises	工业总产值（当年价） Gross Industrial Output Value (At Current Prices)
总计	**Total**	**142**	**39**	**5311005.4**
按隶属关系分	Grouped by Jurisdiction of Management			
中央企业	Central Enterprises	3		101345.6
省属企业	Provincial Enterprises	9	3	656336.1
市属企业	Municipal Enterprises	130	36	4553323.7
按登记注册类型分组	Grouped by Registion Status			
港、澳、台商投资企业	Enterprises with Funds from Hong Kong, Macao and Taiwan	30	5	271815.9
与港、澳、台商合资经营	Co-investment with businessman from Hong Kong,Macao and Taiwan	24	4	167579.5
与港、澳、台商合作经营	Partnership with businessman from Hong Kong,Macao and Taiwan			
港澳台商独资	Wholly Funded from Hong Kong, Macao and Taiwan	5	1	103754.6
港澳台商投资股份有限公司	Share-holding Corporation with Funds from Hong Kong,Macao and Taiwan	1		481.8
外商投资企业	Enterprises with Foreign Investment	112	34	5039189.5
中外合资经营企业	Joint Ownership Operation With Overseas	73	21	4078109.2
中外合作经营企业	Co-operation With Overseas	2		4486.1
外资企业	Foreign Funded Enterprises	32	10	810405.1
外商投资股份有限公司	Foreign funded Share-holding Corporations	5	3	146189.1
在总计中:亏损企业	Deficit Enterprises	39	39	179255.0
按轻重工业分	Grouped by Ligth Industry and Heavy Industry			
轻工业	Light Industry	50	13	2016452.5
重工业	Heavy Industry	92	26	3294552.9
按企业规模分	Grouped by Size of Enterprises			
大型工业	Large-size	3		2542326.6
中型工业	Medium-sized	29	6	1648461.3
小型工业	Small-size	110	33	1120217.5
按工业行业大类分	Grouped by Sector			
煤炭开采和洗选业	Mining and Washing of Coal			
石油和天然气开采业	Extraction of Petroleum and Natural Gas			
黑色金属矿采选业	Mining and Processing of Ferrous Metal Ores			
有色金属矿采选业	Mining and Processing of Non-ferroous Metal Ores			
非金属矿采选业	Mining and Processing of Nonmetal Ores			
其他采矿业	Mining of Other Ores			
农副食品加工业	Processing of Food from Agricultural Porducts	5	1	152070.0
食品制造业	Manufacture of Foods	5		480442.8
饮料制造业	Manufacture of Beverages	10	3	428216.4

Economic Indicators of Foreign Fund Industrial Enterprises Above Designafed size（2009）

（10 000 yuan）

工业销售产值（当年价）Value of Industry Products Sales (At Current Prices)	从业人员年平均人数（人）Annual Average Employers (person)	资产合计 Total Assets	流动资产小计 Total Working Capitals	固定资产小计 Total Fixed Assets	固定资产原价合计 Origing Value of Fixed Assets	累计折旧 Accumulative Total Depreciation
5244336.7	**60779**	**3901682.0**	**2335813.5**	**1248486.5**	**1741489.3**	**590863.1**
106490.9	1396	76909.3	41309.2	33255.0	70166.4	38772.3
639954.0	5252	347852.9	252256.8	55769.5	113106.6	57212.1
4497891.8	54131	3476919.8	2042247.5	1159462.0	1558216.3	494878.7
249096.0	6305	326612.9	169045.4	71535.3	142113.5	70580.3
149912.5	4358	241041.1	130893.6	43968.1	90130.0	45063.6
98701.7	1730	81279.6	35381.2	26045.7	50388.6	24965.4
481.8	217	4292.2	2770.6	1521.5	1594.9	551.3
4995240.7	54474	3575069.1	2166768.1	1176951.2	1599375.8	520282.8
4051464.4	41285	2539743.2	1628148.8	751643.4	1021674.0	336430.1
4081.5	135	6341.5	3623.3	1275.1	1460.2	185.1
787109.3	10484	698815.6	374443.6	269150.2	393416.0	147700.7
152585.5	2570	330168.8	160552.4	154882.5	182825.6	35966.9
173080.9	5652	386643.0	188107.1	143825.8	208749.4	76688.3
1938357.3	21753	1438709.4	754925.3	512410.3	796235.5	295908.3
3305979.4	39026	2462972.6	1580888.2	736076.2	945253.8	294954.8
2627995.6	26522	1153841.3	766638.1	316808.3	414093.0	142001.5
1556079.9	21779	1600054.5	781459.9	684416.7	892035.2	252550.0
1060261.2	12478	1147786.2	787715.5	247261.5	435361.1	196311.6
151207.3	1145	48132.8	37498.7	9338.0	22759.6	13448.4
454439.6	4750	203333.2	100833.1	60340.3	104209.6	49217.9
416256.7	5714	550797.8	211246.1	278408.2	376355.2	98621.8

11-8 续表1

单位：万元

分组	Item	负债合计 Total Liabilites	流动负债 小计 Total Working Liabilities	长期负债 小计 Long-term Liabilities
总计	**Total**	**1958860.3**	**1759735.9**	**178769.9**
按隶属关系分	Grouped by Jurisdiction of Management			
中央企业	Central Enterprises	19222.6	18557.8	
省属企业	Provincial Enterprises	199251.8	193269.5	5967.1
市属企业	Municipal Enterprises	1740385.9	1547908.6	172802.8
按登记注册类型分组	Grouped by Registion Status			
港、澳、台商投资企业	Enterprises with Funds from Hong Kong, Macao and Taiwan	164793.2	157137.6	6453.5
与港、澳、台商合资经营	Co-investment with businessman from Hong Kong,Macao and Taiwan	138435.7	130980.1	6253.5
与港、澳、台商合作经营	Partnership with businessman from Hong Kong,Macao and Taiwan			
港澳台商独资	Wholly Funded from Hong Kong, Macao and Taiwan	24243.7	24043.7	200.0
港澳台商投资股份有限公司	Share-holding Corporation with Funds from Hong Kong,Macao and Taiwan	2113.8	2113.8	
外商投资企业	Enterprises with Foreign Investment	1794067.1	1602598.3	172316.4
中外合资经营企业	Joint Ownership Operation With Overseas	1332442.3	1241235.6	73057.2
中外合作经营企业	Co-operation With Overseas	976.6	717.7	258.9
外资企业	Foreign Funded Enterprises	261703.6	228718.4	32172.1
外商投资股份有限公司	Foreign funded Share-holding Corporations	198944.6	131926.6	66828.2
在总计中:亏损企业	Deficit Enterprises	226037.8	155856.2	54106.9
按轻重工业分	Grouped by Ligth Industry and Heavy Industry			
轻工业	Light Industry	736526.1	617927.0	100811.7
重工业	Heavy Industry	1222334.2	1141808.9	77958.2
按企业规模分	Grouped by Size of Enterprises			
大型工业	Large-size	612527.5	611876.1	651.4
中型工业	Medium-sized	787915.0	633820.5	152331.4
小型工业	Small-size	558417.8	514039.3	25787.1
按工业行业大类分	Grouped by Sector			
煤炭开采和洗选业	Mining and Washing of Coal			
石油和天然气开采业	Extraction of Petroleum and Natural Gas			
黑色金属矿采选业	Mining and Processing of Ferrous Metal Ores			
有色金属矿采选业	Mining and Processing of Non-ferrous Metal Ores			
非金属矿采选业	Mining and Processing of Nonmetal Ores			
其他采矿业	Mining of Other Ores			
农副食品加工业	Processing of Food from Agricultural Porducts	21739.1	21625.8	113.3
食品制造业	Manufacture of Foods	89271.7	88448.8	9.9
饮料制造业	Manufacture of Beverages	309687.3	226875.9	82811.4

continued 1

(10 000 yuan)

所有者权益合计 Total Owners' Equities	实收资本 Total Capital Hold	主营业务收入 Revenue from Principal Business	主营业务成本 Cost of Principal Business	主营业务税金及附加 Taxes and Other Charges on Principal Business
1933594.3	**1069897.6**	**5141207.6**	**3963512.8**	**73058.3**
57686.7	34194.0	106523.3	89256.0	8.6
148601.1	81212.9	621973.8	369930.2	17.5
1727306.5	954490.7	4412710.5	3504326.6	73032.2
161819.7	122656.7	250407.8	185805.8	41.6
102605.4	92046.8	151923.8	114851.3	37.6
57035.9	28809.9	94365.7	67324.8	4.0
2178.4	1800.0	4118.3	3629.7	
1771774.6	947240.9	4890799.8	3777707.0	73016.7
1203408.3	661493.6	3968946.8	3093687.6	70906.8
5364.7	3028.0	4081.5	1651.5	15.8
431777.4	252870.8	767000.2	559285.3	2086.7
131224.2	29848.5	150771.3	123082.6	7.4
154304.5	198147.2	183372.3	159424.2	1613.3
694553.6	387017.4	1885629.3	1323769.9	1754.0
1239040.7	682880.2	3255578.3	2639742.9	71304.3
541313.7	181431.7	2534582.3	1902754.7	65447.2
806319.6	470464.3	1505977.6	1173754.2	3262.9
585961.0	418001.6	1100647.7	887003.9	4348.2
26393.7	15289.7	152517.5	134709.0	156.1
112732.8	71651.3	428309.0	323710.8	4.0
237399.9	116769.2	416793.9	307926.1	1533.7

11-8 续表2

单位：万元

分　　组	Item	营业费用 Expenses for Operation	管理费用 Expenses for Management
总　　计	**Total**	**420434.7**	**163054.6**
按隶属关系分	Grouped by Jurisdiction of Management		
中央企业	Central Enterprises	870.8	4202.8
省属企业	Provincial Enterprises	171326.7	18389.1
市属企业	Municipal Enterprises	248237.2	140462.7
按登记注册类型分组	Grouped by Registion Status		
港、澳、台商投资企业	Enterprises with Funds from Hong Kong, Macao and Taiwan	28216.1	16586.1
与港、澳、台商合资经营	Co-investment with businessman from Hong Kong,Macao and Taiwan	8961.6	11497.3
与港、澳、台商合作经营	Partnership with businessman from Hong Kong,Macao and Taiwan		
港澳台商独资	Wholly Funded from Hong Kong, Macao and Taiwan	19085.1	4823.6
港澳台商投资股份有限公司	Share-holding Corporation with Funds from Hong Kong,Macao and Taiwan	169.4	265.2
外商投资企业	Enterprises with Foreign Investment	392218.6	146468.5
中外合资经营企业	Joint Ownership Operation With Overseas	289108.4	96765.4
中外合作经营企业	Co-operation With Overseas	247.5	1504.9
外资企业	Foreign Funded Enterprises	95443.2	38639.7
外商投资股份有限公司	Foreign funded Share-holding Corporations	7419.5	9558.5
在总计中:亏损企业	Deficit Enterprises	20309.5	22575.1
按轻重工业分	Grouped by Ligth Industry and Heavy Industry		
轻工业	Light Industry	350611.4	66277.3
重工业	Heavy Industry	69823.3	96777.3
按企业规模分	Grouped by Size of Enterprises		
大型工业	Large-size	213297.5	38265.5
中型工业	Medium-sized	164438.1	63109.7
小型工业	Small-size	42699.1	61679.4
按工业行业大类分	Grouped by Sector		
煤炭开采和洗选业	Mining and Washing of Coal		
石油和天然气开采业	Extraction of Petroleum and Natural Gas		
黑色金属矿采选业	Mining and Processing of Ferrous Metal Ores		
有色金属矿采选业	Mining and Processing of Non-ferroous Metal Ores		
非金属矿采选业	Mining and Processing of Nonmetal Ores		
其他采矿业	Mining of Other Ores		
农副食品加工业	Processing of Food from Agricultural Porducts	6005.8	2829.1
食品制造业	Manufacture of Foods	66978.3	10099.4
饮料制造业	Manufacture of Beverages	74739.8	17022.9

continued 2

(10 000 yuan)

财务费用 Financial cost	营业利润 Operating Profit	利润总额 Total Profits	亏损企业亏损总额 Total Loss of Deficit Enterprises	利税总额 Total Pre-tax Profits	本年应交增值税 Value Added Tax Payable
29802.7	**632591.1**	**565418.6**	**22959.6**	**933845.7**	**295368.8**
128.4	13074.0	13014.6		18387.2	5364.0
9975.2	59975.8	59884.0	5833.4	137099.0	77197.5
19699.1	559541.3	492520.0	17126.2	778359.5	212807.3
501.0	20456.1	21173.5	1586.0	32072.7	10857.6
552.8	17086.1	17504.6	1491.0	24407.5	6865.3
-50.9	3268.9	3567.8	95.0	7373.8	3802.0
-0.9	101.1	101.1		291.4	190.3
29301.7	612135.0	544245.1	21373.6	901773.0	284511.2
20434.6	473893.0	446316.8	10924.6	749362.5	232138.9
33.1	868.3	878.2		929.4	35.4
1214.7	134565.1	92529.9	9429.9	138789.5	44172.9
7619.3	2808.6	4520.2	1019.1	12691.6	8164.0
3603.9	-23623.4	-22959.6	22959.6	-14422.3	6924.0
18440.1	240694.2	154706.8	6798.2	295674.2	139213.4
11362.6	391896.9	410711.8	16161.4	638171.5	156155.4
14990.6	316180.5	318456.8		571588.3	187684.3
8569.9	206713.3	139863.0	7501.7	205806.0	62680.1
6242.2	109697.3	107098.8	15457.9	156451.4	45004.4
84.8	9531.0	9421.8	243.3	11459.0	1881.1
-113.3	112991.7	28011.8		48983.2	20967.4
6222.0	26127.7	26739.4	4362.0	48979.2	20706.1

11-8 续表3

单位：万元

分　组	Item	企业单位数（个）Number of Enterprises (unit)	亏损企业 Loss Making Enterprises	工业总产值（当年价）Gross Industrial Output Value (At Current Prices)
烟草加工业	Manufacture of Tobacco			
纺织业	Manufacture of Textile	1		2431.3
纺织服装、鞋、帽制造业	Manufacture of Textile Wearing Apparel, Footwearand Caps			
皮革、毛皮、羽毛(绒)及其制品业	Manufacture of Leather, Fur, Feather (eiderdown) and Related Products			
木材加工及竹、藤、棕、草制品业	Processing of Timber,Manufacture of Wood,Plam and Straw Products	1	1	878.4
家具制造业	Manufacture of Furniture			
造纸及纸制品业	Manufacture of Paper and Paper Products	2		21622.0
印刷业、记录媒介的复制	Printing,Reproduction of Recording Media	2	1	25739.6
文教体育用品制造业	Manufacture of Articles For Cultural, Educational and Sports Activities			
石油加工、炼焦及核燃料加工业	Processing of Petroleum, Cokeing,Processing of Nuclear and Nuclear Fuel	1		18886.6
化学原料及化学制品制造业	Manufacture of Raw Chemical Materials and Chemical Products	7	4	39092.6
医药制造业	Manufacture of Medicines	10	3	593033.9
化学纤维制造业	Manufacture of Chemical Fibers	1		82238.9
橡胶制品业	Manufacture of Rubber	1		3940.0
塑料制品业	Manufacture of Plastics	5	1	18573.7
非金属矿物制品业	Manufacture of Non-metallic Mineral Products	7	1	229468.9
黑色金属冶炼及压延加工业	Smelting and Pressing of Ferrous Metals	1		13569.0
有色金属冶炼及压延加工业	Smelting and Pressing of Non-ferrou Metals	6	2	96702.4
金属制品业	Manufacture of Metal Products	5	2	9310.1
通用设备制造业	Manufacture of General Purpose Machinery	11	3	81405.1
专用设备制造业	Manufacture of Special Equipment	13	4	129553.6
交通运输设备制造业	Manufacture of Transport Equipment	9	3	2170061.4
电气机械及器材制造业	Manufacture of Electric Equipment and Machinery	17	5	302533.8
通信设备、计算机及其他电子设备制造业	Manufacture of Communication Equipment, Computers and other Electronic Equipment	9	1	202342.6
仪器仪表及文化办公用	Manufacture of Measuring Instruments and Machinery for Cultural Activity and Office Work	8	2	67013.8
工艺品及其他制造业	Manufacture of Artwork and Other Manufacturing	2		999.7
废弃资源和废旧材料回收加工业	Recycling and Disposal of Waste			
电力、热力的生产和供应业	Production and Supply of Electric Power and Heat Power	1	1	8330.2
燃气生产和供应业	Gas mining and supplying industry	1		129526.3
水的生产和供应业	Production and Supply of Water	1	1	3022.3

continued 3

（10 000 yuan）

工业销售产值（当年价） Value of Industry Products Sales (At Current Prices)	从业人员年平均人数（人） Annual Average Employers (person)	资产合计 Total Assets	流动资产小计 Total Working Capitals	固定资产小计 Total Fixed Assets	固定资产原价合计 Origing Value of Fixed Assets	累计折旧 Accumulative Total Depreciation
2500.5	236	5229.8	2865.5	1190.4	6948.1	5795.7
878.4	30	628.0	443.0	185.0	299.4	114.4
21202.2	323	13404.6	8315.7	4525.4	6593.7	2068.3
25929.3	865	59701.8	20861.0	14848.0	23645.7	9058.1
18792.3	58	9566.9	6339.9	2879.5	4279.4	1410.6
34910.8	471	22698.3	15327.7	5050.7	9011.4	3988.8
593827.1	6547	364328.2	248064.8	79382.3	151366.4	75971.1
86995.2	230	50540.2	24393.4	26001.7	56034.5	30068.0
2940.0	157	3804.5	2010.4	1068.9	1484.6	415.7
16901.6	527	37847.8	26201.8	11096.4	17625.6	7505.6
219628.1	1034	179398.5	112387.8	66753.0	82587.7	21169.8
12001.3	47	3606.8	2201.8	1404.9	4842.7	3437.8
78118.5	884	161116.4	99913.2	51261.9	56662.8	13243.8
9630.9	305	13789.4	8075.5	5078.4	13107.1	8345.0
77626.6	1785	95518.6	65628.6	25767.9	52015.8	26264.4
119361.8	3042	201342.4	147107.4	47843.7	91227.0	51338.7
2251671.6	22855	982715.3	644355.2	278201.8	321301.0	84192.5
244862.4	2674	259594.3	205786.0	38025.2	59904.3	22687.2
197208.5	3446	264510.4	168730.5	82952.6	97706.6	33850.1
68897.8	1173	93617.0	73153.5	15174.9	21563.3	8419.0
924.4	255	4814.5	3213.4	1601.0	1712.8	589.7
8330.2	120	14162.8	9772.6	1906.2	754.7	92.6
126271.3	1974	238518.5	90384.5	120915.4	140205.5	19290.1
3022.3	132	18963.2	702.4	17284.8	17284.8	258.0

11-8 续表4

单位：万元

分组	Item	负债合计 Total Liabilites	流动负债小计 Total Working Liabilities	长期负债小计 Long-term Liabilities
烟草加工业	Manufacture of Tobacco			
纺织业	Manufacture of Textile	1302.0	128.1	
纺织服装、鞋、帽制造业	Manufacture of Textile Wearing Apparel, Footwearand Caps			
皮革、毛皮、羽毛(绒)及其制品业	Manufacture of Leather, Fur, Feather (eiderdown) and Related Products			
木材加工及竹、藤、棕、草制品业	Processing of Timber,Manufacture of Wood,Plam and Straw Products	577.5	577.5	
家具制造业	Manufacture of Furniture			
造纸及纸制品业	Manufacture of Paper and Paper Products	5174.1	5174.1	
印刷业、记录媒介的复制	Printing,Reproduction of Recording Media	38630.4	32599.5	6030.9
文教体育用品制造业	Manufacture of Articles For Cultural, Educational and Sports Activities			
石油加工、炼焦及核燃料加工业	Processing of Petroleum, Cokeing,Processing of Nuclear and Nuclear Fuel	2067.1	2067.1	
化学原料及化学制品制造业	Manufacture of Raw Chemical Materials and Chemical Products	12960.5	8945.3	1233.8
医药制造业	Manufacture of Medicines	165635.5	159952.3	5683.2
化学纤维制造业	Manufacture of Chemical Fibers	10677.4	10677.4	
橡胶制品业	Manufacture of Rubber	2148.9	1879.6	269.3
塑料制品业	Manufacture of Plastics	19229.4	15429.4	3800.0
非金属矿物制品业	Manufacture of Non-metallic Mineral Products	49927.5	47999.5	1928.0
黑色金属冶炼及压延加工业	Smelting and Pressing of Ferrous Metals	1803.4	1803.4	
有色金属冶炼及压延加工业	Smelting and Pressing of Non-ferrou Metals	101642.3	72961.3	28680.9
金属制品业	Manufacture of Metal Products	4775.6	4730.2	45.4
通用设备制造业	Manufacture of General Purpose Machinery	29787.4	28782.5	909.4
专用设备制造业	Manufacture of Special Equipment	93136.4	92457.9	-1.5
交通运输设备制造业	Manufacture of Transport Equipment	553603.4	552782.4	792.9
电气机械及器材制造业	Manufacture of Electric Equipment and Machinery	139346.6	133756.9	4016.1
通信设备、计算机及其他电子设备制造业	Manufacture of Communication Equipment, Computers and other Electronic Equipment	114273.3	103824.6	10258.9
仪器仪表及文化办公用	Manufacture of Measuring Instruments and Machinery for Cultural Activity and Office Work	42342.4	42010.4	332.0
工艺品及其他制造业	Manufacture of Artwork and Other Manufacturing	2538.6	2538.6	
废弃资源和废旧材料回收加工业	Recycling and Disposal of Waste			
电力、热力的生产和供应业	Production and Supply of Electric Power and Heat Power	6929.1	6929.1	
燃气生产和供应业	Gas mining and supplying industry	126634.3	94778.3	31856.0
水的生产和供应业	Production and Supply of Water	13019.1		

continued 4

(10 000 yuan)

所有者权益合计 Total Owners' Equities	实收资本 Total Capital Hold	主营业务收入 Revenue from Principal Business	主营业务成本 Cost of Principal Business	主营业务税金及附加 Taxes and Other Charges on Principal Business
3927.8	3768.7	2451.7	1606.7	
50.5	100.0	878.4	828.4	
8230.5	2738.2	21531.9	15948.3	
21071.4	23978.7	23469.7	18294.8	
7499.8	6840.6	19735.9	16342.9	
9737.7	8525.9	33173.4	26900.5	16.0
198692.6	91432.2	573025.7	282616.9	11.2
39862.8	24800.0	86995.2	73193.6	
1299.3	1030.0	2043.8	1636.2	
18618.2	17442.4	15530.1	10915.5	14.7
129471.0	30938.1	220603.4	161633.2	3433.1
1344.6	150.0	10752.2	8826.2	212.7
59474.1	48795.4	87746.9	67841.0	
9012.1	7826.5	9595.6	6596.8	5.6
65731.0	40112.9	82987.5	70332.4	3.2
108206.0	65512.7	123571.4	98855.0	29.4
429111.9	165594.3	2166775.7	1781495.6	65518.6
120247.7	84887.2	254833.5	214936.1	621.1
149456.5	100995.4	191143.5	162706.7	132.8
51274.6	26958.2	74620.7	52901.0	48.1
2275.9	1960.0	4587.0	4035.8	0.2
7233.7	7800.0	8230.2	6546.3	5.2
111884.2	100000.0	126281.5	109191.2	1294.5
3354.0	4000.0	3022.3	2985.8	18.1

11-8 续表5

单位：万元

分　　组	Item	营业费用 Expenses for Operation	管理费用 Expenses for Management
烟草加工业	Manufacture of Tobacco		
纺织业	Manufacture of Textile	364.3	418.3
纺织服装、鞋、帽制造业	Manufacture of Textile Wearing Apparel, Footwearand Caps		
皮革、毛皮、羽毛(绒)及其制品业	Manufacture of Leather, Fur, Feather (eiderdown) and Related Products		
木材加工及竹、藤、棕、草制品业	Processing of Timber,Manufacture of Wood,Plam and Straw Products	31.8	37.2
家具制造业	Manufacture of Furniture		
造纸及纸制品业	Manufacture of Paper and Paper Products	593.2	578.0
印刷业、记录媒介的复制	Printing,Reproduction of Recording Media	1662.2	2896.2
文教体育用品制造业	Manufacture of Articles For Cultural, Educational and Sports Activities		
石油加工、炼焦及核燃料加工业	Processing of Petroleum, Cokeing,Processing of Nuclear and Nuclear Fuel	179.3	1817.2
化学原料及化学制品制造业	Manufacture of Raw Chemical Materials and Chemical Products	1516.1	1978.3
医药制造业	Manufacture of Medicines	196883.9	25001.0
化学纤维制造业	Manufacture of Chemical Fibers	153.5	1894.3
橡胶制品业	Manufacture of Rubber	81.8	239.0
塑料制品业	Manufacture of Plastics	574.0	2042.3
非金属矿物制品业	Manufacture of Non-metallic Mineral Products	3064.5	2447.3
黑色金属冶炼及压延加工业	Smelting and Pressing of Ferrous Metals	219.5	376.4
有色金属冶炼及压延加工业	Smelting and Pressing of Non-ferrou Metals	3419.3	5846.7
金属制品业	Manufacture of Metal Products	282.5	1343.1
通用设备制造业	Manufacture of General Purpose Machinery	4168.8	6232.6
专用设备制造业	Manufacture of Special Equipment	4627.3	12455.8
交通运输设备制造业	Manufacture of Transport Equipment	26392.6	26412.3
电气机械及器材制造业	Manufacture of Electric Equipment and Machinery	8788.3	11933.7
通信设备、计算机及其他电子设备制造业	Manufacture of Communication Equipment, Computers and other Electronic Equipment	4592.0	9405.8
仪器仪表及文化办公用	Manufacture of Measuring Instruments and Machinery for Cultural Activity and Office Work	6583.3	7293.8
工艺品及其他制造业	Manufacture of Artwork and Other Manufacturing	197.9	305.6
废弃资源和废旧材料回收加工业	Recycling and Disposal of Waste		
电力、热力的生产和供应业	Production and Supply of Electric Power and Heat Power	912.8	1085.0
燃气生产和供应业	Gas mining and supplying industry	6922.3	10483.7
水的生产和供应业	Production and Supply of Water	499.6	579.6

continued 5

(10 000 yuan)

财务费用 Financial cost	营业利润 Operating Profit	利润总额 Total Profits	亏损企业亏损总额 Total Loss of Deficit Enterprises	利税总额 Total Pre-tax Profits	本年应交增值税 Value Added Tax Payable
0.4	10.2	6.2		255.5	249.3
6.3	-25.3	-12.1	12.1	67.5	79.6
84.2	5585.6	5953.1		9254.8	3301.7
225.2	1275.9	1322.6	1189.4	2982.3	1659.7
181.5	1397.0	1383.0		2752.4	1369.4
215.1	3176.7	131.6	383.4	1151.6	1004.0
11243.0	64264.2	64735.7	585.8	149179.4	84432.5
197.2	12557.7	12441.3		16297.7	3856.4
27.3	5.5	5.5		129.6	124.1
386.0	1854.3	2106.1	46.9	3210.1	1089.3
442.0	49151.4	52514.1	95.0	67891.2	11944.0
25.4	1992.0	1033.3		1660.0	414.0
2280.3	7810.7	8632.2	251.2	11533.9	2901.7
22.8	1084.4	1045.6	89.0	1682.2	631.0
277.8	3005.9	3156.7	256.9	5848.2	2688.3
-45.7	8426.2	9446.7	2780.0	14815.5	5339.4
5713.1	270534.9	272731.1	4929.7	451484.6	113234.9
1424.3	20539.7	20149.5	2076.4	26367.4	5596.8
1770.5	13731.3	26848.9	530.3	30828.7	3847.0
-147.5	8017.4	8228.1	4261.1	11416.4	3140.2
-16.5	110.2	110.2		304.1	193.7
283.2	-602.3	-638.6	638.6	-337.1	296.3
-1111.2	10269.6	10143.3		15732.7	4294.9
124.5	-232.5	-228.5	228.5	-84.4	126.0

11-9 规模以上大中型工业企业主要经济指标（2009年）

单位：万元

分组	Item	企业单位数（个）Number of Enterprises (unit)	亏损企业 Loss Making Enterprises	工业总产值（当年价）Gross Industrial Output Value (At Current Prices)
总计	**Total**	**190**	**32**	**18495586.5**
按隶属关系分	Grouped by Jurisdiction of Management			
中央企业	Central Enterprises	42	4	7286636.3
省属企业	Provincial Enterprises	25	5	4023298.8
市属企业	Municipal Enterprises	123	23	7185651.4
按登记注册类型分组	Grouped by Registion Status			
内资企业	Domestic Investment Enterprises	158	26	14304798.6
国有经济	State-owned Enterprises	42	8	5375480.5
集体经济	Collective-owned Enterprises	4	1	66987.3
股份合作	Share-holding Corperative	1		18661.1
联营企业	Joint Ownership Enterprises			
有限责任公司	Limited company	72	12	7338680.3
国有独资公司	State-owned appropriator ship corporation	18	4	1855647.9
其他有限责任公司	Other limited corporation	54	8	5483032.4
股份有限公司	Share-holding Corperation Ltd.	26	4	1006021.9
私营企业	Private Enterprises	13	1	498967.5
其他内资企业	Other Domestic Funded Enterprises			
港、澳、台商投资企业	Enterprises with Funds from Hong Kong,Macao and Taiwan	4	1	112381.2
外商投资企业	Enterprises with Foreign Investment	28	5	4078406.7
在总计中:亏损企业	Deficit Enterprises	32	32	963021.8
按轻重工业分	Grouped by Ligth Industry and Heavy Industry			
轻工业	Light Industry	55	10	2978831.1
重工业	Heavy Industry	135	22	15516755.4
按工业行业大类分	Grouped by Sector			
煤炭开采和洗选业	Mining and Washing of Coal			
石油和天然气开采业	Extraction of Petroleum and Natural Gas	2		96835.0
黑色金属矿采选业	Mining and Processing of Ferrous Metal Ores			
有色金属矿采选业	Mining and Processing of Non-ferroous Metal Ores	1		25518.7
非金属矿采选业	Mining and Processing of Nonmetal Ores			
其他采矿业	Mining of Other Ores			
农副食品加工业	Processing of Food from Agricultural Porducts	7		378246.3
食品制造业	Manufacture of Foods	5		498892.6
饮料制造业	Manufacture of Beverages	8	4	487634.5

Economic Indicators of Large and Medium-sizd Industrial Enterprises Above Designafed size（2009）

（10 000 yuan）

工业销售产值（当年价）Value of Industry Products Sales (At Current Prices)	从业人员年平均人数（人）Annual Average Employers (person)	资产合计 Total Assets	流动资产小计 Total Working Capitals	固定资产小计 Total Fixed Assets	固定资产原价合计 Origing Value of Fixed Assets	累计折旧 Accumulative Total Depreciation
18165822.1	**329160**	**23958696.7**	**14007254.9**	**8330517.8**	**10618928.3**	**3795886.6**
7048678.3	134172	12405234.9	6857624.1	5036730.7	6165979.0	2195251.8
4002257.7	55946	3975064.1	2734154.7	965948.2	1145467.2	333475.2
7114886.1	139042	7578397.7	4415476.1	2327838.9	3307482.1	1267159.6
13981746.6	280859	21204800.9	12459156.9	7329292.8	9312800.1	3401335.1
5218800.9	74871	8187231.9	4086934.7	3696119.4	4553310.3	1542277.3
55651.2	3802	36465.5	20455.4	15745.6	17993.4	2486.4
21834.6	576	30847.8	15625.8	4227.2	8929.3	4703.9
7286768.0	168160	11059942.7	7348965.2	3011837.8	3926691.4	1503339.8
1786643.0	57472	3218941.3	1852471.8	1168458.5	1630461.3	642917.6
5500125.0	110688	7841001.4	5496493.4	1843379.3	2296230.1	860422.2
960500.9	24130	1560008.0	766278.7	515434.9	688911.4	312758.2
438191.0	9320	330305.0	220897.1	85927.9	116964.3	35769.5
104021.0	2918	88249.0	40710.9	25797.1	52272.6	26618.2
4080054.5	45383	2665646.8	1507387.1	975427.9	1253855.6	367933.3
954574.1	32645	2026750.5	714003.8	1049804.8	1421659.2	543935.9
2942414.5	60488	2543786.6	1238369.6	955304.1	1472025.6	609379.9
15223407.6	268672	21414910.1	12768885.3	7375213.7	9146902.7	3186506.7
78186.3	2324	100357.2	72258.8	15864.5	42161.8	14119.7
25518.7	430	22560.9	8925.9	8287.9	13267.8	4979.9
328494.8	4108	238771.7	153413.9	52884.1	78586.6	28295.4
474184.0	4873	186886.9	106535.6	67498.2	111919.6	49521.8
581333.6	6619	614799.0	238587.4	291260.0	400361.3	110174.6

11-9 续表1

单位：万元

分组	Item	负债合计 Total Liabilites	流动负债 小计 Total Working Liabilities	长期负债 小计 Long-term Liabilities
总　　计	**Total**	**14739524.1**	**11658108.7**	**2715107.2**
按隶属关系分	Grouped by Jurisdiction of Management			
中央企业	Central Enterprises	8252140.6	6057223.2	1972509.8
省属企业	Provincial Enterprises	2509809.4	2203390.1	296984.0
市属企业	Municipal Enterprises	3977574.1	3397495.4	445613.4
按登记注册类型分组	Grouped by Registion Status			
内资企业	Domestic Investment Enterprises	13339081.6	10412412.1	2562124.4
国有经济	State-owned Enterprises	5832134.3	3948550.0	1627678.9
集体经济	Collective-owned Enterprises	20067.1	19567.1	500.0
股份合作	Share-holding Corperative	22206.0	22206.0	
联营企业	Joint Ownership Enterprises			
有限责任公司	Limited company	6510195.0	5624417.7	782307.0
国有独资公司	State-owned appropriator ship corporation	1455001.2	1184133.5	180666.7
其他有限责任公司	Other limited corporation	5055193.8	4440284.2	601640.3
股份有限公司	Share-holding Corperation Ltd.	770428.2	620368.7	145594.1
私营企业	Private Enterprises	184051.0	177302.6	6044.4
其他内资企业	Other Domestic Funded Enterprises			
港、澳、台商投资企业	Enterprises with Funds from Hong Kong,Macao and Taiwan	44458.0	38427.1	6030.9
外商投资企业	Enterprises with Foreign Investment	1355984.5	1207269.5	146951.9
在总计中:亏损企业	Deficit Enterprises	1330318.8	744215.6	497512.8
按轻重工业分	Grouped by Ligth Industry and Heavy Industry			
轻工业	Light Industry	1298160.7	1118814.6	167481.1
重工业	Heavy Industry	13441363.4	10539294.1	2547626.1
按工业行业大类分	Grouped by Sector			
煤炭开采和洗选业	Mining and Washing of Coal			
石油和天然气开采业	Extraction of Petroleum and Natural Gas	51507.9	51507.9	
黑色金属矿采选业	Mining and Processing of Ferrous Metal Ores			
有色金属矿采选业	Mining and Processing of Non-ferroous Metal Ores	13528.9	13399.9	129.0
非金属矿采选业	Mining and Processing of Nonmetal Ores			
其他采矿业	Mining of Other Ores			
农副食品加工业	Processing of Food from Agricultural Porducts	173544.2	167010.8	5829.4
食品制造业	Manufacture of Foods	86475.0	85452.1	209.9
饮料制造业	Manufacture of Beverages	348360.7	265427.0	82933.7

continued 1

（10 000 yuan）

所有者权益合计 Total Owners' Equities	实收资本 Total Capital Hold	主营业务收入 Revenue from Principal Business	主营业务成本 Cost of Principal Business	主营业务税金及附加 Taxes and Other Charges on Principal Business
9206169.7	**3646208.4**	**18007990.7**	**14463704.9**	**228622.5**
4153063.6	1335313.0	7197082.3	5618172.4	125614.7
1463828.6	597154.3	3926733.3	3301156.0	8472.4
3589277.5	1713741.1	6884175.1	5544376.5	94535.4
7858536.4	2994312.4	13967430.8	11387196.0	159912.4
2351016.4	878680.3	5060029.2	3783915.4	125795.5
16398.4	9820.3	59545.3	54405.9	311.4
8641.7	1984.6	20402.7	18259.1	
4546729.7	1678604.5	7448291.7	6371704.3	26719.4
1763940.0	370489.5	1864892.4	1567132.4	5799.1
2782789.7	1308115.0	5583399.3	4804571.9	20920.3
789527.5	349758.4	943002.6	786667.0	4983.1
146222.7	75464.3	436159.3	372244.3	2103.0
43791.0	35249.0	99578.2	69208.1	
1303842.3	616647.0	3940981.7	3007300.8	68710.1
691269.2	489746.2	905265.9	829535.8	4322.5
1240534.0	631123.9	2850320.8	2083139.3	14788.4
7965635.7	3015084.5	15157669.9	12380565.6	213834.1
48849.3	15908.6	75775.8	62321.9	1444.9
9031.9	4900.0	25518.7	23036.0	64.3
65227.4	35274.4	325221.2	290447.7	389.8
99083.1	53534.7	445722.9	338806.1	111.1
262727.7	128624.5	583936.9	439184.8	9220.6

11-9 续表2

单位：万元

分　组	Item	营业费用 Expenses for Operation	管理费用 Expenses for Management
总　计	**Total**	**837154.9**	**1003768.5**
按隶属关系分	Grouped by Jurisdiction of Management		
中央企业	Central Enterprises	178651.5	473708.8
省属企业	Provincial Enterprises	273715.9	164839.9
市属企业	Municipal Enterprises	384787.5	365219.8
按登记注册类型分组	Grouped by Registion Status		
内资企业	Domestic Investment Enterprises	459419.3	902393.3
国有经济	State-owned Enterprises	151837.8	335068.7
集体经济	Collective-owned Enterprises	889.2	1546.6
股份合作	Share-holding Corperative	1198.3	1226.5
联营企业	Joint Ownership Enterprises		
有限责任公司	Limited company	229847.2	477439.1
国有独资公司	State-owned appropriator ship corporation	44845.2	165137.9
其他有限责任公司	Other limited corporation	185002.0	312301.2
股份有限公司	Share-holding Corperation Ltd.	53855.1	74547.0
私营企业	Private Enterprises	21791.7	12565.4
其他内资企业	Other Domestic Funded Enterprises		
港、澳、台商投资企业	Enterprises with Funds from Hong Kong,Macao and Taiwan	19346.5	7383.9
外商投资企业	Enterprises with Foreign Investment	358389.1	93991.3
在总计中:亏损企业	Deficit Enterprises	39712.8	84275.7
按轻重工业分	Grouped by Ligth Industry and Heavy Industry		
轻工业	Light Industry	421926.4	135078.0
重工业	Heavy Industry	415228.5	868690.5
按工业行业大类分	Grouped by Sector		
煤炭开采和洗选业	Mining and Washing of Coal		
石油和天然气开采业	Extraction of Petroleum and Natural Gas	990.2	4273.8
黑色金属矿采选业	Mining and Processing of Ferrous Metal Ores		
有色金属矿采选业	Mining and Processing of Non-ferroous Metal Ores	1172.8	694.7
非金属矿采选业	Mining and Processing of Nonmetal Ores		
其他采矿业	Mining of Other Ores		
农副食品加工业	Processing of Food from Agricultural Porducts	16015.2	8105.6
食品制造业	Manufacture of Foods	67848.6	10430.2
饮料制造业	Manufacture of Beverages	87610.0	20014.6

continued 2

（10 000 yuan）

财务费用 Financial cost	营业利润 Operating Profit	利润总额 Total Profits	亏损企业亏损总额 Total Loss of Deficit Enterprises	利税总额 Total Pre-tax Profits	本年应交增值税 Value Added Tax Payable
173895.4	**1553317.2**	**1473902.7**	**118806.5**	**2313330.2**	**610805.0**
103946.9	727495.8	774322.9	7870.2	1060865.1	160927.5
23727.1	137877.4	159743.2	4775.7	309909.8	141694.2
46221.4	687944.0	539836.6	106160.6	942555.3	308183.3
150334.9	1030423.4	1015582.9	111304.8	1535935.9	360440.6
57785.3	692650.9	700836.0	10159.0	1004472.9	177841.4
226.2	1849.6	1824.3	17.5	4215.1	2079.4
53.8	-335.1	7.3		7.3	
67407.3	267489.1	306523.7	22388.5	469956.2	136713.1
11414.5	86063.2	96097.9	5685.3	147958.4	46061.4
55992.8	181425.9	210425.8	16703.2	321997.8	90651.7
19562.1	-17065.8	-18936.8	78387.1	21101.1	35054.8
5300.2	85834.7	25328.4	352.7	36183.3	8751.9
109.1	3709.0	3956.1	1189.4	7448.9	3492.8
23451.4	519184.8	454363.7	6312.3	769945.4	246871.6
40499.0	-120015.5	-118806.5	118806.5	-83154.4	31329.6
34396.6	355231.6	209944.0	14038.2	397008.3	172275.9
139498.8	1198085.6	1263958.7	104768.3	1916321.9	438529.1
181.8	7327.5	7134.6		17614.8	9035.3
271.3	265.0	920.0		1633.0	648.7
2710.0	68715.6	12198.2		15319.2	2731.2
208.2	116640.0	28964.8		50262.2	21186.3
6071.4	39495.6	40196.8	4379.2	77749.3	28331.9

11-9 续表3

单位：万元

分 组	Item	企业单位数(个) Number of Enterprises (unit)	亏损企业 Loss Making Enterprises	工业总产值（当年价） Gross Industrial Output Value (At Current Prices)
烟草加工业	Manufacture of Tobacco			
纺织业	Manufacture of Textile	5	2	107909.4
纺织服装、鞋、帽制造业	Manufacture of Textile Wearing Apparel, Footwearand Caps	1		27205.9
皮革、毛皮、羽毛(绒)及其制品业	Manufacture of Leather, Fur, Feather (eiderdown) and Related Products	1		12428.1
木材加工及竹、藤、棕、草制品业	Processing of Timber,Manufacture of Wood,Plam and Straw Products			
家具制造业	Manufacture of Furniture			
造纸及纸制品业	Manufacture of Paper and Paper Products	4	1	104859.3
印刷业、记录媒介的复制	Printing,Reproduction of Recording Media	8	1	278273.8
文教体育用品制造业	Manufacture of Articles For Cultural, Educational and Sports Activities			
石油加工、炼焦及核燃料加工业	Processing of Petroleum, Cokeing,Processing of Nuclear and Nuclear Fuel	1		608554.0
化学原料及化学制品制造业	Manufacture of Raw Chemical Materials and Chemical Products	8	3	429331.1
医药制造业	Manufacture of Medicines	10	1	731463.3
化学纤维制造业	Manufacture of Chemical Fibers			
橡胶制品业	Manufacture of Rubber			
塑料制品业	Manufacture of Plastics	3	1	126987.8
非金属矿物制品业	Manufacture of Non-metallic Mineral Products	6		221887.8
黑色金属冶炼及压延加工业	Smelting and Pressing of Ferrous Metals	1		8233.9
有色金属冶炼及压延加工业	Smelting and Pressing of Non-ferrou Metals	5		139147.5
金属制品业	Manufacture of Metal Products	5		68802.3
通用设备制造业	Manufacture of General Purpose Machinery	7		612663.4
专用设备制造业	Manufacture of Special Equipment	28	5	1386698.9
交通运输设备制造业	Manufacture of Transport Equipment	24	1	7398987.6
电气机械及器材制造业	Manufacture of Electric Equipment and Machinery	12		2466804.0
通信设备、计算机及其他电子设备制造业	Manufacture of Communication Equipment, Computers and other Electronic Equipment	20	6	524288.4
仪器仪表及文化办公用	Manufacture of Measuring Instruments and Machinery for Cultural Activity and Office Work	8	1	497786.6
工艺品及其他制造业	Manufacture of Artwork and Other Manufacturing			
废弃资源和废旧材料回收加工业	Recycling and Disposal of Waste			
电力、热力的生产和供应业	Production and Supply of Electric Power and Heat Power	8	6	1081251.8
燃气生产和供应业	Gas mining and supplying industry	1		129526.3
水的生产和供应业	Production and Supply of Water	1		45368.2

continued 3

（10 000 yuan）

工业销售产值（当年价） Value of Industry Products Sales (At Current Prices)	从业人员年平均人数（人） Annual Average Employers (person)	资产合计 Total Assets	流动资产小计 Total Working Capitals	固定资产小计 Total Fixed Assets	固定资产原价合计 Origing Value of Fixed Assets	累计折旧 Accumulative Total Depreciation
110178.8	13615	135082.7	58364.6	39906.9	68726.7	32611.2
34118.7	1336	51000.6	45430.9	4374.8	6115.6	2560.1
12500.0	1053	35220.0	12043.1	23176.9	4042.2	1160.2
98605.6	6912	71457.6	14676.7	56780.9	60019.7	5239.7
271043.8	6016	377704.8	155846.3	173735.3	264277.4	130551.8
607780.0	1246	158985.3	63320.0	95665.2	121339.5	43687.8
421097.6	16373	741199.1	295628.3	339242.8	468216.9	181786.2
727400.4	9736	569037.5	309790.3	133392.6	214315.4	95075.7
124330.3	2785	221036.5	133100.5	75046.7	70255.1	18808.6
211142.3	3213	243111.6	74491.5	128203.7	111119.1	17226.2
8233.9	672	7620.5	6401.5	1204.6	1464.6	260.0
123079.6	3741	399442.5	213883.5	72098.6	89965.4	25846.3
67170.7	2291	64041.9	46583.6	14915.8	18742.1	4345.9
625294.1	10830	1227383.2	979464.1	157848.0	241013.5	101989.1
1286543.2	36918	2313014.9	1471708.6	723562.1	873142.1	344178.4
7400492.3	117736	8613888.5	5958177.5	2190043.4	2638617.8	927044.4
2319512.2	27430	2885429.0	2017723.5	831703.4	727290.7	253857.0
523644.4	18982	1088617.1	644962.9	346453.1	530880.5	260704.0
453045.5	15316	846005.9	499186.3	256251.8	388751.5	176280.1
1081251.8	9877	2415852.6	314533.9	2040743.8	2749816.2	828783.3
126271.3	1974	238518.5	90384.5	120915.4	140205.5	19290.1
45368.2	2754	91670.7	21831.2	69457.3	184313.7	117509.1

11-9 续表4

单位：万元

分组	Item	负债合计 Total Liabilites	流动负债小计 Total Working Liabilities	长期负债小计 Long-term Liabilities
烟草加工业	Manufacture of Tobacco			
纺织业	Manufacture of Textile	61387.3	56210.1	5177.2
纺织服装、鞋、帽制造业	Manufacture of Textile Wearing Apparel, Footwearand Caps	39239.5	39239.5	
皮革、毛皮、羽毛(绒)及其制品业	Manufacture of Leather, Fur, Feather (eiderdown) and Related Products	21933.0	14213.3	7719.7
木材加工及竹、藤、棕、草制品业	Processing of Timber,Manufacture of Wood,Plam and Straw Products			
家具制造业	Manufacture of Furniture			
造纸及纸制品业	Manufacture of Paper and Paper Products	29714.2	16297.5	13416.7
印刷业、记录媒介的复制	Printing,Reproduction of Recording Media	117247.3	95577.9	21669.4
文教体育用品制造业	Manufacture of Articles For Cultural, Educational and Sports Activities			
石油加工、炼焦及核燃料加工业	Processing of Petroleum, Cokeing,Processing of Nuclear and Nuclear Fuel	127689.0	127643.5	45.4
化学原料及化学制品制造业	Manufacture of Raw Chemical Materials and Chemical Products	368847.2	284867.2	40678.6
医药制造业	Manufacture of Medicines	271855.3	255502.3	6005.0
化学纤维制造业	Manufacture of Chemical Fibers			
橡胶制品业	Manufacture of Rubber			
塑料制品业	Manufacture of Plastics	143411.7	112781.7	29811.0
非金属矿物制品业	Manufacture of Non-metallic Mineral Products	119581.9	98480.9	21101.0
黑色金属冶炼及压延加工业	Smelting and Pressing of Ferrous Metals	6905.6	6905.6	
有色金属冶炼及压延加工业	Smelting and Pressing of Non-ferrou Metals	206657.3	154176.7	52480.6
金属制品业	Manufacture of Metal Products	51573.7	40058.0	11242.7
通用设备制造业	Manufacture of General Purpose Machinery	753463.5	718749.6	34618.4
专用设备制造业	Manufacture of Special Equipment	1180949.9	1044203.2	135381.8
交通运输设备制造业	Manufacture of Transport Equipment	5199731.8	4512983.2	659480.2
电气机械及器材制造业	Manufacture of Electric Equipment and Machinery	2086360.1	1710791.2	212975.5
通信设备、计算机及其他电子设备制造业	Manufacture of Communication Equipment, Computers and other Electronic Equipment	641702.6	514549.7	123355.1
仪器仪表及文化办公用	Manufacture of Measuring Instruments and Machinery for Cultural Activity and Office Work	413596.9	316684.5	28465.3
工艺品及其他制造业	Manufacture of Artwork and Other Manufacturing			
废弃资源和废旧材料回收加工业	Recycling and Disposal of Waste			
电力、热力的生产和供应业	Production and Supply of Electric Power and Heat Power	2065578.4	836582.7	1182513.1
燃气生产和供应业	Gas mining and supplying industry	126634.3	94778.3	31856.0
水的生产和供应业	Production and Supply of Water	32046.9	24034.4	8012.5

continued 4

(10 000 yuan)

所有者权益合计 Total Owners' Equities	实收资本 Total Capital Hold	主营业务收入 Revenue from Principal Business	主营业务成本 Cost of Principal Business	主营业务税金及附加 Taxes and Other Charges on Principal Business
73695.4	34882.4	112162.9	100660.3	531.6
11761.1	7500.0	41967.7	34863.5	408.7
13287.0	6000.0	13838.3	11999.1	23.8
41743.3	25723.0	89683.6	80562.1	123.5
260457.4	137524.5	273274.1	197812.1	2417.1
31296.3	24583.2	605934.9	484695.4	98550.6
372299.9	136899.7	427130.3	356903.3	1502.2
297182.0	112235.9	667220.8	324495.7	766.7
77593.5	37653.1	129920.0	111901.1	644.0
123529.6	45060.0	232786.5	176885.8	804.4
714.9	1000.0	8111.2	7175.1	52.0
192785.1	55958.6	120589.1	99247.6	1052.2
12468.1	8500.0	55647.8	46523.1	534.4
471264.4	72461.3	585298.7	454688.7	2217.3
1130608.6	490367.2	1292080.6	1079960.8	6109.7
3414156.5	1102232.2	7484431.9	6405081.0	77306.9
796082.3	246176.3	2013117.5	1534568.7	13938.5
446133.8	291551.4	524075.0	450886.2	3320.7
432409.0	232659.1	449152.4	368199.8	2778.0
350274.1	199998.3	1251462.9	831608.1	2677.4
111884.2	100000.0	126281.5	109191.2	1294.5
59623.8	39000.0	47647.5	41999.7	337.6

11-9 续表5

单位：万元

分　　组	Item	营业费用 Expenses for Operation	管理费用 Expenses for Management
烟草加工业	Manufacture of Tobacco		
纺织业	Manufacture of Textile	1397.4	8945.9
纺织服装、鞋、帽制造业	Manufacture of Textile Wearing Apparel, Footwearand Caps	2992.7	3361.1
皮革、毛皮、羽毛(绒)及其制品业	Manufacture of Leather, Fur, Feather (eiderdown) and Related Products	438.8	1135.9
木材加工及竹、藤、棕、草制品业	Processing of Timber,Manufacture of Wood,Plam and Straw Products		
家具制造业	Manufacture of Furniture		
造纸及纸制品业	Manufacture of Paper and Paper Products	1613.9	1805.4
印刷业、记录媒介的复制	Printing,Reproduction of Recording Media	6631.4	33200.1
文教体育用品制造业	Manufacture of Articles For Cultural, Educational and Sports Activities		
石油加工、炼焦及核燃料加工业	Processing of Petroleum, Cokeing,Processing of Nuclear and Nuclear Fuel	1303.8	9914.0
化学原料及化学制品制造业	Manufacture of Raw Chemical Materials and Chemical Products	20257.0	54942.9
医药制造业	Manufacture of Medicines	223262.6	36001.7
化学纤维制造业	Manufacture of Chemical Fibers		
橡胶制品业	Manufacture of Rubber		
塑料制品业	Manufacture of Plastics	8504.5	7147.9
非金属矿物制品业	Manufacture of Non-metallic Mineral Products	8037.8	6641.3
黑色金属冶炼及压延加工业	Smelting and Pressing of Ferrous Metals		937.3
有色金属冶炼及压延加工业	Smelting and Pressing of Non-ferrou Metals	1139.0	8088.5
金属制品业	Manufacture of Metal Products	3739.3	3033.7
通用设备制造业	Manufacture of General Purpose Machinery	21354.9	69504.5
专用设备制造业	Manufacture of Special Equipment	39693.6	128475.5
交通运输设备制造业	Manufacture of Transport Equipment	156344.1	302812.2
电气机械及器材制造业	Manufacture of Electric Equipment and Machinery	125133.4	142901.1
通信设备、计算机及其他电子设备制造业	Manufacture of Communication Equipment, Computers and other Electronic Equipment	24608.8	65514.0
仪器仪表及文化办公用	Manufacture of Measuring Instruments and Machinery for Cultural Activity and Office Work	8310.7	56620.9
工艺品及其他制造业	Manufacture of Artwork and Other Manufacturing		
废弃资源和废旧材料回收加工业	Recycling and Disposal of Waste		
电力、热力的生产和供应业	Production and Supply of Electric Power and Heat Power		6132.2
燃气生产和供应业	Gas mining and supplying industry	6922.3	10483.7
水的生产和供应业	Production and Supply of Water	1832.1	2649.8

continued 5

(10 000 yuan)

财务费用 Financial cost	营业利润 Operating Profit	利润总额 Total Profits	亏损企业亏损总额 Total Loss of Deficit Enterprises	利税总额 Total Pre-tax Profits	本年应交增值税 Value Added Tax Payable
556.8	674.4	1579.8	1472.3	5288.1	3176.7
144.4	181.6	577.4		2253.9	1267.8
93.7	354.2	651.2		675.0	
2439.6	8634.8	479.0	954.1	1782.4	1179.9
526.0	42744.0	42811.4	1189.4	58802.9	13574.4
3438.0	8835.2	8983.8		121457.9	13923.5
6700.2	-5663.9	-1348.3	13166.7	15443.3	15289.4
18796.1	71305.7	70760.6	4905.1	165347.0	93819.7
1705.5	3590.9	3723.6	352.7	8278.6	3911.0
1744.6	43538.6	47587.2		61240.6	12849.0
76.6	302.3	302.3		874.7	520.4
4610.9	8250.3	8690.4		11642.3	1899.7
491.8	7187.4	1630.2		4118.9	1954.3
-6847.9	67513.8	52132.4		78811.1	24461.4
10092.8	80918.2	78070.9	7626.2	119943.2	35762.6
53136.2	448241.2	500703.4	956.6	750222.7	172212.4
22265.5	183070.6	195659.6		282698.8	73100.7
5578.7	-62662.7	-43433.5	73729.0	-24747.0	15365.8
3732.0	20890.0	23624.5	35.9	56687.0	30284.5
36213.6	382017.6	380482.9	10039.3	410324.9	27164.6
-1111.2	10269.6	10143.3		15732.7	4294.9
68.8	679.7	676.2		3872.7	2858.9

11-10 规模以上工业高技术产业企业主要经济指标（2009年）

单位：万元

分组	Item	企业单位数（个）Number of Enterprises (unit)	亏损企业 Loss Making Enterprises	工业总产值（当年价）Gross Industrial Output Value (At Current Prices)
总　计	**Total**	**166**	**40**	**4360287.9**
按高技术产业行业分	**Classification by High-tech Industrial Sector**			
一、信息化学品制造	**Information Chemical Products**			
二、医药制造业	**Medicines Manufacturing**	**54**	**16**	**950925.8**
#化学药品原药制造业	Chemical Medicine Manufacturing	22	5	693669.6
中成药制造业	Traditional Chinese Midicine	22	8	165130.8
生物、生化制品的制造业	Biology,Biochemistry Products	6	2	71358.2
三、航空航天器制造业	**Aviation and Aircrafts Manufacturing**	**13**	**1**	**2000276.8**
1.飞机制造及修理业	Manufacture and Repairing of Aircrafts	8	1	1755999.5
2.航天器制造业	Aircrafts Manufacturing	5		244277.3
四、电子及通讯设备制造业	**Electronic and Communication Equipment**	**46**	**13**	**760178.7**
1.通信设备制造业	Communication Equipment Manufacturing	12	3	153517.3
#通信传输设备制造业	Communication Transmitting Equipment	5	2	74484.5
通信交换设备制造业	Communication Exchanging Equipment	2		8802.4
通信终端设备制造业	Communication Terminal Equipment			
移动通信及终端设备制造业	Mobile Communication and Terminal Equipment	1	1	17022.0
2.雷达及配套设备制造业	Rader Equipments	1		58226.7
3.广播电视设备制造业	Broadcast and Television Equipments	2		11798.6
4.电子器件制造业	Electronic Appliances Manufacturing	17	5	353608.0
电子真空器件制造业	Electronic Vacuum Appliances	4	1	166447.9
半导体分立器件制造	Semiconductor Discreting Appliances	9	2	148661.6
集成电路制造	Integrate Circuit	3	2	30517.9
光电子器件及其他电子器件制造	Photoelectron Appliances and Other Electronic Appliances	1		7980.6
5.电子元件制造	Electronic Components Manufacturing	12	5	169887.1
6.家用视听设备制造	Household Audiovisual			
7.其他电子设备制造	Other Electronic Equipment	2		13141.0
五、电子计算机及办公设备制造业	**Computers and Office Equipment Manufacturing**	**2**		**10365.5**
1.电子计算机整机制造	Entired Computer Manufacturing	1		7300.0
2.计算机网络设备制造	Computer Network Equipment			
3.电子计算机外部设备制造	Computer Peripheral Equipment	1		3065.5
4.办公设备维修	Repairing of Office Equipment			
六、医疗设备及仪器仪表	**Medical Equipments and Meters**	**51**	**10**	**638541.1**
1.医疗仪器设备及器械制造	Medical Equipments and Instruments	4	4	7513.5
2.仪器仪表制造业	Instruments and Meters	47	6	631027.6
七、公共软件服务	**Public software Service**			
八、其他	**Others**			

Economic Indicators of High Technology Industry

Industrial Enterprises Above Designafed size（2009）

（10 000 yuan）

工业销售产值（当年价） Value of Industry Products Sales (At Current Prices)	从业人员年平均人数（人） Annual Average Employers (person)	资产合计 Total Assets	流动资产小计 Total Working Capitals	固定资产小计 Total Fixed Assets	固定资产原价合计 Origing Value of Fixed Assets	累计折旧 Accumulative Total Depreciation
4194530.5	**111112**	**8005011.3**	**5254300.8**	**2108172.2**	**2854774.5**	**1220944.0**
923917.5	15326	851380.5	437684.9	248314.9	361884.5	138621.2
688768.8	9843	460222.3	306352.4	115869.1	195854.7	86437.1
147979.4	3668	199600.1	91051.0	73958.6	97937.3	26677.9
66089.8	1289	176915.3	29843.5	54454.5	62557.3	23490.2
1922971.4	53571	4736483.3	3314327.1	1168200.2	1452405.2	601955.5
1683902.0	45585	4199749.1	3045337.2	928343.8	1198009.0	501900.2
239069.4	7986	536734.2	268989.9	239856.4	254396.2	100055.3
748268.7	22174	1371476.3	863878.4	391603.9	601570.5	289244.3
153921.9	3637	215858.2	161610.2	45264.3	56625.1	28830.3
80639.6	1518	68903.8	51445.4	13968.0	16345.5	7730.9
8994.1	362	39604.6	33396.1	6181.1	17852.2	11671.1
15900.0	610	38252.2	20390.6	12790.8	9282.3	4515.3
58226.7	3555	257742.1	188621.9	68997.8	85450.8	23372.3
10892.6	308	14386.8	11466.5	1684.9	2374.3	1077.9
351055.7	7495	532170.6	313518.0	203434.0	363271.9	191424.8
169656.9	3480	221296.4	128843.9	90371.4	238708.0	148340.2
142678.2	2390	196866.9	133552.7	55759.8	54564.9	21116.6
30740.0	995	107294.3	47923.1	54436.3	66511.4	21346.8
7980.6	630	6713.0	3198.3	2866.5	3487.6	621.2
161051.9	7073	342399.7	181685.9	70630.3	92117.5	43579.2
13119.9	106	8918.9	6975.9	1592.6	1730.9	959.8
9482.3	407	8304.0	6433.2	1713.8	1258.0	260.2
6800.0	300	4486.9	3719.6	767.3	160.8	109.5
2682.3	107	3817.1	2713.6	946.5	1097.2	150.7
589890.6	19634	1037367.2	631977.2	298339.4	437656.3	190862.8
8264.6	631	26777.5	13800.9	10867.9	10523.0	3451.9
581626.0	19003	1010589.7	618176.3	287471.5	427133.3	187410.9

11-10 续表1

单位：万元

分组	Item	负债合计 Total Liabilites	流动负债小计 Total Working Liabilities	长期负债小计 Long-term Liabilities
总　计	**Total**	**4585290.3**	**3854343.3**	**623895.8**
按高技术产业行业分	**Classification by High-tech Industrial Sector**			
一、信息化学品制造	**Information Chemical Products**			
二、医药制造业	**Medicines Manufacturing**	420193.9	379772.2	27159.5
#化学药品原药制造业	Chemical Medicine Manufacturing	215376.7	200592.1	4436.6
中成药制造业	Traditional Chinese Midicine	108109.9	87735.0	17460.7
生物、生化制品的制造业	Biology,Biochemistry Products	88564.0	83589.0	4975.0
三、航空航天器制造业	**Aviation and Aircrafts Manufacturing**	2834082.5	2386934.0	426980.4
1.飞机制造及修理业	Manufacture and Repairing of Aircrafts	2552381.3	2193873.6	358507.6
2.航天器制造业	Aircrafts Manufacturing	281701.2	193060.4	68472.8
四、电子及通讯设备制造业	**Electronic and Communication Equipment**	801363.2	662854.3	133443.1
1.通信设备制造业	Communication Equipment Manufacturing	120713.0	106470.8	10572.7
#通信传输设备制造业	Communication Transmitting Equipment	34615.1	33432.6	
通信交换设备制造业	Communication Exchanging Equipment	24765.4	22251.2	217.0
通信终端设备制造业	Communication Terminal Equipment			
移动通信及终端设备制造业	Mobile Communication and Terminal Equipment	21257.9	11068.1	10000.0
2.雷达及配套设备制造业	Rader Equipments	168000.6	159783.9	8216.7
3.广播电视设备制造业	Broadcast and Television Equipments	8937.3	8937.3	
4.电子器件制造业	Electronic Appliances Manufacturing	263873.8	195585.5	67201.9
电子真空器件制造业	Electronic Vacuum Appliances	125176.1	68780.4	55309.4
半导体分立器件制造	Semiconductor Discreting Appliances	100854.6	89562.0	11292.5
集成电路制造	Integrate Circuit	34194.3	33594.3	600.0
光电子器件及其他电子器件制造	Photoelectron Appliances and Other Electronic Appliances	3648.8	3648.8	
5.电子元件制造	Electronic Components Manufacturing	237968.6	190416.9	47241.8
6.家用视听设备制造	Household Audiovisual			
7.其他电子设备制造	Other Electronic Equipment	1869.9	1659.9	210.0
五、电子计算机及办公设备制造业	**Computers and Office Equipment Manufacturing**	4072.0	3834.9	237.1
1.电子计算机整机制造	Entired Computer Manufacturing	2460.7	2223.6	237.1
2.计算机网络设备制造	Computer Network Equipment			
3.电子计算机外部设备制造	Computer Peripheral Equipment	1611.3	1611.3	
4.办公设备维修	Repairing of Office Equipment			
六、医疗设备及仪器仪表	**Medical Equipments and Meters**	525578.7	420947.9	36075.7
1.医疗仪器设备及器械制造	Medical Equipments and Instruments	12744.5	11288.5	1456.0
2.仪器仪表制造业	Instruments and Meters	512834.2	409659.4	34619.7
七、公共软件服务	**Public software Service**			
八、其他	**Others**			

continued 1

(10 000 yuan)

所有者权益合计 Total Owners' Equities	实收资本 Total Capital Hold	主营业务收入 Revenue from Principal Business	主营业务成本 Cost of Principal Business	主营业务税金及附加 Taxes and Other Charges on Principal Business
3418334.1	**1389383.6**	**4377748.4**	**3392204.8**	**15017.8**
431186.0	241656.9	858904.0	463511.5	1428.1
244845.1	105672.8	653208.6	332881.0	739.7
91490.1	81620.3	141993.4	88246.7	499.7
88351.3	49963.8	42380.5	22735.4	108.5
1902400.7	488141.2	2181688.4	1816521.9	5742.6
1647367.8	452715.9	1941954.5	1623735.4	4943.5
255032.9	35425.3	239733.9	192786.5	799.1
568795.4	367363.6	738800.5	627340.8	4043.0
94608.6	95646.5	148210.5	119325.1	478.4
34288.6	31242.7	77449.7	64309.4	317.7
14839.2	47203.3	8768.9	5047.0	4.5
16994.3	6470.5	13007.0	9755.2	5.1
89741.5	18130.0	72313.9	56340.0	159.2
5449.5	5120.0	10892.6	7957.3	52.6
267515.7	163014.4	345245.4	316595.1	1367.1
96120.2	47180.2	164449.1	152363.4	623.9
95231.3	51930.6	141498.1	123928.6	688.1
73100.0	62303.6	31317.6	33535.3	17.1
3064.2	1600.0	7980.6	6767.8	38.0
104431.1	84502.7	150509.9	119002.8	1927.3
7049.0	950.0	11628.2	8120.5	58.4
4232.0	3500.0	10054.6	7669.8	403.4
2026.2	2000.0	7500.0	6200.0	385.0
2205.8	1500.0	2554.6	1469.8	18.4
511720.0	288721.9	588300.9	477160.8	3400.7
14032.9	13452.7	7278.8	5888.5	46.2
497687.1	275269.2	581022.1	471272.3	3354.5

11-10 续表2

单位：万元

分　　组	Item	营业费用 Expenses for Operation	管理费用 Expenses for Management
总　计	**Total**	**328758.9**	**375652.5**
按高技术产业行业分	**Classification by High-tech Industrial Sector**		
一、信息化学品制造	**Information Chemical Products**		
二、医药制造业	**Medicines Manufacturing**	244238.0	57581.1
#化学药品原药制造业	Chemical Medicine Manufacturing	207471.5	35354.5
中成药制造业	Traditional Chinese Midicine	26885.9	14667.6
生物、生化制品的制造业	Biology,Biochemistry Products	8019.7	6078.8
三、航空航天器制造业	**Aviation and Aircrafts Manufacturing**	34870.1	166203.6
1.飞机制造及修理业	Manufacture and Repairing of Aircrafts	32488.7	137032.3
2.航天器制造业	Aircrafts Manufacturing	2381.4	29171.3
四、电子及通讯设备制造业	**Electronic and Communication Equipment**	31583.1	78164.5
1.通信设备制造业	Communication Equipment Manufacturing	10141.0	12531.4
#通信传输设备制造业	Communication Transmitting Equipment	3645.6	4557.2
通信交换设备制造业	Communication Exchanging Equipment	2865.6	762.9
通信终端设备制造业	Communication Terminal Equipment		
移动通信及终端设备制造业	Mobile Communication and Terminal Equipment	1633.1	1867.7
2.雷达及配套设备制造业	Rader Equipments	776.5	13537.3
3.广播电视设备制造业	Broadcast and Television Equipments	601.8	1172.9
4.电子器件制造业	Electronic Appliances Manufacturing	11891.5	26687.8
电子真空器件制造业	Electronic Vacuum Appliances	8401.9	15743.7
半导体分立器件制造	Semiconductor Discreting Appliances	3295.3	7763.3
集成电路制造	Integrate Circuit	26.2	2198.7
光电子器件及其他电子器件制造	Photoelectron Appliances and Other Electronic Appliances	168.1	982.1
5.电子元件制造	Electronic Components Manufacturing	7562.4	23815.8
6.家用视听设备制造	Household Audiovisual		
7.其他电子设备制造	Other Electronic Equipment	609.9	419.3
五、电子计算机及办公设备制造业	**Computers and Office Equipment Manufacturing**	1007.4	1755.7
1.电子计算机整机制造	Entired Computer Manufacturing	855.1	1185.9
2.计算机网络设备制造	Computer Network Equipment		
3.电子计算机外部设备制造	Computer Peripheral Equipment	152.3	569.8
4.办公设备维修	Repairing of Office Equipment		
六、医疗设备及仪器仪表	**Medical Equipments and Meters**	17060.3	71947.6
1.医疗仪器设备及器械制造	Medical Equipments and Instruments	536.7	1923.7
2.仪器仪表制造业	Instruments and Meters	16523.6	70023.9
七、公共软件服务	**Public software Service**		
八、其他	**Others**		

continued 2

(10 000 yuan)

财务费用 Financial cost	营业利润 Operating Profit	利润总额 Total Profits	亏损企业亏损总额 Total Loss of Deficit Enterprises	利税总额 Total Pre-tax Profits	本年应交增值税 Value Added Tax Payable
72249.0	**166894.0**	**225539.9**	**90506.9**	**406063.4**	**165505.7**
22688.7	79597.0	78631.7	8598.9	180862.1	100802.3
12522.0	71892.5	71734.8	1343.8	162152.8	89678.3
3130.0	8202.3	8331.6	1505.2	15154.4	6323.1
6921.4	-1642.3	-1617.4	5715.0	3002.0	4510.9
38129.5	102904.5	138267.8	283.2	151910.9	7900.5
36905.7	83322.0	110642.7	283.2	121049.9	5463.7
1223.8	19582.5	27625.1		30861.0	2436.8
6896.3	-43898.6	-23300.7	76246.7	1507.7	20765.4
1325.1	8583.1	10976.1	594.5	15542.8	4088.3
192.1	8063.9	8059.3	64.2	9867.5	1490.5
44.4	62.6	208.0		849.9	637.4
1231.3	-1488.9	-530.3	530.3	494.3	1019.5
410.1	1059.4	1120.7		1774.8	494.9
258.8	888.4	986.7		1200.1	160.8
2490.0	-60620.3	-45371.4	73919.2	-35596.7	8407.6
2173.7	-63949.2	-63765.2	70433.3	-56693.8	6447.5
102.6	7055.2	8641.2	1119.9	10892.9	1563.6
213.7	-3821.1	9524.9	2366.0	9713.9	171.9
	94.8	227.7		490.3	224.6
2405.0	4214.8	7081.9	1733.0	16093.3	7084.1
7.3	1976.0	1905.3		2493.4	529.7
125.4	811.7	826.6		1602.3	372.3
81.7	427.0	427.0		1015.0	203.0
43.7	384.7	399.6		587.3	169.3
4409.1	27479.4	31114.5	5378.1	70180.4	35665.2
243.6	-884.1	-646.0	646.0	-148.1	451.7
4165.5	28363.5	31760.5	4732.1	70328.5	35213.5

11-11 分区县规模以上工业企业主要经济指标（2009年）

单位：万元

区县名称	Name of District and County	企业单位数（个）Number of Enterprises (unit)	亏损企业 Loss Making Enterprises	工业总产值（当年价）Gross Industrial Output Value (At Current Prices)	工业销售产值（当年价）Value of Industry Products Sales (At Current Prices)	从业人员年平均人数（人）Annual Average Employers (person)
新城区	Xingcheng	38	12	1954554.1	1910730.3	37594
区属	Under District	30	12	1286279.2	1280260.2	14050
碑林区	Beilin	41	11	585979.8	570087.6	9765
区属	Under District	31	8	495969.4	486134.6	8089
莲湖区	Lianhu	64	19	3998327.9	3867518.9	63116
区属	Under District	58	19	3684307.3	3561284.3	50172
灞桥区	Baqiao	149	10	1788190.9	1745691.3	42151
区属	Under District	144	10	1610206.7	1568654.5	33127
未央区	Weiyang	187	39	3932127.4	3872207.6	64100
区属	Under District	83	18	1616398.0	1685881.2	24623
雁塔区	Yanta	188	44	2496820.1	2373882.7	61427
区属	Under District	56	15	397098.1	383679.7	11213
阎良区	Yanliang	54	1	1289930.4	1220631.5	24334
区属	Under District	50		267941.2	251848.4	3262
临潼区	Lintong	51	20	1657738.6	1621115.7	21074
区属	Under District	51	20	1657738.6	1621115.7	21074
长安区	Chang'an	105	18	2779864.3	2828400.6	43669
区属	Under District	60	11	258444.6	241984.7	9620
蓝田县	Lantian	38	17	234066.7	195912.4	3627
县属	Under County	37	17	226519.4	188394.2	3393
周至县	Zhouzhi	27	4	90297.7	84046.6	2908
县属	Under County	27	4	90297.7	84046.6	2908
户县	Huxian	91	26	815406.4	743164.8	19361
县属	Under County	90	25	664304.4	591551.1	14315
高陵县	Gaoling	98	37	3059347.5	3047119.5	41032
县属	Under County	78	30	478723.5	434561.9	9598

Economic Indicators of Industrial Enterprises Above Designated size by Region（2009）

（10 000 yuan）

资产合计 Total Assets	流动资产小计 Total Working Capitals	固定资产小计 Total Fixed Assets	固定资产原价合计 Origing Value of Fixed Assets	累计折旧 Accumulative Total Depreciation	负债合计 Total Liabilites	流动负债小计 Total Working Liabilities	长期负债小计 Long-term Liabilities
2561929.0	**1172922.7**	**1295349.3**	**1938271.2**	**776310.0**	**1723061.3**	**992507.8**	**727380.9**
1247992.5	405575.8	793823.5	1239055.1	520295.0	1030251.4	385850.4	641228.6
1660294.9	451592.1	1059464.7	1297097.6	336335.6	1169359.9	885868.5	237004.7
1452636.1	382988.0	1013146.1	1243250.3	318295.8	1047382.7	767903.4	232992.6
5164138.7	3351831.9	1563244.7	1942671.7	817520.4	3062023.0	2461188.9	433497.9
4362391.3	2838713.5	1376313.5	1620681.2	652284.3	2624384.9	2155923.7	301125.1
1422453.1	582888.3	729249.9	923984.3	266052.6	873098.3	479249.3	359620.7
961039.3	401464.9	465854.9	643255.5	186535.0	673928.7	352120.2	307748.2
4396733.0	2809617.7	1153298.7	1701140.6	595208.4	2706159.5	2288220.4	396462.8
1223694.3	733318.4	382657.9	560920.7	205584.7	785173.0	680020.4	101028.3
3880242.0	2274068.0	1133882.6	1623718.3	665564.4	2000486.2	1548994.4	352038.4
483036.2	267573.7	150039.6	260867.5	125496.4	284881.4	252533.1	21856.1
2420383.3	1833694.4	551454.7	554527.7	220111.9	1469930.7	1404978.2	42721.2
142812.5	63352.0	56269.5	65754.6	23819.3	67566.4	53917.3	13131.9
1635427.9	1196038.2	322112.2	397198.0	149329.6	948686.5	792378.9	33590.6
1635427.9	1196038.2	322112.2	397198.0	149329.6	948686.5	792378.9	33590.6
1784854.1	1045922.9	618670.8	701695.5	212917.5	965102.4	894479.6	69690.7
181244.6	99043.8	74629.0	99020.9	27027.8	103698.3	92185.4	10803.8
194373.2	87700.8	99596.4	109947.2	23750.5	100746.8	76828.2	18771.6
189506.1	85309.2	97401.1	107065.6	23064.2	97725.9	73807.3	18771.6
75407.1	34367.9	32942.8	40340.3	10182.5	50491.9	35460.6	15031.3
75407.1	34367.9	32942.8	40340.3	10182.5	50491.9	35460.6	15031.3
940207.5	385087.8	454472.7	643272.3	216676.6	610562.3	409300.2	161653.1
618970.6	279775.6	311588.3	452686.1	145570.3	441136.6	278890.1	161542.4
2999151.2	1929320.4	851496.9	892175.5	210524.4	2114110.2	1829294.8	279203.8
542452.0	313382.7	158994.5	223653.9	66042.2	292030.0	254701.5	34247.7

11-11 续表

单位：万元

区县名称	Name of District and County	所有者权益合计 Total Owners' Equities	实收资本 Total Capital Hold	主营业务收入 Revenue from Principal Business	主营业务成本 Cost of Principal Business	主营业务税金及附加 Taxes and Other Charges on Principal Business
新城区	Xingcheng	838867.2	277753.5	2072094.6	1312594.2	3709.0
区属	Under District	217740.7	107522.3	1402121.6	747985.7	2209.0
碑林区	Beilin	490348.8	251157.7	554093.6	472382.6	2309.3
区属	Under District	405203.8	206492.7	495391.2	432847.6	2085.6
莲湖区	Lianhu	2102115.6	713014.4	3634711.0	2852883.0	21591.3
区属	Under District	1738006.3	565646.8	3273764.2	2565736.5	20070.4
灞桥区	Baqiao	546709.5	197477.1	1728960.2	1427798.9	11149.0
区属	Under District	284465.3	166683.5	1556382.7	1305408.8	10530.7
未央区	Weiyang	1682530.8	983763.3	3975206.0	3306956.9	115997.8
区属	Under District	438519.7	321883.6	1657109.4	1391402.7	110067.2
雁塔区	Yanta	1876874.3	998973.5	2357549.9	1910611.2	13660.6
区属	Under District	195841.6	130896.3	381063.6	329670.1	1584.7
阎良区	Yanliang	947132.4	249535.9	1283945.2	1068394.5	4348.5
区属	Under District	74516.0	39353.0	242170.6	192558.3	1578.8
临潼区	Lintong	682364.5	136241.6	1532916.0	1297643.8	2697.7
区属	Under District	682364.5	136241.6	1532916.0	1297643.8	2697.7
长安区	Chang'an	818773.2	403099.3	2791234.6	2304910.9	69339.3
区属	Under District	77375.4	61010.5	237436.7	214558.7	1341.5
蓝田县	Lantian	92129.8	34635.6	191456.2	121502.1	589.7
县属	Under County	90283.6	34193.2	184347.5	115209.8	589.7
周至县	Zhouzhi	24915.0	35741.7	75695.0	65136.2	367.1
县属	Under County	24915.0	35741.7	75695.0	65136.2	367.1
户县	Huxian	329636.1	206683.2	707834.3	629443.7	2479.6
县属	Under County	177824.9	152386.7	553288.5	487066.8	2148.5
高陵县	Gaoling	875178.4	656574.0	2939460.9	2644610.6	5723.7
县属	Under County	240621.2	144498.1	409669.3	354140.7	2402.2

continued

(10 000 yuan)

营业费用 Expenses for Operation	管理费用 Expenses for Management	财务费用 Financial cost	营业利润 Operating Profit	利润总额 Total Profits	亏损企业亏损总额 Total Loss of Deficit Enterprises	利税总额 Total Pre-tax Profits	本年应交增值税 Value Added Tax Payable
186698.8	108284.8	16716.6	462317.4	472949.1	3839.3	587631.3	110973.2
180247.9	30829.3	12349.4	439073.2	440156.6	3308.6	543160.0	100794.4
19200.7	33240.1	27362.8	13324.3	11182.5	11904.9	26704.3	13212.5
15013.1	24561.6	20321.2	14910.8	12680.5	5887.6	23186.5	8420.4
204741.7	259340.6	23030.9	289205.4	306469.3	2391.6	456105.2	128044.6
199608.1	219753.6	16664.3	265863.1	277726.2	2391.6	422439.2	124642.6
48244.8	95025.5	27225.9	130878.4	112942.0	6761.2	173931.8	49840.8
42490.7	63914.0	25181.6	117696.2	97943.9	6761.2	152029.6	43555.0
166235.2	193889.4	36141.8	202089.0	204686.0	17249.6	428420.8	107737.0
36136.7	64732.5	5711.1	61561.2	59547.6	5833.9	225965.2	56350.4
123735.6	214465.7	35304.8	59065.0	76899.4	96071.4	202373.3	111813.3
15641.4	33708.3	3636.8	6265.4	10767.1	13350.3	29930.6	17578.8
30728.9	69816.6	12397.3	71967.6	81704.7	228.5	91708.8	5655.6
8691.7	11212.6	1302.0	23109.5	12817.0	0.0	16738.2	2342.4
87503.9	95064.9	-2556.0	319331.8	73917.0	1806.3	117583.3	40968.6
87503.9	95064.9	-2556.0	319331.8	73917.0	1806.3	117583.3	40968.6
56074.8	67112.3	10643.3	302354.7	319161.6	5936.9	515510.2	127009.3
6937.6	8775.8	2241.7	7847.0	3283.1	1635.6	10352.1	5727.5
2648.9	7547.7	9907.9	29270.2	33089.8	2296.0	42529.9	8850.4
2523.8	6946.2	9839.8	29248.5	32944.9	2296.0	42378.8	8844.2
3049.0	6243.0	759.8	4694.0	2222.8	1050.8	3554.0	964.1
3049.0	6243.0	759.8	4694.0	2222.8	1050.8	3554.0	964.1
25114.6	30643.1	16765.0	30189.4	10887.9	14544.3	36412.3	23044.8
22472.1	17280.5	14988.8	34632.0	13047.1	12385.1	34242.3	19046.7
88765.1	114068.4	20095.8	49057.3	65847.8	15184.7	124345.8	52774.3
11919.8	22055.2	3988.4	16175.6	17626.0	6608.3	42399.3	22371.1

11-12 规模以上工业企业能源购进、消费及库存（2009年）

能源名称	Name(unit)	年初库存 Stock (year-beginning)	购进量 实物量 Quantity
原煤(吨)	Raw Coal（ton）	872646	7612015
洗精煤(吨)	Washing Coal(ton)		1388
其他洗煤(吨)	Other Washed Coals(ton)		7982
型煤(吨)	Briquettes(ton)	1085	15270
焦炭(吨)	Coke(ton)	1707	58493
其他焦化产品(吨)	Other Coking Products(ton)	23	3182
其他煤气(万立方米)	Other Gases(10 000cu.m)		
天然气(万立方米)	Natural Gas(10 000cu.m)		9375
原油(吨)	Crude Oil(ton)	36180	1686264
汽油(吨)	Gasoline(ton)	223	357402
煤油(吨)	Kerosene(ton)	444	11549
柴油(吨)	Diesel Oil(ton)	1653	363245
燃料油(吨)	Fuel Oil(ton)	333	412
液化石油气(吨)	LPG(ton)		896
其他石油制品(吨)	Other Petroleum Products(ton)	117	4930
热力(百万千焦)	Heat (1 million kilo-joule)		8735430
电力(万千瓦时)	Electricity(10 000kwh)		673893
能源合计(吨标准煤)	Total Energy(ton of SCE)		

Energy Purchases Consumption and Inventory of Industrial Enterprises Above Designafed size（2009）

Purchases	消费量			Consumption	年末库存
金额（万元） Sum (10 000 yuan)	合计 Total	工业生产消费 Industrial Production Consume	用于原材料 as raw Material	非工业生产消费 Non-industrial Production Consume	Stock year-end
309347.2	7840721	7741653	54234	99068	637541
114.1	1388	1388			
422.4	7982	4488		3494	
915.6	15167	11769	593	3398	560
9408.7	57750	57750	1207		2450
350.9	2792	2792			413
15553.2	9375	8956	190	419	
633530.6	1688958	1688958			33486
208607.3	357367	352399	1848	4968	258
7972.8	11409	11405	1	4	584
185707.0	363707	360516	201	3191	1191
206.4	515	515			230
409.2	896	890		6	
6969.2	16915	16915	95	0	67
37471.8	10281211	8769835		1511376	
314896.5	750667	732251		18416	
	10169482	10001573		167909	

11-13 主要能源按工业行业分组消费量（2009年）

行　业	Sector	原煤（吨） Raw Coal (ton)
总　计	**Total**	**7840721**
按工业行业大类分列	Grouped by Sector	
煤炭开采和洗选业	Coal Mining and Dressing	
石油和天然气开采业	Petroleum and Natural Gas Extraction	
黑色金属矿采选业	Ferrous Metals Mining and Dressing	
有色金属矿采选业	Nonferrous Metals Mining and Dressing	702
非金属矿采选业	Nonmetal Minerals Mining and Dressing	
其他采矿业	Other mining industry	
农副食品加工业	Agricultural products and non-stable food processing industry	246205
食品制造业	Food Production	60358
饮料制造业	Beverage Production	137179
烟草制品业	Tobacco Processing	7
纺织业	Textile Industry	18103
纺织服装、鞋、帽制造业	Textile clothing, footwear and headgear industry	6
皮革、毛皮、羽毛(绒)及其制品业	Leather, fur, feather (eiderdown) and their products industry	
木材加工及木、竹、藤、棕、草制品制造	Timber Processing,Bamboo,Cane,Palm Fiber and Straw Products	6408
家具制造业	Furniture Manufacturing	
造纸及纸制品业	Papermaking and Paper products	500236
印刷业和记录媒介的复制	Printing,Record Medium Reproduction	276
文教体育用品制造业	Cultural,Educational and Sports Goods	180
石油加工、炼焦及核燃料加工业	Petroleum refining, coke making and nuclear fuel processing industry	20778
化学原料及化学制品制造业	Raw Chemical Materials and Chemical Products	395370
医药制造业	Medical and Pharmaceutical Products	42148
化学纤维制造业	Chemical Fiber	25
橡胶制品业	Rubber Products	400
塑料制品业	Plastic Products	3315
非金属矿物制品业	Nonmetal Mineral Products	391372
黑色金属冶炼及压延加工业	Smelting and Pressing of Ferrous Metals	67259
有色金属冶炼及压延加工业	Smelting and Pressing of Nonferrou Metals	5355
金属制品业	Metal Products	9540
通用设备制造	General equipment manufacturing industry	30336
专用设备制造业	Special Purpose Equipment	85312
交通运输设备制造业	Transport Equipment	333695
电气机械及器材制造业	Electric Equipment and Machinery	6846
通信设备、计算机及其他电子设备制造业	Communication equipment, computer and other electronic equipment manufacturing industry	5567
仪器仪表及文化办公用机械制造业	Instruments,Meters,Cultural and Office	52
工艺品及其他制造业	Handicraft and other stuff manufacturing industry	5008
废弃资源和废旧材料回收加工业	Discarded resources and waste materials salvaging and processing industry	
电力、热力的生产和供应业	Electric power, heating power generating and supplying industry	5468683
燃气生产和供应业	Gas mining and supplying industry	
水的生产和供应业	Water processing and supplying industry	

Majar Energy Consumption by Sector（2009）

天然气(万立方米) Natural Gas(10 000cu.m)	原油(吨) Crude Oil (ton)	汽油（吨） Gasoline (ton)	柴油（吨） Diesel Oil (ton)	热能（百万千焦） Heat (million kilo-joule)	电力（万千瓦时） Electricity (10 000kwh)
9375	**1688958**	**357367**	**363707**	**10281211**	**750667**
40		168	897		328
		6			40
154		72		12505	4942
2		678	1032		16106
48	1	456	319	283071	7805
135		360	246	494113	18942
		12		5895	145
		153	21	483723	32113
4		87			1170
		67		31100	151
		43	16		7060
		137	63		656
		1454	243	37440	27532
174		506	327	67557	6732
		26			152
154	1688953	331053	320385		27050
295		2283	1528	2371199	56560
847		1001	143	338424	9656
		20	15	738723	2787
		61	18		758
186		328	1299	19870	12170
244		2207	14210	49409	47605
56		81	59	106114	38503
291		354	515	104582	12998
5	4	777	240		4222
123		1263	523	40142	21132
478		3166	7200	1043195	30392
2473		6018	9910	812096	101444
1945		2195	1072	921769	30378
1339		747	137	802105	20996
43		586	31	405449	5226
		47	22		1023
					12
		382	3089	1112730	192658
210		306	134		3155
131		264	15		8070

11-14 规模以上工业分行业综合能源消费量（2009年）

Majar Energy Consumption by Sector Above Designated Size（2009）

单位：吨标准煤 (ton of SCE)

指　　标	Item	2009	比上年增长（%） Increase over Preceding Year (%)
合　计	**Total**	**4928305**	**6.0**
煤炭开采和洗选业	Coal Mining and Dressing		
石油和天然气开采业	Petroleum and Natural Gas Extraction	277	18.1
黑色金属矿采选业	Ferrous Metals Mining and Dressing	58	-68.9
有色金属矿采选业	Nonferrous Metals Mining and Dressing	8680	-36.9
非金属矿采选业	Nonmetal Minerals Mining and Dressing	2578	-6.3
其他采矿业	Other mining industry		
农副食品加工业	Agricultural products and non-stable food processing industry	197415	10.7
食品制造业	Food Production	66244	3.0
饮料制造业	Beverage Production	139483	7.0
烟草制品业	Tobacco Processing	402	-10.6
纺织业	Textile Industry	62707	-12.6
纺织服装、鞋、帽制造业	Textile clothing, footwear and headgear industry	1606	-13.0
皮革、毛皮、羽毛(绒)及其制品业	Leather, fur, feather (eiderdown) and their products industry		
木材加工及木、竹、藤、棕、草制品制造	Timber Processing,Bamboo,Cane,Palm Fiber and Straw Products	12243	21.2
家具制造业	Furniture Manufacturing	939	3.3
造纸及纸制品业	Papermaking and Paper products	372508	9.0
印刷业和记录媒介的复制	Printing,Record Medium Reproduction	13572	-4.1
文教体育用品制造业	Cultural,Educational and Sports Goods	346	120.9
石油加工、炼焦及核燃料加工业	Petroleum refining, coke making and nuclear fuel processing industry	273553	-2.6
化学原料及化学制品制造业	Raw Chemical Materials and Chemical Products	273525	-31.0
医药制造业	Medical and Pharmaceutical Products	63577	4.2
化学纤维制造业	Chemical Fiber	28683	-5.1
橡胶制品业	Rubber Products	1869	-51.6
塑料制品业	Plastic Products	22694	20.6
非金属矿物制品业	Nonmetal Mineral Products	360625	6.5
黑色金属冶炼及压延加工业	Smelting and Pressing of Ferrous Metals	105587	86.3
有色金属冶炼及压延加工业	Smelting and Pressing of Nonferrou Metals	27416	-29.4
金属制品业	Metal Products	11965	8.5
通用设备制造	General equipment manufacturing industry	60644	-15.3
专用设备制造业	Special Purpose Equipment	57898	-17.4
交通运输设备制造业	Transport Equipment	187898	4.5
电气机械及器材制造业	Electric Equipment and Machinery	99877	2.8
通信设备、计算机及其他电子设备制造业	Communication equipment, computer and other electronic equipment manufacturing industry	48554	-42.8
仪器仪表及文化办公用机械制造业	Instruments,Meters,Cultural and Office	4215	2.1
工艺品及其他制造业	Handicraft and other stuff manufacturing industry	6250	17.2
废弃资源和废旧材料回收加工业	Discarded resources and waste materials salvaging and processing industry	15	63.1
电力、热力的生产和供应业	Electric power, heating power generating and supplying industry	1991438	20.5
燃气生产和供应业	Gas mining and supplying industry	7103	24.8
水的生产和供应业	Water processing and supplying industry	10472	-18.8

主要统计指标解释

工业 指从事自然资源的开采，对采掘品和农产品进行加工和再加工的物质生产部门。具体包括:（1）对自然资源的开采，如采矿、晒盐等（但不包括禽兽捕猎和水产捕捞）;（2）对农副产品的加工、再加工，如粮油加工、食品加工、轧花、缫丝、纺织、制革等;（3）对采掘品的加工、再加工，如炼铁、炼钢、化工生产、石油加工、机器制造、木材加工等，以及电力、自来水、煤气的生产和供应等;（4）对工业品的修理、翻新，如机器设备的修理、交通运输工具（包括小卧车）的修理等。

1984年以前农村的村及村以下办工业归属农业，1984年以后划归工业。

工业统计调查单位 工业统计调查单位分为两类:独立核算法人工业企业和工业活动单位。

（1）独立核算法人工业企业 是指从事工业生产经营活动的单位。独立核算法人工业企业应同时具备以下条件:①依法成立，有自己的名称、组织机构和场所，能够承担民事责任;②独立拥有和使用资产，承担负债，有权与其他单位签订合同;③独立核算盈亏，并能够编制资产负债表。

（2）工业活动单位 是指在一个场所从事一种或主要从事一种工业生产活动的经济单位。它包括独立核算工业企业按主营业务活动（即工业生产活动）划分的主营业务活动单位和非工业企业所属的工业生产活动单位（即原非独立核算工业生产单位）。工业活动单位，一般应同时具备以下三个条件:①具有一个场所，从事一种或主要从事一种工业活动;②单独组织工业生产、经营或业务活动;③单独核算收入和支出。

本年鉴中涉及的企业登记注册类型:

（1）国有及国有控股企业 指国有企业加上国有控股企业。国有企业（即过去的全民所有制工业或国营工业）是指企业全部资产归国家所有，并按《中华人民共和国企业法人登记管理条例》规定登记注册的非公司制的经济组织。包括国有企业、国有独资公司和国有联营企业。1957年以前的公私合营和私营工业，后均改造为国营工业，这部分工业的资料不单独分列时，均包括在国有企业内。

（2）集体企业 指企业资产归集体所有，并按《中华人民共和国企业法人登记管理条例》规定登记注册的经济组织。是社会主义公有制经济的组成部分。包括城乡所有使用集体投资举办的企业，以及部分个人通过集资自愿放弃所有权并依法经工商行政管理机关认定为集体所有制的企业。

（3）股份合作企业 指以合作制为基础，由企业职工共同出资入股，吸收一定比例的社会资产投资组建，实行自主经营，自负盈亏，共同劳动，民主管理，按劳分配与按股分红相结合的一种集体经济组织。

（4）联营企业 指两个及两个以上相同或不同所有制性质的企业法人或事业单位法人，按自愿、平等、互利的原则，共同投资组成的经济组织。联营企业包括:

国有联营企业指国有企业与国有企业间的联营;

集体联营企业指集体企业与集体企业间的联营;

国有与集体联营企业指国有企业与集体企业间的联营。

（5）有限责任公司 指根据《中华人民共和国公司登记管理条例》规定登记注册，由两个以上，五十个以下的股东共同出资，每个股东以其所认缴的出资额对公司承担有限责任，公司以其全部资产对其债务承担责任的经济组织。

有限责任公司包括国有独资公司以及其他有限责任公司。

（6）股份有限公司 指根据《中华人民共和国企业法人登记管理条例》规定登记注册，其全部注册资本由等额股份构成并通过发行股票筹集资本，股东以其认购的股份对公司承担有限责任，公司以其全部资产对其债务承担责任的经济组织。

（7）私营企业 指由自然人投资设立或由自然人控股，以雇佣劳动为基础的营利性经济组织。包括按照《公司法》、《合伙企业法》、《私营企业暂行条例》规定登记注册的私营有限责任公司、私营股份有限公司、私营合伙企业和私营独资企业。

（8）港、澳、台商投资企业 指企业注册登记类型中的港、澳、台资合资、合作、独资经营企业和股份有限公司之和。

（9）外商投资企业 指企业注册登记类型中的中外合资、合作经营企业、外资企业和外商投资股份有限公司之和。

轻工业 指主要提供生活消费品和制作手工工具的工业。按其所使用的原料不同，可分为两大类:（1）以农产品为原料的轻工业，是指直接或间接以农产品为基本原料的轻工业。主要包括食品制造、饮料制造、烟草加工、纺织、缝纫、皮革和毛皮制作、造纸以及印刷等工业;（2）以非农产品为原料的轻工业，是指以工业品为原料的轻工业。主要包括文教体育用品、化学药品制造、合成纤维制造、日用化学制品、日用玻璃制品、日用金属制品、手工工具制造、医疗器械制造、文化和办公用机械制造等工业。

重工业 是指为国民经济各部门提供物质技术基础的主要生产资料的工业。按其生产性质和产品用途，可以分为下列三类:（1）采掘（伐）工业，是指对自然资源的开采，包括石油开采、煤炭开采、金属矿开采、非金属矿开采和木材采伐等工业;（2）原材料工业，指向国民经济各部门提供基本材料、动力和燃料的工业。包括金属冶炼及加工、炼焦及焦炭、化学、化工原料、水泥、人造板以及电力、石油和煤炭加工等工业;（3）加工工业，是指对工业原材料进行再加工制造的工业。包括装备国民经济各部门的机械设备制造工业、金属结构、水泥制品等工业，以及为农业提供的生产资料如化肥、农药等工业。

根据上述划分原则，修理业中以重工业产品为修理作业对象的划为重工业，反之划为轻工业。

工业总产值 是以货币表现的工业企业在一定时期内生产的已出售或可供出售工业产品总量，它反映一定时间内工业生产的总规模和总水平。它包括：在本企业内不再进行加工，经检验、包装入库（规定不需包装的产品除外）的成品价值，对外加工费收入，自制半成品、在产品期末初差额价值。工业总产值采用“工厂法”计算，即以工业企业作为一个整体，按企业工业生产活动的最终成果来计算，企业内部不允许重复计算，不能把企业内部各个车间（分厂）生产的成果相加。但在企业之间、行业之间、地区之间存在着重复计算。

轻重工业总产值的划分是按“工厂法”计算的，即一个工业企业生产的主要产品性质属于轻工业，则该企业的全部总产值作为轻工业总产值；如它的主要产品性质属于重工业，则该企业的全部总产值作为重工业总产值。

工业增加值 指工业行业在报告期内以货币表现的工业生产活动的最终成果。

实收资本 指企业实际收到的投资人投入的资本。按投资主体可分为国家资本、集体资本、法人资本、个人资本、港澳台资本和外商资本等。

资产合计 指企业拥有或控制的能以货币计量的经济资源。包括各种财产、债权和其他权利。资产按其流动性划分为流动资产、长期投资、固定资产、无形及递延资产和其他资产。

（1）流动资产　指企业可以在一年内或者超过一年的一个生产周期内变现或耗用的资产合计。包括现金及各种存款、短期投资、应收及预付款项、存货等。

（2）固定资产 指企业固定资产净值、固定资产清理、在建工程、待处理固定资产损失所占用的资金合计。

（3）无形资产 指企业长期使用而没有实物形态的资产。包括专利权、非专利技术、商标权、著作权、土地使用权、商誉等。

负债合计 指企业承担的能以货币计量，将以资产或劳务偿付的债务。负债一般按偿还期长短分为流动负债和长期负债、递延税项等。

（1）流动负债　指企业在一年内或者超过一年的一个营业周期内需要偿还的债务合计，其中包括短期借款、应付及预收款项、应付工资、应交税金和应交利润等。

（2）长期负债　指企业在一年以上或者超过一年的一个营业周期以上需要偿还的债务合计，其中包括长期借款、应付债务、长期应付款项等。

所有者权益 指企业投资人对企业净资产的所有权。企业净资产等于企业全部资产减去全部负债后的余额，其中包括投资者对企业的最初投入，以及资本公积金、盈余公积金和未分配利润，对股份制企业即为股东权益。

固定资产原价　指企业在建造、购置、安装、改建、扩建、技术改造某项固定资产时所支出的全部货币总额。它一般包括买价、包装费、运杂费和安装费等。

固定资产净值　是指固定资产原价减去历年已提折旧额后的净额。

流动资产 是指可以在一年或者超过一年的一个营业周期内变现或者耗用的资产，包括现金及各种存款、短期投资、应收及预付货款、存货等。

主营业务收入 根据会计“利润表”中对应指标的本年累计数填列。未执行2001年《企业会计制度》的企业，用“产品销售收入”的本期累计数代替。

主营业务成本 根据会计“利润表”中对应指标的本年累计数填列。未执行2001年《企业会计制度》的企业，用“产品销售成本”的本期累计数代替。

营业费用 根据会计“利润表”中对应指标的本年累计数填列。未执行2001年《企业会计制度》的企业，用“产品销售费用”的本期累计数代替。

主营业务税金及附加 根据会计“利润表”中对应指标的本年累计数填列。未执行2001年《企业会计制度》的企业，用“产品销售税金及附加”的本期累计数代替。

利润总额 指企业实现的利润。

应交增值税 指企业在报告期内应交纳的增值税额。

总资产贡献率 反映企业全部资产的获利能力，是企业经营业绩和管理水平的集中体现，是评价和考核企业盈利能力的核心指标。计算公式为:

总资产贡献率=(利润总额+税金总额+利息支出)/平均资产总额*100%

资本保值增值率 该指标反映企业净资产的变动状况，是企业发展能力的集中体现。计算公式为：

资本保值增值率（％）=报告期期末所有者权益/上年同期期末所有者权益*100%

资产负债率 该指标既反映企业经营风险的大小，也反映企业利用债权人提供的资金从事经营活动的能力。计算公式为:

资产负债率=负债总额/资产总额*100%

工业成本费用利润率 指在一定时期内实现的利润与成本费用之比，是反映工业生产成本及费用投入的经济效益指标，同时也是反映降低成本的经济效益的指标。计算公式为:

工业成本费用利润率(%)=利润总额/成本及费用总额*100%

工业增加值率 指在一定时期内工业增加值占同期工业总产值的比重，反映降低中间消耗的经济效益。计算公式为:

工业增加值率(%)=工业增加值(现价)/工业总产值*100%

流动资产周转次数 指在一定时期内流动资产完成的周转次数，反映流动资产的周转速度。计算公式为:

流动资产周转次数=产品销售收入/全部流动资产平均余额

产品销售率 指报告期工业销售产值与同期全部工业总产值之比，是反映工业产品已实现销售的程度，分析工业产销衔接情况，研究工业产品满足社会需求程度的指标。计算公式为:

产品销售率(%)=工业销售产值/工业总产值(现价)*100%

全员劳动生产率 指根据产品的价值量指标计算的平均每一个就业人员在单位时间内的产品生产量。是考核企业经济活动的重要指标，是企业生产技术水平、经营管理水平、职工技术熟练程度和劳动积极性的综合表现。目前我国的全员劳动生产率是将工业企业的工业增加值除以同一时期全部就业人员的平均人数来计算的。计算公式为:

全员劳动生产率(%)=工业增加值/全部就业人员平均人数*100%

能源消费量 指能源使用单位在报告期内实际消费的一次能源或二次能源的数量。具体包括原煤和原油及其制品、天然气、电力等。

工业生产能源消费 指工业企业为进行工业生产活动所消费的能源。

非工业生产能源消费 指在工业企业能源消费中，除“工业生产能源消费”以外的能源消费，即非工业生产用能和工业企业附属的不从事工业生产活动的非独立核算单位用能。

交通运输工具用能 指在厂区内、外进行交通运输活动的交通运输工具所消费的能源。

能源加工转换投入 能源的加工转换是指为了特定的用途，将一种能源（一般为一次能源），经过一定的工艺，加工或转换成另外一种能源（一般为二次能源）。能源加工转换的投入即能源加工、转换消费。

一次能源 是指自然界中以现成形式存在，不经任何改变或转换的天然能源资源，即从自然界直接取得并不改变其形态和品位的能源。如原煤、原油、天然气、核燃料、植物燃料、风能、水能、太阳能、地热能、海洋能、潮汐能等。

二次能源 是指为了满足生产工艺和生活的特定需要以合理利用能源，将一次能源直接或间接加工转换产生的其它种类和形式的人工能源。如原煤加工产出的洗煤；由煤炭加工转换产出的焦炭，煤气；由原油加工产出的汽油、煤油、柴油、燃料油、液化石油气、炼厂干气等；由煤炭、石油、天然气转换产出的电力。

综合能源消费量 报告期内工业企业在工业生产活动中实际消费的各种能源的总和净值。计算综合能源消费量时，需要先将使用的各种能源折算成标准燃料后再进行计算。

Explanatory Notes on Main Statistical Indicators

Industry refers to the material production sector which is engaged in extraction of natural resources and processing and reprocessing of minerals and agricultural products, including (1) extraction of natural resources, such as mining, salt production, (but not including hunting and fishing); (2) processing and reprocessing of farm and sideline produces, such as rice husking, flour milling, wine making, oil pressing, cotton ginning, silk reeling, spinning and weaving, and leather making; (3) manufacture of industrial products, such as steel making, iron smelting, chemicals manufacturing, petroleum processing, machine building, timber processing; water and gas production and electricity generation and supply; (4)repairing of industrial products such as the repairing of machinery and means of transport (including cars).

Prior to 1984, the rural industry run by villages and cooperative organizations under village was classified into agriculture. Since 1984, it has been grouped into industry.

Units of Industrial Statistics and Inquiry: They are classified into two categories (1) corporate industrial enterprises with independent accounting system (2) industrial establishments.

(1) Corporate industrial enterprises with independent accounting system refer to enterprises engaging in industrial production activities, which meet the following requirements: ① They are established legally, having their own names, organizations, location, able to take civil liability; ②They possess and use their assets independently, assume liabilities, and are entitled to sign contracts with other units; ③They are financially independent and compile their own balance sheets.

(2)Industrial establishments refer to economic units which located in one single place and engaged entirely or primarily in one kind of industrial activity, including financially independent industrial enterprises and units engaged in industrial activities under the non industrial enterprises (or financially dependent). Industrial establishments generally meet the following requirements: ① They have each one location and are engaged in one kind of industrial activity each; ② They operate and manage their industrial production activities separately;③ Theyhave accounts of income and expenditures separately.

(1) State-owned Enterprises refer to industrial enterprises where the means of production or income are owned by the state. Joint state-private industries and private industries, which existed before 1957, have been transformed into state industries. Statistics on these enterprises has been included in the state-owned industries since 1957 when separation of data was no longer necessary.

(2) Collective-owned Enterprises refer to industrial enterprises where the means of production are owned collectively, including urban and rural enterprises invested by collectives and some enterprises which were formerly owned privately but have been registered in industrial and commercial administration agency as collective units through raising fund from the public.

(3) Share-holding Cooperative Enterprises refer to economic units set up on cooperative basis, with funding partly from members of the enterprise and partly from outside investment, where the operation and management is decided by the members who also participate in the production, and the distribution of income is based both on work (labour input) and on shares (capital input).

(4) Joint-operation enterprises refer to economic units that are established by joint investment by two or more corporate enterprises or institutions of the same or different types of ownership on voluntary, equal and mutual-beneficial basis. They include:

a) state-owned joint-operation enterprises (joint operation between state-owned enterprises);

b) collective joint-operation enterprises (joint operation between collective enterprises; and

c) state-collective joint-operation enterprises (joint operation between state and collective enterprises).

(5) Limited Liability Corporations refer to economic units registered in accordance with the Regulation of the People's Republic of China on the Management of Registration of Corporations, with capitals from 2 to 49 investors, each investor bears limited liability to the corporation depending on his/her holding of shares, and the corporation bears liability to its debt to the maximum of its total assets.

(6) Share-holding Corporations Ltd. refer to economic units registered in accordance with the Regulation of the People's Republic of China on the Management of Registration of Corporate Enterprises, with total registered capitals divided into equal shares and raised through issuing stocks. Each investor bears limited liability to the corporation depending on the holding of shares, and the corporation bears liability to its debt to the maximum of its total assets.

(7) Private Enterprises refer to economic unitsinvested or controlled (by holding the majority of the shares) by natural persons who hire labours for profit-making activities. Included in this category are private limited liability corporations, private share-holding corporations Ltd., private partnership enterprises and private sole investment enterprises registered in accordance with the Corporation Law, Partnership Enterprise Law and Tentative Regulation on Private Enterprises.

(8) Enterprises with Funds form Hong Kong, Macao and Taiwan refers to all industrial enterprises registered as the joint-venture, cooperative, sole (exclusive) investment industrial enterprises and limited liability corporations with funds from Hong Kong, Macao and Taiwan.

(9) Foreign Funded Enterprises refers to all industrial enterprises registered as the joint-venture, cooperative, sole (exclusive) investment industrial enterprises and limited liability corporations with foreign funds.

Light Industry refers to the industry that produces consumer goods and hand tools. It consists of two categories, depending on the materials used:

(1)Industries using farm products as raw materials. These are branches of light industry which directly or indirectly use farm products as basic raw materials, including the manufacture of food and beverages, tobacco processing, textile, clothing, fur and leather manufacturing, paper making, printing, etc.

(2)Industries using non farm products as raw materials. These are branches of light industry which use manufactured goods as raw materials, including the manufacture of cultural, educational articles and sports goods, chemicals, synthetic fiber, chemical products for daily use, glass products for daily use, metal products for daily use, hand tools, medical apparatus and instruments, and the manufacture of cultural and clerical machinery.

Heavy Industry refers to the industry which produces capital goods, and provides various sectors of the national economy with necessary material and technical basis. It consists of the following three branches according to the purpose of production or the use of products:

(1)Mining, quarrying and logging industry refers to the industry that extracts natural resources, including extraction of petroleum, coal, metal and non-metal ores and logging.

(2)Raw materials industry refers to the industry that provides various sectors of the national economy with raw materials, fuels and power. It includes smelting and processing of metals, coking and coke chemistry, chemical materials and building materials such as cement, plywood, and power, petroleum refining and coal dressing.

(3)Manufacturing industry refers to the industry that processes raw materials. It includes machine building industry which equips sectors of the national economy, industries of metal structure and cement products, industries producing means of agricultural production, such as chemical fertilizers and pesticides. According to the above principle of classification, the repairing trades which are engaged primarily in repairing products of heavy industry are classified into heavy industry while these engaged in repairing products of light industry are classified into light industry.

Gross Industrial Output Value is the total volume of industrial products sold or available for sale in value terms which reflects the total achievements and overall scale of industrial production during a given period. It includes the value of the finished products, which are not to be further processed in the enterprises and have been inspected, packed and put in storage, the value of industrial services rendered to other units, and the changes in the value of the semi-finished products and products in process between the beginning and closing of the period. The gross industrial output value is calculated with "factory method". No double calculations are to be made within the same enterprise. However, double counting does occur among different enterprises.

Output value of light and heavy industries is based on the "factory" method. If the major products of an industrial enterprise are classified as light industry products, the entire gross output value of that enterprise is classified into the light industry; the same principle applies to heavy industry.

Value-added of Industry refers to the final results of industrial production of the industrial trade in money terms during the reference period.

Capital Obtained refers to capital actually received by the enterprise from investors. It can be further classified by investors as state capital, collective capital, corporate capital, individual capital, capital from Hong Kong, Macau and Taiwan and foreign capital.

Total Assets refer to all economic resources, owned or controlled by enterprises, that could be measured in monetary terms, including properties, creditors equity and other economic rights of all forms. Classified by the degree of equitability, total assets include circulating assets, long term investment, fixed assets, intangible assets anddeferred assets, and other assets.

(1)Circulating assets (working capital) refer to assets which can be cashed in or spent or consumed in anoperating cycle of one year or over one year, including cash, all kinds of deposits, short term investment, receivables, advance payment, stock, etc.

(2)Fixed assets refer to the net value of fixed assets, clearance of fixed assets, project under construction, fixed assets losses in suspense. These are corporations fund holdings.

(3)Intangible assets refer to the assets without material form used by enterprises over a long time, such as patents, non-patent technologies, trade marks, copyright, land use right, business reputation, etc.

Total Liabilities refer to the debts, measured in monetary terms, that enterprises are responsible for repayment in the form of cash, assets or labour. Classified by terms of repayment, liability include liquid liabilities and long-term liabilities.

(1)Liquid liabilities (also called quick liabilities or immediate liabilities) refer to enterprises' total debt payable within an operating cycle of one year or over one year, including short term loans, payable and advance payments, wages payable, taxes payable and profit payable, etc.

(2)Long term liabilities refers to total debt payable within an operating cycle of one year or over one year, including long-term loans, payable liabilities, long-term payable, etc.

Creditors' Equity refers to investors ownership of net assets of the enterprise. It is equal to the total assets of the enterprise minus its total liabilities, including the primary input from investors, capital accumulation fund, surplus accumulation fund and undistributed profit. It is the shareholder's equity in share-holding companies.

Original Value of Fixed Assets refers to the original value of all fixed assets owned by industrial enterprises, calculated at the cost paid at the time of purchase, installation, reconstruction, expansion, and technical innovation and transformation of the said assets, which includes expenses on purchase, package, transportation, and installation, etc.

Net Value of Fixed Assets is obtained by deducting depreciation over years from the original value of fixed assets.

Working Capital (Circulating Assets) refers to assets which can be cashed in or spent or consumed in an operating cycle of one year or over one year, which includes cash, various deposits, short term investment, and receivable payments, and advance payments, stock, etc.

Income from Main Operation Filled by cumulative number of related index in 'profit table' in current year. it is replaced by cumulative number of 'sales revenue' in current period, as to the enterprises not operating by 'Enterprise Accounting System' of 2001.

Cost of Main Operation Filled by cumulative number of related index in 'profit table' in current year. it is replaced by cumulative number of 'cost of sales' in current period, as to the enterprises not operating by 'Enterprise Accounting System' of 2001.

Expenses for Operation Filled by cumulative number of related index in 'profit table' in current year. it is replaced by cumulative number of 'sales of expense' in current period, as to the enterprises not operating by 'Enterprise Accounting System' of 2001.

Main Operation Tax and Extra Charges Filled by cumulative number of related index in 'profit table' in current year. it is replaced by cumulative number of 'sales tax and extra charges' in current period, as to the enterprises not operating by 'Enterprise Accounting System' of 2001.

Total Profits refer to the profits gained by the enterprises.

Value-added Tax Payable refers to the amount of the value added tax which should be paid by the enterprises in the reporting period.

Ratio of Profits, Taxes and Interests to Average Assets reflects the profit-making capability of all assets of the enterprise and is a key indicator manifesting the performance and management and evaluating the profit-making potential of the enterprise. It is calculated as follows:

Ratio of profits, taxes and interests to average assets (%) = [(Total profits+total Taxes+interest payment) / average assets]×100%

The Rate of Value-Sustained and Value-Added Assets reflects the indicator of net assets changes of enterprises and the embodiment of the enterprise development.

The rate of value-sustained and value-added assets=owner's equity at the end of current period/ owner's equity at the same period of last year*100%

Ratio of Debts to Assets reflect both the operation risk and the capability of the enterprise in making use ofthe capital from the creditors. It is calculated as follows:

Ratio of debts to assets (%) = (Total debts / total assets)×100%

Ratio of Profits to Total Industrial Costs refers to the ratio of profits realized in a given period to the total costs in the same period, which reflects the economic efficiency of input cost and is calculated as follows:

Ratio of Profits to Total Industrial Cost(%)=(Total Profits/ Total Costs)×100%

Value-added Rate of Industry refers to the ratio of value added of industry in a given period to the gross output value in the same period, which reflects the economic efficiency of cutting down the intermediate input and is calculated as follows:

Value-added Rate of Industry(%)=[Value-added of Industry (at current prices)] / [Gross Output Value (at Current Prices)]×100%

Turnover of Working Capital refers to the number of times of turnover of working capital in a given period of time, which reflects the speed of the turnover of working capital and is calculated as follows:

Turnover of Working Capital(%)=(Sales Revenue ofProducts) / (Average Balance of Total Working Capital)×100%

Ratio of Sales to Gross Output Value refers to the sales of industrial products to the gross industrial output value during the reference period, and is important in reflecting the linkage between production and sales and the extent of the needs of the society that has been met by the supply of industrial products. It is calculated as follows:

Ratio of Sales to Gross Output Value=[Industrial sales / Gross industrial output value (at current prices)] × 100%

Overall Labour Productivity of Industrial Enterprises refers to the average output per employed person in industrial enterprises in value terms. At present, the value added and the average number of staff and workers of an industrial enterprises in a given period are used to calculate the overall labour productivity. The formula used is:

Overall Labour Productivity=(Value Added of Industry) / (Average Number of Staff and Workers)

Energy Consumption refers to the volume of primary or secondary energy actually consumed by energy utilization units in the reference period. Including raw coal, crude oil with its products , natural gas, electric power etc.

Industry Consumption Energy refers to the volume of energy consumed by Industrial enterprises for industrial production activities.

Non-industry Consumption Energy refers to the energy consumed by industrial enterprises except for industrial production activities , means that energy consumed by non-industry production and not independent accounting units which was not engaged in industrial production activities affiliated to industrial enterprises.

Vehicle Energy refers to the energy consumed by vehicles which carried out transport activities in and out of factories.

Energy Processing Conversion Devoted energy processing conversion refers to for specialized application , a source of energy (normally primary energy), after a certain technology , processed or converted to another kind of energy (normally secondary energy). The input of energy conversion processing that is energy processing, and conversion consumption.

Primary Energy Source refers to natural energy resources as found naturally in the form of ready-made , without any change or conversion , as energy obtained directly from natural and not change its shape and grade, such as raw coal, crude oil, natural gas, nuclear fuel, plant fuel, wind energy, water energy, solar energy, geothermal energy, oceanic energy, tidal energy and so on .

Secondary Energy refers to other types and forms of artificial energy which was processed and conversed from primary energy sources directly or indirectly , in order to meet the specific needs in production process and life to use energy more effectively. Such as washing coal processed from raw coal; coke and coal gas processed and transformed from raw coal; gasoline, kerosene, diesel oil, fuel oil, liquefied petroleum gas, dry gas refinery processed from crude oil; electric power conversed from coal, oil and natural gas.

Comprehensive energy consumption refers to the total and net energy actually consumed in industrial production activities by industrial enterprises in the reference period. When calculated the volume of consumption of comprehensive energy , should converted sorts of energy which was used into standards fuel firstly.

12 建筑业

CONSTRUCTION

资料整理：陈海生
Data management:Chen Haisheng

第十二部分 建筑业

一、简要说明

本章资料主要包括建筑业基本情况，建筑业施工企业生产情况和财务状况，由西安市统计局固定资产投资处提供。

二、主要指标

企业个数（个）	326	比上年减少	2个
建筑业总产值（亿元）	1296.58	比上年增长	41.6%
#国有及国有控股企业	1067.22	比上年增长	57.8%
房屋建筑竣工面积（万平方米）	2419.75	比上年增长	129.0%
房屋建筑面积竣工率（%）	61.3	比上年提高	27个百分点

12 CONSTRUCTION

Ⅰ.Brief Introduction

This chapter consists of primarily the data basic situation of the construction industry, production situation and financial situation of the construction enterprises, provided by Fixed Asset Investment Division of the Xi'an Bureau of Statistics.

Ⅱ.Major Indicators

		Increase over Preceding Year
Number of Enterprises(item)	326	-2
Total Output Value of Construction(100 mil. yuan)	1296.58	41.6%
State-owned Or State Holding Majority Shares	1067.22	57.8%
Floor Space of Buildings Completed(10 000 sq.m)	2419.75	129.0%
Rate of Floor Space of Buildings Completed(%)	61.3	27 percentage points

12-1 全市建筑施工企业基本情况（2009年）

Main Indicators on Construction Enterprise of Xi'an（2009）

指　　标	Item	合　计 Total	国有及国有控股 State-owned Or State Holding Majority Shares
企业个数(个)	Number of Enterprises (unit)	326	79
#二级以上企业（施工总承包）	First and Second Class Enterprise(Overall Cortractor For Construction)	225	68
计算劳动生产率的平均人数（人）	Average Number of Employed Persons in Calculation of Labor Productivity (person)	453580	324016
#二级以上企业（施工总承包）	First and Second Class Enterprise(Overall Cortractor For Construction)	424307	320831
建筑业总产值（千元）	Total Output Value of Construction(1 000 yuan)	129657875	106721780
#二级以上企业（施工总承包）	First and Second Class Enterprise(Overall Cortractor For Construction)	124657634	106176344
全员劳动生产率(元/人)	Overall Labor Productivity (yuan/person)	285854	329371
按总产值计算	Calculated by Total Output Value		

12-2 施工总承包和专业承包建筑业企业生产情况（2009年）

分　组	Item	签定的合同额（千元）Contract Value (1 000 yuan)
总　计	**Total**	**316636171**
#国有及国有控股	State-Owned and State Holding Majority Shares	276128763
一、按登记注册类型分	**Grouped by Registion Status**	
内资	Domestic Investment Enterprises	316628018
国有企业	State-owned Enterprises	140650173
集体企业	Collective-owned Enterprises	8454727
股份合作企业	Share-holding Corperative Enterprises	8080
联营企业	Joint Ownership Enterprises	158683
有限责任公司	Limited Liability Corporations	155977580
股份有限公司	Share-holding Corperation Ltd	7055449
私营企业	Private Enterprises	4323326
其他企业	Others	
港澳台商投资企业	Enterprises with Funds from Hong Kong,Macao and Taiwan	8153
外商投资企业	Enterprises with Foreign Investment	
二、按国民经济行业分	**Grouped by Sector**	
房屋和土木工程建筑业	Building Engineering and Civil Engineering Construction	304002304
房屋工程建筑	Building Engineering Construction	55960053
土木工程建筑	Civil Engineering Construction	248042251
建筑安装业	Installation of Construction	8853072
建筑装饰业	Fitting and Decoration	1246472
其他建筑业	Others	2534323
三、按隶属关系分	**Grouped by Administrative Relationship**	
中　央	Central	240229535
地　方	Region	76406636
四、按企业资质等级分	**Grouped by Class of Enterprises**	
1.施工总承包	Overall Contractor for Construction	306598164
#特级	Special Class	159981310
一级	First Class	117518445
二级	Second Class	25684648
2.专业承包	Special Contractor	10038007
#一级以上	First Class	5830554

Main Indicators on Overall Constructing Contractors and Professional Contractors by Registration Status（2009）

建筑业总产值（千元）Total Output Value of Constrution (1 000 yuan)	建筑工程产值 Output Value of Constrution	安装工程产值 Output Value of Installation	其他产值 Others	计算劳动生产率的平均人数（人）Average Number of Employed Persons in Calculation of Labour Productivity(person)	期末从业人数（人）Number of Employment at Year-end (person)	工程技术人员 Technical Personnel	企业总产值（千元）Total Output Value of Enterprises (1 000 yuan)
129657875	**113232091**	**12493691**	**3932093**	**461080**	**443069**	**52222**	**135491130**
106721780	93845676	9521162	3354942	331516	319540	36456	109955748
129649722	113223941	12493688	3932093	461015	443004	52206	135482977
60725315	54532389	4390663	1802263	189063	177917	19658	61950505
4715334	4195177	439144	81013	36941	38648	4250	4721756
5500	5500			75	70	32	5500
110096	105296	4000	800	998	912	226	110096
56634575	48878715	6179406	1576454	204989	199223	21699	59438341
4392775	3096476	889473	406826	9944	8319	3876	6100146
3066127	2410388	591002	64737	19005	17915	2465	3156633
8153	8150	3		65	65	16	8153
120113238	108287216	8726798	3099224	427346	413213	47912	125610847
33065826	29524845	3169677	371304	168437	166635	19682	37258211
87047412	78762371	5557121	2727920	258909	246578	28230	88352636
6507429	2942106	3292996	272327	22442	21105	3018	6777879
1157784	217783	382209	557792	5173	3177	504	1222980
1879424	1784986	91688	2750	6119	5574	788	1879424
84744076	75762297	6055653	2926126	254186	244282	26234	87748544
44913799	37469794	6438038	1005967	206894	198787	25988	47742586
122165076	109168745	9780938	3215393	429399	417022	49144	127851319
46912544	42651042	1984415	2277087	139251	141231	12261	47754820
57602853	53591801	3722127	288925	196733	183880	24660	60466555
15039708	10723290	3825695	490723	70188	68301	9328	16860208
7492799	4063346	2712753	716700	31681	26047	3078	7639811
3896185	1765356	1551814	579015	13935	11461	1675	3962208

12-2 续表

分　组	Item	房屋建筑施工面积（平方米）Number of Projects under Constrution (sq.m)	本年新开工 Beginning Projects in this year
总　计	**Total**	**39470137**	**16604717**
#国有及国有控股	State-Owned and State Holding Majority Shares	24377018	8601710
一、按登记注册类型分	**Grouped by Registion Status**		
内资	Domestic Investment Enterprises	39470137	16604717
国有企业	State-owned Enterprises	12188874	4181585
集体企业	Collective-owned Enterprises	5440984	3207317
股份合作企业	Share-holding Corperative Enterprises		
联营企业	Joint Ownership Enterprises	135295	90914
有限责任公司	Limited Liability Corporations	19034829	7521532
股份有限公司	Share-holding Corperation Ltd	356581	237110
私营企业	Private Enterprises	2313574	1366259
其他企业	Others		
港澳台商投资企业	Enterprises with Funds from Hong Kong,Macao and Taiwan		
外商投资企业	Enterprises with Foreign Investment		
二、按国民经济行业分	**Grouped by Sector**		
房屋和土木工程建筑业	Building Engineering and Civil Engineering Construction	38782508	16221657
房屋工程建筑	Building Engineering Construction	36242005	15301886
土木工程建筑	Civil Engineering Construction	2540503	919771
建筑安装业	Installation of Construction	605964	331260
建筑装饰业	Fitting and Decoration	6865	
其他建筑业	Others	74800	51800
三、按隶属关系分	**Grouped by Administrative Relationship**		
中　央	Central	6779319	1386552
地　方	Region	32690818	15218165
四、按企业资质等级分	**Grouped by Class of Enterprises**		
1.施工总承包	Overall Contractor for Construction	38356629	15901396
#特级	Special Class	3852352	1727004
一级	First Class	25876110	9167243
二级	Second Class	6258303	3944034
2.专业承包	Special Contractor	1113508	703321
#一级以上	First Class	508587	166660

continued

房屋建筑 竣工面积 (平方米) Floor Space of Buildings under Construction (sq.m)	自有机械设备 年末净值 (千元) Net Value of Mechanical Equipment owned by Constructions Enterprises at Year-end(1 000yuan)	自有机械设备 年末总台数 (台) Number of Mechanical Equipment Owned By Construction Enterprises at Year-end(unit)	自有机械设备 年末总功率 (千瓦) Total Power of Mechanical Equipment Owned by Construction Enterprises at Year-end(kw)
12098754	**5499834**	**146159**	**3569802**
5972351	4444997	114691	2399629
12098754	5499214	146129	3569367
2785770	2517882	28490	1533031
2470935	194047	12285	218971
	94	7	528
47780	26146	1291	10760
5785736	2549927	26601	1714211
180182	85843	75115	35318
828351	125275	2340	56548
	620	30	435
11813854	5302293	138633	3156719
11387399	1089648	35375	1018372
426455	4212645	103258	2138347
271100	115197	5573	144404
	31920	489	36554
13800	50424	1464	232125
1672766	3943094	101446	2009855
10425988	1556740	44713	1559947
11711085	5218762	138089	2888235
818581	2368820	17453	1315366
7664000	1975548	97166	841448
2293392	712539	16197	583393
387669	281072	8070	681567
192253	205837	4854	503727

12-3 施工总承包和专业承包建筑业企业财务状况（2009年）

单位: 千元

指　　标	Item	总　　计 Total
流动资产小计	Circulating Assets	82005455
#存货	Stocks	20405937
长期投资	Long-term Investment	3557210
固定资产合计	Fixed Assets	11115575
固定资产原价	Original Value of Fixed Assets	17600982
#生产经营用	Using for Production and Management	16044398
累计折旧	Accumulative Total Depreciation	7359151
#本年折旧	Depreciation Within the Year	1882641
在建工程	Projects Under Construction	447721
无形及递延资产合计	Intangible and Deferred Assets	1279248
#无形资产	Intangible Assets	1279248
资产合计	Total Assets	101483936
流动负债小计	Liquid Liabilities	78882703
长期负债小计	Long-term Liabilities	3398209
负债合计	Total Liabilities	82280912
所有者权益合计	Owner Rights and Interests	19203024
#实收资本	Actual Capital Hold	13773532
1.国家资本	State Capital	1814663
2.集体资本	Collective Capital	1078132
3.法人资本	Corporation Capital	8167399
4.个人资本	Individual Capital	2634190
5.港澳台资本	Capital from HongKong,Macao and Taiwan	46648
6.外商资本	Foreign Capital	32500
工程结算收入	Revenue of Project Settlement Accounts	138430622
工程结算成本	Costs of Project Settlement Accounts	125912331
工程结算税金及附加	Taxs and Extra Charges on Project Settlement Accounts	4344635
工程结算利润	Profits of Projet Settlement Accounts	7897135
其他业务收入	Other Income from Business	541368
其他业务利润	Other Profits from Business	142109
经营费用	Running Expenses	276521
管理费用	Management Expenses	3756962
#税金	Tax Revenue	171939
财产保险费	Expense of Property and Insurance	36990
财务费用	Financial Expenditures	631178
营业利润	Operating Surplus	3651104
利润总额	Total Profits	3403550
# 应交所得税	Income taxes Payable	472902
应付利润	Profits Payable	1131585
劳动、待业保险费	Expense of Insurance for Laboring、Employment	151355
本年应付工资总额	Total Wages Payable this Year	18245235
本年应付福利费总额	Total Welfare Expense Payable in this Year	1022907
应收工程款	Accounts receivable from project construction	25702660

Financial Status of Overall Constructing Contractors and Professional Contractors（2009）

(1 000yuan)

国有及国有控股 State-Owned and State Holding Majority Shares Enterprises	中央企业 Enterprises Central	省属企业 Province Enterprises	市属企业 Municipal Enterprises
71115927	58694498	9109962	14200995
17886837	16139936	1650197	2615804
2827969	1992370	830801	734039
7689453	6474332	909675	3731568
13497325	11854824	1192868	4553290
12967514	11621127	899693	3523578
6082467	5571951	362849	1424351
1647286	1535001	55763	291877
174787	112200	59804	275717
1034325	683140	253539	342569
1034325	683140	253539	342569
85975115	70846352	11385270	19252314
70989249	59158505	8428405	11295793
2723625	2529481	315066	553662
73712874	61687986	8743471	11849455
12262241	9158366	2641799	7402859
8208673	5962386	2027257	5783889
1754663	892822	517786	404055
658	17700	165701	894731
6227501	4917877	1198256	2051266
158228	66364	145514	2422312
35123	35123		11525
32500	32500		
118959020	98737062	14751462	24942098
108876388	90185792	13720951	22005588
3726865	3104244	460745	779646
6226843	5357074	564110	1975951
472070	399605	42207	99556
119322	86108	24371	31630
128924	89952	5656	180913
3014345	2435458	380538	940966
80375	42744	19588	109607
29984	12418	4650	19922
540890	516201	7397	107580
2790930	2491523	200546	959035
2741059	2492077	153388	758085
363307	322136	24040	126726
1024142	929686	25149	176750
94597	80004	9621	61730
15110237	12468831	1920854	3855550
809932	590928	181400	250579
19155867	10954000	2847207	11901453

12-4 劳务分包建筑业企业基本情况（2009年）

Basic Statistic on Enterprises of Work Subcontractors（2009）

单位: 千元 (1 000yuan)

指　标	Item	2009
一、生产情况	**Main Indicators**	
1.企业个数（个）	Number of Enterprises（unit）	2
2.建筑业总产值	Total Output Value of Constrution	
3.从业人员情况	Employed persons	
计算建筑业劳动生产率的平均人数（人）	Average Number of Employed Persons in Calculation of Labour Productivity (person)	20
年末从业人数（人）	Number of Employment at Year-end (person)	20
#工程技术人员	Technical Personnel	5
二、财务状况	**Finacial Status**	
1.资产负债	Funds and Liabilities	
固定资产原值	Original Value of Fixed Assets	429
本年折旧	In The Year	21
资产总计	Total Assets	1187
负债总计	Total Liabilities	67
实收资本	Paid in Capital	1020
国家资本	State Capital	
集体资本	Collective Capital	
法人资本	Corporation Capital	1020
个人资本	Individual Capital	
港澳台资本	Capital from HongKong,Macao and Taiwan	
外商资本	Foreign Capital	
2.损益及分配	Profits,Loss and Allocation	
营业收入	Income from Operation	480
#主营业务收入	Income from Main Operation	480
主营业务成本	Cost of Main Operation	365
主营业务税金及附加	Sales Tax and Extra Charges	16
费用合计	Total of Expenses	214
营业利润	Business Profits	-3
利润总额	Total Profit	-114
3.从业人员劳动报酬	Earnings of Employed persons	194
4.劳动失业保险费	Expenses of Insurance for laboring and Unemployment	21

12-5 分区县建筑业主要经济指标（2009年）

Main Indicators of Construction Enterprises by Region（2009）

区县名称 Name of District and County		企业个数（个） Number of Enterprises (unit)	总产值（千元） Total Output Value (1 000 yuan)	计算劳动生产率的平均人数（人） Average Number of Employed Persons in Calculation of Labor Productivity(person)	全员劳动生产率（万元/人） Overall Labor Productivity (10 000 yuan/person)	利税总额（千元） Total Pre-tax Profits (1 000 yuan)
新城区	Xincheng	31	15844237	47842	33.12	470151
碑林区	Beilin	32	22001448	65734	33.47	1170798
莲湖区	Lianhu	30	11466510	56153	20.42	367410
灞桥区	Baqiao	19	1211342	4806	25.2	38785
未央区	Weiyang	49	28757376	122323	23.51	413519
雁塔区	Yanta	96	41623232	95269	43.69	1273603
阎良区	Yanliang	15	1402665	9002	15.58	44279
临潼区	Lintong	10	575032	4723	12.18	21325
长安区	Chang'an	17	1871118	10831	17.28	54190
蓝田县	Lantian	9	832132	4787	17.38	30898
周至县	Zhouzhi	5	325420	9060	3.59	10899
户　县	Huxian	7	888688	9971	8.91	29881
高陵县	Gaoling	6	2858675	13079	21.86	140308

主要统计指标解释

建筑业统计单位 指从事房屋、构筑物建造和设备安装活动的法人企业。建筑业法人企业应同时具备的条件是：①依法成立，有自己的名称、组织机构和场所，能够承担民事责任；②独立拥有和使用资产，承担负债，有权与其他单位签订合同；③独立核算盈亏，能够编制资产负债表。

建筑业总产值（即自行完成施工产值） 是以货币表现的建筑安装企业在一定时期内生产的建筑业产品的总和。建筑业总产值包括：

（1）建筑工程产值：指列入建筑工程预算内的各种工程价值。

（2）设备安装工程产值：指设备安装工程价值，不包括被安装设备本身价值。

（3）房屋、构筑物修理产值：指房屋、构筑物修理所完成的价值，但不包括被修理房屋、构筑物本身的价值和生产设备的修理价值。

（4）非标准设备制造产值：指加工制造没有定型的、非标准的生产设备的加工费和原材料价值，以及附属加工厂为本企业承建工程制作的非标准设备的价值。

建筑业增加值 指建筑业企业在报告期内以货币表现的建筑业生产经营活动的最终成果。目前建筑业增加值采用分配法（收入法）计算，即从收入的角度出发，根据生产要素在生产过程中应得的收入份额计算。具体计算公式为：

建筑业增加值 = 本年提取的固定资产折旧+主营业务应付工资+主营业务应付福利费+管理费用中的劳动待业保险金、税金+工程结算税金及附加+营业利润

房屋建筑施工面积 指在报告期内施工的全部房屋建筑面积，包括本期新开工的房屋面积、上期施工跨入本期继续施工的房屋面积、上期停缓建在本期恢复施工的房屋面积、本期竣工的房屋面积及本期施工后又停缓建的房屋面积。

房屋建筑竣工面积 指在报告期内房屋建筑按照设计要求全部完工，达到了住人和使用条件，经验收鉴定合格，正式移交使用单位的房屋建筑面积。

自有机械设备年末总台数 指归本企业所有，属于本企业固定资产的生产性机械设备年末总台数。包括施工机械、生产设备、运输设备以及其他设备。

自有机械设备年末总功率 指本企业自有施工机械、生产设备、运输设备以及其他设备等列为在册固定资产的生产性机械设备年末总功率，按设定能力或查定能力计算。包括机械本身的动力和为该机械服务的单独动力设备，如电动机等。计算单位用千瓦，动力换算可按1马力 = 0.735千瓦折合成千瓦数。电焊机、变压器、锅炉不计算动力。

工程结算收入 指企业承包工程实现的工程价款结算收入，以及向发包单位收取的除工程价款以外的按规定列作营业收入的各种款项，如临时设施费、劳动保险费、施工机械调迁费等以及向发包单位收取的各种索赔款。

工程结算利润 指已结算工程实现的利润，如亏损以“-”号表示。计算公式为：

工程结算利润 = 工程结算收入 - 工程结算成本 - 工程结算税金及附加

企业总收入 指与企业生产经营直接有关的各项收入，包括工程结算收入和其他业务收入。计算公式为：

企业总收入 = 工程结算收入 + 其他业务收入

Explanatory Notes on Main Statistical Indicators

Statistical Unit in Construction refers to corporate enterprise engaged in the construction of buildings and structures and in the installation of equipment. A corporate construction enterprise should meet the following 3 requirements:① being set up in line with relevant legal basis, having its full name, organization and location, and capable of taking civil liabilities;② independently possessing and using its assets and assuming its liabilities, and entitled to sign contracts with other institutions; and ③ making independent accounts of its profits and losses, and capable of compiling its own balance sheet.

Gross Output Value of Construction (Output Value of Projects Under Construction) refers to total of construction products, expressed in money terms, completed by construction and installation enterprises during a given period of time. It includes:

(1)Output value of construction projects, that is the value of projects covered by the project budgets;

(2)Output value of installation projects, that is the value of the installation of equipment, (excluding the value of the equipment to be installed);

(3)Output value of repair of buildings and structures, that is the value created through the repairs of buildings or structures, but does not include the value of buildings or structures being repaired and the value of the repair of production equipment;

(4)Output value of manufactured non-standard equipment, that is the value of non-standard production equipment (including raw materials and manufacturing cost) made for the construction project, and the equipment manufactured by subsidiary workshops.

Value-added of Construction refers to the final result of the activities of production and management of construction in monetary terms in the reference period. At present, the value-added of construction is calculated with the income approach. In other words, it is the sum of income of various production factors in the production process. The formula is as follows:

Value-added of construction=depreciation of fixed assets in the year+wages payable+welfare expensespayable+insurance premium and tax for waiting for employment in the administrative expenses +taxes and surcharges on project settlement+profit gained from project settlement.

Floor Space of Buildings Under Construction refers to floor space of buildings under construction during the reference period, including newly started buildings, buildings started earlier and continued during the reference period, and buildings suspended earlier but restarted during the reference period, buildings completed during the reference period, and buildings under construction and then suspended during the reference period.

Floor Space of Buildings Completed refers to the floor space of buildings that are completed in the reference period in accordance with the requirements of the design, up to the standard for putting them into use, and have been checked and accepted by concerned departments as qualified ones.

Total Number of Machinery and Equipment Owned by the End of Year refers to the number of machines and equipment owned by the enterprises, and listed as the fixed assets of the enterprises by the end of the year, including machinery and equipment for construction, production and transportation.

Total Power of Machinery and Equipment Owned by the End of Year refers to the total power of machinery and equipment owned by the enterprises, and listed as the fixed assets of the enterprises by the end of the year, including machinery and equipment for construction, production and transportation. The power of the machinery is calculated on basis of the designed or verified capacity, covering the power of the machinery/equipment and the separate power equipment serving the machinery/ equipment (such as electric motors), but excluding welders, transformers and boilers. The unit used for the calculation of power is kilowatt, with horsepower converted to kilowatt by 1 horsepower=0.735 kilowatt.

Income from Settlement of Projects refers to the income received by the construction enterprise from the contracted project through settlement procedures, and other charges to the contractoree as operational costs in addition to the value of the project, such as temporary facility fee, labour insurance premium, moving cost of construction equipment, as well as various types of claimsto the contractee.

Profit from Settlement of Projects refers to profit realized through settled projects. It is calculated with the following formula:

Profit from Settlement of Projects=Income from Settlement of Projects-Settled Cost-Settled Taxes and Other Cost

Total Revenue of Enterprises refers to the sum of income from production and operation of enterprises, including income from settlement of projects and other operational income, namely:

Total Revenue of Enterprises=Income from Settlement of Projects+Other Operational Income

13 运输和邮电

TRANSPORTATION AND POSTAL SERVICE

资料整理：曾文元

Data management:Zeng Wenyuan

第十三部分　运输和邮电

一、简要说明

本章资料包括交通运输业和邮电通信业的基本情况，主要是交通运输工具、货物和旅客运输量、邮电业务、邮政局所及服务点等基本情况。资料由西安市统计局社会科技处根据有关部门提供资料整理。

二、主要指标

旅客周转量（亿人公里）	258.20	比上年增长 2.1%
货物周转量（亿吨公里）	376.68	比上年增长 7.9%
电信业务总量（亿元）	298.82	比上年增长 12.9%
全社会车辆数（万辆）	101.29	比上年增长 15.8%
#民用小轿车	37.48	比上年增长 33.0%

13 TRANSPORTATION AND POSTAL SERVICE

Ⅰ.Brief Introduction

Data in this chapter consists of primarily basic data of communication, transportation and postal service industry, transportation facility, amount of goods and passenger transportation, basic data of postal service, post offices and service establishments of Xi'an City. Data in this chapter is compiled by Social & Science and Technology Division of the Xi'an Bureau of Statistics according to the data provided by department concerned of the municipal government.

Ⅱ.Major Indicators

		Increase over Preceding Year
Passenger-Km (100 mil. person-km)	258.20	2.1%
Freight Ton-Km (100 mil. ton-km)	376.68	7.9%
Amount of Telecommunication Service(100 mil. yuan)	298.82	12.9%
Civil Motor Vehicles(10 000 units)	101.29	15.8%
Small Saloon Car	37.48	33.0%

13-1 各种交通线路里程和桥梁数

Length of Transportation Routes and Number of Bridges

指　　标	Item	2008	2009	2009年比2008年增长（%）Increase Rate in 2009 over 2008(%)
铁路营业里程（公里）	**Length of Railways in Operation (km)**	**269**	**269**	
电气化营业里程	Length of Electrified Railways in Operation	205	205	
复线里程	Double-Tracking Length	133	133	
公路里程(公里)	**Length of Highways (km)**	**11895**	**12378**	**4.1**
#晴雨通车里程	Length of Highways in All Weathers			
等级公路	Expressways and Class Ⅰ to Ⅳ Highways	10891	11839	8.7
高速	Expressway	374	377	0.8
一级	First Class	317	317	0.0
二级	Second Class	937	952	1.6
三级	Third Class	1132	1186	4.8
四级	Forth Class	8131	9007	10.8
等外公路	Highways below Class Ⅳ	1004	539	-46.3
桥梁	**Bridges**			
座 (座)	Seat (seat)	1710	1856	8.5
长度 (米)	Length (m)	151996	154866	1.9
永久式桥梁	Permanent			
座 (座)	Seat (seat)	1657	1803	8.8
长度 (米)	Length (m)	150980	153850	1.9
半永久式桥梁	Semi Permanent			
座 (座)	Seat (seat)	12	12	
长度 (米)	Length (m)	210	291	38.6
民航通航里程(公里)（重复航线）	**Length of Total Civil Aviation Routes(km)**	**515524**	**587904**	**14.0**

13-2 全社会车辆数

Possession of Civil Vehicles

指　标	Item	2006	2007	2008	2009
合　计	**Total**	**608155**	**840376**	**875005**	**1012937**
民用汽车 (辆)	Motor(unit)	442624	522616	595735	754803
载客汽车	Passenget Vehicles	296078	360081	430472	567326
#大　型	Large	8956	9624	10007	11352
轿　车	Car	182076	229805	281726	374827
普通载货汽车	Ordinary Trucks	89772	97614	89093	113430
#重、中型	Heavy and Medium	35666	38585	37752	48783
其他汽车	Others	56774	64921	76170	74047
#三　轮	Three Wheelers	39114	40454	41309	38739
拖拉机 (台)	Tractors(unit)	33236	32028	30176	31347
#大中型	Large and Medium	10205	10499	11016	11890
小　型	Small-sized	19016	17663	16332	15905
摩托车 (辆)	Motorcycle (unit)	131449	284594	247079	224121
普通摩托车	Bicycle Motor	89270	235833	212581	201302
挂车 (辆)	Articulated Trailers (unit)	671	966	1850	2552
其他类型车 (辆)	Others (unit)	175	172	165	114

13-3　交通运输量及运输周转量

Passenger Traffic and Kilometers and Freight Traffic and Ton-kilometers

指　标	Item	2008	2009	2009年比2008年增长（%）Increase Rate in 2009 over 2008(%)
一、客运量（万人次）	**Passenger Traffic(10 000 person-times)**	**26501**	**28693**	**8.3**
铁　路	Railways	2680	2585	-3.6
公　路	Highways	23175	25271	9.0
民　航	Civil Aviation	646	837	28.3
二、旅客周转量（万人公里）	**Passenger-Km (10 000 person-Km)**	**2529007**	**2582025**	**2.1**
铁　路	Railways	525830	512686	-2.5
公　路	Highways	1125607	1229172	9.2
民　航	Civil Aviation	877570	840167	-4.3
三、货运量（万吨）	**Freight Traffic(10 000 tons)**	**27560**	**30606**	**11.1**
铁　路	Railways	605	614	1.6
公　路	Highways	26949	29986	11.3
民　航	Civil Aviation	6	6	
四、货物周转量（万吨公里）	**Freight Ton-Km (10 000 ton-Km)**	**3490707**	**3766806**	**7.9**
铁　路	Railways	1575038	1650050	4.8
公　路	Highways	1902693	2107236	10.8
民　航	Civil Aviation	12976	9520	-26.6

13-4 邮政业务及服务网点

Postal service and branch post office

指　标	Item	2008	2009	2009年比2008年增长（%）Increase Rate in 2009 over 2008(%)
一、邮政业务总量（万元）	Business Volume of Postal and Telecommunication Services(10 000 yuan)	82138	88410	7.6
二、邮政业务总收入（万元）	Gross Income of Post Services (10 000 yuan)	69619	79460	14.1
三、函件（万件）	Number of Letters (10 000 pcs)	5638	6128	8.7
四、包件（万件）	Parcels (10 000 pcs)	91	81	-10.5
五、汇票（万张）	Money order (10 000 pcs)	190	208	10.0
六、报纸订销累计份数（万份）	Accumulated newspaper prescribing and sales volume (10 000 pcs)	11137	11187	0.4
七、杂志订销累计份数（万份）	Accumulated magazine prescribing and sales volume (10 000 pcs)	553	561	1.5
八、特快专递类业务（万件）	Express mail service volume (10 000 pcs)	396	497	25.4
九、集邮业务量（万枚）	Stamps for Collection (10 000 pcs)	1560	1494	-4.2
十、邮政储蓄余额（万元）	Postal savings deposit balance (10 000 yuan)	1485556	1287892	-13.3
十一、邮政营销网点（处）	Number of post office branch establishments (unit)	298	300	0.7
#设在农村的局所	In it: number of post offices in rural area	92	92	
十二、邮政信筒信箱（个）	Number of mailboxes(unit)	908	998	9.9

13-5 电信业务情况

Telecommunication service

指　标	Item	2008	2009	2009年比2008年增长（%）Increase Rate in 2009 over 2008(%)
一、电信业务总量（万元）	Business Volume of Telecommunication Services (10 000 yuan)	2564524	2900836	13.1
二、电信业务总收入（万元）	Gross Income of Telecommunication Services (10 000 yuan)	822967	951343	15.6
三、固定电话年末户数（户）	Number of Immobile Telephone at Year-end (subscriber)	3068807	2891009	-5.8
#农村电话年末户数	Number of Telephone in Rural Areas at Year-end	383869	358238	-6.7
四、长途电话通话总数（万次）	Number of Long-distance Telephone Call (10 000 times)	32486	30633	-5.7
五、电话交换机容量（门）	Capacity (number) of Telephone Switchboard (line)	4625249	4411059	-4.6
六、移动电话用户年末数（户）	Number of Mobile Phone at Year-end(subscriber)	7377575	11200566	51.8
七、互联网年末宽带用户（户）	Number of Broad Band Net User (subscriber)	813987	1167916	43.5

主 要 统 计 指 标 解 释

铁路营业里程 又称营业长度（包括正式营业和临时营业里程），指办理客货运输业务的铁路正线总长度。凡是全线或部分建成双线及以上的线路，以第一线的实际长度计算;复线、站线、段管线、岔线和特殊用途线以及不计算运费的联络线都不计算营业里程。铁路营业里程是反映铁路运输业基础设施发展水平的重要指标，也是计算客货周转量、运输密度和机车车辆运用效率等指标的基础资料。

铁路正线延展里程 指正线第一线、第二线、第三线和其他正线建筑里程之和，不包括站线、段管线、岔线及特殊用途线的延展里程。它是作为计算铁路线上钢轨、枕木及路基砂石需要量的主要依据。

公路里程 指在一定时期内实际达到《公路工程[WTBZ]技术标准JTJ01-88》规定的等级公路，并经公路主管部门正式验收交付使用的公路里程数。包括大中城市的郊区公路以及通过小城镇街道部分的公路里程和桥梁、隧道渡口的长度，不包括大中城市的街道、厂矿、林区生产用道和农业生产用道的里程。两条或多条公路共同经由同一路段，只计算一次，不得重复计算里程长度。它是反映公路建设发展规模的重要指标，也是计算运输网密度等指标的基础资料。

民用航空航线里程 指民航运输定期班机飞行的航线长度的总和。航线长度按机场之间的距离计算，通常有两种计算方法：一是将每条航线长度相加称为重复计算航线里程；一是将两线或两条以上航线经过同一区段里程，只计算一次航线长度称为不重复计算航线里程。一般常用的是后者，它能确切反映民航运输网的规模，是表明民航事业为国民经济服务和方便人民生活程度的主要指标。

货（客）运量 指在一定时期内，各种运输工具实际运送的货物（旅客）数量。它是反映运输业为国民经济和人民生活服务的数量指标，也是制定和检查运输生产计划、研究运输发展规模和速度的重要指标。货运按吨计算，客运按人计算。货物不论运输距离长短、货物类别，均按实际重量统计。旅客不论行程远近或票价多少，均按一人一次客运量统计;半价票、小孩票也按一人统计。

货物（旅客）周转量 指在一定时期内，由各种运输工具运送的货物（旅客）数量与其相应运输距离的乘积之总和。它是反映运输业生产总成果的重要指标，也是编制和检查运输生产计划，计算运输效率、劳动生产率以及核算运输单位成本的主要基础资料。计算货物周转量通常按发出站与到达站之间的最短距离，也就是计费距离计算。计算公式为:

货物（旅客）周转量 = Σ货物（旅客）运输量 × 运输距离

邮电业务总量 指以价值量形式表现的邮电通信企业为社会提供各类邮电通信服务的总数量。邮电业务量按专业分类包括函件、包件、汇票、报刊发行、邮政快件、特快专递、邮政储蓄、集邮、公众电报、用户电报、传真、长途电话、出租电路、无线寻呼、移动电话、分组交换数据通信、出租代维等。计算方法为各类产品乘以相应的平均单价（不变价）之和，再加上出租电路和设备、代用户维护电话交换机和线路等的服务收入。它综合反映了一定时期邮电业务发展的总成果，是研究邮电业务量构成和发展趋势的重要指标。计算公式为:

邮电业务总量 = Σ（各类邮电业务量 × 不变单价）+ 出租代维及其他业务收入

无线寻呼用户 无线寻呼是指电话用户通过无线寻呼中心，在规定范围内向携带小型寻呼机的用户发出声音、数字或文字显示信息。在寻呼台办理登记手续携带小型寻呼机的用户，称为无线寻呼用户。

移动电话用户 是指通过移动电话交换机进入移动电话网、占用移动电话号码的电话用户。用户数量以报告期末在移动电话营业部门实际办理登记手续进入移动电话网的户数进行计算，一部移动电话统计为一户。

电话用户 指接入国家公众固定电话网，并按固定电话业务进行经营管理的电话用户。1997年以前，电话用户分为市内电话用户和农村电话用户。“市内电话用户”是指接入县城及县以上城市的电话网上的电话用户;“农村电话用户”是指接入县邮电局农话台及县以下农村电话交换点，以县城为中心（除市话用户外）联通县、乡（镇）、行政村、村民小组的用户。从1997年起，电话用户数分组调整为以用户所在区域划分为“城市电话用户”和“乡村电话用户”，与过去的按市内电话和农村电话划分方法不同。而电话用户总数、电话机总部数统计范围不变。

城市电话用户 指直辖市、省辖市、地级市、县级市的市区、市郊区及县城（包括县人民政府所在地的县城关区或行政建制相当于县人民政府所在地的镇）范围内接入局用交换机的电话用户数，包括分布在农村地区的独立工矿区、林区、驻军等接入局用交换机的电话用户数。

乡村电话用户 指县城关区以下的集镇和农村接入局用交换机的电话用户数。

住宅电话用户 是指安装在居民住宅或农民家里并按照住宅电话用户登记注册和收费的电话用户。包括私人付费、单位付费和按规定免费安装的住宅电话用户。

局用交换机容量 是指安装在本地电信运营商内用于接续本地固定电话的电话交换机容量，有倍增设备按倍增后的数量计数。包括现用和备用的人工或自动交换机的全部容量。

Explanatory Notes on Main Statistical Indicators

Length of Railways in Operation refers to the total length of the trunk line under passenger and freight transportation (including both full operation and temporary operation). The calculation is based on the actual length of the first line even if this line has a full or partial double track or more tracks, excluding double tracks, station sidings, tracks under the charge of stations, branch lines, special-purpose lines and the non-payable connecting lines. The length of railways in operation is an important indicator to show the development of the infrastructure for the railway transport, and also the essential data to calculate volume of passenger freight transport, traffic density and utilization efficiency of the locomotives and carriages.

Extenuation Length of Trunk Lines refers to the sum of the first, the second, the third lines and other constructed length of the trunk railways, excluding the extenuation length of the station lines, lines under the jurisdiction of depots, sidings and lines for special purpose. It provides important information for the calculation of the needs for rails, sleepers, sand and stone for the construction of railways.

Length of Highways refers to the length of highways which are built in conformity with the grades specified by the highway engineering standard formulated by the Ministry of Communications, and have been formally checked and accepted by the departments of highways and put into use. The length of highways includes that of the suburb highways at large and medium-sized cities, highways passing through streets at small cities and towns, and also the length of bridges、 tunnel and ferries. It does not include the length of streets in big and medium-sized cities and highways built for the production purpose at factories, mines, forest areas and agricultural areas. If two or more highways go the same section of the way, the length of the section is only calculated for once and no duplication is allowed. The length of highways is an important indicator to show the development of the highway construction and to provide essential information to calculate the transport network density.

Length of Civil Aviation Routes refers to the length of all routes for regular civil aviation flights. There are usually two ways to calculate the distance between airports connected by the route length: one is to put the length of all air routes together, called duplicated calculation of the length of the routes; the other is not to allow the duplication in calculation when two or more routes passing the same section of aviation routes. The latter is usually used, as it can precisely show the size of the civil aviation network and indicate the extent of civil aviation serving the national economy and the people.

Freight (Passenger) Traffic refers to the volume of freight (passenger) transported with various means. Freight transport is calculated in tons and passenger traffic is calculated in the number of persons. Despite the type of freight and travelling distance, the freight transport is calculated in the actual weight of the goods: and despite the travelling distance and ticket price, the passenger traffic is calculated by the principle that one person can be counted only once in one travel. The passenger who travel with a half price ticket or a child ticket is also calculated as one person. The freight (passenger) traffic provides a quantitative measure to show how the transport industry serves the national economy and people, and is also an important indicator for planning the transport industry and for studying the development scale and speed of the transport industry.

Freight Ton-kilometers (Passenger-kilometers) refer to the sum of the products of the volume of transported cargo (passengers) multiplying by the transport distance, usually using ton-kilometer and passenger-kilometer as units for measurement. Normally, the shortest distance between the departure station and the destination station (i.e., the payable distance) is the basis to calculate the freight ton-kilometers. This is an important indicator to show the total results of the transport industry, to prepare and examine the transport plan and to measure the efficiency, the labour productivity and the unit cost of transport.

The formula is as follows:

Freight Ton-kilometers (Passenger-kilometers) =Σ {Freight (Passenger) Traffic x Distance of Transportation}

Measuring unit: ton-kilometer (person-kilometer)

Business Volume of Post and Telecommunications refers to the total amount of post and telecommunications services, expressed in value terms, provided by the post and telecommunications departments for the society. Post and telecommunication services can be classified as letters, parcels, remittance, issue of newspapers and magazines, fast mail service, express mail service, savings deposits, stamps for collection, public and individual telegraph service, facsimiles, long-distance telephone service,leasing of telephone lines, urban paging service, mobile telephone service, data transfer and transmission, etc. The accounting approach is to multiply the service products of all types with their average unit price (constant price) to get sum of business value, plus income from other services such as leasing of telephone lines and equipment, maintenance of telephone switchboards and lines on behalf of customers. This indicator reflects the overall results of post and telecommunications service during a given period, and is important to study the composition of business service and the development of post and telecommunications service.

The formula is as follows:

Business Volume of Post and Telecommunications=Σ (Transaction of Post and Telecommunication Service x Constant Price) + Income from Leasing, Maintenance and other Services

Subscribers of Wireless Paging Services Wireless paging service refers the service by which telephone users send audio, digital or character signals to persons carrying small-size pagers within the designated areas through wireless paging centers. The page carriers who have registered in paging centers are counted as paging subscribers.

Mobile Telephone Subscribers refer to the persons who own mobile telephone numbers and are connected with the mobile telephone communication network through the mobile telephone switchboards. The number of subscribers is calculated by the subscribers who have completed registration at mobile communication business centers and entered into the mobile telephone network. One mobile telephone is taken as a subscriber.

Telephone Subscribers refer to subscribers that are connected to the public line telephone network provided with telephone services. Before 1997, telephone subscribers were classified as city subscribers and village subscribers. City subscribers referred to those connected to city telephone networks in county towns and cities, while village subscribers referred to those connected to village telephone stations at and below counties. Since 1997, the classification of telephone subscribers was modified on the basis of physical location of the subscribers as Urban telephone subscribers and rural telephone subscribers , which is different from the previous classification of categorizing local telephones and rural telephones , while the definition of total subscribers and total number of telephones remain unchanged.

Urban Telephone Subscribers refer to subscribers telephone subscribers, located at municipalities, cities under the jurisdiction of province, cities at prefectural level, downtown and suburb of city at county level town and county towns (including country towns where county government located, and towns of county level according to the administrative organizational system), that are connected to the public line telephone network, including rural mineral area, forest area, military area.

Rural Telephone Subscribers refer to telephone subscribers, located at towns under county town and country, that are connected to the public line telephone network.

Household Telephone Subscribers refer to telephone sets installed in the dwelling units of urban or rural residents, and registered as residence subscribers for payment, including 3 types of payment for the service: private payment, public payment and free service.

Capacity of Office Telephone Exchanges refers to the capacity (measured in gate) of telephone exchanges installed in the offices of local telecommunication service providers for communication between fixed telephones. It includes the capacity of both manual and automatic exchanges in use and for stand-by purpose. Equipment with expansion function is to be counted by the expanded capacity.

14 国内贸易

DOMESTIC TRADE

资料整理：马晓庆　杨　骏　曹志健　左　宇
Data management: Ma Xiaoqing　Yang Jun　Cao Zhijian　Zuo Yu

第十四部分　国内贸易

一、简要说明

本章资料主要包括社会消费品零售总额，批发零售贸易业商品购、销等情况，限额以上批发零售贸易业主要商品销售情况，限额以上批发零售贸易和住宿餐饮企业财务状况、经济效益，以及交易市场情况，由西安市统计局贸易外经处提供。

二、主要指标

批发零售贸易业网点（万个）	19.23	比上年增长　0.4%
餐饮业网点（万个）	3.95	比上年增长　3.7%
社会消费品零售总额（亿元）	1381.12	比上年增长 17.4%
#批发零售贸易业零售额	1222.98	比上年增长 18.4%

14 DOMESTIC TRADE

Ⅰ.Brief Introduction

Content of this chapter consists of total retail sales of consumer goods, sails data on commodity purchasing and sails of wholesale and retail trade, sales data on primary goods exceeds quotation, financial, economic performance and market data on wholesale and retail trade and food services industry exceeds quotation. Data in this chapter is compiled and provided by Trade and Foreign Economy Division of the Xi'an Bureau of Statistics.

Ⅱ.Major Indicators

		Increase over Preceding Year
Establishments Engaged in Whole-sale and Retail Trade(10 000 unit)	19.23	0.4%
Establishments Engaged in Trade(10 000 unit)	3.95	3.7%
Establishments Engaged in Catering Trade(10 000 unit)	1381.12	17.4%
Total Retail Sales of Consumer Goods (100 mil. yuan)	1222.98	18.4%
Retail Sales of Wholesale and Retail Enterprises		

14-1 主要年份社会消费品零售总额

Total Retail Sales of Consumer Goods in Representative Year

单位:亿元 (100 million yuan)

年份 Year	社会消费品零售总额 Total Retail Sales of Consumer Goods	市的零售额 Retail Sales of Urban Area	县及县以下的零售额 Retail Sales of County and Below	批发零售贸易业 Wholesale Trades and Retail Trades	住宿餐饮业 Accommodation and Catering Trade	其他行业 Others
1978	12.70	8.82	3.88	11.01	0.53	0.21
1979	13.94	9.88	4.06	11.88	0.60	0.21
1980	15.88	11.53	4.35	13.05	0.80	0.20
1981	17.41	12.85	4.56	14.31	0.80	0.19
1982	18.54	13.79	4.75	15.25	0.88	0.27
1983	20.82	15.14	5.68	16.95	1.03	0.32
1984	24.87	19.13	5.74	19.47	1.29	0.46
1985	32.92	26.09	6.83	25.04	1.69	0.48
1986	37.50	29.25	8.25	28.88	1.97	0.64
1987	43.86	34.62	9.24	33.32	2.50	0.49
1988	59.65	47.74	11.91	44.84	2.97	0.78
1989	68.05	54.60	13.45	54.41	2.98	0.76
1990	72.77	59.42	13.35	57.46	3.79	0.90
1991	81.04	66.93	14.11	60.35	4.43	1.26
1992	100.84	89.17	11.67	71.86	6.13	2.30
1993	115.38	104.41	10.97	75.99	7.49	2.71
1994	144.64	131.56	13.08	89.79	9.12	3.43
1995	186.60	165.98	20.62	115.46	11.97	3.73
1996	222.94	198.19	24.75	145.05	15.83	4.02
1997	264.47	238.17	26.30	169.08	22.12	4.17
1998	291.45	257.39	34.06	183.43	30.97	4.27
1999	323.37	283.32	40.05	207.96	34.78	4.85
2000	360.42	317.12	43.30	232.89	41.42	5.43
2001	406.21	358.97	47.24	265.25	48.87	5.86
2002	459.76	409.86	49.90	309.36	51.42	6.45
2003	502.65	449.62	53.03	440.28	53.30	9.07
2004	578.60	520.94	57.66	509.60	56.87	12.13
2005	670.56	604.63	65.93	592.77	63.59	14.20
2006	784.95	708.31	76.64	694.03	74.77	16.15
2007	936.21	845.59	90.62	828.63	89.32	18.26
2008	1176.58	1063.93	112.65	1033.00	122.90	20.68
2009	1381.12	1249.79	131.33	1222.98	134.54	23.60

注：依据2008年第二次经济普查数据，对2005-2007年数据进行调整。

Note:According to the Secong Economic Census statistics,datas from 2005 to 2007 were adjusted.

14-2 社会消费品零售总额（2009年）

Total Retail Sales of Consumer Goods（2009）

单位:亿元 (100 million yuan)

分　　类	Classify	金　额 Sum
社会消费品零售总额	**Total Retail Sales of Consumer Goods**	**1381.12**
（一）按销售地区分:	Grouped by Region	
（1）市的零售额	Retail Sales of Urban Area	1249.79
（2）县的零售额	Retail Sales of County	63.50
（3）县以下的零售额	Retail Sales Under County Level	67.83
（二）按行业分:	Grouped by Sector	
（1）批发业	Wholesale Enterprises	180.50
限额以上企业	Enterprises Above Designated Size	70.40
限额以下企业和个体户	Enterprises Below Designated Size and Self-employed Laborers	110.10
#个体户	Self-employed Laborers	29.24
（2）零售业	Retail Enterprises	1042.48
限额以上企业	Enterprises Above Designated Size	673.44
限额以下企业和个体户	Enterprises Below Designated Size and Self-employed Laborers	369.04
#个体户	Self-employed Laborers	160.54
（3）住宿和餐饮业	Accommodation and Catering Trade	134.54
限额以上企业	Enterprises Above Designated Size	63.37
限额以下企业和个体户	Enterprises Below Designated Size and Self-employed Laborers	71.17
#个体户	Self-employed Laborers	44.13
（4）其他行业	Others	23.60

14-3 各区县社会消费品零售总额（2009年）

Total Retail Sales of Consumer Goods by Region（2009）

单位：亿元 (100 million yuan)

区县名称	Name of District and County	社会消费品零售总额 Total Retail Sales of Consumer Goods	批发零售贸易业 Wholesale and Retail Trade of Retail Sales	住宿餐饮业 Accommodation and Catering Trade of Retail Sales
新城区	Xincheng	241.41	225.07	11.43
碑林区	Beilin	241.37	215.08	23.47
莲湖区	Lianhu	197.99	179.54	17.18
灞桥区	Baqiao	31.87	27.26	4.30
未央区	Weiyang	194.27	181.92	11.95
雁塔区	Yanta	267.42	222.63	35.58
阎良区	Yanliang	16.25	13.18	2.85
临潼区	Lintong	34.02	28.85	4.31
长安区	Chang'an	76.47	62.55	12.43
蓝田县	Lantian	24.96	21.34	3.22
周至县	Zhouzhi	16.72	14.58	1.68
户　县	Huxian	27.19	22.47	4.34
高陵县	Gaoling	11.18	8.50	1.79

14-4 主要年份批发零售贸易业、餐饮业网点和人员

Wholesale and retail trade, catering outlets and staff in Representative Years

单位:个、人 (unit,person)

年份 Year	批发业 Wholesale Trade		零售业 Retail Trade		餐饮业 Catering Services	
	网点 Branch Shop	人员 Personnel	网点 Branch Shop	人员 Personnel	网点 Branch Shop	人员 Personnel
1978	586	22136	5862	51462	442	9043
1979	462	14002	5387	49252	815	10349
1980	1505	28320	6312	51927	1893	16297
1981	597	17780	8800	74095	3397	25626
1982	881	25023	9811	68734	6422	25879
1983	1642	32597	17130	77863	6387	28054
1984	1875	34906	27043	136852	8484	25977
1985	1247	43311	35860	223076	11907	41025
1986	1706	42270	37503	241052	11977	48335
1987	3351	44475	42484	260450	13673	51361
1988	1829	40324	44330	282911	9576	47131
1989	1638	80078	46613	229705	10228	46420
1990	1558	37077	43244	219413	9800	34561
1991	1918	45583	48171	236235	10369	36813
1992	1864	36012	48422	258491	9916	38935
1993	5177	54255	43289	226572	11804	38318
1994	6338	58154	60292	318287	14296	56502
1995	6564	63337	69623	364430	15485	68782
1996	8008	67840	76828	437655	15668	78313
1997	8414	71178	80379	468811	20259	82917
1998	10780	85420	95056	515723	22500	100862
1999	10865	86630	96516	516163	24977	118442
2000	10393	81519	93928	492083	27531	124988
2001	10534	78285	95414	497448	28219	128738
2002	12220	107352	96815	465320	29219	140623
2003	13274	117740	99764	490169	32899	150883
2004	19696	102779	106477	281221	27905	132855
2005	20392	106138	112541	298285	30156	142176
2006	21243	110595	117168	312426	31694	148317
2007	21835	114497	122810	330583	34249	161517
2008	26813	148403	164642	470886	38134	201978
2009	26403	154777	165921	507706	39515	205364

14-5 批发贸易业机构、网点、人员（2009年）

单位:个、人

分类	Classify	合计 Total 法人单位 Constitutional Unit	活动单位 Movemental Unit	网点 Branch Shop	人员 Personnel
总计	**Total**	**7370**	**7549**	**26403**	**154777**
一、按登记注册类型分组	**Grouped by Registered Kind**				
内资企业	Civil Funded Enterprises	7328	7503	9568	97875
国有企业	State-owned Enterprises	324	383	612	16814
集体企业	Collective-owned Enterprises	261	268	512	3897
股份合作企业	Cooperative Enterprises	19	21	21	439
联营企业	Joint Ownership Enterprises	17	17	17	229
有限责任公司	Limited Liability Corporations	1690	1740	1938	23388
股份有限公司	Share-holding Corporations Ltd.	84	89	134	6351
私营企业	Private Enterprises	4858	4908	6040	46165
其他企业	Other Enterprises	75	77	294	592
港澳台商投资企业	Enterprises with Funds from Hong Kong，Macao &Taiwan	16	19	19	695
外商投资企业	Foreign Funded Enterprises	26	27	27	355
个体经济	Individuals			16789	55852
二、按国民经济行业分组	**Grouped by Sector**				
农畜产品批发	Wholesale of Farm Produce and Livestock Products	134	147	994	4158
食品、饮料及烟草制品批发	Wholesale of Food,Beverages and Tobaccos	291	311	3922	20452
纺织、服装及日用品批发	Wholesale of Textiles， Garments and Daily Articles	378	391	3145	21537
文化、体育用品及器材批发	Wholesale of Culture , Sports Articles and Equipments	321	334	2701	10863
医药及医疗器材批发	Wholesale of Medicines and Medical Appliances	393	435	1017	8238
矿产品、建材及化工产品批发	Wholesale of Mineral Products,Building Materials and Chemical Products	2034	2072	4958	29000
机械设备、五金交电及电子产品批发	Wholesale of Machinery, Hardwares, Transport Means and Electronic Equipment	3109	3138	6978	44913
贸易经纪与代理	Trade Broker and Agency	73	73	122	746
其他批发	Other Wholesales	637	648	2566	14870

Organizations, Establishments and Persons Engaged in Whole-sale Trade（2009）

（unit,person）

城镇 Urban				城区 County				乡村 Village			
法人单位 Constitutional Unit	活动单位 Movemental Unit	网点 Branch Shop	人员 Personnel	法人单位 Constitutional Unit	活动单位 Movemental Unit	网点 Branch Shop	人员 Personnel	法人单位 Constitutional Unit	活动单位 Movemental Unit	网点 Branch Shop	人员 Personnel
7220	**7383**	**24803**	**149240**	**7012**	**7131**	**22884**	**142167**	**150**	**166**	**1600**	**5537**
7178	7337	9402	95167	6971	7086	9136	91960	150	166	166	2708
279	328	557	15268	236	260	444	13888	45	55	55	1546
215	221	465	3250	175	181	392	2614	46	47	47	647
19	21	21	439	16	18	18	341				
17	17	17	229	17	17	17	229				
1685	1735	1933	23172	1678	1727	1925	23005	5	5	5	216
84	89	134	6351	78	83	128	6326				
4807	4853	5985	45884	4702	4730	5925	45021	51	55	55	281
72	73	290	574	69	70	287	536	3	4	4	18
16	19	19	695	15	18	18	679				
26	27	27	355	26	27	27	355				
		15355	53023			13703	49173			1434	2829
104	112	814	3536	58	58	554	2653	30	35	180	622
262	277	3787	18942	236	246	3334	17283	29	34	135	1510
373	386	3105	21324	357	368	2694	20084	5	5	40	213
321	334	2661	10773	320	333	2631	10713			40	90
393	433	995	8183	388	411	927	7441		2	22	55
1991	2029	4450	27791	1934	1964	4082	26457	43	43	508	1209
3108	3137	6810	44587	3091	3120	6622	44030	1	1	168	326
69	69	94	665	68	68	93	659	4	4	28	81
599	606	2087	13439	560	563	1947	12847	38	42	479	1431

14-6 零售贸易业机构、网点、人员（2009年）

单位：个、人

分类	Classify	合计 法人单位 Constitutional Unit	Total 活动单位 Movemental Unit	网点 Branch Shop	人员 Personnel
总计	**Total**	**5469**	**6222**	**165921**	**507706**
一、按登记注册类型分组	**Grouped by Registered Kind**				
内资企业	Civil Funded Enterprises	5434	6168	6712	116224
国有企业	State-owned Enterprises	212	382	467	17615
集体企业	Collective-owned Enterprises	373	449	558	4217
股份合作企业	Cooperative Enterprises	31	48	48	6275
联营企业	Joint Ownership Enterprises	21	22	22	197
有限责任公司	Limited Liability Corporations	988	1307	1499	37168
股份有限公司	Share-holding Corporations Ltd.	58	76	106	3622
私营企业	Private Enterprises	3657	3785	3913	46125
其他企业	Other Enterprises	94	99	99	1005
港澳台商投资企业	Enterprises with Funds from Hong Kong，Macao &Taiwan	12	28	28	4295
外商投资企业	Foreign Funded Enterprises	23	26	31	7652
个体经济	Individuals			159150	379535
二、按国民经济行业分组	**Grouped by Sector**				
综合零售	Intergrated Retail	551	740	32693	103023
食品、饮料及烟草制品专门零售	Retail of Food,Beverages and Tobaccos	375	475	32698	84030
纺织、服装及日用品专门零售	Special Reail of Textiles,Garments and Daily Consumer Articles	726	775	35834	121688
文化、体育用品及器材专门零售	Retail of Culture,Sports Appliances and Equipments	429	466	7938	27290
医药及医疗器材专门零售	Retail of Medicines and Medical Appliances	510	775	6716	20896
汽车、摩托车、燃料及零售配件专门零售	Retail of Motor Vehicles, Motorcycles, Fuel and Parts	601	646	13106	58317
家用电器及电子产品专门零售	Special Retail of household Electric Appliances and Electronic Products	994	1019	11367	34470
五金、家具及室内装修材料专门零售	Special Retail of Hardware, Furniture and Decoration Materials	858	897	16716	35490
无店铺及其他零售	Non-shop and Other Retail	425	429	8853	22502

Organizations, Establishments and Persons Engaged in Retail Trade（2009）

（unit,person）

城镇 Urban				城区 County				乡村 Village			
法人单位 Constitutional Unit	活动单位 Movemental Unit	网点 Branch Shop	人员 Personnel	法人单位 Constitutional Unit	活动单位 Movemental Unit	网点 Branch Shop	人员 Personnel	法人单位 Constitutional Unit	活动单位 Movemental Unit	网点 Branch Shop	人员 Personnel
5276	**6014**	**133654**	**440037**	**4914**	**5566**	**110950**	**388342**	**193**	**208**	**32267**	**67669**
5241	5960	6418	113346	4879	5512	5913	107794	193	208	294	2878
203	370	439	17080	185	330	359	16610	9	12	28	535
338	414	457	3762	296	324	349	3079	35	35	101	455
31	48	48	6275	26	43	43	6094				
18	19	19	157	17	18	18	151	3	3	3	40
979	1298	1490	37075	952	1271	1463	36813	9	9	9	93
58	76	106	3622	56	61	91	3354				
3529	3645	3769	44541	3274	3387	3512	40979	128	140	144	1584
85	90	90	834	73	78	78	714	9	9	9	171
12	28	28	4295	12	28	28	4295				
23	26	31	7652	23	26	31	7652				
		127177	314744			104978	268601			31973	64791
492	680	19682	77186	370	553	13922	61090	59	60	13011	25837
356	452	26708	73344	338	428	21961	63972	19	23	5990	10686
711	756	32362	116168	668	711	25135	103264	15	19	3472	5520
425	462	7065	25775	409	446	6553	24844	4	4	873	1515
496	758	5896	19138	464	682	4847	16995	14	17	820	1758
554	599	9543	47253	500	521	8142	42737	47	47	3563	11064
975	997	9229	28213	943	965	8277	25723	19	22	2138	6257
855	894	16291	34651	826	860	15837	33393	3	3	425	839
412	416	6878	18309	396	400	6276	16324	13	13	1975	4193

14-7 餐饮业机构、网点、人员（2009年）

单位:个、人

分 类	Classify	合 计 Total			
		法人单位 Constitutional Unit	活动单位 Movemental Unit	网 点 Branch Shop	人 员 Personnel
总计	**Total**	**1611**	**1752**	**39515**	**205364**
一、按登记注册类型分组	**Grouped by Type of Registration**				
内资企业	Domestic Funded Enterprises	1578	1654	1801	68370
国有企业	State-owned Enterprises	58	65	66	5020
集体企业	Collective-owned Enterprises	17	20	20	535
股份合作企业	Share-Holding Cooperative Enterprises	3	3	3	210
联营企业	Joint Ownership Enterprises	21	21	21	763
有限责任公司	Limited Liability Corporations	302	323	373	20690
股份有限公司	Share-holding Corporations Ltd.	19	26	26	3051
私营企业	Private Enterprises	1130	1165	1243	36755
其他企业	Other Enterprises	28	31	49	1346
港、澳、台商投资企业	Enterprises with Funds from Hong Kong，Macao &Taiwan	12	75	75	4078
外商投资企业	Foreign Funded Enterprises	21	23	23	2503
个体经济	Individuals			37616	130413
二、按餐饮业行业分组	**Grouped by Sector of Catering Trade**				
正餐服务	Restaurant	1315	1354	17634	125448
快餐服务	Fast Food	69	146	4018	12873
饮料及冷料服务	Beverages and Cold Drinks	95	96	3133	9177
其他餐饮服务	Others	132	156	14730	57866

Organizations Staff and Branch Shopes of Catering Trade（2009）

(unit,person)

城镇			Urban	城区			County	乡村 Village			
法人单位 Constitutional Unit	活动单位 Movemental Unit	网点 Branch Shop	人员 Personnel	法人单位 Constitutional Unit	活动单位 Movemental Unit	网点 Branch Shop	人员 Personnel	法人单位 Constitutional Unit	活动单位 Movemental Unit	网点 Branch Shop	人员 Personnel
1529	**1667**	**34407**	**187896**	**1352**	**1485**	**27815**	**163095**	**82**	**85**	**5108**	**17468**
1497	1570	1718	66820	1320	1388	1541	62929	81	84	83	1550
57	64	65	4906	53	60	60	4621	1	1	1	114
17	20	20	535	17	20	20	535				
3	3	3	210	2	2	2	200				
19	19	19	694	4	4	4	212	2	2	2	69
301	322	372	20523	296	312	362	19990	1	1	1	167
19	26	26	3051	17	24	24	2994				
1056	1088	1167	35570	909	941	1026	33082	74	77	76	1185
25	28	46	1331	22	25	43	1295	3	3	3	15
12	75	75	4078	12	75	75	4078				
20	22	22	2417	20	22	22	2417	1	1	1	86
		32592	114581			26177	93671			5024	15832
1237	1273	16984	119062	1079	1110	15247	106848	78	81	650	6386
65	142	3356	11674	58	135	1974	10326	4	4	662	1199
95	96	2698	6617	95	96	1793	5637			435	2560
132	156	11369	50543	120	144	8801	40284			3361	7323

14-8 限额以上批发零售贸易企业财务状况（2009年）

单位：万元

分　　类	Classify	单位数（个）Number (unit)	流动资产 小　计 Circulating Funds	存货 Inventories	固定资产原价 Original Value of Fixed Assets
总　　计	**Total**	**422**	**4456113.3**	**844070.9**	**1258409.4**
一、批发企业	**Wholesale Enterprises**	**162**	**2532697.3**	**423288.1**	**352185.2**
#国有控股	State-holding Majority Shares	40	1205122.9	179236.6	204687.6
1.按登记注册类型分组	Grouped by Category of Commodities				
内资企业	Domestic Funded Enterprises	158	2170400.2	378583.6	297907.0
国有企业	State-owned Enterprises	31	895766.9	126337.6	159696.5
集体企业	Collective-owned Enterprises	2	31959.8	2234.5	7918.0
股份合作企业	Corperative Enterprises				
联营企业	Joint Ownership Enterprises	1	1572.8	355.0	8.3
国有联营企业	State Joint Ownership Enterprises				
集体联营企业	Collective Joint Ownership Enterprises	1	1572.8	355.0	8.3
国有与集体联营企业	Joint State-collective Enterprises				
其他联营企业	Others Joint Ownership Enterprises				
有限责任公司	Limited Liability Corporrations	70	697451.4	106838.4	38208.1
国有独资	State Funded Corporations	2	77749.3	3318.4	9304.8
其他有限责任公司	Other Limited Liability Corporrations	68	619702.1	103520.0	28903.3
股份有限公司	Share-holding Corporations Ltd.	4	181203.9	62869.5	40978.4
私营企业	Private Enterprises	48	314312.0	78370.9	46405.6
私营独资企业	Private-funded Enterprises	1	2804.9	3.0	4400.5
私营有限责任公司	Private Limited Liability Corporations	46	310769.6	78367.8	41857.7
私营股份有限公司	Private Share-holding Corporations Ltd.	1	737.5	0.1	147.4
其他企业	Other Enterprises	2	48133.4	1577.7	4692.1
港、澳、台商投资企业	Enterprises with Funds from Hong Kong，Macao &Taiwan	2	13056.3	0.6	657.7
与港澳台商合资经营	Joint-venture Enterprises	1	7401.0		246.8
港澳台商独资	Enterprises with Sole Investment	1	5655.3	0.6	410.9
外商投资企业	Foreign Funded Enterprises	2	349240.8	44703.9	53620.5
中外合资经营	Joint-venture Enterprises	2	349240.8	44703.9	53620.5
外资企业	Foreign Owned Enterprises				
2.按国民经济行业分组	Grouped by Sector				
农畜产品批发业	Wholesale of Farm produce and livestock products	2	36003.1	3104.4	12071.0
食品、饮料及烟草制品批发	Wholesale of Beverages and Tobaccos	5	148871.8	16973.3	64439.8
烟草制品批发业	Wholesale of Tobaccos	2	120888.7	15149.7	57590.6
纺织、服装及日用品批发业	Wholesale of Textiles,Garments and Daily Consumer Articles	12	75977.9	32634.3	13336.9
文化、体育用品及器材批发	Wholesale of Culture,Sports Applionces and Equipments	5	48231.8	14011.4	7188.4

Financial Status of Enterprises Above Designated Size in Wholesale and Retail（2009）

(10 000 yuan)

累计折旧 Accumulated Depreciation	本年折旧 In The Year	资产合计 Total Assets	负债合计 Total Liabilities	实收资本 Paid in Capital	营业收入 Total Revenue	主营业务收入 Revenue from Principal Business	主营业务成本 Cost of Principal Business
302822.0	**47295.2**	**6175432.5**	**4788494.1**	**1003999.5**	**14653737.5**	**14528246.6**	**13293229.2**
97619.3	**17985.1**	**3135962.8**	**2481109.0**	**517600.3**	**7903575.2**	**7879358.0**	**7452710.2**
63083.4	10181.0	1483796.3	1182302.6	186613.9	3919708.3	3906000.5	3629119.0
96719.6	17406.8	2623787.0	2135133.1	374766.5	6741527.7	6717310.5	6316936.8
43747.4	7555.9	1106104.4	862178.5	108386.2	2745674.2	2734666.3	2515141.9
3190.8	109.4	63933.5	66055.0	5098.0	38223.6	37538.6	36933.2
7.8	0.4	1623.3	1347.5	5.0	3466.5	3466.5	3232.2
7.8	0.4	1623.3	1347.5	5.0	3466.5	3466.5	3232.2
13709.3	2930.2	791484.8	664425.7	129690.9	1995753.1	1991360.7	1915491.1
3001.0	443.6	102931.7	97028.5	23405.5	75992.0	74522.2	72906.4
10708.3	2486.6	688553.1	567397.2	106285.4	1919761.1	1916838.5	1842584.7
18336.4	2252.7	229044.7	186396.7	37072.2	628331.2	627061.2	567102.9
16729.3	4181.9	379769.4	298698.0	90914.2	831927.4	825065.5	781742.6
1027.4	189.9	6178.0	4393.8	3500.0	2173.5	2173.5	2067.3
15636.2	3979.0	372162.2	293837.3	86414.2	828876.1	822014.2	778853.4
65.7	13.0	1429.2	466.9	1000.0	877.8	877.8	821.9
998.6	376.3	51826.9	56031.7	3600.0	498151.7	498151.7	497292.9
417.8	308.6	13417.3	15061.4	1973.8	253348.2	253348.2	243489.9
168.4	59.2	7551.0	8787.7	1000.2	180844.5	180844.5	174182.9
249.4	249.4	5866.3	6273.7	973.6	72503.7	72503.7	69307.0
481.9	269.7	498758.5	330914.5	140860.0	908699.3	908699.3	892283.5
481.9	269.7	498758.5	330914.5	140860.0	908699.3	908699.3	892283.5
4335.8	206.6	71297.1	82135.0	6777.5	24806.4	24058.3	23416.3
16360.7	3637.2	217521.0	64882.2	7781.5	507039.5	506084.8	377085.2
13646.9	3361.1	172751.8	44941.4	2622.6	467603.0	467027.2	346805.7
6012.2	583.6	90403.6	73743.0	18671.3	178263.0	176655.1	154344.4
2827.2	407.9	100963.1	45338.2	31000.0	103766.9	103766.9	94489.8

14-8 续表1

单位：万元

分　类	Classify	主营业务税金及附加 Taxs and Other Changes on Principal Business	主营业务利润 Profits from Prinapal Business	营业费用 Expenses for Operation
总　计	**Total**	**103830.2**	**1131187.2**	**524705.3**
一、批发企业	**Wholesale Enterprises**	**33346.3**	**393301.5**	**190172.5**
#国有控股	State-holding Majority Shares	23917.6	252963.9	94588.1
1.按登记注册类型分组	Grouped by Category of Commodities			
内资企业	Domestic Funded Enterprises	33278.8	367094.9	181284.1
国有企业	State-owned Enterprises	22960.6	196563.8	65992.2
集体企业	Collective-owned Enterprises	14.9	590.5	402.7
股份合作企业	Corperative Enterprises			
联营企业	Joint Ownership Enterprises	4.2	230.1	156.2
国有联营企业	State Joint Ownership Enterprises			
集体联营企业	Collective Joint Ownership Enterprises	4.2	230.1	156.2
国有与集体联营企业	Joint State-collective Enterprises			
其他联营企业	Others Joint Ownership Enterprises			
有限责任公司	Limited Liability Corporations	8382.9	67486.7	40070.8
国有独资	State Funded Corporations	90.4	1525.4	638.9
其他有限责任公司	Other Limited Liability Corporrations	8292.5	65961.3	39431.9
股份有限公司	Share-holding Corporations Ltd.	1078.4	58879.9	30769.2
私营企业	Private Enterprises	631.0	42691.9	30693.0
私营独资企业	Private-funded Enterprises	6.8	99.4	548.1
私营有限责任公司	Private Limited Liability Corporations	624.2	42536.6	30103.1
私营股份有限公司	Private Share-holding Corporations Ltd.		55.9	41.8
其他企业	Other Enterprises	206.8	652.0	13200.0
港、澳、台商投资企业	Enterprises with Funds from Hong Kong，Macao &Taiwan	48.0	9810.3	8536.8
与港澳台商合资经营	Joint-venture Enterprises	0.9	6660.7	5429.5
港澳台商独资	Enterprises with Sole Investment	47.1	3149.6	3107.3
外商投资企业	Foreign Funded Enterprises	19.5	16396.3	351.6
中外合资经营	Joint-venture Enterprises	19.5	16396.3	351.6
外资企业	Foreign Owned Enterprises			
2.按国民经济行业分组	Grouped by Sector			
农畜产品批发业	Wholesale of Farm produce and livestock products	12.9	629.1	276.6
食品、饮料及烟草制品批发	Wholesale of Beverages and Tobaccos	18546.7	110452.9	14609.1
烟草制品批发业	Wholesale of Tobaccos	18461.6	101759.9	10995.9
纺织、服装及日用品批发业	Wholesale of Textiles,Garments and Daily Consumer Articles	522.7	21788.0	8316.1
文化、体育用品及器材批发	Wholesale of Culture,Sports Applionces and Equipments	148.8	9128.3	3589.4

continued 1

(10 000 yuan)

管理费用 Managenment Expenses	财务费用 Financial Expenses	利息支出 Interest Expenditure	营业利润 Business Profits	利润总额 Total Profits	应交所得税 Income Tax Payable	应付工资 Salary payable	应付福利费 Welfare funds	全部从业人员年平均人数（人） Average Number of Employed Persons(person)
272588.7	**45243.1**	**22778.8**	**397200.1**	**387876.5**	**67584.2**	**161218.2**	**10952.2**	**71502**
86302.2	**16163.5**	**3535.9**	**114978.3**	**123549.3**	**25157.7**	**52444.2**	**3772.7**	**15741**
53291.5	6735.7	4084.9	107622.4	111842.3	22461.4	32222.4	2009.1	8127
83706.7	11717.3	3633.3	104701.8	113117.0	24677.6	49703.0	3358.4	15336
49464.9	2053.3	1158.0	83108.3	82912.2	21944.7	23055.7	1217.4	4897
888.5	18.8	18.6	-34.5	47.6	15.3	253.2	44.1	201
58.8	12.3		2.8	2.8	0.7	36.5	14.1	10
58.8	12.3		2.8	2.8	0.7	36.5	14.1	10
17014.6	5549.0	2284.8	11540.6	13393.1	1572.8	10205.2	867.6	4089
2142.2	-6.8	-6.8	181.8	292.8	62.5	921.7	113.0	302
14872.4	5555.8	2291.6	11358.8	13100.3	1510.3	9283.5	754.6	3787
5052.9	400.0	362.2	22895.7	27926.5	301.0	10572.2	886.9	3979
10559.8	2859.9	-205.3	1228.1	2850.2	739.7	4473.0	225.8	1712
156.6	27.4	27.1	-632.7	-632.7		124.5	17.4	54
10367.1	2861.9	-203.0	1853.4	3475.5	739.7	4337.8	208.4	1653
36.1	-29.4	-29.4	7.4	7.4		10.7		5
667.2	824.0	15.0	-14039.2	-14015.4	103.4	1107.2	102.5	448
703.2	-23.3	-28.9	593.6	599.3	239.7	2288.0	401.0	289
412.4	-28.5	-28.5	847.3	848.3	239.7	1021.2	114.0	139
290.8	5.2	-0.4	-253.7	-249.0		1266.8	287.0	150
1892.3	4469.5	-68.5	9682.9	9833.0	240.4	453.2	13.3	116
1892.3	4469.5	-68.5	9682.9	9833.0	240.4	453.2	13.3	116
1011.4	460.1	459.9	-370.9	76.5	14.1	216.1	35.3	298
20456.8	-225.3	-292.1	77208.6	77865.2	19666.0	13691.6	471.1	1967
18396.3	-291.4	-292.1	73234.9	73513.0	18802.1	12689.5	393.9	1551
5078.7	222.6	149.6	9441.6	9919.2	435.9	5244.5	500.5	2133
4314.2	-302.1	-334.0	1526.8	1591.0	604.4	423.4	57.1	384

14-8 续表2

单位：万元

分类	Classify	单位数（个）Number (unit)	流动资产 小计 Circulating Funds	存货 Inventories	固定资产原价 Original Value of Fixed Assets
医药及医疗器材批发	Wholesale of Medicines and Medical Appliances	21	124965.5	32455.2	8208.8
矿产品、建材及化工产品批发	Wholesale of Mineral Products, Building Materials and Chemical Products	80	1585242.9	229615.7	223083.8
煤炭及制品批发	Wholesale of Coal and Related Products	6	31156.3	5359.6	2285.9
石油及制品批发业	Wholesale of Petrolem and Related Products	20	371613.7	70755.9	141530.2
金属及金属矿批发业	Wholesale of Metal metals	39	1066095.0	122607.4	71719.9
建材批发业	Wholesale of Building Materials	9	56370.8	15918.4	6329.5
化肥批发业	Wholesale of Chemicel Fertilizer	3	53353.6	13160.0	635.8
其他化工产品批发	Wholesale of Other Chemical Products	3	6653.5	1814.4	582.5
机械设备、五金交电及电子产品批发业	Wholesale of Machinery, Hardware, and Electronic Equipment	36	500419.1	89585.8	23746.7
汽车、摩托车及零配件批发业	Wholesale of Motor Vehicles, Motocycles and Parts	9	253401.9	40463.3	9144.9
家用电器批发业	Wholesale of Household Electrical Appliances	5	114656.9	14083.8	1766.6
计算机、软件及辅助设备批发业	Wholesale of Computers,Software and Peripherals	2	13056.3	0.6	657.7
贸易经纪与代理	Trade Borker and Agency	1	12985.2	4908.0	109.8
其他批发业	Other wholesale not Classified Elsewhere				
二、零售企业	**Retail Trade**	**260**	**1923416.0**	**420782.8**	**906224.2**
#国有控股	State-owned ding Majority Shares	25	193105.4	58154.6	54332.3
1.按登记注册类型分组	Grouped by Category of Commodities				
内资企业	Domestic Funded Enterprises	240	1615950.5	332247.6	784715.7
国有企业	State-owned Enterprises	14	75892.8	27874.0	22329.4
集体企业	Collective-owned Enterprises	15	3856.8	2379.6	2666.2
股份合作企业	Share-Holding Cooperative Enterprises	4	3317.3	809.2	544.5
有限责任公司	Limited Liability Corporrations	92	651898.1	126619.2	393082.1
国有独资	State Funded Corporations	1	22479.8	9083.6	19783.7
其他有限责任公司	Other Limited Liability Corporrations	91	629418.3	117535.6	373298.4
股份有限公司	Share-holding Corporations Ltd.	4	303316.8	70486.4	163192.1
私营企业	Private Enterprises	108	576616.8	103632.2	201346.5
私营独资企业	Private-funded Enterprises	14	16861.8	5689.6	2265.3
私营合伙企业	Private Partnership Enterprises	4	6307.4	3790.4	2273.1
私营有限责任公司	Private Limited Liability Corporations	82	504497.6	86191.3	194561.4
私营股份有限公司	Private Share-holding Corporations Ltd.	8	48950.0	7960.9	2246.7
其他企业	Other Enterprises	3	1051.9	447.0	1554.9

continued 2

(10 000 yuan)

累计折旧 Accumulated Depreciation	本年折旧 In The Year	资产合计 Total Assets	负债合计 Total Liabilities	实收资本 Paid in Capital	营业收入 Total Revenue	主营业务收入 Revenue from Principal Business	主营业务成本 Cost of Principal Business
2977.7	519.0	145140.9	124863.9	35992.1	377415.8	377155.6	356688.7
55580.7	11025.6	1961853.4	1562436.8	386987.0	5414585.0	5398572.1	5219747.1
311.2	190.3	34586.6	18203.6	8800.0	125267.3	125267.3	106278.5
44130.5	8754.1	557510.3	431147.4	149747.2	2541429.7	2532134.8	2442961.9
9220.6	1645.4	1241739.4	1010071.4	209426.3	2549522.4	2543033.9	2478599.2
1371.5	294.3	63640.7	47617.3	13353.5	142377.5	142148.0	134769.4
231.1	99.8	56405.2	48928.5	4600.0	25674.8	25674.8	27367.9
315.8	41.7	7971.2	6468.6	1060.0	30313.3	30313.3	29770.2
9481.6	1599.5	535389.7	515169.1	29467.1	1269378.1	1265056.0	1202301.2
2622.1	519.3	269291.5	260202.4	13115.7	659081.9	658242.0	623843.3
293.0	22.1	116232.9	115294.5	1778.6	160594.7	160400.8	154109.9
417.8	308.6	13417.3	15061.4	1973.8	253348.2	253348.2	243489.9
43.4	5.7	13394.0	12540.8	923.8	28320.5	28009.2	24637.5
205202.7	**29310.1**	**3039469.7**	**2307385.1**	**486399.2**	**6750162.3**	**6648888.6**	**5840519.0**
15808.2	1534.3	247977.7	191809.1	46911.4	543512.2	539997.0	487123.5
177974.9	24870.4	2513364.2	1906425.0	417549.4	5870350.7	5794765.0	5127678.5
5269.2	633.9	96643.6	58503.6	23570.3	223966.1	222610.4	197517.2
716.1	19.2	7224.4	7473.8	1984.8	43066.5	43055.4	39882.1
234.9	10.5	9211.2	8675.2	443.7	48902.1	48902.1	46640.4
72028.4	9165.7	1129278.6	853956.9	208408.4	3202219.6	3175757.9	2807270.4
5999.1	579.8	37438.3	27841.0	2740.0	30039.9	29684.8	22652.5
66029.3	8585.9	1091840.3	826115.9	205668.4	3172179.7	3146073.1	2784617.9
55661.2	7459.3	449553.0	302335.4	50496.4	406141.8	389200.7	327484.1
43919.4	7555.4	818944.0	673556.1	131335.8	1940993.4	1910177.3	1705239.0
508.7	205.3	19059.3	15633.6	2242.9	56823.3	55801.5	46629.7
519.0	139.1	9793.5	6497.9	1578.0	38771.9	38771.9	36823.3
42058.4	6835.7	732168.8	598170.6	120829.9	1724530.8	1694789.7	1511891.0
833.3	375.3	57922.4	53254.0	6685.0	120867.4	120814.2	109895.0
145.7	26.4	2509.4	1924.0	1310.0	5061.2	5061.2	3645.3

14-8 续表3

单位：万元

分　类	Classify	主营业务税金及附加 Taxs and Other Changes on Principal Business	主营业务利润 Profits from Prinapal Business	营业费用 Expenses for Operation
医药及医疗器材批发	Wholesale of Medicines and Medical Appliances	260.9	20206.0	14067.7
矿产品、建材及化工产品批发	Wholesale of Mineral Products, Building Materials and Chemical Products	13259.1	165565.9	102934.0
煤炭及制品批发	Wholesale of Coal and Related Products	229.4	18759.4	16991.2
石油及制品批发业	Wholesale of Petrolem and Related Products	7191.3	81981.6	57519.3
金属及金属矿批发业	Wholesale of Metal metals	5599.1	58835.6	22800.8
建材批发业	Wholesale of Building Materials	224.5	7154.1	4673.7
化肥批发业	Wholesale of Chemicel Fertilizer	8.4	-1701.5	856.3
其他化工产品批发	Wholesale of Other Chemical Products	6.4	536.7	92.7
机械设备、五金交电及电子产品批发业	Wholesale of Machinery, Hardware, and Electronic Equipment	593.8	62161.0	43170.4
汽车、摩托车及零配件批发业	Wholesale of Motor Vehicles, Motocycles and Parts	321.1	34077.6	23267.7
家用电器批发业	Wholesale of Household Electrical Appliances	80.8	6210.1	6095.5
计算机、软件及辅助设备批发业	Wholesale of Computers,Software and Peripherals	48.0	9810.3	8536.8
贸易经纪与代理	Trade Borker and Agency	1.4	3370.3	3209.2
其他批发业	Other wholesale not Classified Elsewhere			
二、零售企业	**Retail Trade**	**70483.9**	**737885.7**	**334532.8**
#国有控股	State-owned ding Majority Shares	1630.5	51243.0	21721.1
1.按登记注册类型分组	Grouped by Category of Commodities			
内资企业	Domestic Funded Enterprises	64410.2	602676.3	253796.0
国有企业	State-owned Enterprises	1026.6	24066.6	8257.2
集体企业	Collective-owned Enterprises	125.7	3047.6	1195.7
股份合作企业	Share-Holding Cooperative Enterprises	219.5	2042.2	1496.4
有限责任公司	Limited Liability Corporrations	45704.8	322782.7	130663.6
国有独资	State Funded Corporations	82.2	6950.1	3529.8
其他有限责任公司	Other Limited Liability Corporrations	45622.6	315832.6	127133.8
股份有限公司	Share-holding Corporations Ltd.	1607.2	60109.4	19955.0
私营企业	Private Enterprises	15476.0	189462.3	91724.0
私营独资企业	Private-funded Enterprises	503.0	8668.8	2188.2
私营合伙企业	Private Partnership Enterprises	24.5	1924.1	459.7
私营有限责任公司	Private Limited Liability Corporations	8623.5	174275.2	85111.5
私营股份有限公司	Private Share-holding Corporations Ltd.	6325.0	4594.2	3964.6
其他企业	Other Enterprises	250	1165.5	504.1

continued 3

(10 000 yuan)

管理费用 Management Expenses	财务费用 Financial Expenses	利息支出 Interest Expenditure	营业利润 Business Profits	利润总额 Total Profits	应交所得税 Income Tax Payable	应付工资 Salary payable	应付福利费 Welfare funds	全部从业人员年平均人数（人） Average Number of Employed Persons(person)
5368.4	8.7	-90.6	922.3	958.5	486.7	3159.7	182.0	1968
31163.2	16357.9	4962.2	24481.0	32245.5	3307.1	21953.9	1647.9	6871
1940.2	283.1	274.2	-455.1	-438.5	122.9	541.9	26.5	144
12755.5	4968.0	694.6	10554.7	15157.4	873.1	13526.3	779.8	4794
13359.5	10611.5	3665.4	17389.3	17537.8	2257.4	6426.1	661.5	1456
2398.1	219.1	56.7	92.0	133.1	49.1	1156.3	155.2	300
469.9	244.3	241.1	-3272.0	-303.4	0.3	196.6	11.9	135
240.0	31.9	30.2	172.1	159.1	4.3	106.7	13.0	42
18711.9	-358.4	-1319.1	1766.7	891.5	643.5	7660.1	878.8	2094
10725.6	-835.8	-1082.7	1720.4	1594.1	72.8	1354.7	119.3	502
1758.0	-495.0	-519.5	-1004.9	-1006.5	107.8	1230.7	206.1	382
703.2	-23.3	-28.9	593.6	599.3	239.7	2288.0	401.0	289
197.6			2.2	1.9		94.9		26
186286.5	**29079.6**	**19242.9**	**282221.8**	**264327.2**	**42426.5**	**108774.0**	**7179.5**	**55761**
26773.3	154.9	-48.9	5660.2	8814.5	1213.0	13039.1	1356.8	5322
154594.5	23190.7	15587.2	240130.9	219586.3	35540.7	88631.8	6430.0	45559
14559.9	376.7	312.5	1805.5	1764.8	320.5	5609.2	658.9	2386
1264.9	35.5	28.1	562.6	551.4	153.3	1041.7	8.8	1016
498.9	7.0	3.7	39.9	45.2	4.3	1806.4	12.9	1325
81320.2	10779.9	6402.5	125345.3	122834.7	17307.5	43871.1	3041.7	20822
3715.7	-91.9	-91.9	151.6	212.5		2555.5	307.2	940
77604.5	10871.8	6494.4	125193.7	122622.2	17307.5	41315.6	2734.5	19882
23781.9	4763.1	4762.9	26672.2	8134.1	2202.5	10630.8	1455.1	5841
32785.0	7190.7	4077.6	85465.5	86053.7	15500.4	25578.4	1248.5	14107
1602.6	172.6	21.1	5526.5	5490.1	239.1	955.9	38.5	784
1045.3	237.9	236.8	181.2	158.8	16.8	451.5	53.8	347
29202.4	6548.7	3693.3	80257.7	78459.6	15205.0	23128.2	1071.2	12476
934.7	231.5	126.4	-499.9	1945.2	39.5	1042.8	85.0	500
383.7	37.8	-0.1	239.9	202.4	52.2	94.2	4.1	62

14-8 续表4

单位：万元

分　　类	Classify	单位数（个）Number (unit)	流动资产 小计 Circulating Funds	存货 Inventories	固定资产原价 Original Value of Fixed Assets
港、澳、台商投资企业	Enterprises with Funds from Hong Kong，Macao &Taiwan	6	220170.2	62917.1	77456.5
与港澳台商合资经营企业	Joint-venture Enterprises	1	7936.6	1786.5	3368.9
港澳抬商独资	Wholly Funded from Hong Kong, Macao and Taiwan	4	102649.9	52130.5	58608.4
外商投资股份有限公司	Share-holding Corporations Ltd.	1	109583.7	9000.1	15479.2
外商投资企业	Foreign Funded Enterprises	14	87295.3	25618.1	44052.0
中外合资经营企业	Joint-venture Enterprises	3	9758.7	4900.4	31074.4
外资企业	Enterprises with Sole Fund	10	67335.8	20526.9	12099.7
外商投资股份有限公司	Share-holding Corporations Ltd.	1	10200.8	190.8	877.9
2.按国民经济行业分组	Grouped by Sector				
综合零售	Integrated Retail	75	671859.3	129434.3	363129.4
百货零售	Retail of General Merchandise	38	454750.8	81103.2	284046.9
超级市场零售	Retail of Supermarkets	28	215208.5	47403.5	77023.0
其他综合零售	Other Integrated Retail	9	1900.0	927.6	2059.5
食品、饮料及烟草制品专门零售	Retail of Food, Beverages and Tobaccos special retail trade	7	102499.1	48386.7	99395.2
纺织、服装及日用品专门零售	Special Retail of Textiles, Garments and Daily Consumer Articles	19	209497.4	31077.2	221171.6
#服装零售	Retail of Garments	11	178950.4	9182.6	217721.7
文化、体育用品及器材专门零售	Retail of Culture,Sports Appliances and Equipments	14	53942.3	21568.6	22067.7
#图书零售	Retail of Book	3	35549.2	18126.3	21319.0
医药及医疗器材专门零售	Retail of Medinces and Medical Appliances Special	10	100931.5	22877.4	8141.1
#药品零售	Retail of Medinces	10	100931.5	22877.4	8141.1
汽车、摩托车、燃料及零配件专门零售	Retail of Motor Vehicles, Motorcycle, Fuel and Parts special retail trade	99	495101.3	127473.7	139975.6
#汽车零售业	Retail of Motorcar Vehicles	81	478998.5	124609.7	125435.7
家用电器及电子产品专门零售	Household Appliances and Electronic products special retail trade	20	202631.2	29239.3	7562.9
#家用电器零售	Retail of Household Electric Appliances	9	174098.2	17619.9	5150.4
计算机、软件及辅助设备零售	Retail of Computer, Software and Peripherals	5	13174.9	4055.6	1619.3
通讯设备零售	Retail of Communication Equipment	3	12718.7	6919.6	627.4
五金、家具及室内装修材料专门零售	Ironware, Furniture and Room fitting stuff special retail trade	14	81397.7	8371.9	43424.3
无店铺及其他零售	Retail of No Stores and Others	2	5556.2	2353.7	1356.4

continued 4

(10 000 yuan)

累计折旧 Accumulated Depreciation	本年折旧 In The Year	资产合计 Total Assets	负债合计 Total Liabilities	实收资本 Paid in Capital	营业收入 Total Revenue	主营业务收入 Revenue from Principal Business	主营业务成本 Cost of Principal Business
18705.9	2275.5	387069.9	292156.1	36059.1	475108.1	456901.0	384294.5
741.7	379.9	11161.2	4829.0	1100.0	59706.3	59496.6	54655.5
15226.7	1256.3	253085.4	183630.6	11409.1	316140.5	300161.0	250832.0
2737.5	639.3	122823.3	103696.5	23550.0	99261.3	97243.4	78807.0
8521.9	2164.2	139035.6	108804.0	32790.7	404703.5	397222.6	328546.0
3836.5	632.8	40730.7	27241.7	11445.1	128424.8	126438.6	110831.4
3871.7	1363.2	88039.9	74252.7	19845.6	234663.3	230728.5	186512.3
813.7	168.2	10265.0	7309.6	1500.0	41615.4	40055.5	31202.3
109614.1	10592.7	1181971.0	867150.8	222710.7	1930420.2	1856627.0	1588874.9
83257.6	7109.0	864082.2	593657.0	196113.5	1210968.6	1178151.4	994133.2
25960.0	3450.2	311824.8	268169.4	25910.2	697149.8	656173.8	576146.0
396.5	33.5	6064.0	5324.4	687.0	22301.8	22301.8	18595.7
23327.4	4629.2	192907.5	145766.2	11563.1	120196.9	120196.9	88759.0
14254.5	4593.0	435694.3	400441.2	24389.4	430169.5	428369.9	277473.8
13395.2	4359.4	401018.0	377073.7	21791.6	360756.9	359736.6	228866.8
7247.3	645.6	81545.4	62389.8	14537.2	124730.1	124234.9	109771.4
6700.9	617.3	51540.5	38441.2	4779.1	49892.7	49397.5	40123.3
4112.1	389.9	113774.9	106828.7	20098.6	163107.5	162163.2	145475.6
4112.1	389.9	113774.9	106828.7	20098.6	163107.5	162163.2	145475.6
29801.1	6138.9	670070.3	489224.1	136364.0	2773110.4	2771394.7	2608468.2
28356.4	5943.0	638664.9	481691.8	111826.7	2729793.6	2728099.2	2571831.3
2644.5	505.0	212722.9	139628.1	19459.2	764610.2	744176.4	647844.4
1560.7	262.7	181911.9	117884.6	11056.6	668609.5	649108.7	561070.8
630.6	155.3	14169.0	9151.4	5709.6	47802.4	47727.5	45200.1
373.9	83.8	13215.1	9661.4	1139.0	44924.8	44150.7	38505.9
13729.6	1739.5	144220.0	90368.0	36797.0	420871.5	419814.0	356408.8
472.1	76.3	6563.4	5588.2	480.0	22946.0	21911.6	17442.9

14-8 续表5

单位：万元

分类	Classify	主营业务税金及附加 Taxs and Other Changes on Principal Business	主营业务利润 Profits from Prinapal Business	营业费用 Expenses for Operation
港、澳、台商投资企业	Enterprises with Funds from Hong Kong, Macao &Taiwan	1384.4	71222.1	47058.1
与港澳台商合资经营企业	Joint-venture Enterprises		4841.1	1709.2
港澳台商独资	Wholly Funded from Hong Kong, Macao and Taiwan	772.3	48556.7	37969.9
港澳台商投资股份有限公司	Share-holding Corporations Ltd.	612.1	17824.3	7379.0
外商投资企业	Foreign Funded Enterprises	4689.3	63987.3	33678.7
中外合资经营企业	Joint-venture Enterprises	190.6	15416.6	8299.7
外资企业	Enterprises with Sole Fund	4259.8	39956.4	23513.5
外商投资股份有限公司	Share-holding Corporations Ltd.	238.9	8614.3	1865.5
2.按国民经济行业分组	Grouped by Sector			
综合零售	Integrated Retail	17080.5	250671.6	170130.3
百货零售	Retail of General Merchandise	7937.2	176081.0	91076.9
超级市场零售	Retail of Supermarkets	8722.1	71305.7	77530.5
其他综合零售	Other Integrated Retail	421.2	3284.9	1522.9
食品、饮料及烟草制品专门零售	Retail of Food, Beverages and Tobaccos special retail trade	6770.6	24667.3	11689.3
纺织、服装及日用品专门零售	Special Retail of Textiles, Garments and Daily Consumer Articles	5350.7	145545.4	32399.5
#服装零售	Retail of Garments	5247.2	125622.6	23265.0
文化、体育用品及器材专门零售	Retail of Culture,Sports Appliances and Equipments	264.1	14199.4	8657.3
#图书零售	Retail of Book	93.0	9181.2	3959.5
医药及医疗器材专门零售	Retail of Medinces and Medical Appliances Special	248.1	16439.5	10043.6
#药品零售	Retail of Medinces	248.1	16439.5	10043.6
汽车、摩托车、燃料及零配件专门零售	Retail of Motor Vehicles, Motorcycle, Fuel and Parts special retail trade	33765.8	129160.7	49771.7
#汽车零售业	Retail of Motorcar Vehicles	33464.9	122803.0	47044.5
家用电器及电子产品专门零售	Household Appliances and Electronic products special retail trade	1922.9	94409.1	34853.1
#家用电器零售	Retail of Household Electric Appliances	1681.7	86356.2	28047.9
计算机、软件及辅助设备零售	Retail of Computer, Software and Peripherals	78.8	2448.6	1777.3
通讯设备零售	Retail of Communication Equipment	143.5	5501.3	5025.4
五金、家具及室内装修材料专门零售	Ironware, Furniture and Room fitting stuff special retail trade	4941.2	58464.0	13677.7
无店铺及其他零售	Retail of No Stores and Others	140.0	4328.7	3310.3

continued 5

(10 000 yuan)

管理费用 Managenment Expenses	财务费用 Financial Expenses	利息支出 Interest Expenditure	营业利润 Business Profits	利润总额 Total Profits	应交所得税 Income Tax Payable	应付工资 Salary payable	应付福利费 Welfare funds	全部从业人员年平均人数（人） Average Number of Employed Persons(person)
16089.4	4607.0	3606.8	21860.8	27068.0	2983.3	14180.0	150.9	6490
1009.3	10.8		2310.8	4210.0	1056.8	856.6		120
9646.2	184.0	-121.6	16932.9	20309.2	1289.3	10620.5	3.8	5897
5433.9	4412.2	3728.4	2617.1	2548.8	637.2	2702.9	147.1	473
15602.6	1281.9	48.9	20230.1	17672.9	3902.5	5962.2	598.6	3712
2362.2	488.0	135.6	6041.8	6245.7	1461.2	1391.6	219.6	961
9726.5	685.0	-86.7	9580.4	6755.4	1707.9	4147.2	372.8	2578
3513.9	108.9		4607.9	4671.8	733.4	423.4	6.2	173
81212.2	9764.8	6643.1	59334.0	58444.7	10891.9	49528.6	2244.8	27209
68033.3	10586.0	7717.0	38468.5	37886.1	8289.8	30570.3	1873.1	14041
12024.9	-829.9	-1073.9	20266.2	19870.5	2443.5	18497.9	362.6	12661
1154.0	8.7		599.3	688.1	158.6	460.4	9.1	507
3836.3	5644.8	5470.4	3501.0	3956.5	416.4	3709.5	347.4	2529
32338.0	2010.2	480.5	80325.0	77662.9	14018.6	11449.9	484.1	6296
27288.7	1651.8	272.6	74165.1	71147.1	13625.5	5154.6	231.1	3028
6671.9	111.6	29.0	-746.2	2045.7	131.6	6367.8	457.5	2091
5673.1	-59.9	-91.9	103.7	103.4		3495.2	440.8	1209
5476.9	-595.3	-637.8	2449.3	4028.3	515.6	3595.0	83.9	3274
5476.9	-595.3	-637.8	2449.3	4028.3	515.6	3595.0	83.9	3274
29449.8	8859.7	4789.8	42528.1	51008.2	9981.6	19108.0	1586.4	7420
26743.3	8808.1	4776.1	41634.4	50163.3	9793.1	18065.0	1397.9	6947
12794.1	639.7	-1.2	64125.0	44813.6	3865.5	10708.5	1509.8	5162
11631.7	497.7	-10.2	63326.0	43904.6	3701.7	7434.5	1287.3	4022
582.5	105.9	5.4	55.5	61.7	46.8	743.4	11.6	276
513.5	35.1	4.0	701.4	700.8	107.5	1468.8	198.0	378
11875.1	2654.5	2481.7	31274.6	22439.2	2586.7	2566.1	260.7	1307
2632.2	-10.4	-12.6	-569.0	-71.9	18.6	1740.6	204.9	473

14-9 限额以上住宿和餐饮业企业主要财务状况（2009年）

单位：万元

分 类	Classify	单位数（个）Number (unit)	流动资产 小 计 Circulating Funds	存 货 Inventories	固定资产原价 Original Value of Fixed Assets
总 计	**Total**	**422**	**416194.4**	**34263.1**	**997019.0**
一、住宿业	**Hotel Services**	**156**	**245635.7**	**16394.4**	**735643.2**
#国有控股	State-holding Majority Shares	54	72126.9	6384.3	243879.2
1.按登记注册类型分组	Grouped by Type of Registration				
内资企业	Domestic Funded Enterprises	142	194605.2	14000.5	474381.2
国有企业	State-owned Enterprises	43	55444.4	5644.6	216358.7
集体企业	Collective-owned Enterprises	2	93.1	13.9	5479.0
股份合作企业	Cooperative Enterprises				
联营企业	Joint Ownership Enterprises				
国有联营企业	State Joint Ownership Enterprises				
集体联营企业	Collective Joint Ownership Enterprises				
国有与集体联营企业	Joint State-collective Enterprises				
其他联营企业	Others Joint Ownership Enterprises				
有限责任公司	Limited Liability Corporrations	51	92637.7	3432.5	134255.5
国有独资企业	State Sole Funded Corporations				
其他有限责任公司	Other Limited Liability Corporrations	51	92637.7	3432.5	134255.5
股份有限公司	Share-holding Corporations Ltd.	5	3040.9	113.7	12983.6
私营企业	Private Enterprises	38	42508.0	4744.6	104440.3
私营独资企业	Private-funded Enterprises	3	980.0	57.9	875.0
私营合伙企业	Private Partnership Enterprises				
私营有限责任公司	Private Limited Liability Corporations	34	38834.3	4250.8	103565.3
私营股份有限公司	Private Share-holding Corporations Ltd.	1	2693.7	435.9	
其他企业	Other Enterprises	3	881.1	51.2	864.1
港、澳、台商投资企业	Enterprises with Funds from Hong Kong, Macao &Taiwan	7	23131.2	1074.0	87422.8
合资经营企业（港或澳、台资）	Joint-venture Enterprises	3	10352.2	645.2	21488.0
合作经营企业（港或澳、台资）	Cooperative enterprises	1	2790.2	234.5	38144.6
港澳台商独资	Enterprise with Sole Fund	3	9988.8	194.3	27790.2
港澳台商独资股份有限公司	Share-holding Corporations Ltd. With their Investment				
外商投资企业	Foreign Funded Enterprises	7	27899.3	1319.9	173839.2
中外合资经营企业	Joint-venture Enterprises	2	5490.3	338.0	59364.4
中外合作经营企业	Cooperation Enterprises	3	5879.0	323.9	44058.5
外资企业	Foreign Funded Enterprises	2	16530.0	658.0	70416.3
外商投资股份有限公司	Share-holding Corporations Ltd. With Foreign funds				
2.按住宿行业中类分组	Grouped by Major Group of Hotel Services				
旅游饭店	Tourist Hotel	122	225273.1	14904.2	700173.0
一般旅馆	Normal Hotel	33	18435.6	1371.0	28675.3
其他住宿服务	Others	1	1927.0	119.2	6794.9

Finacial Status of Catering Enterprises Above Designated Size（2009）

(10 000 yuan)

累计折旧 Accumulated Depreciation	本年折旧 In The Year	资产合计 Total Assets	负债合计 Total Liabilities	实收资本 Paid in Capital	营业收入 Total Revenue	主营业务收入 Revenue from Principal Business	主营业务成本 Cost of Principal Business
379261.0	**53532.4**	**1283583.1**	**1077679.2**	**674785.9**	**817942.0**	**811474.3**	**357131.5**
277604.3	**34523.6**	**849747.5**	**849622.6**	**440541.4**	**304053.1**	**301435.0**	**90281.2**
99306.3	**9485.7**	**279660.1**	**264442.8**	**125364.5**	**104775.5**	**104370.3**	**33310.3**
158023.8	22684.3	632481.5	578496.4	326892.3	234976.1	233649.0	71505.3
88796.8	9349.8	238327.2	198787.9	113775.3	85635.9	85275.3	27070.7
1662.1	264.2	5225.5	1405.8	1796.4	1723.9	1723.9	1481.8
46477.1	6899.1	225179.7	230782.0	165173.3	88519.9	88309.7	26317.9
46477.1	6899.1	225179.7	230782.0	165173.3	88519.9	88309.7	26317.9
3383.6	545.0	13351.2	10880.4	671.9	5306.4	5292.1	833.5
17613.2	5573.5	148672.5	134003.1	44788.4	52091.9	51349.9	14919.0
601.9	120.1	1258.9	964.9	788.8	2075.1	2075.1	1128.2
17011.3	5453.4	144719.9	131773.5	43999.5	46319.6	45577.6	13090.5
		2693.7	1264.7	0.1	3697.2	3697.2	700.3
91.0	52.7	1725.4	2637.2	687.0	1698.1	1698.1	882.4
40069.6	3913.5	88822.1	60749.5	41714.0	21493.2	21042.3	6990.5
15111.2	1106.9	27347.1	13102.0	14274.0	11442.2	11442.2	2687.0
19157.9	608.4	21776.9	14852.5	6840.0	6492.9	6042.0	2456.0
5800.5	2198.2	39698.1	32795.0	20600.0	3558.1	3558.1	1847.5
79510.9	7925.8	128443.9	210376.7	71935.1	47583.8	46743.7	11785.4
30264.5	1509.8	36277.4	70953.5	15252.7	14879.6	14879.6	3756.4
36186.3	2040.2	13859.4	83686.4	11763.5	8899.3	8899.3	1254.9
13060.1	4375.8	78307.1	55736.8	44918.9	23804.9	22964.8	6774.1
269992.3	31779.9	785676.7	798932.2	313943.7	269601.1	267211.2	79290.1
6257.8	2251.5	50021.0	38186.4	120597.7	30874.8	30646.6	10139.0
1354.2	492.2	14049.8	12504.0	6000.0	3577.2	3577.2	852.1

14-9 续表1

单位：万元

分　类	Classify	主营业务税金及附加 Taxs and Other Changes on Principal Business	主营业务利润 Profits from Prinapal Business	营业费用 Expenses for Operation
总　计	**Total**	**40014.7**	**414328.1**	**246761.9**
一、住宿业	**Hotel Services**	**15395.7**	**195758.1**	**99980.2**
#国有控股	State-holding Majority Shares	5193.2	65866.8	35661.0
1.按登记注册类型分组	Grouped by Type of Registration			
内资企业	Domestic Funded Enterprises	12052.1	150091.6	84162.3
国有企业	State-owned Enterprises	4417.4	53787.2	29261.5
集体企业	Collective-owned Enterprises	62.9	179.2	12.3
股份合作企业	Cooperative Enterprises			
联营企业	Joint Ownership Enterprises			
国有联营企业	State Joint Ownership Enterprises			
集体联营企业	Collective Joint Ownership Enterprises			
国有与集体联营企业	Joint State-collective Enterprises			
其他联营企业	Others Joint Ownership Enterprises			
有限责任公司	Limited Liability Corporrations	4411.2	57580.6	31928.1
国有独资企业	State Sole Funded Corporations			
其他有限责任公司	Other Limited Liability Corporrations	4411.2	57580.6	31928.1
股份有限公司	Share-holding Corporations Ltd.	299.4	4159.2	2778.5
私营企业	Private Enterprises	2814.6	33616.3	19644.5
私营独资企业	Private-funded Enterprises	114.9	832.0	733.5
私营合伙企业	Private Partnership Enterprises			
私营有限责任公司	Private Limited Liability Corporations	2496.4	29990.7	18030.6
私营股份有限公司	Private Share-holding Corporations Ltd.	203.3	2793.6	880.4
其他企业	Other Enterprises	46.6	769.1	537.4
港、澳、台商投资企业	Enterprises with Funds from Hong Kong, Macao &Taiwan	995.7	13056.1	5977.0
合资经营企业（港或澳、台资）	Joint-venture Enterprises	562.2	8193.0	3501.9
合作经营企业（港或澳、台资）	Cooperative enterprises	310.9	3275.1	1446.9
港澳台商独资	Enterprise with Sole Fund	122.6	1588.0	1028.2
港澳台商独资股份有限公司	Share-holding Corporations Ltd. With their Investment			
外商投资企业	Foreign Funded Enterprises	2347.9	32610.4	9840.9
中外合资经营企业	Joint-venture Enterprises	743.1	10380.1	2978.5
中外合作经营企业	Cooperation Enterprises	449.2	7195.2	2741.2
外资企业	Foreign Funded Enterprises	1155.6	15035.1	4121.2
外商投资股份有限公司	Share-holding Corporations Ltd. With Foreign funds			
2.按住宿行业中类分组	Grouped by Major Group of Hotel Services			
旅游饭店	Tourist Hotel	13558.3	174362.8	86955.8
一般旅馆	Normal Hotel	1640.7	18866.9	11653.7
其他住宿服务	Others	197	2528.4	1370.7

continued 1

(10 000 yuan)

管理费用 Managenment Expenses	财务费用 Financial Expenses	利息支出 Interest Expenditure	营业利润 Business Profits	利润总额 Total Profits	应交所得税 Income Tax Payable	应付工资 Salary payable	应付福利费 Welfare funds	全部从业人员年平均人数（人） Average Number of Employed Persons(person)
151132.2	**18116.2**	**9072.9**	**8253.1**	**823.6**	**5951.2**	**132184.4**	**12407.0**	**72215**
106020.4	**13131.2**	**6193.1**	**-21438.2**	**-21447.2**	**1195.3**	**60559.8**	**8309.2**	**30257**
32296.7	5122.3	2679.1	-6943.7	-7480.3	392.8	25264.6	2093.7	12782
73923.7	10068.8	5208.5	-16945.2	-16219.4	540.9	51556.3	6079.6	25948
28485.3	4654.0	2254.6	-8380.5	-8080.8	248.8	21506.2	1822.8	10173
601.8	0.4		-435.3	-435.1		254.9	11.4	139
25409.7	2619.0	2275.2	-2196.9	-2801.5	82.1	17574.5	3129.7	9197
25409.7	2619.0	2275.2	-2196.9	-2801.5	82.1	17574.5	3129.7	9197
471.3	5.6		918.1	918.8	161.3	801.5	109.3	473
17302.4	2764.0	652.9	-5403.3	-4404.6	46.4	10676.3	1004.4	5542
153.4	43.5	33.1	-98.4	-67.2		191.3	10.9	196
15535.5	2717.5	619.8	-5601.6	-4634.1	46.4	9691.9	682.1	4985
1613.5	3.0		296.7	296.7		793.1	311.4	361
1653.2	25.8	25.8	-1447.3	-1416.2	2.3	742.9	2.0	424
10274.5	1772.3	318.5	-4669.9	-5468.6		3175.5	914.8	1439
5597.5	64.2		-974.4	-965.0		1255.4	303.3	698
2310.1	318.5	318.5	-498.8	-528.9		1357.7	592.2	430
2366.9	1389.6		-3196.7	-3974.7		562.4	19.3	311
21822.2	1290.1	666.1	176.9	240.8	654.4	5828.0	1314.8	2870
7869.2	283.1	-296.2	-750.7	-717.3	11.9	1687.3	285.6	917
5517.9	452.0	407.3	-1515.9	-1505.3		1589.3	770.1	1009
8435.1	555.0	555.0	2443.5	2463.4	642.5	2551.4	259.1	944
95502.5	12135.9	5793.6	-18497.8	-18722.8	1161.4	54040.1	8156.4	26338
9583.4	538.9	399.5	-2707.2	-2474.3	33.9	6004.9	152.8	3714
934.5	456.4		-233.2	-250.1		514.8		205

14-9 续表2

单位：万元

分　类	Classify	单位数（个）Number (unit)	流动资产 小计 Circulating Funds	存货 Inventories	固定资产原价 Original Value of Fixed Assets
二、餐饮业	**Catering Trade**	**266**	**170558.7**	**17868.7**	**261375.8**
#国有及国有控股	State-owned and State-holding Majority Shares	9	24436.1	2950.0	84845.3
1.按登记注册类型分组	Grouped by Type of Registration				
内资企业	Domestic Funded Enterprises	248	136406.0	14511.0	220753.6
国有企业	State-owned Enterprises	7	9125.8	891.9	65698.5
集体企业	Collective-owned Enterprises	3	226.9	90.0	221.1
股份合作企业	Share-Holding Cooperative Enterprises	2	794.9	68.9	67.8
有限责任公司	Limited Liability Corporrations	89	52131.1	4985.9	65930.8
其他有限责任公司	Others Limited Liability Corporrations	89	52131.1	4985.9	65930.8
股份有限公司	Corporations Ltd.	3	15269.5	2183.9	40662.9
私营企业	Private Enterprises	138	56029.8	5855.7	40784.2
私营独资企业	Private-funded Enterprises	29	3401.1	798.4	4837.9
私营合伙企业	Private Partnership Enterprises	6	1580.8	171.5	270.1
私营有限责任公司	Private Limited Liability Corporations	94	48612.3	4518.5	33753.3
私营股份有限公司	Private Share-holding Corporations Ltd.	9	2435.6	367.3	1922.9
其他企业	Other Enterprises	6	2828.0	434.7	7388.3
港、澳、台商投资企业	Enterprises with Funds from Hong Kong，Macao &Taiwan	6	19574.9	2622.9	20202.6
合资经营企业（港或澳、台资）	Joint-venture Enterprises	2	3344.6	707.4	4019.3
合作经营企业（港或澳、台资）	Cooperative enterprises	1	590.5	209.4	3249.8
独资经营企业	Enterprise with Sole Fund	3	15639.8	1706.1	12933.5
外商投资企业	Foreign Funded Enterprises	12	14577.8	734.8	20419.6
中外合资经营企业	Joint-venture Enterprises	4	3063.8	207.9	4323.7
中外合作经营企业	Cooperation Enterprises	1	9.0	7.8	67.3
外资企业	Foreign Funded Enterprises	7	11505.0	519.1	16028.6
2.按国民经济行业分组	Grouped by Sector				
正餐服务业	Dinner	255	148837.1	15818.5	241757.6
快餐服务业	Fast Food	10	21700.7	2046.7	19558.3
其他餐饮服务业	Other Catering Services	1	20.9	3.5	59.9

continued 2

(10 000 yuan)

累计折旧 Accumulated Depreciation	本年折旧 In The Year	资产合计 Total Assets	负债合计 Total Liabilities	实收资本 Paid in Capital	营业收入 Total Revenue	主营业务收入 Revenue from Principal Business	主营业务成本 Cost of Principal Business
101656.7	**19008.8**	**433835.6**	**228056.6**	**234244.5**	**513888.9**	**510039.3**	**266850.3**
27830.6	3833.3	117623.9	45519.4	51215.4	56631.0	56631.0	20556.8
81632.2	16887.0	363345.4	203132.0	189882.7	431043.0	430347.8	233752.1
14649.0	2447.9	66758.7	18104.5	52321.8	18118.8	18118.8	5237.8
51.9	49.7	445.8	662.5	175.0	2789.7	2789.7	2278.2
27.1	10.2	840.3	586.2	250.5	2545.6	2545.6	1238.8
31000.9	7971.3	111122.8	71779.9	44105.5	178261.7	178252.3	96708.0
31000.9	7971.3	111122.8	71779.9	44105.5	178261.7	178252.3	96708.0
15722.1	2071.9	71912.0	30321.9	20652.8	38900.6	38900.6	14977.0
16446.8	3882.8	102638.7	78671.5	66707.9	178947.9	178262.1	106897.4
1445.9	405.0	8038.9	5877.7	4448.8	23920.6	23373.4	15064.0
120.3	57.8	1869.9	1443.5	843.0	6818.8	6818.8	4672.8
14339.7	3264.3	87981.4	67686.3	58685.1	137825.6	137688.6	80156.4
540.9	155.7	4748.5	3664.0	2731.0	10382.9	10381.3	7004.2
3734.4	453.2	9627.1	3005.5	5669.2	11478.7	11478.7	6414.9
11347.0	1263.4	40092.6	9258.3	26209.8	64203.4	64046.9	25203.0
2641.9	396.9	5710.4	2092.9	2000.0	14559.7	14559.7	7184.2
907.9	90.7	6496.6	3572.8	1731.8	9567.0	9567.0	3510.3
7797.2	775.8	27885.6	3592.6	22478.0	40076.7	39920.2	14508.5
8677.5	858.4	30397.6	15666.3	18152.0	18642.5	15644.6	7895.2
1815.8	190.4	6639.8	6787.1	3319.8	3554.9	3554.9	1317.7
58.7	12.3	144.5	64.3	100.0	546.1	546.1	244.6
6803.0	655.7	23613.3	8814.9	14732.2	14541.5	11543.6	6332.9
91933.0	17882.5	390279.2	214044.4	212565.7	460265.4	459570.2	246754.6
9696.6	1114.3	43483.9	13976.1	21598.8	53375.8	50221.4	19917.7
27.1	12.0	72.5	36.1	80.0	247.7	247.7	178.0

14-9 续表3

单位：万元

分 类	Classify	主营业务税金及附加 Taxs and Other Changes on Principal Business	主营业务利润 Profits from Prinapal Business	营业费用 Expenses for Operation
二、餐饮业	**Catering Trade**	24619.0	218570.0	146781.7
#国有及国有控股	State-owned and State-holding Majority Shares	2874.8	33199.4	23043.0
1.按登记注册类型分组	Grouped by Type of Registration			
内资企业	Domestic Funded Enterprises	20975.0	175620.7	116278.1
国有企业	State-owned Enterprises	912.0	11969.0	8085.6
集体企业	Collective-owned Enterprises	74.9	436.6	54.3
股份合作企业	Share-Holding Cooperative Enterprises	140.0	1166.8	596.0
有限责任公司	Limited Liability Corporrations	8877.5	72666.8	43462.4
其他有限责任公司	Others Limited Liability Corporrations	8877.5	72666.8	43462.4
股份有限公司	Corporations Ltd.	1975.9	21947.7	16497.5
私营企业	Private Enterprises	8504.7	62860.0	44424.0
私营独资企业	Private-funded Enterprises	1191.7	7117.7	4833.2
私营合伙企业	Private Partnership Enterprises	250.4	1895.6	1578.0
私营有限责任公司	Private Limited Liability Corporations	6711.7	50820.5	36039.3
私营股份有限公司	Private Share-holding Corporations Ltd.	350.9	3026.2	1973.5
其他企业	Other Enterprises	490.0	4573.8	3158.3
港、澳、台商投资企业	Enterprises with Funds from Hong Kong，Macao &Taiwan	2946.6	35897.3	25060.1
合资经营企业（港或澳、台资）	Joint-venture Enterprises	727.6	6647.9	5838.5
合作经营企业（港或澳、台资）	Cooperative enterprises	478.4	5578.3	4763.6
独资经营企业	Enterprise with Sole Fund	1740.6	23671.1	14458.0
外商投资企业	Foreign Funded Enterprises	697.4	7052.0	5443.5
中外合资经营企业	Joint-venture Enterprises	186.5	2050.7	2168.4
中外合作经营企业	Cooperation Enterprises	27.3	274.2	26.8
外资企业	Foreign Funded Enterprises	483.6	4727.1	3248.3
2.按国民经济行业分组	Grouped by Sector			
正餐服务业	Dinner	22072.8	190742.8	125250.0
快餐服务业	Fast Food	2532.6	27771.1	21478.5
其他餐饮服务业	Other Catering Services	13.6	56.1	53.2

continued 3

(10 000 yuan)

管理费用 Management Expenses	财务费用 Financial Expenses	利息支出 Interest Expenditure	营业利润 Business Profits	利润总额 Total Profits	应交所得税 Income Tax Payable	应付工资 Salary payable	应付福利费 Welfare funds	全部从业人员年平均人数（人） Average Number of Employed Persons(person)
45111.8	4985.0	2879.8	29691.3	22270.8	4755.9	71624.6	4097.8	41958
7247.2	2004.6	1936.1	6407.1	6407.0	1656.0	10266.4	776.2	5296
38850.5	4668.7	2934.6	21423.6	15690.6	3381.3	59539.4	3874.3	35527
4688.4	415.7	342.4	-1220.7	-1366.5	40.9	4465.1	202.4	1984
440.5	4.2		-62.4	-62.9	4.2	259.9	10.9	184
428.2	1.5		141.1	143.2	35.7	401.9	5.2	243
15361.0	833.0	198.8	13015.6	6525.4	1318.0	25022.0	1845.7	14770
15361.0	833.0	198.8	13015.6	6525.4	1318.0	25022.0	1845.7	14770
2890.0	1606.4	1603.8	6456.3	6534.1	1581.2	6165.6	581.8	3630
14405.4	1798.7	792.5	2329.2	3132.7	392.9	21890.1	1200.5	13866
1144.1	89.3	44.8	1052.0	1122.0	135.3	3186.6	125.5	1877
342.9	49.0	30.1	-74.3	254.1	5.3	552.6	26.7	479
12142.5	1631.9	707.3	1103.6	1508.5	247.3	17156.2	984.7	10867
775.9	28.5	10.3	247.9	248.1	5.0	994.7	63.6	643
637.0	9.2	-2.9	764.5	784.6	8.4	1334.8	27.8	850
3244.0	243.2	33.9	7499.5	7452.2	1007.6	6564.9	69.5	3930
498.4	115.5	54.9	195.5	196.2	58.6	2658.5	55.9	1339
282.9	111.6		420.2	369.6	202.3	108.4	12.1	240
2462.7	16.1	-21.0	6883.8	6886.4	746.7	3798.0	1.5	2351
3017.3	73.1	-88.7	768.2	-872.0	367.0	5520.3	154.0	2501
546.4	187.4	52.6	-851.5	-2536.1	0.1	715.4	18.0	486
287.5			-40.1	-40.1		116.6		47
2183.4	-114.3	-141.3	1659.8	1704.2	366.9	4688.3	136.0	1968
41039.0	4947.3	3010.7	25106.7	17666.5	3480.3	66705.4	3975.6	38938
4049.6	37.7	-130.9	4604.9	4624.4	1275.6	4859.3	118.6	2993
23.2			-20.3	-20.1		59.9	3.6	27

14-10 限额以上批发和零售业商品购进、销售和库存总额（2009年）

Total Sales of Enterprises Above Designated Size in Wholesale and Retail Trades Grouped by Category of Commodities（2009）

单位：个、万元　　　　(unit,10 000 yuan)

分　类	Classify	法人单位 Number of Enterprises	销售合计 Total	批发额 Wholesale Trade	零售额 Retail Trade
总　计	**Total**	**422**	**15897062.1**	**8677267.9**	**7219794.2**
一、批发企业	**Wholesale Enterprises**	**162**	**8576937.1**	**8047737.5**	**529199.6**
#国有控股	State-holding Enterprises	40	4411190.1	4041604.2	369585.9
1.按登记注册类型分组	Grouped by Registration Status				
内资企业	Domestic Funded Enterprises	158	7403465.3	6926482.5	476982.8
国有企业	State-owned Enterprises	31	3075258.7	2813429.9	261828.8
集体企业	Collective-owned Enterprises	2	43834.7	43235.0	599.7
股份合作企业	Cooperative Enterprises				
联营企业	Joint Ownership Enterprises	1	4055.8	4055.8	
国有联营企业	State Joint Ownership Enterprises				
集体联营企业	Collective Joint Ownership Enterprises	1	4055.8	4055.8	
国有与集体联营企业	Joint State-collective Ownership Enterprises				
其他联营企业	Other Joint Ownership Enterprises				
有限责任公司	Limited Liability Corporrations	70	2197311.5	2130357.1	66954.4
国有独资公司	State-funded Corporations	2	81614.3	81614.3	
其他有限责任公司	Other Limited Liability Corporations	68	2115697.2	2048742.8	66954.4
股份有限公司	Stock Limited Corporation	4	709514.5	602086.0	107428.5
私营企业	Private Enterprises	48	875338.4	857229.7	18108.7
私营独资企业	Private-funded Enterprises	1	2173.5	2137.9	35.6
私营合伙	Private Partnership Enterprises				
私营有限责任公司	Private Limited Liability Corporations	46	872287.1	854214.0	18073.1
私营股份有限公司	Private Share Holding Corporations	1	877.8	877.8	
其他	Others	2	498151.7	476089.0	22062.7
港、澳、台商投资企业	Enterprises Funded by Hong Kong, Macao and Taiwan	2	253348.2	201880.8	51467.4
与港澳台商合资经营	Joint-venture with Funds from Hong Kong, Macao and Taiwan	1	180844.5	129377.1	51467.4
与港澳台商合作经营	Cooperative Enterprises with Funds from Hong Kong Macau and Taiwan				
港澳台商独资	Enterprises with Sole Investment from Hong Kong Macau and Taiwan	1	72503.7	72503.7	
港澳台商投资股份有限公司	Share Holding Enterprises Funded by Overseas Chinese from Hong Kong, Macao & Taiwan				
外商投资企业	Foreign Funded Enterprises	2	908699.3	908699.3	
中外合资企业	Sino-foreign Joint Ventures	2	908699.3	908699.3	
中外合作企业	Sino-Foreign Cooperative Operation Enterprises				
外资企业	Foreign Owned Enterprises				
外商投资股份有限公司	Limited Company Funded by Foreign Investment				
个体工商户	Individually-owned Business		11424.3	10674.9	749.4

14-10 续表1 continued 1

单位：个、万元 (unit、10 000 yuan)

分类	Classify	法人单位 Number of Enterprises	销售合计 Total	批发额 Wholesale Trade	零售额 Retail Trade
2.按国民经济行业分组	Grouped by Economic Sector				
农畜产品批发业	Wholesale of Agricultural and Livestock Products	2	29073.2	29073.2	
#谷物、豆及薯类批发	Wholesale of Cereal, Bean and Tuber	1	5800.8	5800.8	
食品、饮料及烟草制品批发	Wholesale of Food, Beverages and Tobacco Products	5	587457.8	584537.8	2920.0
#烟草制品批发业	Wholesale of Tobacco and Tobacco Products	2	544939.6	542339.6	2600.0
纺织、服装及日用品批发业	Wholesale of Textiles, Garments and Daily Articles	12	186955.9	186955.9	
文化、体育用品及器材批发	Wholesale of Culture, Sports Articles and Equipments	5	105890.3	104459.8	1430.5
医药及医疗器材批发	Wholesale of Medicines and Medical Appliances	21	420932.5	406087.8	14844.7
矿产品、建材及化工产品批发	Wholesale of Mineral Products, Building Materials and Chemical Products	80	5878744.1	5527618.4	351125.7
#煤炭及制品批发	Wholesale of Coal and Related Products	6	145537.3	144181.2	1356.1
石油及制品批发业	Wholesale of Petroleum and Related Products	20	2787528.8	2438087.8	349441.0
金属及金属矿批发业	Wholesale of Metals and Metal Minerals	39	2736757.9	2736429.3	328.6
建材批发业	Wholesale of Building Materials	9	146650.3	146650.3	
其他化工产品批发	Wholesale of Other Chemical Products	3	36595.0	36595.0	
机械设备、五金交电及电子产品批发业	Wholesale of Machinery, Hardwares, Transport Means and Electronic Products	36	1329774.1	1170995.4	158778.7
#汽车、摩托车及零配件批发业	Wholesale of Motor Vehicles, Motorcycles and Parts	9	710554.1	613572.2	96981.9
家用电器批发	Wholesale of Electronic Household Equipments	5	168292.8	167610.2	682.6
计算机、软件及辅助设备批发业	Wholesale of Motor Vehicles, Motorcycles and Parts	2	253348.2	201880.8	51467.4
贸易经纪与代理	Trade Manage and Agent	1	38109.2	38009.2	100.0
其他批发	Other Wholesales				
3.经营形式分组	Grouped by Means of Operation				
独立门店	Independent shop	110	3637617.6	3484571.7	153045.9
连锁总店	Headquarter of chain store	1	536126.0	536126.0	
连锁门店	Chain store	2	571535.2	464106.7	107428.5
其他	other	49	3831658.3	3562933.1	268725.2
二、零售企业	**Retail Trade**	**260**	**7320125.0**	**629530.4**	**6690594.6**
#国有控股	State-holding Enterprises	25	569368.8	45527.1	523841.7
1.按登记注册类型分组	Grouped by Registration Status				
内资企业	Domestic Funded Enterprises	240	6325166.9	623924.3	5701242.6
国有企业	State-owned Enterprises	14	227583.6	155.3	227428.3
集体企业	Collective-owned Enterprises	15	45279.1	839.0	44440.1
股份合作企业	Cooperative Enterprises	4	49169.6		49169.6

14-10 续表2 continued 2

单位：个、万元 (unit,10 000 yuan)

分　　类	Classify	法人单位 Number of Enterprises	销售合计 Total	批发额 Wholesale Trade	零售额 Retail Trade
联营企业	Joint Ownership Enterprises				
国有联营企业	State Joint Ownership Enterprises				
集体联营企业	Collective Joint Ownership Enterprises				
国有与集体联营企业	Joint State-collective Ownership Enterprises				
其他联营企业	Other Joint Ownership Enterprises				
有限责任公司	Limited Liability Corporrations	92	3577572.9	535316.7	3042256.2
国有独资公司	State-funded Corporations	1	35957.0		35957.0
其他有限责任公司	Other Limited Liability Corporations	91	3541615.9	535316.7	3006299.2
股份有限公司	Stock Limited Corporation	4	441227.6	42998.9	398228.7
私营企业	Private Enterprises	108	1979272.9	44614.4	1934658.5
私营独资企业	Private-funded Enterprises	14	59117.8		59117.8
私营合伙企业	Private Partnership Enterprises	4	38895.4		38895.4
私营有限责任公司	Private Limited Liability Corporations	82	1755536.4	44584.9	1710951.5
私营股份有限公司	Private Share Holding Corporations	8	125723.3	29.5	125693.8
其他企业	Others	3	5061.2		5061.2
港、澳、台商投资企业	Enterprises Funded by Hong Kong, Macao and Taiwan	6	483979.1	3622.3	480356.8
与港澳台商合资经营	Joint-venture with Funds from Hong Kong, Macao and Taiwan	1	59496.6		59496.6
与港澳台商合作经营	Cooperative Enterprises with Funds from Hong Kong Macau and Taiwan				
港澳台商独资	Enterprises with Sole Investment from Hong Kong Macau and Taiwan	4	309922.5	3622.3	306300.2
港澳台商投资股份有限公司	Share Holding Enterprises Funded by Overseas Chinese from Hong Kong, Macao & Taiwan	1	114560.0		114560.0
外商投资企业	Foreign Funded Enterprises	14	419222.6		419222.6
中外合资营企业	Sino-foreign Joint Ventures	3	130532.2		130532.2
中外合作企业	Sino-Foreign Cooperative Operation Enterprises				
外资企业	Foreign Owned Enterprises	10	242219.9		242219.9
外商投资股份有限公司	Limited Company Funded by Foreign Investment	1	46470.5		46470.5
个体工商户	Individually-owned Business		91756.4	1983.8	89772.6
2.按国民经济行业分组	Grouped by Registered Kind				
综合零售	General Retail Sales Trade	75	2021499.6	1050.9	2020448.7
#百货零售	Retail of Daily Goods	38	1276623.9	278.0	1276345.9
超级市场零售	Retail of Supermarkets	28	700652.6	211.9	700440.7
食品、饮料及烟草制品专门零售	Retail of Food，Beverage and Tobaccos	7	129219.4	463.3	128756.1
纺织、服装及日用品专门零售	Retail of Textiles，Garments and Daily Articles	19	474625.8	59734.9	414890.9
#服装零售	Retail of Garments	11	387928.9	55531.8	332397.1

14-10 续表3 continued 3

单位：个、万元 (unit,10 000 yuan)

分　　类	Classify	法人单位 Number of Enterprises	销售合计 Total	批发额 Wholesale Trade	零售额 Retail Trade
文化、体育用品及器材专门零售	Retail of Culture , Sports Articles and Equipments	14	136515.0		136515.0
#图书零售	Retail of Books and Mangzines	3	55669.7		55669.7
医药及医疗器材专门零售	Retail of Medicines and Medical Appliances	10	188091.6	45922.5	142169.1
#药品零售	Retail of Medicines	10	188091.6	45922.5	142169.1
汽车、摩托车、燃料及零配件专门零售	Retail of Motor Vehicles，Motorcycles, Feuls and Parts	99	3035682.4	388003.5	2647678.9
#汽车零售业	Retailof Motor Vehicles	81	2986295.8	387428.0	2598867.8
家用电器及电子产品专门零售	Retail of Household Electronic Equipments and Products	20	849913.9	119159.3	730754.6
#家用电器零售	Retail of Household Electronic Equipments	9	747007.4	102953.4	644054.0
计算机、软件及辅助设备零售	Retail of Computer , Software and Auxiliary Equipments	5	47782.1	3001.9	44780.2
通讯设备零售	Retail of Communications	3	51562.7	13204.0	38358.7
五金、家具及室内装修材料专门零售	Retail of Hardwares , Furniture and Room Decorative Building	14	429708.8	15136.0	414572.8
无店铺及其他零售	No Fixed Stores and Other Retails	2	54868.5	60.0	54808.5
3.按经营形式分	Grouped by Means of Operation				
独立门店	Independent Shop	219	4631472.0	219860.4	4411611.6
连锁总店	Headquarter of Chain Store	15	815048.0	12426.8	802621.2
连锁门店	Chain Store	9	808668.8	30572.1	778096.7
其他	Other	17	1064936.2	366671.1	698265.1
4.按零售业态分	Grouped by Retail Size				
有店铺零售	Retail of Shop	258	7274136.3	629530.4	6644605.9
食杂店	Grocery Store	10	537027.1	73994.6	463032.5
便利店	Convenience Store	1	1630.2		1630.2
折扣店	Dime Store	1	850.0		850.0
超市	Supermarket	19	139291.1	182.4	139108.7
大型超市	Larget Supermarket	20	796021.7	550.3	795471.4
仓储会员店	Warehouse Club				
百货店	Department Store	36	868369.2	839.0	867530.2
专业店	Special Store	55	1702893.8	413533.1	1289360.7
专卖店	Monopoly Store	89	2110585.0	69763.2	2040821.8
家居建材商店	Home-building Material Store				
购物中心	Shopping Center	18	882168.9	55531.8	826637.1
厂家直销中心	Factory Outlet Center	9	235299.3	15136.0	220163.3
无店铺零售	Retail of No-shop	2	45988.7		45988.7
电视购物	TV Shopping	2	45988.7		45988.7
邮购	Mail Order				
网上商店	Online Stores				
自动售货亭	Vending Machine				
电话购物	Tele Shopping				

14-11 限额以上住宿和餐饮业经营情况（2009年）

Statistic on Hotel Services and Catering Services above Designed Size（2009）

单位：个、万元 (unit、10 000 yuan)

分　　类	Classify	法人单位 Number of Enterprises	营业额 Business Revenue	客房收入 From Hotel Room	餐费收入 From Meals	商品销售收入 From Commodities
总　计	**Total**	**422**	**856941.5**	**189329.1**	**582090.1**	**38973.7**
一、住宿业	**Lodging Services**	**156**	**297209.2**	**151019.7**	**121044.6**	**7017.5**
#国有控股	State-holding Enterprises	54	93525.4	41401.0	38910.3	3543.2
（一）按登记注册类型分组	Grouped by Registration Status					
内资企业	Domestic Funded Enterprises	142	227927.5	114856.0	93152.5	6126.4
国有企业	State-owned Enterprises	43	90768.7	41822.5	38055.4	3905.1
集体企业	Collective-owned Enterprises	2	1723.9	534.6	1170.4	8.8
股份合作企业	Cooperative Enterprises					
有限责任公司	Limited Liability Corporrations	51	85095.9	45740.3	34198.4	1354.0
国有独资企业	State-funded Corporations					
其他有限责任公司	Other Limited Liability Corporations	51	85095.9	45740.3	34198.4	1354.0
股份有限公司	Stock Limited Corporation	5	5306.4	2841.2	564.9	298.9
私营企业	Private Enterprises	38	44284.9	23636.2	18732.0	529.7
私营独资企业	Private-funded Enterprises	3	704.5	297.7	370.3	36.5
私营有限责任公司	Private Limited Liability Corporations	34	39883.2	21594.4	16471.8	493.2
私营股份有限公司	Private Share Holding Corporations	1	3697.2	1744.1	1889.9	
其他企业	Others	3	747.7	281.2	431.4	29.9
港、澳、台商投资企业	Enterprises Funded by Hong Kong, Macao and Taiwan	7	21493.2	10312.5	8342.3	416.7
合资经营企业(港或澳、台资)	Joint-venture with Funds from Hong Kong, Macao and Taiwan	3	11442.2	4835.5	4332.5	322.0
合作经营企业(港或澳、台资)	Cooperative Enterprises with Funds from Hong Kong Macau and Taiwan	1	6492.9	3639.4	2402.6	1.1
外商投资企业	Foreign Funded Enterprises	7	47586.5	25701.2	19497.8	474.4
中外合资经营企业	Sino-foreign Joint Ventures	2	14879.6	8074.5	5733.0	109.8
中外合作经营企业	Sino-Foreign Cooperative Operation Enterprises	3	8902.0	4476.2	4064.0	
个体工商户	Individually-owned Business		202.0	150.0	52.0	
（二）按住宿行业中类分组	Grouped in classes according to Lodging Industry					
旅游饭店	Tour Restaurant	122	271685.2	137406.5	110232.9	6441.5
一般旅馆	Common Hotel	33	25524.0	13613.2	10811.7	576.0

14-11 续表 continued

单位：个、万元 (unit、10 000 yuan)

分类	Classify	法人单位 Number of Enterprises	营业额 Business Revenue	客房收入 From Hotel Room	餐费收入 From Meals	商品销售收入 From Commodities
二、餐饮业	**Catering Trade**	**266**	**559732.3**	**38309.4**	**461045.5**	**31956.2**
#国有控股	State-holding Enterprises	9	54565.3	10225.5	30509.6	7359.8
1.按登记注册类型分组	Grouped by Registration Status					
内资企业	Domestic Funded Enterprises	248	440152.9	33086.9	356784.6	26120.5
国有企业	State-owned Enterprises	7	21976.0	7739.6	8086.1	4105.8
集体企业	Collective-owned Enterprises	3	2584.7		2584.7	
股份合作企业	Cooperative Enterprises	2	457.6		457.6	
联营企业	Joint Ownership Enterprises					
集体联营企业	Collective Joint Ownership Enterprises					
有限责任公司	Limited Liability Corporrations	89	193026.4	17179.6	149632.5	12959.4
国有独资公司	State-funded Corporations		3131.3		3131.3	
其他有限责任公司	Other Limited Liability Corporations	89	189895.1	17179.6	146501.2	12959.4
股份有限公司	Stock Limited Corporation	3	38900.6	3802.1	24197.1	6159.2
私营企业	Private Enterprises	138	171523.9	4319.6	161749.2	2762.6
私营独资企业	Private-funded Enterprises	29	18941.9	891.0	17811.7	237.4
私营合伙企业	Private Partnership Enterprises	6	6277.0		6277.0	
私营有限责任公司	Private Limited Liability Corporations	94	137262.9	3244.3	128809.9	2523.1
私营股份有限公司	Private Share Holding Corporations	9	9042.1	184.3	8850.6	2.1
其他企业	Others	6	11683.7	46.0	10077.4	133.5
港、澳、台商投资企业	Enterprises Funded by Hong Kong, Macao and Taiwan	6	64203.4	948.1	60725.4	2309.7
合资经营企业(港或澳、台资)	Joint-venture with Funds from Hong Kong, Macao and Taiwan	2	14559.7	538.6	11647.7	2309.7
合作经营企业(港或澳、台资)	Cooperative Enterprises with Funds from Hong Kong Macau and Taiwan	1	9567.0		9567.0	
独资经营企业	Enterprises with Sole Investment	3	40076.7	409.5	39510.7	
外商投资企业	Foreign Funded Enterprises	12	19138.9	299.4	14375.5	765.8
中外合资经营企业	Sino-foreign Joint Ventures	4	3348.3		2649.7	
中外合作经营企业	Sino-Foreign Cooperative Operation Enterprises	1	546.1		546.1	
外资企业	Foreign Owned Enterprises	7	15244.5	299.4	11179.7	765.8
个体工商户	Individually-owned Business		36237.1	3975.0	29160.0	2760.2
2.按餐饮行业中类分组	Grouped by Catering Middle Sector					
正餐服务	Dinner Services	255	502748.4	37894.9	409268.8	30433.6
快餐服务	Fast Food Services	10	55086.2	409.5	50034.0	1487.6
饮料及冷饮服务	Beverage and Cold Beverage Services					
其他餐饮服务	Other Catering Services	1	1897.7	5.0	1742.7	35.0

14-12 限额以上批发和零售业主要商品分类销售额（2009年）

Sale Values of Enterprises above Designated Size of Wholesale and Retail Trades by Category of Main Commodities（2009）

单位：万元 (10 000 yuan)

分　类	Classify	销售合计 Total Sales Value	批发 Wholesale Value	零售 Retail Value
粮油、食品饮料、烟酒类	Grain and Oil, Food and Beverages, Alcoholic Drinks and Tobacco	1317037.3	635982.4	681054.9
粮油、食品类	Cereals, Oils and Foodstuffs	572904.9	65753.3	507151.6
#粮油类	Grain and Oil	191440.2	27941.2	163499.0
肉禽蛋类	Meat, Poultry and Eggs	126979.1		126979.1
水产品类	Aquatic Products	27230.2		27230.2
蔬菜类	Vegetables	19291.2	74.5	19216.7
干鲜瓜果类	Fresh and Dried Fruit Category	27921.7	3567.4	24354.3
饮料类	Beverages	78679.3	19964.2	58715.1
烟酒类	Tobacco and Liquor	665453.1	550264.9	115188.2
服装、鞋帽、针、纺织品类	Clothing, Shoes, Hats and Textiles	1178412.4	132362.2	1046050.2
服装类	Clothing	853706.7	80711.4	772995.3
鞋帽类	Shoes and Hats	199356.6	12131.2	187225.4
针、纺织品类	Knitwear and Textiles	125349.1	39519.6	85829.5
化妆品类	Cosmetics	183882.4	38243.0	145639.4
金银珠宝类	Gold,Silver and Jewelry	186695.2	11714.0	174981.2
日用品类	Articles for Daily Use	329334.2	59009.3	270324.9
#洗涤用品类	Bathing and Washing	126473.0	40526.5	85946.5
儿童玩具类	Children's Toys	47225.9	9951.4	37274.5
五金、电料类	Hardwear and Electrical Materials	99220.0	44460.2	54759.8
体育、娱乐用品类	Sports and Recreation Articles	84950.4	4766.1	80184.3
书报杂志类	Newspapers and Magazines	140003.4	76208.6	63794.8
电子出版物及音像制品类	E-journal and Video Products	8138.9		8138.9
家用电器和音像器材类	Household Appliances and Video Products	650795.4	214590.0	436205.4
中西药品类	Traditional Chinese and Western Medicine	601593.6	438963.9	162629.7
#西药	Western medicine	426235.7	292438.3	133797.4
中草药及中成药	Chinese Herbal Medicine and Mid-product Medicine	47112.5	38181.1	8931.4
文化办公用品类	Cultural and Official Goods	350875.5	166774.8	184100.7
家具类	Furniture	304672.2	5050.0	299622.2
通讯器材类	Communication Appliances	146380.6	62893.6	83487.0
煤炭及制品类	Coal and Related Products	149913.7	148996.5	917.2
木材及制品类	Wood and Wooden Products	216.7	216.7	
石油及制品类	Petroleum and Related Products	3558860.3	2731462.9	827397.4
化工材料及制品类	Raw Chemical Materials	10647.5	10647.5	
#化肥类	Chemical Fertilizers			
金属材料类	Metal Materials	1993622.1	1993622.1	
建筑及装潢材料类	Buildings and Decoration Materials	283282.1	14510.2	268771.9
机电产品及设备类	Mechanical and Electrical Products	587349.2	586104.8	1244.4
#农机类	Agricultural Machinery			
汽车类	Automobile	3104043.0	608545.2	2495497.8
种子饲料类	Seeds and Feedstuff			
棉麻类	Cotton,Hemp	19794.1	19794.1	
其他类	Others	35221.5	8014.2	27207.3

14-13 亿元以上商品交易市场成交情况（2009年）

Basic Statistics on Commodity Exchange Markets of Transaction Value over 100 Million Yuan

分 类	Classify	年末出租摊位数（个）Number of Rental Booths at Year-end (unit)	成交额（万元）Turnover (10 000 yuan)
粮油、食品饮料、烟酒类	Grain and Oil, Food and Beverages, Alcoholic Drinks and Tobacco	2588	447069
粮油、食品类	Cereals, Oils and Foodstuffs	2236	426425
#粮油类	Grain and Oil	437	179807
肉禽蛋类	Meat, Poultry and Eggs	247	55255
水产品类	Aquatic Products	125	11300
蔬菜类	Vegetables	910	128370
干鲜瓜果类	Fresh and Dried Fruit Category	517	51693
饮料类	Beverages	256	8060
烟酒类	Tobacco and Liquor	96	12584
服装、鞋帽、针、纺织品类	Clothing, Shoes, Hats and Textiles	10341	1119859
服装类	Clothing	6704	549895
鞋帽类	Shoes and Hats	1622	304243
针、纺织品类	Knitwear and Textiles	2015	265721
化妆品类	Cosmetics	101	43332
金银珠宝类	Gold,Silver and Jewelry	48	33349
日用品类	Articles for Daily Use	1043	329157
#洗涤用品类	Bathing and Washing	339	137906
儿童玩具类	Children's Toys	67	33222
五金、电料类	Hardwear and Electrical Materials	424	107631
体育、娱乐用品类	Sports and Recreation Articles	299	45171
书报杂志类	Newspapers and Magazines		
电子出版物及音像制品类	E-journal and Video Products	273	5088
家用电器和音像器材类	Household Appliances and Video Products	1991	201920
中西药品类	Traditional Chinese and Western Medicine	337	182432
#西药	Western medicine		
中草药及中成药	Chinese Herbal Medicine and Mid-product Medicine	337	182432
文化办公用品类	Cultural and Official Goods	479	56804
家具类	Furniture		
通讯器材类	Communication Appliances	27	540
煤炭及制品类	Coal and Related Products		
木材及制品类	Wood and Wooden Products		
石油及制品类	Petroleum and Related Products		
化工材料及制品类	Raw Chemical Materials		
#化肥类	Chemical Fertilizers		
金属材料类	Metal Materials		
建筑及装潢材料类	Buildings and Decoration Materials	816	41720
机电产品及设备类	Mechanical and Electrical Products	210	14600
#农机类	Agricultural Machinery		
汽车类	Automobile		
种子饲料类	Seeds and Feedstuff		
棉麻类	Cotton,Hemp		
其他类	Others	17	612

14-14 批发和零售业连锁经营情况（2009）

Basic Statistics on Chain Business of Wholesale and Retail Trades

指 标	Item	本年合计 Total	上年合计 Total Last Year	本年直营店 Ragular Chain
一、门店总数（个）	**Number of Stores(unit)**	**472**	**377**	**420**
二、年末从业人员数（人）	**Employees at Year-end(person)**	**16443**	**16727**	**15675**
三、年末零售营业面积（平方米）	**Operating Area of Retail at Year-end(sq.m)**	**683191**	**597386**	**589591**
四、连锁门店商品购进额（千元）	**Purchases Value of Chain Stores(1 000 yuan)**	**11074283**	**9988087**	**10874610**
#统一配送商品购进额	Centralized Purchases and Delivery	7172715	6522363	7144610
#自有配送中心配送商品购进额	Self Centralized Purchases and Delivery	4686875	4094692	4658770
非自有配送中心配送商品购进额	Non-self Centralized Purchases and Delivery	2197023	2156004	2197023
五、连锁门店商品销售额（千元）	**Sales Value of Chain Store(1 000 yuan)**	**13159103**	**11592879**	**12942068**
#零售额	Retail Value	7797843	6987119	7580808

14-14 续表 continued

指 标	Item	上年直营店 Ragular Chain Last Year	本年加盟店 Franchise	上年加盟店 Franchise Last Year
一、门店总数（个）	**Number of Stores(unit)**	**333**	**52**	**44**
二、年末从业人员数（人）	**Employees at Year-end(person)**	**16095**	**768**	**632**
三、年末零售营业面积（平方米）	**Operating Area of Retail at Year-end(sq.m)**	**564346**	**93600**	**33040**
四、连锁门店商品购进额（千元）	**Purchases Value of Chain Stores(1 000 yuan)**	**9871267**	**199673**	**116820**
#统一配送商品购进额	Centralized Purchases and Delivery	6512710	28105	9653
#自有配送中心配送商品购进额	Self Centralized Purchases and Delivery	4085039	28105	9653
非自有配送中心配送商品购进额	Non-self Centralized Purchases and Delivery	2156004		
五、连锁门店商品销售额（千元）	**Sales Value of Chain Store(1 000 yuan)**	**11409677**	**217035**	**183202**
#零售额	Retail Value	6803917	217035	183202

14-15 住宿和餐饮业连锁经营情况（2009）

Basic Statistics on Chain Business of Hotels and Catering Services

指　　标	Item	本年合计 Total	上年合计 Total Last Year	本年直营店 Ragular Chain
一、门店总数（个）	**Number of Stores(unit)**	**39**	**29**	**39**
二、年末从业人员数（人）	**Employees at Year-end(person)**	**2730**	**2390**	**2730**
三、年末餐饮营业面积（平方米）	**Operating Area of Retail at Year-end(sq.m)**	**25724**	**20649**	**25724**
四、客房总数（间）	**Guest Rooms(room)**			
五、床位数（张）	**Guest Beds(bed)**			
六、餐位数（位）	**Dining Seats(set)**	**6934**	**5374**	**6934**
七、连锁门店商品购进额（千元）	**Operating Area of Catering Services at Year end(room)**	**111722**	**86705**	**111722**
#统一配送商品购进额	Centralized Purchases and Delivery	67200	51947	67200
#自有配送中心配送商品购进额	Self Centralized Purchases and Delivery	67200	51947	67200
非自有配送中心配送商品购进额	Non-self Centralized Purchases and Delivery			
八、连锁门店商品营业额（千元）	**Sales Value of Chain Store(1 000 yuan)**	**178953**	**132216**	**178953**
#餐费收入	Catering Revenues	176342	131150	176342
商品销售额	Sales Value	2392	1066	2392

14-15 续表 continued

指　　标	Item	上年直营店 Ragular Chain Last Year	本年加盟店 Franchise	上年加盟店 Franchise Last Year
一、门店总数（个）	**Number of Stores(unit)**	**29**		
二、年末从业人员数（人）	**Employees at Year-end(person)**	**2390**		
三、年末餐饮营业面积（平方米）	**Operating Area of Retail at Year-end(sq.m)**	**20649**		
四、客房总数（间）	**Guest Rooms(room)**			
五、床位数（张）	**Guest Beds(bed)**			
六、餐位数（位）	**Dining Seats(set)**	**5374**		
七、连锁门店商品购进额（千元）	**Operating Area of Catering Services at Year end(room)**	**86705**		
#统一配送商品购进额	Centralized Purchases and Delivery	51947		
#自有配送中心配送商品购进额	Self Centralized Purchases and Delivery	51947		
非自有配送中心配送商品购进额	Non-self Centralized Purchases and Delivery			
八、连锁门店商品营业额（千元）	**Sales Value of Chain Store(1 000 yuan)**	**132216**		
#餐费收入	Catering Revenues	131150		
商品销售额	Sales Value	1066		

14-16 成品油批发企业（单位）能源购进、销售与库存（2009）

Purchases,Sales and Stock of Refined Oil Wholesale Enterprises（2009）

指　　标	Item	年初库存量 Stock at Beginning of the Year	本年购进量 Purchases This Year	购自省（区、市））From Other Provinces（Regions,Cities）	本年销售量 Sales This Year	销往省(区、市)外 For Other Provinces（Regions,Cities）	售予批发和零售业 For Wholesale and Retail Trades	年末库存量 Stock at End of the Year
汽油(吨)	Gasoline(ton)	205413.2	3274447.3	192949.6	3356886.6	1062007.1	1558172.5	123736.8
＃93〃	＃93〃	18348.4	869901.0	42485.2	863341.5	109338.6	441602.6	25771.1
柴油(吨)	Diesel Oil(ton)	159401.5	5281738.8	666929.8	5313711.4	1316565.1	1707991.4	132064.2
＃0〃	＃0〃	102965.6	3772361.4	474214.2	3802907.0	797914.2	1051143.8	79609.3
煤油(吨)	Kerosene(ton)	16393.0	466318.0	466318.0	466318.0	145884.0	320434.0	17264.0
燃料油(吨)	Fuel Oil(ton)							
润滑油(吨)	Lube(ton)	1035.3	14562.3	10842.0	14715.5	8025.0	4299.6	880.9

14-17 成品油零售企业（单位）能源商品销售与库存（2009）

Purchases,Sales and Stock of Refined Oil Retail Enterprises（2009）

指　　标	Item	年初库存量 Stock at Beginning of the Year	本年销售量 Sales This Year	年末库存量 Stock at End of the Year
汽油(吨)	Gasoline(ton)	11519.1	338179.6	11295.1
#93〃	#93〃	5180.3	235485.3	6399.4
柴油(吨)	Diesel Oil(ton)	8571.2	352569.4	14212.5
#0〃	#0〃	5273.6	236683.8	10079.0
煤油(吨)	Kerosene(ton)	6.0	331.7	3.7
燃料油(吨)	Fuel Oil(ton)			
润滑油(吨)	Lube(ton)	149.7	3726.6	122.8

主要统计指标解释

社会消费品零售额 指各种经济类型的批发零售贸易业、餐饮业和其他行业对城乡居民和社会集团的消费品零售额总和。这个指标反映通过各种商品流通渠道向居民和社会集团供应的生活消费品来满足他们生活需要，是研究人民生活、社会消费品购买力，货币流通等问题的重要指标。对居民的消费品零售额：指售给城乡居民用于生活消费的商品。对社会集团的消费品零售额：指售给机关、团体、部队、学校、企业、事业单位和城市街道居民委员会，农村村民委员会用公款购买的用作非生产、非经营使用的消费品。

社会消费品零售额包括：

售给社会集团的办公用品、纸张、账册、文印用品和纺织品、针织品；学校用的教学用具；文体用品；非专用的劳动保护用品，如工作服、套袖、围群、手套、毛巾、肥皂等；日用百货和杂品，包括职工食堂用的餐具、炊具、设备和清洁卫生工具等；家具、设备、日用电器、电讯设备、电影器材和照相器材等；取暖用的设备和燃料，防暑、降温的饮料；非生产经营用的交通工具如小轿车、面包车、工具车、卡车和油料；零星修理用的各种零配件、材料、工具、建筑材料等；举办各种招待会、茶话会、宴会用的烟酒茶和各种食品及馈赠的礼品；从公费医疗经费中开支的中、西药品、中药材和医疗器材以及其他非生产性设备和用品。

商品销售总额 指对本企业（单位）以外的单位和个人出售（包括对境外直接出口）的商品总额。它反映批发零售贸易业在国内市场上销售商品以及出口商品的总量。商品销售总额包括:（1）售给城乡居民和社会集团消费用的商品;（2）售给工业、农业、建筑业、运输邮电业、批发零售贸易业、餐饮业、服务业等作为生产、经营使用的商品;（3）售给批发零售贸易业作为转卖或加工后转卖的商品;（4）对国（境）外直接出口的商品。不包括出售本企业（单位）自用的废旧包装用品;未通过买卖行为付出的商品;经本单位介绍，由买卖双方直接结算，本单位只收取手续费的业务;购货退出的商品以及商品损耗和损失等。

住宿和餐饮业营业额 指住宿和餐饮业法人企业、产业活动单位在经营活动中的因提供服务或销售商品等取得的收入。包括：客房收入、餐费收入、商品销售收入和其它收入。

客房收入 指住宿和餐饮业法人企业、产业活动单位在经营活动中因提供住宿服务取得的客房收入。

餐费收入 指住宿和餐饮业法人企业、产业活动因为顾客提供就餐服务取得的收入。包括：经烹饪、调制加工之后出售的各种食品，如主食、炒菜、凉拌菜等的收入。

商品销售收入 指住宿和餐饮业法人企业、产业活动单位伴随服务而出售商品所取得的收入。

其他收入 指营业收入中除客房收入、餐费收入、商品销售收入以外的其它收入。包括：娱乐、健身和商业服务等。

客房数 指宾馆、饭店、酒店、旅馆等用于或主要用于旅客就餐的房间数，不包括宾馆、饭店、酒店、旅馆等内作其他用途的房间、储藏室、会议室等。该指标按年内正常情况下的实有数统计。

床位数 指宾馆、饭店、酒店、旅馆等供应旅客使用的床位数，不包括临时加的床位和宾馆、饭店、酒店、旅馆等内部工作人员使用的床位，该指标按年内正常情况下的实有数统计。

餐位数 指住宿和餐饮业法人企业、产业活动单位为顾客提供就餐服务时，正常可同时容纳就餐人员的餐位数量，不包括临时加的餐位。该指标年内正常情况下的实有数统计。

年末餐饮业营业面积 指住宿和餐饮业法人企业、产业活动单位对外提供就餐服务的门店建筑面积和从事食品加工、烹饪、调制的厨房面积，不包括办公用房和仓库等面积，该指标按年末实有面积统计。

Explanatory Notes on Main Statistical Indicators

Total Retail Sales of Consumer Goods it refers to sum of retail amount of consumer goods sold by wholesale and retail trade in all kinds of economic type, accommodation trade and other industry sold to urban and countryside citizens and social groups. This indicator reflects all living consumer goods supplied by all kinds of commodity channel to residents and social group to meet the needs of their life, and it is an important indicator to study people's life, social consumer goods purchasing power and circulation of currency and so on. Volume of retail sales of consumer goods to residents: it refers to commodities sold to residents of urban and rural area used for daily consuming. Volume of retail sales of consumer goods to social groups: it refers to the amount of consumer goods bought by government functionary office, groups, army, schools, enterprises, institutions, residents committees in urban area and villagers committees in rural area using public money, used for non-productive, non-operational purposes.

Volume of retail sales of social consumer goods consists of items sold to social groups such as stationery, papers, account books, printing articles, computing instruments, books, newspapers, magazines and awards; public facilities, dry goods and hosiery; teaching instruments for schools; recreation and sports facilities; non-special labor safety articles, such as work clothes, over sleeves, apron, gloves, towels, soaps etc.; articles for everyday use, commodities and sundry goods, include table wares, cooking utensils, equipment and cleaning and sanitary facilities for staff eateries; furniture, equipment, electrical appliances of daily use, telecommunication equipment, film equipment, photo equipment etc.; equipment and fuel for heating, drinks for sunstroke prevention and lowering the temperature; non-productive and operational vehicles such as sedans, vans, tool cars, trucks and fuels; various parts, fittings, materials, tools, building materials for fragmentary repairing; cigarettes, alcoholic drinks and tea leafs for various receptions, tea parties and banquets and all kinds of foods and gifts for present; Chinese traditional medicine, Western medicine, Chinese traditional medicinal materials, medical treatment equipment paid by public health service outlays and other non-productive equipment and facilities.

Total Sales of Commodities refer to value of commodities sold by the establishments to other establishments and individuals (including direct export). This indicator is used to show the total value of sales of commodities at domestic markets and export. The total sales include: (1) commodities sold to urban and rural residents and social groups for their consumption; (2) commodities sold to establishments in industry, agriculture, construction, transportation, post and telecommunications, wholesale and retail trades, catering trade and public utility for their production and operation; (3) commodities sold to wholesale and retail establishments for re selling, with or without further processing; and (4)commodities for direct export to other countries. Excluded are selling of waste packaging materials used by the establishments (units) themselves, commodities transferred without buying or selling procedures, commission income from brokerage in transactions whose settlement is directly handled by buyers and sellers, rejected commodities in the purchase, loss in commodities, etc.

Turnover of Hotel and Catering refers to revenue from providing services or selling products by Hotel and Catering corporate enterprises and economic active units. It includes revenue of guest room, revenue of meal cost, revenue of products sale and other revenue.

Revenue of guest room refers to revenue from providing hotel services by Hotel and Catering corporate enterprises and economic active units.

Revenue of meal cost refers to revenue from providing catering services by Hotel and Catering corporate enterprises and economic active units. It includes revenue from selling sorts of food after cooking and processing, for example: staple food, cooking dish, cold and dressed dish, etc.

Revenue of product sale refers to revenue from product sale by Hotel and Catering corporate enterprises and economic active units.

Other revenue refers to other revenue from deducting revenue of guest room, revenue of meal cost and revenue of product sale from total operating revenue. It includes revenue of entertainment, body-building, commercial services, etc.

Number of guest rooms refers to number of room that used for or mainly for catering services in hotel, restaurant, drinkery and rest house, it excludes number of room, storeroom, meeting room, etc. that used for other services in hotel, restaurant, drinkery and rest house. It is accounted by actually-owned-number on normal condition in a year.

Number of beds refers to number of beds used for tourists in hotel, restaurant, drinkery and rest house, it excludes number of temporary beds or beds used for internal staffs. It is accounted by actually-owned- number on normal condition in a year.

Number of meal tables refers to number of meal tables to accommodate guests on normal condition while providing catering services by Hotel and Catering corporate enterprises and economic active units, it excludes temporary meal tables. It is accounted by actually-owned-number on normal condition.

Year-end operational area of catering industry refers to building area of stores to provide catering services by Hotel and Catering corporate enterprises and economic active units and kitchen area involving with food processing, cooking and processing. It excludes area of office room , storehouse, etc and is accounted by actually-owned-area by end of year.

15 对外经济贸易和旅游

FOREIGN TRADE AND ECONOMIC COOPERATION TOURISM

资料整理：马晓庆　赵琳瑛
Data management:Ma Xiaoqing　Zhao Linying

第十五部分　对外经济贸易和旅游

一、简要说明

本章资料包括对外经济贸易、利用外资以及与国外友好城市交流和旅游等方面资料，由西安市统计局贸易外经处根据西安市商务局、海关、政府对外办公室和旅游局提供资料整理。

二、主要指标

进出口总额（亿美元）	72.46	比上年增长	2.9%
#出　口	33.31	比上年增长	-25.5%
实际利用外商直接投资额（亿美元）	12.19	比上年增长	6.2%
国际旅游人数（万人）	67.29	比上年增长	6.5%
国际旅游收入（亿元）	31.05	比上年增长	8.1%

15 FOREIGN TRADE AND ECONOMIC COOPERATION,TOURISM

Ⅰ.Brief Introduction

Data in this chapter consists of data on foreign trade, using of foreign capital and fund and tourism. Data on foreign economy and trade, intercommunion to foreign cities of friendship and tourism are compiled and provided by Foreign Economy Division of the Xi'an Bureau of Statistics according to the data from Xi'an Bureau of Commerce, Xi'an Custom Office, Foreign Affairs Office of the Xi'an Municipal Government and Xi'an Bureau of Tourism.

Ⅱ.Major Indicators

		Increase over Preceding Year
Total Imports and Exports (USD 100 mil.)	72.46	2.9%
Toal Exports	33.31	-25.5%
Total Amount of Foreign Capital Actually Used(USD 100 mil.)	12.19	6.2%
Total Number of International Tourists (10 000 persons)	67.29	6.5%
Total Foreign Exchange Earnings (100 mil. Yuan)	31.05	8.1%

15-1 主要年份外资、外贸和国际旅游基本情况

Main Indicators on Foreign Investments,International Trading and International Tourism In Representative Years

指标	Item	1990	1995	2000	2004
一、利用外资签订协议项目(个)	**Number of Projects of Foreign Capital Used through the Signed Agreements and Contracts (unit)**	**11**	**184**	**135**	**159**
利用外资签订协议金额(万美元)	Value of Foreign Capital Used through the Signed Agreements and Contracts(USD 10 000)	415	28956	54123	78312
外商实际直接投资额(万美元)	Value of Foreign Direct Investment (USD 10 000)	1154	18653	15633	27595
年末已建成投产企业数(个)	Number of Enterprises Completed and put into use at Year-end(unit)			808	
二、进出口总额(万美元)	**Total Imports and Exports (USD 10 000)**	**38229**	**137510**	**173696**	**309295**
#进口总额	Total Imports	9939	27347	67634	105756
出口总额	Total Exports	28290	110163	106062	203539
进出口差额	Balance of Imports and Exports	18351	82816	38428	97783
三、国际旅游人数总计(万人次)	**Total Number of International Tourists (10 000 person-times)**	**25.88**	**41.35**	**65.03**	**65.03**
#外国人	Foreigners	15.40	37.11	54.65	52.75
港澳台同胞	Chinese Compatriot From Hong Kong, Macao and Taiwan	10.07	4.16	10.38	12.28
四、国际旅游者人天数总计(万人天)	**Total number of days of international tourists (10 000 person/day)**	**55.03**	**84.44**	**162.69**	**186.80**
#外国人	Foreigners	33.48	75.71	131.44	151.11
港澳台同胞	Chinese Compatriot From Hong Kong, Macao and Taiwan	21.55	8.56	31.15	35.69
五、国际旅游收入(亿元)	**Earning of International Tourism (100 millon yuan)**	**1.96**	**10.38**	**22.41**	**27.39**
#商品收入	Income from Mercantile	0.44	2.57	7.71	10.44
劳务收入	Income from Labour Service	1.52	7.81	14.70	16.95
六、旅游者在西安人均停留天数(天)	**Number of Days of Average Tourists Staying in Xi'an (day)**	**2.1**	**2.0**	**2.5**	**2.9**
七、旅游者在西安人均消费(元)	**Consumption of Average Tourists in Xi'an (yuan)**	**759**	**2511**	**3445**	**4212**

注：1990年和1995年国际旅游者中含华侨。

Note:The international tourists included overseas Chinese in 1990 and 1995.

15-1 续表 continued

指　　标	Item	2005	2006	2007	2008	2009
一、利用外资签订协议项目(个)	**Number of Projects of Foreign Capital Used through the Signed Agreements and Contracts (unit)**	**157**	**190**	**135**	**100**	**65**
利用外资签订协议金额(万美元)	Value of Foreign Capital Used through the Signed Agreements and Contracts(USD 10 000)	121499	182525	143978	118230	60027
外商实际直接投资额(万美元)	Value of Foreign Direct Investment (USD 10 000)	57113	82463	111567	114738	121872
年末已建成投产企业数(个)	Number of Enterprises Completed and put into use at Year-end(unit)					
二、进出口总额(万美元)	**Total Imports and Exports (USD 10 000)**	**390146**	**415403**	**536162**	**704029**	**724618**
#进口总额	Total Imports	126705	142541	189029	256916	391504
出口总额	Total Exports	263441	272862	347133	447113	333114
进出口差额	Balance of Imports and Exports	136736	130321	158104	190197	-58391
三、国际旅游人数总计(万人次)	**Total Number of International Tourists (10 000 person-times)**	**77.56**	**86.73**	**100.01**	**63.20**	**67.29**
#外国人	Foreigners	65.86	73.40	85.09	53.58	59.09
港澳台同胞	Chinese Compatriot From Hong Kong, Macao and Taiwan	11.70	13.33	14.92	9.62	8.20
四、国际旅游者人天数总计(万人天)	**Total number of days of international tourists (10 000 person/day)**	**224.93**	**253.17**	**290.02**	**162.93**	**195.14**
#外国人	Foreigners	190.99	214.10	246.76	138.72	171.36
港澳台同胞	Chinese Compatriot From Hong Kong, Macao and Taiwan	33.94	39.07	43.26	24.21	23.78
五、国际旅游收入(亿元)	**Earning of International Tourism (100 millon yuan)**	**33.54**	**37.83**	**42.43**	**28.72**	**31.05**
#商品收入	Income from Mercantile	11.25	15.93	15.19	9.74	8.94
劳务收入	Income from Labour Service	22.29	21.90	27.24	18.98	22.11
六、旅游者在西安人均停留天数(天)	**Number of Days of Average Tourists Staying in Xi'an (day)**	**2.9**	**2.9**	**2.9**	**2.6**	**2.9**
七、旅游者在西安人均消费(元)	**Consumption of Average Tourists in Xi'an (yuan)**	**4324**	**4353**	**4242**	**4544**	**4614**

15-2 主要年份利用外资情况

Utilization of Foreign Capital In Representative Years

单位：万美元 (USD 10 000)

年 份 Year	利用外资签定协议金额 Value of Foreign Capital Used through the Signed Agreements and Contracts	外商实际直接投资额 Direct Foreign Investment
1983	3500	800
1984	8	
1985	8361	1106
1986	19919	4010
1987	3218	5552
1988	2423	6758
1989	1645	11632
1990	415	1154
1991	591	1094
1992	24165	5200
1993	57289	8996
1994	20321	15240
1995	28956	18653
1996	35978	20510
1997	27214	22057
1998	40034	22286
1999	40390	13801
2000	54123	15633
2001	60736	17687
2002	70692	20281
2003	96380	25557
2004	78312	27595
2005	121499	57113
2006	182525	82463
2007	143978	111567
2008	118230	114738
2009	60027	121872

15-3 外国和港澳台地区在西安直接投资（2009年）

Direct Investments from Foreign Countries and Hong Kong, Macao and Taiwan in Xi'an（2009）

分　类	Classity	新签协议情况 New-signed Agreement Circumstances 合同数(个) Number of Constracts (unit)	利用外资签订协议金额(万美元) Value of Foreign Captial Used through the Signed (USD10 000)	外商实际直接投资额（万美元）Value of Foreign Direct Investment (USD10 000)
合　计	**Total**	**65**	**60027.0**	**121872.4**
一、按投资方式分	**Grouped by Investment Mode**			
1.中外合资经营企业	Joint-venture Enterprises	20	4906.5	21756.6
2.中外合作经营企业	Cooperation Enterprises	1	1573.4	1760.7
3.外资企业	Wholly Foreign-owned Enterprises	44	53547.1	90390.1
4.外资企业再投资	Re-investment from Foreign-funded Enterprises			
二、按国民经济行业分组	**Grouped by Sector**			
1.农林牧渔水利业	Agriculture,Forestry,Animal,Husbandy and Fishery	1	35.0	262.0
2.制造业	Manufacturing	29	12439.0	37143.9
3.电力、煤气及水的生产和供应业	Production and Distribution of Electricity,Gas and Water			2917.0
4.建筑业	Construction	1	256.1	
5.交通运输、仓储及邮电通信业	Transporation,Storage,Postal and Telecommunications	1	100.0	1360.0
6.批发和零售贸易、餐饮业	Wholesale, Retail Trads and Catering Services	2	3.0	16930.7
7.房地产业	Real Estate	7	29254.4	54093.1
8.社会服务业	Social Services	10	7018.8	8295.7
9.其他行业	Others	14	10920.7	870.0
三、按投资国别、地区分组	**Grouped by Different Countries and Regions**			
香港	Hong Kong	32	36506.0	74388.8
澳门	Macao			1260.0
台湾	Taiwan	5	108.9	80.5
日本	Japan	4	709.0	1804.5
泰国	Tailand			
马来西亚	Malaysia	1	1000.0	170.0
新加坡	Singapore	4	5280.1	7639.4
韩国	Korea	1	742.8	3649.9
德国	Germany	1	7.6	441.0
意大利	Italy		38.4	
法国	France			
英国	England			509.0
捷克	Czechoslovakia			
加拿大	Canada	1	-1.6	198.7
美国	America	8	10258.2	10881.1
澳大利亚	Australia		-19.9	
维尔京群岛	Virgin Islands	1	-682.0	
其它	Others	7	6079.5	20849.5

15-4 主要年份进出口总额

Total Imports and Exports In Representative Years

单位：万美元 (USD 10 000)

年 份 Year	进出口总额 Total Imports and Exports	出口总额 Total Exports	进口总额 Total Imports
1987	13596	7540	6056
1988	36750	24632	12118
1989	32715	21564	11151
1990	38229	28290	9939
1991	55356	41511	13845
1992	70467	53060	17407
1993	93330	62393	30937
1994	104752	76897	27855
1995	137510	110163	27347
1996	143187	91745	51442
1997	150668	107753	42915
1998	180589	100492	80097
1999	172919	94495	78424
2000	173696	106062	67634
2001	169914	87948	81966
2002	186966	112479	74487
2003	230932	140327	90605
2004	309295	203539	105756
2005	390146	263441	126705
2006	415403	272862	142541
2007	536162	347133	189029
2008	704029	447113	256916
2009	724618	333114	391504

15-5 外贸商品进出口总额分国别和地区（2009年）

Total Value of Imports and Exports by Country and Region（2009）

单位：万美元 (USD10 000)

国别和地区	Country and Region	进出口总额 Total Imports and Exports	出口 Exports
亚洲	**Asia**	**203645**	**107461**
#香港	Hong kong	15730	14788
台湾	Taiwan	24916	2467
日本	Japan	49199	22182
菲律宾	Phiilippines	4170	3301
马来西亚	Malaysia	5583	4337
韩国	Korea	24862	10398
非洲	**Africa**	**71737**	**67417**
#埃及	Egypt	2552	2551
突尼斯	Tunisia	235	234
埃塞俄比亚	Ethiopia	140	140
博茨瓦那	Botswana	28	24
南非	South Africa	6545	5227
欧洲	**Europe**	**220249**	**73388**
#德国	Germany	76085	21047
法国	France	10504	3622
意大利	Italy	11966	4113
荷兰	Netherland	15003	11769
英国	England	13664	8214
瑞士	Switzerland	9144	155
西班牙	Spain	6132	4783
俄罗斯联邦	Russia	4828	4077
拉丁美洲	**Latin America**	**58030**	**11529**
#哥伦比亚	Colombia	525	525
巴西	Brazil	17855	1072
阿根廷	Argentina	774	774
北美洲	**North America**	**131612**	**54149**
#加拿大	Canada	14320	4763
美国	America	117292	49386
大洋洲及太平洋岛屿	**Oceanic and Pacific Islands**	**39346**	**19170**
#澳大利亚	Australia	24385	4512
新西兰	New Zealand	733	430

15-6 主要商品分大类出口金额

Export Value of Major Merchandise by Type

单位：万美元 (USD 10 000)

商品分类	HS Section and Division	2000	2001	2002
食用蔬菜、根及块茎	Edible Vegetables, Certain,Roots amd Tubers	1095	1957	1275
蔬菜、水果、坚果或植物其它部分的制品	Vegetables, Fruits, Nuts, or products made of other parts of plants	2076	2684	3470
矿砂、矿渣及矿灰	Ores,Slags and Ash	4083	4649	8714
无机化学品；贵金属、稀土金属、放射性元素及其同位素的有机及无机化合物	Inorganic Chemicals,Organic or Inorganic Compounds of Precious Metals,of Rare Earth Metals,of Radioactive Elements or of Isotopes	3714	4141	4141
有机化学品	Organic Chemicals	2367	3279	4883
羊毛、动物细毛或粗毛、马毛纱线及其机织物	Wod ,Fine or Coarse Animal Hair; Horsehair Yarn and Woven Fabric	810	829	1313
棉花	Cotton	3197	2734	3826
化学纤维短纤	Short staple chemicd fibers	5061	3612	2512
针织或钩编的服装及衣着附件	Articles of Apparel and Clothing Accessories, Knitted or Crocheted	6753	1632	2660
非针织或非钩编的服装及衣着附件	Articles of Apparel and Clothing Accessories, not Knitted or Crocheted	7269	3319	3629
其它纺织制成品；成套物品；旧衣着及旧纺织品	Other Made Up Textile Articles;Sets;Worn Clothing and Worn Textile Articles;Rags Articles	1649	1002	1432
鞋靴、护腿和类似品及其零件	Footwear,Gaiters and The Like;Parts of Such Articles Headgear and Parts Thereof	1347	279	296
玻璃及其制品	Glass and Glassware	3376	3838	5542
钢铁	Iron and Steel	3534	1197	2167
钢铁制品	Articles of Iron or Steel	5535	6401	7414
铅及制品	Lead Areticles Thereof	1371	1363	444
锌及制品	Zinc Areticles Thereof	4031	1945	1895
其它贱金属、金属陶瓷及其制品	Other Base Metals,Germets;Areticles Thereof	1066	1704	1546
贱金属工具、器具、利口器、餐匙、餐叉及其零件	Tools,Implements,Cutlery,Spons and Forks, of Base Metal;Parts Thereof of Base Metal	2933	2669	2613
核反应堆、锅炉、机器、机械器具及其零件	Nuclear Reactors ,Boilers, Machinery and Mechanical Appliances; and Parts Thereof	10915	11979	16140
电机、电气设备及其零件；录音机及放声机、电视图像、声音的录制和重放设备及其零件、附件	Electrical Machinery and Equipment and Parts Thereof;Sound Recorders and Repreducers, Television Image and Sound Recordes and Repreducers,and Parts and Accessories of Such Articles	8339	8696	8962
光学、照相、电影、计量、检验、医疗或外科用仪器及设备、精密仪器及设备；上述物品的零件、附件	Optical,Photographic,Cinematographic,Measuring, Checking,Precision Medical or Surgical Instruments and Apparatus;Parts and Accessories Thereof	2020	2818	5395
家具、寝具、褥垫、弹簧床垫、软床垫及类似的填充制品；未列名灯具及照明装置；发光标志、发光名牌及类似品；活动房屋	Mattresses,Mattress Supports,Cushions and Similar Stuffed Furnishings;Lamps and Lighting Fittings, not Elsewhere Spcified or Included;Illumihated Signs,Illuminated	2587	2150	2715

15-6 续表1 continued 1

单位：万美元 (USD 10 000)

商品分类	HS Section and Division	2003	2004	2005
食用蔬菜、根及块茎	Edible Vegetables, Certain,Roots amd Tubers	1379	1386	1190
蔬菜、水果、坚果或植物其它部分的制品	Vegetables, Fruits, Nuts, or products made of other parts of plants	4490	7786	10531
矿砂、矿渣及矿灰	Ores,Slags and Ash	11224	30590	63247
无机化学品；贵金属、稀土金属、放射性元素及其同位素的有机及无机化合物	Inorganic Chemicals,Organic or Inorganic Compounds of Precious Metals,of Rare Earth Metals,of Radioactive Elements or of Isotopes	5814	5806	10997
有机化学品	Organic Chemicals	4757	4837	8569
羊毛、动物细毛或粗毛、马毛纱线及其机织物	Wod ,Fine or Coarse Animal Hair; Horsehair Yarn and Woven Fabric	1600	1640	903
棉花	Cotton	3984	3133	3240
化学纤维短纤	Short staple chemicd fibers	2120	1987	1471
针织或钩编的服装及衣着附件	Articles of Apparel and Clothing Accessories, Knitted or Crocheted	341	7465	5736
非针织或非钩编的服装及衣着附件	Articles of Apparel and Clothing Accessories, not Knitted or Crocheted	4981	5543	5068
其它纺织制成品；成套物品；旧衣着及旧纺织品	Other Made Up Textile Articles;Sets;Worn Clothing and Worn Textile Articles;Rags Articles	2203	2667	3000
鞋靴、护腿和类似品及其零件	Footwear,Gaiters and The Like;Parts of Such Articles Headgear and Parts Thereof	585	2687	1368
玻璃及其制品	Glass and Glassware	6667	8083	8576
钢铁	Iron and Steel	2779	5244	5314
钢铁制品	Articles of Iron or Steel	8474	10398	13959
铅及制品	Lead Areticles Thereof	232	43	12
锌及制品	Zinc Areticles Thereof	2200	522	135
其它贱金属、金属陶瓷及其制品	Other Base Metals,Germets;Areticles Thereof	3150	6419	11233
贱金属工具、器具、利口器、餐匙、餐叉及其零件	Tools,Implements,Cutlery,Spons and Forks, of Base Metal;Parts Thereof of Base Metal	3232	3406	3052
核反应堆、锅炉、机器、机械器具及其零件	Nuclear Reactors ,Boilers, Machinery and Mechanical Appliances; and Parts Thereof	21281	24696	30832
电机、电气设备及其零件；录音机及放声机、电视图像、声音的录制和重放设备及其零件、附件	Electrical Machinery and Equipment and Parts Thereof;Sound Recorders and Repreducers, Television Image and Sound Recordes and Repreducers,and Parts and Accessories of Such Articles	15106	19812	23605
光学、照相、电影、计量、检验、医疗或外科用仪器及设备、精密仪器及设备；上述物品的零件、附件	Optical,Photographic,Cinematographic,Measuring, Checking,Precision Medical or Surgical Instruments and Apparatus;Parts and Accessories Thereof	3339	1847	2341
家具、寝具、褥垫、弹簧床垫、软床垫及类似的填充制品；未列名灯具及照明装置；发光标志、发光名牌及类似品；活动房屋	Mattresses,Mattress Supports,Cushions and Similar Stuffed Furnishings;Lamps and Lighting Fittings, not Elsewhere Spcified or Included;Illumihated Signs,Illuminated	3994	4955	4773

15-6 续表2 continued 2

单位：万美元 (USD 10 000)

商品分类	HS Section and Division	2006	2007	2008	2009
食用蔬菜、根及块茎	Edible Vegetables, Certain,Roots amd Tubers	1136	1232	1374	803
蔬菜、水果、坚果或植物其它部分的制品	Vegetables, Fruits, Nuts, or products made of other parts of plants	15374	37426	29270	21920
矿砂、矿渣及矿灰	Ores,Slags and Ash	52046	47378	40502	6141
无机化学品；贵金属、稀土金属、放射性元素及其同位素的有机及无机化合物	Inorganic Chemicals,Organic or Inorganic Compounds of Precious Metals,of Rare Earth Metals,of Radioactive Elements or of Isotopes	10916	16508	15882	9774
有机化学品	Organic Chemicals	11923	11182	13954	16294
羊毛、动物细毛或粗毛、马毛纱线及其机织物	Wod ,Fine or Coarse Animal Hair; Horsehair Yarn and Woven Fabric	1400	1065	720	460
棉花	Cotton	3808	3255	3213	2346
化学纤维短纤	Short staple chemicd fibers	1556	1767	1181	2217
针织或钩编的服装及衣着附件	Articles of Apparel and Clothing Accessories, Knitted or Crocheted	5332	5345	4371	3617
非针织或非钩编的服装及衣着附件	Articles of Apparel and Clothing Accessories, not Knitted or Crocheted	4078	3875	3623	2919
其它纺织制成品；成套物品；旧衣着及旧纺织品	Other Made Up Textile Articles;Sets;Worn Clothing and Worn Textile Articles;Rags Articles	3342	3090	3187	2813
鞋靴、护腿和类似品及其零件	Footwear,Gaiters and The Like;Parts of Such Articles Headgear and Parts Thereof	216	348	380	367
玻璃及其制品	Glass and Glassware	8272	6246	6538	5574
钢铁	Iron and Steel	4900	11366	11966	4254
钢铁制品	Articles of Iron or Steel	16903	17329	26568	11943
铅及制品	Lead Areticles Thereof	158	1650	2	1
锌及制品	Zinc Areticles Thereof	4119	2470	46	78
其它贱金属、金属陶瓷及其制品	Other Base Metals,Germets;Areticles Thereof	17695	23414	27576	11276
贱金属工具、器具、利口器、餐匙、餐叉及其零件	Tools,Implements,Cutlery,Spons and Forks, of Base Metal;Parts Thereof of Base Metal	3607	3917	4083	2777
核反应堆、锅炉、机器、机械器具及其零件	Nuclear Reactors ,Boilers, Machinery and Mechanical Appliances; and Parts Thereof	36174	47381	75911	52372
电机、电气设备及其零件；录音机及放声机、电视图像、声音的录制和重放设备及其零件、附件	Electrical Machinery and Equipment and Parts Thereof;Sound Recorders and Repreducers, Television Image and Sound Recordes and Repreducers,and Parts and Accessories of Such Articles	22801	33393	56758	53355
光学、照相、电影、计量、检验、医疗或外科用仪器及设备、精密仪器及设备；上述物品的零件、附件	Optical,Photographic,Cinematographic,Measuring, Checking,Precision Medical or Surgical Instruments and Apparatus;Parts and Accessories Thereof	3521	4230	6348	5255
家具、寝具、褥垫、弹簧床垫、软床垫及类似的填充制品；未列名灯具及照明装置；发光标志、发光名牌及类似品；活动房屋	Mattresses,Mattress Supports,Cushions and Similar Stuffed Furnishings;Lamps and Lighting Fittings, not Elsewhere Spcified or Included;Illumihated Signs,Illuminated	5086	8301	8296	4769

15-7 主要商品分大类进口金额

Import Value of Major Merchandise by Type

单位:万美元 (USD 10 000)

商品分类	HS Section and Division	2000	2003	2004	2005
无机化学品；贵金属、稀土金属、放射性元素及其同位素的有机及无机化合物	Inorganic Chemicals,Organic or Inorganic Compounds of Precious Metals,of Rare Earth Metals,of Radioactive Elements or of Isotopes	1467	4082	89	317
有机化学品	Organic Chemicals	7257	11852	14829	15237
塑料及其制品	Plastic and Articles Thereof	2559	2358	2560	4317
钢铁	Iron and Steel	2467	2086	1205	752
铜及制品	Copper and Articles Thereof	2367	1487	842	689
铝及制品	Aluminium and Articles Thereof	2652	1194	1634	3627
核反应堆、锅炉、机器、机械器具及其零件	Nuclear Reactors ,Boilers, Machinery and Mechanical Appliances; and Parts Thereof	12990	31100	37185	38050
电机、电气设备及其零件；录音机及放声机、电视图像、声音的录制和重放设备及其零件、附件	Electrical Machinery and Equipment and Parts Thereof;Sound Recorders and Repreducers, Television Image and Sound Recordes and Repreducers,and Parts and Accessories of Such Articles	5911	12200	16102	23337
车辆及其零件、附件，铁道及电车道车辆除外	Vehicles Other Than Railway or Tramway Rolling-Stock, and Rarts and Accessories Thereof	1530	2759	3291	1387
航空器、航天器及其零件	Aircraft,Spacecraft and Parts Thereof	10443	768	814	8800
光学、照相、电影、计量、检验、医疗或外科用仪器及设备、精密仪器及设备	Optical,Photographic,Cinematographic,Measuring, Checking,Precision Medical or Surgical	3673	8111	10358	10424

15-7 续表 continued

单位:万美元 (USD 10 000)

商品分类	HS Section and Division	2006	2007	2008	2009
无机化学品；贵金属、稀土金属、放射性元素及其同位素的有机及无机化合物	Inorganic Chemicals,Organic or Inorganic Compounds of Precious Metals,of Rare Earth Metals,of Radioactive Elements or of Isotopes	709	1039	6001	5040
有机化学品	Organic Chemicals	13521	14536	15692	14186
塑料及其制品	Plastic and Articles Thereof	2889	5149	2553	3134
钢铁	Iron and Steel	1014	1270	3888	2537
铜及制品	Copper and Articles Thereof	8035	22683	11097	41195
铝及制品	Aluminium and Articles Thereof	3172	3223	4767	6505
核反应堆、锅炉、机器、机械器具及其零件	Nuclear Reactors ,Boilers, Machinery and Mechanical Appliances; and Parts Thereof	33065	55243	68504	87493
电机、电气设备及其零件；录音机及放声机、电视图像、声音的录制和重放设备及其零件、附件	Electrical Machinery and Equipment and Parts Thereof;Sound Recorders and Repreducers, Television Image and Sound Recordes and Repreducers,and Parts and Accessories of Such Articles	21279	25164	48008	113034
车辆及其零件、附件，铁道及电车道车辆除外	Vehicles Other Than Railway or Tramway Rolling-Stock, and Rarts and Accessories Thereof	1228	1529	3789	1798
航空器、航天器及其零件	Aircraft,Spacecraft and Parts Thereof	17879	2463	26148	13057
光学、照相、电影、计量、检验、医疗或外科用仪器及设备、精密仪器及设备	Optical,Photographic,Cinematographic,Measuring, Checking,Precision Medical or Surgical	12152	17026	17737	24210

15-8 主要年份旅游人数及收入

Number of Tourists and Tourism Earnings In Representative Years

年 份 Year	接待旅游人数（万人次） Number of Tourists (10 000 person-times)	#国际人数旅游 Number of International Tourists	旅游总收入（万元） Totalm Tourism Earnings (10 000 yuan)	#国际旅游收入 Earning of International Tourists	国际旅游者在西安人均停留天数（天） Number of Days of Average International Tourists Staying in Xi'an(day)	国际旅游者在西安人均消费（元/人） Consumption of Average International Tourists in Xi'an (yuan/person)
1980	4.00	4.00	1757	1757	3.8	438.7
1981	6.71	6.71	2314	2314	3.4	345.2
1982	9.09	9.09	3172	3172	2.8	348.3
1983	12.38	12.38	3720	3720	2.5	300.6
1984	15.13	15.13	4579	4579	2.3	302.6
1985	21.15	21.15	7029	7029	2.2	332.3
1986	25.78	25.78	10886	10886	2.2	422.2
1987	30.15	30.15	16588	16588	2.1	550.3
1988	36.58	36.58	21152	21152	2.0	578.3
1989	21.20	21.20	14125	14125	1.9	666.2
1990	25.88	25.88	19628	19628	2.1	758.5
1991	31.00	31.00	29051	29051	2.3	936.9
1992	40.16	40.16	40966	40966	2.2	1020.2
1993	43.50	43.50	48951	48951	1.9	1125.2
1994	41.49	41.49	82000	82000	2.2	1975.9
1995	791.35	41.35	440000	103818	2.0	2510.8
1996	925.39	45.39	470000	149400	2.6	3291.8
1997	1010.53	48.53	510000	166359	2.6	3428.2
1998	1105.80	47.98	560000	160244	2.6	3393.8
1999	1260.40	55.41	830000	186282	2.5	3362.0
2000	1567.00	65.03	1050000	224100	2.5	3445.0
2001	1752.20	67.20	1130000	240700	2.4	3582.0
2002	1984.13	74.13	1310000	260000	2.2	3507.3
2003	1647.67	33.66	1064200	121200	2.5	3584.0
2004	2149.03	65.03	1544000	273900	2.9	4212.0
2005	2423.60	77.56	1785000	335380	2.9	4324.0
2006	2738.70	86.73	2043000	378270	2.9	4353.0
2007	3118.01	100.01	2372000	424263	2.9	4242.0
2008	3232.20	63.20	2435200	287200	2.6	4544.3
2009	3929.29	67.29	2974000	310500	2.9	4614.4

15-9 主要年份国际旅游收入

Earning of International Tourism In Representative Years

单位:万美元 (USD10 000)

项 目	Item	2000	2001	2002	2003	2004	2005	2006	2007	2008	2009
合 计	**Total**	**27000**	**29002**	**32000**	**14600**	**33000**	**40900**	**46700**	**54323**	**35900**	**39000**
一、长途交通费	**Long Distance Transportation**	**7047**	**7946**	**6816**	**3109**	**8415**	**12311**	**11442**	**14286**	**10016**	**12597**
1.飞机	Airplane	6011	7395	5536	2526	7524	9407	9527	10918	7467	9438
2.火车	Train	273	203	288	131	264	858	561	2009	1436	2262
3.汽车	Highway	763	348	992	452	627	2046	1354	1359	1113	897
二、游览	**Sightseeing**	**1296**	**1276**	**1120**	**511**	**1155**	**2045**	**2335**	**2335**	**1831**	**2262**
三、住宿	**Accommodation**	**3051**	**3684**	**4480**	**2044**	**4752**	**4621**	**5977**	**6573**	**4523**	**5343**
四、餐饮	**Food and Beverage**	**2673**	**3074**	**3264**	**1489**	**2673**	**3823**	**2195**	**3804**	**2908**	**3471**
五、娱乐	**Entertainment**	**1512**	**1074**	**896**	**409**	**990**	**1779**	**747**	**1847**	**2046**	**1833**
六、购物	**Shopping**	**6615**	**7047**	**9600**	**4380**	**9900**	**9897**	**17466**	**15645**	**9262**	**7761**
七、邮电通讯	**Post and Communication Services**	**1350**	**899**	**1120**	**512**	**957**	**2454**	**1261**	**1794**	**1652**	**1131**
八、市内交通	**Local Transportation**	**1566**	**899**	**768**	**350**	**726**	**858**	**841**	**1249**	**1041**	**975**
九、其他	**Others**	**1890**	**3103**	**3936**	**1796**	**3432**	**3112**	**4436**	**6790**	**2621**	**3627**

15-10 主要涉外星级宾馆接待海外旅游者情况

Mainly Concerning Oversea Tourists Reception in Star Hotels

单位：人次 (person-time)

项　　目	Item	2004	2005	2006	2007	2008	2009
海外旅游者人数合计	**International Tourists**	**650325**	**775620**	**867273**	**1000063**	**632036**	**672909**
外国人	Foreigners	527480	658578	733963	850905	535837	590870
#日本	Japan	99614	75639	85708	93135	43017	60192
菲律宾	Philippines	876	2165	1910	2162	1466	1708
新加坡	Singapore	3990	6148	6395	7309	6335	7570
美国	America	89499	116913	121788	146089	104742	100445
加拿大	Canada	13132	16807	20075	29193	19047	21901
英国	England	36279	45956	50046	56560	40299	43068
法国	France	30837	49414	49113	58216	37415	39350
德国	Germany	29051	37527	41446	50882	32892	36371
意大利	Italy	7693	16909	16493	21444	9445	15316
瑞士	Switzerland	2390	3748	4080	5047	3763	4479
澳大利亚	Australia	19231	28645	30146	36581	24784	26349
新西兰	New Zealand	2451	4522	3296	4978	4027	4238
港澳和台湾同胞	Chinese Compatriots from Hong Kong, Macao and Taiwan	122845	117042	133310	149158	96199	82039
#台湾同胞	Taiwan	64209	57958	66601	74962	44552	37464

主要统计指标解释

进出口总额 海关进出口总额指实际进出我国国境的货物总金额。包括对外贸易实际进出口货物，来料加工装配进出口货物，国家间、联合国及国际组织无偿援助物资和赠送品，华侨、港澳台同胞和外籍华人捐赠品，租赁期满归承租人所有的租赁货物，进料加工进出口货物，边境地方贸易及边境地区小额贸易进出口货物（边民互市贸易除外），中外合资企业、中外合作经营企业、外商独资经营企业进出口货物和公用物品，到、离岸价格在规定限额以上的进出口货样和广告品（无商业价值、无使用价值和免费提供出口的除外），从保税仓库提取在中国境内销售的进口货物，以及其他进出口货物。进出口总额用以观察一个国家在对外贸易方面的总规模。我国规定出口货物按离岸价格统计，进口货物按到岸价格统计。

利用外资 指我国各级政府、部门、企业和其他经济组织通过对外借款、吸收外商直接投资以及用其他方式筹措的境外现汇、设备、技术等。

对外借款 是我国利用外资的重要部分。指通过对外正式签订借款协议，从境外筹措的资金，包括外国政府贷款、国际金融组织贷款、外国银行商业贷款、出口信贷以及对外发行债券等。1996年及以前还包括对外发行股票。

外商直接投资 指外国企业和经济组织或个人（包括华侨、港澳台胞以及我国在境外注册的企业）按我国有关政策、法规，用现汇、实物、技术等在我国境内开办外商独资企业、与我国境内的企业或经济组织共同举办中外合资经营企业、合作经营企业或合作开发资源的投资（包括外商投资收益的再投资），以及经政府有关部门批准的项目投资总额内企业从境外借入的资金。

外商其他投资 指除对外借款和外商直接投资以外的各种利用外资的形式。包括企业在境内外股票市场公开发行的以外币计价的股票（目前主要是在香港证券市场发行的H股和在境内证券市场发行的B股）发行价总额，国际租赁进口设备的应付款，补偿贸易中外商提供的进口设备、技术、物料的价款，加工装配贸易中外商提供的进口设备、物料的价款。

对外承包工程 指各对外承包公司以招标议标承包方式承揽的下列业务:（1）承包国外工程建设项目，（2）承包我国对外经援项目，（3）承包我国驻外机构的工程建设项目，（4）承包我国境内利用外资进行建设的工程项目，（5）与外国承包公司合营或联合承包工程项目时我国公司分包部分，（6）对外承包兼营的房屋开发业务。对外承包工程的营业额是以货币表现的本期内完成的对外承包工程的工作量，包括以前年度签订的合同和本年度新签订的合同在报告期内完成的工作量。

对外劳务合作 指以收取工资的形式向业主或承包商提供技术和劳动服务的活动。我国对外承包公司在境外开办的合营企业，中国公司同时又提供劳务的，其劳务部分也纳入劳务合作统计。劳务合作营业额按报告期内向雇主提交的结算数（包括工资、加班费和奖金等）统计。

旅游者人数

（1）入境国际旅游者人数:指来中国参观、访问、旅行、探亲、访友、休养、考察、参加会议和从事经济、科技、文化、教育、宗教等活动的外国人、华侨、港澳同胞和台湾同胞的人数。不包括外国在我国的常驻机构，如使领馆、通讯社、企业办事处的工作人员;来我国常住的外国专家、留学生以及在岸逗留不过夜人员。

（2）出境居民人数:指大陆居民因公务活动或私人事务短期出境的人数。公务活动出境居民人数包括在国际交通工具上的中国服务员工，因私出境居民人数不包括在国际交通工具上的中国服务员工。

（3）国内旅游者人数:指我国大陆居民和在我国常住1年以上的外国人、华侨、港澳台同胞离开常住地在境内其他地方的旅游设施内至少停留一夜，最长不超过6个月的人数。

国际旅游（外汇）收入 指入境旅游的外国人、华侨、港澳同胞和台湾同胞在中国大陆旅游过程中发生的一切旅游支出，对于国家来说就是国际旅游（外汇）收入。

国际旅行社 指经营对外招徕并接待外国人、华侨、港澳同胞和台湾同胞来中国、归国或回内地旅游业务的旅行社。

国内旅行社 指负责经营招徕、组团、接待国内旅客的旅游业务，以及不对外招徕，负责经营接待国际旅行社或其它涉外部门组织的外国人、华侨、港澳同胞和台湾同胞来中国、归国或回内地的旅游业务的旅行社。

涉外饭店 指经有关部门批准，允许接待外国人、华侨、港澳同胞和台湾同胞的饭店。

Explanatory Notes on Main Statistical Indicators

Total Imports and Exports at Customs refer to the value of commodities imported into and exported from the boundary of China. They include the actual imports and exports through foreign trade, imported and exported goods under the processing and assembling trades and materials, supplies and gifts as aid given gratis between governments and by the United Nations and other international organizations, and contributions donated by overseas Chinese, compatriots in Hong Kong and Macao and Chinese with foreign citizenship, leasing commodities owned by tenant at the expiration of leasing period, the imported and exported commodities processed with imported materials, commodities trading in border areas (excluding mutual exchange goods), the imported and exported commodities and articles for public use of the Sino-foreign joint ventures, cooperative enterprises and ventures exclusively with foreign own investment. Also included are import or export of samples and advertising goods for whose CIF or FOB value are beyond the permitted ceiling (excluding goods of no trading or use value and free commodities for export), imported goods sold in China from bonded warehouses and other imported or exported goods. The indicator of the total imports and exports at customs can be used to observe the total size of external trade in a country. In accordance with the stipulation of the Chinese government, imports are calculated at CIF, while exports are calculated at FOB

Utilization of Foreign Capital refers to remittance, equipment and technology financed from abroad, by loans, foreign direct investment and other forms undertaken by the Chinese governments at all levels, by various departments, enterprises and other economic units.

Foreign Borrowings an important part of Chinas utilization of foreign capital, it refer to funds borrowed from abroad through formal signing of borrowing agreements with foreign institutions, including loans of foreign governments, loans of international financial institutions, commercial loans of foreign banks, export credit, and funds raised by Chinese bonds (and shares before 1996) issued abroad.

Direct Investment by Foreign Entrepreneurs refers to the investments inside China by foreign enterprises and economic organizations or individuals (including overseas Chinese, compatriots from Hong Kong and Macao, and Chinese enterprises registered abroad), following the relevant policies and laws of China, for the establishment of ventures exclusively with foreign own investment, Sino-foreign joint ventures and cooperative enterprises or for co-operative exploration of resources with enterprises or economic organizations in China. It includes the re investment of the foreign entrepreneurs with the profits gained from the investment and the funds that enterprises borrow from abroad in the total investment of projects which are approved by the relevant department of the government.

Other Investment by Foreign Entrepreneurs refers to all forms of utilization of foreign capitals other than foreign borrowings and foreign direct investment. It includes the total value of stock shares in foreign currencies issued by enterprises at domestic or foreign stock exchanges (now mainly consisting of H shares issued at Hong Kong Security Market and B shares issued at domestic security markets), rent payable for the imported equipment through international leasing arrangement, cost of imported equipment, technology and materials provided by foreign counterparts in compensation trade and processing and assembly trade.

Contracted Projects with Foreign Countries refer to projects undertaken by Chinese contractors (project contracting companies) through bidding process. They include: (1)overseas civil engineering construction projects financed by foreign investors; (2)overseas projects financed by the Chinese government through its foreign aid programs; (3)construction projects of Chinese diplomatic missions, trade offices and other institutions stationed abroad; (4)construction projects in China financed by foreign investment; (5)sub-contracted projects to be taken by Chinese contractors through a joint umbrella project with foreign contractor(s); (6)housing development projects. The business income from international contracted projects is the work volume of contracted projects completed during the reference period, expressed in monetary terms, including completed work on projects signed in previous years.

Service Cooperation with Foreign Countries refers to the activities of providing technology and labour services to employers or contractors in the forms of receiving salaries and wages. Labour services providing by contractual joint ventures of Chinese international contracting corporations should be included in the statistics of service co-operation with foreign countries. The business income of labour service co operation is theincome in the form of wages and salaries, overtime pay, bonuses and other remuneration received from the employers during the reference period.

Number of Tourists

(1) International tourists refer to foreigners, overseas Chinese, Chinese compatriots from Hong Kong, Macao and Taiwan coming to China for sight-seeing, visits, tours, family reunions, vacations, study tours, conferences and other activities of a business, scientific and technological, cultural, educational and religious nature. It does not include representatives and employees of resident institutions of foreign countries in China such as embassies, consulates, news agencies and offices of foreign companies and organizations, nor does it include long-term foreign experts or students residing in China, or persons in transition without spending a night in China.

(2) Chinese residents going abroad refer to Chinese residents going abroad for short terms for either public business or private purposes. Chinese employees working on international transport carriers are included in those going abroad for public business purpose, not in those for private purpose.

(3) Domestic tourists refer to residents of the mainland of China who stay for one night at least but no more than 6 months at tourist facilities in other places than their permanent residence within the territory of the mainland China, including foreigners, overseas Chinese and Chinese compatriots from Hong Kong, Macao and Taiwan who have resided in China for over one year.

Foreign Exchange Earnings from International Tourism refer to the total expenditures of foreigners, overseas Chinese, Chinese compatriots from Hong Kong, Macao and Taiwan during their stay in the mainland of China, which are earnings of foreign exchange from international tourism from the point of view from China.

International Travel Agencies refer to travel agencies engaged in the promotion, solicitation, organization and reception of tours to the mainland of China by foreigners, overseas Chinese, Chinese compatriots from Hong Kong, Macao and Taiwan.

Domestic Travel Agencies refer to travel agencies engaged in the promotion, solicitation, organization and reception of domestic tourists, and in the reception of foreigners, overseas Chinese, Chinese compatriots from Hong Kong, Macao and Taiwan organized by international travel agencies or other departments concerned, without their own promotion and solicitation programmes.

Tourist Hotels refer to hotels that are able, with the approval of departments concerned, to accommodate foreigners, overseas Chinese, Chinese compatriots from Hong Kong, Macao and Taiwan Province.

16 金融和保险

BANKING AND INSURANCE

资料整理：刘　婷　张小文
Data management:Liu Ting Zhang Xiaowen

第十六部分　金融和保险

一、简要说明

本章资料包括金融、证券和保险业情况，由西安市统计局综合处根据省银监局、人民银行西安分行营业管理部、省证监局和省保监局提供资料整理。

二、主要指标

金融机构人民币（含外资）存款余额（亿元）	7622.93	比年初增加	1790.07亿元
金融机构人民币（含外资）贷款余额（亿元）	4539.75	比年初增加	1224.21亿元
金融机构现金收入（亿元）	9121.40	比上年增长	12.39%
金融机构现金支出（亿元）	8842.75	比上年增长	12.74%
保费收入（亿元）	122.11	比上年增长	20.4%

16 BANKING AND INSURANCE

Ⅰ.Brief Introduction

This chapter includes information of the financial, securities and insurance, compiled by Integration Division of the Xi'an Bureau of Statistics, according to data from Xi'an Branch Management Department of the People's Bank of China, Provincial Banking Bureau, Securities Supervisory Authority and Insurance Supervisory Authority.

Ⅱ.Major Indicators

		Increase over Preceding Year
Deposit in Financial Institution(100 mil. yuan)	7622.93	1790.07
Loans in Financial Institutions(100 mil. yuan)	4539.75	1224.21
Cash Income of Financial Institutions(100 mil. yuan)	9121.40	12.39%
Cash Expenditure of Financial Institutions(100 mil. yuan)	8842.75	12.74%
Premiums(100 mil. yuan)	122.11	20.4%

16-1 西安银行系统机构、人员数

Number of Institution and Employed Person in Finance System in Xi'an

机构名称	Name of Institution	2008		2009	
		机构数（个） Number of Institution (unit)	年末人数（人） Number of Staff and Workers (person)	机构数（个） Number of Institution (unit)	年末人数（人） Number of Staff and Workers (person)
合 计	**Total**	**921**	**21570**	**935**	**22253**
人民银行西安分行营业管理部	Management Department of the People's Bank of China Xi'an Branch	1	394	1	400
国家开发银行陕西省分行	National Development Bank Shaanxi Branch	1	145	1	159
进出口银行陕西省分行	Export Import Bank of Shaanxi Branch	1	46	1	57
农业发展银行陕西省分行	Agricultural Development Bank of China Shaanxi Branch	8	236	12	257
工商银行陕西省分行	Industrial and Commercial Bank of China Shaanxi Branch	193	4223	194	4212
农业银行陕西省分行	Agricultural Bank of China Shaanxi Branch	165	3077	166	3055
中国银行陕西省分行	Bank of China Shaanxi Branch	120	2924	122	3106
建设银行陕西省分行	Construction Bank of China Shaanxi Branch	174	3797	174	3898
中国光大银行西安分行	China Everbright Bank Xi'an Branch	13	407	14	431
华夏银行西安分行	China Huaxia Bank Xi'an Branch	7	237	8	243
招商银行西安分行	China Merchants Bank Xi'an Branch	21	904	22	957
浦发银行西安分行	Pufa Bank Xi'an Branch	10	325	9	350
民生银行西安分行	China Minsheng Banking Corp., Ltd Xi'an Branch	13	495	13	612
福建兴业银行西安分行	Fujian Industrial Bank Xi'an Branch	9	286	10	299
西安市商业银行	Xi'an City Commercial Bank	114	2248	114	2286
东亚银行西安分行	Dongya Bank Xi'an Branch	4	201	5	201
汇丰银行西安分行	Huifeng Bank Xi'an Branch	2	63	3	61
交通银行西安分行	Bank of Communication Xi'an Branch	50	1048	50	1063
中信实业银行西安分行	CITIC Industrial Bank Xi'an Branch	14	437	15	508
浙商银行西安分行	China Zheshang Bank Xi'an Branch	1	77	1	98

16-2 金融机构（含外资）本外币存贷款年末余额（2009年）

Financial institution Including Foreign-funded balance of bisic currency and foreign currency at Year-end（2009）

单位：亿元 (100 million yuan)

指 标	Item	2009	比年初增减数 Increase or decrease compared with the beginning of the Year
存款余额合计（汇率：6.8282）	**Total Deposit （Exchange Rate：6.8282）**	**7622.93**	**1790.07**
一、企事业单位存款	**Enterprise and Institution Deposit**	**3123.75**	**877.32**
1.活期存款	Demand Deposits	2167.43	495.85
2.定期存款	Time Deposits	956.32	381.47
二、储蓄存款	**Savings Deposits**	**3125.29**	**573.64**
1.活期储蓄	Current Saving	1116.06	262.45
2.定期储蓄	Time Saving	2009.23	311.19
三、信托存款	**Trusted Deposits**		
四、委托存款	**Consignment Deposits**	**274.57**	**174.81**
五、其他存款	**Other Deposits**	**1099.31**	**164.29**
贷款余额合计（汇率：6.8282）	**Total Loans（Exchange Rate：6.8282）**	**4539.75**	**1224.21**
一、短期贷款	**Short-term Loans**	**1168.25**	**131.92**
二、中长期贷款	**Medium-term and Long-term loans**	**2928.57**	**1006.88**
三、信托贷款	**Trusted Loans**		
四、委托贷款	**Consignment Loans**	**64.99**	**23.97**
五、其他贷款	**Other Loans**	**27.93**	**2.75**
六、票据融资	**Bill Financing**	**349.27**	**59.13**
七、各项垫款	**Various Advance Funds**	**0.75**	**-0.44**

注：金融机构贷款余额（含国家开发银行）为4866.17亿元。

Note:Financial institution loan balance(including China Development Bank) is 486.617 billion yuan.

16-3 金融机构（不含外资）本外币存贷款年末余额（2009年）

Domestic Funded Financial institution balance of bisic currency and foreign currency at Year-end（2009）

单位：亿元 (100 million yuan)

指　　标	Item	2009	比年初增减数 Increase or decrease compared with the beginning of the Year
存款余额合计	**Total Deposit**	**7554.55**	**1766.11**
一、企事业单位存款	**Enterprise and Institution Deposit**	**3069.41**	**856.45**
1.活期存款	Demand Deposits	2143.37	493.02
2.定期存款	Time Deposits	926.04	363.43
二、储蓄存款	**Savings Deposits**	**3112.38**	**571.00**
1.活期储蓄	Current Saving	1112.35	260.77
2.定期储蓄	Time Saving	2000.04	310.23
三、信托存款	**Trusted Deposits**		
四、委托存款	**Consignment Deposits**	**274.57**	**174.81**
五、其他存款	**Other Deposits**	**1098.19**	**163.86**
贷款余额合计	**Total Loans**	**4487.18**	**1219.29**
一、短期贷款	**Short-term Loans**	**1160.13**	**128.03**
二、中长期贷款	**Medium-term and Long-term loans**	**2884.14**	**1005.68**
三、信托贷款	**Trusted Loans**		
四、委托贷款	**Consignment Loans**	**64.99**	**23.97**
五、其他贷款	**Other Loans**	**27.92**	**2.83**
六、票据融资	**Bill Financing**	**349.27**	**59.23**
七、各项垫款	**Various Advance Funds**	**0.75**	**-0.44**

16-4 金融机构（含外资）人民币存贷款年末余额（2009年）

Year-end Balance of Deposit and Loans in Financial Institutions Including Foreign-funded（2009）

单位：亿元 (100 million yuan)

指 标	Item	2009	比年初增减数 Increase or decrease compared with the beginning of the Year
存款余额合计（汇率：6.8282）	**Total Deposit （Exchange Rate：6.8282）**	**7522.08**	**1772.71**
一、企业存款	**Deposits by Enterprses**	**3077.99**	**869.32**
1 .活期存款	Demand Deposits	2135.00	494.00
2 .定期存款	Time Deposits	942.98	375.31
二、财政存款	**Fiscal Deposits**	**80.12**	**35.34**
三、机关团体存款	**Deposits of Government Departments and Organizations**	**424.19**	**34.59**
四、储蓄存款	**Savings Deposits**	**3084.20**	**570.49**
#定期储蓄	Time Savings	1979.22	309.18
五、农业存款	**Agricultural Deposits**	**131.14**	**33.28**
六、信托存款	**Credit Deposits**		
七、委托存款	**Trusted Deposits**	**274.24**	**174.55**
八、其他存款	**Other Deposits**	**450.22**	**55.14**
贷款余额合计（汇率：6.8282）	**Total Loans（Exchange Rate：6.8282）**	**4482.63**	**1207.52**
一、短期贷款	**Short-term Loans**	**1155.83**	**124.05**
1 .工业贷款	Industrial Loans	416.59	65.67
2. 商业贷款	Commercial Loans	89.63	1.25
3.建筑业贷款	Construction Loans	34.91	-8.80
4.农业贷款	Agricultural Loans	69.42	12.33
5.乡镇企业贷款	Loans to Township Enterprises	67.59	6.17
6.三资企业贷款	Loans to Enterprises with Foreign Funds	4.43	-2.15
7.私营企业及个体贷款	Loans to Private Enterprises and Self-employed Individuals	9.32	4.43
8.其他短期贷款	Other Short-term Loans	463.93	45.15
#个人短期消费贷款	Individual short-term consumer loan	3.82	-0.99
二、中长期贷款	**Medium-term &Long-term Loans**	**2908.75**	**1003.84**
1 .基本建设贷款	Loans to Capital Construction	1031.58	264.66
2. 技术改造贷款	Loans to Technical Innovation	67.54	11.73
3.其他中长期贷款	Other Medium-term&Long-term Loans	1809.63	727.45
#个人中长期消费贷款	Individual medium-long-term consumer loan	565.94	215.36
三、信托贷款	**Credit Loans**		
四、融资租赁	**Financial Leasing**	**4.73**	**-1.39**
五、委托贷款	**Trusted Loans**	**64.99**	**23.97**
六、票据融资	**Bill Financing**	**347.59**	**57.49**
七、各项垫款	**Various Advance Funds**	**0.75**	**-0.44**

16-5 金融机构（不含外资）人民币存贷款年末余额（2009年）

Year-end Balance of Deposit and Loans in Domestic Funded Financial Institutions（2009）

单位：亿元 (100 million yuan)

指　　标	Item	2009	比年初增减数 Increase or decrease compared with the beginning of the Year
存款余额合计	**Total Deposit**	**7457.71**	**1746.44**
一、企业存款	**Deposits by Enterprses**	**3025.54**	**845.61**
1.活期存款	Demand Deposits	2112.81	488.32
2.定期存款	Time Deposits	912.73	357.30
二、财政存款	**Fiscal Deposits**	**80.12**	**35.34**
三、机关团体存款	**Deposits of Government Departments and Organizations**	**424.19**	**34.59**
四、储蓄存款	**Savings Deposits**	**3072.41**	**568.00**
#定期储蓄	Time Savings	1970.78	308.25
五、农业存款	**Agricultural Deposits**	**131.14**	**33.28**
六、信托存款	**Credit Deposits**		
七、委托存款	**Trusted Deposits**	**274.24**	**174.55**
八、其他存款	**Other Deposits**	**450.09**	**55.06**
贷款余额合计	**Total Loans**	**4436.50**	**1200.66**
一、短期贷款	**Short-term Loans**	**1151.74**	**122.80**
1.工业贷款	Industrial Loans	416.59	65.67
2.商业贷款	Commercial Loans	89.63	1.25
3.建筑业贷款	Construction Loans	34.91	-8.80
4.农业贷款	Agricultural Loans	69.42	12.33
5.乡镇企业贷款	Loans to Township Enterprises	67.59	6.17
6.三资企业贷款	Loans to Enterprises with Foreign Funds	4.43	-2.15
7.私营企业及个体贷款	Loans to Private Enterprises and Self-employed Individuals	9.32	4.43
8.其他短期贷款	Other Short-term Loans	459.84	43.91
#个人短期消费贷款	Individual short-term consumer loan	3.58	-0.88
二、中长期贷款	**Medium-term &Long-term Loans**	**2866.71**	**998.12**
1.基本建设贷款	Loans to Capital Construction	1031.58	264.66
2.技术改造贷款	Loans to Technical Innovation	67.54	11.73
3.其他中长期贷款	Other Medium-term&Long-term Loans	1767.59	721.73
#个人中长期消费贷款	Individual medium-long-term consumer loan	562.53	213.78
三、信托贷款	**Credit Loans**		
四、融资租赁	**Financial Leasing**	**4.73**	**-1.39**
五、委托贷款	**Trusted Loans**	**64.99**	**23.97**
六、票据融资	**Bill Financing**	**347.59**	**57.59**
七、各项垫款	**Various Advance Funds**	**0.75**	**-0.44**

16-6 金融机构现金收入、支出（2009年）

Cash Income and Expenditure of Domestic Funded Financial Institutions（2009）

单位：亿元 (100 million yuan)

指　标	Item	2009	比去年同期增减（%） Increase or down over the some period of Preceding Year(%)
现金收入合计	**Total Cash Income**	**9121.40**	**12.4**
一、商品销售收入	**Income from Commodity Sales**	**786.67**	**4.2**
二、服务业收入	**Income from Service Trade**	**293.38**	**3.6**
三、行政税费收入	**The Tax and Fee Income**	**65.34**	**4.2**
四、城乡个体经营收入	**Income from Urban and Rural Individual Business**	**211.70**	**-4.9**
五、储蓄存款收入	**Income from Savings Deposits**	**6872.53**	**15.8**
六、其他金融性公司收入	**Income from Other Financial Institutions**	**32.33**	**-37.1**
七、居民归还贷款收入	**Income from Repayment of Loans by Residents**	**48.42**	**-13.3**
八、汇兑收入	**Income from Remittances**	**75.64**	**-10.7**
九、有价证券及其他投资性收入	**Income from Securities and Other Investment**	**7.84**	**-43.5**
十、其他收入	**Other Income**	**727.55**	**11.9**
现金支出合计	**Total Cash Expenditure**	**8842.75**	**12.7**
一、工资性及个人其他支出	**Wages and Other Personal Expenses**	**347.72**	**15.4**
二、农副产品采购支出	**Purchases of Agricultural and Sideline Products**	**101.18**	**-5.3**
三、工矿及其他产品采购支出	**Expenditure for Purchases of Individual Business**	**71.87**	**25.9**
四、行政企业管理与经营费支出	**Expenditure for Administration Overhead and Management**	**486.48**	**3.8**
五、城乡个体经营支出	**Expenditure for Individual Business**	**297.96**	**7.9**
六、储蓄存款支出	**Expenditure for Savings Deposits**	**6858.08**	**17.0**
七、其他金融性公司支出	**Expenditure for Other Financial Companies**	**9.86**	**-56.9**
八、居民提取贷款支出	**Expenditure for Loans by Residents**	**26.52**	**-37.6**
九、汇兑支出	**Expenditure for Remittances**	**50.24**	**-25.4**
十、有价证券支出	**Expenditure for Securities**	**11.14**	**2.3**
十一、其他支出	**Other Expenditure**	**581.69**	**-7.6**
投放（+）回笼（-）	**Currency Issue(+)cash withdrawn(-)**	**-278.66**	**2.3**

16-7 保险业务情况

Indicators of Insurance Business

指 标	Item	2008	2009
保险金额（亿元）	**Amount Insured(100 million yuan)**	**30224.5**	**18999.6**
保费收入（万元）	**Premiums(10 000 yuan)**	**1014454.7**	**1221132.7**
一、财产险	**Property Insurance**	**193468.0**	**258976.3**
（一）财产保险	Property Insurance	186568.8	249582.3
1.机动车辆及第三者责任	Motor Vehicle and Outside Person Liability	151284.5	211182.1
2.企业财产险	Enterprise Property Insurance	20438.8	18826.6
3.货物运输保险	Freight Transport Insurance	3853.0	3443.2
4.家庭财产保险	Family Property Insurance	471.0	448.4
5.建工及安工保险及其责任险	Construction and Installation Projects Insurance and Related Libility Insurance	6690.3	13330.8
6.其他	Others	3831.2	2351.2
（二）责任保险	Liability Insurance	3296.2	4313.4
（三）信用保险	Export Credit Insurance	2434.6	3896.1
（四）保证保险	Guarantee Insurance		-444.9
（五）农业保险	Agriculture Insurance	1698.7	1629.3
二、人身险	**Personnel Insurance**	**820986.6**	**962156.5**
（一）人寿保险	Life Insurance	750648.0	852259.0
1.普通寿险	Ordinary Life Insurance	87052.4	89159.3
2.分红保险	Dividend Insurance	439349.2	624794.8
3.投资连接保险	Insurance Connection Insurance	70255.4	7252.6
4.万能保险	Universal Insurance	154001.4	131052.4
（二）意外伤害保险	Unforeseen Injury Insurance	18273.3	23189.7
（三）健康保险	Health Insurance	52065.4	86707.7
赔款支出和各项给付（万元）	**Indemnity and Other Expenditure(10 000 yuan)**	**259205.1**	**251562.6**
一、财产险	**Property Insurance**	**112816.0**	**126091.3**
（一）财产保险	Property Insurance	108114.9	120205.7
1.机动车辆及第三者责任	Motor Vehicle and Outside Person Liability	88463.5	99329.9
2.企业财产险	Enterprise Property Insurance	14556.7	15177.0
3.家庭财产保险	Freight Transport Insurance	112.5	78.3
4.货物运输保险	Family Property Insurance	1328.4	1548.8
5.建工及安工保险及其责任险	Construction and Installation Projects Insurance and Related Libility Insurance	3147.8	2869.1
6.其他	Others	506.1	1202.7
（二）责任保险	Liability Insurance	2386.1	1247.7
（三）信用保险	Export Credit Insurance	125.3	868.9
（四）保证保险	Guarantee Insurance	1721.3	2053.0
（五）农业保险	Agriculture Insurance	468.5	1716.1
二、人身险	**Personnel Insurance**	**146389.1**	**125471.3**
（一）人寿保险	Life Insurance	129397.6	101989.5
1.普通寿险	Ordinary Life Insurance	28314.5	28996.4
2.分红保险	Dividend Insurance	100267.4	59740.4
3.投资连接保险	Insurance Connection Insurance	101.7	51.7
4.万能保险	Universal Insurance	714.1	13200.9
（二）意外伤害保险	Unforeseen Injury Insurance	4623.9	5531.8
（三）健康保险	Health Insurance	12367.6	17950.0
退保金（万元）	**Withdrawal(10 000 yuan)**	**142572.9**	**129091.2**
#人寿保险	Life Insurance	139336.3	120209.0
1.普通寿险	Ordinary Life Insurance	9089.6	7310.9
2.分红保险	Dividend Insurance	111262.8	72283.0
3.投资连接保险	Insurance Connection Insurance	8428.7	26520.0
4.万能保险	Universal Insurance	10555.1	14095.1

16-8 西安证券期货系统机构、人员数

Number of Institution and Employed Person in Securities and Futures System in Xi'an

机构名称	Name of Institution	2008		2009	
		机构数（个）Number of Institution (unit)	年末人数（人）Number of Staff and Workers (person)	机构数（个）Number of Institution (unit)	年末人数（人）Number of Staff and Workers (person)
合 计	**Total**	**74**	**3303**	**78**	**4184**
证券经营机构	**Securities Company and the Sales Department**	**71**	**3133**	**75**	**3997**
一、证券公司及营业部	**Securities Company**	**19**	**1553**	**20**	**1940**
西部证券股份有限公司及营业部	Western Securities Company Ltd.	13	1325	14	1626
陕西开源证券经纪有限责任公司及营业部	Shaanxi KaiYuan Securities Company Ltd.	3	108	3	132
西安华弘证券经纪有限责任公司及营业部	Xi□An HuaHong Securities Company Ltd.	3	120	3	182
二、证券营业部	**the Sales Department**	**52**	**1580**	**55**	**2057**
期货经纪机构	**Futures Company**	**3**	**170**	**3**	**187**
迈科期货经纪有限公司	Maike Futures Company Ltd.	1	83	1	84
陕西长安期货经纪有限公司	Shaanxi ChangAn Futures Company Ltd.	1	38	1	46
西部期货经纪有限公司	Western Futures Brokerage Co., Ltd.	1	49	1	57

16-9 证券期货市场基本情况

Basic Facts on Securities and Futures Markets

指 标	Item	2007	2008	2009
一、上市证券公司情况	**Listed Securities Companies**			
拥有上市股份公司（个）	Number of Listed Share-holding Companies(unit)	17	20	22
占全国比重（%）	Percentage to National Total(%)	1.1	1.3	1.3
上市股份公司总股本（亿股）	Total Capital of Listed Share-holding Companies (100 millon shares)	43.75	88.26	115.27
#流通股（亿股）	Negotiable shares(100 million shares)	26.96	38.44	63.99
总市值（亿元）	Total Market Capitalization(100 million yuan)	694.15	698.77	1749.15
累计证券市场筹措资金（亿元）	Accumulated Capital Raised by Securities Markets (100 millon yuan)	80.62	262.61	325.20
二、证券经营机构情况	**Securities Trading Organizations**			
拥有证券公司（个）	Number of Securities Companies(unit)	3	3	3
证券营业部（个）	Number of Securities Business Departments(unit)	51	52	55
投资者开户数（万户）	Number of Investors Who have Opened an Account (10 000 accounts)	124.0	130.3	147.5
证券交易总额（亿元）	Total Turnover(100 million yuan)	12100.10	7323.55	13841.70
三、期货市场情况	**Futures Market**			
拥有期货经纪公司（个）	Number of Futures Business Management Companies(unit)	3	3	3
期货营业部（个）	Number of Futures Business Departments(unit)	2	3	6
期货代理交易额（亿元）	Total Transaction Value in Futures Commissioning (100 million yuan)	2931.55	4992.37	7327.23
每个经纪公司平均拥有注册资金（万元）	Average Registered Capital of Each Business Management Company(10 000 yuan)	7666.67	7666.70	7666.70

主要统计指标解释

信贷资金 指金融机构以信用方式积聚和分配的货币资金。金融机构信贷资金的来源有各项存款、对国际金融机构负债、流通中货币、银行自有资金及当年结益等;信贷资金的运用有各项贷款、黄金占款、外汇占款、财政借款及在国际金融机构中的资产等。

存款 指企业、机关、团体或居民根据资金必须收回的原则，把货币资金存入银行或其他信用机构保管并取得一定利息的一种信用活动形式。根据存款对象的不同可划分为企业存款、财政存款、机关团体存款、基本建设存款、城镇储蓄存款、农村存款等科目。它是银行信贷资金的主要来源。

贷款 指银行或其他信用机构根据资金必须归还的原则，按一定利率，为企业、个人等提供资金的一种信用活动形式。我国银行贷款分为流动资金贷款、固定资产贷款、城乡个体工商户贷款以及农业贷款等科目。

保险金额 指保险人承担赔偿或者给付保险金责任的最高限额。

保费 指投保人为取得保险人在约定范围内所承担赔偿责任而支付给保险人的费用。

赔款 指保险人根据保险合同的规定，向被保险人支付的赔偿保险责任损失的金额。

给付 包括死伤医疗给付和满期给付。死伤医疗给付是指保险人根据人寿保险及长期健康保险合同的规定，因被保险人在保险期内发生保险责任范围内的保险事故支付给被保险人（或受益人）的金额。满期给付是指被保险人生存期满，保险人按人寿保险合同规定支付给被保险人的满期保险金额。

Explanatory Notes on Main Statistical Indicators

Credit Funds refer to the funds issued as loans by banking institutions. The sources of credit funds of the banking institutions included deposits, liabilities to international financial institutions, currency in circulation, self-owned funds and current retained profits, etc. The credit funds can be used in forms of loans, gold, foreign exchange, government debt and assets in the international financial institutions.

Deposit is a form of credit by which enterprises, institutions, organizations or households can put money into banks and other credit institutions for safekeeping and interest earning under the principle of free withdrawal. According to different depositors, deposits are divided into enterprise deposits, treasury deposits, deposits of government agencies and organizations, capital construction deposits, urban savings deposits, rural deposits and other deposits. Deposits are major sources of the credit funds of banks.

Loan is a form of credit by which banks and other credit institutions provide funds at certain interest rate to enterprises and individuals in the light of the principle of unconditional repayment. Loans from Chinese banks include circulating capital loans, fixed assets loans, loans to urban and rural individuals engaged in industrial and commercial business and agricultural loans.

Amount Insured refers to the maximum that the insurant will get for the claim of the case insured.

Premium is the fee paid by the insurant to the insurer to obtain the obligation of compensation from the insurance within the agreed terms.

Settled Claim is the compensation paid by the insurer to the insurant in accordance with the insurance contract.

Payment includes payment for death, injury or medical treatment and mature payment. Payment for death, injury or medical treatment refers to the money paid to the insurant (or the beneficiary) in accordance with the life orhealth insurance contract when the insurant encounters accidents within the insured period covered in the contract. Mature payment refers to the mature payment to the insurant in accordance with the life insurance contract at the end of the insured period.

17 教育和科技

EDUCATION,SCIENCE AND TECHNOLOGY

资料整理：陈超毅　郝　静　蔺秀玲　齐昆峰
Data management:Chen Chaoyi　Hao Jing　Lin Xiuling　Qi Kunfeng

第十七部分　教育和科技

一、简要说明

本章资料包括教育事业、科技事业基本情况，由西安市统计局社会科技处根据西安市教委等有关部门提供资料整理。科技部分由于全国科技普查资料整理尚未完成，暂无数据。

二、主要指标

普通高等学校数（所）	49	比上年增加　1所
普通高等学校在校学生（万人）	63.22	比上年增长　5.2%
研究生人数（万人）	7.24	比上年增长　7.5%

17　EDUCATION,SCIENCE AND TECHNOLOGY

Ⅰ.Brief Introduction

Data in this chapter consists of primarily data of educational undertakings, science and technology Activities of Xi'an city, compiled by Social & Science and Technology Division of the Xi'an Bureau of Statistics according to data from Xi'an Municipal Government Departments concerned.As the data of national science and technology census was sorting out ,there was no data.

Ⅱ.Major Indicators

		Increase over Preceding Year
Number of Schools Regular Institutions of Higher Education(unit)	49	1
Student Enrollment of Regular Institutions of Higher Education(10 000 persons)	63.22	5.2%
Postgraduates(10 000 persons)	7.24	7.5%

17-1 主要年份各类普通教育基本情况

Basic Statistics on Regular Eduction in Representative Years

指　　标	Item	2000	2005	2006	2007	2008	2009
学校数(所)	**Number of Schools (unit)**						
普通高等教育	Regular Institutions of Higher Education	25	44	47	48	48	49
中等学校	Secondary Schools	671	648	660	648	637	678
#专业学校	Specialized Secondary Schools	47	32	31	30	29	28
普通中学	Regular Secondary Schools	466	460	457	453	442	439
小学	Primary Schools	2323	1980	1929	1872	1781	1666
幼儿园	Kindergartens	367	737	863	830	905	896
毕业生数(万人)	**Graduates (10 000 persons)**						
普通高等教育	Regular Institutions of Higher Education	3.03	11.12	13.01	15.84	17.55	16.90
中等学校	Secondary Schools	15.09	23.26	23.00	23.70	24.67	25.67
#专业学校	Specialized Secondary Schools	1.63	1.44	1.84	2.03	2.58	2.70
普通中学	Regular Secondary Schools	12.01	18.82	18.04	18.37	17.99	17.80
小学	Primary Schools	13.83	11.92	11.53	11.38	10.58	9.96
招生数(万人)	**New Enrollment (10 000 persons)**						
普通高等教育	Regular Institutions of Higher Education	7.49	16.54	17.06	18.98	21.46	21.28
中等学校	Secondary Schools	21.58	25.87	26.83	27.93	27.75	28.33
#专业学校	Specialized Secondary Schools	1.90	2.26	2.61	2.91	2.55	2.15
普通中学	Regular Secondary Schools	17.88	18.53	18.61	17.96	17.16	16.57
小学	Primary Schools	11.51	8.47	9.16	8.67	8.33	7.84
幼儿园	Kindergartens	8.71	6.57	6.87	6.67	7.68	7.20
在校学生(万人)	**Total Enrollment (10 000 persons)**						
普通高等教育	Regular Institutions of Higher Education	19.41	53.06	57.10	62.31	66.68	70.31
中等学校	Secondary Schools	58.75	72.81	76.70	77.20	78.39	80.66
#专业学校	Specialized Secondary Schools	6.02	6.16	7.30	7.97	8.06	7.44
普通中学	Regular Secondary Schools	48.31	55.74	56.11	54.68	52.83	50.63
小学	Primary Schools	77.81	60.47	59.33	56.83	54.66	52.52
幼儿园	Kindergartens	12.85	12.75	13.38	14.11	15.46	16.30
教职工（人）	**Staff and Teachers (person)**						
普通高等教育	Regular Institutions of Higher Education	38067	57285	61414	65624	69048	70818
中等学校	Secondary Schools	48194	52674	53722	53462	56059	57477
#专业学校	Specialized Secondary Schools	6964	3924	3621	3548	3417	2965
普通中学	Regular Secondary Schools	34385	39456	39341	39171	39088	39002
小学	Primary Schools	35336	33907	34460	34901	34653	34389
幼儿园	Kindergartens	6346	10528	12335	13468	14932	15928
专任教师(人)	**Number of Full-time Teachers (person)**						
普通高等教育	Regular Institutions of Higher Education	15679	29498	32891	36717	38926	40605
中等学校	Secondary Schools	32923	39416	37399	38613	41321	44137
#专业学校	Specialized Secondary Schools	3172	2130	2014	2011	1904	1720
普通中学	Regular Secondary Schools	26230	31094	31203	31373	31425	31415
小学	Primary Schools	30215	29674	30018	30533	30382	30334
幼儿园	Kindergartens	2995	5959	7106	7951	8704	9240

注：幼儿园中包括学前班；普通高等教育含高校研究生。

Note:'Kindergartens' here including units providing pre-school education;Regular institution of higher education includes postgraduates .

17–2 各级普通教育基本情况（2009年）

Basic Facts on Regular Education by School Type（2009）

指 标	Item	学校数（所） Number of schools (unit)	毕业生数(人) Number of Graduates (person)	招生数(人) New enrollment (person)
一、研究生	**Postgraduates**	**(46)**	**19025**	**24879**
1.普通高校	Regular Institutions of Higher Education	(20)	18574	24400
2.科研机构	Scientific Research Institution	(26)	451	479
二、普通高等学校	**Regular Institutions of Higher Education**	**49**	**150389**	**188395**
三、普通中等学校	**Regular Institutions of Secondary Schools**	**678**	**256725**	**283257**
1.中等专业学校	Specialized Secondary Schools	28	27022	21518
2.普通中学	Regular Secondary Schools	439	177981	165694
3.技工学校	Technical Schools	126	37002	64993
4.职业高中	Vocational Middle Schools	84	14691	31042
5.工读学校	Reformatory Schools	1	29	10
四、小学	**Primary Schools**	**1666**	**99646**	**78411**
五、特殊教育学校	**Special Education Schools**	**7**	**311**	**202**
六、幼儿园及学前班	**Kindergartens**	**896**	**56288**	**71975**

注：（）为含研究生教育的普通高等学校和科研机构数。

Note:Institutions of regular higher education and scientific research which contain post-graduate education.

17-2 续表 continued

指 标	Item	在校学生数(人) Total Enrollment (person)	教职工数(人) Number of Staff and Teachers(person)	专任教师 Full-time Teachers
一、研究生	**Postgraduates**	**72366**		
1.普通高校	Regular Institutions of Higher Education	70908		
2.科研机构	Scientific Research Institution	1458		
二、普通高等学校	**Regular Institutions of Higher Education**	**632200**	**70818**	**40605**
三、普通中等学校	**Regular Institutions of Secondary Schools**	**806586**	**57477**	**44137**
1.中等专业学校	Specialized Secondary Schools	74356	2965	1720
2.普通中学	Regular Secondary Schools	506317	39002	31415
3.技工学校	Technical Schools	153454	10335	7786
4.职业高中	Vocational Middle Schools	72388	5129	3179
5.工读学校	Reformatory Schools	71	46	37
四、小学	**Primary Schools**	**525197**	**34389**	**30334**
五、特殊教育学校	**Special Education Schools**	**1523**	**335**	**234**
六、幼儿园及学前班	**Kindergartens**	**162993**	**15928**	**9240**

17-3 主要年份普通高等教育基本情况

Number of Schools by Level and Type of School in Representative Years

年 份 Year	学校数(所) Number of Schools (unit)	毕业生数(万人) Number of Graduates (10 000 persons)	招生数(万人) New Enrollment (10 000 persons)	在校学生数(万人) Total Enrollment (10 000 persons)	教职工数(万人) Number of Staff and Teachers (10 000 persons)	专任教师 Full-time Teachers
1978	21			2.88		0.87
1980	25			4.17		0.97
1985	28			6.49		1.28
1990	31	2.17	2.15	8.02	4.15	1.56
1995	32	3.04	3.40	10.87	4.21	1.59
1997	29	3.04	3.54	11.89	4.00	1.51
1998	29	2.84	3.69	12.66	3.91	1.50
1999	29	3.13	5.62	15.09	3.95	1.52
2000	25	3.03	7.49	19.41	3.80	1.57
2001	32	3.69	9.24	25.49	4.30	1.75
2002	35	4.23	11.88	33.00	4.67	2.06
2003	37	6.49	13.65	40.12	4.92	2.21
2004	41	7.66	13.17	40.29	5.45	2.69
2005	44	10.08	14.68	47.79	5.73	2.95
2006	47	11.75	15.15	51.40	6.14	3.29
2007	48	14.33	16.96	56.03	6.56	3.67
2008	48	15.82	19.31	60.10	6.90	3.89
2009	49	15.04	18.84	63.22	7.08	4.06

注：本表不含研究生。

Note:Graduate students educatedare not included.

17-4 主要年份研究生情况

Basic Situation of the major Year on Post-graduates in Representative Years

单位：人 （person）

年 份 Year	毕业生数 Graduates	高等学校 Institution of Higher Education	招生数 New Enrollment	高等学校 Institution of Higher Education	在校人数 Total Enrollment	高等学校 Institution of Higher Education
1978						
1980					651	651
1985					4799	4799
1990	2051	2051	1662	1662	5275	5275
1995	1769	1769	2712	2712	7974	7974
1996	2172	2172	3003	3003	8647	8647
1997	2619	2619	3423	3423	9393	9393
1998	2316	2316	3888	3888	10833	10833
1999	2903	2903	5020	5020	12986	12986
2000	3236	3236	6924	6924	16620	16620
2001	3881	3770	9274	8966	22564	21855
2002	4103	3952	11282	10882	28446	27471
2003	5971	5765	14322	13882	36936	35790
2004	8384	8127	17310	16871	45402	44169
2005	10416	10127	18583	18106	52699	51310
2006	12914	12552	19581	19105	58433	56951
2007	15506	15124	20570	20167	64137	62801
2008	17234	16788	21892	21443	67296	65834
2009	19025	18574	24879	24400	72366	70908

注：2000年以前不含科研机构研究生。

Note:Graduate students educated in scientific research institutions are not included in the data before 2000.

17-5 普通高等学校分学校研究生（2009年）

Post-graduates in Regular Institutions of Higher Education（2009）

单位：人 （person）

校　名	毕业生 Graduates	招　生 New Enrollment	在校学生 Total Enrollment	博　士 Doctor	硕　士 Master	毕业班学生数 Number of Students in Graduate-class
西安交通大学	3776	4195	12848	3933	8915	4875
陕西师范大学	1565	2389	6470	708	5762	1993
西北工业大学	2379	2714	9128	2951	6177	3956
西安理工大学	1259	1595	4519	429	4090	1414
西安电子科技大学	2374	3181	9219	1614	7605	3326
西安工业大学	250	709	1741		1741	590
西安建筑科技大学	1275	1690	5109	789	4320	1927
西安科技大学	569	735	2126	169	1957	709
西安石油大学	250	410	1038		1038	295
长安大学	1432	1864	5484	830	4654	1990
西安工程大学	253	500	1179	11	1168	306
西北政法大学	631	817	2302		2302	678
西安体育学院	113	202	459		459	117
西北大学	1616	2041	5707	677	5030	1859
西安外国语大学	258	403	1043		1043	297
西安音乐学院	66	79	213		213	65
西安美术学院	89	106	306	44	262	107
西安邮电学院	40	169	336		336	63
陕西科技大学	379	508	1496	80	1416	462
西安财经学院		93	185		185	35

17-6 全市普通高等学校分学校情况（2009年）

Basic Facts on Regular Higher Education by Unit（2009）

单位：人 （person）

校 名 Name of Schools	在校学生数 合计 Total Enrollment Total	本科 Regular College	专科 Junior College	教职工 合计 Staff and Teachers Total	#专任教师 Full-time Teachers
合 计	**632200**	**389928**	**242272**	**70818**	**40605**
一、国家部委直属院校	**91134**	**90212**	**922**	**18083**	**9237**
西安交通大学	16337			5458	2391
西北工业大学	14183			3355	1891
西安电子科技大学	20946			3142	1824
长安大学	22780			3525	1695
陕西师范大学	16888		922	2603	1436
二、陕西省属院校	**437827**	**227251**	**210576**	**44815**	**26568**
西北大学	19326	12721	6605	2418	1316
西安理工大学	18040	15598	2442	2396	1293
西安工业大学	8210	8210		2411	1462
西安建筑科技大学	14692	13826	866	1381	944
西安科技大学	18173	16820	1353	1821	1041
西安石油大学	17079	15420	1659	1563	1016
陕西科技大学	17455	16002	1453	1961	1166
西安工程大学	19505	17527	1978	1693	1105
西安外国语大学	18369	14587	3782	1501	965
西北政法大学	12905	11827	1078	1319	841
西安体育学院	7342	7292	50	830	565
西安音乐学院	3034	3034		483	278
西安美术学院	5976	5387	589	897	683
西安培华学院	20279	9888	10391	1566	883
西安财经学院	18926	14712	4214	1474	1060
西安邮电学院	15098	14338	760	1237	983
西安医学院	12035	5392	6643	1943	1085
西安欧亚学院	18668	5301	13367	1397	805
西安外事学院	18729	5749	12980	1707	1082
西安翻译学院	18500	6031	12469	2314	1152
西京学院	20640	6631	14009	1787	1083
西安航空技术高等专科学校	11103		11103	746	471
西安电力高等专科学校	4773		4773	1152	279
陕西电子信息职业技术学院	2234		2234	287	186
陕西国防工业职业技术学院	9187		9187	579	506
西安航空职业技术学院	8156		8156	615	476
陕西省交通职业技术学院	6980		6980	382	240
陕西职业技术学院	8755		8755	627	425
西安思源职业学院	13826	976	12850	1356	693
西安高新科技职业学院	5679		5679	466	249
西安三资职业学院	4561		4561	389	163
西安科技商贸职业学院	6617		6617	606	352
西安海棠职业学院	6211		6211	672	242
西安汽车科技职业学院	6518		6518	748	369

注:军校只包括地方招生计划招收的部分。其他院校属成人学校，只统计按普通高校招生计划招收的部分。

Note: Military school includes only that recruited under local recruiting plan. Other schools mean adult schools, only that recruited under ordinary colleges and universities` recruiting plan are taken into account.

17-6 续表 continued

单位：人 (person)

校 名 Name of Schools	在校学生数 Total Enrollment 合计 Total	本科 Regular College	专科 Junior College	教职工 Staff and Teachers 合计 Total	#专任教师 Full-time Teachers
西安东方亚太职业技术学院	138		138	116	85
陕西警官职业学院	4468		4468	339	201
陕西经济管理职业技术学院	3626		3626	425	163
陕西青年职业学院	5502		5502	277	184
陕西电子科技职业学院	3885		3885	613	278
陕西旅游烹饪职业学院	937		937	130	88
西安医科高等专科学校	1708		1708	191	110
三、西安市直属院校	**20144**	**8523**	**11621**	**2306**	**1304**
西安文理学院	9603	8523	1080	1115	718
西安铁路职业技术学院	6125		6125	669	306
西安职业技术学院	4416		4416	522	280
西安师范学院大专班					
四、其他院校	**65514**	**63942**	**1572**	**5614**	**3496**
武警工程学院	11	11			
空军工程大学					
西安通信学院					
第四军医大学	350	350			
第二炮兵工程学院					
西安陆军学院					
西安交通大学城市学院	7321	7321		468	296
西北大学现代学院	5937	5937		451	320
西安建筑科技大学华清学院	10545	10545		929	600
西安财经学院行知学院	5055	5055		465	260
西安工业学院北方信息工程学院	7691	7691		657	480
延安大学西安创新学院	6562	6562		701	397
西安电子科技大学长安学院	4084	4084		328	228
西北工业大学明德学院	7240	7240		546	315
长安大学兴华学院	1965	1965		115	80
西安理工大学高科学院	2665	2665		293	164
西安科技大学高新学院	6088	4516	1572	661	356
五、成人高校举办的普专班	**17581**		**17581**		
陕西航天职工大学	1416		1416		
西安航空职工大学	2417		2417		
西安飞机工业公司职工学院	1354		1354		
陕西兵器工业职工大学					
西安铁路工程职工大学	1814		1814		
西安电力机械制造公司机电学院	1192		1192		
陕西省建筑工程总公司职工大学	1797		1797		
西安市职工大学	197		197		
西安外贸职工大学	597		597		
陕西工运学院	964		964		
陕西教育学院	5833		5833		
陕西省广播电视大学					
西安市广播电视大学					

17-7 主要年份博士后、博士、硕士流动站情况

Mobile research centers for post-doctors, doctors and masters in Representative Years

指　标 Item	2005	2006	2007	2008	2009
博士后流动站（个）	66	62	87	88	94
Mobile Postdoctoral Centers(unit)					
博士点（个）	355	436	494	505	516
Ph.D Programs(unit)					
硕士点（个）	832	1097	1201	1208	1243
Master Programs(unit)					
本科专业（个）	981	1077	1215	1176	1197
Undergraduate Specialties(unit)					
重点学科（个）	409	401	459	419	491
Important Fields of Study(unit)					
院士（人事关系在学校）（人）	22	25	25	22	20
Academicians (organizational affiliation with educational institutions)(person)					

17-8 主要年份普通中等专业学校基本情况

Basic Statistics on Specialized Secondary Schools In Representative Years

年 份 Year	学校数(所) Number of Schools (unit)	毕业生数(万人) Number of Graduates (10 000 persons)	招生数(万人) New Enrollment (10 000 persons)	在校学生数(万人) Total Enrollment (10 000 persons)	教职工数(人) Number of Staff and Teachers (person)	专任教师 Full-time Teachers
1978	19			0.87		1110
1980	33			1.50		1474
1985	37			1.70		2363
1990	44	0.56	0.68	2.09	7136	2891
1995	46	0.97	1.37	3.74	5903	2533
1996	47	1.15	1.61	4.18	5940	2573
1997	47	1.20	1.65	4.63	6124	2731
1998	47	1.26	1.62	5.08	6181	2840
1999	46	1.42	2.11	5.75	6385	2865
2000	47	1.63	1.90	6.02	6964	3172
2001	47	1.70	1.58	5.63	5252	2467
2002	46	1.60	1.69	5.57	5170	2508
2003	34	1.62	1.80	5.28	4562	2302
2004	35	1.40	2.09	5.71	4676	2388
2005	32	1.44	2.26	6.16	3924	2130
2006	31	1.84	2.61	7.30	3621	2014
2007	30	2.03	2.91	7.97	3548	2011
2008	29	2.58	2.55	8.06	3278	1814
2009	28	2.70	2.15	7.44	2965	1720

17-9 中等技术（中等专业）学校分学校基本情况（2009年）

Situation of every secondary technical and Specialized Secondary school（2009）

单位：人 （person）

校　名 Name of Schools	毕业生数 Number of graduates	招生数 New Enrollment	在校学生数 Total Enrollment	教职工数 Number of Staff and Teachers	专任教师 Full-time Teachers
总　计	**27022**	21518	74356	2965	1720
一、中央部门属学校	1187	1038	3714	394	187
1.西安军需工业学校	160	132	537	76	55
2.西安交大医学院附设卫生学校	281	595	1482	47	16
3.西安航天工业学校	746	311	1695	271	116
二、陕西省属学校	**19950**	15406	53048	2188	1316
4.西安体育学院附属竞技体校	53	57	150		
5.西安体育学院附属体校	41		102		
6.西安电力工业学校	236	119	726		
7.陕西省城市经济学校	566	148	825	90	55
8.陕西省城乡建设学校	341	293	946	64	41
9.陕西省对外贸易学校	621	194	838		
10.陕西省体育运动学校	135	183	489	76	45
11.陕西省电影电视学校	94	41	159	56	28
12.陕西省旅游学校	389	544	1646	83	53
13.陕西省电子信息学校	3450	1630	8287	217	125
14.西安环境信息工程学校	55	5	105	25	10
15.陕西省理工学校	3016	1521	5406	237	125
16.西安音乐学院附属中专	64	125	295	24	17
17.西安美术学院附属中专	158	185	508	36	30
18.陕西省石油化工学校	2276	784	4697	257	145
19.陕西省经贸学校	980	1038	3843	171	122
20.陕西银行学校	928	1065	3141	124	82
21.陕西省商贸学校	445	207	1166	94	60
22.陕西省建筑材料工业学校	2491	1605	5905	90	70
23.陕西医科学校	1021	2365	4939	248	144
24.陕西科技卫生学校	2191	2947	7517	163	82
25.陕西省艺术学校	399	350	1358	133	82
三、西安市属学校	**2957**	2578	9511	383	217
26.西安市体育运动学校	17	46	77	116	44
27.西安市艺术学校	180	228	693	101	70
28.西安市卫生学校	1268	980	4417	166	103
西安文理学院	248	252	707		
西安职业技术学院	699	568	2174		
西安铁路职业技术学院	545	504	1443		
四、其他机构	**2928**	2496	8083		
西安外国语大学高职部	829	581	1945		
陕西职业技术学院	98	69	122		
陕西交通职业技术学院	275		475		
西安医学院	696	1136	2812		
陕西工运学院	102	57	226		
西安航空职业技术学院	230		408		
陕西国防工业职业技术学院	380	240	960		
西安外事学院	214	238	461		
西安三资职业学院	19	65	231		
西安科技商贸职业学院	85	110	443		

17-10　主要年份普通中学基本情况

Baisc Statistics on Regular Secondary Schools in Representative Years

年 份 Year	学校数(所) Number of Schools (unit)	毕业生数(万人) Number of Graduates (10 000 person)	招生数(万人) New Enrollment (10 000 person)	在校学生数(万人) Total Enrollment (10 000 person)	教职工数(人) Number of Staff and Teachers(person)	专任教师 Full-time Teachers
1978	962			44.16		20660
1980	1002	12.33	14.03	44.08	29867	22530
1985	563	10.72	13.05	38.24	30063	22050
1990	518	9.11	10.49	30.03	30739	22386
1995	485	8.13	12.40	32.32	30423	21984
1996	462	8.67	13.03	35.25	30902	22478
1997	466	9.96	13.83	37.16	31682	23129
1998	467	10.64	15.00	39.79	32371	23884
1999	469	11.21	16.58	43.49	33387	25114
2000	466	12.01	17.88	48.31	34385	26230
2001	470	13.85	18.98	52.50	35442	27190
2002	467	15.76	19.68	55.36	36706	28335
2003	467	16.76	18.78	56.44	38252	29887
2004	461	18.01	18.85	56.54	39121	30600
2005	460	18.82	18.83	55.74	39456	31094
2006	457	18.04	18.61	56.11	39341	31203
2007	453	18.37	17.96	54.68	39171	31373
2008	442	17.99	17.16	52.83	39088	31425
2009	439	17.80	16.57	50.63	39002	31415

17-11　各区县普通中学基本情况（2009年）

Baisc Statistics on Regular Secondary Schools by Region （2009）

单位：所、人　　(unit,person)

区 县	Region	学校数 Number of Schools	毕业生数 Number of Graduates	高中 Senior	招生数 New Enrollment	高中 Senior	在 校 学生数 Total Enrollment	高中 Senior	教职工数 Number of Staff and Teachers	专任教师 Full-time Teachers
合　计	**Total**	**439**	**177981**	**62397**	**165694**	**64298**	**506317**	**183637**	**39002**	**31415**
新城区	Xincheng	25	12856	4860	12946	4642	37941	13179	2632	1996
碑林区	Beilin	38	15169	7025	16684	7239	49724	21602	3811	2739
莲湖区	Lianhu	21	11341	4115	12113	4307	36635	13139	2755	2130
灞桥区	Baqiao	31	8964	2888	8386	3102	25330	8713	2191	1718
未央区	Weiyang	35	10891	4289	11435	4333	33071	12673	3058	2255
雁塔区	Yanta	48	14887	5571	16568	6226	46895	17170	3767	2915
阎良区	Yanliang	12	6574	2555	5129	2342	15921	6540	1328	1075
临潼区	Lintong	38	16537	4607	14880	4994	46394	14318	3417	3010
长安区	Chang'an	54	23858	8059	18644	7820	59620	22248	4745	4080
蓝田县	Lantian	46	14461	4381	14640	4879	43770	13534	3215	2510
周至县	Zhouzhi	37	20189	5777	16080	6291	52925	17829	3551	2973
户　县	Huxian	39	16496	6648	13184	5874	42678	17160	3271	2925
高陵县	Gaoling	15	5758	1622	5005	2249	15413	5532	1261	1089

17-12 主要年份职业中学基本情况

Basic Statistics on Vocational Secondary Schools in Representative Years

年 份 Year	学校数(所) Number of Schools (unit)	毕业生数（人) Number of Graduates (person)	招生数（人) New Enrollment (person)	在校学生数（人） Total Enrollment (person)	教职工数（人） Number of Teachers and Staff (person)	专任教师 Full-time Teachers
1985	40	1661	8346	17621	1375	868
1990	58	5936	8095	20151	2674	1574
1995	71	8976	12490	32673	2394	1877
1996	67	9235	10563	25955	3098	1735
1997	73	8756	13390	29068	2993	1709
1998	89	7753	13949	31264	3152	1823
1999	91	8480	13062	31973	3217	1908
2000	95	9949	13903	32188	3311	1997
2001	85	10300	15591	34336	3517	2113
2002	78	8659	17231	39428	3461	2192
2003	87	10755	17310	44033	4036	2458
2004	83	12177	17865	46358	4101	2515
2005	91	15092	20603	51766	4750	2892
2006	96	14887	21158	53828	5193	3126
2007	86	14881	24434	56012	4899	3064
2008	84	15813	30201	62963	4878	3008
2009	84	14691	31042	72388	5129	3179

17-13 各区县职业中学基本情况（2009年）

Baisc Statistics on Vocational Secondary Schools by Region （2009）

区 县	Region	学校数 (所) Number of Schools (unit)	毕业生数（人） Number of Graduates (person)	招生数（人） New Enrollment (person)	在校学生数（人） Total Enrollment (person)	教职工数（人) Number of Teachers and Staff (person)	专任教师 Full-time Teachers
合 计	**Total**	**84**	**14691**	**31042**	**72388**	**5129**	**3179**
新城区	Xincheng	10	2053	4219	11913	800	509
碑林区	Beilin	8	2154	3440	7694	634	303
莲湖区	Lianhu	6	1482	2867	6708	509	296
灞桥区	Baqiao	10	909	2040	4698	581	289
未央区	Weiyang	7	969	2985	6713	357	233
雁塔区	Yanta	18	1657	3790	9192	651	370
阎良区	Yanliang	1	530	1277	2259	110	97
临潼区	Lintong	5	1672	2026	4950	271	192
长安区	Chang'an	7	1055	3313	7172	709	474
蓝田县	Lantian	1	737	700	2217	17	13
周至县	Zhouzhi	5	833	1568	3200	174	140
户 县	Huxian	5	405	1920	3484	251	212
高陵县	Gaoling	1	235	897	2188	65	51

17-14 主要年份小学基本情况

Basic Statistics on Primary Schools in Representative Years

年 份 Year	学校数(所) Number of Schools (unit)	毕业生数（万人） Number of Graduates (10 000 person)	招生数（万人） New Enrollment (10 000 person)	在校学生数（万人） Total Enrollment (10 000 person)	教职工数（人） Number of Teachers and Staff (person)	专任教师 Full-time Teachers
1978	2667			74.03	29744	26428
1980	2337	11.91	12.57	73.36	31770	28360
1985	2337	11.21	9.57	62.16	31075	26430
1990	2343	8.67	10.85	61.87	37788	29090
1995	2360	9.93	14.09	79.36	35568	30270
1996	2362	10.48	13.63	81.81	35821	30267
1997	2368	10.98	12.48	82.67	35767	30117
1998	2361	12.18	11.88	82.03	35576	30089
1999	2354	13.65	11.61	79.81	35639	30196
2000	2323	13.83	11.51	77.81	35336	30215
2001	2277	14.20	11.07	74.51	34257	29281
2002	2137	13.89	10.13	70.78	34143	29428
2003	2084	12.97	9.28	66.78	34080	29531
2004	2016	12.37	9.12	63.75	33794	29367
2005	1980	11.92	8.47	60.47	33907	29674
2006	1929	11.53	9.16	59.33	34460	30018
2007	1872	11.38	8.67	56.83	34901	30533
2008	1781	10.58	8.33	54.66	34653	30382
2009	1666	9.96	7.84	52.52	34389	30334

17-15 各区县小学基本情况（2009年）

Basic Statistics on Primary Schools by Region （2009）

单位：所、人 (unit、person)

区 县	Region	学校数 Number of Schools	毕业生数 Number of Graduates	招生数 New Enrollment	在校学生数 Total Enrollment	教职工数 Number of Teachers and Staff	专任教师 Full-time Teachers
合 计	**Total**	**1666**	**99646**	**78411**	**525197**	**34389**	**30334**
新城区	Xincheng	37	7142	5757	40955	2073	1773
碑林区	Beilin	46	6829	5631	38526	2158	1764
莲湖区	Lianhu	48	7542	6595	44349	2522	2149
灞桥区	Baqiao	81	5536	5121	31669	2195	1813
未央区	Weiyang	73	7796	8420	51096	2931	2537
雁塔区	Yanta	66	10614	10498	65731	3419	2926
阎良区	Yanliang	44	2731	2100	14285	1169	1047
临潼区	Lintong	237	10421	6698	46475	3684	3335
长安区	Chang'an	243	11585	8375	53324	4242	3664
蓝田县	Lantian	333	9969	5425	46758	3137	2988
周至县	Zhouzhi	207	9306	6357	41521	2876	2600
户 县	Huxian	164	7353	5354	36409	2518	2413
高陵县	Gaoling	87	2822	2080	14099	1465	1325

17-16 主要年份幼儿园基本情况

Basic Statistics on Kindergartens in Representative Years

年 份 Year	园 数(所) Number of Kindergartens (unit)	班 数(个) Number of Class (unit)	在园幼儿数(万人) Student Enrollment (10000 person)	教职工数(人) Number of Staff and Teachers (person)	专任教师 Full-time Teachers
1978	363		4	3568	1315
1980	186		10	5525	2657
1985	310	3135	10	6887	2770
1990	256	3816	14	6123	2058
1995	257	4464	16	6173	2659
1996	244	4313	15	5918	2661
1997	228	4243	15	6065	2748
1998	235	4195	13	6272	2910
1999	234	4222	13	6329	2982
2000	367	4142	13	6346	2995
2001	366	4306	12	6224	3069
2002	378	4186	12	6541	3397
2003	610	4470	12	8959	4853
2004	660	4507	12	9870	5577
2005	737	4712	13	10528	5959
2006	863	5037	13	12335	7106
2007	830	5081	14	13468	7951
2008	905	5506	15	14932	8704
2009	896	5710	16	15928	9240

注:幼儿园中包括学前班。

Note:"Kindergartens" here including units providing pre-school education.

17-17 主要年份特殊教育学校基本情况

Basic Statistics on Special Education Schools in Representative Years

单位：所、人 (unit、person)

年 份 Year	学校数 Number of Schools	毕业生数 Number of Graduates	招生数 New Enrollment	在校学生数 Total Enrollment	教职工数 Number of Teachers and Staff	专任教师 Full-time Teachers
1978						
1980	1	48	64	315	66	43
1985	2	14	36	318	94	59
1990	5	35	111	451	142	96
1995	5	27	147	1363	204	141
1996	5	60	164	1520	210	150
1997	5	153	164	1655	210	148
1998	5	266	140	2145	232	157
1999	5	349	115	1912	235	160
2000	5	269	145	1880	230	156
2001	5	237	209	1915	238	162
2002	5	216	148	1661	232	157
2003	5	156	161	1380	237	166
2004	5	137	142	1290	236	167
2005	5	184	182	1445	240	169
2006	6	171	143	1425	254	178
2007	6	169	114	1342	259	190
2008	6	83	96	1286	259	190
2009	7	311	202	1523	335	234

注:包括盲、聋、哑、弱智儿童教育在内。

Note:Including schools providing education for blind, deaf and dumb children and children with weak intelligence .

17-18 主要年份小学、初中升学率

Rate of Graduates from Junior Schools and Primary Schools Entering Higher Level Schools in Representative Years

年 份 Year	小 学 Primary Schools		
	小学毕结业生数（万人） Graduates of Primary Schools (10 000 person)	升学人数（万人） Number of Graduates from Primary Schools (10 000 persons)	升学率 (%) Percentage of Graduates from Primary Schools Entering Junior Secondary Schools (%)
1978			
1980	11.91	10.43	87.60
1985	11.21	9.56	85.30
1990	8.68	8.09	91.50
1995	10.02	9.50	94.85
1996	10.62	10.15	95.62
1997	11.04	10.56	95.65
1998	12.25	11.76	96.02
1999	13.77	13.23	96.04
2000	13.83	13.44	97.21
2001	14.22	13.83	97.25
2002	13.92	13.54	97.25
2003	12.97	12.61	97.26
2004	12.37	11.98	96.79
2005	11.92	11.84	99.31
2006	11.53	12.22	104.23
2007	11.38	11.69	102.70
2008	10.58	10.98	103.81
2009	9.96	10.14	101.76

17-18 续表 continued

年 份 Year	初 中 JunionSchools		
	初中毕结业生数(万人) Graduates from Junior Secondary Schools (10 000 persons)	升学人数（万人） Number of Graduates from Junior Secondary （10 000persons）	升学率 (%) Percentage of Graduates from Junior Secondary Schools Entering Senior Secondary Schools (%)
1978			
1980			60.71
1985	8.36	4.63	55.30
1990	6.86	2.39	52.70
1995	6.35	4.60	72.35
1996	6.66	5.39	81.00
1997	7.98	6.14	76.93
1998	8.53	6.56	76.90
1999	9.19	7.08	77.00
2000	9.35	7.53	80.50
2001	10.88	8.77	80.56
2002	12.31	10.19	82.80
2003	12.66	10.16	80.26
2004	12.90	10.53	81.60
2005	12.93	10.52	81.39
2006	12.17	10.52	86.06
2007	12.04	10.68	88.70
2008	11.88	10.69	90.03
2009	11.67	10.52	90.09

注：小学升学率的分子项含外地转学生，故升学率大于100，本数据为市教育局部门统计数据。

Note:As the molecular item of percentage of graduates from primary schools entering junior secondery schools includes outland transfer students, the percentage is bigger than 100.The number comes from the City Board of Education.

17-19 主要年份小学学龄儿童入学率

Percentage of School-Age Children Enrolled in Representative Years

年 份 Year	学龄儿童总数 (万人) Total School-Age Children (10 000 persons)	农 村 Rural Areas	入学儿童总数 (万人) Total School-Age Children (10 000 persons)	农 村 Rural Areas	入学率 (%) Enrollment Rate (%)	农 村 Rural Areas
1978						
1980					98.42	
1985	63.02	32.57	62.16	31.95	98.62	98.10
1990	62.42	34.35	61.87	33.88	99.11	98.66
1995	77.86	29.12	77.62	28.98	99.69	99.49
1996	81.40	27.69	81.19	27.58	99.75	99.61
1997	82.45	24.30	82.24	24.21	99.74	99.65
1998	81.69	22.52	81.54	22.44	99.82	99.66
1999	79.66	21.67	79.55	21.61	99.86	99.75
2000	77.68	20.44	77.56	20.37	99.85	99.68
2001	69.69	41.31	69.58	41.22	99.84	99.77
2002	65.76	36.59	65.66	36.50	99.85	99.75
2003	62.44	33.78	62.37	33.72	99.88	99.81
2004	59.95	35.49	59.87	35.43	99.87	99.83
2005	57.00	31.53	56.95	31.49	99.90	99.85
2006	56.05	31.50	56.01	31.46	99.92	99.88
2007	53.71	28.97	53.68	28.95	99.94	99.90
2008	52.00	27.03	51.97	27.01	99.95	99.91
2009	50.26	25.19	50.24	25.17	99.96	99.92

17-20 主要年份平均每万人口在校学生数和大中小学生构成

Student Enrollment Per 10000 Populations and Composition of Students Enrolled in Representative Years

年 份 Year	占全市人口(%) Percentage of Population of Whole City (%)	平均每万人口中 Students Per 10 000 Population		
		大学生（人） University and College Students(person)	中学生（人） Secondary School Students(person)	小学生（人） Primary School Students(person)
1978	25.37	58	886	1486
1980	25.92	84	906	1434
1985	22.24	117	692	1124
1990	19.84	123	493	1016
1995	22.86	168	639	1224
1996	23.37	177	672	1249
1997	23.54	180	701	1249
1998	23.62	189	740	1228
1999	24.06	224	798	1183
2000	24.56	282	854	1131
2001	25.17	366	903	1072
2002	25.84	470	940	1007
2003	27.84	560	939	932
2004	27.83	618	980	879
2005	27.10	715	981	815
2006	27.46	760	1018	788
2007	27.57	817	1009	744
2008	27.88	863	1015	708
2009	28.16	901	1032	672

17-20 续表 continued

年 份 Year	大中小学生各占学生总数比重(%) Students of Different Level as Percentage of Total Students (%)		
	大学生 University and College Students	中学生 Secondary School Students	小学生 Primary School Students
1978	2.28	34.94	58.57
1980	3.14	33.21	55.27
1985	5.32	31.34	50.93
1990	6.71	25.10	51.71
1995	7.33	27.96	53.55
1996	7.57	28.78	53.46
1997	7.63	29.77	53.05
1998	8.01	31.34	52.01
1999	9.30	33.18	49.18
2000	11.48	34.77	46.04
2001	14.57	35.88	42.59
2002	18.17	36.40	38.99
2003	20.11	33.75	33.47
2004	22.22	35.23	31.59
2005	26.39	36.22	30.08
2006	27.68	37.09	28.69
2007	29.30	36.32	26.67
2008	30.77	36.09	25.17
2009	31.84	36.46	23.74

注：本表计算使用的全市人口数为户籍人口数。

Note:'Population of the whole city ' in this form is the household population.

17-21　成人教育情况（2009年）

Adult Education （2009）

分　类	Classify	学校数（所）Number of Schools (unit)	毕业生数（人）Graduates (person)	招生数（人）New Enrollment (person)
合　计	**Total**	**3211**	**675931**	**53023**
一、成人高等学校	**Adult Higher Education Institution**	**16**	**8190**	**8401**
1.广播电视大学	Radio and TV Universities	2	2201	3338
2.职工高等学校	Schools of Higher Education for Staff and Workers	11	3503	4641
3.管理干部学院	Colleges for Management Cadres	2	234	214
4.教育学院	Pedagogical Colleges	1	2252	208
二、普通高校成教学院	**Adult Education Units in Regular Institutions**		**36743**	**41908**
1.函授部	Correspondence Divisions	(20)	23164	29743
2.夜大学	Evening Schools	(18)	5566	12165
3.成人脱产班	Short-cycle Courses for Adults	(21)	8013	
三、成人中等学校	**Adult middle school**	**3195**	**630998**	**2714**
1.成人中等专业学校	Specialized Secondary Schools for Adults	11	2168	2714
（1）广播电视中专	Radio and TV Specialized Secondary School	(4)	1892	2220
（2）职工、干部、函授中专	Schools for Workers, Cadres and Correspondence Secondary	(7)	276	494
2.成人中学	Adult middle school			
3.成人技术培训学校	Adult technology training school	3184	628830	
#教师进校	Teacher Training Schools	13	16009	
四、成人初等学校	**Adult elementary school**			

注:1.本表是西安市行政辖区内各级各类成人学校的全口径数据；2.( )内数因与普通高校重复,不加入总计数。

a):First,The table Shows the Data of All the Adult Education Schools in Xi′an Administrative Region (Party Schools not included);

b): Number in brackets overlapped over that of Regular Schools for higher education, so it is not excluded from the total.

17-21 续表 continued

分 类	Classify	在校学生数（人）Total Enrollment (person)	教职工数（人）Teachers and Staff (person)	专任教师 Full-time Teachers
合 计	**Total**	**849843**	**20243**	**10097**
一、成人高等学校	**Adult Higher Education Institution**	**21970**	**3378**	**2063**
1.广播电视大学	Radio and TV Universities	7024	521	269
2.职工高等学校	Schools of Higher Education for Staff and Workers	13097	2010	1272
3.管理干部学院	Colleges for Management Cadres	419	175	137
4.教育学院	Pedagogical Colleges	1430	672	385
二、普通高校成教学院	**Adult Education Units in Regular Institutions**	**108898**		
1.函授部	Correspondence Divisions	79754		
2.夜大学	Evening Schools	22309		
3.成人脱产班	Short-cycle Courses for Adults	6835		
三、成人中等学校	**Adult middle school**	**718975**	**16865**	**8034**
1.成人中等专业学校	Specialized Secondary Schools for Adults	8622	1322	683
（1）广播电视中专	Radio and TV Specialized Secondary School	7327	1024	544
（2）职工、干部、函授中专	Schools for Workers, Cadres and Correspondence Secondary	1295	298	139
2.成人中学	Adult middle school			
3.成人技术培训学校	Adult technology training school	710353	15543	7351
#教师进校	Teacher Training Schools	20102	540	316
四、成人初等学校	**Adult elementary school**			

主要统计指标解释

普通高等学校 指按照国家规定的设置标准和审批程序批准举办，通过国家统一招生考试，招收高中毕业生为主要培养对象，实施高等教育的全日制大学、独立设置的学院和高等专科学校、短期职业大学。

成人高等学校 指按照国家有关规定审批，招收通过全国成人高教统一招生考试的具有高中毕业或同等学历的在职从业人员，利用脱产、半脱产、业余或函授等多种形式对其实施高等学历教育，培养高等教育专科或本科毕业水平的专门人才，修业年限、课程设置和总学时数均按高等学历教育要求付诸实施的学校。包括广播电视大学、职工高等学校、农民高等学校、管理干部学院、教育学院、独立设置的函授学院等。

小学学龄儿童入学率 指调查范围内已入小学学习的学龄儿童占校内外学龄儿童总数（包括弱智儿童，不包括盲聋哑儿童）的比重。计算公式为:

小学学龄儿童入学率=已入学的小学学龄儿童数/校内外小学学龄儿童总数*100%

科技活动 指在自然科学、农业科学、医药科学、工程与技术科学、人文与社会科学领域（简称科学技术领域）中，与科技知识的产生、发展、传播和应用密切相关的有组织的活动。可分为研究与试验发展（R&D）、研究与试验发展成果应用及相关的科技服务三类活动。

科技活动人员 指直接从事科技活动、以及专门从事科技活动管理和为科技活动提供直接服务的人员。累计从事科技活动的实际工作时间占全年制度工作时间10%及以上的人员。（1）直接从事科技活动的人员包括:在独立核算的科学研究与技术开发机构、高等学校、各类企业及其他事业单位内设的研究室、实验室、技术开发中心及中试车间（基地）等机构中从事科技活动的研究人员、工程技术人员、技术工人及其它人员;虽不在上述机构工作，但编入科技活动项目（课题）组的人员;科技信息与文献机构中的专业技术人员;从事论文设计的研究生等。（2）专门从事科技活动管理和为科技活动提供直接服务的人员包括:独立核算的科学研究与技术开发机构、科技信息与文献机构、高等学校、各类企业及其他事业单位主管科技工作的负责人，专门从事科技活动的计划、行政、人事、财务、物资供应、设备维护、图书资料管理等工作的各类人员，但不包括保卫、医疗保健人员、司机、食堂人员、茶炉工、水暖工、清洁工等为科技活动提供间接服务的人员。

科学家与工程师 指科技活动人员中具有高、中级技术职称（职务）的人员和不具有高、中级技术职称（职务）的大学本科及以上学历人员。

研究与试验发展（R&D） 指在科学技术领域，为增加知识总量、以及运用这些知识去创造新的应用而进行的系统的创造性的活动，包括基础研究、应用研究、试验发展三类活动。

基础研究 指为了获得关于现象和可观察事实的基本原理的新知识（揭示客观事物的本质、运动规律，获得新发现、新学说）而进行的实验性或理论性研究，它不以任何专门或特定的应用或使用为目的。其成果以科学论文和科学著作为主要形式。

应用研究 指为获得新知识而进行的创造性研究，主要针对某一特定的目的或目标。应用研究是为了确定基础研究成果可能的用途，或是为达到预定的目标探索应采取的新方法（原理性）或新途径。其成果形式以科学论文、专著、原理性模型或发明专利为主。

试验发展 指利用从基础研究、应用研究和实际经验所获得的现有知识，为产生新的产品、材料和装置，建立新的工艺、系统和服务，以及对已产生和建立的上述各项作实质性的改进而进行的系统性工作。其成果形式主要是专利、专有技术、具有新产品基本特征的产品原型或具有新装置基本特征的原始样机等。在社会科学领域，试验发展是指把通过基础研究、应用研究获得的知识转变成可以实施的计划（包括为进行检验和评估实施示范项目）的过程。人文科学领域没有对应的试验发展活动。

研究与试验发展人员 指参与研究与试验发展项目研究、管理和辅助工作的人员，包括项目（课题）组人员，企业科技行政管理人员和直接为项目（课题）活动提供服务的辅助人员。

研究与试验发展人员全时当量 指全时人员数加非全时人员按工作量折算为全时人员数的总和。例如:有两个全时人员和三个非全时人员（工作时间分别为20%、30%和70%），则全时当量为2+0.2+0.3+0.7=3.2人年。

专业技术人员 指从事专业技术工作和专业技术管理工作的人员，即企事业单位中已经聘任专业技术职务从事专业技术工作和专业技术管理工作的人员，以及未聘任专业技术职务，现在专业技术岗位上工作的人员。包括工程技术人员、农业技术人员、科学研究人员、卫生技术人员、教学人员、经济人员、会计人员、统计人员、翻译人员、图书资料、档案、文博人员、新闻出版人员、律师、公证人员、广播电视播音人员、工艺美术人员、体育人员、艺术人员及企业政治思想工作人员，共十七个专业技术职务类别。

科技活动经费筹集 指从各种渠道筹集到的计划用于科技活动的经费，包括政府资金、企业资金、事业单位资金、金融机构贷款、国外资金和其他资金等。

政府资金 指从各级政府部门获得的计划用于科技活动的经费，包括科学事业费、科技三项费、科研基建费、科学基金、教育等部门事业费中计划用于科技活动的经费以及政府部门预算外资金中计划用于科技活动的经费等。

企业资金 指从自有资金中提取或接受其他企业委托的、科研院所和高校等事业单位接受企业委托获得的，计划用于科研和技术开发的经费。不包括来自政府、金融机构及国外的计划用于科技活动的资金。

金融机构贷款 指从各类金融机构获得的用于科技活动的贷款。

科技活动经费内部支出 指报告年内用于科技活动的实际支出包括劳务费、科研业务费、科研管理费，非基建投资购建的固定资产、科研基建支出以及其他用于科技活动的支出。不包括生产性活动支出、归还贷款支出及转拨外单位支出。

劳务费 指以货币或实物形式直接或间接支付给从事科技活动人员的劳动报酬及各种费用。包括各种形式的工资、津贴、奖金、奖金、福利、离退休人员费用、人民助学金等。

固定资产购建费 指报告年内使用非基建投资购建的固定资产和用于科研基建投资的实际支出额，即固定资产实际支出和科研基建投资实际完成额之和。固定资产是指长期使用而不改变原有实物形态的主要物资设备、图书资料、实验材料和标本以及其他设备和家具、房屋、建筑物。

新产品 指采用新技术原理、新设计构思研制、生产的全新产品，或在结构、材质、工艺等某一方面比原有产品有明显改进，从而显著提高了产品性能或扩大了使用功能的产品。既包括政府有关部门认定并在有效期内的新产品，也包括企业自行研制开发，未经政府有关部门认定，从投产之日起一年之内的新产品。

专利 是专利权的简称，是对发明人的发明创造经审查合格后，由专利局依据专利法授予发明人和设计人对该项发明创造享有的专有权。包括发明、实用新型和外观设计。

发明 指对产品、方法或者其改进所提出的新的技术方案。

实用新型 指对产品的形状、构造或者其结合所提出的适于实用的新的技术方案。

外观设计 指对产品的形状、图案、色彩或者其结合所作出的富有美感并适于工业上应用的新设计。

Explanatory Notes on Main Statistical Indicators

Regular Institutions of Higher Learning refer to educational establishments set up according to the government evaluation and approval procedures, enrolling graduates from senior secondary schools and providing higher education courses and training for senior professionals. They include full-time universities, colleges, high professional schools and short-term professional universities.

Institutions of Higher Learning for Adults refer to educational establishments, set up in line with relevant rules approved by the government, enrolling staff and workers with senior secondary school or equivalent education ,and providing higher education courses in many forms of full time, part time, spare time, or correspondence for adults. Professionals thus trained receive a qualification equivalent to graduates studying regular courses at regular universities, colleges and professional colleges. Institutions of higher learning for adults include Radio and TV universities, schools of high education for staff and workers and peasants, colleges for management cadres, pedagogical colleges, independent correspondence colleges.

Enrollment Rate of Primary School Age Children refers to the proportion of school age children enrolled at schools to the total number of school age children both in and outside schools (including retarded children ,but excluding blind, deaf and mute children). The formula is:

Enrollment Rate of Primary School-age Children = (Total Primary School-age Children at Schools) (Total Primary School age Children Both at and Outside Schools) 100%

Scientific and Technological Activities (S&T Activities) refer to organized activities which are closely related with the creation, development, dissemination and application of the scientific and technical knowledge in the fields of natural sciences, agricultural science, medical science, engineering and technological science, humanities and social sciences (referred to as scientific and technological fields). S&T activities can be classified in to 3 categories: research and development (R&D) activities, application of R&D results, and related S&T services.

Personnel Engaged in S&T Activities refer to personnel directly engaged in S&T activities, in the management of S&T activities, and in providing direct service to S&T activities, who spend over 10% of the total working hours in a year in S&T activities. (1) Personnel directly engaged in S&T activities include researchers, engineers, technicians and other related personnel engaged in S&T activities in independent-accounting R&D institutions, institutions of higher learning, and in research institutes, laboratories, technology development centers and central experiment workshops under enterprises and institutions. Also included are people working in S&T research project teams, professional and technical personnel working in S&T information archiving institutes, and graduate students working on the design of their thesis. (2) Personnel engaged in the management of S&T activities and in providing direct service to S&T activities include senior management people responsible for S&T activities in independent-accounting R&D institutions, S&T information archiving institutes, institutions of higher learning, and in enterprises and institutions where S&T activities are undertaken. Also included are people responsible for the planning, administration, personnel management, financial management, logistics supply, equipment maintenance, information and library management that are related with S&T activities. People providing indirect services are excluded, such as security, medical service, drivers, plumbers, cleaners and those providing catering and related service.

Scientists and Engineers refer to persons engaged in S&T activities who have obtained titles of senior and middle level professional positions, and those without such position but have completed university or higher education.

Research and Development (R&D) refers to systematic and creative activities in the field of science and technology aiming at increasing the knowledge and using the knowledge for new application. R&D includes 3 categories of activities: basic research, applied research and experiments and development.

Basic Research refers to empirical or theoretical research aiming at obtaining new knowledge on the fundamental principles of phenomena of observable facts reveal the nature and law of movement of objects and to acquire new discoveries or new theories. basic research takes no specific or designated application as the aim of the research. Results of basic research are mainly released or disseminated in the form of scientific papers or monographs.

Applied research refers to creative research aimingat obtaining new knowledge on a specific objective or target. Purpose of the applied research is to identify the possible use of results from basic research, or to explore new (fundamental) methods or new approaches. Results of applied research are expressed in the form of scientific papers, monographs, fundamental models or invention patents.

Experiments and Development refer to systematic activities aiming at using the knowledge from basic and applied researches or from practical experience to develop new products, materials and equipment, to establish new production process, systems and services, or to make substantial improvement on the existing products, process or services. Results of experiment and development activities are embodied in patents, exclusive technology, monotype of new products or equipment. In social sciences, experiment and development activities refer to the process of converting the knowledge from basic or applied researches into feasible programmes (including conduct of demonstration projects for assessment and evaluation). There is no experiment and development activities in the science of humanities.

R&D Personnel refer to persons engaged in research, management and supporting activities of R&D, including persons in the project teams, persons engaged in the management of S&T activities of enterprises and supporting staff providing direct service to the research projects.

Full-time Equivalent of R&D Personnel refers to the sum of the full-time persons and the full-time equivalent of part-time persons converted by workload. For instance, if there are 2 full-time persons and 3 part-time workers (20%, 30% and 70% of working hours respectively on R&D activities), the full-time equivalent is 2+0.2+0.3+0.7=3.2person-years.

Professional and Technical Personnel refer to person engaged in professional and technical work or in the management of professional and technical activities, i.e., people with professional or technical positions who are engaged in professional and technical work or in the management of professional and technical activities, and people without professional or technical positions but are working on professional or technical posts. They include professionals and technicians working in 17 categories of technical occupations including engineering, agriculture, scientific researches, medical service, teaching, economic research and application, accounting, statistics, translation, libraries, archives, cultural and museum service, journalism and publication, lawyers, notarization service, radio and television broadcasting, handicraft and fine arts, sports, performing art, and political workers in enterprises.

Funding for S&T Activities refers to funds obtained from various sources for S&T activities, including government funds, self-raised funds by enterprises, self-raised funds by institutions, loans from financial institutions, foreign funds and other funds.

Government Funds refer to funds obtained from government agencies at all levels to be used for S&T activities, including fund for scientific undertakings, 3 kinds of fund for S&T activities, fund for capital construction for scientific researches, science fund, funds from education expenditures by education departments for S&T activities, and extra-budget fund from government agencies for S&T activities.

Self-raised Funds by Enterprises refers to self-raised funds by enterprises from their own expenditure or from other enterprises and funds received by universities or research institutions from enterprises for scientific research or technical development projects. Excluded in this category are funds from government agencies, financial institutions or from foreign institutions.

Loans from Financial Institutions refer to loans from various financial institutions for S&T activities.

Internal Expenditures on S&T activities refer to the actual expenditures on S&T activities during the reference year, including service fees, expenditure on research activities, expenditure on research management, purchase or construction of fixed assets not included in the activities, expenditure on research management, purchase or construction of fixed assets not included in the investment for capital construction, expenditure on capital construction for scientific researches, and other expenditures on S&T activities. Not included are expenditure on production activities, repayment of loans and transfer expenditure.

Service Fees refer to direct or indirect payment, in cash or in kind, made to personnel engaged in S&T activities as remuneration and other fees. They include, in various forms, salaries, subsidies, bonus, benefits, retirement pension, stipend, etc.

Purchase or Construction of Fixed Assets refers to the fixed assets purchased or constructed using funds other than the investment in capital construction, and the actual expenditure on capital construction for scientific researches. In other words, it is the sum of the actual expenditure on fixed assets and the accomplished investment in capital construction for scientific researches. Fixed assets refer to main materials and equipment, literatures and documents in libraries, materials for experiments, specimen, instruments, furniture, buildingsand constructions that can be used for a long time without changing the form and shape of those articles or constructions.

New Products refer to new products produced with new technology and new design, or products that representnoticeable improvement in terms of structure,material, or production process so as to improve significantly the character or function of the older versions. They include new products certified by relevant government agencies within the period of certification, as well as new products designed and produced by enterprises within a year without certification by government agencies.

Patent is an abbreviation for the patent right and refers to the exclusive right of ownership by the inventors or designers for the creation or inventions, given from the patent offices after due process of assessment and approval in accordance with the Patent Law. Patents are granted for inventions, utility models and designs.

Inventions refer to the new technical proposals to the products or methods or their modifications.

Utility Models refer to the practical and new technical proposals on the shape and structure of the product or the combination of both.

Designs refer to the aesthetics and industrially applicable new designs for the shape, pattern and color of the product, or their combinations.

18 文化、体育、卫生、社会福利和其他

CULTURE,PUBLIC HEALTH,SOCIAL WELFAREINSTITUTIONS AND OTHER SOCIAL ACTIVITIES

资料整理：陈超毅　郝　静

Data management:Chen Chaoyi　Hao Jing

第十八部分　文化、体育、卫生、社会福利和其他

一、简要说明

本章资料主要包括文化、卫生、民政、劳动保障、体育、计划生育、共青团、妇联以及公、检、法等方面内容，由西安市统计局社会科技处根据西安市文化局、卫生局等有关部门提供资料整理。

二、主要指标

图书馆总藏量（千册件）	4324	比上年增加　767千册件
医院数（所）	261	比上年减少　15所
医院床位数（万张）	3.24	比上年增加　1789张

18 CULTURE,SPORTS,PUBLIC HEALTH,SOCIAL WELFARE INSTITUTIONS AND OTHER SOCIAL ACTIVITIES

Ⅰ.Brief Introduction

Data in this chapter consists of primarily data of culture, sanitation, civil administration, labor ensure, physical education, family planning, Communist Youth League, the Women's Federation, public security organs, procuratorial organs and people's court, compiled and provided by Social & Science and Technology Division of the Xi'an Bureau of Statistics ,according to data from Xi'an Municipal Government Department concerned.

Ⅱ.Major Indicators

		Increase over Preceding Year
Number of Collections in Libraries (1 000 volumes)	4324	767
Number of Hospitals(unit)	261	-15
Number of Beds(10 000 units)	3.24	1789 units

18-1 文化事业机构和人数（2009年）

Number of Institutions and Personnel in Culture and Art（2009）

项　　目	Item	机构数(个) Number of Institutions (unit)	人员数（人） Number of Personnel (person)
一、电影事业	**Career of Film**		
制片厂	Studio	1	
发行放映管理机构	Number of Film Projection and Publication Administrating Institutions	2	
电影放映单位	Unit of Film shows	588	
#电影院	Cinema	26	
影剧院	Theaters	13	
放映队	Film Projection Team	393	
二、艺术事业	**Art**		
表演团体	Performance Troupes	18	2279
表演场所	Artcenters	18	246
三、图书馆事业	**Libraries**	**15**	**481**
四、群众文化事业	**Mass Culture**	**197**	**938**
#文化馆	Cultural Centers	15	360
文化站	Culture Stations	182	578
五、教育事业	**Educations**	**2**	**266**

18-2 文化事业发展情况

Basic Statistics on Culture Development

指　　标	Item	2005	2006	2007	2008	2009
电影放映场数 (千场)	Number of Film shows (1 000 shows)	33	32	29	25	44
观众人数(千人次)	Number of Spectators (1 000 person-times)	3186	2568	1890	1295	1299
艺术表演团体演出场次(国内)(千场)	Number of Art Performance Troupes Performers (1 000 shows)	4	4	4	4	5
观众人数(千人次)	Number of Spectators (1 000 person-times)	6138	22765	4416	3972	5573
图书馆总藏量(千册件)	Number of Collections in Libraries (1000 volumes)	3671	3807	3893	4040	4324
书刊文献外借人次(千人次)	Books, Journals and Documents Borrowing (1 000 person-times)	384	416	432	478	435
书刊文献外借册次(千册)	Books, Journals and Documents Borrowing (1 000 Volume-time)	656	884	813	917	727

18-3 群众艺术馆、文化馆（站）活动情况

Basic Statistics on Activities of Mass Art Centers and Cultural Centers

指　　标	Item	2005	2006	2007	2008	2009
机构数(个)	Number of Insititutions (unit)	192	193	197	197	197
举办展览个数(个)	Number of Exhibitions (unit)	458	667	511	520	716
组织文艺活动次数(次)	Art Performances and Story-telling Sessions (time)	1439	2251	2884	2378	3158
举办训练班班次(个)	Number of Training Courses (unit)	1137	1327	1625	1109	1467
培训人次(千人次)	Number of Training Persons (1 000 person-times)	37	43	67	87	96
藏　书(千册)	Collections (1 000 volumes)	322	336	227	270	299
本年收入(千元)	Income of this year (1 000 yuan)	11257	12981	21111	22571	40891
本年支出(千元)	Expenditure of this year (1 000 yuan)	10924	12706	21007	22458	42826

18-4 文物保护业基本情况（2009年）

Basic Statistics on Cultural Relics Protection（2009）

指　标	Item	机构（个）Insititution (unit)	人员（人）Personnel (person)	文物藏品实际数量（件）Factual Number of Collections(piece)	一级品 Grade One	参观人员（千人次）Number of Visitors (1000 person-times)
总　计	**Total**	**55**	**3080**	**599393**	**4833**	**5272**
文物保护管理机构	Protection and Management Agencies	26	381	14360	34	379
其他文物机构	Other Agencies	7	219			
博物馆	Museums	19	2229	561155	4591	4893
文物商店	Cultural Relics Agencies					
文物科研机构	Scientific Research of Historical Relics Preservation	3	251	23878	208	

注：文物科研机构文物藏品数2009年统计口径发生变化，与往年不可比。

Note:As statistical caliber of scientific research of historical relics preservation and number of relics has changed since 2009,so they couldn't be compared with those of former years.

18-5 广播电台及节目制作情况

Basic Statistics of Broadcasting Stations and Program Production

指　标	Item	2004	2005	2006	2007	2008	2009
省、地广播电台(座)	Broadcasting Stations at the Province and Disstrict Level(set)	2	2	2	2	2	2
县级广播电视台(座)	Number of Wire Broadcasting Stations and TV Relaying Stations(set)	6	6	6	6	6	6
中短波、调频发射台及转播台(座)	Medium/Short Ware and FM Broadcast Transmission Stations and Relaying Stations(set)	280	280	290	40	46	51
节目(套)	Number of Programs(set)	14	14	15	17	17	18
平均每日播出时间(时)	Broadcasting Hours per Day(hour:minute)	233	244	248	297	311	337
广播人口覆盖率(%)	Listener Rating(%)	98.85	99.35	99.36	99.37	99.37	99.37
制作广播节目(时)	Productions of Broadcasting(hour)	74696	81840	84083	97013	103328	110455
#新闻节目	News Programs	10918	12189	11013	12274	9139	10586
专题节目	Special Subject Programs	18831	23196	31662	33182	17539	29764
文艺节目	Literature Programs	29161	29837	32698	32270	48014	46859
服务节目	Service Programs	14628	12056	8710	19287	28636	23246

18-6 电视台及节目制作情况

Basic Statistics of TV Stations and Production of TV Program

指　　标	Item	2004	2005	2006	2007	2008	2009
电视台(座)	Number of Television Stations（set）	2	2	2	2	2	2
发射台及转播台(座)	Number of Television Transmission Stations and Relaying Stations（set）	297	297	297	8	8	10
无线电视节目(套)	Program Productions of Non-cable television Stations（set）	5	6	5	5	5	7
有线电视节目(套)	Program Productions of cable television Stations（set）	10	9	10	16	17	15
平均每周播出时间(时)	Average Broadcasting Hours per Week（hour）	1733	2294	2289	2504	2704	2661
电视人口覆盖率(%)	Viewer Rating（%）	97.07	97.67	97.85	98.33	98.35	98.41
卫星电视地面站(座)	Earth Stations of Satellite TV（set）	1338	1319	1251		32638	26167
制作电视节目 (时)	Productions of TV Programs(hour)	18643	27377	36337	25883	26897	27131
#新闻节目	News Programs	6386	9031	9918	6596	6726	6520
专题节目	Special Subject Programs	3830	7378	10593	9646	10819	9652
文艺节目	Literature Programs	3539	5136	10526	3880	4774	5805
服务节目	Service Programs	4641	3032	5300	5761	4578	5154
有线电视用户(万户)	Users of Cable television Stations（10 000 households）	91.4	102.21	115.16	125.28	138.79	146.84

注：1.2007年中短波、调频发射台及转播台功率50瓦以下不计算在内，故数据与往年不可比。
2.卫星电视地面站（座）2007年无数据。

Notes:1.2007 years,MW and SW,FM transmitters and relay stations,power of 50 watts is not taken into account,so the data are not comparable with previous years.
2. Satellite TV stations (Block) 2007 no data.

18-7 体育事业基本情况（市属）（2009年）

The Basic Situations of Sports (Under Municipality)（2009）

单位：人、枚 (person、unit)

指　　标	Item	2009
一、体育系统职工人数	**Number of Staffs and Workers in Physical Education System**	**661**
#运动员	Athletes	290
教练员	Coaches	98
二、等级裁判员发展人数	**Number of the Development of Grade Referees**	**59**
三、等级运动员发展人数	**Number of the Development of Grade Athletes**	**88**
四、全年获得奖牌数	**Number of Full-year Medals**	**309**
#国家级金牌	National Gold	26
国家级银牌	National Silver	21
省级金牌	Provincial Gold	76
省级银牌	Provincial Silver	68

18-8 少年儿童分项业余体校情况（市属）（2009年）

Basic Statistics of Youth Part-time Physical Training School（2009）

单位：人 (person)

指　　标	Items	2009
一、在读学生数	**Total Enrollment**	
总　计	**Total**	**2727**
田　径	Track and Field	1100
游　泳	Swimming	120
体　操	Gymnastics	40
举　重	Weightlifting	98
国际式摔跤	Wrestling	20
柔　道	Judo	21
射　击	Shooting	128
射　箭	Archery	60
足　球	Football	180
蓝　球	Basketball	260
排　球	Volleyball	40
兵乓球	Table Tennis	230
拳　击	Box	40
武　术	Wu Shu	260
跆拳道	Kickboxing	60
跳　水	Diving	20
棒　球	Baseball	50
二、职工数	**Number of Staff and Workers**	**230**

18-9 卫生机构、床位及人员数（2009年）

卫生机构	Health Care Institutions	机构数(个) Number of Institutions (unit)	床位数(张) Number of Beds (unit)
总　计	**Total**	**2162**	**36849**
一、医院	**Hospitals**	**261**	**32371**
综合医院	General Hospitals	200	26404
中医医院	Hospitals Specialized in Traditional Chinese Medicine	35	2324
中西医结合医院	Hospitals Integrating Traditional Chinese Medicine with Western Therapeutics in Practice	1	
民族医院	Nationalities Hospitals		
专科医院	Specialized Hospitals	25	3643
口腔医院	Dental Hospitals	3	76
眼科医院	Eye Hospitals	3	151
耳鼻喉科医院	ENT Hospitals		
肿瘤医院	Cancer Hospitals	2	630
心血管病医院	Cardiovascular Hospitals		
胸科医院	Chest Hospitals		
血液病医院	Blood Disease Hospitals		
妇产（科）医院	Obstetrics and Gynecologist Hospitals	2	102
儿童医院	Children's Hospitals	1	674
精神病医院	Psychiatric Hospitals	4	850
传染病医院	Hospitals for Infectious Diseases	1	200
皮肤病医院	Skin Hospitals		
结核病医院	Tuberculosis Hospitals	1	490
麻风病医院	Leprosy Hospitals		
职业病医院	Occupational Diseases Hospitals		
骨科医院	Orthopedic Hospitals	1	80
康复医院	Rehabilitation Hospitals	3	28

Number of Health Care Institutions，Beds and Employed Persons in Health Care Institutions（2009）

人员合计(人) Total Number of Employed Persons (person)	卫生技术人员 Medical Technical Personnel	其他技术人员 Other Technical Personnel	管理人员 Administrative Personnel	工勤人员 Logistics Technical Workers
65003	**51641**	**1325**	**6067**	**5970**
48306	**37848**	**877**	**4808**	**4773**
40131	31655	704	3756	4016
3340	2569	138	356	277
48	43		4	1
4787	3581	35	692	479
330	249	3	51	27
193	155		31	7
802	619	10	101	72
116	101		10	5
1225	993	4	147	81
556	357	6	94	99
381	245	2	89	45
406	288	3	73	42
96	91		5	
108	52		11	45

18-9 续表

卫生机构	Health Care Institutions	机构数(个) Number of Institutions (unit)	床位数(张) Number of Beds (unit)
整形外科医院	Plastic Surgery Hospitals		
美容医院	Beauty Hospitals		
其他专科医院	Other Specialized Hospitals	4	362
护理院	Nursmg Centets		
二、疗养院	**Sanitary**	**3**	**375**
三、社区卫生服务中心	**Commuting health care service centre**	**91**	**344**
社区卫生服务中心	Community Health Care Center	46	335
社区卫生服务站	Community Health Care Station	45	9
四、卫生院	**Small hospital**	**154**	**2533**
街道卫生院	Urban Township Health Centers	16	369
乡镇卫生院	Rural Twnship Heatth Centers	138	2164
五、门诊部	**Policlinic**	**150**	**17**
六、急救中心（站）	**Emergency centre (station)**	**1**	
七、采供血机构	**Blood collect and supply institution**	**1**	
八、妇幼保健院（所、站）	**Health center for women and children (institute, station)**	**15**	**809**
九、专科疾病防治院（所、站）	**Special disease prevention and cure hospital (institute, station)**	**1**	**400**
十、疾病预防控制中心（防疫站）	**Disease prevention and control centre (epidemic prevention station)**	**17**	
十一、卫生监督所	**Hygiene supervision centre**	**14**	
十二、医学科学研究机构	**Medicine science research institution**	**4**	
十三、医学在职培训机构	**Medicine incumbency training institution**	**5**	
十四、健康教育所（站、中心）	**Health education centre**	**2**	
十五、其他卫生机构	**Other hygiene institution**	**1437**	
诊所	Clinic	1145	
卫生所、医务室	Clinic	292	
十八、社区卫生服务站	**Community hygiene service station**	**6**	

continued

人员合计(人) Total Number of Employed Persons (person)	卫生技术人员 Medical Technical Personnel	其他技术人员 Other Technical Personnel	管理人员 Administrative Personnel	工勤人员 Logistics Technical Workers
574	431	7	80	56
210	**150**	**2**	**29**	**29**
1741	**1467**	**46**	**106**	**122**
1414	1169	44	90	111
327	298	2	16	11
4104	**3409**	**91**	**299**	**305**
373	315	3	32	23
3731	3094	88	267	282
2065	**1795**	**33**	**156**	**81**
100	**34**	**10**	**26**	**30**
150	**90**	**11**	**38**	**11**
1857	**1491**	**40**	**162**	**164**
297	**199**	**6**	**22**	**70**
1057	**727**	**70**	**126**	**134**
706	**418**	**25**	**197**	**66**
180	**98**	**23**	**29**	**30**
217	**83**	**71**	**40**	**23**
60	**19**	**13**	**24**	**4**
3874	**3752**			**122**
2832	2751			81
1042	1001			41
79	**61**	**7**	**5**	**6**

18-10 各区县卫生机构、床位及人员数（2009年）

Number of Health Care Institutions， Beds and Employed Persons in Health Care Institutions By Region（2009）

区 县	Region	机构数(个) Number of Health Care Institutions (unit)	床位数合计(张) Number of Beds (unit)	人员合计(人) Total Number of Employed Persons （person）	卫生技术人员 Total Number of Employed Persons
全 市	**Total**	**2162**	**36849**	**65003**	**51641**
新城区	Xincheng	278	6123	12117	9461
碑林区	Beilin	298	5374	10263	7674
莲湖区	Lianhu	342	4610	8419	6745
灞桥区	Baqiao	179	1658	2350	1969
未央区	Weiyang	131	2235	3793	3153
雁塔区	Yanta	364	7397	12547	10002
阎良区	Yanliang	64	1221	1739	1377
临潼区	Lintong	71	1445	2245	1749
长安区	Chang'an	142	2335	3942	3395
蓝田县	Lantian	72	1112	1522	1231
周至县	Zhouzhi	83	668	1989	1593
户 县	Huxian	82	1849	2873	2320
高陵县	Gaoling	56	822	1204	972

18–11 卫生机构各类人员数

Number of Employed Persons in Health Care Institutions

单位：人　　(person)

指　　标	Item	2000	2005	2006	2007	2008	2009
人员总数	**Total**	**53111**	**52821**	**54912**	**55551**	**59934**	**65003**
卫生技术人员	Medical Technical Personnel	41836	42255	43862	43707	47433	51641
执业（助理）医师	Licensed（Assistant） Doctors	18750	17730	18007	17266	18066	19284
#执业医师	Chartered Doctors	16146	15533	15778	15142	15975	17286
注册护士	Registered Nurses	14344	14004	15538	15337	17186	20167
药师（士）	Junior Paramedics	3475	3084	2987	2707	2721	2814
技　师（士）	Technicians	2179	2252	2242	3046	3168	3350
#检验师	Laboratory Technicians	2179	2252	2242	2150	2204	2290
其　他	Other	3088	5185	5088	5351	6292	6026
其他技术人员	Other Technical Personnel	855	1425	1601	1399	1051	1325
管理人员	Administrative Personnel	5647	5199	5309	5532	6007	6067
工勤人员	Logistics Technical Workers	4773	3942	4140	4913	5443	5970

18-12 医院、卫生院诊疗人次及诊疗情况（2009年）

卫生机构	Health Care Institutions	诊疗人次数总计 总 计 Total	合计（人） Count(person)
总 计	**Total**	**29764940**	**29373668**
在总计中：	**Among the Total:**		
一、医院	**Hospitals**	**18777528**	**18557342**
综合医院	General Hospitals	15785014	15571334
中医医院	Hospitals Specialized in Traditional Chinese Medicine	1502158	1495867
中西医结合医院	Hospitals Integrating Traditional Chinese Medicine with Western Therapeutics in Practice	5000	5000
民族医院	Nationalities Hospitals		
专科医院	Specialized Hospitals	1485356	1485141
口腔医院	Dental Hospitals	180239	180239
眼科医院	Eye Hospitals	93882	93882
耳鼻喉科医院	ENT Hospitals		
肿瘤医院	Cancer Hospitals	20685	20685
心血管病医院	Cardiovascular Hospitals		
胸科医院	Chest Hospitals		
血液病医院	Blood Disease Hospitals		
妇产（科）医院	Obstetrics and Gynecologist Hospitals	56344	56344
儿童医院	Children□s Hospitals	747689	747674
精神病医院	Psychiatric Hospitals	73224	73024
传染病医院	Hospitals for Infectious Diseases	22641	22641
皮肤病医院	Skin Hospitals		
结核病医院	Tuberculosis Hospitals	55823	55823
麻风病医院	Leprosy Hospitals		
职业病医院	Occupational Diseases Hospitals		
骨科医院	Orthopedic Hospitals	25608	25608
康复医院	Rehabilitation Hospitals	21140	21140
整形外科医院	Plastic Surgery Hospitals		
美容医院	Beauty Hospitals		
其他专科医院	Other Specialty Hospitals	188081	188081
护理院	Nursing Centers		
二、卫生院	**Health Centers**	**1915487**	**1886194**
街道卫生院	Urban Health Centers	282170	264585
乡镇卫生院	Rural Health Centers	1633317	1621609
中心卫生院	Town Health Centers	805188	801205
乡村卫生院	Village Health Centers	828129	820404

Number of Visits and Inpatients in Medical Institutions（2009）

Total Number of Clinics			观察室 Observation Room	
其中:门、急诊人次数 Number of Outpatient and Emergency			收容病人数（人）Number of Patients Receiving(person)	死亡人数（人）Number of Deaths (person)
门诊人次数 Number of Outpatients	急诊人次数 Number of Emergency 小计 Subtotal	死亡人数 Number of Deaths		
27418102	**1955566**	**1827**	**159982**	**207**
16881539	**1675803**	**1782**	**30619**	**202**
14199596	1371738	1741	29212	198
1444013	51854	25	643	2
4860	140			
1233070	252071	16	764	2
177600	2639			
92477	1405		10	
20644	41	2	18	2
34719	21625		18	
553746	193928	7		
72616	408			
15872	6769	1	505	
55412	411			
25569	39			
20960	180		25	
163455	24626	6	188	
1814900	**71294**	**13**	**40381**	**4**
245103	19482		155	
1569797	51812	13	40226	4
775250	25955	11	32916	
794547	25857	2	7310	4

18-13 医院、卫生院床位及病人治疗情况（2009年）

Beds and Patients Treated Conditions in Health Care Institutions（2009）

卫生机构	Health Care Institutions	实有病床数（张） Number Hospital Beds (unit)	平均开放病床数（张） Average Daily Number of Open Beds (unit)	治愈率(%) Curative Ratio (%)	好转率(%) Improvement Rate (%)	死亡率(%) Mortality Rate (%)
总计	**Total**	**36849**	**35573**	**62.37**	**35.19**	**0.83**
在总计中：	**Among the Total:**					
一、医院	**Hospitals**	**32371**	**31330**	**59.67**	**37.83**	**0.94**
综合医院	General Hospitals	26404	25599	59.99	37.57	1.01
中医医院	Hospitals Specialized in Traditional Chinese Medicine	2324	2188	46.17	51.25	0.65
中西医结合医院	Hospitals Integrating Traditional Chinese Medicine with Western Therapeutics in Practice					
民族医院	Nationalities Hospitals					
专科医院	Specialized Hospitals	3643	3543	64.72	32.28	0.44
口腔医院	Dental Hospitals	76	76	89.05	10.49	0.09
眼科医院	Eye Hospitals	151	151	97.66	2.07	
耳鼻喉科医院	ENT Hospitals					
肿瘤医院	Cancer Hospitals	630	589	63.89	30.71	1.32
心血管病医院	Cardiovascular Hospitals					
胸科医院	Chest Hospitals					
血液病医院	Blood Disease Hospitals					
妇产（科）医院	Obstetrics and Gynecologist Hospitals	102	94	96.07	2.72	0.32
儿童医院	Children's Hospitals	674	656	75.22	22.94	0.24

18-13 续表 continued

卫生机构	Health Care Institutions	实有病床数（张）Number Hospital Beds (unit)	平均开放病床数（张）Average Daily Number of Open Beds (unit)	治愈率(%) Curative Ratio (%)	好转率(%) Improvement Rate (%)	死亡率(%) Mortality Rate (%)
精神病医院	Psychiatric Hospitals	850	834	42.99	54.02	0.02
传染病医院	Hospitals for Infectious Diseases	200	200	60.93	35.28	0.48
皮肤病医院	Skin Hospitals					
结核病医院	Tuberculosis Hospitals	490	490	4.96	89.80	0.42
麻风病医院	Leprosy Hospitals					
职业病医院	Occupational Diseases Hospitals					
骨科医院	Orthopedic Hospitals	80	80	38.87	45.50	
康复医院	Rehabilitation Hospitals	28	26	60.87	28.35	
整形外科医院	Plastic Surgery Hospitals					
美容医院	Beauty Hospitals					
其他专科医院	Other Specialty Hospitals	362	347	68.12	30.63	0.38
护理院	Nursing Centers					
二、卫生院	**Health Centers**	**2533**	**2380**	**81.91**	**16.31**	**0.02**
街道卫生院	Urban Health Centers	369	330	81.61	16.10	
乡镇卫生院	Rural Health Centers	2164	2050	81.95	16.34	0.02
中心卫生院	Town Health Centers	1280	1222	80.11	18.12	0.02
乡村卫生院	Village Health Centers	884	828	85.40	12.98	0.04

18-14 县（区）村卫生室基本情况（2009年）

单位：个、人、次

指标	Item	总计 Total	村办 Run by Village
机构数	Number of Health Care Institutions	3122	2322
执业（助理）医师	Licensed（Assistant） Doctors	789	638
注册护士	Registered Nurses	190	128
乡村医生和卫生员	Village Doctors and Medics	4549	3257
乡村医生数	Number of Village Doctors	4143	3026
#大专及以上学历	College Degree or Above	401	303
中专学历及中专水平	Vocational Education and Secondary School Level	3216	2281
在职培训合格者	Qualified Job Training	493	414
卫生员	Number of Medics	406	231
诊疗人次数	Number of Treatment	8498896	6079296

The Market Circumstance of the Consumer Goods Wholesales（2009）

(unit、person、time)

按设置/主办单位分 Grouped by Setering/Owner				按行医方式分 Grouped by Medical Mode		
乡卫生院设点 Division of Township Health Center	联合办 Collectively	私人办 Privately	其他 Others	西医为主 Mainly Western Medicine	中医为主 Mainly Chinese Medicine	中西医结合 Integrating Chinese Medicine with Western Medicine
19	214	526	41	51	2367	704
	43	98	10	14	621	154
	28	33	1	3	154	33
19	369	849	55	79	3283	1187
16	338	715	48	70	3124	949
5	40	49	4	7	289	105
10	273	617	35	55	2408	753
1	24	47	7	8	399	86
3	31	134	7	9	159	238
64753	693424	1584197	77226	136149	6240293	2122454

18-15 社会福利事业单位基本情况（2009年）

Basic Statistics on Social Welfare Insititutions（2009）

单位：个、人 （unit,person）

指 标	Item	福利院数 Number of Homes	工作人员 Number of Staff	床位数 Number of Bed	年末在院人数 Number of Persons Housed at the Year-end
一、社会福利院情况	**Statistics on Social Welfare**	**55**	**970**	**6291**	**5117**
1.社会福利院	Social Welfare Homes	5	91	848	494
2.儿童福利院	Baby Welfare Homes	1	77	700	763
3.社会福利医院	Social Welfare Hospitals	1	149	500	474
4.收养性老年福利机构	Adopting Elderly Welfare Units	48	653	4243	3386
城镇	Urban	29	578	3238	2616
农村	Rural	19	75	1005	770

18-16 社会福利事业单位机构、人员数

Number of Social Welfare Institutions and Employed Persons

单位：个、人 （unit，person）

项 目	Item	2000	2005	2006	2007	2008	2009
一、机构	**Insititutions**						
烈士纪念建筑物管理单位	Institutions Managing Memorial Buildings of Martyrs	2	2	2	2	2	2
救助类单位	Units Providing Assistance	8	8	8	8	8	8
殡仪服务单位	Funeral Service Unit	18	20	22	21	20	20
殡仪馆	Funeral Home	4	4	4	5	4	4
公墓	Cemetery	12	13	14	13	12	12
殡葬管理单位	Funeral Management Units	2	3	4	3	4	4
二、人员	**Staff**						
烈士纪念建筑物管理单位	Institutions Managing Memorial Buildings of Martyrs	43	43	40	37	39	39
救助类单位	Units Providing Assistance	99	112	116	113	110	118
殡仪服务单位	Funeral Service Unit	613	756	765	902	1015	1046
殡仪馆	Funeral Home	164	204	177	239	220	218
公墓	Cemetery	425	516	533	624	745	776
殡葬管理单位	Funeral Management Units	24	36	55	39	50	52

18-17 各区县优抚对象人员情况（2009年）

Statistics on Persons Enjoying Favoured Treatment by Region（2009）

单位：人 （person）

指　标	Item	全市 Total	新城区 Xincheng	碑林区 Beilin	莲湖区 Lianhu
合　计	**Total**	**26459**	**805**	**901**	**1021**
1.革命伤残人员	Number of Disabled Veterans	4819	606	537	692
2.烈军属人员	Number of Family Members of Martyrs and Soldiers	1202	52	43	73
3.在乡红军老战士	Old Red Army Men in Hometown	6		2	1
4.在乡复原军人	Demobilized Soldiers in Hometown	7614	19	15	35
5.在乡退伍军人	Veterans in Hometown	1532		6	12

18-17 续表1 continued 1

单位：人 （person）

指　标	Item	灞桥区 Baqiao	未央区 Weiyang	雁塔区 Yanta	阎良区 Yanliang	临潼区 Lintong
合　计	**Total**	**1994**	**1021**	**1224**	**1097**	**3211**
1.革命伤残人员	Number of Disabled Veterans	271	244	582	91	327
2.烈军属人员	Number of Family Members of Martyrs and Soldiers	77	58	39	42	164
3.在乡红军老战士	Old Red Army Men in Hometown					
4.在乡复原军人	Demobilized Soldiers in Hometown	642	241	140	321	1442
5.在乡退伍军人	Veterans in Hometown	246	5	122	55	233

18-17 续表2 continued 2

单位：人 （person）

指　标	Item	长安区 Chang'an	蓝田县 Lantian	周至县 Zhouzhi	户　县 Huxian	高陵县 Gaoling
合　计	**Total**	**4850**	**2191**	**3777**	**2605**	**1675**
1.革命伤残人员	Number of Disabled Veterans	404	225	346	284	123
2.烈军属人员	Number of Family Members of Martyrs and Soldiers	191	108	186	96	73
3.在乡红军老战士	Old Red Army Men in Hometown	0		1	1	1
4.在乡复原军人	Demobilized Soldiers in Hometown	1203	795	1138	964	659
5.在乡退伍军人	Veterans in Hometown	164	204	192	135	158

18-18 计划生育和婚姻情况（2009年）

Conditions of Birth Control and Marriage Registration（2009）

区 县	Region	晚婚率(%) Late Marriage Rate	计划生育率(%) Family Planning Rate	综合节育率(%) Cntraceptive Rate
全 市	**Total**	**78.5**	**98.4**	**91.4**
新城区	Xingcheng	99.2	99.8	89.8
碑林区	Beilin	99.9	99.8	87.3
莲湖区	Lianhu	87.7	99.8	88.9
灞桥区	Baqiao	68.3	99.5	93.8
未央区	Weiyang	64.6	99.7	90.4
雁塔区	Yanta	61.6	99.7	88.8
阎良区	Yanliang	60.2	98.9	88.2
临潼区	Lintong	91.7	97.1	92.8
长安区	Chang'an	69.6	97.4	93.1
蓝田县	Lantian	88.3	97.3	91.7
周至县	Zhouzhi	61.3	96.7	92.8
户 县	Huxian	77.1	97.9	94.4
高陵县	Gaoling	64.0	98.9	91.8

18-18 续表 continued

区 县	Region	独生子女领证率(%) Only-child Certificate Rate	结婚对数（对） Marriages (coaple)	再婚数（人） Remarriages	离婚对数（对） Divorced (coaple)
全 市	**Total**	**45.4**	**88138**	**22598**	**15796**
新城区	Xingcheng	48.6	6198	1953	1595
碑林区	Beilin	57.8	11920	120	1931
莲湖区	Lianhu	39.6	8053	2208	2069
灞桥区	Baqiao	47.8	3846	310	711
未央区	Weiyang	63.7	7101	1492	1401
雁塔区	Yanta	59.4	9352	5514	2026
阎良区	Yanliang	63.0	2780	1080	564
临潼区	Lintong	30.0	7206	252	1219
长安区	Chang'an	37.5	10647	2477	1468
蓝田县	Lantian	19.7	6185	222	863
周至县	Zhouzhi	12.3	5902	4550	617
户 县	Huxian	34.3	5139	1128	797
高陵县	Gaoling	28.9	3809	1292	535

18-19 律师、公证及调解基本情况

Basic Statistics on Lawyers、Notaries and Mediation

指　　标	Item	2000	2005	2006	2007	2008	2009
一、律师工作	**Lawyers**						
律师事务所（个）	Number of Law Offices（unit)	46	65	70	71	73	79
律师（人）	Lawyers(person)	534	866	902	864	940	1058
#专职	Full-time	469	825	851	808	865	1001
兼职	Part-time	65	41	51	56	66	55
二、公证工作	**Notarization**						
公证处（个）	Number of Notary Offices（unit)	14	14	14	14	14	14
公证人员（人）	Notarial Personnel（person）	158	192	205	243	189	194
#公证员	Notaries	96	93	102	156	100	102
办理公证件数（件）	Number of Notarized Documents Issued（case）	79199	68110	70777	70863	74440	88637
国内	Domestic	62060	46427	45717	42996	43640	57190
民事	Civil	24576	11737	13258	15466	15782	22337
经济	Economics	37484	34690	32459	27530	27858	34853
涉外	Foreign-related	16990	21451	24857	27616	30481	31082
涉港、澳、台	Hong Kong、Macco and Taiwan related	149	232	203	251	319	365
三、人民调解工作	**Number of People Mediations**						
已建调委会数（个）	Number of Mediation Committees（unit）	4379	3904	3952	3952	3961	3961
调解人员数（人）	Number of Mediators（person）	13059	16156	15930	15525	15424	17198
调解纠纷数（件）	Number of Civil Disputes Mediated（case）	34212	17770	17608	14986	12223	23185
#调解成功数	Number of Cases Successfully Mediated	31574	14084	14597	13756	11201	21373

18–20 共青团组织情况

Basic Facts on Communist Youth League

单位：个、人 (unit,person)

指标	Item	2000	2005	2006	2007	2008	2009
一、基层团组织	**Grass-root Youth League organisations**	**10323**	**7726**	**9560**	**9329**	**10985**	**9054**
二、共青团员	**Youth League Members**	**278165**	**344035**	**329669**	**327332**	**348141**	**324785**
#女团员	Female Youth League Members	134289	153493	142431	141271	145777	144027
三、专职团干部	**Full-time Youth League Cadre**	**845**	**537**	**524**	**576**	**601**	**387**

18–21 妇联组织状况

Women's Organizations Status

单位：个 (unit)

项目	Item	2009
一、妇联组织	**Women's Organizations**	
市级妇联	Municipal Women's Federation	1
街道妇联	Street Women's Federation	99
社区妇联	Community Women's Federation	544
县（区）妇联	County (district) Women's Federation	13
乡（镇)妇联	Township (town) Women's Federation	90
村妇代会	Village Women's Representative Conference	3105
二、非公有制经济组织中妇女组织	**Women's Organizations in Non-public Economic Organizations**	
个体劳动者协会中的妇女组织	Women's Organizations in Association of Individual Workers	6
专业市场中的妇女组织	Women's Organizations in the Professional Market	
私营企业中的妇女组织	Women's Organizations in the Private Sector	40
三资企业中的妇女组织	Foreign-funded Enterprises in the Women's Organizations	
三、机关事业单位妇女组织	**Women's Organizations in Government Departments and Institutions**	
直属机关妇委会（妇工委）	Women's Committee of Direct-affiliated Departments	21
部门机关妇委会（妇工委）	Women's Committee of Affiliated Departments	261
事业单位妇委会（妇工委）	Women's Committee of Government Institutions	2
四、民主党派妇女组织	**Women's Organizations of Democratic Parties**	
民主党派妇委会	Women's Committee of Democratic Parties	7
五、团体会员	**Members of Organisation**	
工会女职工委员会	Women Staff Committee of Labor Unions	2233
民政部门登记注册的妇女社团	Women's Communities Registered at Civil Administration Departments	3

18-22 妇联工作情况

Basic Facts on Women's Federation

单位：人、个 （person,unit）

项　　目	Item	2009
一、双学双比活动	**Double Learning and Double Competition Activities**	
(一)科技培训	Scientific and Technical Training	
接受技术培训人数	Number of People Receiving Technical Training	115448
获绿色证书人数	Number of People Gaining Green Certificates	296
妇代会主任中农民技术员数	Number of Farmer in Women's Head Technicians	136
(二)巾帼扶贫	Women Aid-the-poor Project	
脱贫户数	Households out of Poverty	632
扶贫项目数	Number of Poverty Alleviation Projects	9
二、巾帼建功活动	**Women Make Achievements**	
(一)巾帼建功	Women Make Achievements	
评选巾帼建功标兵数	Number of Pacemakes	149
巾帼建功先进工作者数	Number of Advanced Workers	100
巾帼建功先进协调单位数	Number of Advanced Supporting Units	0
巾帼文明示范岗数	Number of Model Workers	141
(二)下岗失业妇女再就业	Re-employment of Laid-off and Unemployed Women	
妇女就业服务机构数	Number of Institutions for Women's Employment Services	14
妇联主办的劳务市场	Labor Markets Sponsored by Women's Federation	3
三、三八红旗手	**Models of Women**	**205**
四、三八红旗集体	**Models of Women Group**	**58**
五、实施春蕾计划	**Carrying out of CHUNLEI Project**	
资助女童入学或返校数	Helping Women Children Enter School or Back School	127
社会捐资总额(万元)	Amount of Money That Social Attribates（10 000yuan）	27
六、来信来访情况	**Conditions of Letters and Visits**	
女职工劳动保护信访案件	Cases about Labor Protection of Employed Women through Letters and Visits	30
侵犯妇女财产权利信访案件	Cases about Encroachment of Women's Property through Letters and Visits	227

18-23　交通事故情况

Statistics on Traffic Accidents

指　　标	Item	2000	2005	2006	2007	2008	2009
次　数(起)	Number of Traffic Accidents（case）	4099	4903	3709	3643	2576	2702
死亡人数（人）	Number of Deaths（person）	589	617	617	597	551	531
受伤人数 （人）	Number of Injuries（person）	2884	3081	3075	3002	2464	2247
直接财产损失（万元）	Direct Property Loss（10 000yuan）	1116.1	2024.4	1328.3	1038.0	522.8	851.7

注：2006年及以前道路交通数据不含高速公路数据,故年度数据不可比。

Note:As road data of traffic didn't include expressways, annual data were not comparable.

18-24　火灾情况

Statistics on Fires

指　　标	Item	2000	2005	2006	2007	2008	2009
次　数（起）	Number of Traffic Accidents（case）	1040	2664	2310	2009	1537	1485
死亡人数（人）	Number of Deaths（person）	17	13	9	13	11	17
受伤人数（人）	Number of Injuries（person）	12	15	9	11	4	3
直接财产损失(万元）	Direct Property Loss（10 000yuan）	472.4	1565.5	1376.0	773.9	1907.7	1850.6

18-25 安全生产情况

Dato on Sasfety in Production

指　　标	Item	2006	2007	2008	2009
全市合计	**Sum of Erntire City**				
起数（起）	Number of Cases（case）	6065	5685	4138	4225
死亡人数（人）	Number of Deaths（person）	676	648	591	586
受伤人数（人）	Number of Injuries（person）	3090	3013	2472	2264
损失（万元）	Economic Loss（10 000yuan）	3004.1	2308.4	2802.0	3128.9
道路交通事故	**Road Accidents**				
起数（起）	Number of Cases（case）	3709	3643	2576	2702
死亡人数（人）	Number of Deaths（person）	617	597	551	531
受伤人数（人）	Number of Injuries（person）	3075	3002	2464	2247
损失（万元）	Economic Loss（10 000yuan）	1328.3	1038.0	522.8	851.7
火灾事故	**Fire Accidents**				
起数（起）	Number of Cases（case）	2310	2009	1537	1485
死亡人数（人）	Number of Deaths（person）	9	13	11	17
受伤人数（人）	Number of Injuries（person）	9	11	4	3
损失（万元）	Economic Loss（10 000yuan）	1376.0	773.9	1907.7	1850.6
农机事故	**Farm Machinery Accidents**				
起数（起）	Number of Cases（case）	2	3	2	11
死亡人数（人）	Number of Deaths（person）	1	3	1	
受伤人数（人）	Number of Injuries（person）	1		1	2
损失（万元）	Economic Loss（10 000yuan）				1.1
工矿商贸事故	**Accidents in Industry,Mine, Business and Trade**				
起数（起）	Number of Cases（case）	42	30	22	27
死亡人数（人）	Number of Deaths（person）	47	35	27	38
受伤人数（人）	Number of Injuries（person）	5		3	12
损失（万元）	Economic Loss（10 000yuan）	293.0	496.5	366.5	425.5
特种设备	**Special Accidents**				
起数（起）	Number of Cases（case）	2		1	
死亡人数（人）	Number of Deaths（person）	2		1	
受伤人数（人）	Number of Injuries（person）				
损失（万元）	Economic Loss（10 000yuan）	6.8		5.0	

注：1.2006年及以前道路交通数据不含高速公路数据,故年度数据不可比.

2.2007年、2009年工矿商贸事故数据含特种设备数据.

Note: 1.As statistical range of economic loss due to fire extended in 2005, the indexes of economic loss were not comparable with the indexes in corresponding period.

2.Data of accidents in industry , mine, business and trade include special equipment in 2007 and 2009.

18-26 刑事案件情况

Data on Criminal Cases

指　　标	Item	2005	2006	2007	2008	2009
一、案件数情况	**Data on Number of Cases**					
立案数（起）	Number of Registered Cases(caes)	23537	43856	43583	41811	42321
破案数（起）	Number of Cleared up Cases(caes)	13145	13952	17241	19284	21921
破案率（%）	Percent of Cleared up Cases(%)	56	32	40	46	52
抓获作案人员（人）	Number of Criminals Caught(person)	10690	11068	12717	12364	11870
二、查获犯罪集团情况	**Data on Hunted down and Seized Criminal Gangs**					
查获犯罪集团个数（个）	Number of Hunted down and Seized Criminal Gangs（person）	221	203	230	211	154
查获犯罪集团人数（人）	Number of Members of Hunted down and Seized Criminal Gangs（person）	985	938	1061	916	663
涉及案件（起）	Number of Cases Involved(case)	1102	847	1225	1328	622
三、涉枪案件情况	**Data on Cases with Guns Involved**					
立案数（起）	Number of Registered Cases(caes)	34	37	10	11	25
破案数（起）	Number of Cleared up Cases(caes)	32	35	8	9	24
破案率（%）	Percent of Cleared up Cases(%)	94.1	94.6	80.0	81.8	96.0

18-27 治安案件情况

Data on Public Order Cases

指　　标	Item	2005	2006	2007	2008	2009
案件数情况	**Data on Number of Cases**					
受理数（起）	Number of Accepted(caes)	45484	40550	41213	45226	45925
查处数（起）	Number of Investigated and Prosecuted(caes)	40743	35598	38737	44202	45871
查处率（%）	Percent of Investigated and Prosecuted Cases(%)	89.6	87.8	94.0	97.7	99.9
查处违法犯罪人数（人）	Number of Investigated and Prosecuted Laws Breakers and Crime Committer(person)	48949	37109	36739	38606	39214

18-28 分区县刑事、治安案件情况（2009年）

Data on criminal cases and public order cases grouped by districts and counties（2009）

单位：件 (case)

区县 Region	刑事案件 Criminal cases			治安案件 Public order cases		
	立案数 Number of Registered Cases	破案数 Number of Cleared up Cases	破案率 Percent of Ceared up Cases (%)	受理数 Number of Accepted Cases	查处数 Number of Investigated and Prosecuted Cases	查处率 Percent of Investigated and Prosecuted Cases(%)
新城区 Xincheng	5254	2191	41.7	5152	5152	100.0
碑林区 Beilin	5262	2997	57.0	5285	5375	
莲湖区 Lianhu	6085	3955	65.0	4558	4646	
灞桥区 Baqiao	2088	1239	59.3	4576	4586	
未央区 Weiyang	3354	2454	73.2	2503	2444	97.6
雁塔区 Yanta	8265	2445	29.6	13532	13532	100.0
阎良区 Yanliang	940	507	53.9	398	398	100.0
临潼区 Lintong	1533	1284	83.8	923	921	99.8
长安区 Chang'an	2634	1707	64.8	2546	2583	
蓝田县 Lantian	548	413	75.4	929	874	94.1
周至县 Zhouzhi	670	397	59.3	390	390	100.0
户　县 Huxian	672	362	53.9	1379	1380	
高陵县 Gaoling	771	386	50.1	516	516	100.0

18-29 西安市人民检察院案件受理情况

Data on Acceptance of Cases of Xi'an People's Procuratorate

指　　标	Item	受案 Acceptance of Cases			
		2006	2007	2008	2009
总　计	**Toatl**	**7354**	**7972**	**8924**	**8462**
一、贪污贿赂案件（件）	**Cases about Corporation and Bribery（case）**	**425**	**383**	**431**	**316**
二、渎职、侵权案件（件）	**Cases about Misprision and Tortious（case）**	**99**	**83**	**115**	**89**
三、审查逮捕（件）	**EXamination and Arresting（case)**	**3175**	**3497**	**3835**	**3656**
决定逮捕贪污贿赂犯罪嫌疑人（人）	Suspects of Corporation and Bribery to be Arrested（person）	101	73	104	97
决定逮捕渎职、侵权犯罪嫌疑人（人）	Suspects of Misprision and Tortious to be Arrested（person）	16	4	11	11
批准逮捕刑事犯罪嫌疑人（人）	Suspects of Criminal to be Arrested（person）	4480	4935	5702	5321
四、刑事立案监督、侦查活动监督（件）	**Supervision of Acceptance of Criminal Cases and Investigation（case）**	**163**	**204**	**218**	**159**
五、审查起诉（件）	**EXamination and Prosecution（case)**	**3492**	**3805**	**4325**	**4242**
起诉贪污贿赂犯罪被告人（人）	Prosecution of Corporation and Bribery to be Defendants（person）	169	126	158	159
起诉渎职、侵权犯罪被告人（人）	Prosecution of Misprision and Tortious to be Defendants（person）	16	23	15	11
起诉刑事犯罪被告人（人）	Prosecution of Criminal to be Defendants（person）	4524	4947	5435	5444

18-30 西安市中级人民法院案件基本情况（2009年）

Xi'an Intermediate People's Court Basic Data of the Law Cases（2009）

单位：件 (case)

指 标	Item	陪审员参加 Number of Jurors Partcipating	回避 Withdrawn	诉讼财产保全 Preserving of Property of Lawsuit	先予执行 Execute in Advance
合 计	**Total**	**3985**	**6**	**64**	**2**
一、刑 事	**Criminal**	**1623**			
二、婚姻家庭、继承	**Marriage，Family and Inheritance**	**679**			
三、合 同	**Contract**	**1060**	**3**	**51**	**2**
四、权属、侵权及其他民事案件	**Tort and Other Civil Cases**	**592**	**3**	**13**	
五、行 政	**Administration**	**31**			
六、申诉、申请再审	**Appeals，Apply for Retrial**				
七、司法赔偿	**Judicial Indemnification**				
八、执 行	**Execution**				
合计中	Collegiating	3985	6	64	2
海事海商	Maritime Affairs & Business				
知识产权	Intellectual Property	4			
一 审	First Instance	3985	6	64	2
二 审	Second Instance				
审判监督	Trial Supervision				

18-30 续表

指标	Item	审委会讨论（件）Under Discussing of Judicial Board (case)	法律援助（件）Legal Aids (case)	结案合计（件）Wound up Cases（case）	诉讼标的总总额合计（万元）Amount of Lawsuit object (10 000 yuan)
合　计	**Total**	**497**	**9**	**66299**	**1188671.6**
一、刑　事	**Criminal**	**142**	**2**	**4325**	**13287.8**
二、婚姻家庭、继承	**Marriage，Family and Inheritance**	**30**	**4**	**11068**	**28482.7**
三、合　同	**Contract**	**140**	**1**	**21493**	**563049.0**
四、权属、侵权及其他民事案件	**Tort and Other Civil Cases**	**77**	**2**	**10882**	**110143.6**
五、行　政	**Administration**	**20**		**541**	
六、申诉、申请再审	**Appeals，Apply for Retrial**	**5**		**372**	
七、司法赔偿	**Judicial Indemnification**			**4**	**28.2**
八、执　行	**Execution**	**83**		**17614**	**473680.3**
合计中	Collegiating	497	9	66299	1188671.6
海事海商	Maritime Affairs & Business				
知识产权	Intellectual Property			457	9098.3
一　审	First Instance	339	8	42522	590204.0
二　审	Second Instance			5621	121488.4
审判监督	Trial Supervision	70	1	166	3270.7

continued

中级人民法院结案（件）Intermediate People's Court closed（case）	中级人民法院诉讼标的总金额（万元）Intermediate People's Court subject matter of litigation the total amount (10 000 yuan)	基层人民法院结案（件）Primary People's Courts Closed（case）	基层人民法院诉讼标的总金额（万元）Primary People's Courtsubject matter of litigation the total amount (10 000 yuan)	其中人民法庭结案（件）Courtroom Closed（case）	其中人民法庭诉讼标的总金额（万元）Courtroom subject matter of litigation the total amount (10 000 yuan)
8562	**751526.5**	**57737**	**437145.1**	**12053**	**44959.1**
865	**7426.2**	**3460**	**5861.6**		
477	**8427.4**	**10591**	**20055.3**	**5211**	**9530.0**
3540	**355308.2**	**17953**	**207740.8**	**2984**	**21006.5**
1766	**75402.9**	**9116**	**34740.7**	**3792**	**14371.1**
185		**356**			
351		**21**			
2	**15.0**	**2**	**13.2**		
1376	**304946.8**	**16238**	**168733.5**	**66**	**51.5**
8562	751526.5	57737	437145.1	12053	44959.1
444	9089.9	13	8.3		
1142	323656.9	41380	266547.1	11987	44907.7
5621	121488.4				
70	1419.4	96	1851.3		

主要统计指标解释

文化事业机构 指从事专业文化工作和为专业文化工作服务的独立建制的单位。不包括这些单位另外举办独立核算的其他机构和各部门的业余文化组织。

艺术表演团体 指从事戏曲、音乐、舞蹈、杂技等专业艺术表演，有独立帐户的单位，不包括半工半艺、半农半艺和民间职业剧团。

电影放映单位 指具有放映机器设备、固定或不固定的放映场所与专职或兼职的放映技术人员，经有关部门登记批准，经常为一定的观众对象放映电影的机构。包括经批准对外开放进行营业，并与电影发行放映管理机构分帐的专用放映单位和军委系统租片单位。

艺术表演观众人数（人次） 指售票、包场演出或民族地区免费演出的艺术表演观众人次数，不包括彩排审查和内部观摩演出的观看人次数。

等级运动员人数 指经考核正式批准授予等级运动员称号的人数。运动员等级分为国际级运动健将、运动健将、一级运动员、二级运动员、三级运动员、少年级运动员。

等级裁判员人数 指经考核正式批准授予等级裁判员称号的人数。裁判员等级分为国际裁判、国家级裁判、一级裁判、二级裁判、三级裁判。

体育场 指有400米跑道（中心含足球场），有固定道牙，跑道6条以上，并有固定看台的室外田径场地。体育场按看台容纳观众人数分为:甲级25000人以上，乙级15000-25000人，丙级5000-15000人，丁级5000人以下。

体育馆 指有固定看台，可供篮球、排球、羽毛球、乒乓球、体操等项目训练比赛活动用的室内运动场地。体育馆按看台容纳观众人数分为:甲级6000人以上，乙级4000-6000人，丙级2000-4000人，丁级2000人以下。

卫生机构 包括医院、疗养院、社区服务中心（站）、卫生院、门诊部、急救中心（站）、采供血机构、妇幼保健院（站、所）、专科疾病防治院（站、所）、疾病预防控制中心（防疫站）、卫生监督所、卫生监督检验（监测、检测）所（站）、医学科学研究机构、医学在职培训机构、健康教育所（站、中心）、诊所、卫生所、医务室、村卫生所。不包括卫生新闻出版社、卫生社会团体、卫生行政机关、教育部门登记注册的高中等医学（药）院校、军队编制内卫生机构、香港澳门特别行政区和台湾所属卫生机构。

医院 指设有固定床位，能收容病人住院并能为病人提供医疗、护理服务的医疗机构，包括县及县以上医院、农村乡卫生院和其他医院三部分。医院按所属性质不同分为卫生部门、工业及其他部门和集体经济单位三类。县及县以上医院按业务性质不同分为综合医院和专科医院。

卫生技术人员 包括执业（助理）医师、注册护士、药剂人员、检验和影像技师（士、员）等卫生专业人员。

社会福利事业单位 指集中收养社会孤老、残、幼的机构，包括由民政部门管理的社会福利院、儿童福利院、精神病人福利院和城镇集体举办的福利院及农村集体举办的敬老院。

社会福利事业单位收养人数 包括民政部门管理和城镇、农村集体举办的社会福利事业单位中收养的老人、少年儿童、缺乏生活自理能力的残疾人员和精神病人。

社会福利企业单位 指以安置城镇有一定劳动能力的盲、聋、哑和肢体残疾人员就业为目的，享受国家减免税待遇的国有或集体企业。包括福利工厂、福利商业和服务业、假肢厂和安置农场等单位。

律师 指受聘参加法律顾问处工作，担任法律顾问、刑（民）事代理人、刑事辩护人，办理非诉讼事件、解答法律询问，代写法律事务文书等主要从事律师业务的专职法律工作者和兼职律师。

公证人员 指在国家公证机关依法办理公证事务的司法人员，包括公证员、助理公证员和在公证处工作的其他人员。

办理公证文书 指公证处在一定时期内办结的公证文书件数。公证文书按司法部规定或批准的格式制作，包括国内公证和涉外公证两部分。国内公证分为经济合同公证和民事法律关系公证两大类。

调解人员 指在人民调解委员会担负调解民间一般民事纠纷和轻微违法行为引起纠纷的工作人员，包括调解委员会的委员和调解小组的调解员。

调解民间纠纷 指调解委员会依照法律规定，根据自愿原则，用说服教育的方法调解民间发生的有关民事权利和义务的争执，促成当事双方达到协议和谅解，解决纠纷。包括婚姻家庭纠纷，财产权益纠纷等，不包括法院受理调解的民事案件数。

受理劳动争议案件数 指劳动争议仲裁委员会根据国家有关规定，对劳动争议当事人的申请予以审查，符合受理条件而正式立案、准备处理的劳动争议案件数。

立案 指检察机关对犯罪线索进行初步调查后，认为存在职务犯罪事实并需要追究刑事责任时，依法决定作为刑事案件进行侦查的诉讼活动，是追究犯罪的开始。

离休、退休、退职人员 指正式办理了离休、退休、退职手续，并享受相应的离休、退休、退职待遇的人员。

保险福利费用 指企业、事业、机关单位在工资以外实际支付给职工和离休、退休、退职人员个人以及用于集体的劳动保险和福利费用。

Explanatory Notes on Main Statistical Indicators

Cultural Institutions refer to units which have their own organizational system and independent accounting system and specialize in or serve cultural development. They exclude other establishments run by these cultural institutions and amateur cultural groups established by various departments.

Art Troupe refers to the troupe which is engaged in drama, opera, music, dance, acrobatics or other art performance, opens independent accounts with banks and has self-supporting accounting system; excluding the troupes which are engaged partly in industrial or agricultural activities, partly in art performance and the professional troupes organized by the people.

Film Projection Units refer to units with film projection equipment, full or part time projectionists, permanent or non permanent places, approved by related administrative departments to show films regularly for certain groups of audience, including those film projection units which have been approved to give commercial shows and run business with independent accounting system as well as those film-renting units of the military system.

Number of Spectators at Art Performance refers to the number of attendants at commercial shows, completely booked shows or free shows given in minority national areas, and does not include the number of spectators at rehearsals for examination and internal shows for study.

Number of Athletes in Grades refers to the number of athletes who have been given titles through examination. The titles of athletes include international masters of sports, masters of sports, first-grade, second-grade and third-grade sportsmen and young athletes.

Number of Referees in Grades refers to the number of referees who have been given titles after examination. They are classified as international referees, national referees and referees of the first, second and third grades.

Stadiums refer to stadiums for track and field events with six lane 400-meter tracks around soccer fields, permanent track marks and permanent bleachers. Stadiums are classified according to seating capacity. they include: class a stadiums seating 25000 people each. class b stadiums seating 15000 to 25000 people each. Class C stadiums seating 5000 to 15000 people each, and Class D stadiums seating fewer than 5000 people.

Gymnasiums refer to indoor sports grounds with permanent seats in which basketball, volleyball. badminton, table tennis and gymnastics competitions can be held. Gymnasiums are classified according to seating capacity. They include Class A gymnasiums seating over 6000 people. Class B gymnasiums seating 4000 to 6000 people. Class C gymnasiums seating 2000 to 4000 people, and Class D gymnasiums seating fewer than 2000 people.

Health institution includes hospital, sanitarium, community service center (station), health center, emergency aid centers(station), blood gathering or supplying institution, maternity and child care center, disease prevention and control institution(epidemic prevention station), health supervision institution, health supervision and testing (monitory, detecting) institution, medical research institution, medical on-the-job training agency, health education center, clinic, health station, dispensary, health center in village. It excludes health news press, health social community, health administration, high-and-medium level medical (pharmic) college registered in educational administration, health institution in army, health institution belong to Hong Kong Special Administration Region or Taiwan.

Hospitals refer to medical institutions with permanent hospital beds, which are able to take in patients and provide them with medical and nursing services. Hospitals are classified into three categories: hospitals at or above the county level, hospitals of rural townships, and other hospitals. According to their ownership, hospitals can be classified into three categories: hospitals under the public health departments, hospitals under industrial and other departments and collective-owned hospitals. Hospitals at or above county level are divided into comprehensive and specialized hospitals.

Medical Technical Personnel includes practicing (assistant) doctor, certified nurse, pharmacist, laboratory and photographic technician, other technicians working in medical institution.

Social Welfare Institutions refer to institutions taking care of old people without children, handicapped people and orphans. They include social welfare institutions run by civil affairs departments, children welfare institutions, social welfare institutions for mental patients, and collective-owned old peoples homes in rural areas.

Number of People Taken in by Social Welfare Institutions refers to the number of old people, children, totally dependent handicapped people and mental patientsTaken in by social welfare institutions run by civil affairs departments and those run by collective units in urban and rural areas.

Social Welfare Enterprises are collective owned enterprises which employ the blind, deaf-mute, and other handicapped people who are able to work in cities and towns and enjoy exemption from state taxes, including welfare plants, welfare commercial services, artificial limb plants and farms, etc.

Lawyers are legal workers who are employed full time by legal counseling firms to act as legal advisers, agents in criminal or civil lawsuits, or defenders in criminal lawsuits, or to handle non-litigious legal affairs, to advise on matters of law or to write legal papers for others. Both full-time and part time lawyers are included.

Notary Personnel refers to judicial workers of the state notary offices handling notarization work according to law. They include notaries, assistant notaries, and other people working for notary offices.

Notarized Documents refer to the documents settled by notary offices in a year. The notary documents are drawn up in accordance with the regulations of the Ministry of Justice, including domestic documents and foreign-related documents. Domestic documents are divided into two major categories, documents on economic contracts and documents on civil legal relations.

Mediators refer to workers on peoples mediation committees responsible for mediating in civil disputes and cases of slight infraction of the law. They include members of the mediation committees and mediators of mediation groups.

Mediation of Civil Disputes refers to mediation committees work in mediating in civil disputes concerning civil rights and duties through persuasion and education in accordance with the provisions of law on a voluntary basis, so as to solve disputes by helping the parties involved come to an agreement and understanding. these disputes include divorce cases and disputes over property ownership, but exclude the civil cases to be handled by the court.

Number of Labour Dispute Cases Accepted refers to the number of cases of labour dispute submitted that, after being reviewed by the labour dispute arbitration committees in line with the relevant state regulations, are accepted and registered for treatment.

Acceptance of Case refers to the decision made by the procurators office to confirm the act of crime after initial investigation and to start legal proceedings of the case as criminal case.

Retired or Resigned Personnel refers to the persons who have formally gone through the formalities for their retirement or quitting work and enjoy the corresponding treatments.

Insurance and Welfare Funds refers to labour insurance and welfare fund paid by enterprises, organizations and institutions to their staff and workers as well as retired and resigned persons in addition to their wages and salaries.

19 企业调查

ENTERPRISES INVESTIGATION

资料整理：刘　艳　王文娟

Data management:Liu Yan　Wang Wenjuan

第十九部分　企业调查

一、简要说明

本章资料主要包括各行业企业景气调查指数和企业家信心指数等，由国家统计局西安调查队提供。

二、主要指标

企业景气指数	128.96	比上年提高 20.23点
企业家信心指数	134.16	比上年提高 20.13点

19 ENTERPRISES INVESTIGATION

Ⅰ.Brief Introduction

Data in this chapter consists prosperity survey indices of various industries and Entrepreneur Expectation Indicator, provided by Enterprise Survey Crew of NBS Survey Office in Xi'an.

Ⅱ.Major Indicators

		Increase over Preceding Year
Business Climate Index	128.96	20.23 points
Entrepreneur Expectation Indicator	134.16	20.13 points

19-1 企业景气指数（2009年）

Business Climate Index（2009）

指标	Item	一季度 First Quarter	二季度 Second Quarter	三季度 Third Quarter	四季度 Forth Quarter
企业景气指数	**Business Climate Index**	**118.95**	**122.11**	**124.62**	**128.96**
按行业门类分	Grouped by Sector				
工业	Industry	88.18	113.93	115.69	123.92
建筑业	Construction	138.19	145.30	142.72	150.76
交通运输、仓储及邮政业	Transport, Storage and Post	114.55	121.08	127.30	117.21
批发和零售业	Wholesale and Retail Sales	131.78	122.82	131.82	135.59
房地产业	Real Estate	122.53	139.54	143.50	138.65
社会服务业	Social Services	108.10	97.92	105.72	94.29
信息传输、计算机服务和软件业	Information transmission, computer service and Safeware service	153.34	144.25	135.15	153.79
住宿和餐饮业	Hotels and Catering Services	120.66	128.84	129.28	121.39
按企业登记注册类型分	Grouped by Registration				
国有企业	State-Owned Enterprises	117.74	124.17	125.40	131.15
集体企业	Collective Enterprises	107.14	122.11	101.18	116.57
股份合作企业	Share-holding Cooperative Enterprises	127.71	131.31	109.21	132.32
联营企业	Joint Ownership Enterprises	100.00	100.00	100.00	100.00
有限责任公司	Limited Liability Corporations	91.96	114.71	116.27	117.48
股份有限公司	Share-holding Corporations Ltd.	110.30	115.65	132.59	141.49
私营企业	Privately Owned Enterprises	100.00	75.00	75.00	66.67
外商及港、澳、台投资企业	Enterprises Invested by Foreigners or Investors from Hongkong,Macro and Taiwan	144.28	149.14	137.17	151.89
按企业规模分	Grouped by Size of Enterprises				
大型企业	Large-size	119.26	140.36	146.07	150.65
中型企业	Medium-size	101.20	107.20	107.20	108.94
小型企业	Small-size	72.55	74.00	63.27	79.59
特殊分组	Special-Grorped				
国家重点企业	State Key Enterprises	85.39	135.44	144.82	141.85
国家试点企业集团成员	Member of Stats Experimental Enterprises Group	84.81	134.72	140.88	140.96
乡镇企业	Town and Township Enterprises	199.89	199.89	150.00	200.00
上市公司	Listed Companies	133.27	133.87	162.38	160.47
国有控股企业	State-holding Enterprises	109.06	123.58	130.33	133.34
生产总量	Total Production	95.31	123.19	122.41	132.76
盈利（亏损）变化	Change of Profits or Losses	81.76	106.87	110.06	117.43
流动资金	Circulating Funds	82.98	73.72	80.12	80.77
货款拖欠	Delinquent Loans	90.45	83.97	89.18	106.19
劳动力需求	Demand of Labor Force	74.58	96.74	102.25	103.57
固定资产投资	Investment of fixed Assets	102.75	105.26	110.42	107.42
产品订货	Product Order	97.10	103.15	116.85	115.57
企业融资	Accommodation	94.94	80.56	77.73	80.84

19-2 企业家信心指数（2009年）

Entrepreneur Expectation Indicator（2009）

指　　标	Item	一季度 First Season	二季度 Second Season	三季度 Third Season	四季度 Fourth Season
企业家信心指数	**Entrepreneur Expectation Indicator**	**124.70**	**115.51**	**131.70**	**134.16**
按行业门类分	Grouped by Sector				
工业	Industry	97.36	105.62	127.57	131.07
建筑业	Construction	135.85	147.24	143.79	137.48
交通运输、仓储及邮政业	Transport, Storage and Post	128.88	123.50	136.66	137.78
批发和零售业	Wholesale and Retail Sales	138.96	110.89	134.78	143.05
房地产业	Real Estate	120.21	131.79	153.34	149.80
社会服务业	Social Services	80.44	85.20	114.03	112.35
信息传输、计算机服务和软件业	Information transmission, computer service and Safeware service	154.55	154.44	128.94	147.12
住宿和餐饮业	Hotels and Catering Services	85.02	111.37	121.75	125.12
按企业登记注册类型分	Grouped by Registration				
国有企业	State-Owned Enterprises	131.08	129.92	139.63	138.39
集体企业	Collective Enterprises	120.29	126.45	123.08	144.28
股份合作企业	Share-holding Cooperative Enterprises	127.71	115.66	133.33	133.33
联营企业	Joint Ownership Enterprises	100.00	100.00	100.00	100.00
有限责任公司	Limited Liability Corporations	94.48	103.59	123.53	132.19
股份有限公司	Share-holding Corporations Ltd.	112.69	104.04	123.35	127.97
私营企业	Privately Owned Enterprises	100.00	100.00	100.00	100.00
外商及港、澳、台投资企业	Enterprises Invested by Foreigners or Investors from Hongkong,Macro and Taiwan	118.36	125.23	140.12	132.41
按企业规模分	Grouped by Size of Enterprises				
大型企业	Large-size	124.22	126.90	148.94	146.65
中型企业	Medium-size	101.20	106.40	115.20	124.39
小型企业	Small-size	78.85	78.00	91.84	104.08
特殊分组	Special-Grorped				
国家重点企业	State Key Enterprises	113.03	118.15	113.32	125.12
国家试点企业集团成员	Member of Stats Experimental Enterprises Group	109.56	114.32	110.02	120.55
乡镇企业	Town and Township Enterprises	166.56	166.56	200.00	200.00
上市公司	Listed Companies	133.79	115.34	133.99	131.97
国有控股企业	State-holding Enterprises	119.12	119.11	134.91	136.49

主要统计指标解释

景气指数：是根据企业家对本企业综合生产经营情况所作的判断与预期（通常是对“良好”、“一般”、“不佳”的选择）而编制的指数，用以综合反映企业的生产经营状况。企业景气指数也称“企业综合生产经营景气指数”。

企业家信心指数：是根据企业家对企业外部市场经济环境与宏观政策的认识、看法所作的判断和预期（通常是对“乐观”、“一般”、“不乐观”的选择）而编制的指数，用以综合反映企业家对宏观经济环境的感受与信心。企业家信心指数也称“宏观经济景气指数”。

景气指数的表示方式：景气指数的表示范围在0～200之间，其含义：100为景气指数的临界值，表明景气状况变化不大；100～200为景气区间，表明景气状况趋于上升或改善，越接近于200，状况越景气；0～100为不景气区间，表明景气状况趋于下降或恶化，越接近于0，状况越不景气。

国家重点企业：是指1999年10月经国务院批准确定的520户国家重点企业。

国家试点企业集团成员：是指由国务院批准组建的国家试点企业集团的成员。

上市公司：是指所发行的股票经国务院授权的中国证券监督管理委员会批准、在境内、外证券交易所（包括上海、深圳、香港、纽约、东京等证券交易所）内上市买卖其有价证券的股份有限公司。

Explanatory Notes on Main Statistical Indicators

Prosperity index of enterprise it is an index worked out according to the judgment and anticipation (normally a choice from good , ordinary , not good) of entrepreneurs made based on synthetic productive and operational situation of the enterprise. It is used to reflect synthetically the productive and operational situation of the enterprise. It is also referred to as synthetic productive and operational prosperity index of enterprise .

Confidence index of entrepreneur it is an index worked out according to the judgment and anticipation (normally a choice from optimistic , ordinary , not optimistic) of entrepreneurs made based on their understandings and views of the market and economic environment outside the enterprise and the macro policies. It is used to reflect synthetically the confidence and feelings of the entrepreneurs to the macro economic environment. It is also referred to as macro-economy prosperity index .

The way to express prosperity index the range of prosperity index is from 0 to 200; 100 is the critical value, and means prosperity situation didn't change largely; from 100 to 200 is the interval of prosperity; and from 0 to 100 is the interval of not prosperity, meaning prosperity situation is going down or worse, the closer to 0, the worse the prosperity situation.

Key enterprise of the state it refers to the 520 key enterprises of the state authorized and confirmed by State Department in Oct., 1999.

Member of state experimental unit enterprise group refers to the members of state experimental unit enterprise groups authorized and formed by State Department.

Company on the market refers to the limited companies with stock authorized by China Securities Regulatory Commission which is authorized by State Department, and their securities can be deal on the market in stock exchanges (include exchanges of Shanghai, Shenzhen, Hong Kong, New York and Tokyo) inside and outside P.R. of China.

中国统计出版社最新图书简目

（仅供参考，以最后出书为准）

统计资料

中国统计年鉴-2010
2010中国发展报告
中国劳动统计年鉴-2010
中国建筑业统计年鉴-2010
中国商品交易市场统计年鉴-2010
中国民政统计年鉴-2010
中国科技统计年鉴-2010
中国高技术产业统计年鉴-2010
全国农产品成本收益资料汇编-2010
第二次全国残疾人抽样调查资料系列
中国县（市）社会经济调查年鉴-2010
中国国内生产总值核算历史资料（1952-2004）
大中型批发零售和住宿餐饮企业统计年鉴-2010

中国统计摘要-2010
中国第三产业统计年鉴-2010
中国社会统计年鉴-2010
中国人口和就业统计年鉴-2010
中国房地产统计年鉴-2010
中国贸易外经统计年鉴-2010
中国农村统计年鉴-2010
中国教育经费统计年鉴-2009
中国科学技术协会统计年鉴-2010
中国棉花年鉴-2008/2009
中国农村住户调查年鉴-2010（中、英文）
中国季度国内生产总值核算历史资料（1992-2005）

国际统计年鉴-2010
中国区域经济统计年鉴-2010
中国城市统计年鉴-2009
中国工业经济统计年鉴-2010
中国能源统计年鉴-2010
2010中国地区经济监测报告
中国农产品价格调查年鉴-2010
中国农村贫困监测报告-2010
工业企业科技活动资料-2010
中国城市(镇)生活与价格年鉴-2010
中国农村全面建设小康监测报告-2010
中国零售和餐饮业连锁企业统计年鉴-2010
2005年中国1%人口抽样调查系列资料

2010年省级综合统计年鉴系列

北京 天津 河北 山西 内蒙古
河南 湖北 湖南 广东 广西
新疆 新疆生产建设兵团

辽宁 吉林 黑龙江 上海 江苏
海南 重庆 四川 贵州 云南

浙江 安徽 福建 江西 山东
西藏 陕西 甘肃 青海 宁夏

2010年市（县）级综合统计年鉴系列

天津滨海新区
运城 忻州 临汾 呼和浩特
黑龙江垦区 上海浦东新区
宁波 绍兴 台州 舟山 温州
厦门经济特区 南昌 上饶
十堰 荆州 黄冈 长沙 广州
贵阳 昆明 西安 庆阳 银川

石家庄 唐山 邯郸 太原 大同
包头 沈阳 大连 长春 吉林市
苏州 无锡 常州 徐州 南通
金华 嘉兴 衢州 安庆 福州
济南 青岛 潍坊 东营 郑州
东莞 惠州 深圳 桂林 南宁
乌鲁木齐 吐鲁番

长治 阳泉 晋城 朔州 晋中
四平 延吉 哈尔滨 齐齐哈尔
盐城 镇江 江阴 丹阳 杭州
福州经济技术开发区
洛阳 三门峡 南阳 武汉 宜昌
柳州 来宾 河池 海口 成都

“十一五”规划教材

非参数统计 医学统计学
多元统计分析 经济计量学教程
统计数据处理概论
企业经营管理统计
统计学:从数据到结论

概率论与数理统计 统计学
应用时间序列分析
质量管理统计方法 社会统计学
市场调查与预测
国民经济核算教程(国民经济统计学)

现代金融投资统计分析
统计指数理论及应用
多元统计分析实验
统计学原理（非统计专业使用）
概率论与数理统计(经济、管理类专业使用）

重点图书

新中国六十年
挑大学选专业2010—高考志愿填报指南
挑大学选专业2010—考研择校指南